American Society of Missiology Series, No. 30

CONSTANTS IN CONTEXT

A Theology of Mission for Today

Stephen B. Bevans, SVD
Roger P. Schroeder, SVD

ORBIS BOOKS

Maryknoll, New York 10545

Founded in 1970, Orbis Books endeavors to publish works that enlighten the mind, nourish the spirit, and challenge the conscience. The publishing arm of the Maryknoll Fathers and Brothers, Orbis seeks to explore the global dimensions of the Christian faith and mission, to invite dialogue with diverse cultures and religious traditions, and to serve the cause of reconciliation and peace. The books published reflect the opinions of their authors and are not meant to represent the official position of the Maryknoll Society. To obtain more information about Maryknoll and Orbis Books, please visit our website at www.maryknoll.org.

Manufactured in the United States of America.

Manuscript editing and typesetting by Joan Weber Laflamme.

The cover art is from a mosaic in the church of St. Apollinaris Nuovo, Via Romea Sud 220, Ravenna, Italy. The creators of the mosaic, known to historians as "In the Presence of Christ, the Holy Spirit Descends on the Apostles at Pentecost," are anonymous. Printed with the permission of Art Resource, New York, N.Y., from the Erich Lessing Collection. According to legend, St. Apollinaris was the first bishop of Ravenna and the church itself was originally the Arian cathedral.

Library of Congress Cataloging in Publication Data

Bevans, Stephen B., 1944-
  Constants in context : a theology of mission for today / Stephen B.
Bevans, Roger P. Schroeder.
      p. cm. — (American Society of Missiology series ; no. 30) Includes bibliographical references and index.
  ISBN 1-57075-517-5 (pbk.)
  1. Missions. I. Schroeder, Roger, 1951- II. Title. III. Series.
  BV2061.3 .B48 2004
  266—dc22
                            2003022781

Stephen Bevans dedicates this book to his mentors and teachers
Eugene Ahner
Roger S. Arnold, SVD
Larry Nemer, SVD

Roger Schroeder dedicates this book to his parents
Alphonse and Angela Schroeder

Contents

PART I
CONSTANTS IN CONTEXT:
BIBLICAL AND THEOLOGICAL FOUNDATIONS

PART III
CONSTANTS IN CONTEXT:
A THEOLOGY OF MISSION FOR TODAY

Maps

Historical-Theological Theme Summary Tables

Foreword

I am honored to write the foreword of a book that promises to make a significant impact in the fields of missiology and theology. I am particularly pleased that its authors have also chosen to use my theological typologies as an interpretative tool for understanding the history of mission. But even more, I am pleased because this book is a prime example of the manner in which the fields of missiology and theology will be intertwined in the future. At the risk of writing an autobiographical foreword to the work of two esteemed colleagues, I believe an account of how I developed the typology that forms the backbone of this book may be helpful.

The typology that the authors of *Constants in Context* employ was first developed as I sought to lecture to beginning students at Candler School of Theology, in Atlanta, in the early 1970s. As I became acquainted with these students, it became apparent that they came to study theology with one of two expectations.

On the one hand, there were those who came with very open minds, looking for answers to the deepest mysteries of life. They wanted life and the world to make sense, and they came to the study of theology hoping that somehow they could find or develop a theological system that would make things fall in place. Theirs was a deep, honest and sometimes agonizing quest for truth. Sometimes, to the point that as they progressed in their studies, the quest itself became the only answer, and the seeker found meaning only in the very act of seeking. When talking with these students, I was often reminded of Kierkegaard's quote from Lessing to the effect that if God were to offer him the fullness of truth in the right hand, and the constant and endless quest after truth in the left, he would choose the left hand, because the fullness of truth belongs to God alone. I would eventually connect these students and their quest with what I would come to call "Type B" theology.

On the other hand, there were some students who did not seem particularly troubled by the mysteries of the universe or of human existence. They had found the truth in the teachings of the church, and they came to school simply to find out more about that truth. They knew and accepted the traditional outline of the gospel and of salvation history: God created all things; humans sinned; therefore we have all fallen short of the glory of God, to whom we owe a great debt; Jesus has come to pay that debt; in order to avail oneself of the benefits of the death of Jesus, one has to accept him. These students knew all these things in broad outline. All they wanted or expected from their education was to fill in the blanks, connect the dots, give them more and better arguments to proclaim these facts. I would eventually connect these students and their attitude with what I would come to call "Type A" theology.

As I taught both of these sorts of students in an introductory course that included both history and theology, it soon became apparent that the first sort had great sympathies toward Origen. Not that they agreed with the contents of Origen's speculations, and much less that they shared his Platonic presuppositions; rather, they liked, as they would say, his "style," his attitude, his quest for sense. When I lectured on Origen, these students would lean forward, all ears, while the others frowned in puzzlement. When the time came for questions and comments, it became obvious that, while following different paths, these students admired Origen's quest after truth—after all, that was why they had come to this school in the first place.

It also became apparent that the second sort of student found Origen quite unhelpful and much preferred Tertullian. In this case, too, it was not so much a matter of agreeing with particular tenets of Tertullian's as it was a matter of liking his assurance, his refusal to speculate, his standing on the teachings of the church. Most of these students would applaud Tertullian's biting and even sarcastic wit. Now they would lean forward, all ears, while the rest of the class shook their heads in disapproval. When the time came for questions and comments, many of these students would applaud what they called the "practical" nature of Tertullian's thought. As time went by, and similar experiences were repeated year after year, it became increasingly clear to me that what these students found so valuable in Tertullian was not just his conservative stance but, even more, his concern for obedience, for doing what God wishes, and for the moral order of the universe.

As a professor in a theological school whose main task was the preparation of pastors for the church, I felt uneasy with both attitudes. In addition, I was under no illusion that my typologies were doing justice to the richness of these great theologians' thought. Indeed, as I now seek to describe them, I must warn the reader that what follows, like any typology, and like my own theological typology, is an oversimplification, even a caricature of the original. My clearly drawn contrasts are written in the effort to achieve clarity. How much help, one can rightly ask, can a pastor be who is always seeking after truth, always moving into new speculations, trying to find meaning for life in existentialism, or in rationalism, or even in nihilism? Could such a pastor offer comfort to the bereaved, guidance to the perplexed, a sense of mission to the church?

And I feared the consequences of unleashing on the church pastors who were convinced that they knew exactly what God wanted, and who would very likely take on the role of prosecutors before the court of the Great Judge.

It was partly as a response to these concerns that I began promoting Irenaeus of Lyon. I had noticed that as I expounded his theology, practically every student seemed puzzled, perhaps even lost. They were particularly puzzled when they realized that, while Irenaeus did not belong in their camp, he did not belong in the other camp either. And then, as I related what Irenaeus was saying to certain passages in the New Testament that many students had always found intriguing, and as I related it also to some of the issues of contemporary life, I was surprised to see the frown on many a forehead disappear and turn into expressions of discovery. Often a new openness to learn and consider ideas really different from anything they had previously considered would be the result. Relating this to my concern for teaching prospective pastors was the fact that of the three, Tertullian, Origen, and Irenaeus, only the last was a pastor—and it was he who saw God essentially as a shepherd leading creation to the green pastures of its consummation. Thus it was that I came to call this "Type C" theology and to seek to infuse all my students, no matter whether "Type A" or "Type B," with a healthy dose of "C"!

All of this, however, is only one side of the story. At the same time as I was lecturing on Origen, Tertullian and Irenaeus, I was reading a great deal of liberation theology. As I read, I realized once again that theology is never done in a vacuum, nor is it ever socially or politically neutral. This helped explain why after the Constantinian settlement Type C theology tended to disappear, while Type A became dominant—even though it had a strong dose of Type B mixed in. Then, when Type A appeared too confining, those who sought to escape it usually opted for Type B. There are subversive dimensions in Type C theology that made it rather unpopular, not only with political leaders, but also with church leaders who valued the support of the powerful. In a way, with this connection it seemed to me that the circle was complete: a certain theological view is more amenable to a certain interest, which in turn promotes that view, which in turn supports that interest, and so on, and on and on.

Although it may not be apparent to the reader of any of the three books I was working on at the same time, they form a sort of trilogy. In the first, *Christian Thought Revisited: Three Types of Theology* (published now by Orbis Books), I propose the typology that the authors of *Constants in Context* have chosen to employ. It serves as a sort of historical and theological framework for the second, *Mañana: Christian Theology from a Hispanic Perspective* (Nashville, Tenn.: Abingdon Press, 1990). This was a contemporary expression of what I thought Type C theology would look like today. The third book, *Faith and Wealth: A History of Early Christian Ideas on the Origin, Significance, and Use of Money* (San Francisco: Harper & Row, 1990), provided the historical proof that the sort of thing that concerned me in *Mañana,* and which was a central concern of all liberation theology, had also been important in the early church.

But I had not really completed the circle. I had not brought in the crucial theme of mission. The question is not simply, How do these three types function in a particular theological system or outlook? Nor is it only, How do these three types serve or subvert certain social, political, cultural or economic agendas? Having asked those two questions, the question that still had to be asked, and I did not, was, How do these three types actually work themselves out in the mission practice of the church? And, conversely, How does the church in mission discover, enrich, modify, strengthen or subvert each of these types? These questions had to be posed and explored, not only along the purely theoretical lines of how this could conceivably happen, but even more so along the historical lines of how it has actually happened. It was necessary to look at particular moments and models of mission and to see how this typology applies or does not apply, how it should be modified, and, most particularly and urgently, how it illumines mission today.

Constants in Context asks these questions and thus enlarges the circle I thought I had completed. It illumines both mission and theology. Full of admiration at the accomplishment of Fathers Bevans and Schroeder, I wish I could have read their book before I wrote about the three types! The book the reader is about to read is both excellent historical theology and an invitation to consider what ought to be the church's mission in the contemporary world. And if Type C is valid, we must take ongoing history as God's shepherding of creation and as the basic category for understanding the good news of the gospel. All our work to make the gospel concrete is building on one another's work, as part of the very nature of things, and even as God's working among us. I commend this book to all as essential reading and a superb example of both historical and constructive theology. It offers an unparalleled study of how the church has responded to the mandate of Jesus since the earliest days of Christianity.

JUSTO L. GONZÁLEZ

Preface to the ASM Series

The purpose of the ASM (American Society of Missiology) Series is to publish—without regard for disciplinary, national, or denominational boundaries—scholarly works of high quality and wide interest on missiological themes from the entire spectrum of scholarly pursuits relevant to Christian mission, which is always the focus of books in the Series.

By *mission* is meant the effort to effect passage over the boundary between faith in Jesus Christ and its absence. In this understanding of mission, the basic functions of Christian proclamation, dialogue, witness, service, worship, liberation, and nurture are of special concern. And in that context questions arise, including, How does the transition from one cultural context to another influence the shape and interaction between these dynamic functions, especially in regard to the cultural and religious plurality that comprises the global context of Christian life and mission?

The promotion of scholarly dialogue among missiologists, and among missiologists and scholars in other fields of inquiry, may involve the publication of views that some missiologists cannot accept, and with which members of the Editorial Committee themselves do not agree. Manuscripts published in the Series, accordingly, reflect the opinions of their authors and are not understood to represent the position of the American Society of Missiology or of the Editorial Committee. Selection is guided by such criteria as intrinsic worth, readability, coherence, and accessibility to a range of interested persons and not merely to experts or specialists.

The ASM Series, in collaboration with Orbis Books, seeks to publish scholarly works of high merit and wide interest on numerous aspects of missiology—the scholarly study of mission. Able presentations on new and creative approaches to the practice and understanding of mission will receive close attention.

The ASM Series Committee
Jonathan J. Bonk
Angelyn Dries, OSF
Scott W. Sunquist

Preface

Since the aim of this book—to propose a contemporary theology of mission in the light of the faithful but always-contextual growth of the Christian movement—is admittedly an ambitious one, there are a number of things of which the reader needs to be aware. While the book has sought to be as inclusive as possible, we are very aware of the need to state clearly and honestly the parameters—indeed the limitations—of what we have accomplished.

Perhaps most fundamental of all are the parameters imposed by our social location, out of which we have researched and written these pages. We are both white, male, Catholic, ordained, fifty-ish, native-born citizens of the United States, both professors in a Catholic graduate school of theology and ministry (Catholic Theological Union at Chicago). We are both men of Christian faith, members of a missionary religious order (the Society of the Divine Word) who have had extensive experience living abroad in cultural situations other than our own, and who are still committed to living and ministering cross-culturally here in North America. We believe passionately in mission.

The very wisdom that we have gained in completing this project has taught us more than ever to recognize our own limitations. We *are* white; we *are* male; we *are* Catholics; we *are* citizens of the United States; we *have* been educated in Western, Enlightenment methods and environments. Nevertheless, we believe that our background in the theory and practice of mission, in having had to learn to live within another world view, and in years of being inspired and challenged by our colleagues in missiology and theology has formed us in ways that have greatly enhanced our capacity to write a book that has not only stretched us, but will—we hope—stretch those who read it.

Although we are indeed products of our social location, we also have been pulled beyond a Eurocentric view of the church's history and have attempted in these pages to present a history that values the contributions of other races, cultures and nations. In fact, we have become persuaded that Christianity is indeed, as Kwame Bediako says, a *non-Western* religion, and that the Western domination of the world Christian movement in the last several hundred years has only been a blip on history's wide screen. The future, as Andrew Walls has so often and so eloquently said, belongs to Africa, Asia, Latin America and the Pacific. In addition, as citizens of what is now the most powerful and most affluent nation in the world, we have been challenged afresh to make our own the commitment to justice, peace and the integrity of creation that will alter the structures which maintain the poverty, violence and ecological disaster from which we U.S. Americans so often profit. We recognize the complexity of these issues, but at the same time we feel conscience-bound to stand in solidarity with our brothers and sisters around the globe.

Although we have written from the perspective of committed Roman Catholics, we have learned from the amazing history and theology of Christians outside our own tradition. Whether East Syriac "Nestorian" Christians, Christians of the Reformation traditions, Evangelicals, Pentecostals or members of the various contemporary indigenous churches, we have not only been enriched by their commitment to Christian faith and the depth of their theology, but we have discovered our Catholicism anew through the diverse ways in which they have sought to confess Christ. Although we are male, our horizons have been broadened by the countless women who have shaped the world Christian movement down through the centuries. Whether leaders of house churches in the early years of the movement, early martyrs like Perpetua and Blandina, church leaders like Hildegard of Bingen and Catherine of Siena, members of the Beguine movement, courageous missionaries like Marie de l'Incarnation or Lottie Moon, lay apostles like Dorothy Day and members of the Grail movement, or the anonymous African, Asian and Latin American women who have kept the faith alive despite poverty and their marginal status in the church and society, we have been challenged to acknowledge our own ignorance of the church's past and our own blindness to women's formative role in both the theology and practice of mission.

Although we are ordained, our study has opened our minds in new ways to the crucial role that lay men and women have played in the twenty centuries of the church's existence. The early Christian community grew primarily through the witness and enthusiasm of people who simply lived out the consequences of their baptismal call; Christianity reached Ethiopia in the fourth century and China as early as the seventh century because merchants, diplomats and even slaves shared the Christian message as they went about their ordinary daily work; the Franciscan movement was one of many lay movements in the Middle Ages that gave ordinary Christians new ways of living out their identity; lay catechists in Vietnam in the seventeenth century, and in China today, are representative of thousands of lay women and men who have faithfully evangelized generations of Christians in Asia, Africa, Latin America and the islands of the Pacific. Although we are committed Christians, we have grown from the witness of Justin Martyr, Alessandro Valignano, E. Stanley Jones and Lesslie Newbigin, all of whom struggled to remain faithful to their Christian faith while at the same time acknowledging the presence of God's Spirit and God's Word in people of other religious ways, and in the traditions of those ways themselves. Our minds and hearts have been enlarged as we have seen the sincerity of Paul Knitter's, Mark Heim's and Jacques Dupuis's attempts to move beyond a simplistic pluralistic understanding of religious truth, and our hearts and minds have been expanded as well by Lesslie Newbigin, John Stott and Peter Beyerhaus, each of whom struggles in his own way to remain faithful to the missionary constant of the centrality of Christ.

Acknowledgments

Our years of experience of living, teaching and ministering cross-culturally have taught us three important lessons. The first is that, when one crosses into another context—cultural, racial, religious or gender—one inevitably learns not only about the other, but—and perhaps most important—about oneself. Second, a valuable part of what we learn about ourselves is that the other's story, struggles and joy are really, in the final analysis, a part of our own story, struggles and joy. Third, in this entire process we also realize how much we do *not* and can never know about the other. Here there is real knowledge in knowing that we do *not* know and *cannot* learn. When one truly participates in God's mission of prophetic dialogue, these are the lessons one learns. In writing this book, both of us have learned these lessons again, as if for the first time.

The experience of writing this book together has been itself an experience, *mutatis mutandis*, of prophetic dialogue. Steve took the lead in writing the chapters in Part I and Part III; Roger took the lead in writing the six historical chapters in Part II. However, the entire book is now a product of our joint effort. After initial writing and mutual critique of the entire manuscript, we spent the better part of two weeks reading it together aloud, listening to one another, challenging each other's content and style, and entering into important discussions about the arrangement within chapters and the key concepts of the book. The first several chapters took shape in the fall of 1997, when we were both in residence at the Overseas Ministries Study Center and research fellows at Yale Divinity School in New Haven, Connecticut. Other venues for our prophetic dialogue included a wonderful cabin in south central Wisconsin and the home of Anne Luther in South Bend, Indiana. The experience of co-authoring is one that we will never forget. It has not only helped us to appreciate one another's scholarship, but it has expanded our minds and hearts in ways we never anticipated when we began this project and has brought us to a greater love of our vocation as scholars, missionaries and ministers. We began this project as friends; the give and take of writing together has deepened that friendship.

We are dedicating this book to people who have supported us in our life's work and have been models for us to imitate as people of faith. Steve dedicates this book to three former teachers and mentors who have shaped his life in very fundamental ways: Gene Ahner, who first taught him to distinguish between church and the reign of God; Roger Arnold, who first introduced him to the work of Bernard Lonergan and continues to be a model of intellectual vitality; and Larry Nemer, who taught him church history and encouraged him to become involved in missiology. Roger dedicates this book to his parents, Alphonse and Angela Schroeder. Through sacrifice, love and prayer, they created a nourishing Christian home for Roger and his ten brothers and sisters in the farmland of northwest Ohio. In addition, his parents' support of a diocesan priest in India taught Roger early on about the world and church beyond Putnam County, Ohio, and planted the seed for his own missionary vocation.

All of those to whom we dedicate this book continue to be a part of God's mission as witnesses of love, faith, and commitment. We are because they are. In a very real way this book is the product of their friendship, love and example.

Theology is always a communal enterprise, and writing this book more than proved this fact. Although we can never name all the friends and colleagues who have helped and inspired us in the writing of this book, we would like particularly to thank a number of people whose friendship and scholarship have been invaluable as we have researched and written this book over the last ten years.

First, we would like to express our gratitude to Dr. Gerald H. Anderson, Dr. Jonathan Bonk and the staff at the Overseas Ministries Study Center (OMSC) in New Haven, Connecticut, for providing an atmosphere of prayer, leisure and scholarship during the fall semester of 1997. It was at OMSC that we began the first serious and extensive work on this book together and were able to avail ourselves of the vast resources of the Day Missions Library at Yale Divinity School. During that same fall we were also able to consult the library at the Research Center of the Franciscan Missionaries of Mary in Providence, Rhode Island, and we would like to especially thank Sr. Mary Motte, FMM, who was then the center's director. In the course of our research and writing, director Ken O'Malley and the wonderful staff of the Bechtold Library at Catholic Theological Union were always ready to help us find that elusive article or bibliographical reference. Steve is especially grateful to Dr. John Nyquist, professor of missions at the School of World Mission at Trinity Evangelical Divinity School, Deerfield, Illinois, for his assistance in providing access to Trinity's marvelous university library. Roger is particularly appreciative of the hospitality and assistance he received from Fr. Jim Knight, SVD, research librarian Siobhan Foster and the library staff at Yarra Theological Union (YTU) in Melbourne, Australia, where he spent the first semester of the 2003 academic year. We are also thankful for the hospitality extended to us by Anne Luther, Bob and Pat Wheeler, Jaime and Lisa Bascuñan, and Mark Weber and the people of St. Anselm's parish in Chicago as we neared the end of our writing.

A number of colleagues have read this manuscript at various stages of its completion and have offered immensely valuable critique and encouragement: Barbara Bowe, David Daniels, José M. de Mesa, Inagrace Dietterich, Maria Homberg, Amy-Jill Levine, Gary B. McGee, Frederick W. Norris, John Roxborogh, James A. Scherer, Susan Smith and Scott W. Sunquist (who also shared the manuscript with two of his students). Although we have not been able to incorporate everything they suggested, we remain immensely honored by the seriousness with which they took our work, and we will be always grateful for the time they spent reading and critiquing what grew to be a very large manuscript.

When Roger was in Australia he had the opportunity to use a draft of this book as a primary text for the course "Introduction to Theology of Mission." This provided him with an opportunity to test the book in the laboratory of a classroom, and he would like to express here his appreciation for the eight students in that class, who by their honest engagement with the ideas in our book really helped in the process of clarifying and refining its contents. Roger also had the opportunity to present parts of this book to faculty members at YTU and to members of the Mission Studies Network in Melbourne. Steve has tested the ideas for this book with a group of pastoral workers in southwest Alaska, with leaders of religious congregations at their annual meeting in 2002 in Philadelphia, and with a number of lay and seminary students in Lexington, Kentucky, in the spring of 2003. The positive reception by all these groups provided wonderful encouragement and helpful criticism.

We are greatly honored by the fact that our book appears in the American Society of Missiology series, and we would like to thank the series committee — Angelyn Dries, Jonathan Bonk and Scott Sunquist.

Among many others, we would like to thank John Markey, Joanne Peters, Charles Weber, Robert Schreiter, John Cockayne, Barbara Reid, Clemens Sedmak, Eleanor Doidge, Anthony Gittins, Dale Irvin, Ogbu Kalu, Richard Bliese, Mark Thomsen and the late Charles Walter. Most especially, however, we would like to thank Bill Burrows, our editor at Orbis Books, for initiating the project, for encouraging us along the way, for gentle prodding and patience, and for challenging us to think in new and exciting ways. Justo González, to whom we owe much inspiration for this book, has graciously written the foreword.

Abbreviations

ABCFM	American Board of Commissioners for Foreign Missions
ACLRI	Australian Conference for Leaders of Religious Institutes
AG	Vatican Council II, *Ad Gentes (Decree on the Church's Missionary Activity)*
AIC	African Initiated Church
AME	African Methodist Episcopal Church
AMECEA	Association of Member Episcopal Conferences of East Africa
BMS	Baptist Missionary Society
CCGM	Chicago Center for Global Ministries
CELAM	Conferencia Episcopal de Latin América (Episcopal Conference of Latin America)
CES	Chinese Evangelical Society
CIM	China Inland Mission
CMA	Christian and Missionary Alliance
CMS	Church Missionary Society
CSMC	Catholic Students' Mission Crusade
CWME	Commission on World Mission and Evangelism
D	Denzinger, *Enchiridion Symbolorum*, 29th edition
DEV	Pope John Paul II, *Dominum et Vivificantem* (encyclical letter)
DH	Vatican Council II, *Dignitatis Humanae (Declaration on Religious Liberty)*
DI	Congregation of the Doctrine of the Faith, *Dominus Iesus*
DP	Congregation for the Evangelization of Peoples and Pontifical Council for Interreligious Dialogue, *Dialogue and Proclamation*
DS	Denzinger-Schönmetzer, *Enchiridion Symbolorum*, 34th edition
ECT	Evangelicals and Catholics Together
EIA	Pope John Paul II, *Ecclesia in Asia* (apostolic exhortation)
EJCSK	L'Eglise de Jésus Christ sur la terre par le prophète Simon Kimbangu (The Church of Jesus Christ on Earth through the Prophet Simon Kimbangu)
EN	Pope Paul VI, *Evangelii Nuntiandi* (apostolic exhortation)
EPCW	"Evangelization, Proselytism and Common Witness" (Pentecostal/Roman Catholic Dialogue, 1997)

E.T.	English translation
FABC	Federation of Asian Bishops' Conferences
GS	Vatican Council II, *Gaudium et Spes (Pastoral Constitution on the Church in the Modern World)*
IMC	International Missionary Conference
INC	Iglesia ni Cristo
IRM	*International Review of Mission(s)*
LCWE	Lausanne Committee for World Evangelization
LFMI	Laymen's Foreign Missions Inquiry
LG	Vatican Council II, *Lumen Gentium (Dogmatic Constitution on the Church)*
LMS	London Missionary Society
MARC	Mission Advanced Research and Communication Center (World Vision International)
MEP	Société des Missions Étrangères (Society of Foreign Missions)
MM	Maryknoll Missioners (Catholic Foreign Mission Society of America)
NA	Vatican Council II, *Nostra Aetate (Declaration on the Relationship of the Church to Non-Christian Religions)*
PG	J.P. Migne, ed., *Patrologia Graeca*
PL	J.P. Migne, ed., *Patrologia Latina*
RH	Pope John Paul II, *Redemptor Hominis* (encyclical letter)
RM	Pope John Paul II, *Redemptoris Missio* (encyclical letter)
SC	Vatican Council II, *Sacrosanctum Concilium (Constitution on the Sacred Liturgy)*
SCPF	Sacred Congregation for the Propagation of the Faith
SEDOS	Servizio di documentazione e studi (Center for Documentation and Study)
SVM	Student Volunteer Movement for Foreign Missions
TCT	*The Church Teaches: Documents of the Church in English Translation*
TEE	United States Catholic Conference, *To the Ends of the Earth* (pastoral statement on world mission)
UR	Vatican Council II, *Unitatis Redintegratio (Decree on Ecumenism)*
USCMA	United States Catholic Mission Association
USCC	United States Catholic Conference
WCC	World Council of Churches
WEF	World Evangelical Fellowship
WFMS	Women's Foreign Missionary Society
WSCF	World's Student Christian Federation
WSCW	"Word and Spirit, Church and World" (Reformed/Pentecostal Dialogue, 2000)

Introduction

WHAT THIS BOOK IS ABOUT

In 1994, Bill Burrows of Orbis Books approached one of us (Roger Schroeder) about writing an introduction to missiology for the Orbis "Introducing . . ." series. In discussing this proposal the two of us thought that it would be an interesting project to do together. Now it is over nine years later and the book that we agreed to write has grown from an introductory text to an in-depth study that has not only taken us far more time than we had initially imagined, but has taken us down paths that we had never anticipated journeying upon. What began as a rather straightforward theological and historical summary led to the discovery of the fundamental importance of mission for theology and theology for mission as well as the dizzying complexity of the church's missionary practice in both past and present.

This book, then, as it has developed and matured, is both a historical, systematic *theology* and a systematic theological *history* of the church's missionary practice. On the one hand, we have conceived this book as a *systematic theology* that has mission at its very core; on the other hand, we have written a *church history* that is not only a collection of facts, persons and events, but one that is shaped by the constant but always contextual Christian biblical and doctrinal traditions. Christian mission is both anchored in fidelity to the past and challenged to fidelity in the present. It must preserve, defend and proclaim the *constants* of the church's traditions; at the same time it must respond creatively and boldly to the *contexts* in which it finds itself. Christian history is a story of the church in mission. It is, to borrow the eloquent phrase of Harvie Conn, a story of the encounter of Eternal Word with changing worlds.[1] As we express it in this book, it is a story of *constants in context*.

The double focus of this book is a response to two important challenges in contemporary theological, missiological and historical scholarship. The first challenge, one articulated by David Bosch in his monumental *Transforming Mission*, and by missiologists J. Andrew Kirk and Wilbert Shenk,[2] is to construct a theology that is inspired by God's constant missionary action in the world and that has as its aim not only greater knowledge of God and God's purposes but more reflective and intelligent participation in those purposes. All theology, in other words, must be a *missionary* theology. The second challenge, expressed best in the ground-breaking two-volume history by Dale T. Irvin and

1

Scott W. Sunquist,[3] is to write a history of the Christian church that is really a history of the world Christian *movement*, one that incorporates all the diverse streams of Christianity and so tells the story of Christianity as it really happened—not as unidirectional (Palestine to Europe to the rest of the world) but as multi-directional (Palestine to Asia, Palestine to Africa, Palestine to Europe), not as simply the expansion of an institution but as the emergence of a movement, not as simply the propagation of ready-made doctrine but as the constant discovery of the gospel's "infinite translatability" and missionary intention.

HOW THIS BOOK IS STRUCTURED

In order to address these challenges adequately, we have structured this book in three major parts. In Part I we lay down the foundation for the two parts that follow. Chapter 1 argues, through a reading of the Acts of the Apostles, that the church only emerges *as* the church when it becomes aware of its boundary-breaking mission not just to Judaism but to all peoples, not just to Jerusalem and Judea but to "Samaria, and to the ends of the earth" (Acts 1:8). The church is "missionary by its very nature" (AG 2) and it becomes missionary by attending to each and every *context* in which it finds itself. Chapter 2 then outlines six *constants*—six doctrinal themes to which the church must be faithful at every boundary crossing and in every context. The interaction and articulation of these six constants—Christology, ecclesiology, eschatology, salvation, anthropology and culture—will determine the way that the church's missionary practice is lived out in the various periods of its history. To assist us in discerning the recurrent patterns of the rich diversity of Christian theological traditions, we have taken as our guides—here and throughout the book—the typologies proposed by Cuban-American theologian Justo L. González and German liberation/feminist theologian Dorothee Sölle.[4]

Part II then focuses on six moments in the history of the Christian movement, from the early church to the end of the twentieth century, situating a particular model of missionary practice within its political, social, religious and institutional context, describing the period's major dynamics, and identifying the principal missionary agents of the time. At the end of each of these six chapters we describe how the six constants are expressed and operative within that particular historical context, after which we draw several implications regarding how this period might enhance and challenge the theology of mission and missionary practice today.

The first of these six periods (Chapter 3) begins with the post-apostolic church in the year 100, as it moves as far as India in the East, northern Africa in the South and the borders of the Roman Empire in Europe. The chapter ends at 301, on the eve of Constantine's move to make Christianity a legitimate religion within the Roman Empire. Chapter 4 begins in 313, the year of Constantine's "Edict of Milan," and ends in 907. It describes the various monastic movements in East and West that characterize mission, whether in the mountains of Syria, the deserts of Egypt and Ethiopia, the hills of Italy, the wilderness of Ireland or the craggy coast of Scotland. In the middle of this period Islam emerged, the religion that would change the face of Christianity, especially in the East. The year 907 marked the fall of the T'ang dynasty in China, a political event that brought to an end several centuries of the East Syrian Church's growth across Asia and into China. The third period that we describe (Chapter 5) deals with the rich and complex life of the church from the year 1000 in both East and West. In Europe this period was marked by a series of crusades to liberate the Holy Land and by the rise of the mendicant orders of both men and women who gave fresh expression to Christianity's missionary existence. This period also saw the painful split between the Latin West and the Greek East and ended, in 1453, with the fall of the Byzantine Empire and its capital of Constantinople.

Chapter 6 begins at 1492, a year that symbolizes the entire "Age of Discovery" and the beginning of a new era of evangelization, particularly in the Americas and in Asia, as Europe began its move to eventual domination of world commerce and politics. This period saw the tragic break in the West as Christians separated under the banners of Protestantism and Catholicism. The period ended in 1773, the year that marked the suppression of the Jesuits in the Catholic Church and the beginning of decades when the church's missionary activity experienced its lowest ebb. This nadir of missionary activity was short lived, however. In Chapter 7 we describe how, first in Protestantism but then in Catholicism and Russian Orthodoxy alike, the nineteenth century saw a new missionary fervor and the emergence of a new missionary model—the society model—beginning in 1792 with William Carey's "Inquiry" and continuing with the Catholic religious and missionary revival some years later. This age of progress, social ferment and Western colonial domination, symbolized by the 1910 Edinburgh World Missionary Conference, came to an end with the marshaling of the "guns of August" at the beginning of World War I in 1914. The final chapter in this section takes us through the tumultuous times of the twentieth century, beginning with Benedict XV's mission encyclical *Maximum Illud* in 1919 and the formation of the International Missionary Council in 1921, through the ferment, transition and chaos in the wake of the Second Vatican Council and the emergence of the Lausanne Movement in the 1960s. It continues with the "rebirth" of the missionary movement after 1975 and the emergence of a vital new "World Christianity," characterized by African Initiated Churches, greater lay involvement in mission, Pentecostalism, the shift of gravity in the Christian population to the Third World and growing numbers of missionaries coming from the South. The chapter ends in 1991, the year after the official publication of John Paul II's encyclical *Redemptoris Missio* and the year of the publication of the Catholic document *Dialogue and Proclamation* as well as David J. Bosch's magisterial summary of missiology and mission theology *Transforming Mission*.

Part III develops a theology of mission for today. In Catholic, Orthodox, Conciliar Protestant, Evangelical and Pentecostal Christianity, we discern three strains of thought that grounded missionary practice and theology in the last quarter of the twentieth century. Each of the first three chapters pairs one major Catholic mission document with documents from Orthodoxy (Chapter 9), Conciliar Protestantism (Chapter 10) and Evangelicalism/Pentecostalism (Chapter 11). Theologians and missiologists who represent the distinctive perspective of each of these sets of documents are then surveyed, and the way that this perspective sheds light on the six missionary constants is explored. Chapter 9 describes a theology, shared by Vatican II's *Ad Gentes* and Orthodoxy, that understands mission as participation in the mission of the triune God *(missio Dei)*. Chapter 10 outlines *Evangelii Nuntiandi*'s and Conciliar Protestantism's vision of mission as the liberating service of the reign of God. And Chapter 11 presents the perspective of *Redemptoris Missio*, and of Evangelical and Pentecostal Christians, a perspective that insists on mission as proclamation of Jesus Christ as universal Savior.

Chapter 12 is the climax of the book. While all three approaches discussed in the previous three chapters are valid, in our opinion, we nevertheless believe that only a *synthesis* of all three can yield a theology that can ground the church in its missionary practice in these first years of the twenty-first century and the new millennium. We call this synthesis *prophetic dialogue*. It is *dialogue* in that it draws from the dialogical nature of God's trinitarian missionary life and from the appreciation of the context of human existence as good, trustworthy and holy. It is *prophetic* in two senses. On the one hand, the church in mission must speak clearly for the world's excluded, against human and ecological violence, and on behalf of God's reign of justice and peace. On the other, even in the face of the "rays of divine truth" within the world's religions, it must proclaim unhesitantly, faithfully—and yet respectfully—the name, the vision and the Lordship of Jesus Christ. Mission as prophetic dialogue must furthermore be conceived as a "single, yet complex reality" (RM 41), and so mission today needs to be understood as comprised of a number of interrelated and mutually critical elements. While church documents and theologians have proposed several sets of such elements, we propose that mission today is composed of the following six: witness and proclamation; liturgy, prayer and contemplation; justice, peace and the integrity of creation; interreligious dialogue; inculturation; and reconciliation. Mission today, we conclude, must be lived out in a bold humility: bold in prophetic witness and speech, humble in attentive dialogue.

WHAT THE READER SHOULD KNOW

As is evident from the paragraphs above, this is a very complex book. To help the reader maintain focus on the "big picture," we have provided charts within each chapter that summarize its contents in a more schematic form. Each chapter in the historical section is also accompanied by a map or maps that show the part of the world with which the chapter deals.

Also because of the book's complexity, we want to stress from the outset that, although the book contains very many details, our aim is to present neither an exhaustive systematic theology nor a comprehensive history of the Christian movement. Not every theological doctrine is treated in historical or systematic detail; not every event, movement, country, person or culture is treated in the six historical chapters. Especially in the historical section, the reader will notice that the beginning and ending dates that form the parameters of each chapter are not contiguous with preceding and following ones. Rather than a complete theology or history, therefore, our aim is to discern and present patterns in Christian theology that have shaped—explicitly or implicitly—the theology and practice of the church's mission, and to discern and present as well particular models of missionary activity that are influenced by and influence in turn the theology and life of the Christian community.

In the six historical chapters of this book it is important to note that the penultimate section of every chapter, entitled "Constants in the Context of . . . ," is written in a way that refers back to Chapter 2, where the six constants of mission are described according to the threefold typology of Justo González and Dorothee Sölle. In the last section of every historical chapter, entitled "Implications for the Theology of Mission Today," we anticipate the more systematic development of mission as prophetic dialogue laid out in Chapter 12.

We have provided abundant references in endnotes so that the reader can study in more detail particular aspects of theology or history that we have not been able to treat in depth. Very often, for example, when we refer to a particular historical person (for example, Henry Venn or Ida S. Scudder), we refer only to an article in Gerald H. Anderson et al.'s *Mission Legacies* or to Anderson's *Biographical Dictionary of Christian Missions*.[5] In these excellent volumes the reader will find ample bibliographical references.

A list of the abbreviations used in this volume can be found on pages xxi-xxii.

Part I

CONSTANTS IN CONTEXT: BIBLICAL AND THEOLOGICAL FOUNDATIONS

One of the most important things Christians need to know about the church is that *the church* is not of ultimate importance. To say this is not to deny the church's divine origin or to believe one whit less that it is "the people made one with the unity of the Father, Son and Holy Spirit" (LG 4).[1] The church is, indeed, the "universal sacrament of salvation" (LG 48; AG 1), "imbued with the hidden presence of God."[2] Nevertheless, the point of the church is not the church itself. The church's foundation and continued existence are not to provide refuge from a sinful world or to provide a warm and supportive community for lonely souls, or even less to be a plank of salvation on a tempestuous sea that threatens damnation. The point of the church is rather to point beyond itself, to be a community that preaches, serves and witnesses to the reign of God. In doing this the church shares in and continues, through the power of God's Spirit, the work of its Lord, Jesus Christ. So completely does the church live for God's reign that, when it finally is fully established, the church will be subsumed into its all-encompassing reality.[3] "Only the Kingdom . . . is absolute and it makes everything else relative" (EN 8).

It is this understanding of the church that the Second Vatican Council expresses when it describes the "pilgrim church" as "missionary by its very nature" (AG 2). Pope Paul VI in his 1975 apostolic exhortation *Evangelii Nuntiandi* expressed the same insight when he spoke of the complex act of evangelization as the church's "deepest identity" (EN 14). In his 1990 encyclical *Redemptoris Missio* Pope John Paul II teaches that missionary activity "belongs to the very nature of the Christian life" (RM 1); the United States bishops express the same thing in the lapidary phrase "to say church is to say mission" (TEE 16). Theologians have also expressed such an understanding, often in memorable phrases. In 1990 the theologians of the Theological Advisory Commission of the Federation of Asian Bishops' Conferences proposed that "the church is a community of disciples bearing witness to the Risen Lord and his Gospel. Therefore it is the process of evangelization that is the *raison d'etre* of the church."[4] Adrian

7

Hastings has written how the church does not so much *have* a mission—as if the church somehow existed *prior* to its task—rather it *is* mission as such;[5] indeed, as the phrase goes, the church of Christ does not so much have a mission as the mission of Christ has a church. Perhaps most memorable of all, theologian Emil Brunner is often quoted as saying that "the Church exists by mission, just as a fire exists by burning."[6]

What mission is exactly, of course, is notoriously difficult to define. Perhaps the best way to begin a definition is to say mission takes the church beyond itself into history, into culture, into people's lives, beckoning it constantly to "cross frontiers."[7] Pope Paul VI taught in *Evangelii Nuntiandi* that mission (or in his words, "evangelization")[8] is a complex and dynamic process by which the church seeks to convert and transform "solely through the divine power of the Message she proclaims, both the personal and collective consciences of people, the activities in which they engage, and the lives and concrete milieux which are theirs" (EN 17). First and "above all" (21), Christians witness, both personally and as a community. Second and essential, "the name, the teaching, the life, the promises, the Kingdom and the mystery of Jesus of Nazareth" (24) are proclaimed. Such proclamation needs to be done with due respect to culture and context (20) and needs to be a clear word that promotes human responsibility, development and liberation (29-31). And although it is only hinted at in the apostolic exhortation (53), evangelical proclamation must sometimes be done in the context of interreligious dialogue.[9] Third, says the pope, mission is communitarian or, better, ecclesial. It is done on behalf of the Christian community and leads to incorporation into that community (23). But it is not ecclesial for its own sake. Once incorporated into the church, Christians are themselves called to witness and proclaim the good news to the world: "It is unthinkable that a person should accept the Word and give himself to the Kingdom without becoming a person who bears witness to it and proclaims it in his turn" (24). Mission is not about recruiting new church members simply for the sake of the church; the fullness of salvation offered by the church involves the wholeness achieved in lives lived in dedication and service to God's purposes. The goal of the church's mission is not the expansion of the church for its own sake; men and women are invited into the church so that they can join a community dedicated to preaching, serving and witnessing to God's reign. It is in such dedication and service that the fullness of salvation is achieved, as men and women participate in the community that is a reflection of what God is in God's deepest identity: a community-in-mission of Father, Son and Spirit / Mystery, Word and Presence. Christians are "saved to save," "reconciled in order to reconcile."[10]

As the CWME expressed it in its 1963 meeting in Mexico City, mission is now on "six continents." In other words, it is not to be understood as certain well-established Christian countries sending women and men to particular "non-Christian" or "underdeveloped" parts of the world. Every country is a sending country, and every country is a receiving country.

The church's mission *ad gentes*, as John Paul II reminded us in 1991, still has the right to be referred to as "missionary activity proper" (RM 34). And it is important to heed Stephen Neill's warning that if everything is mission, then nothing is mission.[11] Nevertheless, we need also to pay attention to David Bosch's warning to "beware of any attempt at delineating mission too sharply."[12] Mission happens wherever the church is; it is how the church exists. Mission is the church preaching Christ for the first time; it is the act of Christians struggling against injustice and oppression; it is the binding of wounds in reconciliation; it is the church learning from other religious ways and being challenged by the world's cultures. "Missions" exist in urban multicultural neighborhoods, rural Ghanaian villages, Brazilian *favelas*, European universities, in the world's cyberspace. Mission is the local church "focusing not on its own, internal problems, but on other human beings, focusing elsewhere, in a world that calls and challenges it."[13]

As we begin this book on the theology and history of the church's mission, the centrality of mission in the church's life is something we want to note and insist on. As we have already intimated and will show in Chapter 1 and in the rest of this book, the church is *only* the church insofar as it focuses on God's reign. The church comes to be the *church* as it realizes and recognizes that it is called beyond itself. The church succeeds, struggles and sometimes fails as church to the extent that it acknowledges and attempts (however awkwardly or even mistakenly) to live out what it most deeply is. If the church focuses too much on its own survival, or its own structural development, or its own perfection, it fails to understand that in its deepest reality it is and is called to be the visible sign and instrument—the sacrament, as Vatican II calls it (LG 1, 48; AG 1)—of the communion that God is and to which all humanity is called.

Although the church has faltered in its task, it has never completely failed to be itself. Throughout varying and conflictive *contexts,* the church has been basically faithful to the *constants* that make up its mission and bestow on it its identity. Chapter 1 will focus on *context* and the church's mission; Chapter 2 will focus on the *constants* to which the church must be faithful in carrying out its mission.

1

"Missionary by Its Very Nature"

Context and the Church's Mission

THE ACTS OF THE APOSTLES:
THE CHURCH EMERGING IN MISSION

This first chapter focuses on the origins of the church as it emerges in the New Testament, particularly in the second of Luke's two-volume history of Jesus and the early community, the Acts of the Apostles. Our thesis is that a study of Acts will confirm that the church only comes to be as it understands and accepts mission anywhere and everywhere in the world. As Acts begins, the community of disciples (scattered at Jesus' arrest but gathered again in the faith that Jesus has been raised from the dead) sees itself as the true Israel, a type of spirituality, religious movement or sect within Judaism, upon which the reign of God will dawn imminently. But as Acts progresses, the community slowly and even painfully begins to realize that something else is going on as the Spirit "drives" or "leads" it to include "half-Jews" (Samaritans), individual Gentile proselytes or "God-fearers" (the Ethiopian official), worthy Gentiles (Cornelius and his household) and, finally, Gentiles *en masse* (in Antioch). Although the mission to Judaism does not cease, it becomes clearer and clearer that the future of this new "way" is not to Judaism, as a part of it, but to the whole world as a separate reality, as church. Even though the word *church* is used to designate the community in Acts occasionally (for example, 5:11; 8:1, 4; 9:31), our contention is that the disciples really do not fully *recognize* themselves as church—a separate reality from Judaism—until they recognize that they are called to a mission that has as its scope "the ends of the earth" (Acts 1:8). In a real sense, then, Pentecost was not, contrary to what is usually said, the "birthday of the church"; rather, the church is born only as the disciples of Jesus gradually and painfully realize that they are called beyond themselves to all peoples until (in Paul's formulation) the "full number of the Gentiles enter in" (Rom 11:25).

10

Mission is not only the "mother of theology," as Martin Kähler said at the turn of the twentieth century and as David Bosch has more recently reminded us.[1] Mission might also be called the "mother of the church," the great task believers have been given that binds them together, provides them with nourishment, focuses their energies, heals their sinfulness and provides them with challenge and vision. "The Christian church grew out of the apostolic proclamation of the gospel and is alive in the act of proclamation."[2]

The struggle to move beyond the centripetal dynamic of Judaism and not only to be *open* to the Gentiles but to *seek them out* was a major concern of Paul in his letters and of much of the gospel tradition.[3] Indeed, as Martin Hengel suggests, the entire history and theology of early Christianity need to be seen as "mission history" and "mission theology."[4] The Acts of the Apostles, however, perhaps more clearly than any other New Testament book, points to the origin of the church *as it engages in missionary activity.* The aim of Luke's two-volume work, contemporary commentators tell us, was to show that the mission of Jesus of preaching, serving and witnessing to the reign of God was authentically shared and continued by the community that emerged in the aftermath of his death and their experience of his resurrection.[5] Acts, it is generally acknowledged, constitutes our principal source of information on the origins of Christian mission.[6] We believe, however, that it is also fair to say that Acts is the principal New Testament source for seeing the emergence of the church's first understanding of itself. "For Luke, what makes the church is mission, and the reality at the heart of the church is the impulse of the Spirit for the increase of the Word."[7]

The Acts of the Apostles, of course, represents just one stream of New Testament theology; there is a vast and rich literature that deals more fully with much that we must take for granted here.[8] We might summarize this biblical theology, however, as follows. First, the church's mission of inclusivity and universality has its roots in the Old Testament, particularly in the vision of the prophets. Israel's election was never for its own sake, but always so that, in it, all nations would receive a blessing (Gen 12:3; Is 45:1-8; 49:1-6).[9] Second, the church's mission has its roots in the ministry and person of Jesus as he preached, served and witnessed to the reign of God and gathered about him a community that assisted him in his work (for example, Mk 1:14-45; 6:7-13; Lk 10:1-20).[10] The church, in other words, is rooted in the mission and person of Jesus (RM 13), who is both "evangel" and "evangelizer."[11] Third, the church's mission has its roots in the post-resurrection faith of the first disciples—that they were called to witness to the gospel *of* Jesus and the gospel *about* Jesus.[12] They held the firm conviction, in other words, of Jesus' universal Lordship as risen Christ, through whom humanity has direct access to God (the gospel *about* Jesus). Indeed, he himself, they believed, was "the image of the invisible God (Col 1:15), the "Word made flesh" (see Jn 1:14). This first aspect of the apostolic faith is clearly evident in Acts (for example, 2:36; 4:8-12; 8:5, 35; 10:34-42; 28:30); it is, however, especially clear in the Pauline literature (for example, Gal 2:15-20; 1 Cor 1:23-24; Rom 5:15-19; 2 Cor 5:19-21; Eph 1:7-10). At the same time, the first disciples were convinced that they were called as well to proclaim, to serve and to embody the same gospel of forgiveness, graciousness, generosity, inclusiveness and justice that Jesus had preached, served and witnessed to in his own earthly ministry (the gospel *of* Jesus). This aspect of the first disciples' faith, while not in any way the exclusive focus of Acts, finds in this New Testament book a particularly clear expression.

Our focus in this chapter, therefore, is on the Acts of the Apostles because we believe that it paints a particularly vivid picture of the church emerging in its response to the mission with which it was entrusted and provides a particularly clear angle from which to view the church being faithful to mission's *constants* in a specific *context*. Readers interested in a more comprehensive study of mission in the New Testament should consult works that deal more generally with the topic.

The Acts of the Apostles is Luke's streamlined, somewhat "unilinear,"[13] "carefully constructed,"[14] idealized and schematized,[15] highly theological history of the earliest days, months and years of the Christian community. As a historian, Luke is regarded today as generally reliable, although by no means to be read uncritically. Neither the nineteenth-century Tübingen School's skepticism nor the more "conservative" viewpoint of Catholics like A. Wickenhauser or Evangelicals like F. F. Bruce holds much sway with contemporary scholarship.[16] At the end of his study of the Gentile mission in Luke-Acts, Stephen G. Wilson concludes that Luke "intends to write good history even if he is not always successful. . . . Luke has undoubtedly made clear his own interpretation of events, but he has also left a sufficient number of lacunae and loose ends for us to be able to construct our own interpretation—and this says a lot for his basic honesty." For the "careful and critical reader Acts contains an immense amount that is of great historical value."[17] As Martin Hengel has insisted, Luke's history is "no less trustworthy than other historians of antiquity. People have done him a great injustice in comparing him too closely with the edifying, largely fictitious, romance-like writings . . . which freely invent facts as they like and when they need them."[18] In the same way that no responsible historian would dismiss Josephus's *Antiquities of the Jews* or Suetonius's *Lives of the Caesars*, no reader of Luke should dismiss his accuracy out of hand. It is true that Luke shapes the narrative, but recognizing the way that he does this is "an important step toward recognizing the *kind* of history he was attempting to write."[19]

The kind of narrative that Luke writes is theological. Wilson would disagree that Luke is a theologian, but he is in the minority.[20] Although all the scholars surveyed by Mark Allan Powell disagree on a number of points (Luke's sources, the literary genre, historical reliability, and so forth), there is one point on which all would agree: "Luke is a theologian. He wrote the book of Acts, not simply to tell interesting stories or to record facts for posterity, but in order to put forth his own distinctive ideas about God's interaction with us through Jesus Christ and the Holy Spirit."[21] While much in Acts may well enjoy historical accuracy, what is most important, says Luke Timothy Johnson, is how Luke used history to "give literary shape to a theological vision."[22] Indeed, says Jacques Dupont, Acts is "a history charged with theological meaning."[23] Luke's task, writes Robert

W. Wall, "is to interpret and grant theological significance to past events rather than to describe them objectively or with factual precision suitable for his modern readers.[24]

Luke's narrative, it must be admitted, is highly selective; his story is told through a highly schematized account of the development of ecclesial consciousness. In the gospel, the movement of the action is toward Jerusalem, where Jesus is put to death and where the community experiences his risen presence (unlike in Matthew's gospel, there are no resurrection appearances in Galilee, but only in Jerusalem). In Acts, the action moves outward from Jerusalem to Judea and Samaria and then to the "ends of the earth" (see Acts 1:8). As the mission takes shape, so does the church.

Our study of Acts in this chapter discerns seven distinct stages in this brilliant theological narrative.[25] Each stage represents a particular moment in the community's understanding of its mission and its corresponding understanding of itself as the *qahal Yahweh, ekklesia tou Theou*—or church. What we hope to show in this study is one aspect of the profound biblical basis for the ideas with which we began this chapter. What we hope emerges from our reading of Acts is, first, a clear realization that the church, even at its origin, is "missionary by its very nature"; mission, in other words, is *prior* to the church, and constitutive of its very existence. Second, we hope to show that the church's missionary nature only emerges as the community engages with particular contexts, under the direction of the Spirit; the Jewish identity of the community is transformed into the church as the community recognizes the Spirit among the Samaritans, in the Ethiopian eunuch, in Cornelius and his household, and in the community of Antioch.

SEVEN STAGES OF MISSION IN ACTS

Stage One:
Before Pentecost (Acts 1)

Stage Two:
Pentecost (Acts 2—5)

Stage Three:
Stephen (Acts 6—7)

Stage Four:
Samaria and the Ethiopian Eunuch (Acts 8)

Stage Five:
Cornelius and His Household (Acts 10:1—11:18)

Stage Six:
Antioch (Acts 11:19-26)

Stage Seven:
The Mission to the Gentiles (Acts 12—28)

Stage One: Before Pentecost

Although the origins of the church are rooted in the ministry and the person of Jesus, his mission, most New Testament scholars agree, was to preach, serve and witness to the reign of God, not to establish a community separate from Israel. Indeed, Jesus and the movement he began represented one of the many contemporary renewal movements within Judaism.[26] Also agreed upon is the fact that what Jesus understood by God's reign is impossible to capture in a clear definition; it is approximated, rather, by reflecting on Jesus' words and deeds as recorded and remembered in the gospel narratives. Jesus *preached* the reign of God mostly through parables, short and vivid stories that spoke of God's almost incredible forgiving love and/or urgent nearness. His ministry of healings and exorcism *served* the reign of God as "parables in action" that demonstrated the love and nearness of God and God's implacable opposition to evil and human suffering. And Jesus' life of inclusion—his free association with women and the poor, and his table fellowship with those thought to be sinners—was a *witness* that God's in-breaking reign was one of new chances, new social relationships and radical equality.[27] Jesus' very life, says Edward Schillebeeckx, was a parable, for in it was embodied the graciousness of the God he lived for and lived with.[28] It was because of his faithfulness to this vision and ministry that Jesus ran afoul of the religious authorities of his day, a conflict that ultimately led to his arrest and execution.[29]

While there is no doubt that this radical, inclusive understanding of God and of God's imminent rule was the foundation upon which the Jesus community built as it moved out to the Gentiles in mission, the evidence shows nevertheless that Jesus himself did not clearly conceive of a mission beyond Judaism. Even less did he foresee his disciples taking up a Gentile mission. Jesus believed, says Stephen G. Wilson in his careful study of the question, that his ministry was heralding the End, and so there was no room or time for such a mission. According to the Judaism of his day, "he maintained a positive hope for the Gentiles, but believed that this hope would be fulfilled in the apocalyptic events of the Endtime; then and only then would the Gentiles enter the kingdom of God."[30] As Stuhlmueller and Senior put it, "Jesus, in effect, was *not* the first missionary to the Gentiles. . . . The connection between the ministry of Jesus and the post-Easter missionary activity of the church is more subtle, more developmental, more rooted in the dynamics of history."[31]

But despite the fact that both the establishment of a community separate from Israel and the idea of a mission beyond Israel were probably far from the thoughts of Jesus, one might still say that Jesus laid a foundation for both. We can say, then, that the movement which began and grew after Jesus' death and resurrection was founded, in a real sense, on his vision and in his person. With the establishment of the Twelve (a symbolic action that anticipated the reconstitution of the whole of Israel—see Mk 3:13-19; Mt 10:1-4; Lk 6:1-5), the bestowal of leadership on Peter (Mt 16:13-19; Jn 21:15-19) and, at the very end, Jesus' command to celebrate a meal in his memory (Lk 22:19), the community was given—perhaps not necessarily in a fully conscious way by Jesus, but given just the same—a real sense of identity and structure. As the disciples came together in the aftermath of their experience of Jesus as raised from the dead, it had a basic shape, a basic structure and, in the witness of the risen Lord, a basic vision and message.[32]

As the Acts of the Apostles opens, we find the Twelve listening to the risen Jesus teaching them about the reign of God and telling them to wait in Jerusalem for the coming of the Holy Spirit "within a few days" (1:5). When Jesus says this, the Twelve ask whether this means that the reign of God will be inaugurated "now" (1:6), that is, with the coming of the Spirit. Jesus replies that the exact time is not theirs to know, but that they will receive power when the Holy Spirit comes, and that they will be witnesses to Jesus "in Jerusalem, throughout Judea and Samaria, yes, even to the ends of the earth" (1:8).

Jesus' command does lay out nicely the plan of the book, for this is how Luke describes the way the Spirit will lead the community in its mission and toward its identity. But it is difficult to believe that this command fits the historical facts.[33] On the one hand, as we have already pointed out, Jesus had no notion of a universal mission. On the other hand—and perhaps more significantly—the rest of the narrative in Acts reveals the community as most hesitant to accept the possibility of a Gentile mission. Perhaps it is more plausible to believe that the disciples were only being loyal to Jesus' expectation of an imminent End. This would explain both the seemingly dumb question that elicits Jesus' command (1:6) and the prediction of the "two men dressed in white" (1:10) that the Jesus who ascended to heaven before their eyes would return in the same way (1:11). That the disciples were expecting an imminent inauguration of God's reign through the returning Jesus also explains the mood of "intense eschatological expectation" that is still detectable beneath these early verses and chapters of the book.[34] The disciples did not go off to "Judea, Samaria and the ends of the earth" immediately. Rather, after Jesus is taken from their sight, they return to Jerusalem, the site of eschatological fulfillment, and wait for him to come again.

Another indication that this waiting in Jerusalem was one of imminent expectation of the reign of God was the decision to fill up the number of the Twelve and the subsequent election of Matthias (1:15-26). The institution of the Twelve was no doubt intended as a symbolic action by which it was declared that the reign of God was even now breaking into human history.[35] The notion of the "restoration" of Israel was a major part of the apocalyptic/eschatological/messianic expectation of Jesus' day, and it appears as a significant theme in Luke's theology.[36] Now, waiting for the End in Jerusalem, the Twelve are reconstituted after the defection and death of Judas, making sure that the one chosen has the same qualifications as they for witnessing to Jesus' resurrection ("one of those who was of our company while the Lord Jesus moved among us, from the baptism of John until the day he was taken up from us" [1:21-22]). Jesus had said that the Twelve would sit on thrones to judge the twelve tribes of Israel (Lk 22:30; Mt 19:28); the action of electing Matthias was to make sure that all of those thrones were occupied![37] Further indication of the significance of this incident in the scheme of Acts is that, a number of years later, when Herod had James (the brother of John and son of Zebedee) put to death (12:1-2), there was no attempt to replace him in the number of the Twelve. By that time, as we shall see, the community had recognized that a nationalistic restoration of Israel was not in its future, and so the symbolic significance and eschatological urgency of the Twelve had faded in importance.[38]

But now they waited. Their "experience of Jesus raised from the dead and his teaching on the kingdom," writes James G. Dunn, "had given them to believe (or confirmed them in their belief) that the kingdom . . . was about to be restored to Israel. Such an expectation indicates a hope fully in continuity with the hope of Israel's prophets (the restoration of Israel), but still constructed by the terms of that earlier hope."[39] There is, however, a sense of emptiness and even awkwardness in these days of prayerful waiting: "uncertainty, awkwardness and powerlessness—just what needed to be remedied by the coming of the Spirit at Pentecost."[40]

Stage Two: Pentecost

"When the day of Pentecost came" (2:1), the community certainly experienced eschatological fulfillment, but it was a fulfillment quite different from what its members had expected. The inauguration of the expected messianic times was not by Jesus' second coming but by the descent of the Spirit. The Spirit endowed the community with the gift of prophecy, and Peter was the community's spokesperson. In his speech (2:14-40) Peter quotes at length the prophet Joel, who spoke about the eschatological times as a pouring of the Spirit on all humanity (2:17), summoning people to call on the name of the Lord, whom Peter equates with the risen Jesus.

The Pentecost experience had not been quite what the community had expected, but it was still enough within the orbit of Jewish thought to be interpreted in Judaism's own terms. The "church" had not yet been born, but the Jerusalem community did take a small step toward its realization. What happened at Pentecost, in the community's new understanding, was not the final end but a fulfillment that made the community of Jesus' disciples the "restored remnant" of Israel.[41] The Jesus community, it now begins to think, had been sent to Israel once more to give Israel a second chance, despite its previous rejection of Jesus as Messiah,[42] and so to be saved "from this generation which has gone astray" (2:40). David Stanley explains the understanding that dawned on the community subsequent to the dramatic events of Pentecost. What it realized at this point, he says, was that

> the "last age" comprised two moments. There was a time of preparation, during which the invisible Lord by the Spirit worked through the community for the building up of a spiritual kingdom. Consequently their role in this period was to assist in aggregating Israel as a whole to the new faith.

The second period was to be marked by Christ's second coming, when he would "bring the times of refreshment" and "the restoration of all things" (Acts 3:20-21). While the disciples did not know the date of this parousia, they were certain of one thing: the Lord's coming was contingent upon the conversion of Israel (Acts 3:19).[43]

The Pentecost narrative recounts in some detail the fact that those who heard Peter's sermon that morning were people from all over the world: "We are Parthians, Medes, and Elamites. We live in Mesopotamia, Judea and Cappadocia, Pontus, the Province of Asia, Phrygia, and Pamphylia, Egypt, and the regions of Libya around Cyrene. There are even visitors from Rome—all Jews, or those who have come over to Judaism; Cretans and Arabs, too" (2:9-11). It is often thought that this internationality, which implied the reversal of the curse of Babel (Gen 11:1-9), was a sign of the birth of the church. It is also thought that Peter's citation of Joel 3:1 and the statement that the promise was made to all present "and to all those still far off whom the Lord our God calls" (2:39) signaled the inauguration of the mission to the Gentiles. But while Pentecost is surely a hint of things to come, the text does say (2:11) that these are all Jews or proselytes—Gentiles who had converted to Judaism, the males of whom had been circumcised and had accepted Jewish customs and dietary regulations. The function of Peter's speech is to show, rather, that what now has arrived is the fulfillment of Judaism itself. Joel's prophecy about the Spirit being poured out on "all humankind" (2:17) need not be taken literally in its Jewish context, and the phrase "to all those still far off" (2:39) is "a minor note in a speech that is mainly concerned to address all Israel."[44] Robert Tannehill suggests that the presence of Jews from all parts of the world and of many languages introduces a symbolic dimension into the narrative that strains "against the limited historical contexts in which they are found." It is the goal of the gospel in the first place "to address all Israel, scattered throughout the world," but the gospel "must also address the gentile inhabitants of the lands from which these Jews came."[45]

But this second development will happen only later. At this point the disciples are convinced that they are in the last days, and that the end and fulfillment of Israel is very near. Their immediate success certainly confirmed them in this opinion. Their number was increasing daily (2:47); they enjoyed an intense and happy community life (2:42-47; 4:32-35)—surely a sign of the End; and they enjoyed the esteem of many in Jerusalem (5:12-16). It seemed right to be content to remain in Jerusalem, live the life of the restored remnant and preach the not-long-delayed restoration of all God's people. Even the fact that they experience persecution from the priests, Sadducees, the leaders, the scribes and the Sanhedrin (4:1-7; 5:17-42) does not deter them. Indeed, it gives them determination to go on preaching and even makes them feel fortunate to have been "judged worthy of ill-treatment for the sake of the Name" (5:41). It certainly seemed like the eschatological time was here.

The notion of a systematic, general Gentile mission or the notion that following Jesus entailed a radical break with Jewish traditions was very far from the disciples' minds. Continuity, not discontinuity, with Judaism was what they strove for, and the idea of receiving Gentiles not yet converted to Judaism was, at this point, inconceivable. To other Jews, as well, this group seemed to be no different from a number of groups with some quirky and yet not unorthodox beliefs and practices. Followers of "the Way" were perceived at this period little differently from groups like the Essenes or the Pharisees.[46] Acts 2—5 presents, despite persecutions and the incident of Ananias and Sapphira (5:1-11), a community that was very much of "one heart and one mind" (4:32). As James G. Dunn points out, the disciples of Jesus were still Jews. They continued to observe the law and did not interpret their traditions of Jesus' words and actions in a way that was hostile to it; they continued to pray at the temple, presumably continuing to be part of the temple sacrificial cult; and they had little concern for the Gentiles or for mission outside the city of Jerusalem.[47]

But this idyllic time would soon be over as the disciples begin to deal with members of the community who have differing ideas about Judaism and its ultimate adequacy.

Stage Three: Stephen

At the beginning of Chapter 6 the idyllic melody of the first five chapters switches abruptly into a minor key "as Luke introduces the first note of serious discord into the history of the Jerusalem church."[48] On the surface, the situation doesn't seem too serious—it's almost as if a mountain is being made out of a mole hill: as the number of disciples grew, the ones who spoke Greek (literally, "Hellenists") complained that their widows were being neglected in the daily food distribution as compared with those widows who spoke Hebrew (literally, "Hebrews"). The Twelve settle the dispute by appointing seven men who would take care of it (see 6:1-6).

As Lucien Legrand says, however, the issue was far more serious than a "demand for a welfare department."[49] Perhaps, he says, we are given a glimpse of the original pluralism of the missionary views of the Jerusalem church, or, as Dunn says, the scene presents a picture of linguistic and cultural diversity, and probably social diversity as well.[50] In any case, what seems to be rumbling beneath the surface in this passage is a theological disagreement between the two groups. The Hellenists were probably Greek-speaking, Hellenized Jews who were living in Jerusalem and had been converted early on to the Way. Being more open to Hellenistic ways of thinking and living than their Jewish sisters and brothers in the community, they may have had a less "traditional" view of Judaism. Perhaps they were even attracted to becoming disciples of Jesus because they recognized that, as Hengel writes, the message of Jesus "had affinities with the universalist Greek-speaking world and perhaps even with some themes in Greek thought. We can see in it not only close connections with Jewish wisdom, but sometimes also echoes of Greek gnomic wisdom and above all of Cynic thought. We find in that the universality which E. Käsemann has described by the phrase 'the call of freedom.'"[51] Hengel goes as far as to claim that the Hellenists in the Jerusalem church seemed to "put forward the offensive claim that the significance of Jesus as the Messiah of Israel essentially super-seded that of Moses in the history of salvation: the gospel of Jesus took the place of the Jewish gospel of exodus and Sinai as God's concluding, incompa-rable eschatological revelation."[52]

Be that as it may, it seems fairly certain from their Greek names that the seven chosen were all Hellenists. In addition, because nothing more is really said about waiting on tables, because the men chosen are "deeply spiritual and prudent" (6:3), and because two of them—Stephen and Philip—are shown to be energetic preachers, commentators agree that the seven may have already been leaders in the Hellenistic part of the Jerusalem community.[53]

As the narrative continues, Stephen is spotlighted as "a man filled with grace and power who worked great wonders and signs among the people" (6:8). Cer-tain Hellenistic Jews from the "Synagogue of Roman Freedmen" are reported to have tried to take Stephen on in debate, "but they proved no match for the wisdom and spirit with which he spoke" (6:9). Obviously scandalized by the brand of Judaism Stephen was preaching but not able to refute him, they did what frustrated people sometimes do in similar circumstances: they played dirty. They persuaded some men to bring false charges against him—they accused him of speaking against Moses, God, the holy place and the law—and this got the people, the elders and the scribes so perturbed that Stephen was arrested and hauled before the Sanhedrin (8:11-15).

Luke has thus set the stage for the speech that, Luke Timothy Johnson says, is "the key Luke provides . . . for the interpretation of his entire two-volume narrative."[54] R. P. C. Hanson says that the speech does not point to the move-ment of the community toward the Gentiles, but it does prepare the reader for the movement away from traditional Judaism.[55] Stephen's speech is Luke's first hint that the community's future does not lie within Judaism or Jewish theol-ogy. Faith in Jesus implies something more. Stephen does not yet grasp fully what that "more" is, but he—and the Hellenist theology his speech probably represents—suspects that the "more" is there. His speech is the first intimation that the Way is a discrete religious system, intimately connected to and yet—because of the centrality of Jesus—distinctly separate from its Jewish roots.[56]

Stephen's speech as skillfully constructed by Luke[57] surveys four crucial periods in Israel's history as represented by four (or five) major characters: Abraham (7:2-8), Joseph (7:9-18), Moses (7:19-44), and David/Solomon (7:45-50). The thread that connects these four periods in the speech, says John Stott, is the fact that "in none of them was God's presence limited to any particular place. On the contrary, the God of the Old Testament was the living God, a God on the move and on the march, who was always calling his people out to fresh adventures, and always accompanying and directing them as they went."[58] But, as Stephen intimates throughout and says with no mincing of words in the speech's conclusion (7:51-53), Israel has consistently opposed God's lead by opposing and murdering God's representatives, including, most recently, "the Just One" (7:52), Jesus. God's Spirit, Stephen seems to be saying, has always pointed Judaism beyond itself as it was called forward—to the land of Canaan (Abraham), to Egypt (Joseph), out of Egypt and into the desert (Moses), and to the building of a temple even though "the Most High does not dwell in buildings made by human hands" (David/Solomon [7:48]). But time and time again Israel settled for the safer way, being jealous of Joseph (7:9), fashioning the golden calf in the desert (7:41-43), and thinking that God's presence was confined to a building (7:48-50)—and so not heeding the promises to Abraham, Joseph, Moses and the line of prophets down to Jesus. "Thus," summarizes John J. Kilgallen, "the speech is overtly a lengthy argument of accusation, contending that a review of Israel's history up to the present generation will show that the children are like their fathers, always stiff-necked and uncircumcised of heart, always in opposition to the Holy Spirit of God. All sections of the speech can be understood as contributing strength to Stephen's argument."[59]

But ultimately, argues Kilgallen, it is Jesus, "the one means necessary for salvation" (Kilgallen makes reference to 4:12), who is "the central proclamation of the Stephen episode taken as a whole."[60] Central to Stephen's conception of Israel's history, says David Stanley, "lies a profound intuition of the central truth of the apostolic preaching: Christ's death at the hands of the Jews and His resurrection by the power of God the Father," a truth that lays bare the "relatively ephemeral nature of Judaism," as well as a "basic incompatibility" between Judaism (which seems destined to turn in on itself) and the new faith in Jesus (which is a step in trust of the God who always calls humanity beyond itself).[61] The centrality of Jesus and the kerygmatic nature of the speech is confirmed by Wilson when he observes that Stephen's arguments from the history of Israel do not appear to be enough to deserve his death. "In the end it is not his attitude to the Law and the Temple, but his confession of Christ which, in Luke's view, is the final cause of his death."[62]

Stephen is dragged outside the city (7:58) and stoned, confessing Jesus as Lord (7:59) and imitating Jesus' forgiveness of his executioners as he dies (7:60). Luke very incidentally mentions that those who stoned Stephen ("the witnesses") "piled their cloaks at the feet of a young man named Saul" (7:58) and that Saul "concurred in the act of killing" (8:1).[63] Thus is introduced the character of Saul/Paul, to whom Luke will give such an important part in the story's latter half. Great things lay in store for him, and for the church. For the moment, however, Luke focuses on the fact that the day of Stephen's death "saw the beginning of a great persecution of the church in Jerusalem" (8:1), with "all except the apostles" scattering throughout Judea and Samaria.

Commentators note the strangeness of this fact. "Could it indeed be the case," Dunn asks, "that the persecution ignored the leaders of the movement being persecuted? Such a claim beggars the imagination."[64] The proposal put forth by a number of scholars is that the persecution was not aimed at the Hebrews (6:1)—those who will later be called "Jewish Christians"[65]—at all. Rather, it was aimed at the Hellenists, those members of the community who, like Stephen, questioned the adequacy of Judaism, and was conducted by Hellenistic Jews in Jerusalem, led by Saul.[66] Luke Timothy Johnson concurs with this opinion but says that even if we take Luke at his word, the persecution seems to have been a short one, for in 9:31 Luke notes that the community throughout all of Judea, Samaria and Galilee was at peace. In any case, he says, "Whatever the historical basis for the persecution, its literary function as a narrative transition device is obvious. The Jerusalem section is now essentially closed."[67] As the disciples scatter, the preaching of the gospel widens in surprising ways, and the community begins to have an inkling of what God is calling it to become.

Stage Four: Samaria and the Ethiopian Eunuch

The Hellenists may have had to flee Jerusalem under persecution, but that did not stop them from preaching the word (8:4). Chapter 8 focuses on the ministry of Philip, who had previously been introduced as one of the "seven" (6:5). This chapter and the next (which recounts the conversion of Saul) are "bridge chapters" to what Luke no doubt considers the great breakthrough of these early years—the full-blown mission to the Gentiles that will call forth the community into its consciousness of being the church. What we see in Chapter 8 is the gospel including, first, "half-Jews"—Samaritans—and then the inclusion of the Ethiopian eunuch, one who is either a Gentile "God-fearer" friendly to Judaism but unable because of his condition to become a Jew, or a proselyte who is, as a eunuch, nevertheless marginalized within his adopted faith. Step by step the circle is becoming wider, and the community is becoming clearer about what God is calling it to be.

John Stott comments that it is hard for contemporary readers to fathom the boldness of Philip in preaching to the Samaritans. They were "despised by the Jews as hybrids in both race and religion, as both heretics and schismatics."[68] In the eyes of Jews from Judea, says Luke Timothy Johnson, the Samaritans "were at best among the 'lost sheep' of Israel."[69] But when Philip preached and performed exorcisms and healings (8:6-8), the Samaritans—these "half-Jews"—responded positively and accepted baptism, apparently in great numbers (8:12). As a kind of confirmation of the activity by the mother community in Jerusalem, Peter and John (two of the Twelve, the leaders of the Jerusalem community) were sent and, as it were, completed Philip's work by imposing hands on the newly baptized Samaritans so that they received the Spirit (8:14-17). Luke, it seems, averts to the dangers to which moving outside Judaism is prey—Simon the Magician certainly misunderstands the meaning of the power that the gospel brings (8:18-24)—but it is clear that the mission is legitimate, since even Peter and John preach to the Samaritans on the way back to Jerusalem (8:25).

In 8:26 Luke begins his marvelous story of the conversion of the Ethiopian eunuch. Philip is again the preacher, but he preaches on divine initiative: it is an angel who tells Philip to go to the road that goes from Jerusalem to Gaza (8:26), and it is the Spirit who tells him to catch up with the eunuch's chariot (8:29) and snatches Philip away when his work was finished (8:39). God is moving the community beyond its borders, much like Stephen, Philip's fellow Hellenist, had said God was constantly doing in Israel's history. And the members of the Way were responding.

There is no unanimity of opinion regarding the identity of the eunuch. Stephen G. Wilson insists that he was a proselyte, and that the word *eunuch* can mean either a person with a physical deformity or a high official or treasurer. Wilson opts for the latter in view of the fact that Luke wants Cornelius to be the first Gentile convert (Acts 10); the Ethiopian eunuch's conversion, in other words, would be that of a semi-Jew.[70] This would make the story one of a step beyond the conversion of the Samaritans but not as far as the conversion of a full Gentile. John Stott believes the man was a physical eunuch but not a Gentile.[71] Luke Timothy Johnson takes a middle position. The man was certainly a eunuch, but one who because of his condition "did not enjoy the full privileges of participation in the people."[72] As such, therefore, his conversion "does not yet represent a formal opening to the Gentiles, but rather to those who were marginalized. . . . He is one of the righteous from among every nation whom God is calling to the restored people."[73]

Tannehill, Dunn and Hengel, however, argue that the Ethiopian is indeed both a eunuch and a Gentile. Although the term *eunuch* can also denote a political and military official, the fact that the text reads "an Ethiopian eunuch, a court official" (8:27) suggests that this official was indeed castrated.[74] That the man was a Gentile is suggested from the fact that he comes from a land that "represented the limit of common geographical knowledge,"[75] and from the fact that according to Deuteronomy 23:1 (verse 2 in the English translation) men without genitals could not be admitted into the "community of the Lord." Isaiah 56:3-4 is a vision of the reversal of Deuteronomy's prohibition, as both foreigners and eunuchs gain access to God's people. Perhaps the story of the eunuch points to the breathtaking fulfillment of Isaiah's prophecy.[76] Here is a man who would be a member of God's people if he could, who makes pilgrimage to Jerusalem, and who reads the scriptures. If he is not a Jew, he is certainly close to Judaism and worthy of inclusion in God's people.

However one chooses to identify the Ethiopian (we would tend to be persuaded by this last set of arguments), the story is clearly one of the expanding vision of the early community, a vision that for the Jerusalem community was probably questionable, even scandalous. Just how difficult these moves are will be made clear in the Cornelius story in chapters 10 and 11.

But to return to the narrative in chapter 8, Philip approaches the man, who is reading from the fifty-third chapter of Isaiah. Philip asks whether he really grasps what he is reading (8:30), and the eunuch replies, "How can I . . . unless someone explains it to me?" (8:31). And so Philip explains the passage to him and uses it as a starting point to tell him "the good news of Jesus" (8:35). When they come to some water, the eunuch asks if anything prevents him from being baptized; and since nothing does—not his physical state, not his foreignness, not his blackness, not his being a Gentile—Philip baptizes him (8:38). The story ends as Philip is snatched away by the Spirit and the eunuch continues on his way to Ethiopia, the "ends of the earth," rejoicing (8:39).

Stage Five: Cornelius and His Household

Chapter 9 might be described as a kind of *entre act* in the drama that Luke is unfolding. It narrates the amazing conversion of Saul/Paul from persecutor of Jesus (9:4) to zealous evangelist of him, with a hint of his later role in the narrative (9:15-16). It also gets Peter out of Jerusalem to Lydda and Joppa, where he is in position for "the most critical phase of the expansion of God's people"[77]—the conversion of Cornelius. As Luke Timothy Johnson describes the setting of the scene:

After the interlude devoted to the call of Saul who would be the elect vessel for carrying the name to the Gentiles (9:1-30), Luke again showed the work of Peter in Judea, healing the lame, raising the dead, and at the same time moving geographically and ethnically closer to the edge, to the place by the sea in Joppa, where he resided with the ritually impure tanner Simon, ready to hear the call from the Gentile city of Caesarea (9:31-42). Now at last Luke is ready to show how the Church made this most fundamental and dangerous step, which would involve the greatest struggle and demand the most fundamental self-reinterpretation for the nascent messianic movement, which in fact would in principle establish its identity as a universal and not simply ethnic religion.[78]

Wilson notes that no other narrative in Acts is given more "epic treatment" than the Cornelius story. Not only is all of chapter 10 and two-thirds of chapter 11 devoted to its telling, but chapter 15 repeats the story once more in shortened form.[79] The story begins in the Roman city of Caesarea, about fifty or sixty miles north of where Peter is staying in Joppa. Luke's readers are introduced to Cornelius, a centurion "of the Roman cohort Italica" (10:1). While "the implication is that he was still a serving officer, with soldiers at his command (10:7),"[80] Dunn is not so sure. There are no records of any Italian cohort stationed at Caesarea, nor would it be likely for Roman troops to be stationed there during the reign of Herod Agrippa. Perhaps Cornelius and his family, together with some loyal former subordinates (10:7), had retired to Caesarea.[81] Cornelius and his household are described as being "religious and God-fearing" (10:1), and he is described as well as being generous to the local people and as a man of constant prayer (10:2). This description may not indicate that Cornelius was a "proselyte of the gate," a God-fearer in the technical sense of a Gentile who had accepted Jewish monotheism and ethical standards and who attended Jewish synagogue without fully accepting Judaism (in other words, circumcision).[82] But it is clear that Cornelius *is* a Gentile, and a very good man. Wilson proposes that Luke is making Cornelius a model for what Gentiles are capable of as human beings, and so worthy of association with Jews and incorporation into God's restored people: "All things considered, there is not much to choose between a Jew and a Gentile. There is no need for Jews to look down their noses as if they were an inferior breed, for God has shown that the pious centurion is subject to his guidance and blessings as much as any thoroughbred Jew."[83]

One afternoon, while at prayer, Cornelius has a vision. A messenger of God comes to him and tells him to send for Peter at Joppa. Accordingly, Cornelius sends two servants and a devout soldier to Joppa, after explaining to them what he had experienced (10:3-8). The narrative then "fast forwards" to noon the next day, as the three men from Cornelius are nearing the city. Peter goes up to the roof to pray, becomes hungry and asks for some food, and while he is waiting for it to be prepared he falls into a trance. The sky opens and a large canvas comes down, and inside "were all the earth's four-legged creatures and reptiles and birds of the sky" (10:12). A voice says that he should kill what he wants of the animals and eat, to which the astonished Peter replies, "Sir, it is unthinkable! I have never eaten anything unclean or impure in my life" (10:14). But the voice answers, "What God has purified you are not to call unclean" (10:15). The vision repeats itself three times, and as Peter puzzles over its meaning, the men from Cornelius arrive at the house, and the Spirit tells Peter to go down and "set out with them unhesitatingly" (10:20). The men tell Peter who has sent them and that Cornelius has asked him to come to Caesarea to hear what he has to say (10:22). Peter, in a gesture that was later to shock the Jerusalem community—for no Jew would dare entertain Gentiles—"invited them in and treated them as guests" (10:23).

The next day Peter sets out with Cornelius's three messengers, and Cornelius is pictured as waiting for them with "his relatives and close friends" (10:24). Cornelius greets Peter in a way that obviously embarrasses the apostle, and Cornelius leads Peter into the crowded house. Dunn significantly entitles this whole section (10:1-29) "The Conversion of Peter,"[84] for while it is the conversion of *Cornelius* that is being narrated, at a whole other level Peter, and with him the whole community, is being transformed. As Peter knows all too well, "it is not proper for a Jew to associate with a Gentile or to have dealings with him," but he also is convinced that "God has made it clear to me that no one should call any person unclean or impure" (10:28). Peter finds out why Cornelius has sent for him, and then he begins to proclaim to Cornelius and those assembled "the good news of peace proclaimed through Jesus Christ who is Lord of all" (10:36).

Practically in the middle of his story, the Spirit descends on all the listeners and—to the surprise of the Jews that had accompanied Peter from Joppa—Peter asks what would prevent these Gentiles from being baptized (10:44-48). Then he gives orders for Cornelius and his household to be "baptized in the name of Jesus Christ" (10:48).

Acceding to their request, Peter stayed with Cornelius and his household a few more days. When he returned to Jerusalem, however, he had some explaining to do. The text is subtle, but it makes a point that not everyone in the Jerusalem community had approved of Peter's decision. Samaritans were one thing; they were, after all, half-Jews. The Ethiopian eunuch was probably considered a rare exception. But here was a whole Gentile household receiving admittance into the community. Luke emphasizes the gravity of the moment by having Peter tell the whole story again. Peter was convinced that he had acting according to the promptings of the Spirit. There was no question about it, he explained. The Holy Spirit had descended upon these Gentiles, "just as it had upon us at the beginning" (11:15). Peter told the community that if God had given the Gentiles the same Spirit, who was he to interfere? (11:17). With this, the Jerusalem community "stopped objecting, and instead began to glorify God in these words: 'If this be so, then God has granted life-giving repentance even to the Gentiles'" (11:18).

Even to the Gentiles! Another major development in the growing consciousness of the community had taken place. The community recognizes that not only must it go to Jews, but that it can also go to Gentiles. Even Gentiles can partake in the blessings of the messianic age, and Jews and Gentiles can live and work together in bringing the message to them. This episode of the conversion of Cornelius is a real breakthrough, says Tannehill. The conversion of the Ethiopian eunuch was a "private and isolated event,"[85] an exception to the general rule, whereas the conversion of Cornelius was public, in the presence of witnesses, a whole group of people, and effected through the instrumentality and, ultimately, however reluctantly, with the approval of the Jerusalem leadership. Tannehill shows quite convincingly how the narrative is a masterpiece of narration in which divine and human efforts intertwine.[86] God is showing the community of Jesus a new way, and the community—like Abraham, Joseph, Moses and David/Solomon in Stephen's defense in chapter 7—is following God's lead. With the baptism of Cornelius and his household, "a redefinition of the religion itself is in process."[87]

Stage Six: Antioch

But the Lucan narrative pushes the consciousness of the community even further. The Cornelius story ends in the middle of chapter 11. Verse 19 starts a new episode, only twenty-one verses long in contrast, but in many ways, perhaps even more significant. Andrew Walls calls this episode "the first real encounter of the Christian faith with the pagan world," and "one of the most critical events in Christian history."[88] After the Cornelius episode, readers are ready for the climax in the drama that Luke is crafting.

In 11:19 the Hellenists who had been scattered because of the persecution after Stephen's death are reintroduced to the readers. Before it was learned that they had scattered throughout Judea and Samaria (8:1); now Luke reveals that some had gone as far as Phoenicia, Cyprus and Antioch. Their evangelization was confined to Jews, presumably the Hellenistic Jews of the Diaspora. "However," we read in two astounding sentences in verses 20 and 21, "some of the men of Cyprus and Cyrene among them who had come to Antioch began to talk even to the Greeks," and "a great number of them believed and were converted to the Lord." In the Cornelius episode, great pains were taken to show how worthy Cornelius and his friends and household were to enter into the community. Here in Antioch, one of the great cities of the Roman Empire,[89] the impression is given that the preaching is more inclusive, more programmatically aimed at Gentiles—former Gentiles or proselytes, Gentiles attracted to Judaism, and other Gentiles.[90] Antioch was where "the complete breakthrough to an open mission to the Gentiles took place,"[91] where Jewish and Gentile converts lived side by side.

The impression given is also that the conversion of Cornelius had not been the cause of this more general Gentile evangelization and inclusive community; indeed, because of the connection of the Hellenists from Cyprus and Cyrene who came to Antioch in the wake of the Jerusalem persecution, one could make the case that this series of events takes place before or simultaneously with the conversion of Cornelius.[92] It is almost as if a new realization is breaking out in several different directions, as the Spirit coaxes the community to recognize the full implications of Jesus' Lordship. In Luke's schematic presentation of the development of this recognition, however, the more general preaching to Gentiles is placed after the more specific Cornelius episode.[93]

The radical nature of what had happened in Antioch is hinted at in several ways. The first hint is that the gospel was presented in terms of the "Lord Jesus" (11:20). Whereas in all previous proclamations, says Andrew Walls, the significance of Jesus had been expressed by the use of the Jewish title "Messiah" (translated in Greek literally as *Christos*), the anonymous Cypriots and Cyrenians speak to Antiochene Gentiles in terms that they could better understand. Jesus was "Lord"—*Kyrios*—"the title Hellenistic pagans gave to their cult divinities."[94] Such a move was as radical as it was vital. It was radical because, for the first time, the gospel message was being presented in terms that moved beyond the pale of Judaism. It was vital because it is doubtful whether the Gentiles to whom the gospel was preached "could have understood the significance of Jesus in any other way."[95] The substitution of one word is perhaps a small indication of a larger program of what we would call today inculturation and a sign that believers in Jesus had seen Jesus' salvific role as one that went far beyond Judaism and was valid for all the world.

A second indication of the significance of this passage is that, when news reached Jerusalem, the community there sent a trusted representative—Barnabas, who like some of the Antioch evangelists was himself a Hellenist from Cyprus (4:36)—to investigate the situation. Like Peter and John, who were sent from Jerusalem to investigate the earlier breakthrough of the gospel to the half-Jew Samaritans (8:14), what Barnabas discovered was that God's grace was truly at work, and, true to his name (Barnabas means "son of encouragement" we are told in 4:36), "he encouraged them all to remain firm in their commitment to the Lord" (11:24). Unsaid, but perhaps quite significant, Barnabas did not have to "complete" the evangelization as Peter and John had needed to do (8:15-17). Barnabas's leadership skill, matched with his own integrity and holiness, was considerable, it seems, for the community flourished and grew (11:24). As subsequent events proved, Barnabas also possessed splendid judgment of character—and we would venture to say a sense of risk—in traveling to Tarsus to find

Saul and persuade him to work with him in Antioch (11:25). He had already sponsored Saul when Saul had returned to Jerusalem after having to flee Damascus (9:27); now his "realization that Saul's talents could best be used in a mixed community like that of Antioch was a stroke of genius, from which both Saul and the Antiochean Christians were to profit."[96]

A third and final sign in the text that the developments at Antioch were a breakthrough for the community's growing consciousness of itself as "church" is the statement in verse 26 that "it was in Antioch that the disciples were called Christians for the first time." Although Luke Timothy Johnson suggests that the name "Christians" as given by outsiders (probably the Roman authorities) has a slightly negative connotation (he compares the designation with the contemporary nickname "Moonies"),[97] and although it is used only twice more in the New Testament (in Acts 26:28 and 1 Pet 4:16),[98] Hengel insists that the name does indicate that the community was perceived as having become "an independent organization over against the Jewish synagogue community. To the outsider, the successful messianic sect could now appear as a group on its own, which had detached itself from Judaism. It was given its own name, the independent character of which made it fundamentally different from earlier designations like 'Galilean' or 'Nazorean' (Acts 24.5) which had referred to Jewish groups."[99] Perhaps this borders on overstatement, but it does seem significant that Luke gives his readers this information at this point. The community has received a distinct name, and it would make sense that Luke is citing the name with approval. Jürgen Moltmann even speculates that it was at Antioch that the word *church* was used for the first time. The word, he says, points to the community's realization that it was different from the synagogue and "contains an element that is critical of the law, and a rejection of the temple cult in Jerusalem."[100]

The Jesus movement has altered itself—always, of course, following the lead of the Spirit—significantly. It has become much more than it understood itself to be before Pentecost or during the idyllic days in Pentecost's aftermath. Stephen's intuitions about the movement's fundamental difference from Judaism have been borne out, as more and more Gentiles come to be added to the number that are being saved (see 2:47). In addition, as more and more Jews (but not all) reject the message—a rejection documented in the remaining chapters of the work—the priority of a longer mission with a worldwide scope emerges with more and more clarity. And with expanding consciousness of mission comes an expanding consciousness of being church.[101] This, however, is the story we will tell in the seventh and final stage of Luke's history.

Stage Seven: The Mission to the Gentiles

The remaining seventeen chapters of Acts (12—28) paint a picture of a steadily expanding mission to the Gentiles, although Luke is careful to show the continuity of this movement with the community's Jewish roots rather than with its discontinuity.[102] The last verses of chapter 11 (27-30) once again establish a link between the new community in Antioch and the community in Jerusalem, and chapter 12 narrates Herod's execution of James (the brother of John [12:2], the son of Zebedee, one of the Twelve), Peter's arrest and subsequent miraculous escape from prison and the grisly death of Herod. This is a last glance at the Jerusalem community. Jerusalem will only figure incidentally in the narrative from now on as the place where the important decision is made regarding Gentile freedom from the law (15:1-35) and where Paul is arrested as he begins his journey in chains to Rome (21:15—23:11). Chapter 13 begins the second half of the book, in which the spotlight will be on Paul and his mission.[103]

Having returned from their relief mission in Jerusalem,[104] Barnabas and Saul are singled out by the community under the direction of the Spirit and are sent off on what will later be recognized as Saul/Paul's "first missionary journey" (12:25—13:3). Although it is clear that they preached to both Jews and Gentiles along the way (13:5-12), the central focus of this section is Paul's preaching in the Roman colony and administrative center of Pisidian Antioch.[105] The sermon that Paul gives is probably typical of one he would have given in synagogues to Jews and Gentile God-fearers and has parallels both with Jesus' inaugural sermon at Nazareth (Lk 4) and Peter's inaugural sermon at Pentecost (Acts 2). The Jews in Paul's audience at first react positively, but then, on the following sabbath, when "almost the entire city gathered to hear the word of God" (13:44), meaning obviously that there were many Gentiles in attendance, the Jews became "very jealous" (13:45), abusive and obstinate. In response, Barnabas and Paul issue the first of three formal declarations in this latter half of Acts (the other two occur in 18:4-7 and 28:25-28) that although the Jews must be preached to first, because they rejected the message, "we now turn to the Gentiles" (13:46). The Gentiles, for their part, were "delighted," and "responded to the word of the Lord with praise" (13:48). Paul will not stop going to the Jews, as the rest of the narrative makes clear, but we do have sounded in this passage a clear warning of what will eventually happen in a more final way: although it is not the fault of the emerging Christian church, the Jews do generally reject the message and the Gentiles accept it. What begins to develop in the community's understanding is the conviction, expressed explicitly by Paul in his agonizing reflections in Romans and more subtly in Luke, that Israel will be converted only when the "full number of Gentiles enter in" (Rom 11:25).[106] The future (for Paul, and maybe even for Luke, somewhat sadly)[107] lay with the Gentiles, and the recognition of this and the response to the mission it entailed would mean the full emergence of the "church."

After they had been driven out of Pisidian Antioch through the treachery of some Jews, and after having preached to both Jews and Greeks at Iconium and narrowly escaping death in Lystra, Paul and Barnabas return home to Antioch, where they report to the congregation there how God "had opened the door of faith to the Gentiles" (14:27). Their return sets up what both Johnson and Wilson call a "watershed" in the theological history Luke is narrating: the council at Jerusalem.[108] Although it has not been stated explicitly in the narrative thus far, the readers now understand the full radicality of the community's practice in Antioch. When some men arrived at Antioch from Judea and began insisting on the necessity of circumcision for Gentile Christians in the community, there was so much controversy that a decision was made to send Paul, Barnabas and several others to Jerusalem so that they could take the matter up with the community's leadership there (15:1-2).

In brief but theologically rich detail, Luke describes this crucial moment in the church's emerging self-realization. The delegation from Antioch was warmly welcomed in Jerusalem and "reported all that God had helped them accomplish" (15:4) but was quickly opposed by some converted Pharisees who demanded that Gentiles be circumcised and be required to keep all the details of the Mosaic law (15:5). The leadership convened, and after much discussion Peter, and then Barnabas and Paul, spoke of their experiences, all of which justified the conclusion that "we are saved by the favor of the Lord Jesus and so are they [the Gentiles]" (15:11). Then James rose and spoke with approval about how God was "taking from among the Gentiles a people to bear his name" (15:14), using the Greek word *laos*, which is almost always used to translate the Hebrew *'am*, the word that is used to refer to Israel's identity as God's specially chosen people.[109] With this preface, which basically said that the uncircumcised Gentiles, like the Hebrew Christians, were now God's true people, the rest is anticlimactic: "we ought not to cause God's Gentile converts any difficulties" (15:19). And so a letter was sent to the Christians of Antioch that, with some relatively simple conditions, they were free from observing the law (15:20-29).

Luke Timothy Johnson may have exaggerated when he says that up until this point in the story the mission to the Jews had had the first priority but that now "attention is given unequivocally to the establishment of Gentile communities."[110] In fact, throughout the rest of the book Paul is consistently pictured as preaching to Jews as well as Gentiles (16:13; 17:1-4, 12, 17; 18:4; 19:8; 28:17-28). Nevertheless, the tone of the story has changed after the apostolic decision in chapter 15. What Luke provides from the end of chapter 15 until Paul is arrested and imprisoned in chapter 21 is a compressed and "vivid account of Paul's missionary work in Europe and Asia, his continuing struggles with Jewish opposition, and his ever more decisive turn to the Gentiles."[111]

The concluding chapters of the book deal with Paul's arrest and trials in Jerusalem, his captivity in Caesarea, and his journey to and arrival in Rome. At Rome, Paul once again preaches to the Jews, once again the gospel is rejected, and once again Paul makes the statement that "this salvation of God has been transmitted to the Gentiles—who will heed it!" (28:28). The last two verses of the work depict Paul welcoming *all* who come to him, preaching the reign of God and teaching about the Lord Jesus Christ (28:30-31).

Stephen G. Wilson suggests that while the ending of Acts is "retrospective" in reference, it points to the fulfillment of Jesus' command in 1:8 that the gospel will be preached to the ends of the earth, represented here by Rome, the center of the world's power. Wilson also suggests, however, that the ending may have a "prospective purpose" as well. Just because the gospel has reached Rome does not mean that everything has been accomplished. On the contrary, "the emphasis on the open and unhindered proclamation of the gospel to the Gentiles, the finality of the rejection of the Jews, and the ending of the story in Rome all point in the same direction: the future of the Church lies among the Gentiles; Christianity is to be a universal religion."[112] Acts ends, therefore, looking toward the future, inviting the church to carry on Paul's work in its own time and context, just as Paul—and before him Stephen and Philip and Peter—carried on Jesus' work.

CONCLUSION

The argument of this chapter has been that, to the extent that the Jesus community responds to the Spirit's call to continue Jesus' mission in new and perhaps unthinkable ways, it becomes the church. We believe that a reading of the Acts of the Apostles shows that the origin of the church is intimately connected to its consciousness of the mission that it saw before it, and so Acts can be claimed to provide a strong biblical basis for the dictum that the church is "missionary by its very nature" (AG 2). Acts is, of course, highly selective and streamlined in presenting its version of what happened in the early church and how the mission to the Gentiles evolved. The price it pays is that of having to ignore both the diversity of the missionary efforts of the early community (for example, where did the community in Damascus come from? Or who planted the community in Rome? Or what happened to the Ethiopian eunuch or the Samaritan community?)[113] and the diversity of theologies within it (Raymond E. Brown discerns *at least* four types of Christian communities within the New Testament).[114] As Dale T. Irvin argues, such "streamlining," when interpreted literally and not theologically, has had severe consequences for the church's historical imagination.[115]

Nevertheless, as James G. Dunn insists in his *Unity and Diversity in the New Testament*, there were certain limits to such diversity over against which the "Great Church" identified itself. In the beginning, Christians were Jews. In many ways they held the same beliefs and practices as groups like the Ebionites, who were eventually considered heretical. But the reason why Ebionism was rejected, Dunn says, was that *"in a developing situation where Christianity had to develop and change, it did not!"*[116] Where Ebionism refused to change was in a conception of Jesus that failed to see Jesus' universal significance; that is, "when it lost the flexibility and openness to a new revelation which questions of law and mission demanded in a developing situation, when it became rigid and exclusive."[117] Ironically, therefore, what was judged an unchristian opinion was a refusal to acknowledge Christianity's fundamental cultural and theological diversity. What was seen as essential to Christian identity, in other words, was not a rigid "orthodoxy" but an acknowledgment of an identity in difference, a unity in diversity.[118] Such an analysis of the growing identity of the church in the context of its early plurality, we would venture to say, is quite similar to the one that can be found in a reading of Luke, particularly his second volume, the Acts of the Apostles.

Dunn's remarks also point to the second aim of the reflections in this chapter, a perspective also central to this book. If a key aspect of orthodoxy, or the identification of the "Great Church" over against heretical groups, consists in the church's having developed an understanding of the universal significance of Jesus Christ and a sense of urgency to preach, serve and witness to the reign of God as he did, perhaps the need to develop in response to particular situations (context) is constitutive of the church as well. In other words, if to be church is to be in mission, to be in mission is to be responsive to the demands of the gospel in particular contexts, to be continually "reinventing" itself as it struggles with and approaches new situations, new peoples, new cultures and new questions. The existence of Christianity seems always to be linked to its expansion beyond itself, across generational and cultural boundaries. Indeed, as Walls says, "the very survival of Christianity as a separate faith has evidently been linked to the process of cross-cultural transmission."[119] There seems to be an inevitable connection, therefore, between the need for Christian mission, on the one hand, and the need for that mission always to be radically contextual. The urgency of mission is linked to the urgency of change, adaptation and translation—in other words, to context. By being faithful to each context the church continues to be called forth by its Lord to share and continue his mission. "Where the retrospective bond with the apostles is concerned," writes Moltmann, "the historical church will ask about continuity and strive for continuity. But where the future its apostolate serves is concerned it will be open to leap forward to what is new and surprising. Here 'the most characteristic thing is not the old things that are preserved but the new ones that take place and come into being.'"[120]

This chapter has focused on the changing *context* in which the church recognizes itself as "missionary by its very nature" ("where the future its apostolate serves is concerned"); the next chapter outlines the *constants* by which the church remains faithful to that nature ("where the retrospective bond with the apostles is concerned").

2

"You Are Witnesses of These Things"

Constants in the Church's Mission

In the first essay of the collection published as *The Missionary Movement in Christian History*, Andrew Walls offers an engaging way of understanding the dazzling variety of the forms of Christianity throughout history.[1] Imagine, he says, a long-living scholar of religion from another planet who periodically receives grants to study Christianity. On his first visit the scholar encounters the newly formed community, about 37 C.E. They are all Jews, and they all practice Judaism in the light of the teachings of Jesus of Nazareth, whom they expect to return imminently. A second visit several hundred years later coincides with the Council of Nicea, where the participants come from all over the Mediterranean world; none is Jewish. While the participants still reverence the Jewish scriptures, another set of writings are also used, and they are debating whether a term that does not appear in either collection of scriptures—the Greek term *homoousios*—can be used to best express their faith in Jesus. Several hundred years later, the scholar's encounter with Christianity takes place in Ireland, where monks express their faith in Jesus by performing bizarre acts of penance and who risk their lives by traveling far and wide to call rough tribes from their worship of nature gods to the worship of Jesus as God. A thousand years later, in the 1840s, the scholar visits earth again, encountering English Christians who are preparing to send missionaries to Africa, and a little over a century later our outer space visitor sees the fruit of their labors—Africans who profess Christianity but hardly in the sober way of Victorian England. These Nigerian Christians are all wearing white robes and are dancing and singing their way to church in a most effervescent and joyous way.

Could all of these people be members of the same religion? The people at Nicea honored the Jewish books but were rather hostile to Judaism. The Irish monks mouthed the Nicene formula but had very different interests. The well-fed British missionaries still spoke of holiness, but they were hardly committed to withdrawal from the world and physical penances. And the ebullient and joyful Nigerian Christians profess the same creed that the missionaries taught, but they are certainly vague about its meaning as they focus on the power of Jesus and his healing presence in their lives. All these people over the centuries called themselves Christians, but did they really share the same faith? Is there any connection between Jews who believed that Jesus was the messiah of Israel, bishops of a newly legitimated faith that spoke of this Jesus as God, scruffy monks, well-fed English clerics and spirit-filled Africans?

Walls answers in the affirmative on two levels. On a first level, there is a *historical* connection. As we have seen in our first chapter, Jewish Christians who had fled Jerusalem had preached to Greeks at Antioch. The Hellenistic culture in which these Antiochene Christians lived was the atmosphere in which the world of the Roman Empire came to understand Christianity. As the civilization of antiquity crumbled, the vitality of Christianity continued on in the culture of Ireland, whose monks evangelized Europe. And Europe's evangelization of the world it had colonized has led to the latest phase of Christianity, the emergence of the World Church. Walls doesn't say it explicitly here, but elsewhere in this same book he seems to say that this historical connection is one maintained by the continuity of Christianity's *missionary* vision.[2] As we saw in Chapter 1, the church is missionary by its very nature; it continues as church as it continues Jesus' mission of preaching, serving and witnessing to God's already-inaugurated yet still-to-be-consummated reign, growing and changing and being transformed in the process.

But Walls sees another level of connection: despite the "wild profusion of the varying statements of these differing groups"[3] as they respond to differing contexts, there is in Christianity an "essential continuity"[4] by which it remains itself as it transforms itself in missionary outreach. Despite differences of language, context and culture, there persist as well certain *constants* that define Christianity in its missionary nature. Walls names several of these, which might be stated generally to be the constant of *Christology* and the constant of *ecclesiology*. First and foremost, "the person of Jesus called the Christ has ultimate significance."[5] Then there is the constant use of the Bible; the sacramental significance of Eucharist and baptism; and a consciousness of continuity with Israel, from which the Christian phenomenon had sprung. Jesus always remains the Christ, although his Christness—the way he is understood as of ultimate significance—is expressed differently and understood more deeply in the church's various historical and cultural embodiments. And although Christians will develop various and even conflicting understandings of who they are, what the significance of the Bible is, and how to celebrate Eucharist and baptism, they will always see themselves as a community that is nourished and equipped for its work in the world by both word and sacrament. The content of these constants is not the same, but Christianity is never without faith in and theology of Jesus as Christ and never without a commitment to and understanding of the community it names church.

To these two constants of the centrality of Jesus the Christ (along with his relation to the Father and the Holy Spirit) and the ecclesial nature of any missionary activity (expressed by fidelity to a common book, a common heritage and a common ritual) we propose an additional four.

First, the missionary church came to consciousness of itself and continues to understand itself over against the future. Questions of *eschatology*—When will God's reign be inaugurated fully? Will the reign of God transform this earth or bring it to fulfillment? How fully does the church already participate in the reign's reality?—play an essential role in shaping the way the church lives out its life and proposes to continue Jesus' mission.

The church's eschatological stance is in turn shaped by what we would propose as a second additional constant: the nature of *salvation*. Is the preaching of the gospel about turning from the world to a wholly spiritual existence outside it or against it? Or is salvation in Christ about wholeness and holistic healing and structural change and transformation?

To propose a third additional constant to Walls's original two, Christianity's identity is always determined by its attitude to and understanding of the human, that is by a particular *anthropology*. Whether humanity is regarded as fallen and wholly corrupt or severely yet not fatally wounded, able or unable to establish "points of contact" with revelation, on its way to greater and greater possibilities and ready to be enlightened or doomed to destruction without revelation all make a difference in establishing church orders and creating ways to evangelize.

Finally, questions as to whether human *culture* can be a vehicle or an obstacle for communicating the gospel, whether it can be a resource for new insights into the reality of God and God's self-giving in Jesus Christ, whether it needs to be destroyed or transformed or explored by the church in mission— these questions regarding the goodness, the wickedness, the value or the menace of culture can never be separated from what defines Christianity or from what the church is about in its missionary task.

The answers to these questions about Jesus, the church, the future, salvation, and human nature and human culture have certainly varied through the two millennia of Christianity's existence, as the church has lived out its missionary nature in various contexts. As *questions*, however, they remain ever present and ever urgent, because how they are answered is how Christianity finds its concrete identity as it constitutes itself in fidelity to Jesus' mission. We propose, therefore, six *constants* in Christianity, six questions that Christianity constantly needs to answer, six questions that shape the way the church will preach, serve and witness to God's reign: (1) Who is Jesus Christ and what is his meaning?[6] (2) What is the nature of the Christian church? (3) How does the church regard its eschatological future? (4) What is the nature of the salvation it preaches? (5) How does the church value the human? and (6) What is the value of human culture as the context in which the gospel is preached?

SIX CONSTANTS OF MISSION, THREE TYPES OF THEOLOGY

This chapter explores the various ways in which these six questions have been answered in the history of theology, and so discovers the ways that the church has lived out its identity as the community that shares and continues Jesus' mission. Our purpose, in other words, is to chart here the various possible theological and missiological routes that Christianity has taken and might take in the future as it strives to be faithful to its essential missionary identity. If Chapter 1 could be summarized by the phrase "missionary by its very nature," this present chapter might be summarized by the Great Commission as it is expressed at the end of Luke's gospel: "You are witnesses of these things" (24:48).

Our guides in this exploration are two contemporary theologians: Cuban American church historian Justo L. González and, to a lesser extent, German liberation/feminist theologian Dorothee Sölle. In *Christian Thought Revisited*, González delineates "three types of theology";[7] Sölle outlines three theological "paradigms" in her 1990 book *Thinking about God*.[8] Each of these types or paradigms has generally been considered to be an orthodox expression of Christian faith; all three can be traced back to the earliest centuries of Christianity, and all three have survived in one form or another through the ages and continue to survive today. These types or paradigms are models, that is, "streamlined, somewhat artificially constructed" cases that can be "useful and illuminating for dealing with realities which are more complex and differentiated."[9] What this means is that, while there are elements of the other two types or paradigms evident in each, there is a certain drift, a certain tendency, a certain perspective in each which is distinct and which tends to determine or color all doctrinal expressions of faith and pastoral decisions that embody it.[10] González compares his types to a caricature sketch of a person: while a particular person obviously does not possess the exaggerated features the sketch portrays (for example, Richard Nixon's nose or Jay Leno's chin), the person's identity is instantly recognizable in stunning, humorous or sometimes shocking clarity. "Likewise, in drawing a typology such as that being presented here, one underscores those elements most characteristic of a particular type. This helps clarify the issues and contrasts, as long as it is not understood as an actual description that makes all nuances superfluous."[11] There may be no "pure" exponents of any of the types, but every church decision, every theological position and therefore every attitude in mission can be seen as a logical consequence of a distinct perspective that is characteristic of one of the three.

Sölle speaks of the three paradigms as "orthodox/conservative," "liberal" and "radical/liberation theology."[12] González names these three distinct perspectives simply Type A, Type B and Type C, and these correspond rather closely to Sölle's three paradigms. Although Type C, or the radical/liberation theology paradigm, is the oldest of the three types or paradigms proposed, both González and Sölle treat them in the order by which they are best known to Christians. This order of treatment also reflects the level of influence that these types have had on the life of the Western church and its mission. González and Sölle write their books with an acknowledged bias toward their third division of theology, and we must admit that it is a bias that we share as well (although we must admit in addition some bias toward *some* forms of Type B).[13] What is important to stress, however, is that all three types have always enjoyed and continue to enjoy, if not full approval in the church, at least relative tolerance. In addition, it is important to acknowledge the basic contextuality of each of these paradigms. If Type A has achieved dominance in the past, it is because its perspectives have helped articulate Christianity in ways that gave meaning and purpose to Christians of those times. If the liberal theology expressed in Type B has remained a close rival to the more dominant Type A, it is because it has always presented a vigorous alternative to what will be described below as a more legalistic vision. If Type C or liberation theology has emerged in our times as a more adequate understanding of Christianity for many, this is because it is rooted in the profound historical and demographic shifts of the late twentieth and early twenty-first centuries, and in striking parallels between the situation of Christianity today and of Christianity in its beginnings. If Philip Jenkins is right that the future of Christianity will be more conservative and more Pentecostal, Type A theology may find a new expression now that the center of gravity has shifted from the affluent North to the poor South.[14]

In the pages that follow, for the sake of simplicity, we have decided to use González's more neutral designations of Type A, Type B, and Type C. Readers, however, should always keep in mind Sölle's more descriptive names. The concern of both González and Sölle in their books is to sketch out three types or paradigms of *theology*. What we are attempting to do in these pages is to illustrate how the typology they develop might play itself out in terms of the theology of *mission*. As the questions that make up the six constants of the church's mission presented above are answered according to each type or paradigm, we try to draw out their missiological implications as clearly as possible. This admittedly long chapter provides the framework for our reflections in both Parts II and III. The table on the next page provides a guide through what follows.

Type A Theology: Mission as Saving Souls and Extending the Church

Type A theology has its origins in the North African city of Carthage, where by the end of the second century we find a flourishing Christian community. Carthage had once been a mortal enemy of Rome, but in 146 B.C.E. Rome conquered and destroyed it and built on its ruins a colony that, by the time Christianity arrived, was thoroughly Roman in architecture, culture and world view. This important Roman town was home to Tertullian, one of the most influential Christian thinkers ever to live, and to whom can be attributed, says González, the origins of this most influential theological type.

OUTLINE OF THREE TYPES OF THEOLOGY

	Type A Theology	Type B Theology	Type C Theology
Origin	Carthage	Alexandria	Antioch
Culture	Roman	Hellenistic	Near Eastern
Key figure	Tertullian	Origen	Irenaeus
Key word	Law	Truth	History
Trajectory	Augustine Anselm of Canterbury Aquinas Protestant Orthodoxy Fundamentalism Neo-Thomism	Abelard Scheiermacher Liberal Protestantism Möhler Lonergan Rahner	Francis of Assisi Early Luther Wesley Barth Teilhard de Chardin Gutiérrez
Christology	Person: high Redemption: satisfaction Exclusive	Person: Premodern: high Modern: low Redemption: exemplar model Inclusive / modified pluralist	Person: low Redemption: liberation Inclusive / moderate pluralist
Ecclesiology	Institutional model	Mystical communion; sacrament	Herald / servant
Eschatology	Futurist Individual	Realized Individual	Inaugurated Historical
Salvation	Spiritual	Premodern: spiritual illumination Modern: holistic	Holistic
Anthropology	Negative Hierarchical	Positive Premodern: hierarchical Modern: equality	Positive Premodern: less hierarchical Modern: equality
Culture	Premodern: classicist Modern: empirical Counter-cultural or translation models	Premodern: classicist Modern: empirical Anthropological model	Premodern: classicist Modern: empirical Praxis or moderate counter-cultural models
Figures in mission	Francis Xavier William Carey	Cyril and Methodius Matteo Ricci Max Warren John Mbiti	East Syrian monks Francis of Assisi Liberation theologians

Although it is uncertain, Tertullian may well have been a lawyer. His works reflect the thinking and language of a legal mind, and such a legal cast of mind was surely reflective of one of Rome's greatest gifts to Western civilization: law. Roman law was rooted in the philosophy of Stoicism, a philosophy that was pervasive of western Roman and North African culture at the time. Stoicism believed in a fundamental order of the universe, and it taught that true happiness could only come when one submitted oneself to this order. Romans saw their own political order as the rational working out of this fundamental natural law, and so to live as a Roman was to live, at least politically, in harmony with universal order.

González suggests that *law* might be the best word to characterize Tertullian's own thinking, and says that *law* might characterize as well the theological type he exemplifies.[15] In Tertullian's writings, God is described as a lawgiver and judge, creation is conceived as wholly complete and ordered, and sin is described as going against this order and breaking divine law. Human beings are born into this world as sinners, having inherited sinfulness from first parents who originally broke God's law and disrupted the world's order.[16] Jesus is depicted as the new Moses and the gospel a new law, which is a new law of repentance. If men and women submit to that law in baptism, they will be saved, and so avoid God's punishment, provided they obey the laws of God's church and the prescriptions of Holy Scripture. At the end, God will resurrect and judge the entire human race, and those to be saved will be with God forever in a state where order will be restored, and all will forever obey the divine commandments.[17]

What Tertullian exemplifies is the understanding of Christian life that became dominant in the West through the works of Augustine, much of medieval Scholastic theology, the thought of the Reformation after Luther, most Catholic and some Protestant theology through the sixteenth to twentieth centuries, and conservative Catholic and fundamentalist thinking today. It will have a definite influence on the way the constants we have named are shaped, and so it will have a strong influence on the shape of the church's mission as well.

Type A Christology

Christology as a theological discipline has usually been divided into the two subcategories of reflection on the *person* and *work* of Jesus Christ. Reflection on the *person* of Jesus asks questions of his identity—Is he fully human? Fully divine? How can he be both? Reflection on Jesus' person inevitably involves one in trinitarian theology. Reflection of Jesus' *work* asks questions about the nature and significance of Jesus as *savior*, and particularly the significance of his death and resurrection.[18] In the last several decades, however, in light of an acknowledgment of the persistence and (for some Christians, at least) genuine value of *other* religious ways, another issue has surfaced as a major issue in Christology: whether and to what extent Jesus' person and work is the *only* way that God offers salvation to humanity. In addition to a sketch of Jesus' person and work in all three types of Christology, therefore, we also point to how each type understands the reality of Jesus in the context of contemporary religious pluralism.

With regard to the person of Christ, the tendency of Type A Christology is to focus less on the meaning of the historical Jesus and the significance of his life and message and more on the orthodoxy of doctrinal descriptions of his reality as eternal Son become truly incarnate. It was Tertullian who was the first to employ the formula (made normative by the Council of Chalcedon in 451 [DS 300-303]) that Jesus was one divine person who possessed two distinct natures, human and divine.[19] This doctrinal expression was developed further and more fully by theologians in the Middle Ages and still remains the orthodox way of expressing the reality of Jesus as the Christ.[20] It might be described as a "high" or "descending" Christology, because although it does acknowledge the humanity of Jesus, its starting point and central concern is his divinity.[21] As this Christology developed, Jesus' gospel miracles and his resurrection from the dead were used as proofs of his divinity, and emphasis was often given to the question of Jesus' knowledge of himself as divine.

The static mentality fostered by Greek philosophy said that what was true and good and beautiful was what remained unchanged. What this meant was that a formula like that of Chalcedon was understood to put an *end* to Christological discussion.[22] The implications of this for mission were far-reaching. Since the formula was considered a privileged one, it was unchangeable. At best it was adaptable or translatable, but there was never any question that new situations and new modes of thought might be able to provide a different perspective on Jesus' identity. Such a doctrinal formula became something learned by rote and often had little impact on people's lives.

Type A Christology also thinks of Jesus' saving work in legalistic terms. Tertullian introduced the word *satisfaction,* which may have come from its use in Roman law, where it meant either to make amends for failing to meet an obligation or even to mete out or to receive punishment.[23] But it was Anselm of Canterbury who was to develop this doctrine in the way that achieved almost normative status in subsequent theological expression. For Anselm, theologizing in the context of traditional Germanic law,[24] Jesus' death on the cross was the ultimate reason for which he became human. Only an act performed by an infinite person could make satisfaction to God for the infinite offense committed by Adam's disobedience. This Jesus was able to do, and his death fully appeased God's justice. So important was this satisfactory, substitutionary death that it was understood as the principal work of Christ in the work of redemption. Redemption had been accomplished, said Bernard of Clairvaux, through Christ's blood, not merely through his word.[25] Not even the resurrection of Christ was as important as this moment of divine satisfaction and victory over the devil.[26] Redemption is "objective"; it was accomplished once and for all on the cross, and for every person, past, present and future. "Subjective" redemption, however, is up to every person, and this could only take place if one heard the message of Jesus, and explicitly confessed Jesus as Lord and Savior.

In today's Christological discussion in the context of the pluralism of the world's religions, three positions are commonly distinguished: an exclusive Christology that confesses Jesus *alone* as Savior, an inclusive Christology that understands God's grace in Christ implicitly present in other religious ways, and a pluralist Christology that recognizes Jesus as merely *one* of many ways to salvation.[27] Type A Christology would probably feel most comfortable with the exclusivist position. This understanding of the significance of Christ for human salvation would say that, while some form of "natural revelation" does exist (Rom 1:18-21), humanity is by itself totally incapable of responding to it, since all humans are heirs to sin. Only through Christ, God's act of "special revelation," can humanity have access to God and God's salvation. Although there has always been a strong tradition in the church that favors a more moderate "inclusive Christology,"[28] there has also been a strong tradition that without explicit faith in Christ one has no hope of salvation. Such was the tradition, for example, that fueled the missionary zeal of Francis Xavier and William Carey, along with countless numbers of missionaries in the eighteenth and nineteenth centuries. According to such a Christology, the aim of mission work was to "save souls" or at least to "plant the church" that would carry on the work of "saving the poor heathen." Even today, particularly among some Evangelical Christians, the explicit confession of Christ is the only way to salvation. In 1974 the Lausanne Covenant said that "there is only one Saviour and one gospel (Gal 1:6-9)" and that "those who reject Christ repudiate the joy of salvation and condemn themselves to eternal separation from God (2 Thess 1:7-9)."[29] In 1989 the *Manila Manifesto* reaffirmed that mission was an urgent task, and that "other religions and ideologies are not alternative paths to God, and that human spirituality, if unredeemed by Christ, leads not to God but to judgement, for Christ is the only way."[30]

Those who ascribe to such an exclusive understanding of Christ's role in the history of salvation would look on present efforts of interreligious dialogue as either futile or dangerous—futile, for they believe they have nothing to learn from such conversation and cooperation, and dangerous because they do violence to the imperative of biblical witness. Dialogue is acceptable only "when its aim is to learn to know other people. . . . Then dialogue serves as the way by which people of other faiths are led to accept God's revelation in Jesus Christ. Christ must be preached. Precisely with this in mind it is of great importance for Christians to get to know their fellow people."[31]

Type A Ecclesiology

The ecclesial nature of mission is expressed in Type A theology by the conviction that the church is the sole agent and protector—or at least the "ordinary means"—of faith in Christ. For Type A theology, the dictum attributed to Cyprian, "extra ecclesiam nulla salus" (outside the church there is no salvation), is understood quite literally. As Boniface VIII expressed it in its most extreme form, salvation is possible only for those who submit to the authority of the Roman pontiff (DS 875). The harshness of this statement has been mollified and even denied in subsequent Roman documents (see D 1647 [TCT 174]), and the phrase "extra ecclesiam . . . " was not even used in Vatican II (see LG 14-16). Nevertheless, in his 1991 encyclical *Redemptoris Missio*, Pope John Paul II admonishes that while interreligious dialogue is an essential aspect of missionary activity, it should "be conducted and implemented with the conviction that *the Church is the ordinary means of salvation* and that *she alone* possesses the fullness of the means of salvation (UR 3; AG 7)" (RM 55; see DI 16-17).

Avery Dulles's classic study *Models of the Church* lays out five models or theological perspectives by which the nature and mission of the church can be understood.[32] The church, he says, can be imaged or modeled as institution, mystical communion, sacrament, herald and servant. The church as institution emphasizes the church's external and often hierarchical aspects, while the church as mystical communion focuses on the church's reality as a community mystically united to Christ and to one another. The sacramental model mediates somewhat between these first two, emphasizing, in the words of Vatican II, the church's nature as visible "sign and instrument" (LG 1) of divine and human unity, while the herald and servant models emphasize the church's task of proclamation and commitment to personal and social transformation, respectively.

The model most operative in Type A theology would almost certainly favor Dulles's institutional model, at least for pre–Vatican II Catholicism and some conservative Catholics today. Protestants, with the exception of "High Church" Anglicans and some Lutheran churches (for example, the Swedish Lutheran Church), have tended to hold a "lower" notion of church in theory, but in fact they too have often been quite concerned about the church's visible structure and polity. In any case, Sölle says that Protestants express this perspective by putting undue emphasis on the importance of proclamation and preaching in the church, to the neglect of action in the world and the development of true community.[33] The emphasis of the institutional model in Roman Catholicism is on the church's visible nature, hierarchical structure and legal status for both its members and in the world at large. Pre–Vatican II Catholic ecclesiology favored the idea that the church was a "perfect society," that is, a visible community with rights over against other "perfect societies" (that is, secular states) and the right to regulate its internal life by its own laws. The institutional model focuses on the hierarchy—bishops and priests or pastors—as those who minister the sacraments that provide the means of salvation and who enforce the laws by which Christians can live out their lives in loyalty to God's law. In 1943 Pius XII issued the encyclical *Mystici Corporis,* which interpreted this institutional model in a much richer way as a communion with Christ so intimate that the church can be understood in more Pauline terms as Christ's (mystical) body. But, as David Bosch has pointed out, the encyclical's explanation not only identified the Mystical Body with the Roman Catholic Church, but "it further strengthened the tendency to absolutize and divinize the church" and reinforced its nature as "perfect society."[34]

Type A ecclesiology tends to view the goal of missionary activity as the extension of the church. Christ's salvation will become accessible to people in particular places to the extent that the church with its full hierarchy and structure can be formally established. Since its understanding of the church is institutional (and institutions are notoriously slow to allow or promote change), the idea that other cultures or new times could develop different structures or improve on present ones is almost inadmissible. Despite the 1659 encouragement of the newly established Propaganda Fide that missionaries respect local customs and uses—"What could be more absurd than to transport France, Spain, Italy, or some other European country to China?"[35]—most missionaries duplicated the structures of the European church, along with its liturgy, church architecture, and often even its language. To become a Christian was to become a member of the church, and to become a member of the church was to become a European or an American. This was the case both in "high" institutional churches like Roman Catholicism and in "low" congregationalist Protestant churches as well. It was what men like Rufus Anderson and Henry Venn were opposed to as they articulated their principles of the "three selfs."[36]

A third trait of Type A ecclesiology that needs to be mentioned is the relation of the church to the reign of God. For the institutional model, the church is basically identified with God's reign. Jesus preached, served and witnessed to the reign of God during his earthly ministry, and this was fulfilled in the establishment of the church. The fullness of salvation that God offers is therefore found only within the church's boundaries, as Christians receive the sacraments from the hands of the church's divinely constituted hierarchical ministers. What the church looks forward to at the end of time is not the coming of the reign of God in a way that will do away with the necessity of the church; rather, it is the full establishment of the church in all lands and the conversion of all peoples to its ranks. But this is getting us into the understanding of mission's third constant: eschatology.

Type A Eschatology

Eschatology is usually articulated from two distinct perspectives. On the one hand, eschatology focuses on the *eschaton*, the end time, the goal and meaning of history. This is often spoken of as general eschatology. Discussion revolves around whether the end time is to come wholly in the future (futurist eschatology); already realized, but as a personal, inner reality (realized eschatology); or already inaugurated, but not yet fully accomplished (inaugurated eschatology).[37] On the other hand, eschatology reflects on the *eschata*, the so-called four last things: death, judgment, heaven and hell. While the former perspective concerns humanity in general and even the whole cosmos, the latter refers to the destiny of individuals.

From the first perspective, Type A theology would tend to think of the eschaton as the time when God's judgment of the world will finally take place, and the good will be rewarded while the evil will be punished. In Tertullian's thinking, which is emblematic of this eschatology, the world's order will once and for all be restored, and all the just will live forever according to God's eternal law.[38] As such, Type A theology is often futurist in orientation and might contain some apocalyptic tendencies as well: this judgment of God is fully in the future and might break in at any time, bringing with it a whole new creation.[39]

Because of these orientations, Type A theology tends to regard the world and human history as ultimately unimportant in the scheme of salvation. In the final analysis, it matters little how the world is developed, or how structures are changed. These will be swept away by God's final judgment and the new world. What matters is rather that men and women keep the divine commands and so prove themselves worthy of inclusion in God's final order.

In the history of the church, the futurist orientation has both eclipsed and instigated missionary activity. David Bosch points out that seventeenth-century Protestant orthodoxy saw the present time merely as a time of waiting for God's judgment, because the gospel had already been preached and those who were predestined to accept it had done so already. "Its philosophy appeared to have been not that all must be saved but that most must be damned."[40] The Pietist breakthrough, however, regarded the time before the parousia "not as a season of waiting but as time allowed for witness and for bringing in as many of the lost as possible."[41] At the present time, much of the zeal for mission of fundamentalist and many Pentecostal Christians is caused by an imminent sense of Christ's second coming. Many of these Christians are motivated by what has come to be called *Dispensationalism,* a belief that the history of salvation is divided into a number of distinct periods. Before the end of time, those to be saved will experience the *rapture,* a belief that is based on 1 Thessalonians 4:15-17 where Paul writes that when Jesus comes again, Christians will be "caught up in the air."[42] Out of the urgency to have as many saved as possible, these Christians are seriously engaged in missionary evangelism.

Type A eschatology is also very preoccupied with the fate of individuals who die in the time before the End. Catholic thought speaks not only about a general judgment at the world's end; it also speaks of a particular judgment of every person immediately after death, at which a person's fate is irrevocably decided by the divine judge. Those judged worthy of eternal life go immediately to their reward; those judged unworthy go immediately to their eternal punishment in the fires of hell. Those who still are in need of purification spend some time of cleansing and "temporal punishment" in purgatory, a time that can be shortened by the prayers and good deeds of Christians on earth.[43] Medieval Christians especially were highly preoccupied with these eschatological questions of death, judgment, heaven, hell and purgatory, and it is to their vivid imaginations, perhaps best expressed in the late medieval poetry and theology of Dante, that we owe much of our own doctrinal images and language today.[44]

While Protestant missionary activity in the past (as with the Pietists) and in the present (as with the Dispensationalists and some fundamentalists) was motivated by the nearness of the end time, Catholic missionaries do not seem to have found this much of a motive at all. Catholics, however, as well as Protestants, were highly motivated by the doctrines of individual eschatology, and there must exist thousands of books, tracts and articles in Catholic and Protestant periodical and devotional literature calling for men and women to devote their lives to saving the majority of humanity from hell and eternal punishment.[45] If missionaries were not motivated by the grim belief in the nearness of the *Dies Irae* (day of wrath, the judgment day),[46] they were certainly motivated by images of innocent yet ignorant people burning in hell because someone had not shared with them the saving message of Jesus. There can be no denying that the "fire and brimstone" thinking of the "New Divinity" in America's Great Awakening was the source of much of the phenomenal missionary movement that flourished in both Europe and America, and among both Catholics and Protestants in the nineteenth century and well into the twentieth.[47] In Type A theology, eschatology, particularly in its more individual perspective, is both motive and object of missionary proclamation.[48]

Salvation in Type A Theology

Mission is always the proclamation of and witness to God's offer of salvation; indeed, "the motif of soteriology is . . . the beating heart of the study of mission,"[49] and the way that salvation is understood in that study is largely determinative of how mission is carried out.[50] Any understanding, of course, is in turn conditioned by the particular perspective of a particular theological type.

Type A theology views human beings as enmeshed in sin, and so, if left on their own, doomed to eternal punishment and damnation. It is through Christ's satisfactory, redeeming work that people become "disentangled" and so are able to live in ways that will ensure eternal life. Though it may in some way have its beginning in this life—Aquinas wrote of sanctifying grace as the "seed of glory"[51]—salvation was conceived as something that is accomplished *after* death and *out of* this world. As theology in the West came more and more under the influence of Anselm's theory of vicarious satisfaction, writes David Bosch, "salvation was the redemption of individual souls in the hereafter, which would take effect at the occasion of the miniature apocalypse of the death of the individual believer."[52] In the same way, Bosch continues, God's "salvific" activities were distinguished from God's "providential" activities; salvation, in other words, referred to spiritual, nonmaterial justification of the sinner before God; salvific activities were what counted ultimately, since they were the conditions of the possibility of avoiding eternal punishment. God's benevolent, everyday providential activities were God's actions on behalf of human, societal and human welfare, but they had nothing to do with salvation. Missionary activity was almost always linked to some kind of charitable work, but this was not seen as witnessing to or bringing God's salvation already now breaking into the world, but as a process of "softening people up," or as it was called in Catholic theology just prior to Vatican II, pre-evangelization.[53]

In Type A theology, salvation is *personal*, in two senses of the word. Often, particularly since the full emergence of the individual with modernity, it is something that happens only to an individual and only with full individual consent; that is, it happens when one accepts Jesus as personal savior. In the other sense of *personal,* salvation is restricted to interior, spiritual renewal and transformation. There is no sense, in other words, that salvation as such includes structural, political or cosmic renewal.[54] In a very sensitive essay, Evangelical theologian John Stott insists that there is certainly a *connection* between salvation, physical and mental health and political and social liberation. "Nevertheless," he concludes, "we still have to affirm that they [health and liberation] are not the salvation which God is offering human beings in Christ now." Stott goes on to quote the Lausanne Covenant to the effect that while both evangelism and sociopolitical involvement are Christian duties, "reconciliation with man is not reconciliation with God, nor is social action evangelism, nor is political liberation salvation."[55]

Type A Anthropology

"Propter nos homines et propter nostram salutem" (for us and for our salvation) is the motive that the Nicene Creed gives for the incarnation, that is, Jesus' mission on earth, the mission the church shares and continues. If the understanding of salvation is foundational to how one does mission, and so a constant in the church's missionary proclamation, a fifth constant is revealed when we realize that the understanding of the nature of humanity is foundational to the notion of salvation. What and who is the human being that is in need of salvation? This is the question of theological anthropology.

Type A theology views human beings as fallen creatures. Humanity was created in the image and likeness of God, but it lost that image and likeness, along with certain powers that came to be called preternatural gifts, when Adam and Eve sinned. Augustine insisted, as he developed his notion of original sin and his doctrine of grace in the context of the Pelagian controversy, that fallen humanity by itself is helpless to achieve any relation with God at all. God must take the first step. God did this objectively in Christ, who brings healing, freedom and pardon;[56] and God offers each person "sufficient grace" to respond personally (although some are offered "efficacious grace," which is irresistible).[57]

Although Tertullian, under the influence of Stoicism, held that the human soul was some kind of material reality ("an extremely subtle sort of body," says González[58]), Augustine, although remaining firmly within the parameters of Type A theology, insisted with Neoplatonism that it was wholly spiritual or immaterial.[59] As Augustine's influence increased within Western expressions of orthodoxy, therefore, human nature was conceived more and more dualistically, composed of body and soul, matter and spirit. In the Platonic/Neoplatonic scheme of things, only spirit was good; matter was of no real value and only served to drag spirit down. The healing, liberation and pardon that God offered to sinful humanity, therefore, was a *spiritual* healing, liberation and pardon. It enabled human beings to transcend or escape the body, which was seen as unworthy of being saved or touched by grace. Augustine's contempt for the body, and particularly for human sexuality, is well known.[60] As theology developed in the West, this dualism persisted. Full humanity, it was believed, was to be achieved by a denial of the body and a flight from the material world. A life of penance and celibacy was seen as the best way to live a life pleasing to God. While Reformation thought mitigated these ideas somewhat, its doctrine of the total corruption of humanity and the absolute need for God's grace reinforced the notion of natural human depravity. In Catholicism, this was echoed in the anthropology implied in Jansenism. And so, as both Catholics and Protestants embarked on a new missionary era in the sixteenth century (Catholics) and nineteenth century (when Protestants had their missionary awakening), they arrived in Asia, Africa, Oceania and Latin America—with a few notable exceptions—bearing very negative notions of the natural goodness of the peoples they were to evangelize.

Another implication of Type A anthropology is the naturally hierarchical order of human beings. Particularly under Neoplatonic influence, the world was seen as ordered in terms of higher and lower beings: God, being pure, uncreated spirit, was the highest being, then came created spirits, angels, then human beings, then animals, then living things, then nonliving matter. Angels existed in a nine-level ranking. Human beings were born into a particular order and worked out their salvation within that order. Thus *inequality* was built into the system: some people were naturally better than others, not because of personal merit, but by accident of birth. As the horizons of the world widened with the discoveries of the fifteenth century, this hierarchical understanding of people carried over into Europeans' attitudes to the peoples of the New World. Europeans were superior; Asians, indigenous Americans and Africans were inferior, perhaps not even fully human and so not worthy of the gospel.[61] Even in the church this hierarchy obtained. Gratian wrote that there are two kinds of Christians:

> One kind, which is linked to divine service, and dedicated to contemplation and prayer, should keep away from all earthly worry, as they are clerics, and devoted, that is, converted, to God. For *Kleros* is Greek for the Latin *sors* (lot). Thus people of this kind are called clerics, that is chosen by lot. For God has chosen them all for God's own. And so they are kings, that is reigning over themselves through virtue, and so they have their kingdom in God. And this assigns a crown for their heads. . . . There is another sort of Christians, who are called lay folk. *Laos* means "people." These are allowed to possess temporal goods, but only what they need for use. For nothing is more wretched than to set God at naught for the sake of money. They are allowed to marry, to till the earth, to pronounce judgment on men's disputes and plead in court, to lay their offerings on the altar, to pay their tithes: and so they can be saved, if they do good and avoid evil.[62]

When missionaries imbued with Type A theology went forth to preach the gospel, they carried with them a sense of their own superiority and condescension toward the "others" to whom they had been sent.[63]

Culture and Type A Theology

The gospel never encounters a people in a vacuum. Human beings are meaning-making animals and work out and express that meaning through human culture. Although he acknowledges that culture is a "notoriously slippery concept," Robert Schreiter, following Jens Loenhoff, proposes a definition that includes three aspects or dimensions. First, culture is "ideational," providing a grid by which the world can be interpreted and according to which life can be lived. Such a grid includes beliefs, values and codes of conduct; it provides the culture's basic world view. Second, culture is "performance"; every culture has ritual ways by which its basic world view can be expressed and through which members of the culture are bound together. Such performances might be cultural celebrations like Thanksgiving Day in the United States or Independence Day (June 12) in the Philippines, or "embodied behaviors" like forms of greeting (shaking hands, bowing, ritual questions of health, and so on) or determined distances for communication (close enough to feel the other's breath, an arm's length away, and so forth). Third, culture has a "material" dimension; every people has distinctive language, food, clothing, music, and so on.[64]

Culture can be conceived, in the famous distinction of Bernard Lonergan, as either classicist or empiricist.[65] From the classicist perspective, culture is normative, universal and permanent. There is really only one culture, and that is the culture of the West. Culture has developed, of course, but in Western modernity it has reached its final achievement. A person of culture, therefore, has constructed his or her world out of the best of Western achievements. For Lonergan, this meant that a person of culture would be steeped in Western classics like Plato and Augustine, Schleiermacher and Kierkegaard, would listen to Bach, Beethoven or Vaughn Williams, and would be enriched by the art of a Michelangelo or a Mary Cassat. Perhaps today, under the reality of globalization, such a classicist understanding of culture might be extended to identity formation by the components of what Benjamin Barber calls the culture of "McWorld"—Levis, Dunkin' Donuts, Michael Jordan, rock music, Hollywood films and movie stars, the Internet.[66]

From the empiricist perspective, however, culture is defined as a set of meanings and values that informs a way of life. As such, therefore, culture is neither normative nor universal, nor is it seen as a permanent achievement. Culture is simply the way people have sought and continue to seek to make sense out of their lives in particular situations. It may not be perfect; it may be seriously flawed. But it is basically something healthy and good. From this perspective, no one culture can be considered better than another.

Stephan B. Bevans has proposed six models that emerge—according to particular contexts and/or persons' theological orientations—in the encounter of Christian faith with human culture.[67] The *translation model* regards culture somewhat positively but focuses more on the faithful transmission of the gospel message. It therefore regards culture as a *means*, as a vehicle of transmission, rather than something good and revelatory in itself. The *anthropological model* starts with a basic trust of culture's goodness and revelatory possibilities, and proposes that the wealth often hidden in a culture might offer new riches to the Christian self-understanding. The *praxis model,* employed particularly by communities struggling for liberation, focuses on the dimensions of culture involved in social change and develops a reinterpretation of Christianity in the midst of reflective action in favor of change that embodies Christian principles. A *synthetic model* focuses on the ambiguity of any culture and looks outward to other cultures and successful Christian expressions of faith for the most adequate expression of Christian faith in cultural context. The *transcendental model* focuses on the authentic individual and his or her ability to spark authentic Christian and cultural thinking in dialogue and conversation. And the *counter-cultural model,* while recognizing the importance of culture, regards it with utmost suspicion as something that needs to be confronted with the culturally specific yet universally valid gospel message.

Type A theology would most likely regard culture from a classicist perspective. Although Tertullian is vividly remembered for his fierce antipathy to culture—"What indeed has Athens to do with Jerusalem?"[68]—even he could not step outside it completely, as his use of Stoic philosophy and Roman legal categories bears witness. But such use was hardly reflective; it was simply regarded as the "normal" way of thinking. As Christianity spread throughout Europe, culture and Christian faith (largely articulated in terms of Type A) were bound together in what has come to be called Christendom. What was Christian was implicitly assumed to be Western, and what was Western, in the same way, was assumed to be Christian. It was only natural, then, that non-Western cultures were looked upon as barbarian, their cultures needing to be "Christianized."

There were always exceptions to this line of thinking. Gregory the Great called for basic respect of Anglo-Saxon traditions; Saints Cyril and Methodius were noted for their cultural sensitivity; the 1659 statement of the Propaganda Fide was extremely far-sighted; there were the "experiments" of de Nobili in India, Valignano, Ricci and de Rhodes in Asia, and some Latin American missionaries approached the indigenous cultures with some toleration. Such openness was the product, as we shall see, of different theological perspectives that left more room for cultural appreciation. In the main, however, Type A thinking prevailed, and Christianity was spread by means of a *tabula rasa* approach, that is, local culture was to be swept aside, so that people would be able to practice Christianity in a "pure" manner. For Thai Christians, for example, it was inconceivable to be Thai culturally and Christian religiously at the same time; Christian Shen in Myanmar were known as American Shen.[69] In nineteenth-century

Britain, missionary activity was caught up with "the white man's burden"—to bring "civilization" to benighted peoples. Since other cultures were basically despised, there was no question of employing the performance or material aspects of culture in Christian expression, and no possibility of seeing Christianity from the perspective of African or Asian world views.

As a more empiricist approach to culture came to prevail in the twentieth century, Type A thinking sometimes was able to accommodate notions of culture into its theological expressions and ecclesial practice, but more along the lines of a translation model. The unchanging message of the gospel, in other words, was regarded as "translatable" into non-Western cultural categories without being compromised. But such efforts, it was argued, needed to be done with extreme caution. Such "ethno-theology" might easily be trapped in syncretism and become instead expressions of "Christopaganism."[70]

Perhaps truer to Type A's trajectory, however, is theology that adopts a more counter-cultural stance. While there exists, we believe, a range of counter-cultural expressions, some Christians even today would view any cultural achievements to be of no value for Christian life. For them, the valuation of anything human is a serious mistake, and the gospel is meant to confront and judge culture, not be enriched by it.[71]

In summary, we might say that Type A theology develops around the insight that true humanity is achieved in submission to an order that is beyond human making but accessible to humanity through God's gracious revelation. *Mission* within the context of Type A theology, therefore, might be characterized as the effort to save souls and extend the church. Without saving knowledge of Christ, offered by the church, human beings cannot be saved; without the structures of the church, the reign of God on earth, men and women cannot avail themselves of the means of salvation. Salvation is found not in the transformation of the world or the enhancement of the human, but in the recognition of the world's transitoriness and the value of eternal life. Culture, although it has no *religious* significance per se, might be used to make Christianity clearer, to better communicate the gospel or to help Christians better express their faith. But it might also be regarded as something to be exorcised, even eliminated altogether, so that Christ might establish his "new creation."

Type A theology has motivated millions of Christians in the two-thousand-year span of Christianity to suffer incredible hardships and to risk their lives so that the world might believe and so be saved. While today its influence may be on the wane in Roman Catholicism, many perspectives of Type A theology are flourishing in some Evangelical circles, particularly in movements like AD 2000 and the Joshua Project II.[72]

Type B Theology: Mission as Discovery of the Truth

González sets the location for the development of Type B theology in the Egyptian city of Alexandria, which, after Rome, was the greatest city of the empire and the intellectual center of Hellenistic thought. Daniel Boorstin quotes the boast of one Hellenistic scholar: "Other cities . . . are but the cities of the country around them; Alexandria is the city of the world."[73] The city received its name from its founder, Alexander the Great, who according to legend had hoped that a great library would be established there. This hope was fulfilled by rulers of the Egyptian Ptolemy dynasty, who established a library that eventually would contain "a reliable text of every work in Greek and a representative collection in other languages."[74] In addition, there was the museum, which González says was more like a modern-day university than a place where exhibits were displayed.[75] We might think of it as one of those cities like Cambridge, England, or New Haven, Connecticut, or even South Bend, Indiana, all of which are dominated by a great university. Like such university towns, Alexandria was the center of a wide variety of thought, particularly religious thought, some of which even bordered on the bizarre. González describes this "religious collage" as including Mesopotamian astrologers, Zoroastrians from Persia, devotees of the gods of ancient Egypt, "and proponents of countless other doctrines and religious theories which often became so intermingled as to be hardly distinguishable from one another."[76] Most important, however, Alexandria was the center of Platonic thought. The great Jewish scholar Philo had lived in Alexandria about the same time that Jesus had lived in Palestine, and he revolutionized Jewish thinking by his allegorical interpretations of scripture. Clement of Alexandria, born in Athens, had been converted in Alexandria when he found in Christianity the "true philosophy," and his writings testify to his conviction that Platonic philosophy was nothing less than the "handmaiden" that God had provided to lead humanity to the truth of Christ.[77] Clement's greatest student and successor at Alexandria was Origen, "the most encyclopedic thinker of early Christianity,"[78] the first Christian systematic theologian, and the person González names as the one who best exemplifies Type B theology.

For Origen, as for all of Platonic philosophy, God was absolutely transcendent, above all change and beyond all time. Human beings were in essence spiritual creatures. They had been created as wholly spiritual beings, but having "strayed from contemplation of the One,"[79] they fell into sin. The divine mercy, however, provided fallen creatures with the material universe where they might find their way back to wholeness. Both reason and revelation were the means that God had given humanity to recover its original holiness, and each was perfectly compatible with the other. Origen's basic insight into Christianity was this perfect compatibility between reason and revelation, philosophy and faith, and he set as his main task the demonstration of this. González says that if Tertullian's (and therefore Type A theology's) watchword was *law,* Origen's (and therefore Type B theology's) was *truth.*

Origen was steeped in Platonic thought, and this, as we will see below, certainly colored his understanding of the six constants we are surveying in this chapter. What is more central to the perspective of Type B theology, however, is not Platonism as such, but the conviction that human reason can indeed come into contact—in partial but nevertheless authentic ways—with ineffable Truth. David Tracy would understand this as an exercise of the "analogical imagination," that conviction that ordinary life, if paid attention to, "manifests itself as the extraordinary revelation of our primordial belonging-to, our radical participation in this body, this Church, this tradition, this history, this planet, this cosmos."[80] Type B is more optimistic—in some of its more modern manifestations perhaps even naively so—about human nature, positing a kind of continuity between human nature and divine mystery.[81] It is based, in other words, on a strong conviction of the validity of the "analogy of being."

For Type B theology, human experience—particularly as enhanced through the power of philosophical reason—can serve "as a basic hermeneutical tool to understand the meaning of Scripture and the nature of Christianity."[82] This is perhaps why Type B theology has tended to be the theology of a more academic or spiritual elite—in universities, seminaries and monasteries—throughout Christian history. It is a tradition that includes great medieval Scholastics like Peter Abelard and mystics like Julian of Norwich, theologians in the tradition of liberal theology like Friedrich Schleiermacher, Albrecht Ritchl and John McCleod Campbell, Catholic theologians like Johann Adam Möhler in the nineteenth century and Bernard Lonergan and Karl Rahner in the twentieth. The theological perspective of Type B is articulated as well by contemporary contextual theologians like José M. de Mesa in the Philippines and John Mbiti in Kenya, both of whom attempt to do theology "in solidarity with the culture."[83] What all these theologians have in common is that they attempt to present Christianity in terms that are compatible with their contemporary mentality.[84] This is the key to Type B theology and will have many ramifications in the theology of mission it implies.

In our survey of how our six constants in mission are articulated in Type B theology, we can hardly do justice to the rich variety of theologies that have emerged as Type B theologians make use of expressions of reason in their contemporary situations. There are, however, among striking differences in expression, some continuities of perspective, and we will try to highlight these especially.

Type B Christology

In the context of the Platonic philosophy that determined the intellectual climate of antiquity, Type B's main concern regarding Jesus is his divinity. Like Type A, but with quite a different approach, Type B theology employs a "high" Christology. The high Christology of Nicea, says González, as well as the Christology hammered out in the controversies in the fourth and fifth centuries, were really results of arguments within the ranks of Type B theologians. While Type A theology certainly accepted these formulas and used them as yardsticks of orthodoxy, it did not get caught up in the minutiae of the disputes from which the formulas emerged.[85]

For Origen, Jesus' principal role in the history of salvation is revelatory. He is the one who, as image of the ineffable God, shows humanity who God is. While Origen would not deny Jesus' true humanity, the impression given, González says, is that his humanity is only important as the instrument whereby the divine mystery is made visible.[86] Even in the Middle Ages, when the humanity of Christ was highly venerated, focus was ultimately on Jesus' divinity. The medieval mystic Mechtild of Hackeborn, for example, speaks of Jesus as the "'door' by which human beings and, indeed, all creation entered into union with divinity."[87]

As culture and thought forms began to change with the dawn of modernity, however, and humanity and human reason began to be the focus of religious life and theological thought, Type B theology took on the forms of a "low" Christology, which focused on the Jesus of history, on his perfection as the ideal human being and on his teachings as important moral principles for authentic human life. This was most evident in nineteenth-century liberal Protestant theology, which saw the appearance of a spate of "lives of Jesus." Walter Kasper points out that by the use of the newly discovered tool of historical research, preoccupation with Jesus' identity as such (that Jesus was God) gave way to preoccupation with Jesus's self-identity (Jesus' human integrity). "The mental life of Jesus was so to speak the mirror in which his divinity was reflected. . . . The distinctive thing about Christ is 'The constant strength of his God-consciousness, which was a very indwelling of God in him' and into which he takes us too in faith."[88] Albert Schweitzer pointed out that these "lives" were really only reflections of their authors' own bourgeois ideas and ideals;[89] nevertheless the promise that Type B Christology holds out is that Jesus can illumine human blindness not by giving new eyes to see but by being a lens through which the world can be seen with precision and sharpness. Jesus' role, therefore, continues to be a revelatory one; in this way we can speak of a real continuity of liberal theology with the thought of a theologian like Origen.

For Type B theology, the work of Christ that culminated in his death and resurrection is not, as in Type A, a work of satisfaction or the relieving of a debt. Rather, as Abelard put it in its classic statement, it is a work of supreme revelation, by which he "instructed and taught us perfectly."[90] Jesus' death and resurrection revealed the depths of God's love for humanity in a way that "he could not have shown by being born." The way Christ died proposed an "example," his resurrection exhibited "a life of immortality," and his ascension taught about the reality of heaven.[91] It was not God who needed reconciliation with humanity; it was humanity that needed reminding of the love of God.[92] Jesus does not effect a legal transaction in his redeeming work; he is an example, the contemplation of whom will draw Christians toward the truth of God's love. Although this exemplary theory of atonement remained a minority theological opinion in Christian theology, it was never declared unorthodox and has appeared in various forms in the centuries since Abelard. Resurfacing in nineteenth-century liberal theology as the moral influence theory of atonement, it was a position held by Schleiermacher and Ritschl in Germany, and by British theologians like Frederick Dennison Maurice and John McCleod Campbell. Douglas John Hall calls this theory "the most popular expression of the atonement in nineteenth- and early twentieth-century liberal Protestant thought in North America."[93]

Within the contemporary discussion of religious pluralism, Type B Christology would certainly be seen to embrace the inclusivist position, and even, in one form or another, the pluralist position as well. We see anticipations of the inclusivist position in Clement of Alexandria, who wrote that "there was always a natural *(phusikès)* manifestation of the one Almighty God, among all right-thinking people,"[94] and insisted that right-thinking people included not only Greeks with their philosophy, but also other philosophers from the non-Hellenic world: "The Indian gymnosophists are also in the number, and the other non-Greek philosophers. And of these there are two classes, some of them are Sarmanae, and others Brahmins. . . . Some, too, of the Indians obey the precepts of Buddha; whom, on account of his extraordinary sanctity, they have raised to divine honour."[95] In his work on the theology of Christian pluralism, Jacques Dupuis also cites the examples of Abelard, Francis of Assisi and Nicholas of Cusa as Christians who had a positive view of non-Christian religions; Dupuis also points out the doctrine of baptism of desire as an important development in Christian thinking about salvation outside the confines of the church and explicit faith in Christ.[96] In a number of articles in the 1950s and 1960s, Karl Rahner developed and refined his theology of "anonymous Christians" and "anonymous Christianity." Rahner's fundamental position was that every person is created with an innate drive and openness toward transcendence that, as part of humanity's created nature, is *already* grace. Furthermore, Rahner argued, since all grace is the communication of God's self, all grace is *the* communication of God's self, whom Christians know as Christ. Therefore, any person who in some way responds to that innate openness by seeking honestly for transcendence in his or her life is implicitly or "anonymously" responding to Christ's presence. And since human beings are social and cultural realities, Rahner would say that the society and cultural structures that shape people's lives are also endowed with Christ's grace. Religious ways other than Christianity in some anonymous fashion bear the grace of Christ.[97] Contemporary Catholic teaching and ecumenical Protestant documents more or less reflect this perspective as well. A sentence often quoted from the Vatican II document on the church in the modern world by Pope John Paul II asserts that the church teaches that "the Holy Spirit offers to all the possibility of being made partners, in a way known to God, in the paschal mystery" (GS 22),[98] and in 1989 in San Antonio, Texas, the World Conference on Mission and Evangelism declared that "we cannot point to any other way of salvation than Jesus Christ; at the same time we cannot set limits to the saving power of God."[99]

In addition, particularly under the influence of nineteenth-century liberal theology, there has even been a tendency in Type B Christology to embrace a kind of pluralist position. In the last years of the twentieth century, Rahner's anonymous Christianity came under strong criticism, especially by Paul F. Knitter, who proposed a Christology that does not focus on Christ as the only way to salvation but as one of many ways that God has offered and continues to offer salvation to humanity. Knitter designates his approach as "theocentric," or, more recently, "soteriocentric" and "regnocentric."[100] Even critics of Knitter such as Jacques Dupuis, David Bosch, William R. Burrows and S. Mark Heim, however, present an opinion that goes beyond Rahner's theory of anonymous Christianity and the Roman Magisterium's cautious fulfillment theology.[101]

Type B Christology lends itself to a model of mission that depicts the missionary as a "treasure hunter," a tutor or a dialogue partner. For Clement of Alexandria, philosophy was a "preparation," a "stepping stone" to full reality of Christ.[102] With Christ's incarnation, even though philosophy has prepared people for Christ, it must now make room for him: "as a lamp loses its raison d'être once the sun is up, so, too, philosophy in Christ's advent (*Stromata*, V, 5). Philosophy is a partial knowledge; Christ alone is the whole truth."[103] "Every wise man," says Origen, "to the extent that he is wise, participates in Christ who is wisdom."[104] But the idea is not so much that the missionary brings Christ *into* a situation; the task of evangelization is rather to bring the good news that the riches of Christ are present already within a particular context and that the knowledge of Christ brings with it the fulfillment and perfection of that context. Missionary activity is vitally necessary, but not to prevent those who have not heard the news from perishing for all eternity. The evangelization of all peoples is necessary, first, so that all peoples can reach their full human potential in Christ, and second, so that all peoples can profit from the full understanding of Christ that comes only when all have been evangelized.[105]

Even for many of those who hold the modest pluralist position we have described above, mission is still necessary. Christians are still convinced of Christ's saving power and want to proclaim this as they learn from others and deepen their faith in dialogue. Frederick E. Crowe writes appreciatively of Bernard Lonergan's understanding of the Holy Spirit present and active in all of humanity's religions, but he says that we cannot shirk the task of evangelization. Referring to 1 Corinthians 9:16 he says, "Woe to us if we do not preach the gospel . . . but our approach will be modified by our new understanding of the situation."[106] Such a new understanding, writes Bosch, is tantamount "to an admission that we do not have all the answers and are prepared to live within the framework of penultimate knowledge, that we regard our involvement in dialogue and mission as an adventure, are prepared to take risks, and are anticipating surprises as the Spirit guides us into fuller understanding."[107] Type B theology would urge that mission be carried out in "bold humility," witnessing to the truth by witnessing to the Lordship of Christ in one's life, and witnessing to the wonderful power of human reason, human experience and human culture to attain it, however vaguely and tentatively.

Type B Ecclesiology

If the Christology of Type B is one of revelation and illumination, Type B ecclesiology might be characterized as the community of those who *know*, those who have been illumined, those who help one another to hold fast to the vision and are called to witness to that vision to all humankind in all parts of the world. Teilhard de Chardin described the church as the "reflexively Christified portion of the world";[108] the church is consciously, in other words, what the rest of humankind is in its deepest aspirations. For Orthodox Christians, writes Alexander Schmemann, the church is "heaven on earth." It is "first of all and before everything else a God-created and God-given reality, the presence of Christ's new life, the manifestation of the new 'aeon' of the Holy Spirit," existing "to manifest and to actualize in this world the *eschaton*, the ultimate reality of salvation and redemption."[109]

Type B ecclesiology would most likely see itself in terms of the model of mystical communion or sacrament. It is a community that is intimately linked to Christ, and through Christ its members are intimately linked to one another. Its sacramental nature points to its essentially missionary nature; the unity it experiences is an anticipation of the unity of all humanity with God and with one another, and the church is called to be instrumental in bringing such unity about (see LG 1 and 48). Even though Cyprian of Carthage might be classified as a Type A theologian, his description of the church as "a people brought into unity from the unity of the Father, the Son and the Holy Spirit"[110] captures the nature of the church as a communion in which Christians have access to the ineffable mystery of God in Godself. At any rate, this phrase is quoted in Vatican II's decree on the church (LG 4), which in many ways exemplifies the best of Type B ecclesiology.

The church is, to use a related image that appears in both Type A and B ecclesiology, the body of Christ. If the human body of Christ is the "door" to union with the divinity, the visible, concrete, structured, sinful-yet-holy church is the "door" to Christ, the way that Christ is encountered today. As Henri de Lubac emphasizes in *Corpus Mysticum*, the Pauline image of the church as Christ's body was a favorite image of the patristic church.[111] Although the image was eclipsed in the Middle Ages by the institutional ecclesiology of Type A, Johann Adam Möhler retrieved it in the beginning of the nineteenth century. Despite the fact that it was interpreted by Pius XII through an institutional lens in his 1943 encyclical *Mystici Corporis*, the encyclical's publication signaled a revolution in Roman ecclesiology. Vatican II preferred the image of the church as the people of God, but the council's document on the church nevertheless gives the image body of Christ rather lengthy treatment in paragraph 7. That the church is the body of Christ means, first, that by baptism Christians share the life of Christ so intimately that they become one with him and so become "members of one another" (Rom 12:4). They are thus Christ's continuing presence in the world and are nourished in this through the celebration of the Eucharist. Second, though the members of the body are many and are endowed with many gifts, they are made one by an equal share of the Spirit. Finally, though the church *is* the body of Christ, Christ transcends the church as its head. While the church continues Christ's presence in the world, his presence is not confined to the visible reality of the church.

As we have pointed out, however, the image favored by the Second Vatican Council was the image of the church as the people of God. First, the people image points to the radical communal nature of the church. Rather than understanding its nature from the institutional perspective of a perfect society, the council begins its reflections on the church by acknowledging its nature as a mystery—"a reality imbued," as Paul VI put it, "with the hidden presence of God."[112] Such a community, second, shares a fundamental equality; there exists prior to any ministerial or hierarchical determination "a common dignity of members deriving from their rebirth in Christ, a common grace as sons and daughters, a common vocation to perfection, one salvation, one hope and undivided charity" (LG 32). Third, the image people of God is described in terms that make it inclusive of all peoples; while Catholic Christians are envisioned to be most fully incorporated into God's people, other Christians are "joined in many ways" (LG 15). Even those who have not yet received the gospel are "related to the People of God in various ways" (LG 16). We see here—and also in the decrees on non-Christian religions (NA 2) and on the church's missionary activity (AG 3)—Type B's confidence in the goodness of human reason and conscience being played out. But we also see articulated, at least implicitly, the motive for missionary activity: to bring humanity to the fullness that it anticipates in its various religious experiences. Finally, the image people of God lends itself to a kind of openness toward the future. In Chapter VII of LG the church is described as a "pilgrim," journeying to the future, with its fulfillment only in heaven (which, from the context, could be interpreted as the time of the full inauguration of the reign of God [see paragraph 48]). The church does not journey blindly, however. While it is not to be identified with the reign of God, it is itself the "seed and the beginning" (LG 5) of it, within which humanity can have a foretaste of what all are called to in the End.

The missionary ramifications of this image point to both the church's mission *ad intra* and *ad extra*. The church, first of all, must work to become what it is called to be and what it is in its deepest nature. The church needs constantly to work on the quality of its community, the vitality of its spiritual life, the integrity of its internal structures—this is its mission *ad intra*, its mission to itself. The internal quality, vitality and integrity are not, however, cultivated for the church itself; they are cultivated, rather, so that the church can be a credible and attractive witness to the gospel in the world. As the church lives as a model of what it preaches and works for in the world, it carries out its mission *ad extra*— to the world.

Type B Eschatology

Perhaps the best way to characterize the eschatology of Type B theology is to highlight its fundamental optimism, or perhaps to be more theologically accurate, its hopefulness, in terms of both universal history and individual human lives. Origen is well known for his theory of universal restoration, when even the devil will be saved. Originally, says Origen, creation was purely spiritual;

physical creation was the result of God's mercy, made as a repository for creatures when they fell from their original state of contemplation of the One. Through
Jesus, the Holy Spirit and the church, God is calling all intellectual creatures
back to the original unity, which will be reestablished at the End. At this time,
physical creation will cease to exist, and although all will have to pass through
the fires of hell to be purified, all will return to their original, wholly spiritual
condition. Of course, there is no guarantee that creatures would not fall again,
and the whole process would have to be repeated—as it may have been repeated
before our own eon of creation.[113]

Origen's vision of hope, like that of the more historical yet equally hopeful
vision of Irenaeus that we will treat as part of Type C eschatology, was never
fully accepted into the theological mainstream. More somber visions of the *dies
irae* prevailed in the eschatological imagination of the West. As Christianity
tried to appropriate the new understandings of the world and humanity proposed by modernity, Origen's hopefulness surfaced in the optimism of liberal
theology. In liberalism, however, focus was on men and women as individuals,
and the end of history was understood not as something that would happen in
the future, but something available to believers *now*. González quotes a striking
example of such eschatological thinking in the work of Adolf Harnack:

> The kingdom of God comes by coming to the individual, by entering into
> his soul and laying hold of it. True, the kingdom of God is the rule of God;
> but it is the rule of the holy God in the hearts of individuals; *it is God
> himself in his power*. From this point of view everything that is dramatic
> in the external and historical sense has vanished; and gone, too, are all the
> external hopes for the future. . . . It is not a question of angels and devils,
> thrones and principalities, but of God and the soul, the soul and its God.[114]

Similar to this kind of "realized eschatology," Rudolf Bultmann in the middle
of the twentieth century employed the existential philosophy of Martin Heidegger
to interpret the gospel that calls individuals to decision for an authentic life
now. For Bultmann, the wild and weird apocalyptic and eschatological imagery
of the Bible and of Christian tradition needs to be "demythologized" and then
reinterpreted in contemporary categories (which were provided by Heidegger's
philosophy).[115] Paul Tillich as well, despite a strong eschatology of the future,
still speaks in terms of Jesus as the "New Being," who meets humanity with full
eschatological power when he is encountered in faith in the midst of history.[116]
The task of mission in the context of this realized eschatology is to call men and
women to the fullness of what they can be already in this life.

The eschatology of most Type B theologians today, however, is much more
of the "inaugurated" version. Rather than understanding God's reign as totally
in the future, or as totally present in individual spiritual encounter, the end of
history is understood as already inaugurated by the death and resurrection of
Jesus but not yet fully present as we "wait with joyful hope the coming of our
Savior, Jesus Christ."[117] This is certainly the eschatology of Vatican II, and it is

with this eschatology that mission is carried out. In the mystical communion of church one can experience already the full reality of God's salvation, and so mission calls men and women to this already inaugurated fullness. While this kind of eschatology certainly does not deny the individual eschatological realities of death, judgment, heaven, purgatory and hell, its focus is less on these than on the final destiny of humanity and the church's role as providing an anticipation of it. But mission is not carried out from the conviction that salvation is wholly dependent on people explicitly accepting the gospel. God will provide opportunities for salvation in ways known only to God (GS 22). Eschatology in Vatican II's version of Type B theology (an eschatology shared also by ecumenical Protestants) provides the time within which the fullness of the gospel can be shared with the world. The hope is that, when the End comes, all will be included in its fullness, but there certainly remains the possibility that individuals may choose to refuse God's grace and spend eternity in separation from communion with God and with humanity.

Salvation in Type B Theology

For Origen, in the context of Platonism, the salvation that Christ brings is both spiritual and intellectual. Sin was essentially a fall from pure spiritual existence, and it is in Christ and through the church that people find their way back to contemplation. Humanity is imprisoned in the material, and salvation is spiritual deliverance. The good news of Jesus Christ was to be preached, therefore, so that humanity might be delivered from the limitations of the material world and darkened intellects might be illumined by the light of divine Truth. Like Type A understandings of salvation, Type B focused on the salvation of the soul.

With the dawn of modernity, however, and the revolution in philosophical, theological and political thinking that modernity's "turn to the subject" entailed, traditional spiritual understandings of salvation were profoundly challenged. As David Bosch describes it, "Salvation now meant liberation from religious superstition, attention to human welfare, and the moral improvement of humanity." This was "an understanding of salvation in which humans were active and responsible agents who utilized science and technology in order to effect material improvements and induce socio-political change in the present."[118]

Some Christians of the Type A variety in both the Catholic and Protestant churches reacted to modernity's "revolution" by ignoring the epochal shift in thinking that was taking place in the modern mind; others openly opposed it. Protestantism reacted with the development of fundamentalism; the rise of neo-Thomism in the nineteenth century, along with the reaction of Pope Pius IX and Pope Pius X (the former with the 1864 Syllabus of Errors and the latter with the 1907 condemnation of modernism) were two major Catholic reactions. Other Christians, however, tried to take the challenges of modernity seriously, and this had profound implications for the notion of salvation. Rather than understanding sin as something that divided humanity from God, this "liberal" approach conceived sin as that which divides humans among themselves. Salvation, then, was that which brought humans together, improved their lot and set them on the road to cultural and material progress. Salvation, true to the Type B thinking, was conceived in terms of enlightenment of ignorance, but now the ignorance was understood in terms of human science for human progress. Mission, caught up in many ways with Western colonial expansion, was part of the "white man's burden," and salvation was all but equated with Western values and civilization. As Bosch puts it, "People only had to be *informed* about what was in their own interest. The Western mission was the great educator, which would mediate salvation to the unenlightened."[119] In the twentieth century, salvation was often too closely connected with development, or even economic and political liberation, based again on Type B's sometimes naive confidence in human possibilities.[120]

Today Type B theology has a much more balanced notion of salvation that in many ways dovetails with what we will see in Type C. What seems to be characteristic, however, is Type B's persistence in regarding human experience and human reason in a very positive light. Nevertheless, like Type C, salvation is understood as holistic and integral.

Type B Anthropology

The Platonic thought underlying Origen's thought is the foundation for a dualistic vision of the human person as composed of body and soul, matter and spirit, the former basically imperfect and even evil, the latter the seat of true personality. To be human, for Origen as for all Platonists, was to rise above the body in the contemplation of the spiritual, unchanging Forms. In this way, Origen's anthropology is quite different from the anthropology of nineteenth-century liberal theology or contemporary Protestant and Catholic efforts to conceive humanity holistically.

The key, however, to Type B anthropology is confidence and trust in human reason—or to put it in more modern terms, human experience—to find Truth. This is what Origen, the Platonist, has in common with Abelard, the medieval rationalist, and what these two premoderns have in common with modern thinkers like Schleiermacher and Rahner or contextual theologians like Mercado or Mbiti. Ultimately, for Type B theology, what is truly human is good, and the truly human is the door to the holy.

Humanity is essentially educable—not, however, in the sense that human minds are empty vessels that need to be filled. Rather, there is a capacity in humanity to build upon what it already knows, to make connections, to be enriched by the new. Mission, therefore, building on this anthropology, is always in the form of education—"leading forth" (literally from the Latin *ex ducere*), bringing to the light, helping to give birth to what is already there. In this process the knowledge of Christ serves as a catalyst, as when people read an article or hear a song that helps them express what they have long thought or felt or known but were never able to articulate. In the famous phrase, grace builds on and perfects nature.

Because Clement, Origen and probably Abelard lived in a world that valued hierarchy, theirs was an anthropology that fostered elitism and favored, if not the rich and powerful, certainly the intelligent and cultivated. For the Alexandrines, wrote R. B. Tollinton, "man at his best was their concern, but they had little regard for the crowd."[121] But, as we should point out once again, as thought and culture at the dawn of modernity turned to the human person and human experience, the anthropology of Type B was much more in tune with Enlightenment values of liberty, fraternity and equality. And as Type B theology gained ascendancy in theological thought in the mid-twentieth century, mission saw itself as engaged in the promotion of what Henry Venn had already articulated as the three selfs—self-supporting, self-governing and self-propagating; it even began to promote a fourth self—self-theologizing.

Culture in Type B Theology

What we have said just above points to the fact that, while premodern versions of Type B theology would espouse more classicist notions of culture, modern expressions would regard culture from the empiricist perspective. In both cases, however, culture is regarded as something good and trustworthy, and a context in which one might encounter the divine. Since the aim of much Type B theology was to demonstrate that Christianity was compatible and ultimately illuminative of the best of philosophy, and that the movement of reason, if followed honestly, would end in the illumination of faith,[122] it would only entail a short step to argue that Type B theology would also aim to show the compatibility of human culture with Christianity. Indeed, culture might even serve as a hermeneutical tool to understand Christianity even more profoundly, as Christianity moves into new cultural contexts.[123] The work of Christians, says Origen, "is to take the materials of the heathen world and fashion from them objects for the worship and glorification of God."[124]

Type B theology would interact with culture, it would seem, through the use of the anthropological model of contextual theology. It would, in other words, begin by listening attentively to the culture in an attempt to discern the presence of God, who, it is convinced, has been in the culture even before Christianity's arrival. It would try to excavate the hidden treasure of Christ that is buried in the warp and woof of cultural patterns and values. Its effort would be to call the culture to its deepest identity by means of the illuminating and ultimately purifying message of the gospel. Its method of evangelization would begin with a thorough "mission in reverse"—it would only dare preach the word of the gospel after it had itself been evangelized by the God who is already there.[125]

The danger of this approach to culture, of course, would be to fall into a pattern that Richard R. Niebuhr characterized as "the Christ of Culture,"[126] an uncritical acceptance of culture that ultimately distorts the gospel which is being preached. There is the danger of a syncretism born of compromise and infidelity to the gospel. But theologians who begin their theologizing with a reverence for culture would say that syncretism as a process is inevitable and that the risk involved is a risk well taken.[127] Type B theology is consistent in its conviction that the best of what is human is, in the last analysis, compatible with the dynamics of God's revelation in the word made flesh.

Type B theology, as González points out, is characterized by a search for Truth, Truth accessible to humanity through attention to human experience and human reason.[128] Summarizing its implications for mission, we might say that mission is carried out as a search for God's grace that is hidden within a people's cultural, religious and historical context; it is a call to people to fulfill their deepest potential as human beings by allowing Christ to be the answer to their deepest human desires. Mission, in other words, is an invitation to discover the Truth. In that Truth lies human salvation, already realized and present in human experience and human culture. The church in mission is the great sacrament of what being human is about; it is a community in which one has access to the mystery and community of God. Contemporary concerns with the inculturation of theology in various contexts find their roots in the confidence in human experience to which Type B theology witnesses.

Type C Theology:
Mission as Commitment to Liberation and Transformation

The third type of theology that we consider in this chapter has its roots in the land that borders the northeast Mediterranean Sea, that is, Asia Minor, or what we now know as Turkey and Syria. The principal city of the area was the Syrian city of Antioch, which, as we pointed out in Chapter 1, was one of the most important cities in the Roman Empire, and perhaps the first place where the Jesus community recognized its full identity as church. González says that the distinct approach to theology that was developed here is both older than Type A or Type B theology and closer in spirit to many of the original witnesses to Christianity collected in the New Testament.[129] Many scholars argue that the Gospel of Matthew is a product of the community of Antioch; Asia Minor is the area from or to which Paul wrote many of his letters, and Ephesus in Asia Minor is linked both with the Gospel of John and the Book of Revelation. In addition, Antioch was the see of Bishop Ignatius, from whom we learn much about the life of the early church; Polycarp, another early witness to Christianity, was bishop of Smyrna, a city also located in Asia Minor. Although this area was a part of the Roman Empire and, like all of the empire, subject to the influence of Hellenistic culture so rooted in Platonic philosophy, it was, González claims, both less Romanized and less Hellenized than either Carthage or Alexandria. Because of this, a way of understanding Christianity developed that was less legalistic and less abstract than the other two theological perspectives we have discussed; it was more concrete, based on events that many of its originators had been eyewitnesses to. The School of Antioch is remembered in the history of theology both for its efforts at literal interpretation of the scriptures and its emphasis on the human nature of Jesus.[130]

The person, says González, who best articulates Type C theology in its origins was not, however, a resident of this area, but Irenaeus, bishop of the Roman frontier city of Lyon, in Gaul. Irenaeus, nevertheless, had been born in Smyrna and had migrated to Gaul with a number of other Christians early in his life. And although he lived in the West, he wrote in Greek and had carried with him the theological traditions of Asia Minor. Unlike both Tertullian and Origen, Irenaeus was heir to the rich sub-apostolic tradition that was based neither on law nor philosophy but on actually witnessed events; unlike them both as well, he was neither a clever lawyer nor a brilliant academic but a pastor in a frontier town and Christian outpost. Irenaeus wrote only two works that we possess in their entirety, but these were seminal works of a theological perspective that stands in contrast to both Type A and Type B. If Type A can be characterized by *law,* and Type B characterized by *truth,* the perspective of Irenaeus in Type C theology might best be characterized by the word *history*—not "in the sense of a faithful narrative of past events . . . but rather in the sense that all takes place within time and is guided toward God's future."[131]

In contrast to Type A and Type B theologies (at least in its Platonic beginnings), history in Type C theology was part of God's plan from the beginning and not a result of a fall from some eternal state of perfection or contemplation. God had created men and women in the *image* of God but with the task of growing into God's full likeness. As such, they were created *imperfect* but were *perfectible.* Adam and Eve had made a mistake in the Garden of Eden. By disobeying God they had, as it were, exceeded their grasp, and so fell into the servitude of the devil. But, despite sin, God as Father and Shepherd continues mercifully to lead and guide humanity throughout history. God sent Jesus to free humanity from Satan's clutches and so to make possible continued growth, until at the End all will be recapitulated in him.

We see here the roots of a tradition that, says González, was forgotten and even suppressed in the history of theology, very likely because of some of the political and economic implications that its acceptance might entail.[132] But it is also a tradition that has resurfaced now and again, and was never entirely eliminated in Christian history. We see some form of it in the work of the missionaries of the East Syriac Church in China in the seventh century, in the radical perspectives of St. Francis of Assisi, in some of the reforming insights of Luther and Wesley and in the powerful theology of Karl Barth and Dietrich Bonhoeffer.[133] In the twentieth century, with a greater appreciation of history and with what is perhaps a more balanced perspective on humanity's nature as both radically sinful and yet fundamentally good, Type C theology emerged once more as a major theological perspective. It has some of its most important expressions in the vision of Pierre Teilhard de Chardin, in the documents of the Second Vatican Council (particularly its *Pastoral Constitution on the Church in the Modern World* [GS]), and in the explosion of liberation theology in its Latin American, Asian, black and feminist varieties.

Type C theology has always been eminently pastoral in outlook and has been the foundation for several creative expressions of the church's missionary nature. It is a theological perspective that remains centered on the mystery of Christ while always acknowledging the importance and dignity of the human.

Type C Christology

Irenaeus speaks of Jesus and the Holy Spirit as the two hands of God.[134] While such language might sound anthropomorphic, González makes the point that such language serves to emphasize that, for Irenaeus—and for Type C theology in general—God relates directly to the world both in Christ and in the Spirit. The freshness of this idea is seen more clearly when we contrast this with the more philosophical notions of some of the earlier expressions of Type B theology. For Origen, for example, the Word and Spirit tend to be used as ways to safeguard the distance between God and creation. Here, however, we have "exactly the opposite";[135] God is engaged in the world's history through the working of the Holy Spirit and the incarnation of the Son. There is no real philosophical speculation as to how mystery can be visible and tangible. God is involved in history and so is manifest in radically historical ways.

Nor is there much concern in Irenaeus's writing about how Jesus' divinity is linked with his humanity. It is enough for him to say that "He is man, the formation of God; and thus took up man into Himself, the invisible becoming visible, the impassible becoming capable of suffering, and the Word being made man, thus summing up all things in Himself."[136] In Irenaeus's perspective, incarnation was not something brought about by human sin as a kind of extreme solution; it was present from the beginning as an expression of God's love. It was always in God's plan to become human, so that humanity might have full communion with the divine. In contrast to a Platonic notion of the impossibility of the spiritual having anything to do with the material, Irenaeus's doctrine of creation sees humanity created for divinity, and divinity open and able to be fully involved with humanity. As such, his perspective is less philosophical and so perhaps less appealing to cultivated Hellenistic minds. As theological reasoning has shifted in our own day to include more appreciation for the Semitic world view of the Bible, Irenaeus's ideas have taken on a new freshness that confirms our need to look at the historical events of Jesus' life to understand his mystery. Liberation theologians like Leonardo Boff and Jon Sobrino insist on beginning their Christological reflections from the historical Jesus, developing a "Christology from below."[137] "They attempt to begin where Jesus began, where he lived, where the people met him—not in churches but in everyday life, and that means in misery. He is not recognizable by his halo."[138]

Irenaeus and Type C theology do not see Jesus' redeeming work as the payment of a debt or the offering of a higher illumination, as would Tertullian and Type A theology or Origen and the theology of Type B. Rather, Jesus is the one whose life, death and resurrection have set us free from our slavery to Satan, a slavery that "keeps us from acting freely and impedes the human growth God had intended."[139] Jesus' work of redemption, in other words, is the accomplishment of our liberation.

As González explains it, for Irenaeus incarnation was something that God had intended from the beginning of creation. After Adam and Eve's sin, however, the incarnation took on an added redemptive dimension. When the Word did finally become flesh, that flesh was not subject to Satan: Jesus was the New Adam, who would live an entire human life as a "recapitulation" or redoing of human history, one who would at the same time undo human history lived under the yoke of Satan and provide new possibilities for humanity henceforth. Irenaeus describes the redemption in terms of a battle: Jesus "fought and conquered; for He was contending for the fathers, and through obedience doing away with disobedience completely: for he bound the strong man, and set free the weak, and endowed His own handiwork with salvation, by destroying sin."[140] The climax of the battle was when Jesus was sentenced to death on the cross. It was as if he lured Satan into believing that he had been conquered; by his resurrection, however, he conquered Satan completely, opening up for us "the gap through which we too can escape from bondage."[141]

Such an interpretation of Jesus' work of redemption was one that persisted into the Middle Ages, only to be supplanted by Anselm's brilliant satisfaction theory, a theory that perhaps captured the mystery more adequately in the context of feudalism and a culture conditioned by Germanic legal systems. In the twentieth century, however, the theory was revived in the context of neo-orthodox theology. The notion that humanity was caught in situations that were totally overwhelming, that systems such as industrialization and colonialism had given rise to conditions that could only be described as enslaving and demonic, made the theology of redemption as victory over such powers one that had new meaning. Jesus redeemed us, wrote Gustav Aulén, as *Christus Victor*, struggling with the powers of death and conquering through his resurrection.[142] The notion of redemption as liberation also found resonance in the various liberation theologies that emerged in the 1970s. Faced with massive institutional violence and systemic oppression, Latin American theologians began to interpret the Jesus of the gospels as one whose siding with the poor and marginalized of his day opened up new possibilities for those who were considered without identity and without hope. Jesus' death was according to no divinely appointed script; the powers that profited from the unjust status quo were responsible for his execution. Sölle quotes Louise Schottroff: "Jesus died as a martyr for his people and for God's righteousness. The Romans understood that the physical embodiment of God's justice in the world is subversive, and threatens the powerful." Sölle adds, "This subversive Jesus had to be eliminated."[143]

Jesus' resurrection, however, stands as a sign that God was irrevocably on Jesus' side and that evil and injustice in the end cannot and will not prevail. In Jesus' life and death God has spoken a final word of life and liberation. "They simply could not do away with him," says Sölle. "That is the resurrection. What his life meant, what his spirit was, what his disciples did, this 'yes' to God's will lived, and lives today, and this life appears on the cross."[144] Such interpretations of Jesus' death and resurrection are the direct legacy of Irenaeus and represent a contemporary, powerful presentation of Type C Christology.

Although the Type C theology of Karl Barth, particularly in its embodiment in the work of Hendrik Kraemer, would include an exclusivist understanding of Christ,[145] in the contemporary context of discussion about the uniqueness of Christ, Type C liberation theologies would take, we believe, a moderately pluralist position. Since Latin America is an overwhelmingly Christian continent, and since liberation theology is rooted in practical and not such theoretical issues, the concern is not so much whether Christ is the unique savior, but what *kind* of salvation is offered. In Asia, however, the question of Jesus' uniqueness enters into the heart of Christology. As Aloysius Pieris has put it, Christianity has to be baptized in the Jordan of Asian religions and crucified upon the cross of Asian poverty.[146] Jacob Kavunkal calls for the cessation of metaphysical claims for Christian uniqueness while at the same time calling for a commitment to live out the message of the gospel in a way that will attract more disciples of Christ. "Instead of brandishing the cross as a sign of might and superiority, it has to become a true sign of the Christian today: a sign of weakness and helplessness of unarmed truth. . . . We are called to be his faithful disciples. That is the mission that the church can render in India."[147] Mission in the light of Type C Christology is not so much the proclamation of a message or a system of doctrines. It is the proclamation of the saving power of Jesus Christ through a life of liberating witness. It is a life lived in a community of freedom and witnessed to by that life in community. This is the ecclesial dimension of mission to which we now turn.

Type C Ecclesiology

For Irenaeus, the church is literally the body of Christ. If in Adam and Eve all humanity became enslaved to the devil, in Christ the New Adam, all are joined to Christ as partakers of his victory. Christ, through his resurrection, already enjoys the fullness of resurrected life; as our head he has gone before us, but "at the proper time," when all will be fully restored in him, we too will rise.[148] As the body of Christ, the church is a sure means of grace: "Where the church is, there is the Spirit of God; and where the Spirit of God is, there is the church, and every kind of grace."[149]

Irenaeus's concern for history is seen in his concern for the connection between the church of his day and the church of the apostles. It is this physical link that distinguishes the true church from the church of heretics. When there was doubt about an issue, Irenaeus recommended that Christians look to a church that had been founded by an apostle. This could easily be done, since "we are in a position to reckon up those who were by the apostles instituted bishops in the church, and to [demonstrate] the succession of these men to our times."[150]

Type C theology's commitment to history only came to full flower in the twentieth century. In many ways the ecclesiology of the Second Vatican Council was influenced by Type B theology. The revolution at the council was the move from an understanding of the church as a hierarchical, perfect society (Type A ecclesiology) to an understanding of the church as a community, the people of God mystically united to Christ (Type B ecclesiology). The seeds of Type C theology, however, were sown already in the designation, in the first paragraph of the council's document on the church, of the church as sacrament—as sign *and* instrument of the unity between God and humanity, and women and men with one another. These seeds came to full flower in two documents that were finalized at the last session of the council and that, in the opinion of several theologians, represent the true trajectory of the council's thought.[151] In these documents the council makes the move from understanding the church in terms of the model of mystical communion or a more static understanding of sacrament to understanding it in terms of the sacramental model's more dynamic interpretations in the context of the models of herald or servant.

The first document is the *Decree on the Church's Missionary Activity*. In a dense theological meditation on the nature of mission, the council speaks of the church as "missionary by its very nature," explaining that this is so because the church has its origin in the "mission of the Son and the Holy Spirit" (AG 2). The council was saying, in other words, that the church, in its essence, is "ec-centric"—involved, like God, in the world and in the ebb and flow of its history. Rather than as a chosen community focused on itself and its own integrity, the church is here described as essentially dynamic, open, discovering integrity in historical action.

The second document in which this dynamic notion of the church appears is in the last document approved by the council, the *Pastoral Constitution on the Church in the Modern World*. The first paragraph of this document sets the tone of the whole document and speaks of the church as committed irrevocably to the world, to the human and to history:

> The joy and hope, the grief and anguish of the men and women of our time, especially of those who are poor or afflicted in any way, are the joy and hope, the grief and anguish of the followers of Christ as well. Nothing that is genuinely human fails to find an echo in their hearts. For theirs is a community composed of women and men who, united in Christ and guided by the holy Spirit, press onwards towards the kingdom of the Father and are bearers of a message of salvation intended for all men. That is why Christians cherish a feeling of deep solidarity with the human race and its history. (GS 1)

In 1968, at the Second General Assembly of the Latin American Bishops' Conference at Medellín, Colombia, these Type C perspectives of Vatican II were further developed, laying the foundation for what began to be called liberation theology. In the book that presented liberation theology's first systematic expression, Gustavo Gutiérrez speaks of the church as the "sacrament of liberation."[152] What the church is, he says, is a community that by its life and by its action in the world witnesses to God's liberating work in history. As liberation theology has developed, it has recognized the central importance of the local community, the base ecclesial community. Such communities, writes Leonardo Boff, are "reinventing the church,"[153] pointing to the church's need to be radically local, to be led by local leaders, to be a church not just *for* the poor but *of* the poor.

Type C Eschatology

Type C's eschatology is one that takes history with utmost seriousness and understands eschatological fullness not as the end of historical process and the inauguration of a timeless, spiritual state, but as history's transformation and fulfillment. Its focus, while not denying realities like heaven, hell and purgatory, is much more that of general and cosmic eschatological concerns. González points out that, in contrast to Tertullian and Origen, history in Irenaeus's theology is not the result of human sin. Even if there had been no sin there would have been history; history was the context in which humanity could develop and grow. Growth to full humanity and maturity, growth as God's *image* into God's *likeness* was part of God's original plan. The goal of history for human beings is their "divinization," as they enter into full communion with God.[154] Irenaeus's theology is eschatological from start to finish.

In Irenaeus's Christology, the movement of history, distorted under Satan's power, is set free once again. Humanity, created in the image of the Word, now has the possibility, through the church, to become a new creation in the New Adam and to continue to grow into his full likeness. The "final consummation" (which González says is really a misnomer, since history, for Irenaeus, does not cease) is cosmic in scope, involving the transformation of all material creation.[155]

Irenaeus's cosmic and evolutionary perspective was largely forgotten as Western theology concentrated on issues of guilt and original sin, and on the eternal destiny of individuals after death. His ideas of growth and development, however, have a particularly contemporary ring and resonate strongly with many contemporary concerns. Although his ideas did not achieve wide circulation until after his death, early in the twentieth century the Jesuit paleontologist Pierre Teilhard de Chardin worked out a powerful vision of history that espoused both the theory of evolution and imagery of cosmic recapitulation in Christ found in both Paul and Irenaeus. History, he said, moved from "cosmogenesis," or creation of the physical world, to "biogenesis," or the emergence of life, to "noogenesis" (or "anthropogenesis"), the development of human consciousness. The next stage, which we are awaiting now and which will bring us to "point Omega" or eschatological fulfillment, is "Christogenesis." Christ's life, death and resurrection have laid the foundation for this final evolutionary leap, and the church as the "reflectively Christian part of the universe" anticipates to some degree this eschatological fullness and is sent to the world to prepare for history's final consummation of cosmic wholeness in Christ.[156]

Although the Catholic Church for some time forbade the publication of his writings, Teilhard's vision exerted a powerful influence on the theological imagination of Christians in the twentieth century, and much of Vatican II's document on the church in the modern world seems inspired by his spirit (see especially GS 45, entitled "Christ: Alpha and Omega"). Teilhard's sense of the holiness of the world, his belief in the divine purpose of human and cosmic history and his conviction that Christian mission involves commitment to human development all exemplify Type C's perspective that Christianity does not so much offer a way to an otherworldly heaven but "a clue that gives us a glimpse into God's purposes for human history and invites us to participate in those purposes."[157] Teilhard's broad cosmic perspective has inspired contemporary efforts to link the church's mission to ecological and environmental concerns.[158]

Type C eschatology today might best be described as "inaugurated eschatology."[159] Jesus' life, death and resurrection inaugurated the reign of God, but the final consummation of that reign is still in the future. We in the church participate in God's reign through our life together and the sacramental life that we share, and we are heartened as well by signs of that reign outside the church's visible boundaries. This consciousness of the reign of God as already inaugurated but not yet fulfilled results in a vision of the church's mission. As David Bosch puts it, "Precisely the vision of that coming kingdom translates itself into a radical concern for the 'penultimate' rather than with the 'ultimate,' into a concern for 'what is at hand' rather than for 'what will be.' . . . Living in the force-field of the assurance of salvation already received and the final victory already secured, the believer gets involved in the urgency of the task at hand."[160] Working for economic and political liberation, for recognition of human rights and equal dignity—all this is part of the church's mission in the perspective of Type C theology, which sees God's saving action taking place in the midst of history, not promising fulfillment outside it.

Salvation in Type C Theology

Much of what we have said in regard to Type C eschatology is applicable to the notion of salvation that underlies it. Salvation is human and cosmic wholeness; it is radically this-worldly, but it is not simply material well-being or prosperity; it is about healing, because the world and humanity have been scarred by sin.

For Irenaeus, salvation meant the ability to grow into greater and greater communion with God. This capacity was arrested when humanity was in the captivity of Satan, but Jesus' work of liberation enabled humanity once more to grow into maturity. Irenaeus understood salvation to be material as well, as the whole of creation lives and grows to its full capacity.[161]

Type C understandings of salvation today, influenced by Teilhard and the various theologies of liberation, also speak of God's and the church's saving activity as human and cosmic healing and wholeness. They acknowledge too, however, that such wholeness involves both material and spiritual dimensions. David Bosch speaks of "comprehensive," "integral," "total" or "universal" salvation as an understanding that avoids the two extremes of (1) regarding it as something that takes us out of the world, or only involves a "personal relation-ship with Jesus Christ" or (2) falling into positions (like that of the Salvation Today conference in Bangkok in 1973) that reduce salvation to economic jus-tice, liberation and human solidarity.[162] On the one hand, he says, "hatred, injus-tice, oppression, war, and other forms of violence are manifestations of evil; concern for humaneness, for the conquering of famine, illness, and meaning-lessness is part of the *salvation* for which we hope and labor."[163] On the other hand, salvation *is* something that transcends human efforts, and perhaps even the human horizon. "Salvation does not come but along the route of repentance and personal faith commitment."[164] In the same way, Pope Paul VI linked salva-tion to liberation but insisted that they should not be identified, nor the latter reduced to the former (EN 35, 32).

Jerald Gort outlines four aspects of the church's mission in the light of the understanding of salvation that we have attributed to Type C theology. First, he says, the church *proclaims* salvation by preaching reconciliation—with God, with humanity, with nature. People "must become acquainted with the good news of acquittal, of forgiveness of sin and guilt, and of the new life that begins in the present and continues beyond the grave with Jesus Christ." Second, mis-sion invites men and women out of their aloneness and into a *community* where "in Christ the dividing walls have been broken down."[165] Third, the church in mission must involve itself in the *ministry of mercy*, by which the community extends help and assistance to the poor and suffering of the world. Finally, mis-sion which preaches, serves and witnesses to salvation will be a *ministry of justice*, a ministry *of* the poor and *with* the poor that addresses itself to the struc-tures that *keep* people poor.

Type C Anthropology

Type C theology provides the basis for a positive appreciation of human beings while at the same time not being naive about human failure and human sinfulness. It represents, we might say, a balance of the perspectives of Type A and Type B. In the theology of Irenaeus, humanity is created good but not yet complete, *perfectible* but not yet *perfect*. The plan of God was to call humanity to constant growth, "not only in the present world, but also in that which is to come, so that God should for ever teach, and man should for ever learn the things taught him."[166] Humanity was created in God's image and called to grow into the divine likeness. The model of that divine likeness was the Word be-come flesh, a process that did not degrade God but showed the full range of God's power and love. There is no sense of dualism, of a chasm between matter and spirit. For humanity to be complete, humanity was to grow into God, who had become flesh. Even sin is not depicted as a "fall" from a higher state to a lower but as a misdirection, a tragic enslavement from which humanity needs to be set free.

Once again, we recognize that Irenaeus's perspective is strangely contempo-rary. Teilhard's vision of humanity in the light of evolution is also one in which the notion of growth is at the core of human identity. While he is often criticized for not paying sufficient attention to the possibilities of human evil, Vatican II's anthropology in its *Pastoral Constitution on the Church in the Modern World* offers more balance. In *Gaudium et Spes* 12 and 13 we read that humanity is the "center and summit" of creation, created in God's image to care for the earth, created essentially as a social being for relationship one with another and with God, but deeply divided by sin. Humanity is distinguished both by its "high calling and deep misery." To be human is both a bodily and a spiritual experience, although both are disoriented by sin (GS 14). To be human, however, is also to experience transcendence in the drive toward understanding and truth (GS 15), towards ethical behavior (GS 16) and toward freedom, that "exceptional sign of the image of God in humanity" (GS 17). This sober view of the nature of humanity is at the center of the thought of Pope John Paul II, who wrote in his first encyclical, *Redemptor Hominis,* that the human person is the route on which the church must travel if it is truly to fulfill its mission (RH 14).

The theologians of liberation share both this high regard for the human and the strong sense of the power of sin. They focus their attention both on calling humanity to full consciousness of it possibilities ("conscientization") and denouncing the greed and selfishness that enslave humanity in dehumanizing structures of institutionalized violence. Citing the sad insight of Paolo Freire that, so often, the oppressed—once liberated—become oppressors, their work for liberation is the development of a vision of the basic dignity and equality of all humanity, and of the responsibility that true freedom entails. The full humanity that liberation makes available is not just for the oppressed who are set free; the humanity of the oppressors is also enslaved by their oppression and is restored when they cease their oppression.

The church's mission is the proclamation, service and witness to the fullness of humanity. It is, in the words of Gustavo Gutiérrez, the "annunciation" of the good news of liberation and the "denunciation" of the situations and structures that hinder human freedom and human development.[167] More and more today, however, humanity is being understood not as the center of creation but as an integral part of it. Humanity is being understood more and more in the context of *cosmic* wholeness. This, too, seems to be within the trajectory of Type C theology, with its deep evolutionary and historical perspective. Mission for the sake of humanity is therefore more and more becoming involved in issues of eco-justice.[168] Only when the cosmos is whole can humanity experience wholeness.

Culture in Type C Theology

Type C theology is rooted in the conviction that history is neither detrimental nor accidental to God's saving action but essential to it. History is the stage on which the drama of salvation is played out. It is not something that will be completed or transcended by eschatological fulfillment, but something healed and perfected as the *sine qua non* of created existence, human life and cosmic wholeness. What this means is that human culture, in the perspective of Type C theology, is regarded as basically good. Because of human sin and the enslavement to overwhelming powers that sin involves, culture needs to be purified, perfected and healed.

It is for this reason that Christian faith might best interact with culture, from the point of view represented by Type C theology, in terms of the "praxis model" of contextual theology, or in terms of the more positive versions of the "counter-cultural model." In the praxis model, culture is conceived much more from the perspective of the dynamics of social change, and humanity responds to the call to have the gospel interact with culture by recognizing that it is involved in culture's very construction. Action, therefore, done out of commitment to gospel values is the beginning and end of such cultural engagement. Christians begin in action, reflect on the quality and effect of that action both by social analysis and a rereading of the scriptural and doctrinal tradition, and then act again in a more enlightened and, it is hoped, a more effective way. This is the method of the variety of liberation theologies that are the legacy of Type C theology. Focus would be on discerning and working for the fullness of salvation within a particular cultural context, and calling that context to greater growth and greater sensitivity to God's saving action in history.

Employment of the counter-cultural model would always be based not only on the recognition of the importance of cultural values and behaviors in shaping attitudes and actions, but also on the recognition of the enslaving and dehumanizing aspects that culture can foster. The task of mission in this situation is, first, to unmask these unsavory aspects of culture and to confront them with the saving (in the full sense that we spoke of above) reality of the gospel. Type C theology recognizes the importance of culture as a factor that shapes human life and human attitudes, but it is also suspicious of culture as a *human* creation. Since all that is human is under the captivity of evil, culture too needs to be liberated by the saving action of Christ. This does not necessarily mean that culture is seen as evil; it is just that the thoroughly ambiguous nature of culture needs to be recognized as such. When culture is judged in the light of the gospel, and healed where healing is necessary, it can be celebrated as a powerful way by which men and women can express and deepen their understanding of God.[169]

We might summarize Type C theology by noting once more its focus on history. On the one hand, Type C appreciates history as the "place" in which real people live and in which they are called to change and grow; on the other hand, it recognizes history's essential ambiguity as a situation enslaved by sin, and so a situation in which growth without God's grace is impossible. Mission, therefore, from the perspective of Type C theology is the commitment of Christians toward the liberation and transformation of humanity, indeed, of the world. Christians proclaim Christ as the true liberator and "transformer of culture." And the church is the community of liberated humanity that finds its identity in its commitment to a liberated world; it is a community-in-mission. The salvation the church proclaims is a salvation already inaugurated in the saving work of Christ, yet one not fully established as the church works with God in confronting the evil of systems and structures, purifying and perfecting human culture, and working for reconciliation of the entire creation. The fulfillment it looks for, therefore, does not take humanity *out* of the world; the liberation and transformation that come from Christ—often by sharing in Christ's suffering—are a liberation and transformation *of* this world. Missionaries see themselves as agents of God's liberating and transforming work.

CONCLUSION

The church only becomes the church as it responds to God's call to mission, and to be in mission means to change continually as the gospel encounters new and diverse contexts. Such change, however, is not arbitrary; rather, there have always existed certain *constants* that, while they might differ in content, are always present as a kind of framework by which the church identifies itself and around which the gospel message takes shape. To our outer-space scholar, the community in Jerusalem might *look* very different from the church of the Council of Nicea, the church of the Irish monks in the seventh century or the church of today. But because it has always responded to God's call to mission, and because that response has always been structured by the centrality of Jesus, lived out as church, preached as life's ultimate meaning, and grounded in understandings of human nature and the nature of history, that community—and its mission—has always been the same. It may have been colored by the Roman or Germanic appreciation of law, by the Greek or the modern love of reason or by the Hebrew intuitions of the importance of the concrete as it appears in history. But because there was always operative a Christology, an ecclesiology, an eschatology, a notion of salvation, an anthropology and a recognition of culture, the church has been recognized as Christian. Sometimes it has been more successful in being itself; sometimes it has faltered. Sometimes it has needed reform; sometimes it has been in the forefront of prophetic denunciation and activity. But as long as it has been faithful in its purpose and in its basic shape, it has been the church.

This chapter has attempted to provide a map, or perhaps better, a grid. Under the guidance of Justo González and Dorothee Sölle, we have presented the various ways that the constants of mission might be conceived while continuing to be "witnesses of these things" (Lk 24:48): "that the Christ should suffer and on the third day rise from the dead, and that repentance and forgiveness of sins should be preached in his name to all nations, beginning from Jerusalem" (Lk 24:46-47). In the six chapters that follow we show in greater detail how these constants change shape and yet remain the same as the church lives out its mission in particular historical contexts. Our hope is that the grid we have developed in this chapter will prove helpful in seeing both the constancy of the church as it lives out its mission and the contextual, changing shape that such constancy requires.

Part II

CONSTANTS IN CONTEXT: HISTORICAL MODELS OF MISSION

As a river twists and turns in its journey toward the sea, both shaping and being shaped by the contour of the land, the geological composition of the soil and the enterprises of humanity, so the church, as a community-in-mission, both forms and is formed by the "lay of the land." In turn, the various *constants* of the church's one mission throughout its history have both shaped and been shaped by the historical-cultural *context* and the corresponding theological thought of particular times and places. The history of mission, the movements of culture and the history of theology intersect, and, depending on the *way* they intersect, various "models" of mission can be discerned.

In reflecting back to the three major theologians of González's typology, for example, the particular historical context influenced each basic theological perspective. The Roman city of Carthage and the Marcion heresy affected Tertullian's concern for law and morals. The intellectual environment of Hellenized Alexandria and Gnosticism helped to shape Origen's concern for truth and metaphysics. The memory of persecution and martyrdom in a less-Hellenized area of Syria and Asia Minor affected Irenaeus's concern for history and the pastoral situation before him.

The next question, then, is, What model of mission would emerge from such theological perspectives? As we now proceed to look at six periods of mission history, González's and Sölle's typologies will be helpful in identifying the dominant type of theology or theological perspective that influenced a distinctive model of mission. In each chapter of Part II we present the historical context, the model of mission which was predominant among others, the theological underpinnings of the period and model and a brief reflection relevant for present issues of mission. We present these historical models of mission as particular "case studies" of how the constants of mission are made concrete in specific changing contexts.

3

Mission in the Early Church (100-301)

Individual Christians in a Variety of Situations

In recent years there has been renewed interest in studying the post-apostolic age—the second and third centuries of Christianity.[1] In an oft-quoted article,[2] Karl Rahner compares the profound theological (and we would add missiological) turning point of the "Council of Jerusalem" (c. 49 C.E.), on the one hand, as Christianity shifted from being a Jewish sect to a Greco-Roman religion of the Gentiles, and the Second Vatican Council, on the other, as the church shifted from being a Western church to being a world church—a phenomenon likewise occurring in other Christian traditions.[3]

During its infancy stage, Christianity spread very rapidly in a variety of ways, particularly in the eastern part of the Roman Empire and in cities. Traveling evangelists, teachers and apologists were all instrumental, but the primary means was through the witness of Christians, who were even willing to die for their faith. The young church in the Roman Empire benefited from the years of religious influence of the Jewish Diaspora communities on their neighbors as it then moved from the Hebrew to the Greek world. The conclusion of the historical period treated in this chapter is marked with the semi-independent kingdom of Armenia officially declaring itself a Christian nation around 301, that is, some years before the Roman Empire would do so.

Further beyond the Roman borders, the news of the Christian faith followed the routes of trade and migration and spread in amazing ways to other cultures and across even greater distances as far east as India. This movement is associated with Christian merchants, emigrants, slaves and wandering ascetics from the Syrian wilderness. While the church here would also be, and in this case would continue to be, a small minority, the foundations were being laid for the church in the East, the ancient church in Asia. Our survey begins here.

THE EASTWARD EXPANSION OF CHRISTIANITY

We usually think of Christianity moving westward from Jerusalem, unaware that it was spreading just as, if not even more, dramatically in the other direction. Until recently, church and mission historians have given little attention, if any, to the eastward spread of Christianity, especially outside the Roman Empire. Even the history of the growth of what would eventually become the Orthodox church has generally been under-represented in Western history.[4] The potential impact of the outstanding contribution of Samuel Moffett[5] in "revealing" the in-depth history of the church in the East—known as Nestorians by other church traditions—is already evident in David Bosch's monumental work.[6] Currently Dale Irvin and Scott Sunquist, working collaboratively with a wide group of consultants, are writing *History of the World Christian Movement*[7] to "retell" the Christian story in such a way that the voices of all Christians— Eastern and Western, women and men representing the diversity of Christian traditions—are heard more equally in this narration. Irvin and Sunquist begin the description of the early Christian movement outside Palestine by looking east to Syria and Mesopotamia.

One of the primary biases that continues to influence the understanding of Christian history is the perspective that, almost from the beginning of the church until the last part of the twentieth century, Christianity has been a Western religion. Speaking against this popular image, Philip Jenkins writes, "Founded in the Near East, Christianity for its first thousand years was stronger in Asia and North Africa than in Europe, and only after about 1400 did Europe (and Europeanized North America) decisively become the Christian heartland."[8]

Another factor affecting this lack of knowledge of the eastward expansion of Christianity is the shortage of written records. Partly for this reason, but also due to the fact that the four major regions outside the Roman Empire to be described below each had its own particular distinct context, we will not present an overall context, but rather briefly present those elements that are most relevant for understanding the early beginnings of Christianity in each area.

Going east through western Syria—with its principal cities of Antioch and Damascus and its importance for Christianity within the Roman Empire (to be treated later)—one moves outside the Roman Empire and finds equally important Christian roots in eastern Syria. By the end of the second century, there was a Christian center in Edessa, a city situated at a strategic junction of two ancient trade highways and the capital of Oshroene, a small buffer kingdom-state between the large warring empires of Rome and Persia. According to a tradition, which cannot be dismissed simply as legend, this people was first evangelized by a Galilean Jewish Christian named Addai, who is considered the founder of the Syrian church (later known as the Nestorians).[9] In those early years, Edessa was predominantly Jewish-Christian.

While Oshroene's claim as the "First Christian Kingdom" needs some qualification, it is quite likely that its king, Abgar VIII, was baptized a Christian a

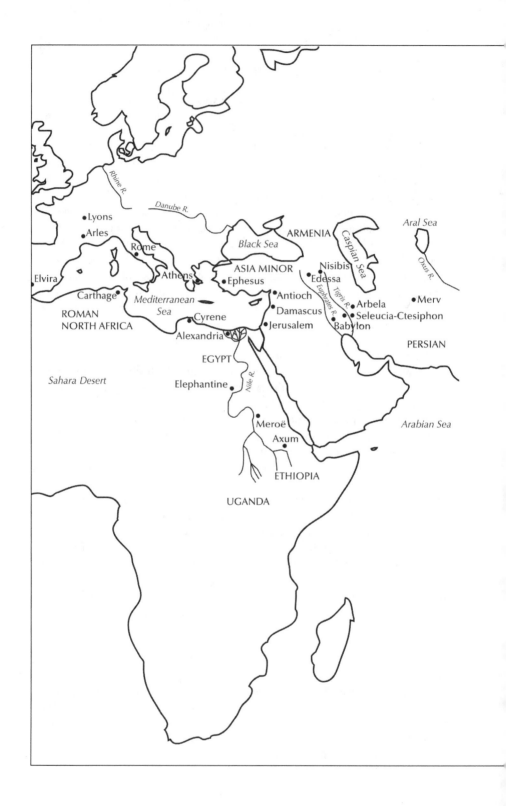

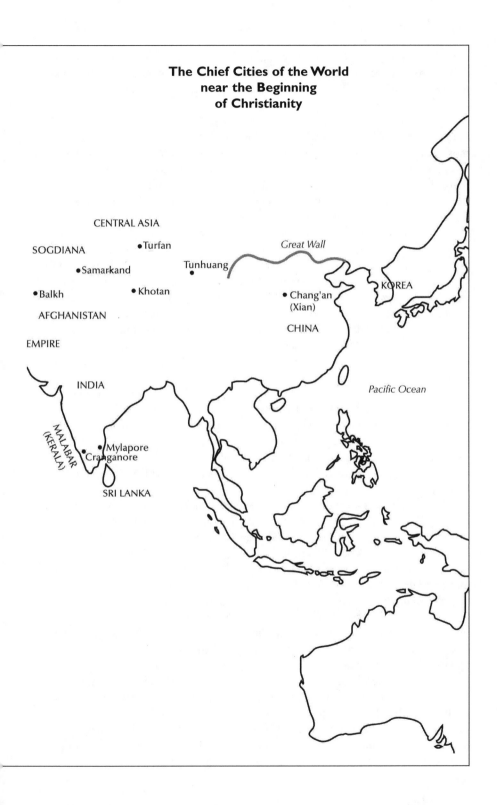

The Chief Cities of the World
near the Beginning
of Christianity

CENTRAL ASIA

SOGDIANA

Turfan

Great Wall

Samarkand

Tunhuang

Balkh

Khotan

KOREA

Chang'an
(Xian)

AFGHANISTAN

CHINA

EMPIRE

INDIA

Pacific Ocean

MALABAR
(KERALA)

Mylapore
Cranganore

SRI LANKA

hundred or more years before Constantine. Also, the Syriac-speaking Christians were so established that one finds the earliest documented record in history of a public church building in Edessa during the reign of Abgar VIII at the end of the second century.[10]

After a short period of political independence from the Parthian dynasty of Persia, Oshroene became a Roman colony in 214. While it remained for the most part under Rome politically, it was closer to Persia religiously and culturally. The Oshroene Christians maintained a sense of fellowship with the Christians of the West and of the East. Their most renowned and controversial philosopher and theologian of the second century, Barbaisan of Edessa, wrote that unity in Christ is stronger than any difference in race or nationality.[11]

During the same period, four hundred miles east of Edessa across the border into present-day Iran, one finds a Christian community in Arbela, the capital of the kingdom of Adiabene in the empire of Persia. While the origins of this Christian community are not known, there is verifiable evidence that in the middle of the second century Tatian the Assyrian—the theologian, linguist, ascetic and ex-pupil of Justin Martyr—brought the Syriac gospels to the church of Asia. Tatian did not directly translate the four Greek gospels but rather arranged them into a harmony, weaving them together into a consecutive history. By the end of the second century, the church of Asia had a Syriac version of the Old Testament, called the Peshitta.

In the radical asceticism of such persons as Tatian, there are claims that ascetic monasticism may actually have had its roots in Syria rather than in Egypt with Anthony. In contrast to the ascetics of Egypt, who retreated from the world into caves and cells, the ascetics of Syria became wandering missionaries. Sources indicate that by the year 225 they preached the gospel and established Christian communities across the Persian Empire as far east as present-day northern Afghanistan.[12]

While 313 marks a dramatic transition for the church in the Roman Empire, the year 226 is similar for Syrian Christianity. When the Parthian kings of Persia were replaced for the next four hundred years by the Sassanid dynasty, the powerful shahs of Persia, Asian church history shifted from the Syrian to the Persian period. While the language of the church remained Syriac, its organizational center shifted to the Persian capital of Seleucia-Ctesiphon, and the theological center would eventually shift from Edessa across the border to the city of Nisibis.

Northwest of Edessa is the kingdom of Armenia, which was caught in a tug of war between Rome and Persia for three hundred years. While it seems that Christian merchants were the first to bring the Christian faith to Armenia, the real founder of Armenian Christianity is Gregory the Illuminator, who was greatly influenced by the church in Cappadocia. He baptized the Armenian king, Tiridates I, at the end of the third century, and around 301 Armenia declared itself officially Christian, the first nation to do so. This is the first occasion of many in which a country became Christian after the baptism of its ruler. From the original preaching of Gregory in Armenian, there has been a very strong link between Christianity and the Armenian language and culture.

One of the most extraordinary stories of Christianity is that of the church in India. In his thorough study of available resources, Samuel Moffett draws the following conclusion: first of all, Jewish colonies were already in India at the time of Christ; second, the Christian church was probably established in India as early as the end of the second century, and certainly by the fourth; third, both the apostle Thomas and the teacher Pantaenus quite possibly had been in India; and fourth, Thomas was possibly in both northwest and southwest India.[13] Underlying these conclusions is the fact that there was much travel, trade and emigration between India and the Roman Empire at this time. "St. Thomas Christians" from southwestern India were to develop into different strands of Christianity over the years, but they all continued to trace their common roots to this ancient Christian tradition.

MISSION IN THE EAST

With the exception of India, the acceptance of Christianity across western Asia occurred mainly in three protectorate kingdoms under the Parthian dynasty of the Persian Empire—Oshroene, Adiabene and Armenia. At first, the Parthian rulers neither brought nor enforced a unified cultural and religious identity. Instead, they seemed to have provided as fertile an environment for the first roots of Asian Christianity as the *Pax Romana* was providing for Christianity in the West. Later, when the Sassanids came to power in Persia in 226, they tried to enforce their strong political, cultural and religious (Zoroastrianism) identity on others.

In this situation of being pulled back and forth between Rome and Persia, these buffer kingdoms often experienced movements toward national and cultural unity. In some situations the adoption of the Christian faith seems to have been partially an expression of this desire for independence. Of probable significance as well for the early spread of Christianity in Asia was the existence of Jewish Diaspora communities in both Oshroene and India. Although Christians remained a small scattered minority, it is important to note that Christianity "was unquestionably spreading across the great continent of the East as vigorously as it moved westward into Europe."[14]

There is not as much clear evidence here for the participation of "ordinary" Christians in the spread of the faith as we will see in the Roman Empire, although Jewish and Christian merchants, migrants and slaves certainly played their part. For example, perhaps trade and emigration were the main reasons for the spread of the Christian faith in India.[15] A second group of missionary agents, under the broad category of "evangelists," includes Addai, Tatian, Gregory the Illuminator, Thomas and Pantaenus. The contribution of teachers, bishops and later patriarchs[16] to mission also was beginning to develop (this will be described in the next chapter).

The third and major type of evangelizers were the various itinerant missionaries, who played a more prominent role for a longer time than in the West, especially through the ascetic movement that began sooner in the East. The wandering hermits and "monks" of the early ascetic communities were very influential in the spread of Christianity in the East; already by 340 there was a network, however tenuous, of missionary monasteries between Edessa and India.[17] This, however, leads us into the next chapter, where we examine the development of monasticism as the primary model of mission in the early Middle Ages both in the West and in the East, which will experience the "Golden Age" of mission for the East Syrian Church.

MISSION WITHIN THE ROMAN EMPIRE

The Social-Political Context

The political situation of the Roman Empire had a very strong impact on the shape of Christianity in these earliest years. On the one hand, the good news traveled quickly because the *Pax Romana* provided a situation of relative stability and peace, an excellent network of roads and trade, and Greek as a language for trade and for communication, at least among educated persons. On the other hand, while there was often basic religious tolerance, this age was marked with persecutions of Christians. Until 250, these persecutions were periodic and local. After that date, however, there were three major systematic attempts to wipe out Christianity, by Decius (250), Valerian (257) and Diocletian (after 303). Underneath a range of personal, religious and political motivations for these persecutions, the Christian movement was often seen as an obstacle to the desire for conformity and for strengthening the sometimes waning central authority of the empire.

In this context the public life of Christians developed around house churches and, to a lesser extent, particularly in Rome, catacombs. A few words need to be added regarding the latter. Instead of cremation, Christians buried their dead. In the beginning they used private Christian property for this purpose, but later larger burial grounds or underground catacombs were built outside city walls. Only in the fourth century would the catacombs become places of worship, and never were they places where Christians would hide. However, they served as a focal point for the identity and life of the church. As for house churches, not every private Christian home was designated for this purpose; rather, certain houses became the accepted places for the regular weekly gathering for prayer, bible study, sharing resources, community discussions and the Eucharist. With time, some houses went through a considerable amount of adaptation as the Christian community increased in size.

A very significant underlying factor of the social context was the shift of the church and mission from the village to the city:

In those early years, then, within a decade of the crucifixion of Jesus, the village culture of Palestine had been left behind, and the Greco-Roman city became the dominant environment of the Christian movement. So it remained, from the dispersion of the "Hellenists" from Jerusalem until well after the time of Constantine. The movement had crossed the most fundamental division in the society of the Roman Empire, that between rural people and city dwellers, and the results were to prove momentous.[18]

Where, how and why Christianity grew was very much influenced by the urbanization process that was creating more and larger cities, in which Jewish communities had already been present for centuries. James Russell asserts that social destabilization of urban centers, particularly in the eastern part of the empire, "contributed to a social, psychological, and religious climate in which alienated individuals sought refuge in socioreligious communities which offered socialization in this world and salvation in the next."[19]

The Religious Context

In many ways Judaism in the Diaspora prepared the way for the spread of the Christian faith. Since the eighth century B.C.E., the Jewish people had been dispersed, both forcefully and voluntarily, throughout the Roman Empire and beyond. Drawn to the major centers of Hellenistic culture such as Antioch, Rome and Alexandria, they organized themselves into tight-knit communities. It is estimated that by the time of Jesus, they made up about 7 percent of the total population of the Roman Empire.[20] They did have some special privileges from the Roman government, and they participated in the dominant Hellenistic culture. Jews of the Diaspora spoke Greek; used a Greek translation of the scriptures, the Septuagint, in their religious gatherings; and some even took Greek names.

Through the influence of the Jewish Diaspora and the availability of the Septuagint, a large number of Gentiles were drawn toward the strongly monotheistic religion of the Jews. While some did join the Jewish religion, it seems that most considered circumcision a major obstacle.[21] However, this group of Gentiles, known as God-fearers, who already knew the God of Abraham and Sarah and the commandments of Moses, were prepared for and responsive to the gospel of Jesus Christ. Stephen Neill maintains that the impact of the God-fearers in this period of the early church makes it almost impossible to compare this time of mission with any other.[22] Furthermore, while the split from Judaism had been more painful and decisive in the Holy Land, the influence of and contact with the Jewish communities in the Diaspora had a longer impact on Christianity. For example, the oldest Christian community in Rome was probably in the Jewish quarter in Trastevere.[23] In this same line of thought, it seems that a significant number of Hellenized Jews became Christians, and Jewish Christianity had an impact into the third century and beyond, that is for a much longer time and at a greater depth than was generally understood in the past.[24]

Perhaps as a sign of an environment of spiritual unrest and searching, the ancient Roman religion and the emperor cult were declining despite periodic attempts to revive them, and a number of mystery religions were being introduced from the East.[25] Another factor that contributed to the demographic and moral degeneration of the Roman Empire was two major epidemics, in 165-180 and in 251, possibly smallpox and measles respectively. In the earlier epidemic, from one-quarter to one-third of the population died. In agreeing with Cyprian, Dionysius, Eusebius and other early church fathers, Rodney Stark suggests that "had classical society not been disrupted and demoralized by these catastrophes, Christianity might never have become so dominant a faith."[26] Quoting the words of the philosopher Víteslav Gordavsky, David Bosch describes this atmosphere as an "odor of decay."[27] In contrast with the urban situation, the popular traditional religions were quite stable and viable in the rural areas, where Christianity was not embraced so quickly during the second and third centuries.

The Institutional Context

The shift in Christianity's development—from being a Jewish sect, to a new religious movement or cult, and eventually into a clearly defined religion—was a rather complex and prolonged process. As the church moved through the post-apostolic age, Christians of a particular city formed a single congregation or local church. Correspondence and representatives were recognized as coming from the church of God in Corinth, Smyrna or Rome. The unity of the congregation was most clearly evident during the eucharistic celebration. In order to defend and foster this unity, the church had to deal with disputes and jealousy on the local level and with divisions within the wider Christian community regarding such issues as the date of Easter and penitential discipline.

In response to what were discerned as popular heresies (for example, Gnosticism, Marcionism and Montanism), the church took up the task of formulating a precise creed, determining the biblical canon and beginning to define the understanding of apostolic succession. Through a number of councils and synods and the writings of fine theologians, such as Tertullian, Origen and Irenaeus, the church was able to find its way through these challenging first years.

Out of the variety of different ministries within local communities, the offices of bishops (episkopoi—literally, "overseers"), elders (presbyteroi) and deacons (diakonoi) developed, and the evidence shows that soon after 150 C.E. the monarchical episcopate became a fairly common ministry in local congregations, at least in Asia Minor. Ignatius of Antioch seems to have been the first to call the universal communion of all Christian communities "the Catholic Church," with Christ as its invisible bishop.[28]

Another ecclesial development that was very significant for the future of the church and mission was the introduction of the catechumenate. Probably due to the increasing missionary success of Christianity at the end of the second century, the church wanted to ensure the proper preparation and instruction of neophytes through an intense transformational initiation process.[29] Evidence of the formalization of the catechumenate by the beginning of the third century in Rome can be found in the writings of Hippolytus and Tertullian.

By the time of Constantine, it is estimated that about 10 percent of the fifty million people of the Roman Empire were Christians.[30] Stark points out that this was a phenomenal growth of about 40 percent per decade.[31]

MODELS OF MISSION

During this early history of Christianity, there was a rich diversity, for example, in theology and church ministry. Likewise, mission was carried out in a wide variety of forms within the social-political, religious and institutional context. In fact, every ministry was missionary, because at this point the entire church saw itself in this way. Mission was not a part of the church's reality, but was its very essence. While we focus most of our attention on the primary model of mission, it is important to identify and briefly describe the other forms as well.

Secondary Models: Evangelists, Bishops, Apologists, Teachers and Martyrs

First of all, there were the *traveling evangelists*, or apostolic preachers, whom Eusebius describes as follows:

> Indeed, most of the disciples of that time, struck in soul by the divine Logos with an ardent love of philosophy, first fulfilled the Saviour's command and distributed their goods among the needy, and then, entering upon long journeys, performed the work of evangelists, being eager to preach everywhere to those who had not yet heard the word of faith and to pass on the writings of the divine Gospels. As soon as they had only laid the foundations of the faith in some foreign lands, they appointed others as pastors and entrusted to them with the nurture of those who had recently been brought in, but they themselves went on to other lands and peoples with the grace and the co-operation of God.[32]

In the *Didache*, these evangelists are described in more detail. They did not stay long in one place (longer than two days already raises suspicions of authenticity); they were dedicated to poverty, were supported by the gifts of the congregations they visited, and were called directly by God rather than being chosen (ordained) by their home churches.[33] While these traveling preachers certainly were important in the early spread of the Christian faith, there were probably never very many, and there is less evidence of this type of evangelization by the end of the second century.

We noted above that the ministry of monarchical *bishop* developed during the post-apostolic age as the Christian congregations became more organized. While the number of itinerant preachers was decreasing, there is evidence that several bishops, such as Ignatius, Polycarp and Irenaeus, embraced the particular responsibility of evangelization outside their Christian community. An example of the seriousness with which Irenaeus undertook his role of mission was that he became fluent in the language of the "despised barbarians" in Gaul so that he could preach more effectively.[34] In the person of Irenaeus, we see the combination of church organizer, evangelist and theologian. Within this general context it is important to note the close identification among the bishop, the local church and the responsibility for mission. The episcopal model of mission, however, will become more prominent in the period of mission history treated in Chapter 4.

The third type of missionaries were the *apologists*.[35] Rather than responding to the immediate concerns of the Christian communities, they took up the task of responding through their writings to non-Christian hostilities, suspicions, misunderstandings and false judgments toward the church. In their endeavors, apologists chose different methods, according to their context. The Greek apologist Justin Martyr represented both González's Type B and Type C theologies,[36] with their emphases on truth and history respectively. He attempted to build a bridge of *continuity* between Hellenistic philosophy and Christianity, especially through the use of the philosophical and Old Testament concept of *logos* to speak of the Word as the intermediary between God and the world, and the *logos spermatikos* ("seed-bearing word") as the divine truth already implanted in classical philosophy:

> We have been taught that Christ is the First-born of God, and we have suggested above that He is the logos of whom every race of men and women were partakers. And they who lived with the logos are Christians, even though they have been thought atheists; as, among the Greeks, Socrates and Heraclitus, and people like them.[37]

In contrast, Tertullian (Type A theology with its more legalistic perspective), who was a strong exponent for the sufficiency of scripture alone for developing apologetics and Christian theology, pointed to the *discontinuity* between Christian faith and secular philosophy:

> What indeed has Athens to do with Jerusalem? What concord is there between the Academy and the Church? what between heretics and Christians? . . . Away with all attempts to produce a mottled Christianity of Stoic, Platonic, and dialectic composition! We want no curious disputation after possessing Christ Jesus, no inquisition after enjoying the gospel![38]

The implications of these two contrasting approaches for mission will be discussed later in this chapter. At this point it is important to note that, although their writings seldom reached their intended non-Christian addressees, they helped establish a natural hypothesis for Christianity in engaging philosophy and culture, without going deeply into the content of the faith.

While the apologists helped to express the faith in a more popular format, a small but influential group of *teachers*, both theologians and philosophers, laid a more academic foundation for the church's understanding of itself, its mission and its relationship with the world. Pantaenus, sometimes considered "the greatest Christian teacher of his age,"[39] was, as we have noted previously, quite possibly himself an evangelizer to India and the founder of the famous theological school of thought in Alexandria, where Clement and Origen succeeded him.

Clement of Alexandria maintained the continuity between Hellenistic philosophy and Christianity. "For philosophy was to the Greek world what the Law was to the Hebrews, a tutor escorting them to Christ. So philosophy is a preparatory process; it opens the road for the person whom Christ brings to his final goal."[40] Origen, considered the greatest theologian of the Alexandrian School, focused much of his attention on the Bible. He wrote critical and philosophical works on the text, scientific commentaries on individual books, and many discourses and homilies. He also instructed catechumens in the Christian faith, first on a private basis and later as the ecclesiastically appointed head of the catechetical school of Alexandria. Converted through the teaching of Origen, Gregory Thaumaturgus ("wonder-worker") became an evangelist and bishop in Pontus (Cappadocia), from which the faith eventually spread outside the Roman Empire to Armenia.

These are clear examples of the important role played by academia—teachers and theologians—in the early church's mission efforts. In the words of Michael Green, "It would be a mistake to think that the apologists and theologians were anything less than evangelists."[41]

While the conversion of members of the elite and educated class to Christianity is often attributed to the work of the apologists and teachers,[42] the conversion of the masses is often associated with *martyrs*, those who gave the ultimate witness *(martyria)*. Although it may not be so common to think of martyrs as evangelists, certainly the powerful witness of those who were willing to suffer and die for their newfound faith provided, first, a strong inspiration for the Christian community, and second, a witness that drew others to the faith.[43]

One of the oldest extant accounts outside the New Testament of a martyrdom of an individual is the description by Eusebius of the martyrdom of Polycarp (70-155?), the eighty-six-year-old bishop of Smyrna.[44] After his execution for refusing to swear by Caesar, the Christians collected his remains, buried them and gathered annually at his grave to honor him on the anniversary of his death. Here we have the earliest evidence in the Christian community for a cult of martyrs, which sees martyrdom as an imitation of the passion of Jesus Christ.

The writings of Eusebius include an eyewitness account of the martyrdom of Blandina, a Gallic slave girl and a recent convert, in Vienne in 177. The parallel drawn between a martyr, in this case a woman, and Christ is very striking:

> But Blandina was suspended on a stake, and exposed to be devoured by the wild beasts who should attack her. And because she appeared as if hanging on a cross, and because of her earnest prayers, she inspired the

combatants with great zeal. For they . . . beheld with their outward eyes, in the form of their sister, him who was crucified for them, that he might persuade those who believe on him, that every one who suffers for the glory of Christ has fellowship always with the living God.[45]

A fine piece of early Christian literature, *The Passion of Perpetua*, describes the martyrdom of an African woman from a prominent family, Perpetua, with her slave, Felicitas, and others, probably in 203 in Carthage. If the first part of this text was written by Perpetua herself, it is one of the earliest in Christian literature written by a woman.[46]

In situating martyrdom within the models of mission, we recall Tertullian's famous phrase, "We become more numerous every time we are hewn down by you: the blood of Christians is seed."[47] The martyr became the ideal of unqualified Christian witness and of protest against worldliness. Even though the actual number of martyrs during this period was smaller than has been popularly believed, most likely under ten thousand and perhaps as few as a thousand, martyrdom had an enormous impact in shaping Christians' self-understanding and the depth of their commitment, in shifting public perception in favor of Christianity, and in attracting many non-Christians to take a closer look at these Christians who were willing to sacrifice so much for their faith.[48]

The Primary Model: Baptism as a Call to Mission

In the survey of various roles in evangelization we now come to the primary model of mission, which is distinctive in the second and third centuries—the mission of "ordinary" Christians. Without jumping to the conclusion that every Christian was actively and explicitly seeking converts, one should think in terms of casual, informal witness. From the viewpoint of Celsus, a second-century critic of Christianity, we get a graphic picture of informal evangelization being carried out by woodcarvers, cobblers, laundry workers and uneducated people both in private homes and during other daily encounters.[49] Michael Green described this situation in the following picturesque way:

> They were scattered from their base in Jerusalem and they went everywhere spreading the good news which had brought joy, release, and a new life to themselves. This must often have been not formal preaching, but the informal chattering to friends and chance acquaintances, in homes and wine shops, on walks, and around market stalls. They went everywhere gossiping the gospel; they did it naturally, enthusiastically, and with the conviction of those who are not paid to say that sort of thing. Consequently, they were taken seriously, and the movement spread, notably among the lower classes.[50]

Several key issues here need further elaboration. First of all, it seems that the Christian faith spread primarily through existing relationships and networks—

family, acquaintances, business associates and the Jewish Diaspora/Gentile God-fearers connections. Stark has pointed out from general sociological theory that new religious movements only continue to grow if they also have an *open* network with the avenues and abilities to reach out into adjacent social networks,[51] which of course was very characteristic of Christianity at this time.

Second, while Green presents a commonly held belief that the majority of early Christians were from the lower classes, recent studies by New Testament historians and others challenge the presupposition that Christianity was a proletarian movement. Their findings seem to indicate that Christianity was based in the middle and upper classes.[52] While many Christians were people with some social privilege and standing, it is also true that many of them were in another way dissatisfied with their situation and on the edges of society—for example, Hellenized Jews, searching God-fearers and women in general. Furthermore, Christianity was neither an elite movement nor overly dependent on its leadership. Government authorities often made the mistake of thinking that they could destroy the church from the top by killing its leaders. Rather, "because Christianity was a mass movement, rooted in a highly committed rank and file, it had the advantage of the best of all marketing techniques: person-to-person influence."[53] This brings us back to Green's point above.

Besides conversations that took place naturally in shops, streets and markets, Green emphatically highlights the home as one of the most important places of evangelization.[54] Continuing from the apostolic tradition where the household was often the venue and focus of mission, formal and informal discussions as well as worship took place in private homes during this house-church period of Christianity. Wayne Meeks confirms that the individual household "was the basic unit in the establishment of Christianity in the city, as it was, indeed, the basic unit of the city itself."[55] It is important to note that the household often extended beyond the immediate family to include slaves, freed persons, hired workers, tenants and partners in trade or craft. Here we have yet another example of the Christian faith moving through established relationships and networks.

Within the Roman Empire, Christianity before the time of Constantine was primarily an urban movement, growing most rapidly in the Greco-Roman cities of Asia Minor in particular, largely due to the influence of the urban Jewish Diaspora in general. Stark offers the following vivid portrait of one particular urban situation, Antioch, whose Christian community was of particular importance:

Any accurate portrait of Antioch in New Testament times must depict a city filled with misery, danger, fear, despair, and hatred. A city where the average family lived a squalid life in filthy and cramped quarters, where at least half the children died at birth or during infancy, and where most of the children who lived lost at least one parent before reaching maturity. A city filled with hatred and fear rooted in intense ethnic antagonisms and exacerbated by a constant stream of strangers. . . . And, perhaps above all, a city repeatedly smashed by cataclysmic catastrophes: where a resident could expect literally to be homeless from time to time, providing that he or she was among the survivors.

People living in such circumstances must often have despaired. Surely it would not be strange for them to have concluded that the end of days drew near. And surely too they must often have longed for relief, for hope, indeed for salvation.[56]

Such a picture points to the precariousness of urban life and the yearnings of urban people—a context of near despair into which the good news of Jesus Christ was proclaimed by the Christian community. It was a lived witness of life in the face of death, inclusive love in the face of antagonism, hope in the face of despair and Christian faith in response to questions of the meaning of life.

Christians also shared the news of the gospel far beyond their homes. Due to the protection provided under the *Pax Romana* and an excellent road system, there was tremendous mobility in the Roman Empire.[57] And so we hear of the spread of Christianity to the far corners of the empire by merchants, artisans, emigrants, soldiers and slaves.[58] The strongest Christian influence in this regard was from Asia Minor—a center for both Christianity and trade. Most of the Christians in Gaul seem to have been from Asia and residents of settlements of Asian merchants.[59] Furthermore, "not only tradesmen but also Oriental immigrants and slaves brought to the West were main factors in carrying Christianity to the heart of the Empire."[60] We recall that Irenaeus was a member of this movement of people from Asia Minor to Gaul.

The missionary idea of "gossiping the gospel" was certainly much more than just a verbal message; rather, it was the message of one's whole life. The conduct of ordinary Christians had the greatest significance and impact for the spread of the gospel.[61] They lived out "the language of love."[62] Aware of the danger of idealizing the early church, Bosch states, "Michael Green perhaps gives too romantic a picture of early Christians, and yet the elements of their lives which he reviews (their example, fellowship, transformed characters, joy, endurance, and power) certainly were crucial factors in the phenomenal growth [of Christianity]."[63] The strong sense of belonging and acceptance strengthened the Christian communities *ad intra*, as well as providing a boundary-crossing witness to others *ad extra*. Living out God's inclusive love propelled Christians to extend their care for the sick, the needy and victims of widespread epidemics to those who were also not Christians—actions that did not go unnoticed by others.[64] Christians absolutely prohibited abortion and infanticide, in contrast to the norm around them. Often the apologists appealed to the high morality of Christian lives as proof of the dignity of Christian faith. "They [Christians] share in all duties like citizens and suffer all hardships like strangers. Every foreign land is for them a fatherland and every fatherland a foreign land. . . . They do not abandon the babies that are born. They share a common board, but not a common bed. In the flesh as they are, they do not live according to the flesh. They dwell on earth, but they are citizens of heaven."[65] In following up this thought, one can easily draw the connection between the witness of a Christian's daily living and of a martyr's dying for his or her faith. Both are seen as imitations of Christ.

Shifting to the sociological perspective, particularly to that of the city, Christianity invited people to a world of order, meaning and community. In response to the situation he portrayed of Antioch, Stark suggests that

> Christianity revitalized life in Greco-Roman cities by providing new norms and new kinds of social relationships able to cope with many urgent urban problems. . . . To cities filled with newcomers and strangers, Christianity offered an immediate basis for attachments. To cities filled with orphans and widows, Christianity provided a new and expanded sense of family. . . . And to cities faced with epidemics, fires, and earthquakes, Christianity offered effective nursing care.[66]

Women and Mission

A distinctive element in the pre-Constantinian church that certainly enhanced and shaped mission during this period was the prominent role of women. On the one hand, one must acknowledge the difficulties involved in getting a complete picture of women in the early church, due to limited sources in general, isolated examples in particular, the prominent male perspective of writers and the current lenses of our time.[67] On the other hand, studies from various perspectives and disciplines continue to contribute to capturing and shaping this very important element of our Christian story. In the first place, more women than men converted to the Christian faith, including a significant number of high-status women. Recognizing that there were a number of factors, most writers recognize "that Christianity was unusually appealing [to women] because within the Christian subculture women enjoyed far higher status than did women in the Greco-Roman world at large."[68] Important aspects of this improved status and human dignity are reflected in the Christian condemnation of infanticide (which was most often female infanticide), divorce, incest, marital infidelity and polygamy—common practices that victimized women in particular. Christians respected and cared for widows instead of applying great pressure on them to remarry. In contrast to the general situation in which women were frequently forced into pre-pubertal, consummated marriages, Christian women "were married at a substantially older age and had more choice about whom they married."[69] Underlying this Christian appreciation of the human dignity of women is the basic belief that all people are equally children of God. Rosemary Radford Ruether describes this dynamic in the following way:

> Over against the patriarchal pattern of the "world," Christians understood themselves as a new community, in which all members shared equally in the freedom of the children of God and in which privileged religious, class and gender roles were abolished. . . . Not only Gentiles and slaves but also women could be full and equal members of this community.[70]

Therefore, the power of the good news in the second and third centuries to a great extent bridged the gender distinctions of its own context, as it had those of class, culture and race.

Being full members of the Christian community—according to basic connection among baptism, church and mission—implied that women were involved in the spread of the Christian faith. Beginning in the household, where much of Christian life was centered, a woman's mission often began with her husband. Since women were in the majority in the Christian community and in a minority within non-Christian society, Christian women often married non-Christian men.[71] Tertullian vividly describes the tension and suspicion between a Christian woman and her non-Christian husband:

> Who, indeed, would permit his wife to go about the streets to houses of strangers, calling at every hovel in town in order to visit the brethren? . . . Or, to take another example, who would not be concerned when she spends the whole night away from the house during the Paschal solemnities? Who, without feeling some suspicion, would let her go to assist at the Lord's Supper, when such vile rumors are spread about it? Who would suffer her to slip into prison to kiss the fetters of a martyr?[72]

In spite of such a situation, Tertullian continues, women were often very influential in the conversion of their husbands: "He sees that his wife is changed into a better person and thus, through reverential awe, he himself becomes a seeker after God."[73] Stark considers such conversions of husbands, and consequently of households, as another significant network of relationships through which the Christian faith spread from one to another.[74]

In Christian homes women also shared responsibility in hosting Christian gatherings for discussions, meetings, worship and what Green refers to as "household evangelism."[75] Moreover, we hear of women serving as heads of house churches—Prisca (Rom 16:5; 1 Cor 16:19), Nympha (Col 4:15), and possibly Phoebe (Rom 16:17), Chloe (1 Cor 1:11), Lydia (Acts 16:14-15, 40), Martha (Lk 10:38) and Mary, the mother of John Mark (Acts 12:12). We assume that some women continued this New Testament tradition through the post-apostolic period. "With a woman's usual role being internal household management, it was a logical development for women to preside over the gatherings of believers in their homes."[76] In addition, women's informal communication of the gospel extended outside their homes to the natural venues where women gathered: the laundry,[77] the marketplace[78] and in the care for the poor.[79] We also noted earlier how women, such as Blandina, Perpetua and Felicitas, witnessed to their Christian faith by dying as martyrs.

Shifting to the area of more "official" roles of ministry, mission and leadership within the early church, we begin with New Testament sources.[80] Paul refers to some women as his "co-workers" and "laborers" for the sake of the gospel.[81] Romans 16 can be seen as a letter of recommendation for Phoebe, a "deacon" or minister *(diakonos)*, to travel as a missionary from one community to another.[82] In the same chapter Paul refers to Junia as an apostle *(apostolos)*—a title he used for himself as "one sent" to proclaim the gospel, that is, an itinerant missionary[83] or a traveling evangelist, mentioned above. Finally, there is reference to official prophesying by the four daughters of Philip.[84]

As we move into the second century and examine the limited sources, we hear of preaching by Maximilla[85] within the Montanist movement and Thecla, whose missionary life is the main focus of the apocryphal *Acts of Paul and Thecla*. While it is difficult to assess the historicity of this apocryphal text, Ben Witherington maintains that "the document does reflect the fact that women in the churches of Asia Minor had a certain amount of freedom and ability to exercise the gift of leadership, as was true in the Montanist movement in the same region."[86] Other apocryphal Acts also indicate that women had prominent roles in the church.[87] According to a disapproving Tertullian,[88] women in Carthage at the beginning of the third century were still appealing to the missionary Thecla for the authority of women to preach and baptize.[89] It is quite interesting that Thecla would also become the apostolic model for ascetic women of the fourth century.[90]

Due to the incomplete collection of reliable written sources from the post-apostolic period, it is difficult to draw an accurate picture of women in official positions of ministry and mission. However, we can conclude that "women were among the most prominent missionaries and leaders in the early Christian movement,"[91] and it does seem that the issue of leadership and ministry by women in the church was still very much alive and controversial in the second and third centuries.[92] As we stated earlier, women were attracted to Christianity because it treated them better and gave them a larger part to play within the community. By the end of the third century, however, these roles would basically disappear in the face of a greater clericalization of the church.

One notable exception to this trend was the development of the ministry of deaconess in the East (excluding Egypt). While speaking against the role of women in teaching and proclaiming Christ, *Didascalia Apostolorum* describes the roles of deaconesses as caring for sick women and assisting at women's baptisms. Quite noteworthy is the fact that the Syrian author of this document draws a parallel between the deaconess and the Holy Spirit as being female.[93]

In looking back at the role of women during the post-apostolic age, it is important not to limit our focus too much to the official positions of ministry and mission, which might be our preference from today's perspective. While this aspect is certainly important and worthy of study, we must situate our evaluation of and appreciation for the role of women within the whole context of the general understanding and models of mission of the time period under consideration. From this perspective we see that women were very much involved in the predominant model of mission, especially within the household, the house churches and the group of martyrs. This is all the more significant given the subordinate role of women in the general society.[94]

As a final comment regarding the study of the contribution of women in mission in the early church, the following statement from Barbara Reid in regards to evaluating the New Testament evidence would likewise apply to the rest of the pre-Constantinian period as well: "One should not presume, then, that if women are not mentioned in the text that they were not present. Nor should those women mentioned in the texts be regarded as unique; rather they should be thought of as representative."[95]

The basic conviction of this primary model of mission of "ordinary" Christian men and women during the second and third centuries is the foundation for all the forms of evangelization. This total commitment in word and deed to one's Christian faith in face of the unbelieving world was most explicit through the persecution and death of martyrs, who became the ideal model for all Christians. However, such personal commitment likewise pervaded the lives and work of the traveling evangelists, missionary bishops, apologists, teachers and heads of house churches—as Christians ministered in times of crisis. One traces this understanding of mission to their idea of baptism and the developing catechumenate process:

> The implications of these facts regarding the motivation of the Christian mission are evident. It was in baptism that converts first learned the meaning of belonging to a people who had made an exclusive covenant with God. By baptism they became soldiers in an army which waged war not through physical force but through spiritual, one that conquered by witness of a holy life and of love, not by the sword.[96]

In summary, "the primary means of its [Christianity's] growth was through the united and motivated efforts of the growing numbers of Christian believers, who invited their friends, relatives, and neighbors to share the 'good news.'"[97]

At the beginning of the fourth century, "Syria, Egypt, and Mesopotamia became the Christian centers that they would remain for many centuries."[98] From there, the Christian message spread further eastward to Persia and India, while Armenia to the north was the first nation to declare itself Christian. It seems that Christianity had spread westward into most if not all of the other main regions of the Roman Empire, but the distribution was quite uneven. Probably about half of the people in parts of Asia Minor and many in Egypt and North Africa had become Christian, while very few Christians lived in inland Greece, the northernmost section of the empire (north of Lyons) and in rural areas in general.

CONSTANTS IN THE CONTEXT OF THE EARLY CHURCH

The passage of the church into the second century and beyond involved a shift from the Hebrew world to multiple cultures—Hellenist, Indian, Syrian, Persian and Armenian—and from being a religious movement within the wider context of Judaism to being a discrete religion, albeit with strong Jewish roots. Particularly in the West, the most significant shift theologically was in terms of

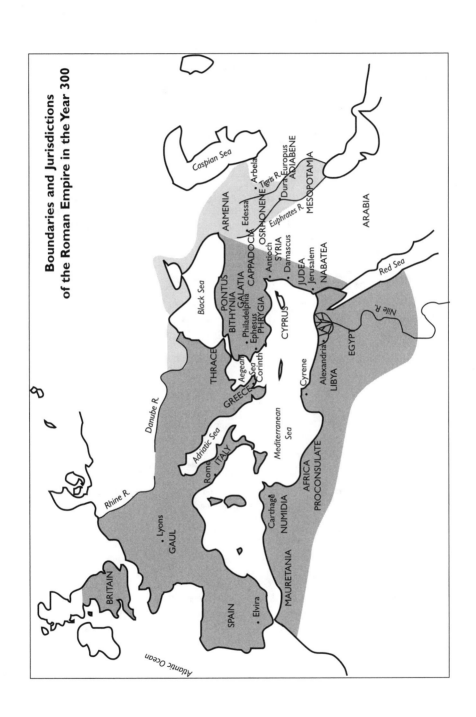

Boundaries and Jurisdictions of the Roman Empire in the Year 300

MISSION IN THE EARLY CHURCH (100-301)

Context	Roman	Hellenistic	Near Eastern
Stream of Christianity	Latin-speaking Strong Jewish influence	Greek-speaking	Syriac-speaking Strong Jewish influence
Primary model	Mission from baptism	Mission from baptism	Mission from baptism
Key figures in mission	Individual Christians; traveling evangelists; bishops, apologists, teachers, martyrs	Individual Christians; traveling evangelists; bishops, apologists, teachers, martyrs	Merchants, migrants and slaves; evangelists; traveling ascetics
Theological typology	A (emphasis on law)	B (emphasis on truth)	C (emphasis on history)
Primary theologians	Tertullian	Justin Martyr Clement of Alexandria Origen	Irenaeus Barbaisan of Edessa Tatian the Assyrian

CONSTANTS

Christology	High	High *Logos* Christology	Low Spirit Christology
Ecclesiology	Missional Institution of salvation	Missional Spiritual elite tendency	Missional Body of Christ
Eschatology	Futurist Individual	Realized Individual	Inaugurated/imminent Historical
Salvation	Spiritual/eternal life	Spiritual/illumination	Holistic
Anthropology	Negative	Positive	Positive
Culture	Negative Counter-cultural model	Positive Anthropological model	Postive/negative Moderate counter-cultural model

eschatology—from primitive Christianity's apocalyptic-eschatological expectation of the immanent return of Christ to a belief in the already consummated eternal reign of Christ. "People's expectations came to be focused on heaven rather than on this world and God's involvement in history; instead of looking forward to the future they looked up to eternity."[99] Through various stages the soul ascended to immortality and perfect union with God. *Salvation* from this world was understood in terms of "eternal life." Alongside these developments, elements of immanent eschatology did continue among some Christians, especially for those facing serious persecution, oppression and martyrdom.[100] While the church eventually rejected apocalypticism, represented by such movements as Montanism, as Per Beskow writes, "we cannot exclude, however, that its [Montanism's] eschatological fervour was an important factor in the rapid expansion of Christianity, esp. in Asia Minor."[101]

With this gradual shift in eschatology and *ecclesiology* away from the apocalyptic overemphasis on the "not yet" aspect of the reign of God, the church had to be careful of the opposite extreme, under the strong influence of Gnosticism, of overemphasizing the "already" aspect, that is, the already actualized salvation of a spiritual elite.[102] Due to this changing self-understanding, the church's mission was carried out less in the Pauline sense of urgency through the missionary fervor of itinerant evangelists. However, the church, more and more as an "institution of salvation," continued to expand rapidly primarily through "ordinary" Christians, as noted above, who were convinced of the good news of forgiveness, love and freedom from evil. The essential identity and interrelatedness of mission, baptism and church provided a theological basis for this primary model of mission in the second and third centuries. Through the catechumenate process and baptism, and frequent references back to both, Christians saw themselves as part of a people who had made an exclusive covenant with God and who would conquer evil by lives lived in holiness and love.[103] God became a human being in Christ, who was central to their faith; in practical terms, this implied a new way of living.

While the theological understandings regarding eschatology, ecclesiology and salvation were fairly commonly held, the budding theological schools expressed more diversity during this post-apostolic time in their *Christologies* and attitudes toward *human nature* and *culture*. All three types of theology were fairly well represented, but Type B theology (with its emphasis on truth) associated with Origen was predominant in the Hellenistic world within the theological-missiological paradigm of this period of the church.[104] Through its openness to and interaction with the *logos spermatikos* (Justin Martyr) in contemporary Greek culture and philosophy, the church associated with Alexandria developed a high Christology, which employed Philo's idea of *logos*. Origen in particular played a central role in this paradigm change in theology by creatively bringing together contemporary culture and Christianity's understanding of itself.[105]

In one of the earliest references regarding the principles of what we refer to today as *inculturation* or *contextualization,* Origen wrote the following around

230 to his former student, Gregory Thaumaturgus, who at that time was a missionary in Cappadocia in Asia Minor:

> I wish to ask you to extract from the philosophy of the Greeks what may serve as a course of study or a preparation for Christianity, and from geometry and astronomy what will serve to explain the sacred Scriptures, in order that all that the sons of philosophers are wont to say about geometry and music, grammar, rhetoric, and astronomy, as fellow-helpers to philosophy, we may say about philosophy itself, in relation to Christianity.[106]

This quotation is representative of Christianity's approach to the surrounding Hellenistic world and representative as well of the mission theology of the prominent Alexandrine church. Some have judged that this Hellenization went too far, but authors like Bosch point out that the early church did avoid extreme Hellenization.[107] Andrew Walls describes Origen as an embodiment of the final stage of the Hellenistic translation of and conversion to the Christian faith, whereby conversion "involves redirecting what is already there, turning it in the direction of Christ."[108]

This form of Hellenistic Christianity and mission theology will continue to develop within the tradition and mission of the Orthodox/Byzantine Church of the Greek East, which we trace in later chapters. In contrast to a commonly held belief that the Orthodox Church lacked a "true missionary dimension," today there is a better appreciation of its mission work and theology.[109] In his presentation and assessment of this paradigm of mission based on the love of God, Bosch identifies the passage of John 3:16 ("For God so loved the world . . . ") as epitomizing this mission theology.[110] On the one hand, this theological perspective of the pre-Constantinian model of mission embraces the essential incarnational aspect of Christianity. On the other hand, however, there is a danger that the equally essential prophetic call-to-conversion aspect may be lost.

In contrast to the theology of Origen, Tertullian expressed strong opposition to entering the cultural world of the Greek *ecumene*. His understanding of theology and mission was very much shaped by his context in Romanized Carthage. While Tertullian absolutely forbade Christians to serve in the army when it was not required, he often used military terms to speak about Christians,[111] especially martyrs,[112] as soldiers of Christ, and Christ as *imperator*.[113] Such imagery associated with *militia Christi* was also used by Origen and Clement of Alexandria and points to an underlying motivation for and understanding of Christian mission.[114] Even the members of the elite Alexandrian School recognized that Christianity is involved in an encounter between good and evil.

While Tertullian was against any type of reconciliation of Christian self-understanding and Greek philosophy, he set out to prove that Christianity was compatible with the highest Roman moral standards. With the so-called Edict of Milan and the influence of Augustine (354-430), this theology of "law and order" would later become the prominent theology of the Latin West.

Differing from the other two types of theology, Irenaeus's (Type C) positive attitude toward history allowed him to adopt the perspective of human nature as a potentiality for Godward growth. Irenaeus, as both theologian and missionary, made cultural accommodations linguistically[115] in his pastoral work that had "evident linguistic and intellectual identification with the world of the gnostic enemies, neophyte Christians, and potential converts."[116] But Irenaeus was not overly interested in making Christianity acceptable and respectable. His interest, rather, was in presenting to Christians the nature of true faith and obedience, especially in the face of persecution and oppression. Such an interest granted few concessions to the surrounding society.

Irenaeus's perspective was not developed so much in the West but was developed in the East through the Syrian church. The Syrian tradition also emphasized the humanity of Jesus and the incarnational character of the Spirit and often spoke of a Spirit Christology rather than a *logos* Christology. "The rich descriptions of the Spirit in relation to Christ are one of the more enduring contributions the early Syriac churches have made to Christian history."[117] In *Ode to Solomon*, a Syriac hymnbook dating back to 80 or 100 C.E., one sees a strong trinitarian theology in which the Holy Spirit is imaged as female, an image that was common in the early tradition of the East.[118]

IMPLICATIONS FOR THE THEOLOGY OF MISSION TODAY

In the middle third of the twentieth century, the church rediscovered the integral theological and missiological relationship of mission, church and baptism so characteristic of the early church. The integration of the International Missionary Council and the World Council of Churches in New Delhi (1961) symbolized this shift in the Protestant world, and the results of the Second Vatican Council (1962-1965) reclaimed a *mission ecclesiology* of the local church within the Catholic Church. The "pilgrim church" is "missionary by its very nature" (AG 2). At the same time, the shift at Vatican II from a hierarchal to a communion ("people of God") ecclesiology reintroduced an awareness of the central role of the laity in the church. In a way reflected in the early church, baptism, not ordination, is recognized as the primary sacrament for being church and therefore for being in mission. David Bosch writes that "it is the community that is the primary bearer of mission. . . . Mission does not proceed directly from the pope, nor from a missionary order, society, or synod, but from the community gathered around the word and the sacraments and sent into the world."[119]

Within this theological framework, both in the Catholic and Protestant churches, the recent recovery of early Christian liturgical practices has reinforced the foundational theology of mission, church and baptism. Such renewal in the Catholic Church has led to a more communal celebration of the Eucharist and other sacraments, restoration of the catechumenate process (RCIA), a revitalization of the importance of scriptures and a rediscovery of the close connection between liturgy and mission.[120] On this latter point, much can be learned from the Orthodox tradition: "The Eucharist is always the End, the sacrament of the *parousia*, and yet it is always the *beginning*, the *starting point*: now the

mission begins. . . . The Eucharist, transforming 'the Church into what it is' —
transforms it into mission."[121] In his introductory chapter for a volume entitled
Inside Out: Worship in an Age of Mission, written by ten professors in Lutheran
seminaries, Thomas Schattauer writes: "More than a place for individuals to
encounter word and sacrament as institutions of grace, the church in its assembly around word and sacrament enacts a ritual symbol of God's gracious purpose for the world and so participates in God's world-encompassing mission."[122]

From our discussion of the role of women in mission, we see that this basic
identification between baptism and mission in the early church extended beyond the boundaries of gender, as well as those of ethnicity and class. In stark
contrast to an Aristotelian "class of slaves," we find a radically different anthropology. Elisabeth Schüssler Fiorenza presents Galatians 3:28 as the key expression of the "theological self-understanding of the Christian missionary movement,"[123] in that "there does not exist among you Jew or Greek, slave or free
person, male or female." In this way Christianity offers the world nothing less
than a *new conception of humanity.* We already have noted that by the end of
the third century restrictions were placed on the official participation of women
in mission, and generally this only began to change in the Late Middle Ages.
The implications of Galatians 3:28 continue to challenge the church in every
age and in every context.

Reflecting upon the various attitudes of the early church toward human culture can shed some light on our present-day concerns about inculturation/
contextualization. On the issue of the interrelationship of Christian faith and
Greek philosophy, Origen stressed continuity between the two, while Tertullian
stressed discontinuity. Theologically speaking, Origen highlights the
incarnational presence of God in society, while Tertullian highlights the demand of the paschal mystery to convert that which is contrary to God's reign.
An overemphasis on either position can lead to blanket divinization or condemnation of culture. While we do not have that much written material on this question by Irenaeus, his approach seems to fall between these two positions in that
he includes both some accommodation to the world of the "other" and also a
lack of interest in conforming to the society around him. Inculturation requires
such a balanced "both/and" approach, discerning in each particular context both
the continuity and discontinuity between gospel and culture/society. However,
the complexity of this dynamic is demonstrated by the fact that both Origen's
and Tertullian's theological traditions, which were opposed to each other on the
issue of Greek philosophy, would eventually be developed in situations that
(while distinct in many ways) would endorse complex church-and-society iden-
tifications — that is, in the two regions of the Roman Empire: the Greek East
(the future Byzantine Empire and Orthodox Church) and the Latin West, respectively. The development of Irenaeus's theology will occur, at least initially,
within the Diaspora situation of the East Syrian Church in Asia, where, of course,
there would never be such an identification between church and society.

4

Mission and the Monastic Movement (313-907)

From Constantine to the Decline of the T'ang Dynasty

At the beginning of the period covered in this chapter,[1] a number of very significant shifts in the history of Christianity can be associated with the actions of Emperor Constantine. Around the year 313, he initiated a process by which Christianity would shift from being a religion of the minority to the official religion of the Roman Empire, marking a historical turning point for Christianity. Soon, in the western part of the empire, the church of the Latin West would shift its primary mission focus from the Mediterranean to the Germanic peoples — who eventually will replace the Western Roman Empire as the political power of Europe — as well as reaching into North Africa. The Christian faith also spread southward in Africa beyond the Roman Empire into the areas of Ethiopia and Nubia.

Another key decision of Constantine was to move the capital of the empire from Rome to Byzantium, which would become a rich and powerful city under its new name of Constantinople, the capital of the Eastern Roman Empire and the center of the Byzantine church of the Greek East for the next eleven hundred years. While the attention of both the Byzantine church and the state was initially focused on the incoming Germanic peoples, they soon were much more preoccupied and affected by the advance of Islam.

The prophet Muhammad stands as one of the most significant figures in world history and world religions.[2] The religion of Islam would arise out of the land of Arabia in the seventh century and extend from India to Spain within one hundred years of the prophet's death — establishing Muslim Arab rule over nearly half of the Christian world by 750. The histories of Christianity and Islam have been intertwined in many ways ever since.

Constantine's decision to identify Christianity more closely with the Roman Empire caused the rival Persian Empire to treat the Christians within their domain—those from the East Syrian Church—less favorably. However, after this period of persecution, the eastward expansion of Christianity through the East Syrian Church would experience a "Golden Age" in missionary outreach as far as China. The primary model of mission during this time period when Christianity continued to spread to the north, south, east and west was that of the monks and nuns of the monastic movement, a movement that developed in a variety of ways in a variety of contexts—from Egypt and Syria to Persia, Ireland, Ethiopia, China, Italy, Asia Minor and England. With the fall in 907 of the Chinese T'ang dynasty, which had been very receptive to Christians, the first period of Christianity in China came to an end, and with it, the end of this dynamic period of mission by the East Syrian Church. The spread of the Christian faith by the churches of the Latin West, the Greek East and Ethiopia were also winding down during the first half of the tenth century, except in Scandinavia.

THE MISSION OF THE EAST SYRIAN CHURCH

The Social-Political Context

Since Constantine somehow assumed that his assistance to Christians extended even beyond the boundaries of his political authority, he sent a letter to the shah of shahs in Persia requesting that he extend benevolent treatment to Christians in his realm as well. Whether or not this letter was actually ever read by the shah of shahs, Constantine's political action in the Roman Empire was the opposite to that experienced by Christians in the Persian Empire. They not only faced strong opposition from the officials of the state religion of Zoroastrianism, but their political loyalty was also questioned. A double tax was levied against Christians, churches were destroyed, forced worship of the sun (the central rite for Zoroastrians) was established, and the estimate of those who died for their Christian faith during this middle period of the fourth century in Persia is in the range of tens of thousands and higher.[3] In 363, Julian as the sole Roman emperor led an army of over fifty thousand troops, the largest army ever assembled, against Persia, but they were defeated even though they had reached the gates of the Persian capital of Seleucia-Ctesiphon. An edict of toleration for Christians was issued in Persia in 409, but persecutions against Christians resumed around 420, and they were even worse than those of the fourth century. One of the most significant factors, which shaped the East Syrian Church and mission, was the experience of persecutions that "were much more severe and extended over a much wider area that any of those which took place under the Roman emperors."[4] Later, Persia's attention was directed toward the attacking Huns, whom they eventually defeated in 571. This period actually provided a moment of relative peace between the empires of Rome and Persia and for the East Syrian Church.

Under Persian rule Christians lived in segregated neighborhoods under a system know as *melet*. Even though Zoroastrians were not permitted by law to become Christians, the church still found ways of witnessing to and sharing the message of Jesus Christ. By the fourth and fifth centuries, monasteries became important centers for preserving Christian identity and life. As educational institutes, they offered not only spiritual and theological training but also taught other subjects, particularly medicine, which was a highly valued contribution by Christians within the empire and beyond.

However, a powerful wave ushering in a new political, social and religious epoch was on the horizon. In the first part of the seventh century, Muslim powers out of Arabia swept across North Africa and into the East Roman and Persian empires. The Muslim forces completed their victory over the Persians in 642, sending the last ruler of the Sassanid dynasty into exile. Christians in Syria and Persia found themselves united under one political domain, while Armenia[5] became a semi-independent state under indirect Arab rule. After a period of some internal instability, the Muslim Arab rule was carried out by the Umayyad dynasty, starting in 661, with the capital of Damascus in Syria. They were overthrown in 750 by the 'Abbasids, who then shifted the capital of the empire to Baghdad.

Under Muslim rule, all Christians—irrespective of theological and ecclesial differences—were classified politically as one community under the category of *dhimmi*.[6] Christians were encouraged to become Muslim but normally were not forced to do so. Mission efforts among Muslims were strictly forbidden, but Christians were allowed to practice their faith, live in community, and use existing houses of worship (although forbidden to build new ones). A tax, which was levied on Christian adult men, was severe enough to sometimes lead them to become Muslim. Under these trying circumstances, Christians not only survived but even sometimes grew in number. They continued to be very valuable in the wider society in the areas of education, medicine, trade and administration—avenues through which they were able to be Christian witnesses.

The Religious Context

Probably much more than other Christians during this period, those of the East Syrian tradition lived as a minority within a very strong interreligious environment. In the west, they lived within first a strong Zoroastrian religious context and later within the fresh religious vigor of Islam. As Christians moved along the trade routes into northeastern Persia and further across central Asia, they encountered not only Zoroastrians and Muslims, but also Buddhist missionaries and monasteries, Manichaean communities following the teachings of Mani, the third-century Persian prophet, and a rich variety of traditional religions among the Turks, Huns and Mongols. In addition, they would meet Taoist and Confucian traditions in China and Hinduism in India. Their mission model would be very much shaped by this context.

Second, the monasteries served not only as a tremendously valuable resource both for Christians and the wider society but also as the primary agent for mission. With their ancient monastic roots in Syria, which stressed mobility and mission more than their Egyptian counterparts, "the ascetic communities became the major dynamic for missions in Asia from the third century on."[7] By the middle of the fourth century, organized communal monasticism appeared and a network of missionary monasteries stretched from Persia to India.[8] Throughout the social and political changes and turmoil from the fourth until the tenth centuries, the East Syrian monastic movement had its share of ups and downs as well, but on the whole it provided a stable and life-giving link for the church of Asia. Christian merchants, artisans, physicians and administrators also benefited from this important network, whether they were traveling through or settling down in that area.

The Institutional Context

Already in the third century Asian church history with its East Syrian Christian tradition had shifted from the Syrian period to the Persian period. The language of the church remained Syriac, but its organizational center moved to the Persian capital of Seleucia-Ctesiphon. Although his exact identity is unclear, one of those who signed the Nicene Creed in 325 identified himself as "John the Persian, of the churches of the whole of Persia and in the great India."[9] Synods held by the Persian church in 410 and 424 confirmed their acceptance of the Council of Nicea and established the bishop of Seleucia-Ctesiphon as the *catholicos* or leader of all the churches in Persia and equal in authority with the other patriarchs, such as the bishops of Rome, Alexandria and Constantinople. However, this relationship with the rest of the Christian world would unfortunately change after the Council of Chalcedon in 451.

Without going into the complex theological, linguistic and political issues and misunderstandings surrounding the Christological debate,[10] the Council of Chalcedon was a turning point for Christianity. In the end, those who considered Cyril of Alexandria as the representative of orthodoxy believed that while there were two natures before the incarnation, Christ was one person with a single united nature after the incarnation. They became known by their opponents as Monophysites ("one nature"),[11] and this view was held in Armenia, western Syria, Egypt, Nubia and Ethiopia. A second group held that two natures and two persons were in union in Christ and so became known by others as Dyophysites ("two natures").[12] They identified with the theological school of Antioch and the teachings of Theodore of Mopsuestia and Nestorius, and this theological position continued in the Persian Church. Due to the role of Nestorius, this church became known as the Nestorian Church, but to avoid using a title directly associated with heresy, we will refer to it rather as the East Syrian Church. While these first two positions are considered non-Chalcedonian positions, the third Christology held the "definition of Chalcedon" of two natures and one person, which combined the insights of the other two and intended to safeguard against tendencies toward overemphasis by either.[13] The churches of the Latin West and Greek East supported this position.

Due to its faithfulness to what was called Nestorianism, the famous school in Edessa (Syria) was closed in 489 and refounded in Nisibis (Persia). Narsai, who was the last director in Edessa, moved with others to Nisibis, where he became its first great teacher and gave the school a strong mission theology from the beginning.[14] It quickly became "the most famous center of learning in all Asia outside China."[15] Including the study of medicine and Greek logic and philosophy, its curriculum was centered around the study of the Bible within a strict, monastic-like environment.

Institutionally, an independent national church of Persia emerged at the end of the fifth century, with the appointment of its patriarch being confirmed by the shah. The delicate Persian church-state relationship shifted back and forth. At times the patriarch was a puppet of the state and the church was concerned primarily with survival, while at other times the patriarch played a key role in political life and the church thrived.

Considering all of the social-political, religious, theological and institutional developments and challenges, it is quite amazing how the influence and authority of the church in Persia would extend across Asia.

MODELS OF MISSION

One of the key moments for mission occurred under the leadership of Yeshuyab II, who was named patriarch of the Persian church in 628. The accomplishments of this great leader include negotiating a moment of peace between Persia and Constantinople, between Byzantine and East Syrian Christians, and later between Christians and Muslims. However, the feats that are even more relevant to our interests here include (probably[16]) establishing the first metropolitanate of India as an independent ecclesial authority directly under the Persian patriarch, and, most important, initiating the first Christian mission to China, which would eventually also lead to the evangelization of Turkish tribes in central Asia. Using Yeshuyab II as the starting point of reference, Samuel Moffett states that the East Syrian Church became "for much of the next seven hundred years in truth as well as in name the Church of the East, the church of Asia."[17]

Christianity in India

As we continue the story of Christianity in India from Chapter 3, we have one of the bishops attending the Council of Nicea in 325 signing on behalf of the churches of Persia and India. The first solid historical evidence of a sustained Christian church in India comes around 350, when Thomas of Cana, a Persian Christian merchant perhaps Armenian by descent, with perhaps up to four hundred Christians, settled in Cranganore (present-day southwestern state of Kerala), where they were welcomed by an already existing but struggling Christian community.[18] In the fifth century the churches of India were placed under the jurisdiction of the metropolitan of Rewardashir in southern Persia. Probably the church was primarily composed of a permanent expatriate merchant community of Persians who perhaps fled persecutions in their homeland. The first clear sign that the church extended beyond Persian to Indian members is found in reports regarding their status in the caste system, indicating that Christianity was entering the Indian cultural context. An Egyptian monk traveling in Asia in the sixth century, known as Cosmas the Indian Navigator, reports visiting a Persian Christian community on the island of present-day Sri Lanka. The community had a complete ecclesiastical ritual and a predominantly Persian Christian community, with a bishop appointed from Persia along the southwestern Malabar coast. His descriptions also indicate that these Christians still were closely related to Jewish culture and faith,[19] which is not surprising in light of the probable role of Jewish Diaspora communities in the earlier, albeit unclear Christian history of India and the stronger Semitic cultural links within the East Syrian Church in general.

While the Indian church barely managed to maintain its link with Persia during the Muslim conquest, later in the seventh century it is established with its own metropolitan, which normally has a minimum of six bishoprics. Through correspondence from Timothy I, famous Persian patriarch of the eighth century, we hear about a monk traveling with a group of immigrants to India and Timothy giving them permission for intermarriage between Persian and Indian Christians. In the ninth century two Armenian brothers come to India as missionaries and local Indian authorities granted land to the Christian communities to build churches in several locations. Irvin and Sunquist describe the situation of these Christian communities, who were still primarily of Persian descent, in this way:

> These were Christians who had come to reside near the spiritual site of St. Thomas, to Crangonore, for instance, the traditional site of the landing of St. Thomas, or even to Mylapore, near Madras in the east, the traditional site of St. Thomas' tomb in India. Eventually they became a separate caste. . . . Like members of other castes in India, they lived in houses near their religious center, in this case their churches, forming distinct Christian neighborhoods.[20]

These communities continued to use Syriac in their liturgies, which enabled them to maintain both that important link with the church and patriarch in Persia and their own distinctive cultural and religious identity in the wider Indian context. At the same time, an indication of their accommodation to their environment was their use of the local products of rice cakes and palm wine for the Eucharist.[21] There are also indications that they attempted missionary outreach to Sri Lanka and possibly to Java, the Malay Peninsula and even up the coast to China.[22]

The First Christian Mission to China

While some Christians following the Silk Route may have been in China earlier, evidence for the first known Christian mission was discovered in China in 1623 on a monument. It verifies that the East Syrian missionary Alopen arrived in the Chinese capital of Chang'an in 635, during the early years of the powerful T'ang dynasty (618-907), often considered the "Golden Age" of China.[23] Fortunately, the Christian mission came during a period of religious toleration aimed at establishing a religious (and political) balance among Buddhism, Taoism, Confucianism and any newly arriving religions. Alopen was received into the emperor's library (one of the best in the world, with its 200,000 volumes) and was ordered to begin translating the Bible into Chinese. In 638 the emperor financed the construction of the first Christian church in China in Chang'an, at that time the largest city in the world, and other churches and monasteries soon followed. There were twenty-one Christian monks, probably all Persian, in China in 638.[24] Four Chinese Christian treatises—the first entitled *Jesus-Messiah Sutra* and the other three grouped under the title *Discourses on Monotheism*—appear to have been written in the seventh century, possibly by Alopen.[25] Irvin and Sunquist point out that while "all four could be works translated in whole or in part from earlier Syriac texts, we cannot rule out that one or more were composed specifically to address questions raised by imperial scholars regarding Christian teachings."[26]

After a period of persecution (683-712) with a change of emperors, Christianity in China experienced a time of recovery (712-781). At that time the East Syrian monks and Persian traders were joined in Chang'an by the Persian crown prince and some of his court, who had fled there for safety from the Muslim Arab invasion of Persia. Missionaries of the East Syrian Church from Persia accompanied Arab embassies to China as interpreters and advisors between 651 and 732. The growth of East Syrian Christianity at this time is closely linked with political connections[27] and noted scholarship.

The most outstanding East Syrian Christian associated with scholarship in this period is Adam, a bishop, missionary and translator from central Asia, who was "so famed for his knowledge of Chinese language and literature that even Buddhist missionaries came to him for help in translating their own sacred books."[28] When Prajna, a well-known Buddhist missionary from northern India, came to Chang'an in 782, he was asked to translate some Buddhist Sutras that he had with him. Unfamiliar with the local languages, Prajna enlisted the help of Adam, and together they translated seven volumes. To add to this intriguing interfaith cooperation, at this time two very famous men of Japanese Buddhism—founders of the Shingon sect of Tantric Buddhism and the Lotus School of Japanese Buddhism respectively—were living in the Buddhist monastery with Prajna. One is left with an unanswerable question: How much contact with or influence upon one another did these four men have? As for the general East Syrian stance toward Buddhism, it appears that "for the purpose of communicating the Christian Message, and for the deepening of

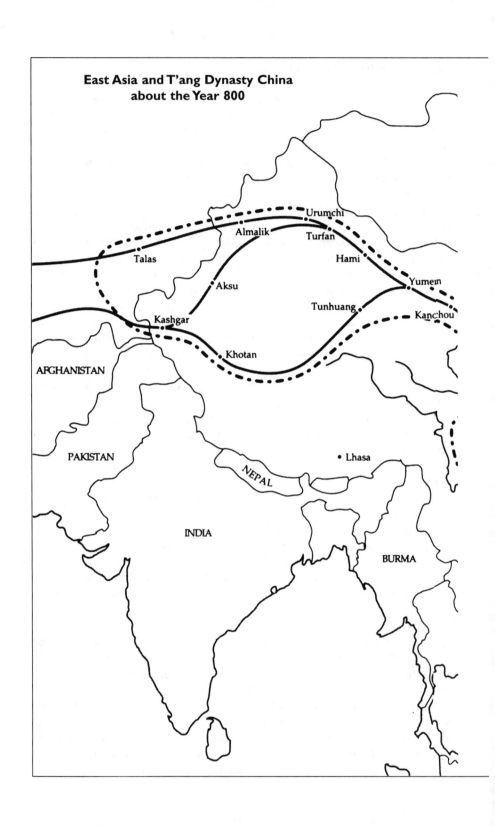

East Asia and T'ang Dynasty China about the Year 800

Urumchi

Almalik

Turfan

Talas

Hami

Aksu

Yumein

Tunhuang

Kanchou

Kashgar

Khotan

AFGHANISTAN

PAKISTAN

NEPAL

Lhasa

INDIA

BURMA

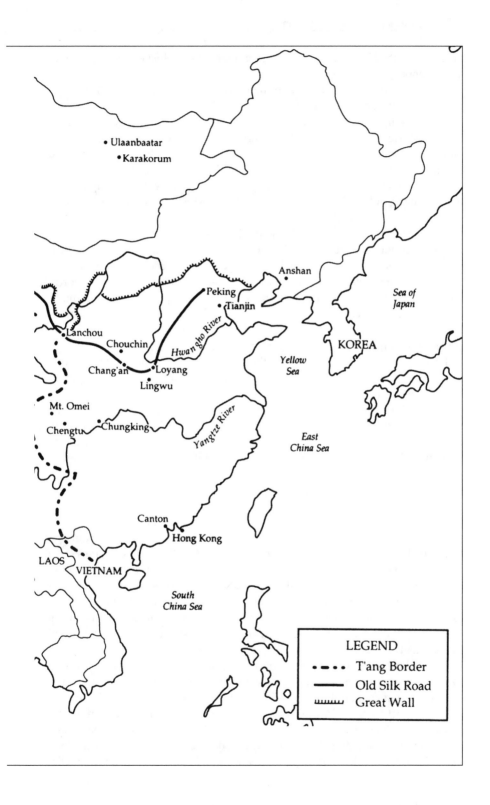

• Ulaanbaatar
• Karakorum

Anshan

Peking
• Tianjin

*Sea of
Japan*

Lanchou
Chouchin
Hwan gho River

KOREA

Chang'an   Loyang
Lingwu

*Yellow
Sea*

Mt. Omei

Chengtu   Chungking

Yangtze River

*East
China Sea*

Canton
Hong Kong

LAOS
VIETNAM

*South
China Sea*

LEGEND
▪▪▪▪ T'ang Border
——   Old Silk Road
ᴖᴖᴖᴖ Great Wall

their own faith-life in the Messiah, they employed Buddhist terms, expressions, and symbols."[29]

From this moment of apparently being on the verge of having a profound impact on Chinese society, Christianity instead would disappear from China in the next two hundred years. While the reasons and circumstances are not clear, Samuel Moffett presents the probable mix of factors under four categories: religious, theological, missiological and political.[30] First of all, religious persecution against all "foreign religions," including Buddhism, arose in proportion to the rise in xenophobia and the decline in political security. For example, in the fall of Canton in 878, it is reported that 120,000 Muslims, Jews, Christians and Zoroastrians were killed.[31]

As for the question of possible theological compromise with Buddhist, Taoist and Confucian concepts, Moffett concludes that "from very different theological perspectives a consensus has emerged that from the limited evidence available T'ang-dynasty Christianity was neither heretically Nestorian nor fatally syncretistic."[32] It is interesting, but not at all surprising, that the importance placed on ancestor veneration stirs up much of present-day discussions of this period of mission history, and this issue will continue to surface in later periods of church and mission history in China.

From a missiological perspective, the question of how much and why Christianity had remained a "foreign," non-Chinese religion is rather complex in light of the strong Chinese flavor in the extant written documents and the fact that Buddhism was also still considered a "foreign religion." The fourth and strongest factor is the political one. Christianity came in with the T'ang dynasty, which promoted religious liberty and toleration, and it would disappear soon after the decline in 907 of that dynasty and its receptive environment.

Early Islam and Christianity in Asia

Soon after the beginning of the first Christian mission in China, the sending Persian church "back home" was encountering the people of the new religion of Islam. In the early years, all Arabs had to become Muslim, but non-Arabs could keep their non-Muslim faith if they lived in a religious ghetto (dhimmi), similar to the Persian melet system, and paid a double tax. To some extent the East Syrians found life better under the Arab Muslims than under the Persian Zoroastrians. As noted earlier, the East Syrian patriarch Yeshuyab II was able to negotiate a fairly favorable agreement with the Muslims, supposedly with Muhammad himself.

When the 'Abbasids Islamic dynasty took over in 750 (it would last until 1258), it moved the capital from Damascus to Baghdad, just twenty miles from the old Persian capital of Seleucia-Ctesiphon. This signaled both a future geographical shift from the Mediterranean to Asia and an ethnic shift from Arab to a more multiethnic identity. Within this context, the third 'Abbasid caliph, Mahdi, invited the Persian patriarch, Timothy I, to a debate on equal terms. This documented dialogue on such topics as Christology and Christianity's understanding of Muhammad is referred to "as the high point in Muslim and Christian relationships in the whole history of Muslim conquest."[33] It is quite interesting that this debate probably happened in the same year (probably 781) that the famous monument was erected in China, marking the height of East Syrian influence in the other great Asian empire at that time.

Similar to Yeshuyab II of another age, the great patriarch Timothy I combined his Christian integrity, intelligence and diplomatic skills with missionary vision and courage. Quite probably educated in a monastery that was the primary source of East Syrian missionary efforts, Timothy I appointed a bishop for Yemen, despite previous Muslim prohibitions, and prayed openly that Christians would be able to share the gospel message with Muslims. Furthermore, the dedication of Timothy I to education and philosophy was typical of the East Syrians' role in handing on Greek science, philosophy and medicine to the Arab world, on the one side, while the Arabs were also receiving astronomical and mathematical knowledge from India, on the other. "One of the greatest contributions of the Asian church to the history of human thought was its key role in transmitting to the Arab empire the heritage of the Greek classics and, through the Arabs, preserving them for rediscovery and transformation of the West in the Renaissance and Reformation."[34] Similar to the situation in China, a number of East Syrians and other Christians were influential in imperial matters due to their valuable "secular" services, such as those in the fields of translation, medicine and education.

People of different religious faiths met along the trade routes across central Asia. The network of East Syrian monasteries provided shelter and religious services for other monks and travelers, and sometimes attracted permanent Christian communities. Those of other faiths often considered the monks holy people and identified the monasteries as places for local medical care. The Christian faith also spread into the central mountains and plains. By the sixth century some nomadic Huns and Turks were identified as Christians, although this does not seem to have been the result of any organized mission effort. Later, Patriarch Timothy I, in response to a request from a Turkish king who said his people had become Christians, sent a bishop and a group of monks to them. This same missionary-minded patriarch assisted and supported the growing number of monasteries, churches and episcopal sees in the areas that are now Uzbekistan, Kazakstan, Tajikistan, Tibet and western China.[35] Evidence indicates that by the year 1000 the northernmost expansion of Christianity had reached the Kerait Turks in north Mongolia, and the easternmost point was probably in Korea and Japan.[36]

Although there had been some persecutions of and restrictions on Christians under the 'Abbasid rule, even by the diplomatic and generous caliph who invited dialogue with Timothy I, the Persian Christians were able to live out their faith fairly openly. However, there was a turning point in 850, when extreme measures taken against Christians included the destruction of their churches, monasteries and graves. At the time of this external persecution, corruption and scandal within the church and monastery also surfaced. Although they were allowed to continue life under the *dhimmi* system, the East Syrian Church would experience a period of decline over the next 150 years. One very significant symptom, consequence and/or cause of this decline, as noted by Moffett, was that the monks were no longer missionaries.[37]

It is interesting to note that Christian fortunes were shifting around this same time in China. In 845, an imperial decree was issued to reduce significantly the total number of monasteries in China, and over 250,000 Buddhist monks and nuns and more than three thousand Christian and Zoroastrian monks and priests were forced to return to secular life.[38] The final blow for this period of mission of the East Syrian Church was the fall of the tolerant T'ang dynasty in 907.

A number of different models of mission surface in this brief overview of the history of the East Syrian Church. To begin with the model that is least documented, the Christian traders, physicians and others who lived and traveled throughout Asia are described as true witnesses to the gospel. "Wherever they went, whether merchants or artisans, clergy or laity, they carried the gospel with them. Supporting themselves by the labour of their own hands, or filling appointments as secretaries, physicians or stewards in the households of the nobles and princes of those lands to which they went, they were one and all missionaries of the Cross."[39] Despite its somewhat flamboyant tone, this statement sounds similar to descriptions of Christians of the early church, and it points to the religious influence of people involved in "secular" affairs, which were very important in Asian societies. As another illustration, it was noted that "there were times when Christian physicians became even more of a Christian influence on Persian culture than the theologians."[40] Finally, this group includes large numbers of refugees fleeing the periodic persecutions of Christians.

The second model of mission is that of the teacher. Drawing in particular upon the strong influence of the School of the Persians in Nisibis, which eventually had an enrollment of a thousand students, East Syrian Christianity had a significant effect on Asian society. As noted above, academic learning and skills were very important within Arab and Chinese societies, and the teacher continues to hold an honorable position within those societies even today. Furthermore, knowledge of the scriptures and intellectual pursuits was essential for such missionary work as that done by seven East Syrian missionaries—two lay men, a bishop and four priests—who provided for the Huns a written language through which the scriptures (and eventually an invitation to baptism) could be presented.[41] The famous School in Nisibis also educated many physicians and some of the Persian patriarchs.

As a minority religion in a much larger political and religious world, the Persian patriarchs played an important role, first of all, in presenting and protecting the interests and values of the Christian community to the wider society, and second, in offering leadership and a sense of connection to and identity within the church of Asia. While the patriarchs varied greatly in their fulfillment of these goals, we have seen the example of two of the finest, Yeshuyab II and Timothy I. It is quite significant that both of them instilled and challenged the church in Asia with the sense of mission. In addition, due to his theological and probable monastic background, Timothy I capably responded to the invitation to dialogue with the Muslim caliph.

The monks are the fourth and primary model, which in some ways builds upon and supports the previous ones. Out of Syrian asceticism, which also produced some fanatical results, the church of the East received a monastic movement, which would continue to provide the missionary impulse for the church. "About these [Syrian] monks it is said that they were people of great faith, well versed in scriptures, large portions of which they knew by heart, fervent in prayer, gentle and humble in manner, full of love of God on the one hand, and love of their neighbor and all human kind on the other."[42]

Already in the fourth century there was a network of monasteries from Persia to India. Alopen and other monks led the first organized Christian mission to China and were received with their impressive written scriptures during a time of religious openness. Similar to the status and role of the teacher model, the monks found immediate acceptance due to their education and its application in learning languages and translation work. Furthermore, the stories of Alopen and Adam point to interreligious exchange and mission on another level. Some of the monks also were bishops, linking them with the important contribution of the patriarch (as a model of mission) on the local level. During the early years under Muslim rule, some wandering mendicants lived alone in the wilderness, but by the ninth century most of them also were living in communities.

East Syrian monasticism included black-robed religious monks and white-robed secular monks. While it is usually not specified in the literature to which type a particular person belonged (and perhaps the distinction was quite fluid), it does indicate the inclusion of a "secular" identity within the parameters of the monastic system, and there may have been some overlap with the professional services offered by Christian laity. East Syrian monks served as interpreters in diplomatic and economic exchanges both for the Persians and Chinese. Issu, one of the most influential East Syrian monks, was a high-ranking general in the Chinese army. It was not uncommon for Christian or Buddhists priests to be in the military.

It is probably not surprising that the East Syrian Church has been called "the 'missionary' church *par excellence* in the overall context of medieval Christianity."[43] In sharp contrast to Western and Byzantine Christianity, the East Syrian Church lived a restricted or diaspora existence within the larger political-religious Asian context. While, on the one hand, this did lead to strict isolation and on occasion hostility from the rest of society, on the other hand, the combined efforts of the various models of mission provided a means of witness to and interaction with people of other faiths and cultures. However, the outlook for mission by the East Syrian Church across Asia was rather dismal in the year 907.

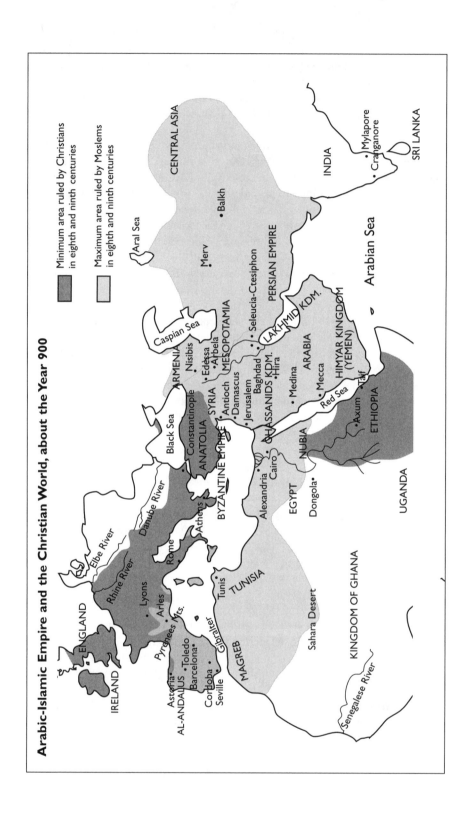

Arabic-Islamic Empire and the Christian World, about the Year 900

Minimum area ruled by Christians in eighth and ninth centuries

Maximum area ruled by Moslems in eighth and ninth centuries

CENTRAL ASIA

INDIA

Mylapore
Cranganore

SRI LANKA

Aral Sea

Balkh

Arabian Sea

Merv

PERSIA N EMPIRE

Caspian Sea

Seleucia-Ctesiphon

LAKHMID KDM.

ARMENIA

Nisibis

MESOPOTAMIA

Edessa
Arbela

HIMYAR KINGDOM (YEMEN)

Antioch

Baghdad

ARABIA

Damascus

Hira

Taif

SYRIA

Jerusalem

Medina

Axum

Constantinople

GHASSANIDS KDM.

Mecca

ETHIOPIA

Black Sea

Red Sea

ANATOLIA

BYZANTINE EMPIRE

NUBIA

Athens

Cairo

Danube River

Alexandria

EGYPT

Dongola

UGANDA

Rome

Elbe River

ENGLAND

Rhine River

Lyons

Arles

Tunis

TUNISIA

Sahara Desert

KINGDOM OF GHANA

IRELAND

Pyrenees Mts.

Gibralter

MAGREB

Astoria
Toledo
Barcelona

AL-ANDALUS

Cordoba
Seville

Senegalese River

THE MISSION OF THE AFRICAN CHURCH

Tatian the Assyrian was associated with the beginnings of a monastic movement in second-century Syria.[44] In a similar development, ascetics were living in the wilderness of Egypt in the third century. Individual Christians moved out of their normal living situations into isolation in order to follow a life of voluntary poverty, sexual continence and strict self-denial. Some lived as lifelong hermits, while others had loose connections with one another. This movement became very well known due to the Greek written account by Athanasius, the bishop of Alexandria, of the life of the desert hermit Antony, who began his eremitical life around 273.[45] In the fourth century the Egyptian ascetic Pachomius drew up a rule for communal monasticism, and within several decades after his death there were tens of thousands of men and women ascetics living according to his rule. In looking at the early years of the two ancient monastic traditions, the Egyptians in general emphasized stability and withdrew from the world,[46] while the Syrians stressed mobility and became wandering missionaries.[47] Egyptian monasticism also tended to have a strong nationalistic character. However, its influence would spread across nations and cultures, take on a variety of forms, and become the primary means of mission in the churches of the Greek East and Latin West through further developments by people like Basil of Caesarea, Martin of Tours, Melania the Younger, Patrick of Ireland and Benedict of Nursia. Moreover, the desert fathers and mothers of Egypt had a broad vision of spirituality and ministry and considered service of one's neighbor of extreme importance.

Following the Nile River farther south and beyond the boundaries of the empires of Rome, Persia and later Constantinople, we come to the city of Axum, the capital of the kingdom known as Ethiopia or Abyssinia—the home of a distinctive African church and an ancient Christian tradition in the world until today. While Ethiopia traces its earliest Christian roots to the Ethiopian eunuch in Acts (8:27) and the apostle Matthew,[48] the first historical evidence comes in the middle of the fourth century with the king and royal court of Axum embracing the Christian faith that was linked with the bishop and church of Alexandria. The central figure of this story is Frumentius, a Syrian youth who was sold into slavery to the king of Axum, ascended through the ranks in the royal court, went to Alexandria to plead the Christian cause and returned as a bishop and missionary to Ethiopia. Frumentius is credited with the conversion of the royal court and translating some sections of scripture into the ancient Ethiopian language of Ge'ez. Explicit mission efforts were carried out in the fifth century by monks from Syria following the rule of Pachomius. The monastic tradition that developed in Ethiopia became and remains a strong characteristic of this ancient church.

In the area between Egypt and Ethiopia, known as Nubia and situated in modern Sudan, there were some Christians in the fifth century quite possibly due to the efforts and presence of Egyptian monasteries. However, the primary missionary efforts would come in the sixth century as Theodora, the wife of the

East Roman emperor Justinian, sent Julian, a priest in Constantinople with a non-Chalcedonian theological perspective, as a missionary to a northern Nubian kingdom. As a result, that royal family accepted Christianity and three other Nubian kingdoms would become Christian by the end of the sixth century. The church of Nubia would develop a much stronger association with the church in Egypt rather than that of Constantinople.

The Muslim invasion had a major impact on Christianity in Africa. In Egypt, it seems that the Arabs were welcomed by many who were dissatisfied with Constantinople's political, economic and ecclesiastical (Chalcedonian position) dominance. The relationship between Muslims and Coptic Christians (*Coptic* is derived from the Arabic word for Egypt) was initially quite friendly, as were relationships in Syria and Persia at the beginning, but the church faced more difficulties starting in the eighth century and became more marginalized. With the rise of Arabic as the official language and the decline of the Coptic language, the latter would survive only in the Coptic liturgy. While new churches were not allowed to be built, new monasteries, including women's monasteries, continued to emerge and flourish in the desert areas.

At the time of the advance of Islamic forces, a united kingdom of Nubia, which stretched from the Aswan to Meroë, handed the Muslim advance its first defeat. However, after a second major attack, the Nubian king negotiated a treaty with the Arabs, guaranteeing political and religious independence for Nubia under certain conditions, which included an annual Nubian payment of three hundred slaves. It appears that Nubia was a thoroughly Christian area during this period of the seventh to the tenth centuries, but the desert sands of the Sahara were beginning to claim many of the churches and towns. The Muslims launched no attack against Ethiopia at this time, partially because Ethiopians had provided refuge to Muslim refugees during the time of Muhammad. Ethiopia's ecclesiastical link with Alexandria became more tenuous because the patriarch in Alexandria was often preoccupied with and restricted by Muslim rule in Egypt, but, even so, Ethiopia did keep this important umbilical-cord link with outside Christianity over the years. Ethiopia did expand politically, economically and religiously farther south during these centuries. While the Ethiopian monastic tradition continued to thrive, it appears that it "ceased being as active a missionary force as it had been in earlier years,"[49] which may have been due to the strong Islamic presence to its east.

Within sixty years after Muhammad's death, Muslim rule extended across what had been Roman North Africa and would become known as *al Maghrib* (Arabic for "the place of sunset"). Eventually, the Arabs formed a coalition with many converted Muslims from indigenous peoples, whom they called *Berbers* (Barbarians). By the tenth century, only a few scattered Christian communities were left along the coastal areas of the Maghrib. The Muslims also developed some commercial relationships across the Sahara into West Africa, and it is reported that by the tenth century some members of the court of the king of Ghana were Muslims.

The emergence of Christianity in Africa during this period is attributed to two basic models of mission. There were, first of all, significant individuals, such as ex-slave Bishop Frumentius and the Theodora-sponsored priest, Julian. Second, the indigenous African monastic movements provided ongoing missionary presence over the years.

Andrew Walls situates the ancient story of Africa in Christian history in the following way:

> Ethiopian stands for Africa indigenously Christian, Africa *primordially* Christian; for a Christianity that was established in Africa not only before the white people came, but before Islam came; for a Christianity that has been continuously in Africa for far longer than it has in Scotland, and infinitely longer than it has in the United States. African Christians today can assert their right to the *whole* history of Christianity in Africa, stretching back almost to the apostolic age.[50]

THE MISSION OF THE CHURCHES
OF THE LATIN WEST AND GREEK EAST

The Social-Political Context

With the events surrounding the conversion of Constantine in 312-313,[51] Christianity received favored religion status and, after an eighty-year, back-and-forth process, it became the official state religion of the Roman Empire by 392 when the Edict of Constantinople banned all private and public "pagan" sacrifices. The actual struggle and interplay between Christianity and "paganism" was very complex, lengthy and sometimes violent (particularly under Justinian in the East Roman Empire) into the eighth century,[52] but in the fourth century the official relationship between the state and Christianity in the West had taken an 180 degree turn. Soon after this, however, the great movement of Germanic peoples over the continent would strike the heart of the empire. Alaric, the Goth, captured and sacked Rome in 410. Such shocking news — like the fall of the Berlin Wall or the collapse of the World Trade Center — marked the beginning of the end of one era and the start of another. Although Roman influence would continue in the cities until the sixth century, the Western Roman Empire was collapsing.

Justinian (482-565), emperor of the Eastern Roman Empire, sought to restore the prestige and domain of the Roman Empire, over which he was the last to rule as a united realm. He oversaw the completion of the major task of the codification of the existing body of Roman law, brought together as never before a synthesis of church and state, and attempted to restore the old imperial boundaries. At this time Slavic peoples began to move into the empire, and Germanic peoples followed after Justinian's time. By 620, Greek had replaced Latin as the official language in the empire of Constantinople.

During this period of upheaval, the new political scene in Western Europe depended upon the outcome of the warring Germanic peoples. The Frankish people would eventually prevail, a development that turned out to be very fortuitous for the church, since King Clovis and the Franks had become Catholic (non-Arian[53]) Christians at the end of the fifth century in the process of their political rise in power.[54] After some years of being separated from political associations with the Roman Empire, Christianity would find itself identified with and supported by the new Frankish state. These developments laid the foundation for the emergence of the new Holy Roman Empire three hundred years later. In 800, Pope Leo III crowned Charlemagne emperor of the Holy Roman Empire, bringing together political and religious authority to establish a European theocratic Christendom.[55] The Church of Rome would then find itself caught between the fierce rivalry of this new Frankish Empire and the longstanding Byzantine (Eastern Roman) Empire of Constantinople. However, this concern was small in relation to the much more serious outside threat from the rapid Muslim expansion, which was moving across Africa and into Spain,[56] on one side, and into Middle East, Asia Minor and beyond, on the other.

Shaped very much by Germanic society and world view, feudalism was well on its way in Europe by the beginning of the tenth century. Under this political-economic system, peasants or serfs worked on properties held by the nobility, who provided protection in return for produce from the land. The aristocracy were related to and dependent upon other aristocracy through oaths of fealty, which included promises to provide military assistance in the form of mounted knights. In this hierarchal system, the king's rule was also dependent upon fealty oaths with high-ranking nobles. Around the time of the fall of the T'ang dynasty, Western Europe was fragmenting into a number of small feudal kingdoms.

The Religious Context

With the support of the Roman state in the fourth century, Christianity gradually spread out from its initial foundations in the cities into the rural areas, especially due to the influence of the rapidly growing number of monks and nuns. Also, the cities themselves were beginning to decline as the world of "antiquity" was doing the same. By the time of the collapse of the Western Roman Empire in the fifth and sixth centuries, the church had absorbed much of the Greco-Roman culture and actually became the vehicle for preserving aspects of this culture of antiquity into the next period of Western history. In this paradoxical turn of events, Christianity would not only survive but would renew itself and the peoples of the North and West through this time of major social-political chaos and change; second, Christianity would bring to this new creation some elements of the cultural tradition of a society that had originally tried to suppress it. Andrew Walls correctly reminds us to look at this period not as the survival of a Roman culture but as an exciting moment of creativity and transformation: "From a Christian point of view it is a period of immense significance in which the traditional cultures of various peoples of the North and West were comprehensively rethought to give them literary expression, intellectual vigor, and a degree of Christian integrity."[57] The Roman Empire died, but Christianity was reborn in a new Western European civilization. In other words, the church of the Latin West shifted from being an imperial church of the Roman Empire to becoming a medieval church of European society of the Middle Ages.

The church accomplished this transition by going through a dynamic of as-similation—as it had done earlier within Greco-Roman society—as a result of its mission to the new tribes entering Europe. Over a period of a thousand years, it moved into the new cultural-religious world of the Germanic peoples.[58] These masses of new Christians were transformed as they appropriated the Christian message they received in such a way that it was meaningful for their day-to-day hopes, concerns and needs. Furthermore, the church itself was profoundly changed and reshaped by Germanic beliefs, practices and world view through a process James Russell calls the "Germanization" of the church.[59] All of this happened because of mission.

While the church of the Latin West was going through this major transfor-mation, the church of the Greek East solidified its presence in and identification with the Byzantine Empire. The close association between Christianity and so-ciety would be reflected in its missionary contact with and outreach to other peoples, especially the Slavic peoples to the north.

The Institutional Context

The fourth and fifth centuries, sometimes referred to as the "Golden Age of the fathers of the church," was a creative period of Christian theology and ma-jor church councils for delineating basic Christian beliefs, for developing a syn-thesis between Christian faith and Greco-Roman language and culture, and for developing classical liturgies. However, while this was a move toward unity within the Roman Empire, the intense theological debates coming out of the church's diversity also led to serious divisions within Christianity.

In Roman North Africa, one party of Christians (known as Donatists), out of concern to maintain the integrity and holiness of the church, was very uneasy with any friendly relationship with a government that had been persecuting Christians; the Donatists also wanted to root out anyone who had betrayed the church by somehow cooperating with the Roman authorities.[60] The split be-tween the Donatists and Catholics in the fourth century would eventually be erased as a result of the Muslim conquest of northern Africa. Second, the Arian controversy of the fourth century focused on the relationship between *logos* and God, that is, it asked whether Jesus Christ was the same God who created the world. The Council of Nicea in 325 condemned Arianism and issued a theologi-cal decision that the three persons of God were of one substance, a position that became the standard of orthodoxy for most churches.[61] The Arian belief, which was held by a number of Germanic Christian peoples, would come to an end when the Visigoths in Spain and the Lombards in northern Italy, in the sixth and seventh centuries respectively, accepted the Nicene formulation. The third area of diversity, which centered around Christological issues, was addressed primarily at the Council of Chalcedon in 451. We already noted earlier how diverse Christological positions continued, and continue until today, to be held by different churches.

Beginning in the urban areas the role of the bishops became more significant and monasticism began to flourish in the rural areas. The term *priest (sacerdos)*, which originally was reserved for bishops, was gradually extended to presbyters until *priest* and *presbyter* become interchangeable terms in the Middle Ages. Large masses of the population became Christian, and the catechumenate process, which was at its height in the third century, was to lose its significance as we move from the fourth century to the beginning of the tenth century.[62] As the church of the Latin West shifted its focus toward the Germanic peoples, their cultural-religious world view influenced Western theology, for example, in shaping the new understanding of salvation in terms of atonement. In the social-political situation of an emerging Western Europe, church life became more organized and uniform under the growing influence of the Church of Rome, especially through the reforms and missionary work of Boniface in the eighth century.

The tensions related to the Christological diversity and the Council of Chalcedon affected Byzantine Christianity more strongly than its Latin counterpart and were still being addressed under the rule of Justinian and Theodora in the sixth century. While Justinian was trying to reconcile proponents of the various theological positions, Theodora turned one of the palaces in Constantinople into a monastery for five hundred monks and nuns who held her "one nature" non-Chalcedonian position. Facing those so-called pagans, Justinian used more forceful means. The bishop of Constantinople began to be called the ecumenical patriarch, to the consternation of the bishop of Rome. Within a hundred years after Justinian, the church of the Greek East faced a situation in which much of the Eastern Roman Empire was now under Muslim rule. Internally, it was dealing with difficult issues regarding the status of images of Christian piety, known as the iconoclastic controversy.

In the Latin West, Charlemagne had secured the support of the Frankish church to add *filioque* to the Nicene creed—with the understanding that the Holy Spirit proceeded from the Father *and* the Son. This phrase had originally been used in Spain since the sixth century to reaffirm the equality of the Son with the Father and to combat Arian tendencies, and Charlemagne applied it for similar reasons. Pope Leo III considered the phrase orthodox but said that it should not be used; actually, it would not be allowed by a bishop of Rome until the eleventh century. However, this unilateral change to the creed on the part of the church of the Latin West would lead to serious conflict with the Greek East, a sign of the growing gap between the two.[63]

MODELS OF MISSION

In the early church, the close identification among baptism, church and mission was most prominently evident in the everyday lives of believers. In the early post-Constantinian era, "the local episcopal church now appeared in focus as the real bearer of the missionary idea and of the day-to-day mission work."[64] While this continued to be manifest and encouraged within the lives of all Christians,[65] the bishop as the leader in the local ecclesial community began to assume greater overall responsibility for mission work, including the all-important catechumenate. While individual bishops showed varying degrees of interest and competence for mission activity, the outstanding examples of Martin of Tours, Victricius of Rouen and John Chrysostom of Constantinople show that some bishops were very instrumental in fostering the spread of the Christian faith beyond their local congregations. Priests and deacons also played an important role in mission under the direction of their bishop.

In contrast with the pre-Constantinian period, there were more mass "conversions" for Christianity—from Clovis and the Franks to Charlemagne's conquest and Christianization of the Saxons. Within this context and while acknowledging the variety of mission efforts, we focus on the primary agents of mission during this period under consideration, that is, the monks and nuns. They succeeded the martyr as the Christian ideal for following Christ, or in other words, "as the expression of unqualified witness and protest against worldliness."[66]

Beginnings of Monasticism in the Roman Empire

The shift from early Christian asceticism to monasticism proper in the West, which occurred after the middle of the fourth century,[67] was greatly influenced by the Eastern forms of monasticism. However, in contrast to monasticism of Egypt, which was characterized particularly in its earlier days as a solitary, individual affair, monasticism in the West would have a much stronger communal and structured character. As a substitute for the wilderness environment of the East, the earliest monastic foundations in the West were founded on islands or remote inlets on the coast. Cases of early monastic communities of women include those established in Italy near Bologna and Verona,[68] and by Melania the Younger in Palestine in 420.[69]

Martin of Tours (316-397), both hermit and bishop, is considered the founder of Gallic monasticism, which had a strong pastoral and missionary character. The famous monastery at Marmoutier grew up from his hermitage. The second phase of the rapid expansion of Gallic monasticism is centered around the influential monastery of Lerins (off the coast of Cannes), from which many monks would be chosen as future bishops. Augustine's monastic rule would have an impact on monastic foundations in his area of North Africa (some thirty male monasteries would be founded before his death), as well as on the creation of

other monastic rules in the future. Although the monks were opposed by some
clergy and bishops in the West at the beginning, they became the primary agents
for deepening and spreading the Christian faith, especially in the rural areas.
Monasticism was upheld as the perfect expression of the Christian ideal in the
midst of what was considered a hostile non-Christian environment.

With their one object "to live in purity and die in peace,"[70] it may seem rather
surprising that monks and nuns would become the predominant model for mission in this early medieval period. Although the monastic communities were
not founded for mission, "their implicitly missionary dimension began to spill
over into explicit missionary efforts."[71] Let us now look more closely at the
particular monastic movements within the context of mission.

Irish Monasticism

While the naming of Palladius as the first bishop of Ireland in 431 points to
some earlier Christian presence, probably in the southern part of Ireland, Patrick
(d. 460) is considered the great missionary from Britain to this land beyond the
boundaries of the declining Roman Empire. At the age of sixteen, Patrick was
captured by Irish raiders at his home on the west coast of Roman Britain and
sold as a slave to a local Irish king. After six years he escaped and returned
home, but his Christian faith, which had become so deeply rooted in him during
his captivity, led him to decide to return to the place of his enslavement, now as
a missionary. While it is sometimes difficult to separate fact from legend, it
appears that Patrick accommodated himself and the Christian message quite
well to the Irish political and social context, in which the gospel was quickly
received. With neither a centralized government nor any urban center, Irish
society consisted of clans ruled by aristocratic kings, a highly developed indigenous oral culture and a learned class of legal specialists and poets. Monasticism was of central importance in the Irish church from the beginning. Although
Patrick was probably not a monk himself, he was familiar with Mediterranean
monasticism and quite possibly spent some time in the monastery of Lerins, the
great center of Gallic monasticism.[72] It appears that Brigid of Kildare (c. 450-
523) with seven other women formed the first women's monastic community in
Ireland. Later, men joined this community, making it the first *double monastery,* one in which women and men lived in separate quarters but shared prayer
and work under one rule.

It is not clear why and how the church took its particular shape after Patrick's
death. However, when the Irish church emerged several generations later in the
sixth century, a strong monastic character had developed in such a way that the
monasteries became the intellectual, spiritual and economic center of life for
the clans, with the abbots as leaders. Bishops were either abbots or subject to
them and ordained for episcopal functions but with no particular territorial jurisdiction. Alongside their work in copying and studying manuscripts, the monks
provided both monastic training and secular education for the youth of the tribe.[73]

Although marked with an extreme asceticism, Irish monasticism was very popular. One reason for this rapid growth is that there seems to have been a certain underlying parallel between monastic and traditional cultures both in Ireland and later among Germanic people on the continent.[74] It was possible for Celts "to pass from the one to the other by a profound change in their beliefs and their system of moral values without losing vital contact with their old social tradition, which was sublimated and transformed, but not destroyed or lost."[75]

Many of the monks were priests who ministered to the clans. Through the close pastoral contacts between the people and the monks, the practice of private confession with immediate absolution began to emerge. The monks developed penitentials, which were adapted from the monastic rule, to spell out the particular penance required for a particular offence. Beyond these great achievements in deepening the faith of Christians, "the greatest service of the Irish monks to Western Christendom was the new movement of missionary expansion which did so much to spread Christianity."[76] The powerful motivation underlying this outreach was the ascetic ideal of pilgrimage, whereby the highest form of renunciation was *peregrinatio pro Christo* ("wandering for the sake of Christ"). In this way, "the concept of pilgrimage often merged into that of mission—even if both pilgrimage and mission remained subordinate to the spiritual perfection of the monk."[77]

The first of two examples of these wandering Irish monks *(peregrini)* is Columba (520-597), known as the Apostle of Scotland. Born of a royal Irish family around 521, he seems to have entered the monastic life at an early age and founded several churches and monasteries in his homeland. In his early forties, Columba with twelve companions set off on pilgrimage to establish a monastery on the Scottish island of Iona. Rather than picturing a grand institution, White Monastery was simply the headquarters for training and sending out monk-missionaries, particularly among the Picts on the Scottish mainland. Stories of spiritual power struggles with their traditional priests, the Druids (and even with the legendary monster of Loch Ness[78]), are complemented by memories of the gentleness, simplicity and holiness of Columba and the many monks who followed him.

While some of the Irish monks traveled north, many crossed the sea to the continent, one of the most well known being Columban (d. 615). At the end of the sixth century, Columban left the Irish monastery of Bangor with twelve fellow *peregrini* for Brittany and eventually settled in the area under Merovingian rule in eastern France. The people there were of a nominal Christian faith, tracing their Christianity back a hundred years to the mass conversion of the Franks through King Clovis. Columban preached a more earnest and austere Christian life, wrote a penitential guide to accompany the practice of private confession and eventually established the monastery of Luxeuil. After conflicts, first of all, with the bishops of Gaul regarding some local church policies, and second, with the Burgundian rulers on the issue of the king's concubines, Columban left this area, where he had worked for twenty years, and went further south into Italy, where he founded a monastery at Bobbio. The importance of Columban for mission extends beyond his death through the many monks who streamed out of his monasteries and through his monastic rule and penitential, which became very prominent and influential. As for women in monasticism, Burgundofara, with the support of the Merovingian queen, founded a contemplative community in 617, two years after Columban's death. She became abbess of this community, which became a double monastery.

Another feature of Celtic monasticism was its tendency not to adapt to the norms of the established local church. The Irish monks and nuns came from a church in which the bishop was subordinate to the authority of the monastery and abbot. They had little understanding of the Roman-inherited territorial diocesan organization, which contrasted with the more fluid style of the Celtic church and society. Therefore, the Irish monks often acted outside the policies of the local bishop and of the Gallo-Frankish monasteries. In addition, there was a general controversy with the continental church over the date of Easter and the shape of the tonsure.[79]

Benedictine Monasticism

As one stream of missionary monasticism was flowing from Ireland, there was another with its source in Benedict of Nursia (480-547), who founded the famous monastery of Monte Cassino in southern Italy in 529. Together with his twin sister, Scholastica (480-543), women's monastic communities were also founded. In comparison with the more austere rule of Columban, the *Rule of St. Benedict* addressed the spiritual, practical and economic details of daily monastic life with the primary aim of giving glory to God.[80] The monastery was to be "a school for the Lord's service," and manual work received a dignified place within this context.

In a famous essay, Cardinal Newman captures the Benedictine spirit and vision of mission within the emerging world of medieval European society in the following way:

He [St. Benedict] found the world, physical and social, in ruins, and his mission was to restore it in the way, not of science, but of nature, not as if setting about to do it, not professing to do it by any set time or by any rare specific or by any series of strokes, but so quietly, patiently, gradually, that often, till the work was done, it was not known to be doing. It was a restoration, rather than a visitation, correction, or conversion. The new world which he helped to create was a growth rather than a structure. Silent men were observed about the country, or discovered in the forest, digging, clearing, and building; and other silent men were sitting in the cold cloister, tiring their eyes, and keeping their attention on the stretch, while they painfully deciphered and copied and re-copied the manuscripts which they had saved. There was no one that "contended, or cried out," or drew attention to what was going on; but by degrees the woody swamp became a hermitage, a religious house, a farm, an abbey, a village, a seminary, a school of learning, and a city.[81]

Benedictine monasticism received a major blow when Monte Cassino was destroyed by the Lombard invaders around 581. However, rather than being a moment of disaster, the subsequent flight of these monks to Rome symbolized a growing association with Rome and the person who would be very instrumental in promoting the rule of Benedict as well as instilling a more explicit missionary dimension to their young tradition: Pope Gregory the Great.

Growing up in a Rome, which was collapsing, Gregory gave up his wealth and became a monk and soon the abbot of a Benedictine monastery. Called to become the bishop of Rome in 590, he soon initiated a plan to send Augustine and forty Benedictine monks as missionaries to England. This direct mission endeavor was quite unique within the Roman Empire, in which Christianity had spread more through a gradual but steady process of diffusion until this time. Such a Rome-directed mission would characterize the developing Benedictine model for mission,[82] and the beginning of how mission would be carried out in later years as well.

On the one hand, the Benedictines shared the concerns for learning and true conversion of their Irish counterparts, while on the other hand, they devoted more energy to church organization and eventually were more dependent upon kings and other political leaders. While Augustine and others would direct their efforts of primary evangelization first of all to the leaders, the monks and nuns were also very close with the ordinary people, especially due to their attitude toward manual work.

According to one of his first letters, Gregory instructed Augustine to follow the general practice of suppressing the traditional religious practices and beliefs of those they wanted to convert. However, perhaps once he realized that the Anglo-Saxons would be very resistant to the Christian message, Gregory fostered a missionary spirit of adaptation and persuasion rather than rejection and coercion. Probably written about a month after the earlier letter, Gregory sent the following message to Augustine through the Abbot Melitus:

The temples of the idols in that nation ought not to be destroyed; but let the idols that are in them be destroyed; let holy water be made and sprinkled in the said temples, let altars be erected, and relics placed. For if those temples are well built, it is requisite that they be converted from the worship of devils to the service of the true God; that the nation, seeing that their temples are not destroyed, may remove error from their hearts, and knowing and adoring the true God, may the more familiarly resort to the places to which they have been accustomed. And because they have been used to slaughter many oxen in the sacrifices to devils, some solemnity must be exchanged for them of this account, as that on the day of the dedication, or the nativities of the holy martyrs, whose relics are deposited there. . . . For there is no doubt that it is impossible to efface every thing at once from their obdurate minds; because he who endeavors to ascend to the highest place, rises by degrees or steps, and not by leaps.[83]

It seems that Gregory saw this as temporary accommodation, that is, until the newly baptized would arrive at the point of abandoning their traditional beliefs and practices completely. However, this shift in missionary approach provided the opportunity for the Anglo-Saxons, and later other Germanic people on the continent, to appropriate more openly their new Christian faith within their traditional world view.[84]

While the Benedictines were involved in mission in the southern part of England, the Irish were evangelizing from the north, moving out from the monastery of Iona. The Anglo-Saxon church would draw from both monastic traditions in developing its own identity and become a prominent missionary church for the next four centuries.

Anglo-Saxon Monasticism

When the Celtic and Benedictine monks eventually came together in England, the major points of dispute were the date of Easter, the form of the tonsure, and more important, the form of church organization. This conflict reached its climax in the English Northumbrian state, which had been primarily evangelized by the Celtic monks and nuns. After hearing both positions at a synod in Whitby in 664, the Northumbrian king decided in favor of the Roman-Benedictine tradition. However, the continual coalescence of and interchange between these two rich Christian traditions produced such a new creation that Dawson states that "it was in Northumbria that Anglo-Saxon culture, and perhaps the whole culture of Western monasticism in the Dark Ages, achieved their climax at the beginning of the eighth century."[85] Regarding the site of the above-mentioned synod, Hilda of Whitby (610-680) was the foundress and abbess of this prestigious double monastery, and she served as spiritual director for its members and for people from the surrounding area.

The Anglo-Saxon monastic tradition carried on the ideal of *peregrinatio pro Christo*, which it received from the rich Irish tradition. However, the primary motivation shifted from one of renunciation to that of mission itself.[86] In contrast with the independent nature of Celtic monasticism, Anglo-Saxon monasticism and mission were more explicitly ecclesiastical in terms of relationship with the local church and the Church of Rome, which was characteristic of the Italian-Benedictine tradition. Also, there was a close affinity between the aristocracy and monasticism. Thirty-three Anglo-Saxon kings and queens spent the last part of their lives in monasteries, and twenty-three of them were venerated as saints.

The most well known of the many Anglo-Saxon monks who had a tremendous impact in the mission history of the church is Wynfrith of Crediton, later known as Boniface (c. 675-754), called the Apostle of Germany. While he was involved directly with the work of conversion during some periods of his life, his most significant contribution was the reform of the Frankish church. Due to his own Benedictine background and several visits to Rome, Boniface concentrated on organizing, strengthening and deepening Christianity in line with the developments out of the Church of Rome, such as filling bishoprics according to church law (not as a mayor's "award" for faithful civil service) and requiring all monks to live according to the Benedictine rule. He founded a number of monasteries, including a large one at Fulda. Still filled with missionary fervor as he neared eighty, he left his administrative responsibilities to others and went to work in Frisia, where he and fifty companions were martyred.

It is quite significant that he called upon women to share explicitly in mission on a wide scale for the first time in the post-Constantinian period. For example, Lioba (Leoba) was called from her cloistered monastery in England and became the abbess of such a women's monastic-mission community at Bischofsheim.

> She [Lioba] was learned not only in Holy Scripture, but in the works of the Church Fathers, in canon law and in the decisions of all the councils. . . . Learning was no mere decoration, it was what made Lioba an abbess-founder, whose disciples and daughter houses spread like good seed over new-plowed fields. Her learning, then, was an aspect of her holiness, for it was the very stuff of that good order, that rootedness in faith and tradition, which the biographer finds so worthy in her monastic foundations.[87]

Boniface requested that Lioba be buried in his tomb, so that as they had shared in the same missionary partnership, they might wait together for the resurrection.[88] This seemingly strange request (and it was considered such by many of Boniface's contemporaries) can be seen as a powerful symbolic statement regarding the collaboration and equality between women and men in mission, and as a challenge that, while not always met in mission history, certainly has resonance today. In this particular case, Boniface's monks did not honor his request, but its significance still stands.

These Anglo-Saxon monks, who cultivated the earth with their own hands, were very close to the peasants. On the one hand, they spread the uniform use of Latin in the liturgy, but at the same time, they supported the preservation of vernacular languages. Also, in line with Gregory the Great's earlier instructions, they encouraged the incorporation of traditionally sacred places and actions into Christian practice, such as the harvest festival of Ember Days during Advent.

Mass Conversions

This period of church history was marked by many mass conversions. The common pattern for this involved a converted king or prince making the choice for Christianity on behalf of his people. While this would often provoke some negative reactions and reversals, eventually masses of people would be baptized and these nominal Christians would then wait for the arrival of bishops, priests, monks and nuns to offer them a further understanding and witness of this new faith. It is important to remember that for a society that more highly values the communal aspect, rather than the individual, such a group choice for a new religion is quite natural. Religion is an integrated part of a holistic cultural system[89] with the ultimate aim of sustaining the well-being of the group—marked, for example, by abundance in fertility, success in war and protection from disaster. In this way, Christianity did over time reach the depth of tribal societies. Such a process was quite common throughout northern Europe, and it had at least begun quite significantly by the end of the tenth century also in Bohemia, Poland, Hungary and Scandinavia. This dynamic link between society and religion lay the groundwork for the emerging concept and identity of a *Christian nation* or *Christendom*—emerging from the tribal appropriation of the Christian faith and determining the future shape of Christianity.

The shadow side of mass conversions is often referred to as the cross-and-sword method. The most disturbing occasions of this took place under Charlemagne, as king of the Frankish state and later as emperor of the Holy Roman Empire. With a combination of political and religious motivation for establishing a Christian theocracy, Charlemagne during a period of over thirty years (772-804) of bloody conflict not only conquered the Saxons but demanded that they be baptized Christians. Following the armies, hundreds of Frankish and Anglo-Saxon priests, monks and nuns attempted to present the gospel to the baptized masses. During this painful period of church history, Alcuin of York, an Anglo-Saxon monk of the Northumbrian tradition and a member of the intellectual court surrounding Charlemagne, raised a prophetic and unheeded plea that adults not be baptized before catechesis.

The Byzantine Mission

As one looks at the changing course of history, it is quite amazing that the Byzantine (Greek East) Empire, with Constantinople as its capital, lasted for eleven centuries, from its foundation by Constantine until its fall to the Turks in 1453. The Byzantine church and state joined together as the eastern form of Christendom.

In the fourth and fifth centuries, monasticism spread from the early beginnings in Egypt into Palestine and the Sinai Peninsula. Basil of Caesarea, known as the father of Eastern Orthodox monasticism, attempted to integrate monasticism into the life of the local church. In contrast with what was seen earlier in the West, Byzantine monasticism from its beginning remained a movement, never becoming an institution.[90] Furthermore, its monasticism "has faithfully preserved its fundamental union of asceticism and mysticism and has remained close to the monasticism of the primitive Church,"[91] while the development of monasticism in the West has been influenced by clericalization and expansion of their activities. In this light, Byzantine monasticism did not develop the strong missionary character of Western or East Syrian traditions, but its mission contribution was significant nevertheless.

The East Gothic tribes were evangelized extensively in the fourth century by Byzantine monks and priests.[92] The most famous of these missionaries, Ulfilas, created an alphabet and translated the scriptures into the Gothic language. The fact that these Germanic peoples had received the Christian message within an Arian theology, which later was judged unorthodox, should not detract from this great missionary work by the church of the Greek East. Less known are monastic mission undertakings that were happening in Palestine, Syria and Mesopotamia during the fourth and fifth centuries.[93] Later in the sixth century we hear of the successful mission work around Smyrna and Ephesus by a monk (known as John of Asia) who had been sent by the emperor Justinian.[94] Justinian's wife, Theodora, was responsible for mission outreach (with a non-Chalcedonian perspective) to Nubia and the area around Edessa. The most significant person in this latter effort was the Syrian monk Jacob Baradeus (500-578), the founder of what would become the Jacobite (West Syrian) Orthodox Church, particularly in the area of Syria and Mesopotamia.[95]

After the sixth century, monastic communities moved to more isolated areas, had less contact with the local bishop and church, and grew in number, spiritual influence and wealth. While acknowledging the earlier mission activity, the Byzantine monastic movement in general did not have such a major impact directly on mission and daily life as it did in the West at this time. "Nevertheless, the spiritual contribution monasticism made overall to the Greek Church and cultural life was an important one, comparable to the contribution monasticism made in other parts of the Christian movement."[96] The monks and nuns in the Byzantine church, as in other Christian traditions, were regarded as the ideal of Christian life.

In addition to the members of the monastic communities, individual Christians who found themselves outside their homeland as merchants, slaves or prisoners of war would sometimes become a diaspora community of Christian witness.[97] However, the bulk of mission and church activity occurred under the umbrella of *imperial mission*, that is, the intermeshing of political and religious motivations to establish and extend the Byzantine imperial church. For example, Emperor Justinian during the sixth century did much to promote a uniform Christian identity both within his traditional domain, including the closing of the Athenian schools of philosophy in 529, and among the new peoples who were becoming part of the empire, such as in North Africa and of the Nile Valley. In the next century, this process would be reversed with the strong advance of Islam. However, to the north during the seventh and eighth centuries, various groups of Slavs, Avars and Bulgars invaded the empire and eventually became Christian, mostly through a process of assimilation into the Christian state.

In the ninth century, after the long and divisive iconoclastic controversy, the imperial church experienced a revival that included missionary efforts among Slavic people of Central Europe, Bulgars of Bulgaria and Russians as far as

Kiev. In a survey of mission models, the work among the Slavic peoples is of particular importance. At the request of the prince of Moravia (Slovakia), the Byzantine emperor selected and sent two Greek brothers, Cyril (Constantine) and Methodius, as missionaries to promote the concerns of both the Byzantine church and the Byzantine state. Through their well-known efforts, they succeeded in developing a Slavonic liturgy, an alphabet for Slavonic languages and the foundations for a Slavic Christian culture, which would find its future home not in Moravia but in Bulgaria. Another major issue in the story of Cyril and Methodius is the destructive rivalry between the Byzantine and Frankish empires and their respective churches.

Without going into great detail in comparing and contrasting the basic mission models of Byzantine and Latin Christianity during this period of the early Middle Ages,[98] several points of comparison would be helpful. While Cyril and Methodius were stressing cultural particularism and the formation of a more independent local church, Boniface and his successors were stressing cultural uniformity and membership in a universal church. In both situations, missionaries were working under the advantages and disadvantages of a favorable relationship with a political state, although the Byzantine church and state were more closely allied.

This preceding survey of almost six hundred years of mission history in the Latin West and Greek East has been characterized by mass conversions, forced baptisms and ambiguous church-state relationships. However, in contrast to this sometimes forceful approach to Christianization, the men and women of the monasteries offered a gentle model, one that combined proclamation and witness. Bosch maintains that "it was because of monasticism that so much authentic Christianity evolved in the course of Europe's 'dark ages' and beyond."[99] Through a process of assimilation (inculturation), the gospel touched the heart of the cultures of recently baptized peoples coming from the north and west, creating something new which in turn, just as decisively, reshaped Western Christianity for years to come.

While monasticism in general initially represented a certain rejection of and noninvolvement in the "world," we have repeatedly noted how instrumental it was in interacting with and shaping the "world." Christopher Dawson claims that monasticism in the West was the center for creating and preserving the new form of Western culture.[100] He also writes:

> By its sanctification of work and poverty it [monasticism] revolutionized both the order of social values which had dominated the slave-owning society of Europe and that which was expressed in the aristocratic warrior ethos of the barbarian conquerors, so that the peasant, who for so long had been the forgotten bearer of the whole social structure, found his way of life recognized and honoured by the highest spiritual authority of the age.[101]

Across Asia, monasteries were resources for the wider society in the areas of medicine, science, philosophy, translation and administration. Furthermore, Samuel Moffett maintains that one of the greatest contributions of the East Syrian Church and monasticism was its transmission of Greek learning to the Arabs, who in time would return it to the West.[102] Within the Byzantine perspective, mission must include involvement in society. "State, society, culture, nature itself, are real *objects* of mission and not a neutral 'milieu' in which the only task of the Church is to preserve its own inner freedom, to maintain its 'religious life.'"[103]

In sum, monastic women and men were identified as ideal realizations of the Christian life and, not coincidentally, were the primary agents of mission in all branches of Christianity during this time period—especially in the East Syrian, Egyptian, Ethiopian, Latin and Greek churches. Acknowledging the diverse expressions and methods, monks and nuns were vehicles for presenting the continual challenging call to conversion to all Christians—no matter how superficial or deep was their faith.

By the year 907, Christianity had spread across central Asia into China, and probably further into northeast and southeast Asia. The fall of the T'ang dynasty marked the end of this first Christian moment in China, although seeds of the Christian faith planted among some Mongol and Turkish peoples would bear fruit during the next Christian period in China. Around the beginning of the tenth century, Christians lived as a religious minority in lands under Muslim rule—Persia, Syria, Mesopotamia, Armenia, Palestine, Egypt, Sicily, the Maghrib and the Iberian Peninsula. Christianity in the West was embraced by most people of Europe, except for those of Scandinavia, Prussia and Lithuania. The Byzantine Christianity of Asia Minor had taken solid root among the Bulgars and initial steps in Russia. The ancient churches in Ethiopia and India were quite isolated from the rest of the Christian world.

CONSTANTS IN THE CONTEXT
OF THE EARLY MEDIEVAL PERIOD

In the early church, there was a close theological, missiological and practical interrelationship among church, mission and baptism; this interrelationship was foundational to the basic models of mission in that period. When Christianity in the Roman Empire became the favored religion and mass conversions followed, Christianity began to lose this foundational mission ecclesiology. However, monasticism arose as a movement that radicalized and symbolized this basic baptismal commitment within the church. The monk and nun replaced the martyr as the ideal in the Christian community.

It is of great significance that the rise in monasticism occurred during a period of decline in the catechumenate. The way in which the church had initiated Christians reflected its understanding of itself. While Augustine still favored

MISSION AND THE MONASTIC MOVEMENT (313-907)

Context	West Roman Empire	East Roman (Byzantine) Empire	Armenia, West Syria, Egypt, Nubia and Ethiopia	Persian Empire and Asia
Stream of Christianity	Latin West	Greek East	Armenian, Jacobite, Coptic and Ethiopian	East Syrian
Primary model	Monks and nuns	Monks and nuns	Monks and nuns	Monks
Key figures in mission	Gallic, Irish, Benedictine, Anglo-Saxon monks and nuns; bishops, priests and deacons	Byzantine monks and nuns; Ulfilas, Cyril and Methodius; merchants, slaves and prisoners of war	Egyptian, Ethiopian and West Syrian monks and nuns; Frumentius and Julian	East Syrian monks; merchants, physicians and refugees; teachers; patriarchs
Theological typology	A (emphasis on law)	B (emphasis on truth)	B (emphasis on truth)	C (emphasis on history)
Primary theologians	Augustine, Anselm	Basil of Caesarea, Macrina, the two Gregories	Cyril of Alexandria	Nestorius, Narsai, Aphraphat the Persian, Ephraem the Syrian
CONSTANTS				
Christology	High; Chalcedonian definition; substitutionary death	High Chalcedonian definition; exemplar model	High Monophysites ("one nature")	Low Dyophysites ("two natures"); "liberation"
Ecclesiology	Institutional model; "City of God"; Universality	Mystical communion, sacrament; Particularity of local church	Mystical communion, sacrament; Particularity of local church	Herald, servant; missional; Diaspora
Eschatology	Futurist (imminent) Individual	Realized Individual	Realized Individual	Inaugurated Historical
Salvation	Spiritual; Atonement; only through church	Spiritual; Pedagogical progression	Spiritual; Pedagogical progression	Holistic
Anthropology	Negative	Positive	Positive	Positive
Culture	Negative; translation model	Positive; anthropological model	Positive; anthropological model	Positive/negative; moderate counter-cultural model

thorough spiritual preparation before baptism, the pre-Constantinian catechumenate was gradually reduced to an intense Lenten period of preparation for baptism in the fourth and fifth centuries. During the sixth century, this special Lenten period became less common, especially with the growing percentage of infant baptisms. Although there were periodic attempts to reinstate a period and process of serious preparation for baptism, especially by people like Martin of Braga, Boniface and Alcuin in missionary situations,[104] the catechumenate practically disappeared during the Middle Ages. Of course, over this same time period, monasticism, with its own form of intense Christian initiation, had grown. Without judging the baptismal commitment of other Christians, the monks and nuns were the predominant living witnesses to the interconnection of church, mission and baptism across the various Christian churches at this time.

Having acknowledged this basic theological stream in the history of monasticism in general, we now need to situate each model of mission more specifically, including its model of monasticism, within its own context and its own contextual theology. Recognizing the advantages and disadvantages of any use of categories, the typology proposed by González and Sölle seems to be helpful in clarifying and understanding the interpretations given to what we have called the *constants* in missionary practice and preaching. While all the constants are present, the perspective on *human nature* seems most fundamental during this period.

With Augustine as its primary theologian at the beginning of this period, Type A theology (with its emphasis on law) became the predominant theology of the Latin West at the beginning of the sixth century with the missionary bishop of Rome, Gregory the Great.[105] At a time of tremendous social upheaval, a theology that emphasized order was very compelling. Type B theology (with its emphasis on truth), which was quite prominent in general during the earlier period of the church and mission, would be associated more with Byzantine Christianity with its strong identification of Christianity and culture.

In refuting Pelagianism's overly optimistic view of human nature, Augustine saw it as depraved and sinful, needing a redemption that can only come from God. God's action and not human achievement would bring salvation. Augustine was struggling more with an anthropological problem than a theological one. The theology of the Greek East, in contrast, held an optimistic view of human nature, which could be taken up into the divine through a pedagogical progression. This difference in their understanding of human nature and salvation was likewise reflected in their *Christological* interpretation of the work of Jesus Christ. The Latin West stressed the cross and atonement, while the Greek East stressed Easter and resurrection. "The theology of the Eastern church was incarnational; its emphasis lay on the 'origin' of Christ, his preexistence. The theology of the Western church was staurological (from *stauros*, Greek for 'cross'); it emphasized the substitutionary death of Christ for the sake of sinners."[106]

Besides his controversies with the Pelagians, Augustine is also noted for his opposition to the Donatists of North Africa. In line with the moral strictness of

Tertullian, the Donatists insisted that Christians should have nothing to do with the world, that sinful individual members of the church would make the church itself unholy, and that church and state must be completely separated. In response, Augustine insisted that the church is not a refuge from the world but existed for the sake of the world, that the holiness of the church is not dependent upon the holiness of its members, and finally, that Christians as members of civil societies must work for building a perfect society, which will only be fully realized with the second coming of Christ. Later, Augustine's strong argument for the holiness of the church would be developed into the belief that salvation itself is equated with membership in the church. In other words, we see the beginnings of the "ecclesiasticization" of *salvation*.[107] With this *ecclesiology,* the act of baptism tends to become more important than a person's appropriation of the faith, which is to be accomplished later through catechesis and sacraments. In addition, we see the rising institutionalization of the church during this period both in the Latin West and Greek East.

Flowing from this Augustinian theology, David Bosch has proposed that *the* text inspiring the church's mission of the Latin West is Luke 14:23 — "and compel them to come in" *(compelle intrare).*[108] Of course, this would be translated into a variety of missionary methods, depending on one's interpretation and context. Charlemagne would force the Saxons to be baptized into the church in his efforts to establish the city of God on earth. Many of the monks and nuns followed a much gentler and less coercive accommodational approach. As a missionary bishop of Rome, Gregory the Great criticized landowners because their laborers were not yet baptized, and he sent missionaries to faraway England to baptize the "barbarians." This latter initiative by Gregory also reflects his positive appreciation of the human dignity of the Germanic people, an attitude not held by most Romans.[109] Some of Gregory's mission motivation also seemed to have been *eschatological,* in that he believed the political-social chaos of his time was an indication that the End was near and that time was running out for people to be saved.[110] David Bosch states that Benedictine and Celtic monasticism also had a strong eschatological emphasis.[111]

Within the Latin West, the monastic life of renunciation influenced not only the rest of the church, such as through the introduction of the practice of individual confessions and penitentials, but also society on the whole. Western monasticism was very instrumental "in asserting in concrete terms the pessimistic concept of human nature and in conveying that message to ever-enlarging circles in the nonmonastic and nonfrontier world."[112] At the same time, the monastic movement upheld the dignity of human labor and education.

In regard to *human culture,* the monks and nuns of the Benedictine/Anglo-Saxon model did not necessarily regard Germanic cultural-religious society that highly, but they were willing, at least initially, to follow what developed into a more accommodational approach. In a significant way, the Germanic people, both appropriated Christianity within their traditional world view and reshaped Christianity in the West. For example, in the area of theology the Germanic cultures, with the central importance of law and custom, would propose new questions to Christianity and prompt Anselm of Canterbury to develop a contextualized theology of atonement.[113] As for Irish monasticism, it is very interesting how some Celtic monks contextualized the gospel by singing *The Heliand*—the song-text of the story of Jesus—in Saxon meadhalls.[114]

In the Byzantine tradition, incarnational theology and the more optimistic view of human nature and human culture are reflected most clearly in the strong accommodational approach of Cyril and Methodius, who responded to the invitation of the Slavic people for evangelization. These two missionaries are pioneers of what we today call "inculturation." Contrary to the more active approach of sending out missionaries, Byzantine Christianity spread more through a gradual progression and synthesis among the peoples who entered the Byzantine domain.

We now turn to East Syrian Christianity during its "Golden Age" of mission, in which its theology seems to align most closely with that of González's Type C theology (with its emphasis on history). While the rest of Christianity at this time was becoming more aligned with and supported by political states in many situations, Christianity in Asia remained a religion of a minority or diaspora, similar to the original context of persecution in Asia Minor and Syria in which Type C theology emerged. Within this environment, Syrian theology and church life stressed the importance of moral rigorism, which helped them to maintain strength and identity as a minority.

Quite different from the Greco-Roman world, Persian Christians were surrounded by Zoroastrianism. Aphrahat the Persian, considered "the greatest Eastern theologian of the early fourth century,"[115] was probably a convert himself from Zoroastrianism, which had an intense dualistic view of the world caught in a warfare between good and evil. In this context, Aphrahat described Christianity as the power against such evil and Christ as the light that withstands the fire, drawing upon central Zoroastrian symbols. Aphrahat also described Jesus Christ in powerful biblical images as the chief shepherd and the living water. Often the understanding of mission "was expressed in terms of struggle, fight, battle and war,"[116] and baptism was seen as "initiation into the army of God for warfare."[117] Obviously, such a mission theology reflects the perspective of a Christian minority within a Zoroastrian context. Their understanding of *Christology* and *salvation* flows from this strong sense of the baptismal responsibility for mission. "The calling of the Christian disciple is to imitate Christ, to follow the footsteps of the master in sacrificing themselves for the salvation of the world. . . . The mission, for the East Syrian theologians, was part of their Christology. The missionary motive permeated the whole Christian life, whether of clergy or laity."[118]

Similar to the situation of the early years of Christianity, the fundamental connection among baptism, mission and church motivated, to various degrees, East Syrian merchants, physicians, administrators and those living in segregated neighborhoods, whether under the Persian *melet* or Muslim *dhimmi* system. The church acted not as an institution, from a position of privilege, but as a diaspora community witnessing to the power of Christ through whatever means were available. Many did this through their professions, daily lives and works of charity. At times this led to martyrdom. Within this context, the monks were held up as ideals. At the core of East Syrian Christianity, one finds the three interrelated dimensions of theology, mission and monasticism.[119]

In contrast to Aphrahat's male imagery of battles and confrontations, Ephraem the Syrian, another important East Syrian theologian of the fourth century, used female imagery for the Holy Spirit, a perspective common in the Syrian tradition, and had a strong incarnational theology with a positive attitude toward *human nature.* "At the center [of his theology] stood the great mystery of God's self-abasement in the incarnation and God's self-giving through the Holy Spirit. . . . Nature, humanity, and especially Mary all shared in the incarnational mystery, which was also at the heart of the sacramental practices of the church."[120] As another indication of Ephraem's high regard for human nature, tradition credits him with overseeing the collection of food during a famine and the establishment of a hospital in Edessa.

In balancing Type A theology's negative perception of *human nature* and *human culture* with Type B's positive one, the dialogue of Timothy I with the Muslim caliph indicates an openness to listen respectfully to the religious world of the other while also upholding the integrity of the Christian faith. It seems that Adam and Alopen attempted to do the same in China. The inclusion, as well, of secular monks within East Syrian Christianity indicates a tendency to avoid the Latin West's temptation of dualism, and their minority status in society indicates a tendency to avoid the Greek East's temptation of complacency.

IMPLICATIONS FOR THE THEOLOGY OF MISSION TODAY

The decline in the catechumenate and the rise in monasticism (and later other types of religious and missionary societies in the Latin West) point to a tendency for mission to be perceived as a particular vocation rather than as an essential part of the baptismal promise. With the revival of the catechumenate process following the Second Vatican Council, there certainly has been a renewal in the *baptismal commitment to mission.* Consequently, there is a challenge to situate the understanding of ordained ministry and religious life within this basic baptismal understanding. At the same time, monasticism points out the possibilities of the *prophetic witness* aspect of the Christian call as a part of God's mission. In an interesting article, Richard Sullivan describes the medieval monk as a frontiersman:

> So convincing is the evidence that I believe one can argue that frontier monasteries constituted virtually the sole source of reform movements between the fifth and twelfth centuries. The monk in the role of frontiersman was almost singlehandedly the provider of leaven in a society that suffered from massive inertia. . . . These movements always focused on a

program that would produce a change of heart among the wicked through a process that involved a simplification of life-styles.[121]

To quote the title of another article, how can the monastic tradition be "a source for unity and renewal today?"[122]

We can learn a lot from the East Syrian model of mission with the underlying theology of the essential interrelationship among baptism, church and mission — as it was in the early church. It seems that the basic *mission ecclesiology* remained prominent, in contrast to the developments we saw in the Latin West and Greek East. Perhaps this is due to the fact that the East Syrian Christians remained a minority (without mass conversions and close state-church affiliations) and that the monastic movement was a part of their history almost from the very beginning. The context of the East Syrian Church provides an interesting point of reference parallel to the situation of the Christian diaspora existing today in many parts of the world, such as in post-Christian Europe.

The moments of *interreligious dialogue* — involving persons such as Alopen, Adam and Timothy I — between Christianity and Islam, Buddhism, Taoism and Confucianism in Asia stand out as quite exceptional not only within this time period, but also within mission history in general. One wonders how they were able to engage in such interchange while maintaining their Christian identity and their minority status. We will later refer to this as *prophetic dialogue*. Asia continues to be the place where such interfaith challenges are most urgent and most hopeful.

Moving back to the European context, a similar dynamic was at work and just as controversial and complex. In comparison with the situation in China, we have more information about both the missionaries and, more important, the Germanic peoples who received and appropriated the Christian message and faith — a process we now call *inculturation*. In his study of this period, Ramsay MacMullen acknowledges the ambiguities and challenges in distinguishing faith and superstition, "popular" religion and the "official" church, religion of the masses and the educated elite, Christianity and "paganism."[123] He concludes that the Western church did not displace "paganism" but assimilated it. From a sociohistorical perspective, James Russell describes this process as the "Germanization" of Christianity: "To the extent that the Christian ideological matrix of sin-repentance-salvation advanced among the Germanic peoples in the early Middle Ages, it may be said that they were Christianized, while to the extent that Christianity accommodated the religiopolitical and magicoreligious orientation of pre-Christian Germanic religiosity during this period, it may be said to have been Germanized."[124] Speaking theologically, Andrew Walls considers this process — inherent to the nature of Christianity — as a series of translations or retranslations of the Christian message in a way that, rather than something new totally replacing something old, the already existing is transformed into something new. "If they [Germanic Christians] took their ideas from the Hellenistic Christian world, they took their attitudes from the primal world; and both ideas and attitudes are components in the complex which makes up a people's religion. As with their predecessors, they appropriated the Christian faith for themselves, and reformulated it with effects which continued amid their successors."[125]

Reflecting upon this particular moment in the history of Christianity, after the fact, offers us some key points as we approach the issue and reality of inculturation today: complexity, ambiguity and "messiness" in the lengthy process; inevitability and necessity of continuity with the past; difficulties and limitations of using categories such as religion and culture/society; acknowledgment of factors operating simultaneously on various "levels" and in different "areas"; recognition of the roles of the "outsider" (missionary) and "insider" (local people); and the importance and challenge of continually discerning new appropriations of the Christian faith, while "letting go" of attitudes of superiority from old appropriations. The delicate interplay of these questions provides important parameters for understanding inculturation as *prophetic dialogue*. Furthermore, missionaries and local communities in diverse *contexts* may be contemporaries, but they shape this process very differently—such as, Alopen and Adam and the Chinese, Cyril and Methodius and the Moravians, Augustine and Boniface and the Germanic peoples, as well as the Christians in Ethiopia, Ireland and India.

This period of missionary activity offers many positive examples, but there are also aspects that are very disturbing. Force under the banner of "Christianization" was used by Charlemagne against the Saxons, by Justinian against the "pagans" and by Augustine against the Donatists. Such events, as distorted expressions of the mission theology of "compel them to come in," are always to be deplored, yet unfortunately they recur throughout Christian history until today.

5

Mission and the Mendicant Movement
(1000-1453)

Crusades, Preachers, Nuns and Mongolian Christianity

The situation for the church and mission at the end of the tenth century looked rather grim—the fall of the T'ang dynasty in China (907) had signaled the end of the "Golden Age" of the East Syrian Church; the church of the Latin West was suffering from corruption and stagnation; and tensions between the Latin West and Greek East were growing. However, at the beginning of the second millennium the overarching challenge facing the church, no matter where it turned, was the ever-present threat of Muslim political and religious power. The East Roman Empire, much reduced in size, was investing the bulk of its energy and resources in a loss-and-gain military struggle with Islamic forces; Spain and Portugal were still under the Moors; the status of the Holy Land was always a major concern; the East Syrian Church continued to face the challenges (fairly well, actually) of surviving under the Muslim 'Abbasid dynasty in east Asia; and the churches of Egypt, Nubia and Ethiopia held their breath (and their faith).

The period this chapter covers was initially characterized by a series of crusades from the West, which, while religious in intent, was marked by cultural insensitivity, wanton violence and ultimate defeat.[1] However, this was also a moment during which Christianity was renewed, particularly through its missionary efforts. The East Syrian Church, for example, reached out to the Turks, Mongols and Chinese; the Byzantine Church to the Russians; and the Latin Church to the Muslims, Scandinavians, Lithuanians and peoples of central Asia and the Far East. In the West, the mendicant movement, in particular the Franciscans and Dominicans, emerged as the primary new missionary model in the second part of the medieval period.

By the last part of the fifteenth century, nevertheless, Christian mission both in the East and the West would come to a standstill, as Turkish and Mongol empires extended the influence of Islam, the church was wracked by corruption and schism, theology became bogged down in a sterile Scholasticism, Europe came to an end of one great epoch and stumbled toward another, and over a thousand years of the glory and endurance of the Byzantine Empire came to an end with the fall of Constantinople in 1453.

THE MISSION OF THE CHURCHES
OF THE LATIN WEST AND GREEK EAST

The Social-Political Context

Western Europe with its feudal states and small kingdoms depended to a great extent upon the Catholic Church for a unifying social and religious identity. The common use of Latin and a developing strong institutional papacy would help to unite an emerging Western civilization, which the Anglo-Saxons began describing in the tenth century as *Christendom*. After they were no longer preoccupied with barbarian invasions from the north, secular powers were ready to respond to another political and religious threat—the Muslims. The army of Alfonso VI of León in 1085 recaptured the important city of Toledo in Spain from the Moors, who had grown quite weak due to internal tensions and divisions. Ten years after this victory in Europe, the Byzantine emperor, despite the bad relations between the Latin West and Greek East, especially after the damaging event in 1054 between the Latin papal delegates and the Greek patriarch, requested military support from the pope against a serious threat from a new Muslim dynasty, known as Seljuk Turks, who had already taken control of Palestine and stopped Christian pilgrimages to Jerusalem for the first time in centuries. While it is not what the emperor had intended, Pope Urban II saw his request from the perspective of the Latin West and in 1095 called a military crusade against the Muslims in the Holy Land.[2]

The crusades are one of the most striking features of medieval European history, and, unfortunately, an image of Christian mission that was to persist into our own age, even though they were not intended to be instruments for spreading the Christian faith or regaining the populations who had become Muslim. Rather, the pope summoned the Christian faithful to take up arms in order to rescue the holy places in Palestine, to defend the Byzantine Christians from the Muslims and to turn back the tide of Muslim conquest. Mixed in with these religious motives were the political aims and ambitions of Western Europe. While the Muslims would eventually be driven out of Europe at the battle of Granada in 1492, most of the other political aims of the crusades were not accomplished in the long run. To the contrary, the second major wave of Muslim advance by its Turkish and Mongol converts during the thirteenth to fifteenth centuries would sweep back against the efforts of the crusades.

As for further negative consequences, the crusades dealt a damaging blow to relationships between the Latin West and the Greek East, especially after the sack of Constantinople by the crusaders in 1204.[3] During the subsequent Latin rule of sixty years, the Byzantine Empire was severely weakened, and even though a Greek emperor did return to the throne, the damage was done. Constantinople and the empire would eventually fall to the Muslim Ottoman Turks in 1453. In addition, the West's invasion of Islamic territories affects the relationships between Christians and Muslims until the present. Despite the original high religious intentions, the behavior of the crusaders, both toward fellow Christians and Muslims, often contradicted the very Christian values they came to defend.

Regarding the social context, Western Europe experienced rapid economic and demographic growth from around the year 1000. These tremendous changes began in the rural areas due to such developments as the wheeled cart, the horse collar and the wool industry. Rice was added to the Mediterranean scene to feed the growing population. Villages grew into towns and cities — the new economic, political and cultural centers. Universities began to spring up. Venice and Genoa became important centers of commerce, which included trade relations with Muslims. In the twelfth and thirteenth centuries, there were clearer signs that the age of feudalism was beginning to pass, as merchants and artisans became more prominent than the landed aristocracy.

Another significant development was the Renaissance, which began in Italy around 1300 and would last about three hundred years.[4] It was a time of great accomplishments in scholarship and the arts. Interest in the study of human nature itself would develop into an understanding of a person more as an individual than as a member of a group. Rather than Latin, writers began using the vernacular languages of Italian, French and English. The full effects of the Renaissance will be described, however, when we move out of the Middle Ages in the next chapter.

During this time of change, one other event that influenced every aspect of the Later Middle Ages was the bubonic plague. It is estimated that the various episodes of this terrible plague of the second half of the fourteenth century claimed one-third of Europe's population.

The Religious Context

Much of what was said above regarding the crusades overlaps the picture of the religious context. "For at least four hundred years they [the crusades] constituted part of the idealism of Western Christendom."[5] The traditional values associated with pilgrimage and martyrdom were combined with the chivalry of fighting in defense of the faith. As we will see below, less forceful alternative approaches to the followers of Islam were also present within the church at this time, especially through the Franciscans, Dominicans and East Syrian missionaries.

Alongside the religious fervor underlying the response to Islam in "far-off lands," an evangelical awakening was also stirring within Europe itself in the twelfth and thirteenth centuries.[6] In the midst of the upheaval brought on by social, economic and demographic changes, people of the emerging towns were hungering for something that they didn't find in the church, which was often corrupted by power, wealth, clericalism and militarism. In response, preachers of new lay apostolic movements, including the Humiliati,[7] the Waldensians[8] and the Franciscans, presented a message focused on the gospel and a life of poverty, as inspired by a reflection on the primitive church. Women and men generously expressed their Christian faith in creative new ways—as penitents, beguines and beghards, and members of third orders and new congregations. To various degrees, this dynamic challenged both the church and the feudal system in which it was situated.

The Institutional Context

The church and mission of the Latin West were at a low point in the year 1000. Lay rulers were appointing priests and bishops, who in return had to give payments for the appointments and take oaths of fealty to these feudal lords. Secular clergy were shackled with their own struggles with worldliness and poor theological training.[9] The Gregorian reform, which actually extended beyond the pontificate of Gregory VII (1073-1085), attempted to address this latter situation, but it also widened the gap between clergy and laity.[10] Celibacy became a requirement for priesthood in the Latin West. Beginning in the tenth century, a variety of other attempts were made to correct the general state of moral corruption and malaise within the church. Most of the early efforts consisted of reformed and stricter monastic movements, such as the Cluniac Reform, Canons Regular, Cistercians, Carthusians and Premonstratensians.[11] It is important to note that in general these well-intentioned reforms stressed isolation from the world and therefore did not contain a strong impetus for mission. Later the Knights Templar, the Hospitallers and other military religious orders were founded as another type of monasticism in response to the situation of the crusades as the militia of Christ.[12] Most of these various movements, up to this point, were generally initiated by the aristocracy, who had the necessary wealth and influence. Probably due to their perspective and vested interest in maintaining the feudal system, they proposed reforms of traditional structures rather than introducing something completely new that might upset the existing order.[13]

Beginning in the twelfth century, the renewal moved more and more into the hands of the town and city dwellers and of the peasants, reflecting the changing of the guard in the social order as well. A chief characteristic of these popular religious movements was the idea of the *vita apostolica* ("evangelical[14] life"). While some of these movements remained within the official church, others wandered away from what was considered orthodox, such as the Cathars.[15] The growing bureaucracy of the church seemed to be more attentive to what it considered aberrant beliefs and practices. Heresy became such a concern that in 1179 the Third Lateran Council granted the same indulgences for participation in the crusades against heresy within Europe as those against Muslims in the Holy Land. "The tragedy of the church was that a real movement of evangelical fervour, which should have been revitalizing the church from inside, was being pushed to and beyond the fringe by a combination of lack of effective understanding and leadership on the part of the official clergy and a serious lack of doctrinal formation on the part of the people."[16] The mendicant orders of Dominic and Francis would not only respond to this dilemma, but they would also instill a new missionary vision and spirit within the church of the Latin West.

The institutional context during this period of five hundred years was marred by two schisms. As we saw in the last chapter, national, cultural and theological tensions had been building up for a long time between the Latin West and the Greek East. The mutual excommunications in 1054 by officials of the two churches are sometimes considered the official break, but it was rather more symbolic of the desperate state of affairs.[17] Later, the "capture" of Constantinople by the Latin crusaders in 1204 was the decisive and final blow. The second schism, that of the West, occurred at the end of the fourteenth century as a result of power struggles in church-state relations, particularly with the French crown. After a seventy-year period of the papacy in Avignon, which was part of the papal states but certainly under the French political sphere, the election of two rival popes (and later a third) marked deeper tensions and problems within the church.[18]

The church of the Greek East struggled as the Byzantine Empire began to collapse in the thirteenth century and finally fell in 1453 at the hands of the Muslim Turks. Its Christian tradition would be renewed through the people of Russia.

MODELS OF MISSION

At the beginning of the second millennium, missionaries from the church of the Greek East began their important work in Russia, which will be described in further detail below. Latin Christianity continued the process begun in the tenth century of spreading northward among the Scandinavian people much in the same way that it had earlier among many of the Germanic tribes. A royal leader often played a central, initial role in his people's choice for Christianity—King Knut (Canute) of Denmark, King Olaf of Norway and King Sverker of Sweden—and the work of evangelization followed. As a notable exception, Iceland approached its decision regarding Christianity in its non-monarchical assembly, considered the oldest parliament in the world. After a long period of debate, the assembly asked its president, or law speaker, to make the decision on behalf of the assembly. After withdrawing "to a full day and night of shamanistic-style divinization,"[19] he returned with the decision that Iceland was to become Christian. That was in the year 1000. In contrast to what we saw in the last chapter, the monks and nuns no longer played a significant role in mission, with the exception of the newly founded Cistercians in Sweden.

The use of military conquest in spreading Christianity—another characteristic of medieval times—remained a part of this period of history. The people of

Finland, the majority of whom were not Scandinavian, were baptized under the threat of the sword of King Eric IX of Sweden, who led a crusade against them in 1155. The religious order of Teutonic Knights shifted its service of the church from regaining the Holy Land to conquering and Christianizing the Prussians, which it accomplished by 1283 after a long, bloody struggle. Political motivation likewise was a part of the story of the last European people to receive the Christian faith, that is, the Lithuanians. In order to secure military assistance from Poland against the dreaded Teutonic Knights, King Jagiello was baptized in 1386.

Today we feel very uncomfortable with the association of political alliances and military conquests for the spread of the Christian faith. However, it is important to remember that the crusades and, to an even greater extent, the military religious orders were founded on an understanding of the Christian ideals of pilgrimage and martyrdom. "The traditional notion of a pilgrimage was combined with the doctrine that to fight for the defense of the faith against the enemies of Christ was not only justifiable but positively meritorious, warranting at least popular martyrdom for those who died on the expedition."[20] Nevertheless, we must insist, as does Frederick W. Norris, that the crusades were, with the possible exception of the Holocaust in the twentieth century, the "worst débâcle" in Christianity's two-thousand-year history.[21]

During this time of the crusades, mass conversions and forced baptisms, the women and men of the mendicant orders replaced the monks and nuns as the primary model of mission. They would be the ones who offer an alternative approach to Islam, who follow up after the Teutonic Knights in Prussia, who facilitate a deeper understanding of and commitment to the Christian faith in Europe and who are witnesses of the gospel across Asia. Let us now focus on these men and women of the mendicant movement, who participate in God's mission in their context. As we have seen so often, the renewal in mission brings a renewal of the church. The church again discovers its identity through mission.

Francis of Assisi

With a well-to-do cloth merchant as his father and a member of a respected French family as his mother, Francis was born around 1181-1182 and educated in the Umbrian town of Assisi in Italy.[22] Several events were significant in his early years—a rather lengthy captivity as a prisoner of war in the neighboring rival city of Perugia, a subsequent serious illness and a life-changing encounter with a leper. Then, while in prayer before a crucifix in San Damiano, Francis received the message, "Francis, go and repair my church!" He terminated his relationship with his father, renounced his social status before the bishop and began a life of austere poverty. At first, he understood this message literally, and he set about repairing the churches in the area around Assisi. However, about three years later, Francis was inspired by reading Matthew 10:5-16 ("Do not take gold . . . no sack for the journey . . . no sandals or walking stick") to combine preaching with poverty in his lifelong striving to imitate Christ. Soon several companions joined him. Even when there were only eight in his group, Francis sent them out (including himself) in four directions, two by two, preaching and begging in the towns and countryside.

Due to some negative experiences of other contemporary lay preaching movements, such as the Cathars and Waldensians, there was some hesitation to give Francis and his movement the official church recognition he sought. However, Pope Innocent III approved the simple rule around 1209 or 1210, and even though Francis did not originally intend to found a new order, many soon were joining the new Order of Friars Minor.[23] Francis began itinerant preaching in Italy but almost immediately directed his attention beyond the Christian world. Although the monks and nuns certainly were agents of mission earlier among those who had not yet heard the gospel, Francis of Assisi is considered "the first of the founders of religious orders who consciously included a mission among non-Christians in his life's program."[24]

Francis and Islam

While most people were caught up in the crusading spirit of the times, Francis's vision offered an alternative approach to the Muslims. His first two attempts to go to Syria and Morocco were unsuccessful. However, after the Whitsun Chapter of Franciscans in 1219, when he officially proposed his more peaceful approach of mission, a few friars were sent to Tunisia and Morocco, and Francis and a few companions set out for and reached Egypt.

After spending a short time in the crusaders' camp outside the city of Damietta, Francis and Brother Illuminato crossed the battle lines and were brought to the sultan, Al-Malik al-Kamil. In this encounter, which is quite significant for mission history, the sultan received Francis with Muslim hospitality, once he realized that Francis was coming as a religious person, not as a crusader.[25] After several days of listening to Francis's gentle words about the Christian faith, the sultan had Francis escorted safely back to the crusaders' camp. Francis had not succeeded in finding a martyr's reward,[26] in converting the sultan or in bringing an end to the war. However, in this human encounter "two men from the two enemy blocks found friendship."[27] Francis was so impressed by the Islamic periodic call to prayer by the muezzin that he proposed the adoption of a similar practice among Christians. "Having no need to exert power over the other, Francis was able to learn more about prayer from the followers of Islam."[28]

Francis's experience shaped the example and instructions for missionary attitudes that he passed on to his community. In the earlier rule of 1221,[29] in chapter 16,[30] addressed to "those who are going among the Saracens and other nonbelievers," two missionary methodologies to "live spiritually" are presented: (1) Christian presence and witness, which does not start with "arguments or disputes" but rather is based on being "subject to every human creature for God's sake (1 Pet 2:13)," and (2) open and explicit proclamation of the word of God, which may lead others to baptism and becoming Christian. The decision of whether one should follow the first or second way was left to the discernment by the missionaries in the particular context. While the dating of chapter 16 is debated, more and more scholars attribute it to the time after Francis's encounter in Egypt.[31] Certainly, the first method reflects Francis's attitudinal approach to the sultan.

Cajetan Esser points explicitly to a third way of mission for Francis as that of enduring opposition, pain and martyrdom, for which chapter 16 of the rule lists eighteen gospel references.[32] The ideal of martyrdom for Francis extended beyond physical martyrdom to include all types of suffering, which "gave everything into the Father's hands for the salvation of the world."[33] In this way, all three ways "to live spiritually among" non-Christians (and Christians) are interrelated. "The preaching of the Word, as Francis saw it, availed little without the sermon of one's life."[34] Or, as in the popular saying attributed to Francis, "Preach always and, if necessary, use words."

Clare of Assisi

Women as well as men were drawn to Francis's vision, the first and most widely known being Clare, born in 1193 into a wealthy family of Assisi. Recognized already during her youth for her spiritual gifts and encouraged through her contacts with Francis, Clare's moment of renouncing her old life and choosing her new occurred on Palm Sunday of 1212. The written accounts tell us that in the morning Clare received a palm branch, a symbol of martyrdom, from the bishop of Assisi, and in the evening she fled secretly from her parents' home to the church of Portiuncula, where Francis and several companions received Clare's commitment to join them in pursuing a gospel life.[35] They escorted her that evening to the Benedictine monastery of San Paolo, but eventually she would take up residence in the church of San Damiano, the first church Francis had repaired. She lived there for over forty years, until her death in 1253.

Through history, Clare has been called *la Pianticella*, the "little plant" of Francis, as his most faithful disciple. However, a flurry of recent studies on Clare—in part sparked by the celebration of the eight-hundredth anniversary of her birth—have shown that she is more than just an "offshoot" of Francis and needs to be understood and appreciated for her own place within Franciscan and church history.[36] For example, Margaret Carney writes:

> We must establish Clare in her rightful place as a threshold figure among medieval women of spirit. She was the first woman to write a *Rule* sanctioned with pontifical approval. She dared to synthesize the evangelical ideals of Francis, the new forms of urban female religiosity, and the best wisdom of the monastic tradition to create a new and enduring order in the Church. She testified to Francis not only by the humility of her faithfulness, but by the authority of her leadership and formative ministry.[37]

Since the time of women like Lioba and Hilda of Whitby within the Anglo-Saxon missionary movement, the role of women in official mission activity was more strictly limited to cloistered life. In the very early days of association with Francis, it is not absolutely clear how much Clare wanted strict enclosure or whether she would have preferred to work among the sick and poor, like the friars.[38] However, within a few years, Clare and her community were certainly following the tradition of the cloister, but at the same time, they were doing so in a unique way.

First, in contrast to the prevalent common practice and understanding of cloister life, the Poor Sisters (originally known as Poor Ladies) committed themselves to a Franciscan radical life of poverty—depending solely on the providence of God for their daily sustenance, rather than the material benefits of endowments and patronage. Second, Clare did not refer to her sisters as *reclusae* (recluses from the world), but rather as *inclusae*. "This meant that the prayer, poverty, and way of life of the Poor Ladies were 'to speak' from a convent culture of silence and were to include the needs of all persons, especially the poor."[39] Through their lives, the sisters were to reflect the life of Christ to one another and to those who were drawn to them from the neighboring towns. To use Clare's image, they were to be a mirror of Christ.[40] In this way Clare and her community developed a "feminine incarnation of the Franciscan evangelical life"[41] in such a complementary way with the friars' life and work that "she and her sisters would be missionaries, preachers, healers, and restorers of churches while remaining behind monastery walls."[42]

Of the numerous miracles attributed to Clare for those both within and outside the monastery, those associated with her successful defense of Assisi against military attacks provide two interesting observations in terms of mission.[43] First of all, one is struck by the strong sense of mutual solidarity between this group of cloistered women and the local community—that sense of mission and church within the local Christian context. Second, a comparison can be drawn between Clare's vulnerable peacemaking approach to the Saracen army, "armed" only with the Blessed Sacrament, and Francis's vulnerable encounter at Damietta, both representing an approach toward the Muslims strikingly contrary to the prevalent approach of the time.

In order to understand the community development of Clare's Second Order of Franciscans (known today as Poor Clares), we return to the first three years of the women's association with the men's community. At this time the women were under the direct guidance of Francis, who fostered a very strong bond and identification between the communities of men and women. However, with the ruling of the Fourth Lateran Council (1215), which forbade the establishment of any new religious orders, Clare's community of San Damiano was compelled to accept the Benedictine rule. Francis then declared Clare the abbess. Clare wanted the women's community to have its own rule based on the rule of the Friars Minor, with evangelical radical poverty as its foundation. For the rest of her life, Clare would struggle within the church to achieve this purpose. Finally, two days before her death (1253), Pope Innocent IV approved the rule, the first rule for religious life written by a woman.

Soon after her death, the Poor Clares divided according to which rule they observed: the original rule of Clare, the rule of Isabel of France (Longchamp) or the rule of Urban IV. Despite these differences, Clare's religious family grew quickly.[44] By 1371, there were about fifteen thousand Poor Clares in 452 monasteries, affiliated either with the First Order of Francis or under more direct episcopal authority. These monasteries stretched from Italy to the British Isles, from Spain to Slavic territories and the Near East. They had their first martyrs when sisters from the monastery in Antioch (Syria) were killed in 1268 during Muslim invasions. All members of the community in Tripoli (Libya) were killed in 1289, and another seventy-four women from the monastery of Tolemaida (Palestine) two years later. The women's communities founded by Clare grew from and beyond the prevalent notion of women's cloistered life to become a female witness of Franciscan evangelical life and mission. Angelyn Dries described this complementarity in the following way: "The Franciscan heritage reminds us that mission is an outer expression (Francis's itinerancy on the crossroads of the world) of an inner reality (Clare's inclusive circle)."[45]

The Beguine Movement

In continuing with the story of the role of women in mission during this time period, it is crucial at this point to introduce the beguines.[46] Scholars often describe the two centuries of the movement's development in terms of four stages.[47] The initial spontaneous development arose out of the context of the evangelical awakening in twelfth-century Europe. Individual women searching for a more intense spiritual life began living an intentional lifestyle that was different from the traditional forms of monasticism. Rather than living separate from the world, they continued to live in households and to support themselves through manual labor, often in the cloth industry. They had no rule or vows and did not necessarily exclude the possibility of marriage. They wore a uniform dress of gray — the same color worn by the Humiliati and early Franciscans.

With the second stage during the early part of the thirteenth century, informal groups of beguines (as they called themselves) became unofficially associated with particular monks and clerics, who supported them. The most significant associations were with the Cistercians and with Jacques de Vitry, who later became bishop, cardinal and spiritual advisor of Pope Gregory IX. During this time, each household began to develop its own pattern of spiritual life, but the beguine life was still unregulated and uncloistered.

In the third period the beguines received quasi-legal recognition in 1223 from Pope Gregory IX, on the one hand, while some of them were judged heretics, on the other.[48] They more and more came under clerical supervision and organization but remained officially lay women.

The fourth development was that the beguine houses (beguinages) were given official religious and civil recognition. With this final move, the beguines lost much of their autonomy and freedom, as they were placed directly under clerical authority. However, they were never seen as an official religious order.

The more developed beguinage was like a small religious settlement in the midst of a city. Entrance to the closed circle of cottages, which served as residences for the beguines, would be through one main gate, and often a surrounding wall or canal would offer further security and identity. A beguinage would also include a church, as well as buildings for community work, dispensing charity and administration.

Let us look at the concrete life of one of the most outstanding and well-known beguine women—Mary of Oignies.[49] Born into a wealthy family in Belgium around 1175, she was forced into marriage at the age of fourteen. However, Mary convinced her husband to respect her desire to live a chaste life, and they turned their house into a hospital for lepers. Many pilgrims began coming to their home due to Mary's growing reputation for holiness. With her husband's permission, she moved to a priory of canons regular in Oignies, which would eventually play a very important role in the developing beguine movement in Belgium, due in a great degree to Mary. She became famous for her voluntary poverty, mystical visions, severe asceticism and zeal for the salvation of souls. She died at the age of thirty-eight.

Two other points should be mentioned in relation to Mary of Oignies and the beguines. First of all, her eucharistic devotion was quite typical within beguine spirituality. Another beguine woman, Juliana of Cornillon, was very instrumental in having the feast of Corpus Christi introduced into the liturgical calendar.[50] Second, although Mary herself never preached, some beguine women were among other women who were preaching at this time.[51]

As we see, the beguines lived out the gospel-based *vita apostolica* in a way that was unique for the twelfth and thirteenth centuries. "Living an acceptable form of the apostolic life, they could remain within the boundaries of traditional spirituality; but being laywomen and free of the restrictions imposed upon cloistered nuns, they had the liberty to experiment and break new ground."[52] The significance of this movement of lay women extends to its impact and influence particularly on women religious orders, which grew in number as the beguine groups dwindled. The famous beguine mystic Mechthild of Magdeburg,[53] who eventually settled into a Cistercian monastery in Helfta (Saxony), is just one example of the strong beguine influence on and similarity with Cistercian women.[54] By the way, Mechtild of Hackeborn (mentioned in Chapter 2) and Gertrude of Helfta lived in the same monastery, which was distinguished by mystics and women of great learning. Some see in Clare's rule and life "a synthesis of elements that can be identified with the beguine movement."[55] Furthermore, even clearer connections can be seen with the Franciscan women of the Third Order and Dominican women. We look at the former in the next section and return to the latter at a later point in this chapter.

The Third Order of Franciscan Women

In order to understand the development of third orders, it is necessary, first of all, to consider another phenomenon of this time of searching for the *vita apostolica*, that is, the penitential movement. For many years, there were groups of penitents who were motivated either by official church penitential discipline or by an individual or communal desire to strive more seriously for evangelical perfection. (Francis, after his conversion, led the life of a penitent.) By the end of the twelfth century, the church officially recognized the Order of Penance. Some of these groups associated themselves as a "third order" of married or celibate lay people to a monastery or a new religious institution, such as the Humiliati or Premonstratensians. Thanks to the Order of Penance and other spiritual institutes for the laity, known collectively as third orders, a woman's rightful aspiration to take an active role in the life of the church outside a monastic structure found an outlet more efficacious than any available in the twelfth century.[56]

Within this context, the preaching of Francis and his friars touched the hearts of women and men who wanted to live a life of "secular holiness," that is, a more radical Christian life within their life of marriage and the home. Many people associated themselves as penitents to Francis's movement. While the actual development is somewhat unclear, the first official rule for the Order of the Brothers and Sisters of Penance (Third Order), associated with Francis, was probably already written by 1221. After a number of years of hot and cold relationships of responsibility and connection between the First Order and the Third Order of Francis, the rule of Pope Nicholas IV in 1289 officially placed the Third Order under the responsibility of the First Order, an arrangement that would last until the nineteenth century. Furthermore, the rule was flexible enough to embrace both lay men and lay women, who continued to live in their homes, and those who lived in community and professed vows. Both groups served the needy. At this point, rather than presenting the overall development of the Third Order,[57] and without denying the importance of men in this movement, we simply highlight those aspects, events and persons that point to the role of women in mission up until 1500.

Born and married in the ranks of royalty, Elizabeth of Hungary at a young age desired to help the less fortunate. She opened several hospitals, in which she personally served the sick and lepers. In the absence of her husband, the king, she opened up the public granaries to feed the poor during a time of hunger. With her husband's death, Elizabeth lost his protection and support in royal circles and was eventually banished from the palace. In 1228, she sold and distributed all her possessions for the sake of the poor and sick, as part of her renouncement of the world and commitment to a life of poverty and charity. She became a penitent within that part of the Franciscan movement that would evolve into the Third Order. Later, a number of congregations of Franciscan sisters, such as the Elizabethan Sisters and Grey Sisters, would consider Elizabeth of Hungary their foundress and patron because of their hospital ministry.

Following a similar pattern, women within the Franciscan spirit and with the support and direction of a bishop or a priest of the First Order would in the future found a new community as a part of the ongoing development of the female Third Order Regular ("regular" religious life). Also, in order to secure church support and recognition in the face of some opposition and accusations, a number of beguine groups became affiliated with the Second Order of Clare, but more often with the Third Order of Francis. Therefore, "community life in the female branch of the Order of Penance had already experienced more than enough development towards the end of the thirteenth century, even before the Rule of Nicholas IV."[58]

Several serious difficulties arose in the early part of the fourteenth century.[59] First of all, religious life for women was still understood exclusively in terms of the cloister. For example, as long as the beguines were not officially "religious," they had a fair bit of latitude. This changed when they placed themselves under an official religious rule. While local interpretations would vary, the church in general was still trying to fit all these "religious" order movements of women within the framework of the cloister. Second, suspicions and accusations of heresy by the Inquisition were often leveled against the beguines and those associated with them.

However, in the second half of the fourteenth century we see the early development of communities of Franciscan Sisters into federations and eventually into congregations.[60] Both the Grey Sisters and the Elizabethan Sisters trace their origins to thirteenth-century lay women who wanted to live a spiritual life in community while continuing their work of charity in hospital work. These developments were among the first to break new ground in the transition from what was considered "secular" to "religious." In 1480, Sixtus IV would officially recognize the vows of the Third Order Regular as those of "true religious."

Two points can be drawn from these descriptions of the interrelated movements associated with Clare, the beguines, the penitents and the Third Order. First of all, in the midst of the social, economic, religious and ecclesial ferment of the High Middle Ages, many people were searching for ways to live a more radical Christian life, ways that often included a commitment to service, charity and mission. Usually mission was lived out within one's own local context.

Second, women in particular struggled to find forms or ways for expressing this evangelical and spiritual fervor that would find an "acceptable" place within the world view and parameters of the society and the official church of that time. Fortunately, one finds this desire for authentic Christian living and mission breaking through into new patterns. We will find similar dynamics when we examine the Dominican movement later.

The First Order of Francis

Francis died in 1226 and was canonized within two years. He had many gifts, but planning and organizational skills were not among them. Even before his death, he had turned over the leadership to others. Within fifteen years, there were signs of the issues that would challenge and divide the Friars Minor, as they attempted to interpret and live out the ideals and mission of Francis.

One of those elements in the early history of the First Order,[61] which likewise affected the entire church, was associated with Joachim of Fiore (d. 1202). The eschatological theories of this Cistercian abbot divided salvation history into three ages—those of the Father, Son and Holy Spirit—whereby in the final period the church of the hierarchy, sacraments and law would be replaced by a "spiritual church" *(ecclesia spiritualis)*. Joachim's writings were very influential among the Spirituals, a group of Franciscans who advocated stricter observance of the ideals of Francis, and later among the Fraticelli, a dissident radical group of Franciscans.[62] These and other non-Franciscan Joachimite movements sometimes contained elements of apocalyptic expectations, social revolution and ecclesial dissension—all of which were confronted by the Inquisition[63] and the mission efforts of the Franciscans and Dominicans. The Friars Minor dealt with these challenges more internally, within their order, and in turn, these eschatological and apocalyptic themes affected their understanding of mission.[64] The Dominicans addressed these issues more externally, within the wider church. Despite their own internal difficulties, it is estimated that the Friars Minor by the year 1300 numbered about forty thousand. Their membership would be half this size in 1385, mostly due to the bubonic plague.

Franciscans and Mission

In the rule of 1221, Francis's exhortations and guidelines for mission extended to the friars "no matter where they are"[65]—whether among the Saracens (chapter 16) or preaching in Christian lands (chapter 17). The understanding of mission was not geographically limited. In Europe, the heart of missionary work for the Friars Minor was preaching and hearing confessions. The long list of well-known preachers includes Anthony of Padua (d. 1231), Berthold of Regensburg (d. 1272) and Bernardine of Siena (d. 1444).[66] Keeping in mind Francis's admonition to maintain integrity in preaching through both one's life and one's word, we recall the witness and mission of the cloistered women of the Second Order as well.

In the social realm the Friars Minor instilled a Christian character in the newly forming trade guilds, acted as peace mediators between rival civil entities, founded charitable institutions, and ministered to the poor, lepers and plague victims. Many of these latter activities were likewise central to the mission of the Third Order, as noted above. One final aspect of the work of the Friars Minor among Christians was their diplomatic and evangelistic efforts to unite those considered schismatics, that is, Christians of the Greek East, to the church of the Latin West.

The mission of the Friars Minor among the Saracens took a variety of forms. Soon after Francis's encounter with the sultan, the first five friars who went to Morocco were martyred in 1220, and other Franciscan martyrs would be added to the list, including the Poor Clares mentioned earlier. Furthermore, ever since Francis's own visit to the Holy Sepulchre in 1220, the Franciscans regarded the guardianship of the Holy Land as a part of their mission. Basically this involved the pastoral care of crusaders and pilgrims, evangelistic efforts among Orthodox Christians and, on occasion, diplomatic efforts on behalf of those captured by Muslims.

An outstanding person who had a major impact on the understanding of mission among the Muslims was Ramón Lull (Llull). Stephen Neill has called him "one of the greatest missionaries in the history of the Church" and "the first to develop a theory of missions."[67] Ramón Lull was born in 1235 on Majorca, just five years after the island had been freed from Muslim political control. Having spent his early years in the frivolity of court life, around the age of thirty he had a conversion to a fully committed Christian life. Lull set aside sufficient resources for his wife and children and gave the rest to the poor. After having contacts with and never quite fitting into the Franciscans or Dominicans, he eventually joined the Third Order of Francis.

Lull's burning desire for mission to the Muslims was expressed in many ways. As a profound scholar, he studied philosophy and Arabic, often visited the University of Paris, lectured at the University of Montpellier, and wrote prolifically in the areas of mysticism, apologetics and philosophy.[68] Based on a belief that the conversion of non-Christians could be accomplished through reason and debate, one of his most famous works is a conversation about the gospel among a Christian, a Muslim and a Jew—a work in that he employed a method which is reminiscent of Francis's approach to the sultan. Lull convinced the king of Aragon to help establish a school for training missionaries in Majorca, but he was less successful in his attempts to have other such schools established by the church. Being a man of his time, he also supported the efforts of the crusades to regain the Holy Land. He himself went as a missionary to North Africa, and on his third trip, near the age of eighty, he was martyred. In many ways Lull is one of the best representatives of the Franciscan model of mission among the Muslims.

The third major focus for mission for the Friars Minor was among the Mongols.[69] When Europe first heard of the large, rapidly growing Mongol Empire over Asia, including a large part of China, in the early part of the thirteenth century, there was hope that the Mongols might be the ones to defeat the Muslims. The Christian West responded through a series of diplomatic efforts, most notably by the Franciscan John of Plano Carpini and the Dominican William of Rubruck. In 1266, the uncles of Marco Polo would bring back a request from the Mongol leader, Kublai Khan, located in present-day Beijing, for one hundred scholars to instruct him in the Christian faith. Unfortunately, the pope would respond only some twenty years later, around 1290, by sending John of Monte Corvino and a Dominican who would die en route. Arriving in China about five years later, John of Monte Corvino met Turks who had become Christians through the East Syrian Church. John reports baptizing six thousand persons by 1305, translating the New Testament and Psalter, and celebrating the Eucharist in the

Ongut Turk language. In the following year he would begin building his second church and organizing a small school. Other Franciscans arrived in China around 1313, 1322, and 1342. The last missionaries of the Latin West from this period of mission history were expelled in 1369, when the Chinese overthrew Mongol rule. However, a much more critical moment in world history had already occurred at the end of the thirteenth century, with the first instances of Mongols choosing Islam rather than Christianity. What if the choice had gone the other way?

Beside the mission methods described above, some Franciscans around the year 1335 were also following an approach of accommodating to the Mongol nomad way of life. Garbed in Mongol dress, they traveled around with their portable altars and few possessions in wagons like those used by the pastoral nomads.

The fourth and final focus of Franciscan mission was the intellectual one.[70] While Francis himself was not a person of high learning, he did see the value and place of theological study, as long as it remained secondary to the spirit of prayer and devotion. Philosophical and theological teaching was offered in most Franciscan communities, and eventually academic centers were established near major universities, the most famous being those of Paris and Oxford. This early Franciscan intellectual tradition is characterized by love over speculation, will over understanding, and God as Good rather than Truth. Franciscan philosophy blended with Neoplatonist and Augustinian traditions.

The great early Franciscan thinkers include Anthony of Padua, Alexander of Hales and of course Bonaventure of Bagnoregio. They were followed by such outstanding people as Roger Bacon, John Duns Scotus and Ramón Lull. Alongside Lull's impact on Europe's approach to Islam, Roger Bacon described a mission model based on presenting the gospel to the Muslims in their own language, rather than using the crusaders' sword. As will be pointed out below, the Franciscans and the Dominicans developed different intellectual traditions, each from its own perspective, but they both responded to the challenge of mission within the newly developing university context.

As we have seen, the three orders of Franciscans responded in various ways within the different mission contexts—whether among Christians, Muslims, Mongols or within academia. Underlying this variety of methodologies was the Franciscan ideal of mission based on martyrdom as the closest expression of the primitive church to witness to and imitate the passion of Christ—"for the sake of the glory of God and the salvation both of the martyr and his neighbor."[71] Martyrdom could be lived through one's choice for poverty, chastity, compassion, forbearance of suffering, or ultimately the giving up of one's life. As in the early church, martyrdom therefore was related to the quality of Christian living, as witnessed in word and deed. Clare's Second Order in the Middle East, friars among the Mongols, women and men of the Third Order in Europe, and the intellectual Ramón Lull all strove to achieve the single mission goal of the Franciscans, which could be summarized as a "renewal of the evangelical life and Christian witness to faithful and non-Christian alike."[72]

Dominic of Caleruega

While the general social-political, religious and ecclesial context was similar for both Francis and Dominic, the particulars of Dominic's world shaped him and his mission in another way.[73] Around 1170, Dominic was born of a noble family in the rugged, mountainous region of Castille, which had only fairly recently been regained from Muslim rule. Several family members joined new military religious orders during Dominic's youth. He came from an area "which was still very much on the frontier of Christendom."[74]

Another element of his context that directly influenced the future direction of Dominic's mission was the presence of the Cathars, or Albigensians, in the nearby Midi area of southern France. This movement of lay preachers had found a very receptive audience among many who felt disillusioned with clergy who seemed more interested in power and wealth than in preaching the gospel. The Cathars, who had organized a counter-church movement by the beginning of the thirteenth century, were considered heretical and so demanded the urgent attention of the church. Unfortunately, the church had not had the appropriate response and personnel until Dominic appeared on the scene.

Educated as a cleric from his youth and having demonstrated his charity and concern for the poor during a time of famine, he was recruited to join the Canons Regular at Osma by its prior, Diego. In 1201, Dominic became subprior and Diego became bishop. Dominic would accompany Diego on two diplomatic trips that would have a tremendous impact on him. During the first, Dominic had his first face-to-face meeting with a Cathar in Toulouse. After an all-night discussion, Dominic was able to convince the Cathar to change his view.

During the second trip, Dominic and Diego were touched by the missionary enthusiasm in Denmark of those preparing to go to Estonia and Livonia. Instead of returning directly to Osma, they went to Rome, where Diego requested leave of his diocese to do missionary work among the Cumans in Hungary. It seems that Dominic wanted to do the same. However, since papal permission was not granted, neither went.

As they continued their journey home in 1206, they met three Cistercian papal legates in Montpellier who were on the verge of abandoning their task of preaching against the Cathars. Diego suggested a change of approach. Rather than traveling around in a fashion typical of church officials, perhaps they would be more successful with a more austere and evangelical style that imitated more closely that of the apostles. On the one hand, the papal legates were resistant to such an approach, which seemed too similar to that of many of those considered heretical preachers, and the idea of begging seemed inappropriate to people of such stature. On the other hand, the Cistercian officials were willing to consider allowing someone else to try this new approach. Diego volunteered, and immediately, without returning to Osma, Diego and Dominic began their mission of itinerant preaching. The initial roots of the Order of Friars Preachers can be traced to this moment.

Circumstances would make such work quite difficult although not impossible. Diego died in 1207, and one of the papal legates was assassinated in 1208. In response to this latter event, the pope called upon the king of France to lead a crusade to restore religious and civil order in the area of Toulouse. In the midst of such conflict and upheaval, Dominic not only continued his preaching but also founded a community of diocesan preachers in Toulouse to assist the bishop in his tasks of confronting what was considered heresy and instructing the believers in their faith. From the beginning, the efforts of the Dominicans would be centered on explaining the faith through what was called doctrinal preaching, which was generally restricted to educated clerics. This is in distinction to penitential preaching on faith, repentance and morals, which was the primary focus of the early Franciscans.

When Dominic attended the Fourth Lateran Council, in 1215, he began the process of getting official recognition for the Order of Preachers. As we saw earlier, the Lateran Council forbade the acceptance of any new religious rule. Dominic and his friars eventually accepted the rule of Augustine with the addition of certain austere elements from various congregations of reformed canons. The shape of the order over the next few years developed from an institute of a single diocese into a mendicant order with a worldwide mission.[75]

Dominican Women and Laity

Monastic convents for women were springing up rapidly as a result of religious motivation and sociological factors. Convent life, for example, provided an acceptable alternative to marriage in a society where, largely due to the crusades and other wars, women outnumbered men. Diego had established a convent in Prouille as a refuge for some of those women who had left the Cathar convents and beliefs. Around 1206-1207, Dominic and a few companions associated themselves with this house, thereby forming a double convent—a tradition that was disappearing in the thirteenth century. The women's community, which shared a common life of poverty, provided center of prayer and hospitality for the community of Dominic's preachers as well as a place for continuing the Cathar custom of educating girls. Along with this first convent in Prouille,[76] three other women's monasteries—in Rome, Madrid and Bologna— were founded directly by the Dominican friars.

However, after Dominic's death (1221), the chapter of the Order of Preachers in 1228 prohibited accepting further responsibility for or affiliation with the rapidly growing number of women's convents. In the following years the relationship between the men's and women's communities went through a difficult up-and-down process. Eventually, more women's convents became associated with the Friars Preachers. In 1259, under Humbert of Romans, the very capable fourth master of the Dominican Order, the constitutions for all the Dominican women's communities were modeled on that of the Dominican men, except for those elements related to ministry. As Suzanne Noffke writes:

The apostolic life, with all its implications for common life, was for Dominican women as for all women religious clearly limited to the evangelical counsels of poverty, chastity, and obedience lived with the discipline of the cloister. And that common life had to embrace women unmarried and widowed as well as young girls, the uneducated as well as the educated, and in some cases even the unwilling as well as the willing.[77]

Acknowledging the limitations and challenges of these early Dominican cloistered monasteries within the context of their day should not distract from, but rather highlight, the important role, witness and relationship of such contemplative communities for the wider Dominican family and for the church and mission in general. In her commentary on the 1984 revision of the *Fundamental Constitutions of the Nuns*, which made explicit what had been true from the beginning for the cloistered Dominicans, Mary of God Kain, OP, stated: "Our 'prophetic mission' is hidden, but no less real than that of our Dominican brothers and sisters."[78] As one other point, it is quite noteworthy that several of the women's monasteries of this Second Order, such as those in Bavaria and Italy,[79] developed the solid Dominican intellectual tradition in these early days within the context of the Middle Ages.

In moving away from the tradition of the cloister, there were other alternatives for women and laity emerging around and within the Dominican movement, similar to what we saw earlier with the Franciscans. First of all, the beguines influenced, associated with and were supported by the Dominican order. The mutuality of this relationship is demonstrated by the fact that just as the beguines, like Mechthild of Magdeburg, "motivated the pastoral labors of the [Dominican] friars, so the latter encouraged women to press on in quest of spiritual perfection."[80] Furthermore, many beguines came under Dominican authority during the fourth stage in their development, which we described earlier. Also, due to similar circumstances with the Franciscans, some beguines associated themselves within the Dominican Third Order.[81]

Second, some penitents very quickly associated themselves with Dominic. In 1285, the Dominicans officially promulgated a rule for an Order of Penance, which would eventually develop into the Third Order Regular. Usually they ran hospitals and hospices and cared for the poor. There were also other Dominican confraternities, which were concerned with strengthening their own faith, doing social work and/or advancing the mission of deepening and correcting the faith of others.[82] "In many different ways, then, we can see how the impetus of St. Dominic's missionary vision attracted men and women to put themselves under his leadership and patronage."[83]

Catherine of Siena

The most famous member of the Dominican Third Order is Catherine of Siena.[84] In 1347, Catherine was born into a world that was being devastated by the bubonic plague, warring city-states, and a struggling papacy. At the age of fifteen, Catherine rejected her family's marriage plans for her and eventually joined the Mantellate—a group of Dominican-associated women (mostly widows) who wore habits, lived in their homes, served the needs of the poor and sick, and were under the direction of a prioress and ultimately the Dominican friars. Then Catherine secluded herself in the "cell" of her room for three years, a period marked by deep mystical experiences of struggle and joy. Around the age of twenty, she had a mystical experience of her betrothal to Christ. Subsequently, Catherine came out of her room, rejoined her family, and began responding to the needs of those around her—the sick, poor, prisoners and victims of the plague. Soon she began attracting followers, both women and men, including some friars and secular priests.

However, in 1374, her life moved into another phase, that is, into the wider political and ecclesiastical world. While she had previously acted as a peacemaker between feuding families in her own Siena, she now applied these efforts to the conflict between the city-states of Pisa, Lucca and Florence and to the situation of the papacy in Avignon. Besides her trips around Italy, she also traveled to Avignon in her mission of reconciliation and of returning the papacy to Rome. Gregory XI did return to Rome, but following his death, a scandalous schism in the Latin West between two rival popes dealt a painful blow to the church and to Catherine. At the explicit request of Urban VI, she eventually came to Rome, where she died in 1380 at the age of thirty-three.

Although Catherine never learned to write, a large part of her life and work spilled out into dictating letters and devotional works, for which she became one of the three women named a doctor of the Catholic Church.[85] Her writings include a collection of prayers, some four hundred letters to state and church officials and *The Dialogue*, her major work consisting of teachings drawn from her mystical conversations with Christ.

Catherine of Siena is quite inspiring for everything she represents in the areas of mysticism, charity, writing and diplomacy. The final two areas are even more striking because during her time women were restricted within the intellectual and public forums of the church and society. Furthermore, Catherine's life is a witness of the integration "of recollection and participation, of contemplation and action."[86] At a time when women were searching for a balanced form of life that would be officially recognized within the church, Catherine of Siena was a fine precursor and model of mission not only for women, but also for men. As for more immediate effects, she certainly shared a large part of the responsibility for the papal approval in 1405 of the rule of the Order of Penance of St. Dominic, the predecessor of the present-day Third Order Regular.

Dominicans and Mission

While the Franciscans were still more of a movement than an order at the time of Francis's death, the Dominicans had benefited from the organizational skills of Dominic, who died in 1221. Some of this clarity in focus would decrease over the next few decades due to the speed and diversity of developments within the order. However, Humbert of Romans, who was elected as the fourth master of the order in 1254, would prove to be a person capable of drawing the different strands together within a common vision and revised structures. He also initiated a missionary revival, supported by centers for oriental studies. However, possibly his greatest achievement was his treatise *On the Formation of Preachers*,[87] in which "the complex, yet coherent, vision that St. Dominic had followed in practice finds its fullest and most balanced theoretical exposition."[88]

Preaching is the origin and aim of the mission of the Friars Preachers, and their spirituality cannot be separated from their mission. While this latter statement was disputed in the twentieth century, there is basic agreement today that "the specific purpose of the Order is its apostolate, and that the urge to preach the gospel to those who need it most ought to be the driving force in Dominican life, and that the contemplative element in Dominican life is neither a higher goal than the apostolate nor an autonomous goal somehow juxtaposed beside the apostolate, but an integral part in the apostolate itself."[89]

In Dominic's world, the ones whom many thought needed to hear the gospel most were people like the Cathars. At a time when the priests and monks in Europe were not able to respond fully both to the yearnings of the evangelical awakening and to the needs for a better understanding of the faith, Dominic and the friars would dedicate themselves to this mission. Dominic quickly highlighted the outward movement of this mission; in 1217 at Whitsun he surprised his little band of companions with the news that he was disbanding them, sending them out in small groups and leaving only a few in the Toulouse area. Within four years they were in France, Italy, Spain, Scandinavia and Hungary.

In order for preachers to perform their task properly, Dominic recognized the essential need for disciplined study. He sent his friars to Paris and Bologna, the two major university centers in Europe at that time, where they would soon become teachers as well as students. By 1229, they held the chair of theology at the University of Paris, where the great scholars Albert the Great and Thomas Aquinas would eventually teach and write. The commitment of the Dominicans to academic excellence is an integral part of their mission of preaching and of understanding the faith. Furthermore, due to their fine theological grounding, they were often employed by the church to serve on the tribunals of the Inquisition. We also noted above that intellectual pursuit was evident as well among some Dominican women, with Catherine of Siena being the most prominent.

This academic perspective likewise is reflected in the Dominicans' approach toward non-Christians, beginning with the Jews and Muslims in Dominic's homeland of Castile and the neighboring kingdom of Aragon. By the beginning of the twelfth century, Toledo had become a point and symbol of intellectual exchange where the philosophical and scientific works of the Jews and Muslims were translated into Latin. In this way, the works of outstanding Jewish and Muslim thinkers, like Maimonides (Moses ben Maimon) and Averroës (Ibn-Rushd), who both had been associated with the famous university of Córdoba, became accessible in the West. In the thirteenth century, the Dominicans joined this intellectual discourse, following Dominic's example of rational disputation as demonstrated by his all-night conversation with the first Cathar he met.

In order to argue with and eventually convert the Muslims and Jews, the Dominicans established missionary colleges in Spain for mastering Arabic and Hebrew. The most prominent Dominicans in this effort included Raymund of Peñafort, Humbert of Romans and Raymond Martí. Peñafort had a big influence on Ramón Lull, who in turn brought this perspective and methodology to the Franciscans, as we saw above, and who also influenced the Dominicans through his participation in three of their general chapters. Such a model of mission likewise encouraged Dominican friars in Palestine, Syria and Armenia—working mostly for reunion with Orthodox Christians—to study Arabic and other oriental languages.

Furthermore, mission work among non-Christian peoples outside Europe, which "grabbed" Dominic and Diego during their second trip to Denmark, was carried out by the Friars Preachers. Within the context of conquest and Christianization, the Dominicans worked as missionaries in Prussia, following up the conquest of the Teutonic Knights, and in present-day Ukraine among the Cumans. About ninety Dominicans died with the Cumans when they were overcome by the Mongol advance, but the Dominicans continued their mission efforts with those Cumans who fled into Hungary. Finally, the Order of Preachers was also involved in various diplomatic and evangelistic efforts among the Mongols, but to a lesser extent than the Franciscans.

To round out the picture of Dominicans and mission until 1453, we recall the prophetic witness of the Second Order of cloistered women, whose emphasis on contemplation may be seen as complementary to the emphasis on the apostolate by the other two orders of Dominicans. From their own more "secular" vantage point, the Order of Penance and confraternities added their dedicated service to that of the friars in addressing the need for deepening and correcting the Christian faith within Europe, as well as responding to certain social and medical needs. In some ways, Catherine of Siena combined many of the different aspects of Dominican mission—contemplation and mysticism, social works of charity, literary works and diplomatic efforts (reminiscent of the friars among the Mongols). In conclusion, the wide variety of activities by all Dominicans are drawn together around Dominic's original call for faithful preachers of the gospel through word and deed.

The Mendicant Model of Mission

Sharing "roots in much the same soil"[90] with the beguines, Waldensians, Humiliati and penitentials, the Dominicans and Franciscans emerged as those who were able to combine evangelical energy and appropriate theological grounding within the official church on a long-term basis. Both responded to the common call for a *vita apostolica*, but in their own ways.[91] For Franciscans, the emphasis was on *vita*—witnessing to and imitating the passion of Christ through austere poverty, with the apostolate or work of mission growing out of the whole *way of life*. For Dominicans, the emphasis was on *apostolica*—responding first of all to the ideal of the activity of mission, and then defining and justifying the way of life in reference to and as a part of the *apostolate*. Furthermore, the Franciscans emphasized lay preaching and the ideal of martyrdom, while the Dominicans emphasized scholarship and preaching by the clergy.

Together, the mendicants were in the forefront of mission—mission with many different facets. For example, in Europe they witnessed to and preached the Christian faith—with the Friars Preachers addressing more those people who were on the edges of what was considered orthodox faith and with the Friars Minor touching a wide strata of society, especially in the cities, through their many pastoral contacts. The primary approach of the former was doctrinal preaching, while that of the latter was penitential preaching. Outside of Europe, the Franciscans directed more attention toward the Mongols, Lithuania and the Holy Land, and the Dominicans toward the Cumans, Prussia and Christians of the church of the Greek East.

Both orders influenced and were influenced by the stimulating intellectual developments of their time, but again each had its particular contributions and perspectives. Recognizing the diversity among individuals at different times within each order, the basic place of theological studies within the mission and vision of the two orders can be seen in the responses of their major thinkers to the question of defining theology as either a speculative or practical discipline. Thomas Aquinas wrote: "Holy doctrine includes both speculation and practice . . . but it is more speculative than practical, for it treats more particularly of divine things than of human actions."[92] Bonaventure wrote: "Theological learning is an emotional habit, half way between speculative and practical knowledge, and its goal is both to foster contemplation and to make us good, and more particularly to make us good."[93] Each focal point runs parallel with the distinctive character highlighted earlier.

Being "children of their times," both orders were involved to some extent in crusade preaching, but on the whole they offered alternatives to the "sword approach" to Islam. Acknowledging the shared importance of preaching and similar expressions in lifestyle and ministry, the Dominicans highlighted a more rational intellectual-philosophical approach, while the Franciscans highlighted a more experiential approach of witness and example. In terms of the societal context of the Latin West, Christopher Dawson maintains that "the creation of the Mendicant Orders together with the foundation of the universities marks the culmination of the movement towards international and superpolitical unity which was the ideal of medieval Christendom."[94]

Furthermore, from the earliest days the visions of Francis and Dominic also attracted the laity to their emerging form of *vita apostolica*, visions which eventually developed into second and third orders. In the historical accounts above, we sense the struggles of women to participate in mission, on the one hand, and also the dedication and service in doing so, on the other. Visionary women like Clare of Assisi, Mary of Oignies, Elizabeth of Hungary and Catherine of Siena pointed to new possibilities. Within this context, the third orders in particular witnessed more clearly to the holistic aspect of preaching with their attention to social "secular" needs.

The Byzantine Mission

Having presented the mendicant mission model of the Latin West in great detail, we now briefly mention the parallel missionary efforts of the church of the Greek East into Russia.[95] While some members of the royal household had become Christian earlier, it was under the rule of Vladimir, around the beginning of the second millennium, that Orthodox Christianity would become established in Russia. Missionary work was primarily carried out by those often referred to as colonial monks.[96] While they were originally searching for solitude in the northern forests, the monks through their lifestyle of contemplation and manual work soon found themselves engaging with their nomadic neighbors. "Their hermitages grew into monasteries, and around the monasteries grew towns. They taught not only the gospel but also what it meant to be a citizen of the Russian state."[97] However, this movement toward Russification did not prevent the use of vernacular languages in liturgy and scriptures—characteristic of the church of the Greek East. Nuns were also founding new communities on Russian soil. An outstanding Orthodox missionary of the Late Middle Ages was the monk Stephen of Perm, who created an alphabet for the Zyrain people of the north forest, translated the liturgy and gospel into the vernacular and almost immediately selected indigenous persons for training to become clergy. The monastic model of mission continued to be the primary one in the Orthodox church at this time.

As the church of the Greek East was being reborn in Russia, it was getting very weak at home in Asia Minor through the fourteenth and fifteenth centuries. The final fall of the Byzantine Empire to the Ottoman Turks was in 1453. The Arab and later the Turkish Muslim powers usually confined the Christians into a ghetto-type existence in the Middle East, but the Mongol rulers of Russia, even after becoming Muslim, allowed the missionary and church activities of the Orthodox Church, which also more and more became an expression of Russian unity. The missionary efforts of the Greek East would continue through the church of Moscow, which became known as the New Constantinople and the Third Rome. Russia and Ethiopia were the only two states outside Western Europe at the end of the fifteenth century where Christian kings held political power.

THE MISSION OF THE EAST SYRIAN CHURCH

We noted in Chapter 4 that the greatest period of the missionary outreach of the East Syrian Church came to an end around the year 907. The two most powerful empires of Asia—the T'ang dynasty of China and the Arab power of Islam—were challenged and eventually replaced by Turkish and Mongol rule.

During this period, the East Syrian Church likewise suffered from this political-social upheaval, contact with the crusaders from the West, and then the new invasions of the Mongols of Genghis Khan. "For the church in Asia the five centuries after the first Christian millennium contained only intermittent periods of growth and expansion. The years 1000 to 1500 could more truthfully be named the period of Christian survival in Asia, not victory."[98]

Within this rather somber overview, it is important to note several significant events and movements of this second, albeit less "glorious," period of the East Syrian Church across Asia.[99] The most enduring Christian influence from the period of the T'ang dynasty was carried on through the Uighurs, a Mongolian people who had received the Christian faith as well as the script for their language from the earlier East Syrian missionaries. Around the year 1000, some unknown lay missionaries — East Syrian merchants — were instrumental in initiating the Christian conversion of the Keraits, a Turkish-Mongolian tribe who had the Uighurs as their neighbors to their south and west. While the Christian faith was embraced by other hunting tribes at this time, the Keraits are most significant for both church and world history because of their influence upon a small Mongol sub-clan and its eventual leader, Genghis Khan (ca. 1162-1227), who would rise to establish the Mongol Empire.

In a few years, Genghis's successors had established a *Pax Mongolica*, which, like the earlier *Pax Romana,* was actually often quite violent. This *Pax Mongolica* "for the first and only time in history . . . gave Asia a continental unity, a short-lived but immensely powerful trans-Eurasian empire that stretched Mongol authority from the shores of the Pacific to the gates of Constantinople and from the Korean border to Moscow and the edge of Poland."[100] During this period of political unity and stability and varying degrees of tolerance for and interest in Christianity, a number of Franciscan and Dominican missionary envoys from the Latin West would travel across Asia with both religious and political hopes of converting the Mongols to the Christian faith and finding a strong ally against the Muslims.[101]

The window of opportunity for Christianity in Asia was most notably under Hulegu (in Persia) and Kublai (in China), two powerful Mongol conquerors, brothers who had a Christian (East Syrian) princess as their mother. As Hulegu led the expansion of the Mongol Empire westward, several famous commanders and troops from Christian tribes of central Asia and southern Russia aided him in the victories against the Muslim rulers in Persia and Syria. The Mongols would eventually be driven out of Syria by the Mamelukes, a Turkish Muslim dynasty out of Egypt, but Persia would remain in the Mongol Empire. Hulegu treated the Persian patriarch and Christian community in Baghdad quite favorably, and there were even reports that Hulegu might be baptized. However, it seems that his attitude to the East Syrian Church was due partially to the influence of his Christian wife but more to his political needs for Christian allies against growing Muslim powers around him. During this seventy-year period of non-Muslim rule, an attempt would be made to reestablish the network of missionary bishoprics across Asia to the Pacific and into India and China.

In the eastern part of the empire, with Kublai Khan's tolerance for all religions, some East Syrians—as they had done during the T'ang dynasty—served in "secular" functions as advisors, physicians and astronomers in the court; monasteries and churches were established in China in a number of cities under Mongol influence and where Persian traders had founded communities; and an East Syrian physician was named president of the newly created department of the Mongol-Chinese government to deal with issues related to the increasing numbers of Christians. Two East Syrian monks, Rabban Sauma and Mark, who had met in Beijing, were sent as the khan's envoys to the courts of Persia and Europe.[102] Perhaps as the clearest sign of the vitality and importance of Christianity in China, the latter—Mark, a monk of Uighur descent, born and raised in the Shaansi province—was enthroned in 1281 as the patriarch of Baghdad to rule over the entire East Syrian Church.[103] As a further sign marking the potentiality of the moment for Christianity in Asia, Kublai even sent a letter with the famous merchants of the Polo family, the first known Europeans to reach China, back to the pope, requesting a hundred missionaries. Unfortunately, the missionaries from the Latin West arrived after Kublai's death.

Two events from opposite ends of the Mongol Empire marked the turning point in the history of Christianity in Asia: Kublai Khan, the protector of Christians in China and beyond, died in 1294; and Genghis's great-great-great-grandson, the ilkhan (emperor) Ghazan, become Muslim the following year at the other end of the empire, in Persia. After the crusaders' devastating defeat at Acre (present-day northwest Israel) several years earlier in 1291, "Mongol enthusiasm for an alliance with the Christian world against the world of Islam had begun to wane."[104] Some began to wonder whether the Allah of Islam was stronger than the God of Christianity. A new wave of violence against Christians began. The ultimate decline of the Asian church would be finalized with, first, the fall of the Mongol-Chinese Empire in 1368 and with it the second period of Christianity in China, and second, the rise of Timur Lenk, better known in the West as Tamerlane (1336-1405), who would lead the second wave of Mongol conquest, one that would be forcefully Muslim and strongly anti-Christian in character.

In a separate and earlier development, Islam had begun taking root in southeastern Asia through Arabic traders in eastern Java by the end of the eleventh century. Over the next four hundred years, this Muslim international network of trade would also include parts of India, Sumatra, the Malay Peninsula and Borneo. Brunei, the independent sultanate on Borneo, extended Islamic influence to what would be called the Philippine Archipelago, from the Sulu Islands and the island of Mindanao to as far north as present-day Manila. Over this same period, East Syrian monks from Persia and Armenia often accompanied merchants through south and southeast Asia, and evidence indicates the presence of Christian communities in Ceylon (Sri Lanka), Burma, Siam (Thailand), Java and quite possibly also in Annam (Vietnam), the Malay Peninsula and Sumatra.[105]

Although there had been a number of hopeful opportunities, East Syrian Christianity disappeared due to a number of factors[106] by the end of the fifteenth

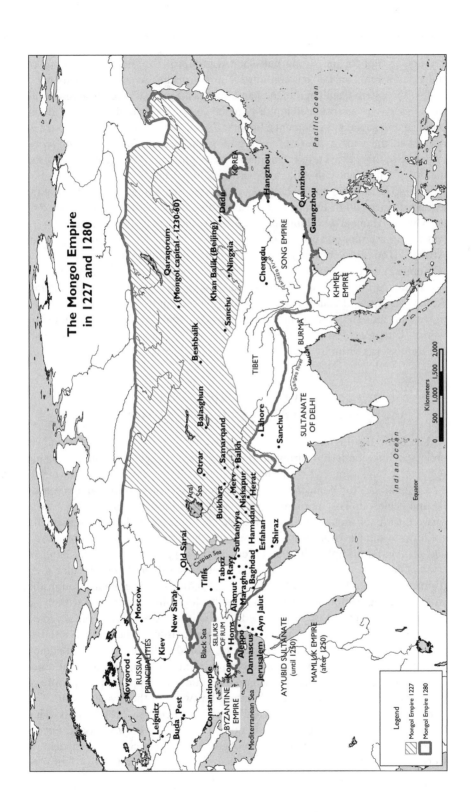

The Mongol Empire
in 1227 and 1280

Pacific Ocean

KOREA
Hangzhou
Quanzhou
Guangzhou

Qaraqorum
(Mongol capital · 1230-60)

Dadu

Khan Baliq (Beijing)

Ningxia
Sanchu

Chengdu

SONG EMPIRE

Beshbaliq

KHMER
EMPIRE

BURMA

TIBET

Balasghun

Ganges River

Samarqand

Otrar

Lahore

Sanchu

SULTANATE
OF DELHI

Aral
Sea

Bukhara

Merv
Balkh

Old Sarai

Sultaniyya
Nishapur
Herat

Hamadan

Esfahan

Shiraz

Caspian Sea

Tiflis

Tabriz
Rayy
Alamut
Maragha
Baghdad

Indian Ocean

New Sarai

Moscow

Kiev

RUSSIAN
PRINCIPALITIES

Novgorod

Leignitz

Buda
Pest

SELJUKS
OF RUM

Konya
Aleppo
Damascus
Jerusalem

Homs

Ayn Jalut

AYYUBID SULTANATE
(until 1250)

MAMLUK EMPIRE
(after 1250)

Constantinople

BYZANTINE
EMPIRE

Black Sea

Mediterranean Sea

Equator

Kilometers

0   500   1,000   1,500   2,000

Legend

Mongol Empire 1227
Mongol Empire 1280

century, except for the strong but isolated group of St. Thomas Christians of India and a remnant Persian community in Kurdistan, Azerbaijan, Armenia[107] and northwestern Iran. On the one hand, the East Syrian Church throughout its long history was an insulated minority in the complex world of Asia's religious, political and social developments, but at the same time, it still was able to reach out across the wide expanse of Asia with missionaries. The year 1498, when Portuguese ships arrived in India, marks the beginning of the next phase of the history of Christianity in Asia, to be covered in our next chapter.

By 1453, the year in which the great Byzantine Empire fell, Christianity extended across all of Europe and most of Russia. As a result of the advance of the Muslim Mamelukes, Nubia had become Muslim, the Coptic Church in Egypt was facing a prolonged crisis, and Ethiopia was the lone Christian kingdom in Africa.[108] The church of India continued its ancient tradition in the current states of Kerala and Tamil Nadu.[109] In other areas of Asia and the Middle East, there survived small diaspora communities, such as those of East Syrian Christians. At the end of the fifteenth century, for the first time in its history "the Christian movement thus found itself in a rather lopsided situation. The majority of the world's Christians resided in the European West. The dominant culture of western Europe was virtually synonymous with Latin Christianity."[110]

CONSTANTS IN THE CONTEXT
OF THE LATER MEDIEVAL PERIOD

The basic theological framework of the church of the Latin West and its understanding of mission during this period marks its beginning with Augustine (Chapter 4) and climaxed with Thomas Aquinas in the thirteenth century. *Salvation* continues to be understood fundamentally as otherworldly, individualistic and ecclesial. The missionary had the responsibility of bringing a person forward for baptism as quickly as possible, and then he or she would gradually conform to the Christian way of living with the help of the instructions, laws and penitential discipline of the church. Since it was understood that baptism left an "indelible mark" on the soul, baptized persons could not renounce their baptism and therefore could be "forced" to return to the church through the work of the Inquisition. However, this was theologically not the same with those who were not baptized. Aquinas stated: "Unbelievers who have never accepted the faith, Jews and pagans, should under no circumstances be coerced into becoming believers; but heretics and apostates should be forced to fulfil what they have promised."[111] There were some exceptions in practice, such as some forcible actions taken toward the Jewish communities in Europe and the people of Finland being baptized under the threat of the sword of the Swedish king. The crusades were not seen as "just wars" intended to convert the Muslims. This theological perspective both shaped and was shaped by the model and understanding of mission of the Late Middle Ages. The Dominicans and Franciscans were very committed to persuading the "heretics" and "apostates" to "return" to

MISSION AND THE MENDICANT MOVEMENT (1000-1453)

Context	Western Europe	Byzantine Empire and Russia	Mongolian Empire
Stream of Christianity	Latin West	Greek East	East Syrian
Primary model	Men and women mendicants	Monks and nuns	East Syriac monks
Key figures in mission	Francis, Clare, Elizabeth of Hungary, Dominic, Catherine of Siena, Ramón Lull, beguines, beghards	Stephen of Perm	Monks; merchants, physicians, astronomers and diplomats
Theological typology	A/C (emphasis on law/history)	B (emphasis on truth)	C (emphasis on history)
Primary theologians	Albert the Great, Thomas Aquinas, Bonaventure, Duns Scotus, William of Ockham		

CONSTANTS

Christology	High: Dominican Low: Franciscan ("Christ of the Poor")	High	Low
Ecclesiology	Institutional model; "Treasury of Merits"; Servant: Franciscans	Mystical communion, sacrament	Herald, servant
Eschatology	Futurist; individual; historical/cosmic (imminent): Franciscans	Realized; individual	Inaugurated; historical
Salvation	Spiritual; only through church	Spiritual	Holistic
Anthropology	Positive	Positive	Positive
Culture	Moderate counter-cultural model: Franciscans; translation model: Dominicans	Positive; anthropological model	Positive/negative; moderate counter-cultural model

the church through their preaching, study and involvement with the Inquisition. They generally followed a much gentler approach with the Muslims, Turks and Mongols.

All of these mission approaches were based on an *ecclesiology* in the Latin West emphasizing that the Catholic Church was the only means to salvation. Furthermore, "if salvation is seen as a process through which we cancel our debt with God, . . . merits become particularly important," and the church was seen as having "a treasury of merits, gained by the saints and by Jesus."[112] With this perspective, the church granted indulgences to the crusaders warring with Muslims and heretics. Much of the spirituality and religiosity of the medieval evangelical awakening, such as the penitential movement, reflected this understanding of salvation.

However, this understanding of church did not go unchallenged. Francis's response to the command "Repair my church!" was to remind the church of the radical simplicity of the gospel. Francis, the beguines (and beghards), and men and women who followed Francis ushered in a glimpse of the church characterized as more servant than institution, more communal than hierarchical, more humble than arrogant. Francis also lived and preached a different *Christology*—Christ of the poor and in the poor, Christ in a leper and speaking to Francis from the crucifix in the dilapidated chapel of San Damiano. This strong incarnational spirituality spilled over into a profound reverence for and wonder of God's love in all creation, which in turn affected his understanding of *human nature.* "Altogether his life and his relationship with the world—including animals, the elements, the poor and sick, as well as princes and prelates, women as well as men, represented the breakthrough of a new model of human and cosmic community."[113] Francis's followers struggled, not always successfully, to live out his vision.

Joachim of Fiore was the most influential figure in the area of general *eschatology* (the final destination of all creation). After his death, his apocalyptic teachings on the coming of the third age attracted many followers, particularly among several more radical Franciscan groups, and the attention of the Inquisition as well. "His method of relating scripture to historical periods and specific crises continued to inspire similar attempts by others to develop their own prophetic interpretation of scripture."[114] In terms of individual eschatology, however, the otherworldly, individualistic understanding focused on the destiny of human beings after death. Masses for the dead and indulgences were ways that the church mediated the shortening of "temporal punishment" of souls in purgatory.

Underlying the mission approach of the Dominican movement was an *anthropology* that stressed the important connection between reason and faith and a positive assessment of *human culture* that highly valued science and philosophy in their intellectual exchanges with Muslims and Jews. Even though he joined the Franciscans and was closer to their model in other ways, Ramón Lull's emphasis on the study of languages of the Muslim world and the potentiality for mission of intellectual exchange in the areas of philosophy, theology and faith situates him more closely with the Dominican model.

A characteristic of the evangelical awakening held in common by both mendicant movements, but expressed differently, was the call for a revival of the text and spirit of the gospel—the *vita apostolica*. The Bible became a sort of textbook for them,[115] leading theology through its own revival. They responded to the challenge of explicitly linking studying, preaching and living out the word of God. While both mendicant orders would establish a balance among these three elements, in the earliest stages the strength of the Dominicans was their direct study of scripture and that of the Franciscans was Francis's clear identification in word and action with the literal spirit of the gospel. "The theology of the word of God could be accomplished only in the transmission of its message. Exegesis, dogmatics, and preaching could not be separated for one who would master the gospels, because they could be fully comprehended only by participation in the immediate action of the word."[116] Theological study and the apostolate defined each other, and both maintained the primacy of the word of God.[117] Within this context, the Franciscans and Dominicans would develop their own rich theological Schools, which also reflected the specific character and mission of each.

For centuries, the theology of the West had developed the thought of Augustine and Plato. The most important contribution of the Dominican School[118] was the constructive way in which Albert the Great (d. 1280) and, to a greater extent, Thomas Aquinas (1225-1274) were able to respond to the challenge of Aristotelianism, a newly rediscovered philosophy that was coming to the West primarily through the translations of the works of several Arabic and Jewish philosophers mentioned earlier.[119] Albert and Thomas were able to produce a theology that was faithful to the authority of scripture and the tradition of the church but framed within the philosophy of Aristotle. This theological perspective both supports and illustrates the strong emphasis placed on the role of philosophical reason and study within the Dominican model of mission as preaching, study and the care of souls.

In contrast to this new theological approach, other theologians maintained the traditional Neoplatonic philosophical framework, while often incorporating some Aristotelian elements. Bonaventure (1221-1274), the main exponent of this attitude, is considered the true founder of the Franciscan School that would be developed later by fellow Franciscans Duns Scotus (c. 1265-1308) and William of Ockham (c. 1280-1349). Drawing its inspiration primarily from Augustinianism and the spirit of Francis, Franciscan theology, for example, "thinks primarily in existential and personal terms as well as in terms of Scripture and redemptive history."[120] Again, such a theological perspective reflects the Franciscan emphasis on the *vita* aspect of *vita apostolica*.

In terms of the typology of Justo González, even with the introduction of the philosophy of Aristotle, the various theological schools of the second half of the Middle Ages in the West all basically developed within Type A theology, with its more legalistic perspective. Francis of Assisi—with his theology of the humanness of his Christ, the primacy of the Trinity and the sacramentality of creation—represented a glimpse of Type C theology, but very quickly this would basically be incorporated into the prevalent theology. While most of our attention in this section has been on the Latin West, it seems that the churches of the Greek East and the East Syrians basically continued to represent developments within Type B (emphasis on truth) and Type C (emphasis on history) theologies, respectively.

IMPLICATIONS FOR THE THEOLOGY OF MISSION TODAY

As a follow-up to the previous section, it seems appropriate to begin our theological reflection by commending the mendicant orders, particularly the Dominicans, for reminding us of the important link between theological study and the apostolate, between *theological reflection* and *missionary practice*. With the centers of learning shifting from the monasteries to the universities, the Franciscans and Dominicans took up their rightful places in the new setting, while continuing to emphasize the importance of study in their other apostolates as well. While most of the academic theological developments were accomplished by members of the First Order, one must not forget the work of such persons as Catherine of Siena and Ramón Lull.

With the primary monastic model of mission in the early part of the Middle Ages, the monasteries in the Latin West, Greek East, Ethiopia and Egypt became the center out of which monks and nuns would carry out their mission. In contrast, with the mendicant movement of the West, we see a model of mission that placed less emphasis on a "monastery" and more focus on going out to people and explicitly preaching the word of God. Perhaps one could characterize the primary emphasis of the monastic model as "See and believe!" and the mendicant model as "Hear and Believe!"

At the same time, such a statement should not detract from the important reminder and challenge regarding the *witness* and integrity of the evangelizers' lives. This was an essential point in the mission of Francis, Dominic and those who followed their founding visions and examples. This aspect of the mendicant movement was lived out in a particular way by the second orders of cloistered women. While the "mainstream" mendicant movement replaced monasticism as the primary model of mission, Clare renewed monasticism with a strong sense of mission. In the first part of the medieval period, the Irish monks saw "wandering for the sake of Christ" as the highest form of asceticism, the East Syrian missionaries were primarily religious and secular monks, and Lioba established female monastic communities as part of the Anglo-Saxon missionary outreach. However, as time passed, the monastic tradition generally lost this explicit mission dimension, and the cloistered life became much stricter, particularly for women. However, "Clare led the way to restore this sense of mission to cloistered life within the Franciscan movement"[121] and, we would add, within the church. *Contemplation and prayer* are essential components for mission today. Just as Clare enfleshed this within her context, the church,

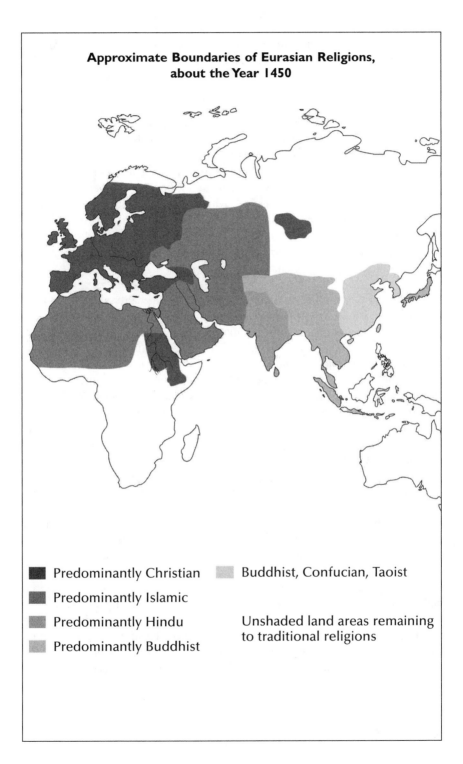

Approximate Boundaries of Eurasian Religions, about the Year 1450

Predominantly Christian

Predominantly Islamic

Predominantly Hindu

Predominantly Buddhist

Buddhist, Confucian, Taoist

Unshaded land areas remaining to traditional religions

missionaries and Christians in general are continually challenged "to keep a balance in the doing/being and contemplation/action aspects of life and work."[122]

Particularly relevant for our situation today is the spirituality and lifestyle of Francis, which Mary Motte describes this way:

> The hermeneutic suggested by Francis's life offers another way [of communicating the gospel message], a model proposed by the Incarnation. The image of God taking on the cloth of humanness seized Francis's imagination and transformed his understanding of himself in relation to God and all creation. He approached the leper and was changed when the leper embraced him. In a person consumed with one of the worst diseases of the time, and a disease that was particularly repugnant for him, Francis discovered the embrace of the suffering God. . . . This led him to the Sultan and eventually led him to learn more about prayer and communicating the Gospel message from this meeting with Islam.[123]

Living during the times of the crusades, Francis's spirituality allowed him not only to approach the sultan in a nonviolent manner—already a great step—but even to be open enough to learn from him. Today we refer to such an approach and attitude as "mission in reverse."[124] Furthermore, what does this mean for mission in terms of *interreligious dialogue* and *reconciliation*, particularly within the current "crusading" environment of the West regarding Islam?[125] Finally, the above quotation also points to an obvious connection between Francis's spirituality and the rediscovered importance of the *integrity of creation* and *ecology* for mission today.

The evangelical awakening in the medieval West represented various creative expressions linking baptism, church and mission. In speaking about the beguines as one example, Saskia Murk-Jansen writes: "The development of the Beguine movement was part of the desire to 'democratize' religion. The desire to bring God to the people, into the market place, flowed from the dawning realization that Christianity was properly a way of life accessible to all, not just a series of rites performed by an inner circle of initiates."[126] The Catholic Church in the Second Vatican Council rediscovered this vision, and although the consequences of this shift are still unfolding, the renewed vocation of all baptized Christians is having a tremendous ripple effect throughout the entire church and, it is to be hoped, society at large. Furthermore, the contemporary search for lay spirituality and the concern of the church and mission to be in dialogue with the modern world can learn from this medieval model of community-in-mission, in that "the spirituality that grew out of the Beguine movement was one that required the business of everyday life in order to be practiced."[127]

6

Mission in the Age of Discovery (1492-1773)

Conquistadors, Prophets and Gurus

The second half of the fifteenth century marked the end of medieval society and church. The evangelical and missionary renewal of the Late Middle Ages lost its energy even earlier. The church of the Latin West was generally preoccupied with and weakened by its own internal problems and tensions, which in great part would lead to the Protestant and Catholic Reformations in the sixteenth century. Politically, Europe was concerned with reestablishing and securing its borders against Muslim domains.

However, this feeling of being hemmed in by Islam, the Sahara and the Atlantic Ocean was shattered by European "discoveries" of other peoples and lands around the world, most notably by Christopher Columbus in 1492. A new missionary movement, particularly in the Catholic Church, would accompany the political-economic expansion and invasion from the West.[1] Such a "partnership" between the church and state will be just one of several major factors that will contribute to the emergence of different models of mission, which will often be in open conflict with one another. Within the context of the Americas, the prophetic, early *convento* and Jesuit "reductions" models will oppose that of the conquistador, imperial mission, while in Asia the accommodational "guru," "scholar" and "dialogue partner" approaches will be in tension with the *tabula rasa* approach. The main attention of this chapter is on these primary models of mission in the Americas and Asia, since they are representative of the major missionary efforts of this period by the Roman Catholic Church under the auspices of Spain and Portugal. We also examine the important missionary activity within early Protestantism. The Russian Orthodox Church was reaching out to Siberia, China and the Middle Volga,[2] and the Catholic Church initiated some missionary efforts along the coast of Africa.[3] These efforts, however, were of limited scope.

171

The event marking the end of the expansive missionary movement during this Age of Discovery for the Catholic Church was the suppression of the Jesuit order in 1773. Europe once again found itself exhausted by interreligious conflict and distracted by the forces of the Enlightenment and the development of the natural sciences.

THE MISSION OF THE CHURCHES OF THE WEST

The Social-Political Context

Around the end of the fifteenth century, feudal governance was being replaced with rising absolute monarchies, spurred on by Machiavelli's "principle of state," which either ignored religion or made it a tool of the state. The power of the throne was overtaking that of the church. Also, important scientific discoveries made it possible, for example, to improve compasses—most likely originally invented in China and Europe independently—and therefore to travel further across the unknown seas. In 1492, Christopher Columbus crossed the Atlantic, and seven years later Vasco da Gama rounded the Cape of Good Hope and reached the west coast of India. The opening up of these new trade routes was important, furthermore, for the commercial revolution in Europe, which was replacing the disintegrating feudal and agricultural systems. These geographical discoveries would be followed by many expeditions of soldiers, colonists and missionaries, especially from Spain and Portugal, but also from England, France, Holland and Scandinavia, to conquer these "new worlds." In addition to all these developments, Copernicus and Galileo were making discoveries in the wider universe and challenging humanity to reconsider its perception of the earth and now see it as a part of a solar system with other planets revolving around the sun. In many different ways, Europe had a new vision of the world, which included both new possibilities and, unfortunately, new conquests.

One horrific aspect of these conquests, which also affected the development of Christianity on both sides of the Atlantic, was the slave trade.[4] Slavery was not new for the Christians of the Iberian Peninsula or the Muslims of northern Africa. However, the increased demand for slaves by the Muslim Ottomans for military and agricultural purposes and by Spain and Portugal for work on sugar cane plantations led the Europeans to look beyond their ordinary sources around the Mediterranean and North African worlds. In the middle of the fifteenth century, a new type of slave trade began as sub-Saharan African people were enslaved by Spaniards and then the Portuguese to work in their newly founded colonies. This African slave trade, which was under Portuguese control after 1493, soon was supplying workers to replace the diminishing number of indigenous peoples of the Caribbean and the Americas. Acknowledging the difficulty of obtaining accurate estimates, it seems that over a four-hundred-year period ten to twelve million Africans were transported to the "New World," another one or two million died in the "middle passage" across the Atlantic, and possibly twelve million more died during the march from inland Africa before even reaching the holding areas on the coast. Such violent and inhumane treatment, which continued after they were "safely" unloaded, was worse than that used earlier against light-skinned slaves. The magnitude of this enslavement and forced movement of peoples makes it one of the worst tragedies in human history.

The Religious Context

The period's new euphoria also touched the religious imagination with the inspiring possibility that all these "new" people would soon become Christian. Just as the Muslims were finally expelled from Europe after seven hundred years in the Iberian Peninsula and Sicily, there were now many "waiting" to embrace the Christian faith in the New World. It was a moment of missionary enthusiasm and optimism.

A parallel religious renewal in Europe was evident in the Protestant and Catholic Reformations. Without denying other political, economic and social factors, certainly Protestantism represented a human spirit that strove for a more radical gospel life. The initial revival of Luther, Zwingli, Calvin and the Anabaptists in the sixteenth century would be followed in the seventeenth century by the emergence of the Puritans, the Quakers and the beginning of Pietism. While it was certainly fueled by anti-Protestant polemic, and so could be called a Counter-Reformation, nevertheless Catholic efforts to reform the church in this context of a general religious renewal might well be called a reformation in its own right (hence the term *Catholic Reformation*). Even before the great reforming Council of Trent (1545-1563), heroic figures like Cajetan and Contarini attempted conciliation with the German reformers, only to be attacked by both sides. Trent itself was a council of sweeping reform at every level of the church, even though it was often motivated by polemics and defensiveness and "missed some remarkable opportunities."[5] In addition, this Catholic Reformation included the renewal of older religious orders and the foundation of new ones—such as Ignatius Loyola and the Jesuits, Angela Merici and the Ursulines, Vincent de Paul and the Vincentians, and Louise de Marillac and the Daughters of Charity. "Both the Protestant and the Roman Catholic wing of the revival strove to lift the level of the masses of Christians more nearly to New Testament standards. In this they resembled the Irish missions to the Continent in the early Middle Ages, with their penitentials as a means of moral discipline for the members of the Church, and the Franciscan and Dominican movements of the thirteenth century."[6]

It was during this period that the term *mission* began to be used in its current sense. Until this time, *mission* was understood in the theological sense of the Father sending the Son and the Father and Son sending the Spirit. The newly founded Jesuits began using *mission* in a generic sense of carrying out whatever task the pope requested. Soon the meaning of *mission* specified the idea of being sent, but not necessary beyond one's local area; mission was directed toward non-Christians and non-Catholic and Catholic Christians, as well. For example, Vincent de Paul and later the Vincentians used this idea to describe their mission to reevangelize Catholics.

The Institutional Context

While the religious movements were stirring and challenging the hearts of Christians in Europe, the institutional church was trying to regain its equilibrium after the fourteenth-century scandal of rival popes, only to find the papacy and other church leaders often overly preoccupied with wealth and politics during the fifteenth and into sixteenth centuries. Columbus would return with news of his discovery when the institutional church was in such a situation. With the two major navigational powers and monarchies of Spain and Portugal quarreling over the newly discovered lands, the pope would draw a line from the North Pole to the South Pole, separating the two domains. Furthermore, he created a *patronatus* (*patronato*: Spanish; *padroado*: Portuguese) system, giving the royal leaders of those two countries the rights and responsibilities for the missionary task. Under such a theocratic mentality, the official goals of the conquest were linked: to annex the conquered lands and to incorporate the baptized people into the Catholic Church. In the second half of the sixteenth century, the popes began to reclaim the church's rightful responsibility for mission, culminating with the foundation of the Sacred Congregation for the Propagation of the Faith (SCPF) in 1622. Protestants of this time were concentrating more on their own organizational structures and doctrinal formulations.

MODELS OF MISSION OF THE CATHOLIC CHURCH IN THE AMERICAS

The primary focus of this section is on the mission models that emerged within the Spanish *patronato* context, which influenced the largest number of indigenous peoples in the Americas. Furthermore, the Portuguese situation in their two vast colonies of Maranho and Brazil (together forming present-day Brazil) was very similar and tightly interwoven with the Spanish one.[7] A very similar pattern was carried out by the Spanish in the Philippines, which is the only present-day Asian country with a Christian majority.[8]

With the *reconquista* of the Iberian Peninsula from the Muslims at the final victory of Granada in 1492 (and the eventual expulsion of the remaining Moors and Jews who refused baptism), Spain turned its crusading spirit toward the *conquista* of the "pagans"—the "new" peoples who were discovered by Columbus that same year. Reunited for the first time in seven hundred years, Spain brought together the sword and the cross to meet the political and religious challenges before it; this was combined with its economic search for gold and silver. The initial conquest moved from the Caribbean area to "New Spain" (Mexico) and later the Peruvian region. In these latter two areas, the Spanish encountered the large established societies of the Aztecs and the Incas, respectively.

The varied intersecting contexts of the peoples of the Americas in 1492 were as complex as those of Europe.[9] In the Maya region of Central America, the Spaniards encountered a people who at that time did not have a centralized political power capable of resisting their invasion. But these people were descendants of the ancient Mayan culture, which was at its height in Central America from 300 to 900 C.E. and afterwards was greatly influenced by the Toltecs as well. The Incas of the Peruvian area, who had inherited more than three thousand years of ethno-history in the Andean region, were at this time united as a theocratic empire with strong economic, political and religious foundations. The multicultural population of central Mexico, which owed much to Teotihuacan and Toltec cultures, had recently been subjugated and unified within the Aztec-Nahuatl Empire, which extended as far as Guatemala.

The traumatic meeting of the peoples of Europe and the peoples of the Americas within the context of a military conquest was clearly a cultural clash on many different levels, at the basis of which are two different ways of being in and understanding the world.[10]

> The collision that occurred in the sixteenth century was not just between opposing cultures, or between races, or between different historical products; it was not between "more advanced" and "backward" cultures, or "civilized" people and "barbarians." It was, essentially, between two states of consciousness, and this is perhaps why it is so painful.[11]

A concrete, devastating consequence of this encounter was that many indigenous people died—perhaps as many as sixty million[12]—as a result of malnutrition and dietary changes, new sicknesses (to which they had no immunity), armed conflict and hard labor. Social disintegration and deculturation were likewise contributing factors.

To carry out the second and third of their tripartite goals—conquest, settlement and evangelization—the Spaniards in 1503 established the *encomienda* system, by which indigenous peoples became charges of particular Spanish settlers, who had the responsibility to take care of them and teach them the Christian faith—and the right to benefit from their labor. The *encomienda*, intended to be a form of indentured labor, at best, became a system of slavery, in fact. The underlying theological motivation was that "outside the church there is no salvation." Thus some Europeans believed that people who refused the "invitation" to Christian faith could be reduced to slavery.

Many missionaries supported and worked within this official state-church "mission." However, others would, through their voices and actions, speak out against the abuses and injustices of such a situation and become the institutional conscience of the Spanish crown. We now proceed to examine these other approaches as alternative models of mission that opposed the official one to various degrees.

The Prophetic Model of Bartolomé de Las Casas

Quite a number of missionaries raised up prophetic voices of compassion on behalf of the indigenous peoples.[13] As a representative, the focus here is on the most well known, Bartolomé de Las Casas. However, we need to begin by situating him within the context of the earliest Dominicans in the Americas.

In response to the cruelty and abuse during the first stage of the conquest in Hispaniola (present-day Haiti and the Dominican Republic), the Dominican vicar, Pedro de Córdoba, chose Antón (Antonio) de Montesinos to deliver a powerful sermon before Christmas of 1511 condemning the perpetrators of these practices and the *encomienda* system itself:

> You are all in mortal sin! You live in it and die in it! Why? Because of the cruelty and tyranny you use with these innocent people. Tell me, with what right, with what justice, do you hold these Indians in such cruel and horrible servitude? On what authority have you waged such detestable wars on these people, in their mild, peaceful lands, where you have consumed such infinitudes of them, wreaking upon them this death and unheard-of havoc? . . . Are they not human beings? Have they no rational souls? Are you not obligated to love them as you love yourselves? Do you not understand this? . . . Know for a certainty that in the state in which you are you can no more be saved than Moors or Turks who have not, nor wish to have, the faith of Jesus Christ.[14]

Despite the strong negative response from the settlers, Montesinos was unwilling to recant. He was summoned before the king to debate these issues with the Franciscan Alonso de Espinar, representing the *encomenderos*.[15] The resulting Burgos Laws of 1512 at least provided a statement on paper against the abuses of *encomiendas*, but they upheld the system itself and made it clear that the Dominicans and other missionaries were not to oppose the use of the indigenous peoples to mine gold.

Bartolomé de Las Casas had already been in Hispaniola in 1502, and later he returned as a secular priest and chaplain in the Spanish conquest in Cuba. As a result, he even became the owner of an *encomienda*. However, in 1514 he went through a major conversion, due to the cruelty he witnessed and the prophetic witness of the Dominicans (whom he later joined); he eventually became widely known as "Defender of the Indians." For the next fifty-two years, he traveled back and forth between Spain and the Americas denouncing the conquest and war itself and the evils that followed—in particular the *encomienda* system— through his writing and preaching.[16]

The theologian Juan Ginés de Sepúlveda was the most articulate of many theologians (and other Europeans) who, first of all, supported armed conquest before evangelization, and second, considered the indigenous peoples inferior and "slaves by nature" according to Aristotelian thought.[17] In response, Las Casas constantly emphasized an evangelization not by force but by peaceful proclamation, persuasion and dialogue, based on "an acknowledgment of the rights of a people to their own way of life and their own religion."[18] Las Casas felt that a major obstacle to evangelization was the counter-witness of Christians.

Las Casas's impact extended to both sides of the Atlantic. For example, he greatly influenced the thought of Pope Paul III in the papal bull of 1537, entitled *Sublimis Deus*, considered the most important papal statement on the fundamental human dignity of indigenous people.[19] Likewise, Las Casas played a very significant role in the promulgation of the New Laws (1542-1543) to combat the major abuses and dangers of the *encomienda* system. Unfortunately, Charles V very quickly bent under the pressure from the *encomenderos* and revoked the primary thrust of this legislation. While this sudden turn of events certainly discouraged Las Casas and others, the issue of the human dignity of the indigenous peoples was at least being addressed on the systemic level. In 1543, Las Casas was appointed bishop of Chiapas in Mexico, partly in an attempt to remove him from the political scene in Spain. In Mexico, however, Las Casas continued his campaign for the rights of indigenous peoples, denying sacramental absolution to any Spaniard who refused to free indigenous slaves. But opposition followed as well, leading soon to his resignation from the see.

One of the disturbing aspects of the life of Las Casas is that for a long time he supported African slavery. However, later in his life he deeply repented his "blindness" as he realized that the situation of injustice and prejudice was the same for the indigenous peoples of both the Americas and Africa, therefore making him the first of his time to do so.[20]

The voice of Las Casas was certainly the clearest and most widely known. However, it is important to note that approximately one-third of the bishops in the Americas until 1620 likewise defended the human rights and freedom of the indigenous people.[21] "In this, the voices of compassion of the Iberian conquest are unique, not only for their prophetic stance vis-à-vis the abuses that were being committed against the aboriginal population of this hemisphere, but also because at a time of increasing nationalism—indeed, at the very apex of Spanish power—they took a critical stance toward their nation and its policies of expansion."[22]

The *Convento* Model

Evangelization was likewise realized through preaching, conversion and baptism—within a pattern referred to as the *convento* model. In this case, four or five missionaries would establish a *convento* with perhaps several Spanish families and hundreds of indigenous people living together in new "Christian villages," which often eventually included a church, school, hospital and orphanage. In Mexico, this approach was initially represented by the arrival of twelve Franciscans in 1524, twelve Dominicans (including Las Casas) in 1526 and a group of Augustinians in 1533. The flow of missionaries for this process was so steady that it would eventually empty many of the men's religious houses in Spain.

In contrast to the secular clergy, who often were chaplains to the Spanish settlers and frequently landholders themselves, these early missionaries attempted to keep distance from the conquest. In this regard, the Dominicans succeeded fairly well in the area of Verapaz in Guatemala, and two Franciscans with three lay persons likewise carried out a conquest-free evangelization in part of Uruguay, where the indigenous people themselves "became active agents of evangelization."[23] However, in most cases it was quite difficult to avoid the consequences of the conquest, although the missionaries of this first phase of the *convento* model are to be admired for their attempt to do so.

Some early attempts were made to learn the local languages and some grammars and dictionaries were written. The missionaries followed a *tabula rasa* approach; that is, people could become Christian only if their cultural-religious beliefs and practices were first destroyed, sometimes but not always by force. At the same time, several bishops, like Juan de Zumárraga and Vasco de Quiroga, were considered "protectors of the Indians" and their cultures.

In the face of the military/cultural conquest and this *tabula rasa* perspective, the appearance of the Virgin of Guadalupe to Juan Diego (canonized by John Paul II in 2002) on the hill of Tepeyac in 1531 linked Spain and New Spain, Christian faith and the Nahuatl world. This phenomenon became a symbol of cultural resistance and unity—affirming the cultural, religious and human dignity of the indigenous people at a time of chaos. Since the rapid acceptance of Christianity was greatly influenced by this event, La Virgen de Guadalupe is often spoken of as the evangelizer of the Americas.[24]

In the beginning, baptism was administered *en masse* followed by some catechesis. However, around 1526 an extended pre-baptismal catechumenate-like process was employed. This change in practice also sparked discussion in Spain, especially among a number of Salamancan theologians who gave it their support. Unfortunately, the later councils of Mexico (1582) and Lima (1585) did not prescribe anything regarding a catechumenate, perhaps since the earlier Council of Trent (1545-1563) had not said anything on this issue. As a result, this movement for pre-baptismal catechesis dwindled toward the end of the sixteenth century.

In terms of women and mission, it is significant that female teachers came from Spain to teach girls.[25] Women's religious orders included the Poor Clares, Dominicans, Carmelites, Conceptionists and Capuchinesses. Some of them became involved in teaching the daughters of the Spanish and creole (mixed blood) families and in caring for orphan children. Along with these female contemplative orders, "many pious and charitably active women also assembled in religious communities without canonical recognition."[26]

The creative energy of this initial phase of evangelization began to wane after 1550 for the following reasons:

The evangelization of America began to decline with the demise of the spirit of genuine mendicant reform that the religious had brought from Spain at the beginning of the sixteenth century. The plan of Philip II's government upon reinstating the *patronato* . . . to attempt to fill the empty or half-empty coffers of the crown, also contributed to this decline. Finally, the hierarchy lost the spirit of the defense of the indigenous people and set in place an authoritarian ecclesiastical structure over against the more charismatic spirit of religious.[27]

Consequently, the modified form of the *convento* model, which continued for more than two hundred years, compromised itself more and more with the conquest. For example, in the areas that are now the southern and western parts of the United States, dedicated and well-intentioned missionaries—also plagued with the paternalism of their time—strove to present Christianity and to help the indigenous people. On the one hand, the indigenous people suffered within the political-economic exploitative environment that strongly influenced, shaped, and often profited from the mission efforts. On the other hand, "the missions protected the Indians from total extermination and prepared them to participate in a Europeanized society."[28] The current controversy around Junipero Serra, the Franciscan founder of the California missions, reflects some of the painful contradictions from today's perspective.[29]

A related criticism of this period of mission history is that due to the general prejudice that questioned the human status, dignity and ability of the indigenous Americans, the Catholic Church did not allow them to be ordained, and the king of Spain for some time extended this exclusion to mestizos as well. While there was some disagreement among the various parties involved, the ban against ordination for indigenous men was officially lifted only in 1772 at the Third Council of Lima.

The Jesuit Reductions Model

To carry on the colonization process, the Spanish crown already in 1503 ordered the indigenous peoples to be gathered into settlements or reductions[30]— to "humanize," "civilize" and eventually "evangelize" them. Rather than the reductions being under the authority of the Spanish settlers, a number of missionaries—such as Las Casas and bishops Zumárraga and Quiroga—favored an alternative type of reduction, in which the indigenous peoples would be protected from the worst aspects of the conquest. After a number of failed attempts, the Dominicans did succeed in establishing such a reduction in Guatemala in an area renamed Verapaz[31] ("land of true peace"). However, soon after this in 1570 the viceroy of Peru, Francisco de Toledo, ordered all the indigenous peoples to be gathered forcibly into settlements or reductions under the control of *encomenderos.*

A new form of these reductions was established for the Gauranís in Paraguay around 1606; a missionary would replace the *encomenderos,* and the indigenous peoples were freed from service in an *encomienda* for the first ten years spent in the reduction.[32] The Franciscans took the lead in this initiative, which was an attempt to avoid the worst abuses of the *encomienda* system. However, the

North and South America in the Late Eighteenth Century

Hudson's Bay Company

Province of Quebec

Boston
New York

San Francisco
CALIFORNIA

Saint Louis

Indian Reserve

Thirteen Colonies

Viceroyalty of New Spain

New Orleans

ZACATECAS

GULF OF MEXICO

ATLANTIC OCEAN

Havana

Guanajuato
Guadalajera
Mexico City
Acapulco
Guatemala

Cuba
Porta u Prince
Jamaica

Saint Domingue
Santo Domingo
Santo Domingo

CARIBBEAN SEA

Santa Marta
Nombre de Dios
Cartagena
Santa Fe

Caracas

Viceroyalty of New Granada

Guiana

Equator

Quito

Pará

PACIFIC OCEAN

Viceroyalty of Peru

Callao Lima
Huancavelica Cuzco

Chuquisaca
Potosi

Asuncion

Viceroyalty of Brazil

MATTO GROSSO

GOIAS

Olinda
Pernambuco
Bahia

Santos
Sao Paulo
Sao Vicente
Rio de Janeiro

Viceroyalty of Peru

Santiago

Viceroyalty of Rio de la Plata

Buenos Aires
Montevideo

San Julian

British territory

Thirteen Colonies

Indian Reserve

Portuguese territory

Spanish territory

Kilometers
0   750   1,500   2,250   3,000

reductions would reach the height of their development under the newly founded Society of Jesus. In contrast to the Franciscans, who collaborated with the colonial system while also raising a prophetic voice to protect the indigenous peoples, the Jesuits established their reductions in such a way that the Guarinís would be freed from the *encomienda* system completely. Without denying the contribution of and similarities with the Franciscans and other missionaries, we focus on these Jesuit reductions as another alternative to the dominant conquest model of mission.

As for the physical structure, the Jesuit reductions had the church, school and workshops on one side of the large central square, and a Council House on the other side. The indigenous peoples lived in rows of uniform housing with doors opening toward the square. These reductions also had the missionary's residence, storerooms, a music school, hospital, cemetery, an inn for visitors and a house set aside for widows and orphans. Drums or a bell would summon people to the regulated communal activities of the daily routine. All children received religious instruction and some elementary education, including a study of both Latin and their vernacular language, while the sons of the *caciques* (indigenous leaders) also learned to read and write in Spanish. The inhabitants of the Jesuit reductions were responsible for the agricultural work both on their individual family plots and on the property dedicated to the support of the entire community. A Jesuit was in charge of the overall life, with the assistance of a *cacique,* second in authority, and an elected council. People were subject to strict discipline, including public flogging, which took place at a large stone or tree trunk in the middle of the square.[33] Due to armed attacks and growing hostility from some of the colonists, the reductions were moved to more isolated areas and surrounded by high walls. The residents were given permission in 1644 to bear arms for their own protection. When the Jesuits were expelled in 1767 (to be followed with the suppression of their entire society in 1773), their reductions were handed over to other missionaries for a short time before they fell apart.

This particular effort by the Jesuits reflected the influence of Renaissance humanism with a more positive, sometimes utopian, attitude toward human nature and culture; it represented another attempt to combat some of the evils of the conquest. However, at the same time, the Jesuits were still guilty of paternalism, in that they did not empower or prepare the indigenous peoples for leadership and full participation in shaping their future. While the strict isolation did provide more safety, it offered less opportunity for eventually adapting to the new wider society. The Jesuit reductions prefigure later attempts in mission history to establish various forms of Christian villages.[34]

French Mission Approaches

Without going into much detail, it is important to note the particular form that missionary activity took in "New France" in North America. Beginning in 1611, the Jesuits (known as blackrobes because of their soutanes) would take the lead in the evangelization efforts which had to contend with the aggressive colonial fur-trading enterprise and the fighting between the English and Iroquois on one side, and the French, Huron and Algonquin, on the other. In contrast to the Spanish and Portuguese situation, the French missionaries were dependent upon benefactors rather than the French government. While their total number only reached fifty-one by 1748, they had managed to extend their work from Canada to Louisiana.

Rather than bringing the indigenous peoples into a mission community, the Jesuits usually went out into the Native American world. The missionaries would often begin by setting up a house in a main village and then going out to preach in other villages. Among nomadic people, like the Iroquois, the missionaries moved with them. This more accommodational approach was similar to that of their fellow-Jesuits in Asia, which we will study below. At the same time, due to the experience of the Jesuits in Paraguay, four small reduction-type communities were established—one of which was begun by an indigenous woman, Catherine Ganneaktena, and one was home to (Blessed) Kateri Tekakwitha, an Iroquois woman well known for her Christian faith.

French lay men *(donnés)* contributed significantly to the missionary efforts as dedicated catechists and co-workers with the Jesuits. Marie de l'Incarnation, a member of the Ursulines, arrived in Quebec in 1639 to found the first school for girls in northern America. The Ursulines and Daughters of Charity are representative of the Catholic Reformation developments in France (and other countries) of apostolates for women in the areas of works of charity, nursing, teaching and missionary work.[35] Of course, this is very significant for continuing the story of our previous chapter regarding the shifting roles of women in mission.

The Jesuits working among the Iroquois, Huron and Algonquin endured many hardships, including martyrdom. The Jesuit Isaac Jogues arrived in New France in 1636 and began his missionary work among the Hurons. In 1642, he was captured, tortured and enslaved by a group of Mohawks of the Iroquois confederation. After escaping the following year, he went to France but soon begged for permission to return to North America. For two years he ministered among the French colonists in Montreal, before he went back to the Mohawks as a French ambassador to negotiate a peace treaty. At this time the Mohawks experienced a crop failure and epidemic, which they attributed to the box of liturgical materials Jogues had left with them after his first diplomatic visit. He was killed when he returned. Jogues is one of the eight canonized North American martyrs, among whom was one French lay man.

Evangelization in the Americas during this time period fell under the shadow of the conquest by "the cross and the sword."[36] However, one notes the complexity and plurality of mission approaches. For example, during the initial stage in the Spanish and Portuguese areas, the prophetic model of Las Casas and others and the early *convento* model were important alternatives to the conquest ideology. However, sometime in the 1550s, these two approaches began to lose their strong "counter-conquest" character. In fact, the prophetic aspect disappeared almost completely. Later, the Jesuit reductions emerged as the strongest anti-conquest model of mission. In the long run, these efforts toward peaceful evangelization were "defeated by the evangelizing programme of the crown, which was to convert the Indies into a colonial Christendom."[37] The accompanying theological debate will be discussed later in this chapter.

In reviewing these alternative missionary approaches, we see that, first of all, they were based on the belief of the human dignity of the indigenous peoples and of their necessary freedom in choosing the Christian faith. Second, these dedicated missionaries remained children of their time, as demonstrated by Las Casas's early attitude toward African slavery and the paternalism of the Jesuits in their reductions. Also, while these alternative models were generally strong in terms of peaceful evangelization, they basically followed a *tabula rasa* methodology in terms of the local cultures and certainly in terms of the local religions. In contrast, the event of the Virgin of Guadalupe stands out as an indigenous inculturated synthesis of Christian faith and the indigenous peoples' religious-cultural world view.

The small group of Jesuits in New France followed a more accommodational approach, which we will later see more strongly developed in Asia. Therefore, these missionaries stood for an anthropology that was radically different from the prominent conquest one, while their perspective on indigenous culture was more in line with the status quo. However, also on this point, these missionaries generally had more appreciation for local languages and cultures than other Europeans in the Americas.

As with any historical study, it is important to remember the complexity of any historical moment and the difficulty of recapturing and understanding its meaning. Since 1980, various attempts have been made to understand and relate mission history with more emphasis on the indigenous perspective and experience, as well as the wider political and economic context. Such a collection of ethnohistorical studies,[38] for example, points out both the variety of variables that determined the degree and type of social-religious disruption and change attributed partially to the impact of missionaries, and the active role of the indigenous peoples in assimilating and adjusting to a new world and a new religion. Therefore, there is much more to the picture than such misleading generalizations that missionaries were simply protectors of the indigenous peoples or that the indigenous peoples were mere victims. Nevertheless, missionaries and political leaders alike were embroiled in a particular theology. They had a Eurocentric world view and a very narrow anthropology, and their soteriology was still largely ecclesiocentric. Prophets like Las Casas and the Jesuit missionaries called the church beyond this, however. Missionaries in many ways were moving beyond the theology of their time.

MODELS OF MISSION OF THE CATHOLIC CHURCH IN ASIA

In contrast to the pattern of conquest and colonization in the Americas, the Portuguese extended their power in Asia first through the use of naval rather than land forces; second, by establishing unlinked coastal strongholds rather than inland control; and third, by being accompanied by only a very small number of European settlers, who remained in the coastal towns. The Europeans were surprised to find, first of all, the St. Thomas Christians in India, with a longer history of Christianity than their own. And they were surprised as well by people like the Chinese and Japanese, in particular, who were to a great extent able to withstand and determine the impact of the political, economic and religious power of these European foreigners.

While the Franciscans, Dominicans and Augustinians were very involved in missionary work in Asia (especially as part of the Spanish conquest in the Philippines), from the beginning of this period the Jesuits played a predominant role in shaping an accommodational missionary approach. Reflecting Roman Catholic Renaissance humanism, the Jesuits would often stand in opposition to the *tabula rasa* perspective of many Franciscan and Dominican missionaries and to the Portuguese conquest mentality and methods.[39] We will trace the development and practice of this accommodational model in Asia by looking at the work of a number of key individual Jesuit missionaries.

Francis Xavier

Raised in a Spanish noble family in Basque territory, educated in the University of Paris, and one of the "charter members" of the Jesuits, Francis Xavier is one of the most famous Roman Catholic missionaries.[40] Xavier left Lisbon in 1541 as a representative of both the king and the pope; his thirteen-month trip included six months on an island off the coast of Mozambique while waiting for favorable monsoons to cross the Indian Ocean. After a short time in the Portuguese settlement of Goa (western coast of India), Xavier went to work among the pearl-fishing Paravas on the southeastern shore of India in the present-day state of Tamil Nadu. The Paravas had been baptized *en masse* about six years earlier, primarily to gain Portuguese protection from local rulers and Arab raiders. It appears that Xavier was a charismatic evangelist but he was not at all the gifted linguist of his legend. His mission approach to the Paravas and their oral culture included teaching young people prayers, which had been translated and set to music, as well as the creed and the Ten Commandments. They would, in turn, teach other villagers what they learned through memorization. Xavier also wrote against the colonizers' scandalous behavior, greed and failure to protect innocent victims in India. After finding more Jesuits and catechists to continue the missionary work among the Paravas and several other neighboring low-caste peoples who requested baptism, Xavier moved on to Malacca on the southwest coast of the Malay Peninsula and parts of present-day Indonesia for two years. At this point, Xavier's missionary drive pushed him further toward Japan, which was even beyond the authority and protection of the Portuguese *padroado*.

During the first part of his missionary career, Xavier stressed the importance of translation, which is already a form of adaptation.[41] Andrew Ross points out that "Xavier's insistence on the translation of prayers and hymns into the local languages broke with the situation hitherto of having, in practice, to accept Portuguese language and culture along with the faith."[42] Recognizing this important element of a new mission approach, Xavier still basically followed the *tabula rasa* perspective—having contempt for Hinduism, Islam and traditional religions. However, this changed after his arrival in Japan in 1549, as indicated in the following excerpt from his letter to Loyola:

> Firstly the people whom we have met so far are the best who have yet been discovered, and it seems to me that we shall never find among heathen another race to equal the Japanese. . . . They are a people of very good will, very sociable and very desirous of knowledge; they are very fond of hearing about the things of God, chiefly when they understand them. . . . They like to hear things propounded according to reason; and, granted that there are sins and vices among them, when one reasons with them, pointing out that what they do is evil, they are convinced by this reasoning.[43]

At this time, Japan was politically and religiously divided. With the breakdown of the central authority, *daimyo* (local feudal-like lords) with their *samurai* armies and some individual Buddhist abbots with their armies of monks were in constant conflict and competition. These local Japanese leaders were very interested in trade with the Portuguese, especially for guns. Realizing the overriding influence of the *daimyo*, Xavier shifted his approach from the poor to these local lords. This change of style involved wearing fine silk clothes rather than ordinary cotton clothing, and presenting the local leaders with Western gifts. Favorably impressed, the *daimyo* Yoshitaka gave the Jesuits permission to preach, and he also gave them an old Buddhist temple for their central house in Yamaguchi. Xavier did engage in discussion with a number of Buddhist monks, a small number of whom were baptized and who were very helpful in bridging the religious and cultural gap between the missionaries and the Japanese people. It is also important to note that a wandering professional minstrel became the first Japanese Jesuit (as a brother) in these early years. This minstrel, who took the religious name of Lourenço, was very significant in spreading the Christian message in a Japanese form through the composition and singing of Christian songs and in debates with Buddhist monks and other educated persons.[44] After Xavier's twenty-seven months in Japan, approximately one thousand people had been baptized.

Now Xavier's missionary energy and passion would shift to China. This was in response, first of all, to an oft-asked question in Japan—Why was the Christian gospel not known in the great influential Chinese Empire? In addition, Xavier felt compelled to investigate a situation in which a number of Portuguese were being held captive in Canton. However, Xavier would die in 1552 on Sancian, a small uninhabited island off the coast of China, leaving to others who followed the beginning of the third Christian missionary moment in China.[45]

Alessandro Valignano

Only recently has the essential role of Alessandro Valignano been recognized in the Jesuit accommodational model of mission. The first challenge facing the thirty-four-year-old Valignano upon his appointment as papal visitor to the East by the Jesuit superior general, Everard Mercurian, was to break free from the *padroado* system and the conquistador mentality. The three most influential leaders of the Portuguese Province of the Jesuits had closely associated "the crown and the altar." In his first confrontation with them,[46] Valignano was successful in selecting and preparing a group of forty-one Jesuit missionaries (twenty of whom were of Jewish ancestry) according to his style of mission—what he called *il modo soave* ("the sweet or gentle way"). Furthermore, Valignano followed the directive of the superior general of the Jesuits in establishing a procurator in Portugal to deal directly with the missionaries working in Asia—an arrangement that would prevent interference from civil or ecclesial authorities in Portugal. Having completed this first phase of his responsibilities as papal visitor to the East, he left from Lisbon in 1574 with this new group of Jesuit missionaries.

Over the next twenty years, Valignano would develop a model of mission founded upon *il modo soave*. Beginning in Japan, he insisted on the importance of preparing and accepting Japanese for priesthood; translating the scripture, catechisms, and prayers into the local languages, a practice that had been initiated by Xavier; and accommodating the style of the mission and church in terms of architecture, clothing, diet and social formalities. Furthermore, some Japanese became *irmao*, new recruits into the Jesuit society. Some *irmao* would eventually be ordained; others would become the *dojuku*, a group of men who joined a community modeled on the monastic organization and lifestyle of Zen Buddhism and who committed themselves to the ministry of the word through preaching, catechesis and other services for the church. Finally, the *kambo* were the local elders of the mushrooming new Christian communities. Many of the *kambo,* along with the women and men of the confraternities established by the Jesuits, would become the backbone of the Japanese church when the missionaries and priests were killed or deported and the Japanese church would go through a long period of persecution.

While Valignano inherited some of the mistakes made in the translation of key Christian terms in the earliest years in Japan, he was able to direct a fresh start in China. Rather than making decisions too hastily regarding translation, he insisted that the Jesuit missionaries begin with an in-depth study of the language, religion, culture and politics of China. Eventually, for example, the Confucian term for God was chosen. This accommodational approach of Valignano, which shaped the mission model of the sixteenth-century Jesuits in China, was based on the Society's principle that "a Jesuit be open and responsive to the situation to which he was called."[47] In order to avoid the influence of the conquistador and *tabula rasa* mentality of mission, Valignano did not want any missionaries from the Philippines or New Spain, including Jesuits, to enter the other countries of Asia.

Matteo Ricci

To make his vision a reality in China, Valignano chose and guided a number of very capable missionaries. At the beginning, he appointed Michele Ruggieri to prepare by first learning Chinese in the Portuguese enclave of Macao at a time when foreigners were not even allowed to reside within the Chinese Empire. In contrast to the behavior and attitude of a number of European missionaries and traders who paid short visits to China before him, Ruggieri gained respect from some Chinese officials because he observed their social etiquette, in particular the *kow tow* (bowing), which many Europeans considered inappropriate to their ethnic dignity. Eventually, he was given permission to establish a house and chapel in Canton.

In 1583, Ruggieri was joined by Matteo Ricci, who would become the most prominent Jesuit missionary in China during this period. At first, they adopted the dress and lifestyle of a Buddhist monk *(bonze)*, since this seemed to be the most appropriate identification in Chinese society to reflect the religious nature of their presence. Gifted with a remarkable mind and memory, Ricci branched out further by devoting himself to learning Mandarin Chinese and studying Confucian classical literature. Due to his intense conversations and contact with Chinese scholars *(literati)* and his own writings and translation work, Ricci would shift from the *bonze* identification to living as, and over time being recognized as, a member of the *literati,* known by the Chinese name of Li Madou. Also, it so happened that he found himself in an open intellectual environment of stimulating discussions and different interpretations of Confucianism. Within this context, Ricci had the "opportunity to lay the foundation for the same sort of marriage between a philosophy, Confucianism, and the Christian faith as Thomas Aquinas had performed with Aristotelianism."[48]

Furthermore, Ricci's Western scientific knowledge of sundials, clocks, mapmaking and mathematics provided another link with the *literati* and eventually with the emperor's court. In 1598, after fifteen years in China, Ricci and his companions finally were able to go to Beijing, the capital of the empire. However, their visit was cut short due to growing anti-foreign sentiment provoked by the renewed fighting of the Japanese in Korea. Finally, in 1601, Ricci and three Jesuit companions (including two Chinese *irmao*) returned to Beijing and were given imperial permission to stay in the capital. When he died in 1610, the emperor donated a site for his burial, which was unheard of for an ordinary Chinese and even more so for a foreigner. Later, some Chinese histories referred to Ricci as the "wise man from the West."

During Ricci's lifetime, small communities of baptized Christians of both *literati* and ordinary Chinese—totaling approximately two thousand people—grew up around the various Jesuit residences. While Ricci was always open to

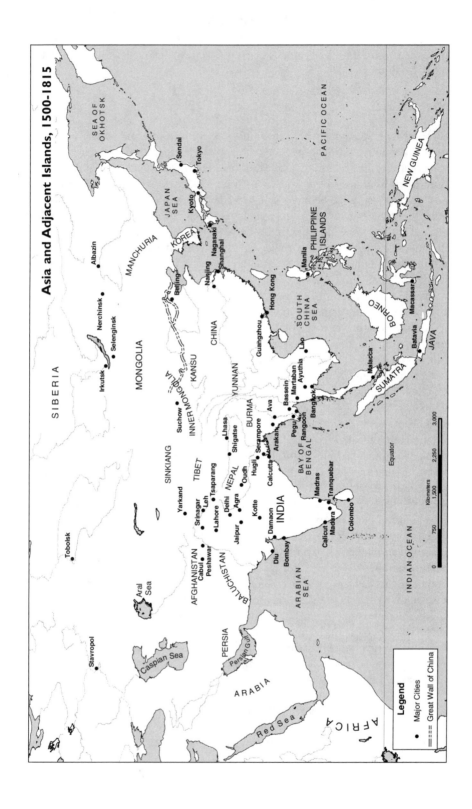

Asia and Adjacent Islands, 1500-1815

SIBERIA

SEA OF OKHOTSK

Albazin
Nerchinsk
Selenginsk
Irkutsk

MANCHURIA

MONGOLIA

JAPAN SEA

Sendai
Tokyo
Kyoto

KOREA

Beijing

Nanjing
Shanghai
Nagasaki

INNER MONGOLIA

KANSU

CHINA

Suchow

PACIFIC OCEAN

NEW GUINEA

PHILIPPINE ISLANDS

Manila

Hong Kong

Guangzhou

SOUTH CHINA SEA

BORNEO

Macassar

Batavia

JAVA

SUMATRA

Malacca

YUNNAN

Lao

Ava

Bassein
Martaban
Pegu
Rangoon
Arakan

Ayuthia

Bangkok

BURMA

Tobolsk

SINKIANG

TIBET

Yarkand

Leh
Srinagar
Tsaparang

Lhasa
Shigatse

NEPAL

Oudh
Agra
Delhi
Lahore
Peshawar
Cabul
AFGHANISTAN

Jaipur
Kotte

INDIA

Serampore
Hugli
Calcutta

BAY OF BENGAL

Madras
Tranquebar

Madura
Calicut
Colombo

Damaon
Bombay
Diu

ARABIAN SEA

BALUCHISTAN

PERSIA

Caspian Sea

Aral Sea

Stavropol

Persian Gulf

ARABIA

Red Sea

AFRICA

INDIAN OCEAN

Equator

Kilometers

0   750   1,500   2,250   3,000

Legend

• Major Cities
--- Great Wall of China

those of sincere Christian faith, his main goal was to shape the mission so that "when the Jesuits and the faith they proclaimed were no longer alien but in some sense Chinese, then a truly Chinese and Christian Church could be built which could then take up the task of the conversion of the nation."[49] In order to accomplish this, Ricci placed great importance on the intellectual, cultural and political realms—Confucianism, the *literati*, the *literati* administrators and imperial favor. One of the key issues facing Ricci was ancestral veneration. Central to Chinese society and Confucianism is the fundamental importance of obedience and respect for one's parents, that is, filial piety, which developed into a system of ancestral rites and is considered the foundation of Chinese morality and identity. After long and serious study with the *literati*, Ricci judged the rites to be cultural and social rather than religious, and therefore not idolatrous. With Valignano's agreement, Ricci decided that Christians could participate in the majority of these rites with some slight modifications. He hoped that later a more mature Chinese church would make its own decisions and adaptations in this regard. This issue of ancestral veneration will resurface later with the "Rites Controversy."

In closing, it is quite interesting to note that Valignano did not think that his policy for accommodation with the Japanese and Chinese could be applied to the peoples of Africa, India and southwest Asia.[50] The next two missionaries to be considered will promote his mission vision beyond his blind spot.

Robert de Nobili

In 1606, Italian Jesuit Robert de Nobili arrived in Madurai in the Indian state of Tamil Nadu. Gonzalvo Fernández was ministering there with people from the pearl-fishery coast, where Francis Xavier had worked some years earlier. De Nobili discovered that becoming Christian was equated with becoming a foreigner, that is, following the Portuguese way of life, eating meat and so on. Fernández considered Indian customs superstitions and therefore contrary to the gospel.

In the spirit of Valignano and Ricci, de Nobili believed that being Indian and being Christian were not incompatible, and that he needed to adapt himself to Indian society. As for the latter point, he was over time able to master the state and local languages of Tamil and Telugu, as well as Sanskrit, the language of the sacred Hindu writings. He took on the austere lifestyle of an Indian holy person *(sannyasi)*—dressing in the saffron robes, living on alms, and devoting himself to a life of meditation and prayer. He became known as a spiritual master of the "true religion" (Christianity).

De Nobili allowed Indian Christians to continue with their customs and habits of dress, for example, the tuft of hair and the sacred cotton thread,[51] which he considered cultural rather than religious. Furthermore, he accepted the ancient caste system, with its social discrimination and strict separation. The consequence of this, since he associated primarily with the Brahmins and upper castes, was that he had to cut himself off more and more from the other castes and even from fellow Europeans. However, de Nobili never lost sight of the lower castes, and he eventually formed two groups of missionaries—the *Brahmanasannyasis* for the upper castes and the *Pandaraswamis* for the lower.

By learning Sanskrit—the first European to do so—and by studying and discussing many of the sacred Hindu texts, de Nobili was able to begin to understand the depths of the Hindu world of thought. Although his dream was not realized, he proposed establishing a seminary in India and teaching Christian dogma based on certain principles of Hindu philosophy. In addition to his writings in European languages, his extensive philosophical and theological works in three Indian languages further established him as a scholar.

Although he had the approval of his Jesuit provincial, Albert Laerzio, and the archbishop of Cranganore, Francis Ros, de Nobili's approach was often attacked by others, both by some within the church and by some Brahmins. In 1623, Pope Gregory XV approved de Nobili's methods, but they would eventually be condemned under the Rites Controversy. Even though the number of Brahmin converts to Christianity was small, de Nobili succeeded in witnessing the Christian faith to them in a way that has not been duplicated. Since his time, those becoming Christian have come mainly from the lower social groups— "tribal" people, who are outside the caste system, and Dalits, so-called untouchables of the lowest caste. Today, Dalits represent 60 percent of India's sixteen million Roman Catholics, 90 percent of the membership of the Protestant Church of North India and approximately 50 percent of the Church of South India.[52]

Alexandre de Rhodes

By the end of the sixteenth century, a few sporadic missionary efforts by Franciscans and Dominicans had had little impact on Vietnam, which was considered by Europeans as part of China. The arrival of the first three Jesuits in Vietnam in 1615, in response to a request of a Portuguese ship captain, marks the real beginning of Christianity there. Soon after this, the Jesuits began sending more missionaries to other parts of the Far East, including Vietnam, as persecutions increased in Japan. One of those new missionaries, Alexandre de Rhodes, who entered Vietnam in 1624, would become the founder of Vietnamese Christianity.

Building upon his excellent linguistic skills and the work of several other Jesuits, de Rhodes developed a system for writing Vietnamese with Roman alphabetization, which is the national script today. The first books written in that alphabet were his French-Vietnamese dictionary, a Vietnamese grammar and the famous catechism, the first Vietnamese Christian theological work.[53] Beyond language, de Rhodes's personal adaptation to Vietnamese culture included dress, food, folk medicine and wearing long, braided hair.

To avoid having Christianity equated with a foreign culture, he attempted to build upon and transform elements of Vietnamese culture, as long as he did not consider them totally unacceptable to the Christian faith. For example, de Rhodes gave Christian meaning to the important celebration of lunar new year by having a crucifix attached to the central bamboo pole and dedicating the three days of new year to the Trinity. In terms of Confucianism and ancestor veneration, he had a less appreciative attitude than Ricci and his fellow Jesuits in China. Part of this is due to the fact that de Rhodes's perspective was drawn from that of the common people, not the scholars and philosophers. However, he did recognize that filial piety is such a central value in Vietnamese culture, and so he substituted alternative Christian practices. De Rhodes also adapted traditional Christian liturgy within the Vietnamese context.

Another significant aspect of his missionary method was empowering lay leaders within the young Christian communities in the areas of worship, preaching, teaching and in becoming missionaries themselves by evangelizing and baptizing non-Christians. It is also noteworthy and surprising that many women[54] also served in this capacity within their patriarchal society. With lives of deep faith, miracles, Christian witness and courage under persecution, these Vietnamese Christian lay leaders are considered "the cofounders of Vietnamese Christianity."[55] A predominant role was played by the catechists, whom de Rhodes organized into quasi-religious communities.[56] From this group of catechists would come the first Vietnamese priests and martyrs.

De Rhodes was permanently expelled from Vietnam in 1645. Due to his strong advocacy for Vietnamese clergy and bishops, a measure contrary to the *padroado* system, the local Portuguese authorities denied de Rhodes access to the sea route around the Cape of Good Hope. He therefore had to travel overland to Europe. After spending some time in Rome and Paris, he was appointed superior of the Jesuit mission in Persia, where he continued his mission work with the same spirit that he had in Vietnam. De Rhodes learned the language well enough to speak with the shah, who attended his state funeral in 1660.

Christianity grew quickly on the foundations laid by de Rhodes, his fellow Jesuits and Vietnamese Catholics. It is estimated that there were 300,000 Vietnamese Christians by 1650.

The Congregation for the Propagation of the Faith

Under the *patronatus* agreement at the end of the fifteenth century, the church had given civil authorities the rights and responsibilities for carrying out the missionary efforts. In the second half of the sixteenth century, as Spain and Portugal were losing their commitment to it, the papacy began trying to reclaim its rightful role in directing the missionary activity. It finally succeeded with the establishment in 1622 of the Sacred Congregation for the Propagation of the Faith (SCPF). As its first secretary, Francesco Ingoli gathered information about the current state of missionary activity and began addressing some of the problem areas, such as the involvement of European political and economic powers in mission, rivalries among missionaries based on national and religious order affiliation, and the lack of diocesan clergy and bishops in missionary activity. In relation to this latter point, a seminary for the Society of Foreign Missions (MEP) was eventually established in Paris in 1663 to prepare French diocesan clergy to do mission work and to promote indigenous clergy and bishops in every part of the world.

Since the church was not able to name the bishops in Asia, Africa and the Americas—this was still a legal right of the civil authorities of Spain and Portugal—the papacy appointed vicars apostolic, who could exercise episcopal duties but did not have territorial authority. While this action was necessary for the church to reclaim its rightful responsibility, conflict between the *patronatus* bishops and the Rome-appointed vicars apostolic would continue for many years in some areas. Furthermore, the efforts of the SCPF were directed not only to the peoples of the new colonial lands but to all non-Catholics, including Protestant and Orthodox Christians. For example, the Roman Catholic dioceses in Scandinavia were under the SCPF into the twentieth century.

The initial concern to prevent Christianity from being associated with foreign political powers and foreignness in general is reflected in the following instruction sent out in 1659 to the vicars apostolic:

> Do not regard it as your task, and do not bring any pressure to bear on the peoples, to change their manners, customs, and uses, unless they are evidently contrary to religion and sound morals. What could be more absurd than to transport France, Spain, Italy, or some other European country to China? Do not introduce all that to them, but only the faith, which does not despise or destroy the manners and customs of any people, always supposing that they are not evil, but rather wishes to see them preserved unharmed. . . . Do not draw invidious contrasts between the customs of the peoples and those of Europe; do your utmost to adapt yourselves to them.[57]

As seen in this letter, the SCPF began with an openness toward non-Western cultures and a spirit of adaptation. However, the situation for mission would become very complex and difficult as the Catholic Church became entangled in the Rites Controversy.

The Rites Controversy and the Decline in Missionary Activity

A variety of factors in both Asia and Europe contributed to the context of the confrontation that would become known as the Rites Controversy.[58] In terms of jurisdiction, the Portuguese were in opposition to the French, the *patronatus* system to the SCPF, and the Jesuits to the MEP. Regarding models of mission, the accommodational approach, primarily represented by the Jesuits, was in tension with the *tabula rasa* approach of many members of other missionary orders. The Jesuits thought that the others had no regard for non-Western cultures, while the others thought that the Jesuits had "sold out" and compromised Christianity. The Jesuits adhered basically to a theology of probabilism, with its positive attitude toward human nature and culture, influenced by the Renaissance and humanism. Moving to the theological debate in Europe at this time, probabilism was seriously opposed by Jansenist theology, with its more negative attitude toward human nature and culture, its concern with predestination and its strong base in France. The primary issues, which triggered the wider debate, involved missionary methods in China and India: first, the term to be used for God in China; second, the extent to which a Christian could participate in certain rituals regarding funerals and ancestor veneration in China and in the caste system in India; and third, the extent to which sacramental rituals could be adapted to cultural sensibilities.

While the first Dominican missionary who came to China from the Philippines was in favor of the approach of Ricci and Valignano, many of the Spanish mendicants who followed were not.[59] As a representative of the latter, Juan Bautista de Morales was sent to Rome to present "twelve doubts" *(dubia)* to the SCPF, which condemned Ricci's method in 1645. In response, Jesuit Martino Martini presented the other side to the Vatican's Holy Office, which then approved the Jesuit position in 1656. While most of the missionaries in China were imprisoned together in Canton in 1667-1668 due to some political and religious factors in the Chinese imperial court, the missionaries of all the orders eventually found a workable agreement regarding the Riccian model. In 1669, Pope Clement IX declared the earlier rulings of both the SCPF and the Holy Office were to be upheld as much as each was true in reality. If Morales's presentation was correct, in other words, then the ruling of the SCPF was to be observed, and the same for the case of Martini and the Holy Office. Judgment was therefore left to the missionaries in Asia, who had reached some type of common understanding in Canton. The church in China prospered over the next twenty years.

However, the issue didn't end there. Domingo de Navarette, a Dominican who had participated in the Canton decision, continued to feel very uneasy about the Jesuit approach.[60] He eventually returned to Europe, where in 1676 he published in Madrid the first of his two volumes against the Jesuits. At this point, the controversy picked up more steam due to factors and tensions in Europe itself, mentioned above, and would return in 1693 to the Asian scene with a condemnation of the Valignano-Ricci approach by Bishop Maigrot, the French MEP vicar apostolic of Fujian, China. The Chinese Kangxi emperor entered the picture when, in response to the appeal of the Jesuits, he declared in 1700 that the ancestral rituals were civil, not religious.

The new pope, Clement XI, sent Bishop Maillard de Tournon to Asia as a papal legate without notifying the Portuguese. Tournon exacerbated the tensions between the Portuguese and the French when he went by French ship to Madurai via the French colony of Pondicherry without paying any diplomatic attention to the Portuguese ecclesiastical or civil authorities in Lisbon, Goa or Macao. Tournon condemned missionary accommodation in India in 1704, the same year that the pope declared the same for China. Tournon then proceeded to China and Beijing. The emperor declared that missionaries could remain in China only if they received an imperial *biao (piao)* by assuring the Chinese officials that they would follow the approach of Ricci. Despite instructions to the contrary from de Tournon, four bishops and a number of missionaries received the *biao*. While under house arrest in Macao by Portuguese authorities, Tournon died in 1710. In 1715, Pope Clement XI published his official support of Tournon, and the emperor responded in 1717 by forbidding Christianity, expelling all missionaries and closing all the churches. Despite a process of further appeals, Tournon's position in the Indian context was likewise upheld and solidified with later papal declarations.

By looking back at the Rites Controversy, one sees that a number of factors, many of them unrelated to the Asian reality, led to the eventual condemnation of the accommodational approach and the expulsion of missionaries from China: lack of communication and understanding, political and national agendas in Europe, rivalries among missionary orders, the involvement of the Chinese emperor, and the conflict between the *patronatus* system and the SCPF. Furthermore, the Jesuit order was dissolved in 1773 due to a number of complex political, economic, theological, ecclesiastical and social factors and events. This was the final major blow to mission efforts at this time. By the end of the eighteenth century, there were probably only about three hundred Roman Catholic active missionaries in the world.

One hundred years earlier, in 1692, an edict of toleration had been granted to Christians in China by Emperor Kang Xi, who ruled over a population which was then approximately equal to that of Europe and Russia combined. (We remember that an edict of toleration by a benevolent emperor had initiated a major turnaround for Christianity in the Roman Empire.) The first Chinese Catholic bishop was consecrated in 1685, and there were 200,000 Catholics in China in 1700. That was the same year in which the emperor entered the Rites Controversy. "The Catholic missions in China can be regarded as one of the greatest might-have-beens in world history."[61]

As seen earlier in this chapter, the conquistador mentality very strongly dominated the context and pattern for mission in the Americas, although alternative missionary approaches were certainly always represented and extremely important. The expansion of European Christendom—that ideal union of state and church—naturally encompassed the political, economic, cultural and religious aspects of life. In contrast to the Americas, its impact in Asia (excluding the Philippines) was in general limited to certain European coastal strongholds. It did not include extensive conquest and settlement.

Also, the missionaries who took the lead in Asia brought a different perspective. The foundation of the Jesuits and the later establishment of the SCPF were both attempts by the church to break the identification of Christianity with a European political agenda.[62] This was evident in the Americas in the missionary efforts in the Jesuit reductions. Andrew Ross identifies three additional elements that prompted the Jesuits to move from the *tabula rasa* to the accommodational approach.[63] First of all, several of the Jesuit pioneers—notably Xavier and Valignano—considered the Japanese and Chinese civilizations similar to the ancient Greco-Roman world and therefore meriting a more mutually enriching intellectual and spiritual disposition. As was previously noted with Las Casas, we again see how very caring and open missionaries are still shaped by the prejudices of their context, but we also recall that other missionaries, like de Nobili and de Rhodes, extended this approach to other peoples of Asia as well. Second, spiritual training through Loyola's *Spiritual Exercises* developed personalities with confidence, self-reflection and self-critical awareness, which enabled the missionaries to "reflect on any situation in ways that could and did challenge conventional wisdom whether in Church or state."[64] Third, the key Jesuit figures were greatly influenced by Italian humanism rather than by the Spanish conquistador environment. Within this overall characterization, it is important not to identify or limit this missionary profile strictly to Jesuits, since not all Jesuits followed it and a number of non-Jesuit missionaries did.

In sum, the primary mission approach in Asia was accommodation, that is, *il modo soave* of Valignano. In this light, William Burrows rightfully suggests that this model, which he calls a "Catholic inculturation paradigm,"[65] should be added to those paradigms presented in David Bosch's monumental work *Transforming Mission*. This image of the missionary as guru, scholar and dialogue partner would disappear after the Rites Controversy.

MODELS OF MISSION WITHIN PROTESTANTISM

Many Catholic and Protestant writers over the years have promoted the view that the Reformers were not at all interested in and sometimes even hostile toward mission. More recently a number of scholars have contended that such an interpretation overlooks the basic direction of their theology.[66] The Reformers' primary emphasis was on what God has done in Christ, not what humans can do to "bring about" salvation, that is, the primacy of faith over good works. However, this does not imply passivity on the part of Christians. Martin Luther believed that a living faith could not remain inactive, and John Calvin went further in describing Christians' responsibility in the world. In addition, the Reformers were totally against the use of force in mission. James Scherer describes Luther as "a creative and original missionary thinker."[67]

While accepting the fact that the theological foundations for mission were there, very little missionary activity occurred during the first two hundred years of Protestantism for a number of reasons. First of all, most of the energy and focus was on mere survival and reforming the church, which involved defending themselves and developing their own identity and doctrine. Second, the countries in which the churches of the Reformation were situated were not initially in much contact with non-Christian peoples. Third, it would take time to develop their own models of mission to replace those of monasticism and religious orders, which they rejected.

Within the restrictions of these early years, the Reformers initiated some missionary outreach in Brazil in 1555 and among the Lapps in Scandinavia in 1559. Both of these efforts were done in collaboration with civil authorities, similar to the Roman Catholic situation. However, another type of mission model emerged in the Anabaptist movement, which, in contrast, insisted on absolute separation between church and state. Furthermore, Anabaptists rejected the idea of territorially defined parishes and ecclesial offices within those boundaries. They sent out traveling preachers, and at the same time insisted that the Great Commission was mandatory for all believers. The Anabaptists discounted all current expressions of Christianity—Catholic and Protestant—as apostate. Instead of reforming the church, they wanted to replace it by restoring early Christian communities. In this way, the Anabaptist local church congregation "is the fully Protestant version of the monastery, with husbands, wives, and children all committed to a Christian style of life."[68]

Within later developments of Lutheran orthodoxy, motivation for mission disappeared. However, as with the Anabaptists earlier, the Pietist movement would break through to provide an active missionary response. Sparked by the theology of Philipp Jakob Spener, the leadership of August Hermann Franke and the establishment of the new University of Halle, the first two Pietist missionaries from Halle, Bartholomew Ziegenbalg and Henry Plütschau, arrived in 1706 in Tranquebar in southeastern India. There they would develop a model of mission that became very significant for future Protestant missionary work. Another significant figure within the Pietist movement, Nikolaus von Zinzendorf, founded Moravianism,[69] whose missionaries likewise broke the link between church and state and stressed the importance of individual personal decisions in becoming Christian. Bosch describes the Moravians as "Protestantism's 'answer' to the very best there was in Catholic monasticism."[70]

As a result of the "Second Reformation" in Holland and Puritanism in England, Scotland and the American colonies, Dutch and Anglo-Saxon Calvinism was able to keep alive the missionary vision better than Lutheranism. This is also due to the fact that Holland and England both were expanding colonial powers. Gisbertus Voetius, the first Protestant to develop a comprehensive theology of mission, was one of several influential theologians within this context. Before the Pietist movement, Reformed missionaries were sent to the Dutch colonies of Indonesia, Ceylon (Sri Lanka) and Formosa (Taiwan), and John Eliot in the 1640s began his pioneer Puritan mission work of establishing "Praying Towns" with the Native Americans in Massachusetts.[71] Founded in 1649 in England to support missionary activity financially, the New England Company was the first Protestant society exclusively devoted to missionary purposes.[72] It is very interesting to note that there was a discussion about Protestant missionary efforts and a connection between English Puritanism and German Pietists through the correspondence and material support of Cotton Mather, the famous Puritan New Englander, with August Hermann Franke and missionaries of Halle in southern India.[73]

Classical Puritanism lasted until the beginning of the Great Awakening around 1735. Jonathan Edwards was its leading theologian-preacher, and David Brainerd, Edwards's friend, became one of its most well-known missionaries among the Native American people, particularly due to Edwards's publication of Brainerd's biography. John Woolman, an outstanding Quaker who advocated very strongly against slavery, refused to pay a war tax for the French and Indian War and approached Native Americans with what we today would call a "mission in reverse" attitude. The Great Awakening and the birth of Methodism, which both occur chronologically within the time frame of this chapter, will be presented in the next chapter because they are major transitional movements sparking the next Protestant missionary model/paradigm of the nineteenth-century period.

David Bosch describes the characteristics of the mission model of these first two centuries of Protestantism—as fluctuating between opposing approaches.[74] For example, while the majority of Protestants accepted the close interconnection between the church and state, notable exceptions were found among the Anabaptists, Pietists and some members of the Second Reformation and Quakers (such as John Woolman). Among the Catholic missionaries of this same period, we noted a similar dynamic, with the notable exceptions being Las Casas, Valignano, Ricci, and the Jesuit reductions.

When the Jesuits were suppressed in 1773, Christianity had spread beyond Europe, Russia, India and Ethiopia[75] to the Americas and the Philippines, to minority populations in other parts of Asia, and to a few small pockets along the coast of Africa (with the emergence of Kongolese Christianity being the most significant[76]). What seemed a promising future, however, was destroyed by intra-church bickering and a faulty understanding of the missionary purpose of the church. While Rome wrote how absurd it was to transplant France or Spain to other cultures, in effect that is what it did. The gospel was preached, of course, but its fruits remained stunted.

CONSTANTS IN THE CONTEXT OF THE AGE OF DISCOVERY

While there has certainly been a pluriformity of mission models during every period of Christianity, the contrast and tension is probably most evident and painful in the time period covered by this chapter. Naturally, this contrast and opposition is reflected in the theological tensions of the age. We will begin by looking at the situation in the Americas and using Las Casas as the primary proponent of missionary models, which were alternatives to the conquest approach.

The predominant mission theology was based on the text "Compel them to come in" (Lk 14:23) and situated within a just-war perspective, both politically and religiously. The Spanish theologian Ginés de Sepúlveda was a strong representative of this widely held position and the primary theological opponent of Las Casas on many key issues. In the face of a theology that justified the use of force and coercion, Las Casas "championed a peaceful proclamation based on persuasion and dialogue."[77] At the heart of this debate was the theological question of *salvation*.

MISSION IN THE AGE OF DISCOVERY (1492-1773)

Context	Americas	Americas
Stream of Christianity	Roman Catholic imperial	Roman Catholic prophetic
Primary model	Imperial	Prophetic
Key figures in mission	Men and women of state-church mission	Las Casas, early *convento*, reductions, De l'Incarnation, Jogues
Theological typology	A (emphasis on law)	C/A (B: reductions) (emphasis on history/law [truth])
Primary theologians	Ginés de Sepúlveda	De Vittorio, De Soto, Vega

CONSTANTS

Christology	High Christ the King	Low Christ of the Poor
Ecclesiology	Institutional model; visible society	Herald, servant, pilgrim church
Eschatology	Futurist Individual	Inaugurated (imminent) Historical
Salvation	Spiritual; only through church	Holistic; implicit faith
Anthropology	Negative	Positive
Culture	Negative; Counter-cultural model	Positive; Translation model

MISSION IN THE AGE OF DISCOVERY (1492-1773)

Context	Asia	Asia	Americas, Asia and Scandinavia
Stream of Christianity	Roman Catholic imperial	Roman Catholic accommodational	Protestant
Primary model	*Tabula rasa*	Accommodational	Evangelists
Key figures in mission	Dominicans, MEP	Valignano, Ricci, De Nobili, De Rhodes	Ziegenbalg, Plütchau, Zinzendorf, Brainerd, Woolman, Eliot
Theological typology	A (emphasis on law)	B (emphasis on truth)	A/C (emphasis on law/history)
Primary theologians	Bañez	Suárez, Molina	Luther, Voetius, Wesley

CONSTANTS

Christology	High	High	High/low
Ecclesiology	Institutional model	Mystical communion, Sacrament	Institutional model, herald
Eschatology	Futurist; individual	Realized; individual	Futurist (imminent); individual
Salvation	Spiritual; only through church	Spiritual	Spiritual
Anthropology	Negative	Positive	Negative
Culture	Negative; Counter-cultural model	Positive; Translation model	Negative; Counter-cultural model

During the Middle Ages, the axiom "outside the church there is no salvation" was understood within a world view where the church was coexistent with the known world and rejection of the church was equated with the rejection of Christ and salvation. At the beginning of the sixteenth century, this context changed drastically with the internal division of the church itself and the discovery of new peoples and new worlds. New theological questions would arise. Regarding salvation, a number of outstanding theologians from the prominent University of Salamanca attempted to break new ground within academic theology. Influenced by Spanish humanists of the Renaissance and reports about the reality of the indigenous peoples in the Americas, Dominicans Francisco de Vittoria and Domingo de Soto and Franciscan Andrés Vega introduced various nuanced understandings regarding the relationships between "implicit faith" and salvation.[78]

While Las Casas did not develop a systematic soteriology, his writings provide the framework for one. Drawing upon the image of the Day of Judgment presented in Matthew 25:31-46 and confronting the inhumane and unjust reality in the Americas, Las Casas points to the decisive importance of works on behalf of the reign of God for the salvation of *both* the baptized and the non-baptized. In other words, baptism is not a guarantee of eternal life. Second, the consequence of his respect for the human dignity of the indigenous peoples—that is, Las Casas's positive *anthropology*—was that their response to the invitation to baptism was to be left "to the free will of each one to believe or not to believe, as each one may wish."[79] Therefore, people were to be given the time and space to accept or not to accept the grace of salvation, rather than having it imposed upon them. This, of course, was in opposition to the theology underlying the conquest mind set, with an accompanying *Christology* of Christ as king and Robert Bellarmine's *ecclesiology* of the church as "visible society." In contrast, Las Casas identified the Christ of the Poor[80] with the indigenous people, and his ecclesiology was that of a church of the poor and a humble, sinful church.[81]

According to the predominant medieval understanding of salvation, adults were baptized *en masse*, by force, with little if any pre-baptismal instruction. Due to the influence of Las Casas and others, a catechetical process before and after baptism was developed over time, in particular by the Dominicans, Augustinians and Jesuits, and supported by the Salamanca theologians.[82] Besides the pressure of the conquest, the tendency of some Franciscans to perform mass baptisms, especially in the early years in the Americas, was partially linked with another understanding of church and *eschatology*, as illustrated by the approach of the Franciscan missionary Toribio de Motolinía:

> For Motolinia, influenced by the millennial expectations of Joachim de Fiore, the mass conversion of the Indians of New Spain announced the advent of the sixth age of the Church. Time was short and all speed was necessary if the great work was to be completed. Moreover, with the associated ideas of a world emperor overthrowing the forces of Satan in armed conflict, it was presumed that salvation was to be found in history before

the Last Day. By contrast, for Las Casas, with his Augustinian conviction of the predestined salvation of the elect, embodied in a pilgrim church, all hopes of universal salvation were a delusion. How could the Indians enter the kingdom or even understand the gospel if they were filled with terror or hatred?[83]

Despite these theological differences underlying the "prophetic" model of the early Dominicans and the "apostolic" model of the early Franciscans, they both strove to one degree or another to protect the indigenous peoples from the violence and abuse of a crusading mentality and a European theocratic ecclesiology.[84] The development of the *convento* and later the reductions by the Franciscans reflected their utopian motivation of reforming the *church* by returning to its primitive era, by establishing a millennial Christian kingdom (which had failed in Europe), and, to some extent, by building upon the traditional sense of community of the indigenous peoples.[85]

An offshoot of Las Casas's concern for religious freedom and human dignity was his respect for *human culture*, that is, the social and religious customs of the Native Americans. "What is at stake is an authentic norm of conduct in the proclamation of the gospel: an acknowledgment of the rights of a people, to their own way of life and their own religion."[86] In this way Las Casas and other outstanding missionaries—such as Franciscans Bishop Juan Zumárraga, Jacobo de Tastera, Bernardino de Sahagún, and the Jesuit theologian José de Acosta—challenged the presuppositions of the predominant *tabula rasa* attitude. Furthermore, many early missionaries learned the local languages and cultures very well. However, the only major manifestation of an explicit inculturation of the gospel and culture, that is, a phenomenon initiated by the Native Americans not by the missionaries, was the event of the Virgin of Guadalupe.

After the first hundred years in the Americas, the conquest pattern of missionary activity would prevail, although there would always be some attempts, such as those of the Jesuits reductions, to keep an alternative alive. As for applying the typology of Justo González to mission theology, the predominant conquest perspective held a Type A theology (emphasis on law) with its high Christology, institutional ecclesiology, negative anthropology, ecclesiocentric soteriology, futuristic and individual eschatology, and pessimistic view of indigenous culture. Las Casas and the early Dominicans represented many elements of a Type C theology (emphasis on history) with a low Christology, the image of a pilgrim church, a positive anthropology and the call for justice in today's historical reality. The method of the Jesuits in the reductions is more reflective of a Type B theology (emphasis on truth).

In moving to Asia (excluding the Philippines), a different type of mission theology was able to develop, since the goals and efforts of the missionaries were not determined to such a degree by and in response to the political, economic and religious conquest ideology, as in the Americas. Besides a very different external context, the Jesuits were also a different type of missionary, formed in a particular way by Italian humanism and an Ignatian mystical-activist spirituality. The open attitude regarding accommodation in the early years of the SCPF was also encouraging to and supportive of the Jesuits' efforts.

As the main architect of this new missionary approach, Valignano developed *il modo soave*, by which the missionaries would, first of all, enter the world of the "other" not with force, but with gentleness, and second, adapt themselves and the Christian message to the host culture. Due to their positive assessment of *culture*, Ricci, de Nobili and de Rhodes, in their own ways and contexts, attempted to identify and nurture the "seeds of the word" in particular Asian cultures, reminiscent of the earlier "mission theologies" of Origen, Justin Martyr and Cyril and Methodius—that is, examples of González's Type B theology. Francis Xavier's experience in Japan had deeply challenged his "mainstream" theology.

Following this "Catholic inculturation paradigm," to use the term of William Burrows, implied severing the link between Christian faith and European power, dialoguing between equals in studying Confucian and Hindu classics, identifying oneself within the cultural-religious world of the "other," and laying the foundations for a contextualized Christian faith and church. The Jesuits also lived out this paradigm among the Quechua and Guarani in South America and native peoples in Canada.

This positive attitude toward *human nature*, culture and the world was eventually developed by some Jesuit theologians in Europe as probabilism. Furthermore, the works of prominent Jesuit theologians like Francisco Suárez and Luis de Molina reflected and developed other aspects of this perspective. Suárez "brought philosophers from vastly different backgrounds—Greeks, Jews, Moslems, Scholastics, and Renaissance scholars—into dialogue with one another,"[87] and Molina stressed the importance of decision by free will, without coercion nor necessity, within the wider discussion of grace, predestination, and *salvation*. Many of the theologians of the Dominican School and Jansenism were in opposition to the developments of Jesuit theology.

In acknowledging the distinguishing dialogical dimension of the Jesuits' approach, it is important to note that it applied explicitly to what they considered the cultural and not the religious world view. For example, Ricci and de Nobili could appreciate and enter the world of Confucius and the caste system, because they saw them as basically cultural and societal phenomena. If considered purely religious, they would fall within the realm of idolatry. From this point of view, the Jesuits' theology of religion would be considered exclusivist by today's categories. However, even in respect to what they considered religious, their approach was less confrontational, as shown in the catechetical method of de Rhodes. "A critique of these religious traditions is, de Rhodes concedes, *necessary* since they do contain doctrinal errors and superstitious practices, but it should not be undertaken as the *preliminary* step before one teaches the truths of Christianity."[88]

Having made this qualification, it cannot be denied that they were actually bridging "religious" or, from today's understanding, "cultural-religious" worlds as they learned from and dialogued with Confucian *literati*, Hindu Brahmins and Buddhist monks. In this sense we see a glimpse of interreligious dialogue, although they did not have an explicit theology of religions to support or guide them. Furthermore, the uniqueness and importance of this ground-breaking Jesuit model of mission are that during a time when the *tabula rasa* mentality was dominant, these missionaries realized that they needed to approach these cultures from within. "Evangelization from within a culture necessitated a profound dialogue with that culture, a capacity for clear discernment, and the assumption that the missionary's goal was a new cultural creation in Christ."[89]

Just as there were opposing theological perspectives in Catholic missionary efforts, David Bosch describes a similar dynamic for Protestantism's missionary paradigm, which "tended to fluctuate between various extremes."[90] The doctrine of predestination led some, at least initially, to deny the need for mission at all, while a new understanding of this led many to see the necessity of human participation in God's mission of *salvation*. In terms of *eschatology*, some believed that God's reign would break in gradually, while most Puritans thought they were living in the last days. While most viewed *human nature* quite negatively, some emphasized Christ's love, so "people were judged to be redeemable and worthy of redemption."[91] John Woolman was a prophetic voice for the human dignity of slaves. Some viewed the *church* as an institution within a tight church-state relationship with Christ as king of both; others saw the church as a herald in opposition to such a theocratic perception and Jesus Christ as overflowing love. As for the attitude toward indigenous *culture*, Protestants in general followed the predominant *tabula rasa* approach.

Understanding this diversity from the framework of theological typologies, the theological underpinnings of Protestant missionary efforts during this time period would generally follow the primary theology of Tertullian, although there were glimpses of Irenaeus's theological tradition in early Luther and in the Pietist, Anabaptist and Quaker movements.

IMPLICATIONS FOR THE THEOLOGY OF MISSION TODAY

Studying this period of history exposes painful points of tension and polarity in mission: conquest, genocide and coercion *vs.* justice, survival and gentleness; exploitation, competition and foreignness *vs.* respect, mutuality and accommodation. There were controversies and conflicts regarding Asian rites, national interests, human rights, missionary affiliations, theological differences and economic concerns. What missiological reflections can we draw in relation to our situation today?

The response of Las Casas and other missionaries to the situation of conquest and violence points both to the necessity of opposition to such tactics and the various forms such opposition would take. Missionaries like Las Casas stood outside the system to confront the systemic evils of the conquest, the *encomienda* system and racism—raising a prophetic voice for *justice* to both the state and church. The Franciscans, through variations of the *convento* model, worked to varying degrees within the system to promote and protect the dignity, culture and lives of the indigenous peoples. The Jesuit reductions fell somewhere between the two approaches. To varying degrees, they gave witness on behalf of the human dignity and religious freedom of all people. "Here is the core of what we call today a liberating evangelization."[92]

Coming out of his alternative view of the human nature of the indigenous peoples, Las Casas the missionary and the theologian dealt with the consequential, relevant theological issues — "from the question of evangelization and ultimately from respect for the religious convictions of non-Christians to the question of the possibility of salvation beyond the visible frontiers of the church."[93] During the Second Vatican Council, the Roman Catholic Church returned to this challenging question of the relationship among religious freedom, salvation and ecclesiology in the document *Dignitatis Humanae (Declaration on Religious Liberty)*. It is probably not a coincidence that this document went through more preparatory schemata than any other Vatican II document, and it is considered by many to be the Vatican II document with the most far-reaching significance. In revising its centuries-old understanding of these central theological issues, the church drew from the wells of the tradition of the early church, much as Las Casas had done as he tried to address the reality around him. The understanding of religious freedom, human nature, salvation and ecclesiology continues to be pivotal for shaping one's model of mission.

We turn to the Jesuits in Asia, who were (although not completely) more successful than their counterparts in the Americas, first of all, in separating mission from coercion and conquest, and second, in accommodating themselves and the Christian message to the host society and culture. While speaking about Ricci in particular, Burrows situates the Jesuit effort in general within the context of *inculturation/contextualization*:

> In retrospect, one sees that Ricci had embarked on a program of reconceptualizing Christian identity for the Chinese world in ways as radical as the Hellenization that was Christianity's first major hermeneutic and inculturational milestone. It would be anachronistic to say that the Jesuits in China were consciously carrying on what we today call "inculturation," but *mutatis mutandis* that was the effect of their entire posture, and they were doing it at a depth analogous to that of early Greek and Latin Church Fathers.[94]

While the situation in Asia certainly was complex and is different from Asia today, many of the same challenging questions stand before the church and mission today, such as ancestor veneration. Without denying mistakes, limitations and differing circumstances, much can be learned from the Jesuits' model of mission in relation to both inculturation and what we know today as *interreligious dialogue*.

The final point is a lesson in humility. Even the great prophetic missionaries who challenged the prejudices and injustices of their time were restricted by those same "blinders" in other areas. Las Casas, the staunch defender of Native Americans, supported the slavery of Africans, and Valignano did not consider other non-Western peoples as "advanced" and "worthy" as the Chinese and Japanese. Las Casas did eventually acknowledge his prejudice, while Valignano didn't live long enough to see his judgment proven wrong. We are reminded that we are all children of our time and approach the constants of Christian misisonary practice within our own historical, cultural and religious contexts.

7

Mission in the Age of Progress
(1792-1914)

Civilizers, Evangelizers and Volunteer Societies

As we saw in the last chapter, the missionary movement was in a state of serious decline in the second half of the eighteenth century. For the Catholic Church, this was linked with the Rites Controversy; the suppression of the Jesuits; the political situations of China, Japan and Europe; and the decline of Spain and Portugal as world powers. However, a new missionary moment was on the horizon[1]—a moment marked with such vitality and optimism that Latourette labeled it the "Great Century."[2] Protestant Christians were the initiators and primary agents of this period of mission. The foundation of the Baptist Missionary Society (BMS) in 1792 marked the beginning, the World Mission Conference of Edinburgh of 1910 its culmination, and the beginning of World War I in 1914 its end. The contribution to this missionary revival by the Roman Catholic Church was delayed due to such factors as the disruptive impact of the French Revolution in 1789 and the Napoleonic Wars, which ended in 1815. Both Protestants and Catholics of this nineteenth-century missionary movement followed what can be generally called a *society model,* that is, missionary organizations consisting of volunteers. To round out the picture, the nineteenth-century renewal of piety and identity by the Orthodox Church included the establishment of the Orthodox Missionary Society in 1870 and missionary activity in Russia, Alaska and east Asia.

The most significant factor affecting the church and mission during this period—much more profoundly the Protestants than the Catholics—was the Enlightenment or modern era, the origins of which can be traced to the seventeenth century. As stated by David Bosch, "The entire modern missionary enterprise is, to a very real extent, a child of the Enlightenment."[3] The parameters of our treatment of this distinct missionary period in the Age of Progress are the foundation of the BMS and the beginning of World War I, which symbolized the breakdown of the Enlightenment's overly optimistic faith in human reason and technical, scientific and intellectual achievement.[4]

THE MISSION OF THE CHURCHES OF THE WEST

The Social-Political Context

In contrast to the symbiosis of ecclesial and political powers of the Middle Ages, one of the significant consequences of the Enlightenment was the eventual separation of church and state. Religion was relegated to the private sphere of opinion and belief, while secular affairs were concerned with the public arena of facts and knowledge. This separation occurred first rather mildly in England and then a century later on the continent, the most dramatic and violent event being the French Revolution (1789). Furthermore, this separation pointed to the shift from the absolute authority of the monarchy to the authority of the people to participate and shape the emerging nation-states—Louis XIV's "L'Etat, c'est moi" ("I am the state") *vs.* Abraham Lincoln's "the government of, by, and for the people."[5] Also, after the Napoleonic wars, Europe would experience a century of relative peace and stability, during which Europe could and would extend its will and influence into the rest of the world.

One of the consequences of the development of nationalism was the idea of *manifest destiny*, whereby individual nations of Europe and the United States regarded themselves as being chosen with a unique destiny in history, to the extent that, for example, leaders of Germany, Britain and France would lay out the rules of colonialization in the "scramble for Africa" during meetings in Berlin in 1884-1885. While these ideas and values were not strong among the missionaries of the eighteenth and early nineteenth centuries, manifest destiny would have a much stronger impact on the missionaries who followed them. In a parallel fashion, colonial expansion was initially seen primarily as a secular activity; however, in the second half of the nineteenth century, "colonial expansion would once again acquire religious overtones and also be intimately linked with mission!"[6] Whatever their explicit intentions, missionaries became agents of the Western imperialistic enterprise as the three "Cs" of colonialism became Christianity, commerce and civilization.

Steam engines, electricity and railroads dramatically improved transportation and communication. Simultaneously, the industrial revolution in Europe created demand for new materials from the colonies. Cities began to grow exponentially, and new social classes made their appearance in Europe. Church responses to the new type of poverty included the Protestant Social Gospel movement and Pope Leo XIII's 1891 encyclical *Rerum Novarum*. It is interesting that the majority of missionaries from Europe in the first part of the nineteenth century came from the growing middle class, the product of the industrial revolution, but in the second half of the century, university-trained persons played a bigger role in the missionary movement.[7]

As for the third "C" of colonialism—civilization—the task of advancing Western technological civilization out of the Enlightenment's pursuit of progress was being carried out by white Europeans. "Whereas in earlier centuries the essential factor that divided people was *religious*, people were now divided according to the levels of *civilization* (as interpreted by the West). This led to the next criterion of division—*ethnicity* or *race*—now interpreted as the matrix out of which civilization (or the lack of it) was born. The 'civilized,' however, not only felt superior to the 'uncivilized,' but also responsible for them."[8]

The Religious Context

The Catholic Church to a large degree, but not totally, withstood and postponed the influence of the Enlightenment until the Second Vatican Council. Protestant churches, however, were more deeply influenced by the modern era. Even in the eighteenth century the Enlightenment certainly had had a great impact on Christian faith, theology and religious life. At the same time, within Protestantism, there was a burst of religious movements in opposition to the spirit of the age. These included the Great Awakenings in the American colonies, and the birth of Methodism and the Evangelical Revival in England. "The religious and cultural background of the Protestant missionary movement includes on the one hand the Enlightenment, liberalism, and cultural optimism, and on the other hand Pietism and Neopietism, that is, the 'free' churches and the evangelical revival within the established churches."[9] In the United States, the initial enthusiasm for overseas missionary work waned after 1845, but by 1885 there was a dramatic resurgence that corresponded with the increased missionary efforts in the colonies of England, France, Germany and Belgium during the period of high imperialism.

In opposition to rationalism and the Enlightenment, the religious context of the Catholic Church at this time was marked, first of all, by a rise in new popular devotions around the Sacred Heart, the Blessed Virgin Mary and the Blessed Sacrament, and second, by the renewal of older religious orders and the founding of many new ones, including many missionary orders of men and women.

The Institutional Context

Due to its recognition of the need and potential for denominational cooperation and interdenominational efforts, mission became the primary motivation for ecumenical openness within Protestantism in the nineteenth century. "It was not cooperation for the sake of unity, but unity in order to better pursue the task of evangelism."[10] This was carried out through ecumenical cooperation among mission boards and missionaries in the field, international mission conferences, the establishment of permanent interdenominational mission organs like the Evangelical Alliance in 1846, and ecumenical youth and student mission movements. The World Missionary Conference in Edinburgh in 1910 is often considered the high point of this nineteenth-century ecumenical mission movement and the beginning of the modern ecumenical movement that culminated in the founding of the World Council of Churches (WCC) in 1948.

The persecution of the Catholic Church during the French Revolution continued under Napoleon. The SCPF was forced to move to France to serve Napoleon's imperialistic agenda, and popes Pius VI and Pius VII were harassed. However, following this humiliation, the papacy acquired a place of prestige and stability in a world of chaos and change. The Syllabus of Errors (1864) condemned the beliefs and practices associated with the liberalism of the Enlightenment and French Revolution, and the First Vatican Council (1870) affirmed the Ultramontane movement to strengthen the Vatican's authority with the doctrine of papal infallibility. Pope Gregory XVI, who had been the prefect of the SCPF, was the first of several popes to use personal initiative and vision to reinvigorate Catholic missionary activity in the nineteenth century.

MODELS OF MISSION WITHIN PROTESTANTISM

Three particular events sparked the nineteenth-century missionary renewal within Protestantism. First, the Great Awakening consisted of a series of revivals in the North American colonies between 1726 and 1760, beginning within the Dutch Reformed congregations and later spreading to others. Jonathan Edwards, the famous Calvinist theologian and preacher, was the leader of this movement, which brought together the emphasis of Protestant Orthodoxy on the scriptures and the importance of personal spiritual experience from the Pietists (mentioned in Chapter 6). Its immediate impact on mission was felt within the colonies themselves through the efforts of many itinerant preachers and such persons as David Brainerd, well-known missionary among various Native American communities and good friend of Edwards. Although no overseas missionary activity began directly as a result of this First Great Awakening, the important theological foundations were laid.

The second major force that influenced this missionary movement was the birth of Methodism. In 1735 Anglicans John Wesley and his older brother, Charles, went as missionaries of the Society for the Propagation of the Gospel to the British colony of Georgia. Although John was sent to minister to the British settlers, he also reached out to the Choctaws, Chickasaws, African Americans and Jews. Influenced by their cross-cultural mission experience[11] and inspired by their contacts with the Moravian missionaries, the brothers returned to England, where they both experienced a spiritual rebirth and became itinerant preachers. John became the founder of the movement that eventually emerged as Methodism. Recognizing the decline of Christendom and the influence of the Enlightenment, Methodism did not distinguish between domestic and foreign missions. John Wesley himself was very outspoken against the social sins of slavery, illiteracy and poverty, and he did not separate evangelism and social action. Later, however, Methodism would consider the goal of societal change a result of, not a parallel activity with, the primary goal of the salvation of souls.

Very much influenced by the Wesleys, George Whitefield was a famous Calvinist Evangelical preacher, who worked primarily in England, Scotland and North America, whose style of revivals redefined Evangelicalism, and who influenced Jonathan Edwards.

The third significant event that set the stage for this missionary period is called the Evangelical Revival (in England) and the Second Great Awakening (in the United States). It took place approximately between 1787 and 1825. First of all, the Methodist revival had a major impact in ushering in the Evangelical Revival, accompanied with tremendous missionary vigor and dedication, particularly among Anglicans and Presbyterians in England. Despite the French Revolution, Napoleon and the full force of the Enlightenment, the ripples from this renewal spread to the European continent fairly quickly. Coming out of the Pietist tradition, Johann August Urlsperger had founded the *Deutsche Christentumsgesellschaft* (Germany Society for Christianity) in 1780, with its headquarters in Basel, Switzerland. This organization would eventually be a resource for German mission societies. Just to mention a few others, Johannes Theodorus van der Kemp was a key figure for mission renewal in Holland, and Johann Jänicke founded a mission school in Berlin in 1800. More will be added to this picture when we enter into the development of the missionary societies below.

Due in great extent to the influence of the American Revolution and the recent arrival of Enlightenment ideas to the American colonies, church attendance in the United States was extremely low at the time of independence (1776). However, the churches of the new nation soon experienced a dramatic renewal and a new passion for foreign missionary work.[12] "By the end of the nineteenth century more missionaries were being sent from the USA than from any other country, which is a testimony to missionary enthusiasm especially among Congregationalists, Presbyterians, and Baptists."[13]

The Society Model and William Carey

One of the most significant developments to emerge out of this dynamic renewal movement was the founding of societies that were devoted explicitly to foreign mission. The key characteristic of this phenomenon was *voluntarism*. Instead of waiting for a signal from an official church, individual Christians, often across denominational affiliations, joined such societies to commit themselves to the task of world mission. Lay people as well as clergy were involved in these associations, which were based on mass membership, and felt responsible for and generously supported them. This represented a major shift within Protestantism, a shift that Andrew Walls calls a "fortunate subversion"[14] of the traditional structures, and the primary model of mission for the nineteenth century. Furthermore, this marks a shift from the Roman Catholic model of the preceding missionary period, which was normally dependent on the state and usually centered around the clergy.

The name of William Carey is normally associated with the beginning of the modern missionary movement and the foundation in 1792 of the BMS. "Whilst there is some validity to thus singling him out, it has to be remembered that he was only one of many similar figures from this period and as much a product as a shaper of the spirit of the time."[15] With this is mind, let us look at Carey as representative of this new missionary period.

Born in Northamptonshire, England, William Carey (1761-1834) was a primary schoolteacher for some time and apprenticed as a shoemaker. Although he was originally an Anglican, he later became a Baptist. Carey was influenced by reading about the American Revolution and the discovery voyages of James Cook in the Pacific and by the preaching of Anglican and Baptist pastor-theologians who passed on the wisdom of the late Jonathan Edwards. In response to a hyper-Calvinism, which denied the need for human efforts to bring people to God, Carey, now a young Baptist pastor, wrote an eighty-seven-page booklet in 1792 entitled *An Inquiry into the Obligations of Christians to Use Means for the Conversion of the Heathens*. This pamphlet contributed greatly to the formation of a voluntary missionary society that would become the BMS. It is noteworthy that this new model was initially shaped by pragmatic, not theological, reasoning. In order to "use means" to effectively accomplish the missionary goal, Carey looked outside the ecclesiastical structures available at that time and drew upon an analogy from commerce: organizing a volunteer "instrumentalist" society is like floating a company. With time, the theology underlying this new mission model would develop. Carey used his context to develop an approach that was appropriate for his time, as missionaries have done throughout history.

As the first BMS missionary, Carey and his family arrived in Calcutta in 1793 without official travel permits and managed to survive by his acceptance of a position as superintendent of an indigo plantation. A major shift occurred with the arrival in 1799 of two colleagues, Joshua Marshman and William Ward, who together with Carey would become known as the Serampore Trio for their joint efforts in the Serampore Mission, located in a village twelve miles from Calcutta. Serampore was a Danish crown colony and, partially due to their positive experience of Pietists Ziegenbalg and Plütschau, the Danes were more favorably disposed to missionaries than was the British East Indian Company.

In collaboration with learned scholars in Bengal and fellow missionaries, Carey devoted himself mostly to Bible translations, establishing Serampore College (1818), securing financial support for the mission and its press, and teaching Bengali and Sanskrit. The Serampore Trio, their wives and other missionaries who later joined them contributed to such activities as running the printing/publishing press and many schools, developing mission strategy and theory,[16] managing public relations, promoting evangelization and social reform, and caring for a large household, including orphans, missionary widows and servants. As time went on, there was growing disagreement between the Serampore Trio and the London-based BMS committee regarding issues of administration, mission promotion and missionary personnel. These factors, combined with the stress caused by tensions between the younger and older missionaries in India, led to an official break between Serampore Mission and the BMS in 1827.

In attempting to differentiate between the "Carey of tradition" and the "historical Carey," current historical research points out that his significance for mission must be understood within the context of the circles of people and circumstances surrounding him.[17] With this understanding, Carey and his Serampore colleagues were transitional figures into the nineteenth-century missionary movement. They brought together in some ways the North American and British concerns for missionary outreach, and they "operated in creative tension between the poles of what are now labeled pragmatism and dogmatism, liberalism and conservatism, ecumenism and evangelicalism, imperialism and independency."[18]

Furthermore, Carey's significance in mission history is related to his involvement in the historic foundation of the BMS. Building upon some historical predecessors,[19] this Protestant archetype became *the* model for mission and was quickly followed by the formation of the London Missionary Society (LMS) in 1795, the Scottish Missionary Society in 1796, the Netherlands Missionary Society in 1797, the Church Missionary Society in 1799, the British and Foreign Missionary Society in 1804, the American Board of Commissioners for Foreign Missions (ABCFM) in 1810, the American Baptist Foreign Mission Society in 1814, the Basel Mission in 1816, the Wesleyan Methodist Missionary Society in 1817-1818, the Danish Missionary Society in 1821, the Berlin Missionary Society in 1824, the Rhenish Missionary Society in 1828, the Swedish Missionary Society in 1835 and the North German Missionary Society in 1836, to mention only a few.

One of the significant influences for the formation of such voluntary societies can be traced to the ideology of the Enlightenment and the French Revolution, that is, "the social and political egalitarianism of the emerging democracies."[20] Rather than depending on the authority of the institutional church and its official ministers, individual Christians could band together for a common cause. Also, the Enlightenment's optimistic view of humanity further supported the motivation to make a difference in the world either from one's home or by leaving it. It is important to see that, contrary to some perspectives, both the Enlightenment and the stream of "revivalist" occurrences together shaped the nineteenth-century missionary movement. Of course, this also built upon previous foundations, such as the earlier Pietist movement.

Another important characteristic of this mission model was that, at least in the beginning, the missionary societies were not denominationally exclusive or confessional. Even a "denominational" society like the BMS was primarily seen as the pragmatic "instrument" for evangelizing other peoples. This outlook was shared with the founders of such interdenominational or nondenominational missionary societies as the LMS, the ABCFM, and the Basel Mission.[21] This dynamic shaped the ecumenical movement within Protestantism. However, there was a shift in this ecumenical understanding in the 1830s, which shaped the society model of mission and the underlying theology. The understanding of the relationship between missionary activity and human society also changed around this time. We shall now look at three individuals who represent these particular elements and developments.

Henry Venn, Samuel Ajayi Crowther and David Livingstone

While the first wave of nineteenth-century Protestant missionaries was often considered fanatic or subversive by mainstream European society, the second wave was regarded as essential for churches and beneficial for governments. All churches embraced the central importance of mission, but the purpose of mission was shifting from the earlier emphasis on individual conversion to the planting of distinctly confessional churches. In this regard, Henry Venn,[22] as the secretary of the Church Missionary Society (CMS) from 1841 until 1872, provided the theology of mission underlying this development in terms of the widely known three-self formula. According to the formula, the goal of mission was to establish churches that were self-supporting, self-governing, and self-propagating. This idea of indigenous churches was being developed at the same time by Rufus Anderson,[23] who served as the long-time secretary of the ABCFM. Underlying this theory was a deep respect and trust of indigenous peoples, an attitude that unfortunately was to diminish in the latter part—the more imperialistic stage—of the nineteenth century. Henry Venn also represented the shifting role of mission and church in exerting Christian influence on public policy. First of all, he was part of the movement that worked through the British government to pass legislation to abolish the slave trade. Second, Venn stressed the importance of education for political, social and economic development. Regarding this latter aspect, he tried to initiate alternative economic endeavors that would undermine the slavery business. Henry Venn contributed to this modern missionary movement as a capable theorist, administrator and statesman.

A remarkable representative of non-Western peoples in mission was Samuel Ajayi Crowther, considered the foremost church leader in nineteenth-century Africa.[24] Crowther, born in 1807, was taken from his birthplace in western Nigeria as a slave but was rescued from a Portuguese slave ship by a British squadron and brought to Freetown in Sierra Leone. Andrew Walls calls Sierra Leone "the first success story of the modern missionary movement."[25] The Clapham philanthropists purchased land in Sierra Leone as a Province of Freedom, and the first residents consisted of eleven hundred African people who had become Christians as plantation slaves, as soldiers in the British army, or, later, as farmers in Nova Scotia. They arrived in 1792—another reason to consider this year the beginning of this missionary period—with their own preachers, and they would not see missionaries there for almost twenty years. Freed slaves, such as Crowther, came to this Christian community, which eventually supplied African missionaries to the rest of West Africa. Crowther himself went as a missionary to Yorubaland and later led an all-African group of missionaries to the Niger Delta, where he eventually presided as bishop. Lamin Sanneh has pointed out the further importance of Crowther for the Africanization of Christianity through both his acknowledgment of the richness of African culture and his role in the antislavery movement.[26] It is also significant to note that Crowther avoided using the common language of denunciation and allegation in his encounters with Muslims. "Crowther seems to have had courteous and friendly relations with Muslim rulers, and to have nourished a hope of reaching beyond them, through the Christian community, to the as yet barely Islamized peasantry under their control."[27] In 1841, there were 107 European and 9 African and Asian missionaries in the CMS, while thirty-two years later, under Venn's leadership, the CMS had 230 European and 148 African and Asian missionaries. In addition, African catechists, evangelists, traders and clerks played important roles in spreading the Christian faith across Africa.[28] During this same period, in another part of the world, Pacific Islanders were also making a significant contribution to evangelization.[29]

If asked to name a nineteenth-century missionary, the name David Livingstone would be the first to come to mind for most people.[30] He became a national figure and representative missionary, albeit extraordinary one, of his time. His famous explorations to "open up" the interior of Africa were seen by him as a prerequisite for the evangelization of its people. Livingstone wanted to get away from the horrific slave trade and other negative influences of the coastal settlements and ports. He still believed that the trilogy of Christianity, commerce and civilization would pave the way for a prosperous, free and nonviolent life for Africans. Always a missionary, Livingstone, like Venn, saw the importance of Africans taking on the responsibility of evangelization. Andrew Walls adds a further comparison: "Livingstone, like Venn, represents a sturdy, confident evangelicalism, secure in its place in national life, sure of its right and duty to influence public and government opinion, and, for all its emphasis on personal regeneration and personal religion, looking to the transformation of society as a normal fruit of Christian activity."[31] Venn and Livingstone are representatives of the wave of missionaries during a time that would later be called *benevolent colonialism*. The next phase of this missionary period was to be shaped by the advent of high imperialism.

Imperialism, Faith Missions, Student Movements and the Social Gospel

Beginning in the late 1870s, Germany, Belgium, England and France aggressively expanded their colonial domains, initiating a period of high imperialism. During this decade, the German statesman Bismarck gathered together in Berlin representatives of a few European colonial powers to divide the continent of Africa. Churches and mission organizations in these countries also showed a dramatic growth at this time. Although the United States was not involved in this colonial expansion, increased missionary activity "provided Americans with an important 'moral equivalent' for imperialism."[32] Manifest destiny was a strong motivation on both sides of the Atlantic. It became almost impossible to separate and distinguish political and religious motivations. On a number of occasions, missionaries petitioned their government to annex a particular territory before a rival could do so. In contrast to the more respectful attitudes toward Africans by Venn and Livingstone, representative of the previous colonial stage, racism reared its ugly head during this imperialistic era among all involved, even among

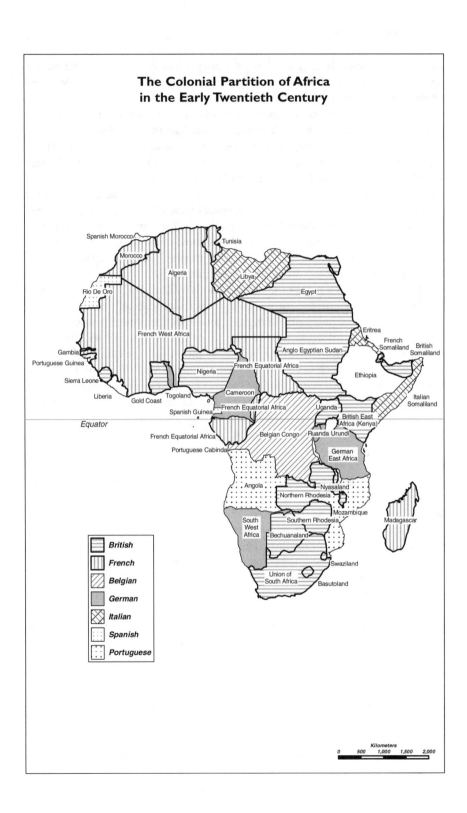

The Colonial Partition of Africa in the Early Twentieth Century

Spanish Morocco
Tunisia
Morocco
Algeria
Libya
Rio De Oro
Egypt
French West Africa
Eritrea
French Somaliland
British Somaliland
Gambia
Anglo Egyptian Sudan
Portuguese Guinea
Nigeria
French Equatorial Africa
Sierra Leone
Ethiopia
Liberia
Togoland
Cameroon
Gold Coast
Italian Somaliland
Spanish Guinea
French Equatorial Africa
Uganda
Equator
British East Africa (Kenya)
French Equatorial Africa
Belgian Congo
Ruanda Urundi
Portuguese Cabinda
German East Africa
Angola
Nyasaland
Northern Rhodesia
Mozambique
Madagascar
South West Africa
Southern Rhodesia
Bechuanaland
Swaziland
Union of South Africa
Basutoland

British
French
Belgian
German
Italian
Spanish
Portuguese

Kilometers
0   500   1,000   1,500   2,000

missionaries themselves. The ideas of Henry Venn and Rufus Anderson for founding indigenous churches were eroded by this attitude that non-Western peoples were inferior, incapable and untrustworthy.

Within such a situation of complicity between mission and imperialism, a number of missionary voices were raised on behalf of the rights of the indigenous peoples. For example, within the German context, A. Reichel and J. Hesse spoke about the incompatibility of mission and colonialism, and after the Herero Rebellion in Namibia in 1904, the Rhenish Mission sided with the Africans and cited the exploitative colonial system and business practices as the reasons for the rebellion.[33] On the whole, the missionaries were children of their time; that is, they normally did not question colonialism in itself or the attitudes associated with manifest destiny. At the same time, most missionaries were very concerned about the welfare of the non-Western peoples, although today we would label their approach paternalistic and ethnocentric.

The tremendous increase of missionary activity at the end of the nineteenth century and into the twentieth was not simply a product of imperialism and nationalism. Experiencing other religious renewals, the older mission societies found new life and new societies emerged. Many of the new societies were known as faith missions. The first and most famous was the China Inland Mission (CIM; today the Overseas Missionary Fellowship), founded by J. Hudson Taylor.[34] Born in a Methodist family, Taylor first went as a missionary to China when he was twenty-one years old with the Chinese Evangelization Society (CES). After resigning from CES and eventually returning to England, he continued to feel burdened for the Chinese in the eleven inland provinces where there were no missionaries. This led him to found CIM in 1865. A year later, he sent a group of inexperienced women and men missionaries two by two into the interior area of China, beyond colonial "control." Despite formidable hardships and predictions of disaster by others, CIM would eventually grow to be the largest mission in China. CIM, like other faith missions that followed it, insisted on a *radical voluntarism*—going on mission with no financial guarantees. In reaction to the imperialistic situation, Taylor insisted that his missionaries not seek protection or favor from a foreign colonial government. They wore Chinese clothing and a braid of hair or pigtail, which symbolized submission to the Chinese government. As a result of its vulnerability in the interior, CIM had the largest number of missionary martyrs in the Boxer Rebellion (1900). Its mission was primarily focused on evangelism for the "salvation of souls," and its hospitals and schools were considered secondary. Each missionary was free to establish a denominational polity, which could only be changed by the churches themselves, not by later missionaries, and the churches were never organized into a national body. In this way, this type of mission society represented a shift to a more ecumenical spirit of the first part of the nineteenth century. Elements of faith missions are foundational for the Evangelical missionary movement of the twentieth century.

A second phenomenon that had a major impact in shaping the growing mission interest and activity during this period was the youth and student movements.

Until 1890, most of the missionary efforts by the Protestant churches in the United States were focused within home missions. However, in 1886, the famous evangelist Dwight L. Moody[35] organized the first Mount Hermon summer conference for college students in Northfield, Massachusetts; at that gathering the Presbyterian A. T. Pierson[36] brought the concern for foreign missions to center stage. As a follow-up, the Student Volunteer Movement for Foreign Missions (SVM) was formed in 1888, with John R. Mott as its chairperson.[37] A year later, SVM chose the motto "The Evangelization of the World in This Generation!" Within its second year, three thousand young people volunteered to be foreign missionaries. In 1895, Mott formed the World's Student Christian Federation (WSCF), which had ecumenical and international influence. These two youth movements and many similar ones provided recruits and enthusiasm for foreign mission within the churches and formed future leaders of world mission, like John R. Mott, J. H. Oldham,[38] Robert Speer,[39] and W. A. Visser 't Hooft.[40] John R. Mott also served the YMCA for forty-four years, first as student secretary and later as general secretary.

While faith missions considered social outreach secondary, other Christians were concerned primarily with addressing the social ills of society and the world. Such efforts would give birth to the Social Gospel movement. Drawing upon the European nineteenth-century theological thought of such theologians as Albrecht Ritschl, this development would become particularly strong in the United States. Its members understood God's reign to be a present ethical reality in this world, one "which would be introduced step by step through successful labors in missionary endeavor abroad and through creating an egalitarian society at home."[41] Progress, efficiency and scientific planning were highly valued. Jesus Christ became the loving and wise teacher, in whom the religious potentiality of humanity was developed. The writing of Baptist minister Walter Rauschenbusch, coming out of his experience in the Hell's Kitchen area of New York City, was very influential in further shaping the Social Gospel movement. This development would eventually influence SVM and missionary-founded churches, and aspects of the Social Gospel would be found in Conciliar Protestantism in the twentieth century.

The sixteen missionary societies of the United States in the 1860s had grown to about ninety by 1900,[42] including faith missions founded by A. T. Pierson and Adoniram Judson Gordon.[43] In that same year, while the British supported the largest number of missionaries, the United States had twice as many Protestant missionaries as those coming from the European continent;[44] the total number of Protestant missionaries in the world was about fifteen thousand. The Ecumenical Missionary Conference, held in New York in 1900, was the largest missionary conference that had ever been held,[45] with participation by two hundred mission societies and 170,000 to 200,000 people from Europe, England and the United States. This event pointed to the intensity of the century's missionary activity and to the importance of interdenominational cooperation. At the same time, the identification of the missionary movement in the United States with a national sense of manifest destiny was symbolized by the following three consecutive speakers at the opening of the New York Missionary Conference: President William McKinley, New York governor Theodore Roosevelt and former president Benjamin Harrison.[46]

Women in Mission

An integral part of the mission history of the nineteenth century is the story of women in this process. On the one hand, their particular roles were usually determined, limited and under-acknowledged due to their subordination within the official male-dominated church structures and social context. On the other hand, women's contributions to the missionary efforts were constant, both qualitatively and quantitatively. By 1890, women represented 60 percent of the Protestant missionaries from the United States.[47]

After the Second Great Awakening in the United States, that is, at the beginning of the modern missionary movement, many women's church-related organizations were founded for charitable and religious purposes. In 1800, Mary Webb founded the Boston Female Society for Missionary Purposes, through which Congregational and Baptist women supported British and United States mission efforts financially and spiritually. At this time, a woman could only take part directly in foreign mission work as the wife of a missionary, and even in these cases the wives were not counted as missionaries at first. In addition to sharing the same theological and religious background as their husbands, women were also motivated for mission through their "desires for usefulness, concern for women and children, and the necessity of serving their husbands."[48]

Within mission history, Mary Lyon was "the female counterpart of Rufus Anderson."[49] In 1837, she founded Mount Holyoke Female Seminary in South Hadley, Massachusetts, to provide an affordable and well-rounded higher education for preparing young women primarily as teachers. Influenced by Lyon's commitment to mission, many graduates of Mount Holyoke became actively involved in both home and foreign missionary work. In the 1820s, primarily in response to the need for the education of girls and young women, the ABCFM had reluctantly begun to send single women as missionaries to serve among Native Americans and to serve as well in Hawaii and India. Mount Holyoke would send Fidelia Fiske as its first of many well-prepared unmarried teachers as a foreign missionary in 1843. The role of missionary teacher opened up a new avenue for single women. While Mount Holyoke emphasized teacher training, this model likewise "affirmed the ideal of the Christian home as a basis for a full-blown mission theory."[50] As time went on, many disagreed with the perspective of the three-self theory of Rufus Anderson and the ABCFM, which viewed education (and other goals related to "civilization") and women's role in mission as subordinate to direct evangelization and not goods in themselves. In 1861 a group of women led by Mrs. Sarah Doremus of the Reformed tradition founded the Woman's Union Missionary Society, an independent, interdenominational mission board run by women to send out single women missionaries, who by this time formed the vast majority of Protestant women in mission.

Across the Atlantic, the British Society for Promoting Female Education in the East was founded in 1834 to send women teachers as missionaries, particularly to India. Several initial women's American Methodist societies supported a number of single women in mission in the 1830s and 1850s. More long-lasting denominational women's missionary societies were founded in the 1860s and 1870s, so that by 1890 there were about forty. The Woman's Foreign Missionary Society (WFMS) of the Methodist Episcopal Church was a prime example. What emerged in this process was a women's missiology, called "Woman's Work for Woman," through which Christianity brought both salvation and "civilization," that is, social advancement for women from a Western perspective. In this regard, this mission model was a part of the cultural imperialism of the West, but at the same time, "its focus on global sisterhood and the essential unity of humankind was a valuable corrective to patriarchal notions that valued men over women, and boys over girls in many parts of the world."[51] With a more holistic sense of mission, women missionaries who were sent, for example by WFMS, were involved in education, health, social reform and evangelization (in certain situations[52]). Regarding this latter area, it is important to note the predominant role of indigenous "Bible women" in India, who were trained and employed by Western missionary women.

Charlotte (Lottie) Moon is probably the most famous North American woman missionary of this time period.[53] During her forty years in northern China, with more than her share of trials and challenges, Lottie was not satisfied with only teaching Chinese children but also became a very effective evangelist of Chinese women. She used her influence to prompt Southern Baptist women to form their own missionary organization, to encourage young women to come to China as missionaries and to inspire the Southern Baptist Convention into becoming one of the major mission bodies in the world.

In the last phase of the nineteenth-century missionary movement, women were also integral to the faith missions and the youth/student movements. In focusing on the former, Hudson Taylor from the very beginning had sent women two by two as evangelists in China. By the early twentieth century, women often outnumbered men three to one in faith missions.[54] The foundation of the Evangelical Missionary Alliance in 1887 was a historic event in the United States "because it stated explicitly that women could work as evangelists under the same terms as men, going wherever God called them to people of both sexes."[55] On the one hand, the nondenominational faith missions opened up new possibilities for women in mission, but at the same time, in reality, women often found themselves eventually working in areas that were not "pure" evangelism. Evangelical independent missionary activity developed further with the emergence of the holiness movement, with its more Wesleyan orientation, and of Pentecostalism. In these two movements, women had a numerical preponderance as well as a greater leadership role.

In 1888, women missionary leaders from North America and England founded the World's Missionary Committee of Christian Women, described by R. Pierce Beaver as "the first international ecumenical missionary agency intended to be universal in scope."[56] They organized meetings and programs in conjunction with the Chicago World's Fair of 1893 and the Ecumenical Missionary Conference of New York in 1900. In many ways, the high point was the Woman's Missionary Jubilee of 1910-1911, a series of two-day local celebrations across the United States that built upon and strengthened the grassroots character of the women's missionary movement. "Probably the most important result of the 1910 Jubilee was that it stimulated further ecumenical action and pulled women together behind common causes."[57] However, 1910 also marked the beginning of the decline of women's missionary agencies, as the first, and eventually most, of women's agencies were forced to merge into general male-dominated denominational mission boards.

The World Missionary Conference of Edinburgh

In addition to the Ecumenical Mission Congress in New York in 1900, another public gathering that formed part of the context for Edinburgh was the 1893 World Parliament of Religions.[58] People representing the major religions of the world gathered in Chicago for the first-time event, which was a showcase of Christian pride. This same Christian optimism carried into Edinburgh.

John R. Mott headed the planning and served as the chairperson for the famous 1910 World Missionary Conference of Edinburgh, as well as later leading the continuation committee. Questions of doctrine and polity were deliberately excluded in order to provide a wide ecumenical forum. The twelve hundred participants representing some 160 boards or societies, including faith missions, focused on consultation, cooperation and strategy for the sake of world mission. As the culmination of the nineteenth-century missionary movement, the Edinburgh conference represented the height of missionary optimism, pragmatism and enthusiasm for the speedy Christianization of the world. William Richey Hogg wrote that the 1910 conference "symbolized Carey's hope and reflected the most dynamic and creative forces in a century of missionary endeavor."[59] Later generations considered it a watershed event separating the nineteenth- and twentieth-century missionary movements. The optimistic mood of Edinburgh would soon be shattered by the 1914 outbreak of World War I particularly in continental Europe, and the church would enter a new missionary period.

The immediate source and inspiration for Latourette's "Great Century" of Protestant missionary activity can be traced to the Great Awakenings, the birth of Methodism and the Evangelical Revival. At the same time, David Bosch rightfully reminds us that this modern missionary movement was a child of the Enlightenment. Within this context, William Carey and others would take the lead in the development of the society model of mission—Christians volunteering to work together, often across denominational affiliations, in responding to the common call of world evangelization. Faith missions would later emerge as a new adaptation of the society model, and youth, student and women's movements in the West would continue to energize the missionary endeavor, soon to be joined by many indigenous Christians. While a variety of denominational, interdenominational and nondenominational organizations existed, ecumenism and unity were basically promoted for the sake of mission.

Against the background of growing nationalism, missionaries often found themselves in close relationship with colonialism and imperialism, which usually but not always (such as with the CIM) implied dependence and collaboration. The pervading spirit of manifest destiny and religious fervor instilled within them a desire to promote their culture and religion, a sense of responsibility for other peoples, a willingness to sacrifice and to trust, and a hope fueled by enthusiastic optimism. For example, John R. Mott "really succeeded, in a masterful way, in combining his faith in God's revelation in Christ with his faith in the 'providential' achievements of modern science."[60] In this way, proclamation and social "advancement," Christianity and "civilization," often went hand in hand. Many mission efforts were in the areas of education and health. Later generations would criticize them for their paternalism, superiority complex and collaboration with imperialism, but one should not overlook their dedication and sacrifice in proclaiming the gospel in the way that made sense to them as children of their time. In 1911, the number of Protestant foreign missionaries around the world had grown to approximately twenty-one thousand, one-third from North America.

The nineteenth century also saw the birth of the academic discipline of missiology. Scottish missionary Alexander Duff developed a systematic theory of mission and was appointed in 1867 to a new chair of Evangelistic Theology in Edinburgh.[61] This first chair of missiology was eliminated after Duff's departure, but the path was laid. It would be Gustav Warneck who would be recognized as the founder of missiology as a discipline in its own right.[62] Warneck founded the *Allgemeine Missions Zeitschrift*, the first scientific missionary periodical, in 1874. In 1897, he was appointed to the chair of missionary science at the University of Halle, Germany. His three-volume work on Protestant mission theory and his survey of the history of Protestant missionary work were extremely important for the young discipline. Influenced by Warneck's work, Catholic Church historian Joseph Schmidlin began lecturing in missiology in 1910 at the University of Münster and was appointed to the first chair of Catholic missiology at the same university in 1914.[63] Schmidlin is considered the founder of missiology for the Catholic tradition, to which we now turn.

MODELS OF MISSION OF THE CATHOLIC CHURCH

As seen in the last chapter, during the second half of the eighteenth century the missionary activity of the Catholic Church was almost nonexistent. On top of that, the French Revolution, liberalism and the Napoleonic wars further paralyzed the Catholic Church, much more than Protestant churches. This was true particularly for the church in France, which was assuming Spain and Portugal's former role as the world's most prominent "Catholic nation." The pope and the SCPF were held captive in France; the authority of the pope, church and religion in general were called into question; religious orders were suppressed in France; and Napoleon wanted Catholic mission efforts to serve his imperialistic ambitions. After the defeat of Napoleon, a struggle between liberalism and conservatism would ensue within the Catholic Church in Europe. The struggle would be over issues of authority, jurisdiction and responsibilities of the church over against the state. The Syllabus of Errors in 1864 would condemn the alleged beliefs and practices of liberalism, such as children being educated by the state, divine revelation being subject to human knowledge, and church and state being separate. In a certain sense, the document is summed up in the final proposition, condemning the notion that "the Roman Pontiff can, and ought to, reconcile himself to, and reach agreement with, progress, liberalism, and modern civilization" (DS 2980). Furthermore, the papacy emerged from suffering under Napoleon into an eventual position of prestige and stability during a time of political, social and religious upheaval and change. The proclamation of the doctrine of infallibility by the First Vatican Council in 1870 would highlight this movement (Ultramontanism[64]) for increasing the authority of the pope and, together with the Syllabus of Errors, signal the defeat of liberalism. In terms of the Enlightenment, Bosch states that while Catholicism certainly was affected by it, "it can, however, hardly be denied that, on the whole, Catholic theology and the Catholic Church withstood Enlightenment influences more effectively than did Protestantism and succeeded longer than the latter to remain intact."[65]

Within the above context, the first signs of the renewal of missionary activity were the restoration of the Jesuits in 1814, the reconstitution of the SCPF in 1817, and the leadership and missionary enthusiasm of Pope Gregory XVI (1831-1846),[66] who had earlier served as the prefect of the SCPF. The general characteristics of the Catholic modern missionary movement included, first of all, the revived role of the SCPF and the personal support and direction by four successive popes during a period of over eighty years: Gregory XVI, Pius IX, Leo XIII and Pius X. Second, some financial support for mission was developed on the popular level, primarily Leopoldinenstiftung, Ludwigsmissionsverein and Holy Childhood. This financial assistance was accompanied by spiritual support and stimulated by mission magazines and popular mission literature from these associations and missionary congregations.

While the society model was a new development within Protestantism, the Catholic Church had a long tradition of religious orders and congregations. During the nineteenth century the Catholic Church experienced an amazing proliferation in the number and variety of newly founded societies with specific purposes and (local and/or wider) contexts in mind. Many were open to and/or committed specifically to missionary work. Some of the earlier ones included the Congregation of the Holy Hearts of Jesus and Mary (1805); Sisters of St. Joseph of Cluny (1807); Oblates of Mary Immaculate (1816/1826); Marist Fathers (1816/1836), Sisters (1817), and Brothers (1817/1863); Pontifical Institute for Foreign Missions (1850); Missionaries of the Sacred Heart (1855); Congregation of the Immaculate Heart of Mary (1862); and Mill Hill Missionaries (1866). These congregations and orders provided the personnel, creativity and energy to adapt earlier traditional religious communities into the Catholic nineteenth-century society model of mission. In addition, older religious congregations—such as the Franciscans, Dominicans, Capuchins, Jesuits and Augustinians—brought renewed vision and energy to mission at this time. These societies, old and new, emphasized team effort and offered a variety of services out of concern for holistic and social advancement in the areas of education, health and economics. This is linked with the context of colonialism and manifest destiny mentioned above. In the next two sections, we look, first of all, at three significant representatives of the earlier nineteenth-century missionary societies, and second, at three models of the later period.

Anne-Marie Javouhey, François Libermann and Rose Duchesne

While Protestant women participated actively in mission as missionary wives and later as single, widowed and married missionaries through volunteer societies, the avenue for Catholic women to participate directly in missionary work continued to be as sisters in religious orders and congregations. During the French Revolution, ten-year-old Anne-Marie Javouhey aided clergy who refused to take an oath of allegiance to the revolutionary government and were in hiding,[67] and she began giving religious instruction to young children. As her interest in education grew, she founded the Sisters of St. Joseph of Cluny (in 1807). She had to deal with much misunderstanding and opposition, mostly from within the church. However, at the request of the French government, she sent sisters first to present-day Reunion Island in the Indian Ocean and later to the French West Indies, French Guiana, and the west coast of Africa. In order to overcome the situation of slavery that she witnessed, Javouhey contributed to developing a system of agricultural and family education. Under her direction, a nearly independent colony of freed slaves was established in French Guiana. When she died in 1851, about nine hundred women of the Sisters of St. Joseph of Cluny were working around the world. Javouhey is credited with initiating nineteenth-century Catholic mission efforts in Africa.

François Marie Paul Libermann was an Orthodox Jew who intended to become a rabbi like his father.[68] However, influenced by the conversions of leading Jews to Christianity, he became a Catholic, entered the seminary, but was not allowed to continue preparing for ordination due to epilepsy. Not to be overcome by obstacles, Libermann founded the Missionaries of the Holy Heart of Mary for the evangelization of Africa in 1840 and was ordained the following year. The first missionaries were sent to Maritius and West Africa. At the request of the SCPF, Libermann agreed in 1848 to merge his new society with the congregation of the Holy Ghost Fathers, who had been founded in 1703 by Claude-François Poullart-des-Places but had been devastated by the French Revolution. While losing its name, Libermann's society provided new life for the Holy Ghost Fathers (known today as the Spiritans). Libermann promoted missionary accommodation to African customs, formation of indigenous clergy and subsequently bishops, and evangelization of Africans by Africans. Although he never visited his missionaries, he kept in very close contact through extensive correspondence. While the Spiritans eventually became involved in different activities, the focus of their missionary work was in Africa, to which they sent more missionaries than any other Catholic organization between 1860 and 1960.

After the disruption caused by the French Revolution, Rose Philippine Duchesne professed vows in 1805 in the Society of the Sacred Heart of Jesus, newly founded by Sophie Barat to provide religious education for young women.[69] Duchesne's childhood desire for mission work had been nurtured by stories of Jesuit missionaries, and she had the opportunity to fulfill her dream when she was chosen to be the superior of the society's first mission to the United States. In response to the directions of the bishop, in 1818 the sisters began to establish schools for the children of settlers in the former Louisiana Territory. Later, Duchesne was also responsible for initiating her society's work with Native Americans; her approach was to have the sisters live with them rather than have the Native American children come to the town schools. She wasn't free to do so herself until, at the age of seventy-one, she went to live with the Potawatomis in Kansas. "Duchesne struggled throughout her life with the tension between the cloister and the needs of the missions, as well as with the prevailing attitude that missions were the work of men and not of women."[70] In the first part of the nineteenth century, Catholic women in the United States were able to participate in domestic mission work only by joining European-founded women's societies like the Society of the Sacred Heart of Jesus, the Sisters of Saint Joseph, the Sisters of Notre Dame of Namur and the Missionary Sisters of the Sacred Heart, all of which came to the United States to fulfill their mission.[71] While the primary role of Catholic women in mission at this time, similar to their Protestant counterparts, was teaching, they also were involved in a variety of charitable works and in the area of health, through nursing and establishing hospitals.

Charles Lavigerie, Daniel Comboni and Katherine Drexel

Many new religious societies of men and women dedicated to missionary activity were founded in the second half of the nineteenth century. One of the most influential people of this second wave was Charles Lavigerie.[72] The name of this Frenchman is associated with the revival of the North African church, where he served as archbishop of Algiers and Carthage. He was named a cardinal in 1882 by Pope Leo XIII. In 1868 he had founded a society of men called the Missionaries of Our Lady of Africa, later popularly known as the White Fathers due to their white robes; a year later he founded a parallel women's society. While their initial focus was on the evangelization of Muslims in North Africa, these two societies extended their work into Central Africa. Lavigerie stressed the importance of learning the language and culture, founded Christian villages for children orphaned after epidemics of cholera and typhus, and established an extensive communal catechetical process that would eventually influence the reinstatement of the catechumenate after the Second Vatican Council. On the international level, Lavigerie's influential efforts in fighting against slavery culminated in the 1889 Brussels Conference, which led to the first international agreement for the abolition of the slave trade. At the same time, under the pervasive influence of the high imperial period, Lavigerie reminded his missionaries that they were working for France as well as for the reign of God.[73]

Another person who contributed greatly to the shape of Catholic missionary efforts in Africa was Daniel Comboni.[74] Born in Italy, Comboni went to Africa for the first time as a missionary to Sudan with the Mazza Institute at Verona, but he had to return to Italy due to the closure of the mission and his own poor health. His concern for Africa led to his involvement in ransoming Africans from slavery and bringing them to Europe for education. Then, in 1864, he conceived his "Plan for the Regeneration of Africa by Africa," which included the foundation of centers in Africa for preparing both Africans and Europeans for evangelization. With the support of Pius IX, Comboni founded a mission institute, out of which eventually developed two missionary societies, one for men and another for women. Comboni was disappointed by the lack of support for his appeal for missionary efforts in Africa at the First Vatican Council in 1870, but he continued to work tirelessly to build international interest. Comboni was appointed pro-vicar apostolic of Central Africa in 1872, and vicar apostolic and bishop five years later. Although his early death in Africa in 1881 prevented him from further developing his missionary vision, Comboni had laid a foundation for recognizing the human dignity of indigenous peoples and their role in evangelization.

While Lavigerie and Comboni are representative of many Catholic women and men from Europe who served as foreign missionaries, Katherine Drexel focused her efforts within her home country, the United States.[75] As an heir of a very wealthy banking family in Philadelphia, Katherine provided influence and financial support particularly in the area of education for those most marginalized in U.S. society—Native Americans and African Americans. In 1891, she founded the Sisters of the Blessed Sacrament to further this work. Katherine insisted that the benefits from the financial resources of her family extend beyond her own congregation to other orders and projects for the sake of the black community, including the eventual founding of Xavier University in New Orleans as the first African American Catholic institution of higher learning. Furthermore, Katherine Drexel became a strong voice for interracial justice and for women and mission in the United States.

The first involvement of U.S. Catholic men and women in mission beyond their national boundaries included some Redemptorists, Passionists, Franciscan sisters of Allegheny and Syracuse (New York), Jesuits and Sisters of the Holy Family of New Orleans. However, two events triggered the beginning of a vigorous *ad gentes* missionary movement: the Spanish-American War in 1898 and the removal of the United States (and Australia) from the list of "mission countries" in 1908. Many Catholics began joining the ranks of missionary societies that were newly founded in Europe—like the Franciscan Missionaries of Mary, the Society of the Divine Word, and the Holy Spirit Missionary Sisters—and that had recently established houses in the States. A major breakthrough came with the foundations of the Catholic Foreign Mission Society of America (Maryknoll Priests and Brothers) in 1911 by James A. Walsh and Thomas Frederick Price,[76] and the Mission Sisters of St. Dominic (Maryknoll Sisters) by Mother Mary Joseph Rogers in 1912 (with canonical approval in 1920).[77] Canadian Catholics would found La Société des Missions Étrangères de la Province de Quebec in 1921 to send diocesan priests in mission overseas. These events marked the beginning of North American–founded Catholic missionary institutes.

The Roman Catholic missionary movement had been at a low point at the end of the eighteenth century, and the situation got worse as a result of the French Revolution and related events. As noted above, a strong Protestant missionary movement came on the scene at this time and would become the predominant Christian mission outreach throughout the nineteenth century. At the beginning of the nineteenth century there were also signs of a vibrant renewal of the Catholic missionary movement, which would grow throughout the century. Coming out of the Catholic roots and heritage, the number of new orders and congregations, including many devoted implicitly or explicitly to mission, exploded. Drawing upon a similar spirit of voluntarism, many Catholics joined the ranks of these new missionary societies, which represented the Catholic equivalent of the nineteenth-century society model. The approximate number of Catholic missionaries worldwide jumped from three hundred in 1800 to seventy-five hundred in 1920.

As for differences, the Protestant society model cut across denominational lines and often distanced itself from official church bodies at home, while the Catholic society model, out of a different ecclesiology, maintained a strong link with the institutional church, particularly through the Vatican. Also, while the Protestant mission movement opened up more opportunities to non-ordained and married persons for involvement in mission, Catholic missionaries consisted almost exclusively of priests, brothers and sisters, all of whom lived celibate lives. While the nineteenth century was characterized by a spirit of ecumenism within Protestantism, the opposition between Catholics and Protestants was very strong both at home and overseas, and this divisiveness was often compounded by nationalistic agendas. A very clear example can be drawn from the history of Christianity in Oceania, where French Catholic missionaries and British Protestant missionaries were part of the competitive colonial enterprise of France and Britain claiming islands across the Pacific.[78]

The nineteenth-century agents of Roman Catholic mission also included non-Western peoples. It is important to note, for example, the work of catechists of the Pacific Islands; the lay foundations of the church in Korea; the role of catechists and the development of "The House of God" institutions as a continuation of the tradition of Alexandre de Rhodes in Vietnam; and the formation of a local Catholic Chinese church through Chinese priests, Lazarists (Vincentians), lay leaders and "Christian virgins" (women who had taken private vows, lived in the homes of their families, and did work in the areas of teaching, catechesis and medical care[79]). Unfortunately, the arrival of Western missionaries in some of these situations hindered these indigenous movements.[80] As within the Protestant missionary movement, Roman Catholic missionaries from North America and Europe were strongly shaped by the colonial, ethnocentric and national influences around them, particularly with the onslaught of imperialism during the period from 1878 to 1914.

MODELS OF MISSION OF THE ORTHODOX CHURCH

While not comparable in scale to the missionary work of the Protestant and Catholic churches, the nineteenth century can also be considered the "Great Century" for the Orthodox Church, since it marked the beginning of a new period of mission.[81] In 1828, the Holy Synod issued a call for missionaries to reverse a movement of eastern Russians who were leaving their Christian faith. One of those to respond immediately was the monk Macarius Gloukharev (Glukharev), who with two companions went to some nomadic peoples in the Altai mountain area of Siberia.[82] In the tradition of the Greek East, he began learning several of their languages and translating some parts of scripture into the vernacular. After receiving little positive response, he began to focus on medicine and hygiene, and his witness of service to the people went as far as his sweeping their homes himself. Contrary to contemporary Orthodox practice, he insisted on a long pre-baptismal preparation and later encouraged them to live in newly established Christian villages. Macarius eventually left this missionary work in the hands of many capable successors in order to devote himself to instilling a mission interest in the Orthodox Church as a whole, developing in the process an Orthodox mission theory.

As Orthodox missionaries traveled across central Russia and Siberia to a new mission in Alaska, they saw how often previous Orthodox missionaries had dealt well with different cultures and languages.[83] One of the greatest Russian missionaries was John (Innocent) Veniaminov.[84] In 1822 he took his family on a fourteen-month journey to reach the Aleutian Islands, where he mastered the local language, developed an alphabet for it and proceeded with scriptural translations. He eventually extended his missionary efforts to the Alaskan mainland among peoples who had had no previous contacts with Europeans. After fifteen years, he returned to St. Petersburg to present a mission strategy to the Holy Synod. His wife died during this visit, a sad fact that nevertheless made him eligible to be ordained bishop of an area stretching from Siberia and the Aleutians to California. After years of episcopal service, blind and physically weak, Veniaminov became metropolitan of Moscow and used his influence to establish the Orthodox Missionary Society (1870). The Orthodox Church in America honored him in 1977 as the "Evangelizer of the Aleuts and Apostle to America," and the Russian Orthodox Church designated 1997, the two-hundredth anniversary of his birth, as the "Year of St. Innocent." One of the lasting legacies of the Orthodox mission is the number of indigenous Alaskan men who serve as priests today in many Orthodox parishes.

Orthodox mission efforts also extended outside Russian territory to East Asia. Nicholas Kassatkin, as chaplain to the Russian consulate in Japan, baptized three Japanese in 1868—at a time when Japanese were not allowed even to study Christianity.[85] He then went to Moscow to get approval for a mission organization in which newly baptized Japanese Christians would serve as catechists and evangelists. Kassatkin returned to Japan in 1871 to carry out this plan. Despite the difficult years during the Russo-Japanese War (1904-1905), by the time of his death in 1912, then archbishop of Japan, the Japanese Orthodox Church included over thirty-three thousand members, who were served by Japanese priests, deacons, and catechists. In China, a small Orthodox community traced it roots to Russians captured by Chinese in the late seventeenth century.[86] A shift occurred in 1858 when a monk, Isaias Polikin, initiated a mission approach that would become known primarily for its Orientalists and scientific research—reminding us of the earlier East Syrian mission work in China. The Orthodox church would suffer greatly during the Boxer Rebellion (1900), and afterward it would devote much energy to caring for the thousands of Orthodox railroad workers in Manchuria. As for entering Korea, missionaries received permission only in 1900 to care for Koreans who returned to Korea after they had become Orthodox during their time as emigrants in Russia.[87] The Russo-Japanese War would also impede mission efforts here.

This survey of Orthodox mission points to an incarnational approach with importance placed on the vernacular, cultural understanding and indigenous church leadership in developing local churches. In some contexts, the missionaries (including the Japanese catechists) directed evangelization; in other situations, such as in China and at the beginning in Japan, they could not do so. However, in most situations the Orthodox church followed a more holistic approach to mission, which was characteristic of Protestant and Catholic mission as well. Similar to their counterparts, the Orthodox missionaries often found themselves closely linked with the national political interests of Russia, particularly in the case of China.[88]

With a few exceptions, such as Tibet, Afghanistan, Nepal and the interior regions of Papua New Guinea, Christian missionaries had set foot in almost every part of the world by 1914, and at least a small community of baptized Christians remained in their wake in most places. World War I shattered the optimism represented at Edinburgh and brought the Age of Progress to a close.

CONSTANTS IN THE CONTEXT OF THE AGE OF PROGRESS

A good starting point for understanding the theological roots of the Protestant missionary burst of the nineteenth century is Johannes van den Berg's *Constrained*

MISSION IN THE AGE OF PROGRESS (1792-1914)

Context	Africa, Asia, Oceania and Americas	Africa, Asia, Oceania and Americas	Siberia, Alaska and East Asia
Stream of Christianity	Protestant	Roman Catholic	Orthodox
Primary model	Society model	Society model	Monks
Key figures in mission	Carey, Serampore Trio, Venn, Anderson, Crowther, Taylor, Livingstone, Pierson, Mott, Oldham, Rauschenbusch, Webb, Lyon, Doremus, Moon, Duff and Warneck	Javoughey, Libermann, Duchesne, Lavigerie, Comboni, Drexel, Janssen, Walsh, Price, Rogers, Schmidlin	Gloukharev, Veniaminov, Kassatkin, Polikin
Theological typology	A/B (emphasis on law/truth)	A (emphasis on law)	B (emphasis on truth)
Primary theologians	Schleiermacher, Ritschl, Maurice, Herrmann, Forsythe	Franzelin, Scheeben	

CONSTANTS

Christology	High	High	High
Ecclesiology	Institutional and herald models	Institutional model	Mystical communion, sacrament
Eschatology	Imminent, individual, premillennial: "Evangelicals"; realized, societal, postmillennial, amillennial: liberals	Futurist Individual	Realized Individual
Salvation	Spiritual: "Evangelicals" Holistic: liberals	Spiritual; only through church	Spiritual
Anthropology	Negative: "Evangelicals" Positive: liberals	Negative	Positive
Culture	Negative; Counter-cultural	Positive/negative; Moderate counter-	Positive; Anthropological model

by Jesus' Love, an excellent study of the missionary motives in Great Britain between 1698 and 1815. In the title, which he drew from 2 Corinthians 5:14, van den Berg points out that love was a "powerful incentive" and "indispensable element" for missionary motivation during that period, but at the same time he is quick to note that it took on a variety of forms.[89] In a positive sense, this love led to compassion, tremendous missionary dedication and "a genuine feeling of concern for others."[90] Tightly knit within this attitude was the ultimate motivation of *salvation*—saving souls before it was too late.[91] However, there was not a serious separation between soteriological and humanitarian goals, at least initially, through the eighteenth and early nineteenth centuries, although sharp distinctions in this regard would lead to tension in the second half of this missionary period.

On the negative side, the missionary motivation of love was influenced by the overly optimistic views of *human nature*, characterized by Rousseau's depiction of the "noble savage." Such optimism often led to a condescending attitude of the missionary toward the "innocent" *tabula rasa*. On the other hand, an overly pessimistic attitude coming out of the Calvinistic doctrine of the radical corruption of humanity likewise tended to place the recipients of the missionary efforts in an inferior position. Another new element was that, as a result of the breakdown of the overarching Christian environment in the missionaries' homelands due to such factors as the Enlightenment, the missionaries understood salvation for themselves and others more on an individual rather than a communal basis. "The individual responsibility of missionaries to proclaim salvation to individuals became the hallmark of nineteenth-century missions."[92] Furthermore, Bosch describes the developments in the missionary theory and practice of this period by examining how the image of the man from Macedonia (Acts 16:9), who said, "Come over . . . and help us," became the archetype of non-Christians,[93] who "in their helplessness and poverty were calling upon the benevolent help of the Christian nations."[94] Therefore, as the missionary motivation of love developed, there was a shift: "The pagans' pitiable state became the dominant motive for mission, not the conviction that they were objects of the love of Christ."[95]

Particularly during this missionary period, there was a very strong link between the fifth and sixth theological constants, that is, the church's valuation of the *human nature* and *culture* of the non-Christian, non-Western peoples. Feelings of religious and human superiority quite naturally led to cultural superiority. While these attitudes were already evident in a significant way during the period from the sixteenth century to the first part of the eighteenth, they became much more pronounced. "The Enlightenment . . . together with the scientific and technological advances that followed in its wake, put the West at an unparalleled advantage over the rest of the world."[96] The missionaries from Europe and North America came out of a context that assumed the supremacy of Western culture and "Western religion," that is, Christianity, in a single breath. Even among theologians, who differed in their theological appreciation of world religions, their shared presuppositions included the following: "a common inability to take seriously any norms or testimonies not originating in Western Christendom

[and] an unwillingness to grant exotic cultures the kind of hearing automatically expected for Christian and Western values."[97]

Within such a context, both Protestant and Roman Catholic missionaries in general were blind to their own ethnocentrism and followed a more *tabula rasa* approach in terms of the interaction between gospel and culture. Even when *indigenization* (the Protestant term for what Catholics called *accommodation*) became the official policy for many Protestant mission societies, "it was usually taken for granted that it was the missionaries, not the members of the young churches, who would determine the limits of indigenization."[98]

While there was a growing separation of church and state during this time, the political and economic forces of colonialism, manifest destiny, and imperialism reflected and reinforced the world view and theology outlined above. Within this context, William Carey easily saw civilization and the spread of the gospel as hand-in-hand goals to be accomplished. Cardinal Lavigerie reminded his missionaries on their way to Africa that they were working for France as well as for the reign of God. Samuel Worcester described the objectives of the ABCFM as "civilizing and christianizing," in that order.[99] In his massive three-volume work *Christian Missions and Social Progress*, James Dennis spelled out in great detail the social evils of the non-Christian world and the role of "missions as a factor in the social regeneration of the world."[100] The rift and tension regarding the overall aim of mission grew within the missionary movement during the nineteenth century, with persons like Rufus Anderson strongly stressing evangelizing over civilizing and the Social Gospel movement stressing social justice over explicit proclamation. However, they all were basically operating out of a perspective of Western cultural superiority.

As is clear from our study of all missionary periods, the gospel is always presented through and affected by the cultural lens of the missionary to some extent. At the same time, a few missionaries were against imposing Western culture; many missionaries defended the interests and dignity of the colonized peoples; and others understood their efforts as a positive response to past sins of the West, particularly regarding its part in the slave trade — "striving toward restitution for the wrongs inflicted on other races."[101] Rufus Anderson strongly promoted the establishment of self-reliant Christian communities free of the Western idea of Christianity. In addition, it is important to remember that, first of all, the culture brought by the missionaries also had positive consequences for non-Western peoples, who, second, were not simply passive recipients but rather active participants in incorporating Christianity and Western culture within their changing world. Lamin Sanneh and Andrew Walls have reminded us that local people themselves have been the primary agents of evangelization, and that the translation of the scriptures into local languages has afforded an opportunity to preserve their languages and the cultures that they embody.[102]

The *ecclesiology* underlying the Roman Catholic understanding of mission basically remained the same as it had been in the previous missionary period, that is, the extension of the church as an institution. Within Protestantism, the understanding of church in mission took on several forms at this time, but here also "the doctrine of the church functioned primarily in defense of the church as institution."[103] The Protestant missionary movement coming out of the Evangelical awakenings was predominantly nondenominational and ecumenical, with the primary emphasis on saving the souls of individuals; "the formation of Church on the mission-field was a corollary of their labours, but not their primary target."[104] However, beginning with the Lutherans around 1830, with the three-hundredth anniversary of the adoption of the Augsburg Confession, denominational identity, mission and competition emerged, and with them, the mission theology of church-planting *(plantatio ecclesiae)*. For example, even the ABCFM and the LMS eventually became "denominational."[105]

Within this context, Henry Venn and Rufus Anderson, as mentioned above, were the major promoters of establishing "self-governing, self-expanding and self-supporting churches." Among other things, this three-self formula reflected a greater respect for the role and status of non-Western Christians. Furthermore, this strong ecclesiocentric missionary perspective implied "that churches in other lands achieved selfhood, authenticity, and maturity insofar as they themselves became missionary."[106] Unfortunately, these ideals did not often turn out as expected. Bosch offers the following description and critique:

> So the Protestant variant of *plantatio ecclesiae* was the carving out of small, exclusive "territories" of Anglicanism, Presbyterianism, Lutheranism, and the like. The "advance of the gospel" was measured by counting tangible things such as the number of baptisms, confessions, and communions, and the opening of new mission stations and outposts.
>
> The church had, in a sense, ceased to point to God or to the future; instead it was pointing to itself. Mission was the road from the institutional church to the church that still had to be instituted.[107]

The development of the faith missions in the second half of the nineteenth century represented a swing back to a more ecumenical spirit and a nondenominational model, which was more interested in eschatology than ecclesiology. The church was seen not so much as a body but more as a group of individuals. Wilbert Shenk summarizes this situation in this way:

> This was the theological womb of the modern missionary movement: missionary theory based on soteriology as personal experience. . . . As a result, the emphasis in missionary practice fell largely on the ecclesiastical and sociological aspects of the church—its organization, growth toward independence of foreign sponsorship, numerical expansion, and affiliations with other church bodies, rather than its ecclesiological dimension.[108]

While recognizing the limitations of this ecclesiology, Andrew Walls describes several aspects of the positive impact of nineteenth-century missionary societies and faith missions on the Protestant understanding of church in the following way:

They [faith missions] continued the revolutionary effect of the voluntary society on the Church, assisting its declericalization, giving new scope for women's energies and gifts, adding an international dimension which hardly any of the churches, growing as they did within a national framework, had any means of expressing. After the age of the voluntary society, the Western Church could never be the same again.[109]

Turning now to *eschatology*, within Protestantism "there was an intimate correlation between mission and millennial expectations,"[110] with millennialism defined as "the biblical vision of a final golden age within history."[111] During the early part of the nineteenth-century missionary movement, millennial concerns were both the motivation for mission and the sign of the dawn of the millennium. With the movement of denominationalism in North America beginning around 1830, eschatological positions would begin to shape and characterize two different models of mission that find their roots in the nineteenth century but become more distinctive after the Conference of Edinburgh in 1910 and up to the present day.

First of all, the premillennialists shared to some degree the following: the right and duty of private judgment in interpreting scriptures, the doctrine of biblical inerrancy and literal truth, and a very strong emphasis on the imminence of the parousia.[112] Seventh-Day Adventism had its roots here in the mid-nineteenth century, and missionaries like J. Hudson Taylor began using Matthew 24:14 as their central text, with the understanding that Christ's return was dependent upon the successful fulfillment of the missionary task and that the latter could hasten the former (see 2 Pet 3:12). Evangelist Dwight L. Moody, a prominent example of this perspective as it developed toward the end of the nineteenth century, stressed the importance of individual choice, personal rather than structural sin, and a more negative view of non-Christian religions. Twentieth-century Christian traditions that trace their roots to this movement/model are Adventism, the holiness movement, Pentecostalism, fundamentalism and conservative Evangelicalism.[113]

Second, the postmillennialists and the amillennialists had little or no interest in focusing on the cataclysmic end of the world and history but rather were concerned with what should be done now for "building the kingdom."[114] As things evolved in time, they committed themselves more to the societal rather than the individual elements of salvation and mission, tended to have a more positive attitude toward other religions, and were influenced by the historical-critical method in biblical studies and the importance of history[115] for theology in general—both of which had been developing primarily in Germany for some time. "Belief in Christ's return on the clouds was superseded by the idea of God's kingdom in this world, which would be introduced step by step through successful labors in missionary endeavor abroad and through creating an egalitarian society at home."[116] In this understanding, Jesus became "the benevolent and wise teacher,"[117] while Christ the Redeemer remained the primary image within the soteriological perspective of premillennialism. This second model was mainly represented by the so-called mainline Protestant churches and agencies and the Social Gospel movement.

While these two mission models will become more distinct and distant from each other as we move through the twentieth century, during the nineteenth-century missionary period they were held together within one missionary effort by the gifted leadership of such people as Robert Wilder,[118] John R. Mott, Robert Speer and J. H. Oldham, who served as excellent mediators and are eloquently described by Bosch in the following way:

> Each of them could look back upon a profound religious experience, a factor which might have caused him to be at odds with some of the more radical elements of the Social Gospel, but each also elected to stay within "mainline" American church life, which often made him suspect in fundamentalist and other extreme premillennialist circles. Frequently, however, their stature and personal integrity helped them bridge gaps where no communication appeared possible. The result was that the movements they helped to create or in which they participated, succeeded in winning the loyalty and support of groups at both ends of the spectrum.[119]

The World Missionary Conference in Edinburgh in 1910 was another key example of their ability at that time to bring together postmillennialists, premillennialists, mainline and Evangelical mission agencies.

Despite their differences in perspective and aim, both models assumed the superiority of Western culture and were influenced by the Enlightenment, with its rationalism, pragmatism, secularism and optimism. "Even where the proponents of pre-, post-, and amillennialism disagreed fiercely about missionary programs and priorities, they did so on the shared assumptions of the Enlightenment frame of mind."[120]

While women, the majority of missionaries in most cases, were working within both mission models and therefore shared this Western ethnocentrism, Dana Robert points out that one of the consistent general characteristics of North American women's mission thought and practice was holism, which avoided the separation of the evangelizing and civilizing aims of mission.[121] As noted above, this led to conflict with the policy of Rufus Anderson and the ABCFM, which minimized the value of women's work in education and "social uplift." In the second half of the nineteenth century, "Woman's Work for Woman," with its "belief in the inseparability of body and soul, of social context and personal religion, and of evangelistic, educational, and medical work was a central contribution to the mission theory of the period."[122]

Let us now turn our attention to the theological underpinnings for the Roman Catholic mission model of this time period. The two major Catholic theological issues at this time were, first, the nature and scope of the pope's authority, and second, the manner of the church's response to new trends in the world. The stance of the church on the second point had a major influence on the shape of mission. Relying heavily on deductive reasoning and neo-Thomistic philosophy and theology, the Catholic Church defended its traditional position and rejected the ideas and movements associated with the Enlightenment, the French Revolution and rationalism. Officially, this was most clearly stated through the Syllabus of Errors in 1864 by Pius IX and the condemnation of modernism in 1907 by Pius X, which "also meant that the claims of history, culture and religious experience were ignored."[123] While this certainly had a strong formative impact on Catholic missionaries, people like Libermann, Lavigerie and Comboni promoted a more positive appreciation of and adaptation to indigenous *cultures*.[124] Although their approach was certainly much less accommodational in comparison with that of the earlier generation of Valignano, Ricci and de Nobili, they were stretching beyond the parameters of the official church in Europe in their time.

As with the Protestants, Catholic missionaries assumed the superiority of Western culture and were very much influenced by the spirit of colonialism and imperialism. Most understood "civilizing" and "evangelizing" to go hand in hand, which led to a holistic approach in mission, and that their missionary work contributed substantially to their national interests, as reflected in Lavigerie's comment above regarding working for France. Javouhey, Duchesne and Drexel are representative of the mission work of women in the areas of education, health, agriculture and charitable works. Many missionaries fought against slavery and defended the human dignity of indigenous peoples. People like Libermann and Comboni envisioned Africans being missionaries to Africans. Arnold Janssen,[125] the founder of the Society of the Divine Word and two women's missionary orders, emphasized the importance of incorporating the social sciences, particularly anthropology, which had begun developing as an academic discipline during the nineteenth century, into mission preparation and mission work.

Regarding *ecclesiology* and *soteriology*, the Catholic Church continued with the operative though not official theology of "outside the church, no salvation."[126] "Church" here meant the Roman Catholic Church, and such an understanding was an underlying motivation for competition between Catholics and Protestants. With the Christendom understanding, the primary goals of Roman Catholic missionary efforts were the Christianization of non-Christians and *plantatio ecclesiae*, that is, establishing local churches within the unity of the Roman Catholic Church and under the leadership of the pope. Catechists played important roles as lay leaders in many areas. Furthermore, the process of the Catholic Church reclaiming the right and responsibility for mission for itself, and not for the state, as in the previous missionary period, also began finding its way "into the pews." Catholic adults and children began explicitly to support mission efforts with money and prayer and to be better informed through the large number of newly established mission associations and mission publications. However, mission was still primarily seen as something done "in the missions by experts," who were celibate, whether as priests and/or members of religious societies/congregations. The theological link among church, mission and baptism would only arrive at center stage with the Second Vatican Council.

Christology for Catholics as well as for Protestants certainly had a central place in missionary motivation and preaching. For the most part, however, the Christ of the nineteenth-century missionaries was more divine than human, and missionary motivation was fueled by the theology of Jesus' atoning death on the cross. For missionaries of the Social Gospel and other practitioners of postmillennialism, Jesus' commitment to justice was an important motivating factor.

In terms of overall theological development, Justo González considers the nineteenth century—jointly with the sixteenth—as one of the two great moments of Protestant theology. and the most conservative century in the history of Roman Catholicism.[127] Roman Catholics (and Eastern Orthodox[128]) were trying to maintain traditional orthodoxy, but quite a number of Protestant theologians were trying to relate theology to the new thoughts and developments within their context, often by compromising the gospel message. The great religious awakenings within Protestantism during the nineteenth century sparked vitality and creativity in both theology and missionary activity.

As for Gonzalez's typology, Wesley came close to reflecting the vision of Type C theology (emphasis on history)[129] with, for example, his insistence on sanctification with a social and collective dimension, rather than justification on a purely individual basis. However, in mainstream developments in the nineteenth century, Protestant premillennialists and Roman Catholics strongly reaffirmed Type A theology (emphasis on law), which, on the negative side, tended to reduce the faith "to a series of rules of action and belief."[130] Post- and amillennialist missionaries were eventually influenced by some elements of Type B theology (emphasis on truth) "as they sought, within the historical process of Scripture, the eternal, universal, and immutable truths,"[131] and they often saw Jesus Christ more as a teacher than as a redeemer. The Eastern Orthodox Church with its positive attitude toward human nature and culture continued to develop within Type B theology.

IMPLICATIONS FOR THE THEOLOGY OF MISSION TODAY

Mentioning nineteenth-century missionary activity normally provokes images of colonialism and imperialism and points to the inherent danger of close affiliations between church and state. Without denying that "only too often, the religious and the national impulses were fundamentally not separable,"[132] they can not be blindly equated in all situations, since every context had its share of ambiguities, complexities, and variations.[133] Missionaries often were the ones who defended the rights of the indigenous peoples, and several others were skeptical of the correlation of mission with nationalism. Both circumstances at times led to tension between the missionaries and colonial agencies.[134] So, while these missionaries were primarily shaped by their context, with their blind spots and superiority complexes, their general concern for indigenous peoples often provided a much-needed *prophetic* conscience to the colonial movement.

Furthermore, some recent voices calling for a reinterpretation of the nineteenth-century missionary period belong to non-Western peoples who became Christians as a result of this missionary activity.[135] As one of his overall theses, Lamin Sanneh (from Gambia) maintains "that Christianity from its origin identified itself with the need to translate"[136] out of one cultural-linguistic world to another, and this translatability of the gospel into another culture and language has over and over again shown its dynamic potential to create something new, which in turn relativizes the previous translation. No translation can or should be absolutized. Turning his attention to the nineteenth century, Sanneh shows how people like Carey and Livingstone,[137] without realizing the full consequences of their actions, were agents in this process of providing and entrusting vernacular translations of the Christian message to peoples in India and Africa, often leading to indigenous self-affirmation, and what today we call *inculturation:*

> Armed with a written vernacular Scripture, converts to Christianity invariably called into question the legitimacy of all schemes of foreign domination—cultural, political and religious. Here was an acute paradox: the vernacular Scriptures and the wider cultural and linguistic enterprise on which the translation rested provided the means and occasion for arousing a sense of national pride, yet it was the missionaries—foreign agents— who were the creators of that entire process. I am convinced that this paradox decisively undercuts the alleged connection often drawn between missions and colonialism. Colonial rule was irreparably damaged by the consequences of vernacular translation—and often by the other activities of missionaries.[138]

This dynamic is at work both through the Protestant emphasis on translation of the scriptures and the Catholic emphasis on cultural assimilation and adaptation.

Related to this discussion is the repeated accusation that missionaries destroyed non-Western cultures. Certainly, prejudice and ethnocentrism based on the superiority complex of Western culture and the white race were reflected to various degrees in missionary attitudes and practices; this is not to be denied or condoned. However, as noted above, certain missionary activities explicitly or implicitly also affirmed certain aspects of the indigenous cultures. On another point, this accusation portrays non-Western peoples as helpless and incapable of resisting and/or accepting Western cultural, political and/or religious elements. On this score, Sanneh states that "to view Africans as a victimized projection of Western ill will is to leave them with too little initiative to be arbiters of their destiny and meaningful players on the historical stage."[139] To use Peter Berger's sociology of religion language,[140] one should not forget that Africans (as all peoples) are active social beings constantly involved in, not only maintaining, but also constructing and reconstructing their world (world view). Andrew Walls describes this dynamic in religious terms:

While some of the features of the evangelical religion that originated the missionary movement—certainly the high place given to Scripture and the recognition of immediacy of personal experience—have been regular features of African Christianity, it is important to note that the fruit of the work of evangelical missionaries has not simply been a replication of Western evangelicalism. The Christian message that they set loose in Africa has its own dynamic, as it comes into creative and critical encounter with African life with its needs and hurts. . . . Africans have responded to the gospel from where *they* were, not from where the missionaries were; they have responded to the Christian message as they heard it, not to the missionaries' experience of the message.[141]

These missiological reflections are all founded upon the theological basis of the *missio Dei*. First of all, it reminds us that God's word has its own energy and power to spark ever-new inculturations, which can both enrich and challenge other inculturations. Second, while missionaries need continually to critique their own context—world view, culture, nation and church—in the light of the gospel, God's mission is at work with or without missionaries in surprising ways. Third, the invitation to and participation in the *missio Dei* continues the pattern described in the Acts of the Apostles of passing over human-made distinctions of culture, race, gender and class. The contribution of *non-Western peoples* to mission, noted throughout this chapter, will continue to increase as we move into the twentieth century in the next chapter. As we know, this was a common phenomenon in earlier periods of Christianity.

In concluding these reflections and this chapter, rather than entering into the particular discussion[142] of the missiological significance of William Carey and the Serampore Trio, we make a few general comments regarding the society model. First of all, it provided the new means and structure—supra-congregational and supra-parish—within the Protestant traditions to tap and direct the tremendous missionary vigor of thousands of committed Christian individuals. Second, the ecclesiology question of the interconnection among the congregation/denomination, the mission agency, and the "mission field"/new congregation caused a lot of tension. These two points raise the challenge of reconciling the movement of the spirit with the institutional church. Third, this new model opened up new avenues of direct mission involvement to laity and women in unprecedented ways, although it proceeded through a movement of ebbs and flows. Fourth, as with all cases of contextualization, the society "business" model that emerged out of that particular Western world view brought short-term and long-term benefits and deficiencies to the missionary effort.[143]

Wilbert Shenk observes that the "Great Century" of Latourette "meant less in terms of the actual numbers of new adherents won to the Christian faith . . . than in the formative impact the movement had on the Christian world," and claims that "the nineteenth century remains crucial because of the way it shaped the twentieth."[144] We will move on to the missionary period of the twentieth century in the next chapter.

8

Mission in the Twentieth Century (1919-1991)

The Emergence of World Christianity

World War I (1914-1918) broke the heart of Europe and the United States—diminishing the high hopes placed on the ability of science, "progress" and the Enlightenment to create the world the way it was meant to be. The "Great War" also deflated the optimism represented at Edinburgh, marking the end of the nineteenth-century period of mission. While the political forces struggled to rebuild, but in many ways set up a situation that made World War II inevitable, a new missionary movement began to emerge slowly but surely.[1] This period had less naive optimism and Western cultural certainty but plenty of energetic commitment. Benedict XV's mission encyclical *Maximum Illud* in 1919 and the establishment of the International Missionary Council (IMC) in 1921 marked the starting point of this new missionary moment, which in many ways began as a continuation of the society model but also included indications that something new was brewing. The missionary movement within Catholicism and Protestantism passed through a phase of ferment, transition and chaos during the sixties and early seventies before it experienced a tremendous rebirth, which also signaled the emergence of a new "World Christianity." The period covered in this chapter ends at 1991, the year after the encyclical *Redemptoris Missio* and the year the Catholic document *Proclamation and Dialogue* and David Bosch's monumental work *Transforming Mission* were published.[2]

Many new obstacles faced Christianity: the East Orthodox Church faced the consequences of the 1917 Russian Revolution, missionaries lost their lives during Communist-associated violence in China in the 1920s, the churches in Europe saw the rise of Hitler in 1933, the ancient Ethiopian church found itself in the grasp of Mussolini in 1935, and the Second World War (1939-1945) affected more of the world and the missionary movement than the First. As dramatic as these events were, the world would see many more changes before the end of the second millennium with the end of colonialism, the rise and fall of the Berlin Wall, the proliferation of many "local" wars, massive migrations of people, the reemergence of Muslim faith and influence, new economic and political centers, and the computer and Internet "revolutions."

In the midst of this whirlwind of change, which witnessed both the interconnectedness and unity of the world as never before, and the destructiveness and division caused by all forms of "tribalism" (from Hitler to Rwanda), the Christian faith continued to emerge in ways beyond human expectations. While Latourette called the nineteenth century the "Great Century" regarding mission, Andrew Walls asserts that "the most remarkable century in the history of the expansion of Christianity has been the twentieth."[3] Many observers would be shocked by such a statement as they look at the rapid erosion of the church in Europe. However, while Christianity was declining in one locality (the West), it was rising in many others. The end of the second Christian millennium marked the emergence of World Christianity, which will be more and more associated with the faith, action and thought of the Christians of Africa, Latin America, Asia and the Pacific. Not only did this represent a dramatic shift in demographics but also in Christian expression and experience. While evident within Catholic, Protestant and Orthodox traditions, it is particularly striking in the rapid emergence of new streams of Christianity, particularly within the movements of Pentecostalism and African Initiated Churches (AICs). And all of this is a result of the missionary movement carried out by both Western and non-Western Christians in a variety of ways.

THE TWENTIETH-CENTURY WORLD

The Social-Political Context

In the early 1900s, at the height of the age of imperialism and colonialism and after a hundred years (1815-1914) of relative peace in Europe, the social-political-economic power and prestige of Western Europe in the world were at a peak. Their decline began with World War I and continued with the rise of Hitler and Mussolini, the economic depression of the 1930s, the fall of Singapore in 1942, the devastation of World War II and the breakdown of colonialism. During this same period, the Russian Revolution of 1917 signaled the entrance onto the world stage of Marxist Communism, which by 1953 had extended its influence from Russia into most of eastern Europe, central Asia, North Korea and China. By this time, the United States had survived the crash of Wall Street (1929) and the Second World War to emerge as the prominent political, economic, military and ideological power in the Cold War against Communism, the primary antagonist of Christianity. Accompanying these political developments, the horror of human tragedies included the deaths of ten million victims of Stalin's social reconstruction and six million Jews during the Holocaust, and the destruction of two-thirds of the city area of Hiroshima and half of Nagasaki by atomic bombs. In former colonies, the movement toward political independence began in Asia with India and Pakistan in 1947 under the leadership of Mahatma Gandhi, Mohammed Ali Jinnah and Jawaharlal Nehru; in sub-Saharan Africa with Ghana in 1957 under Kwame Nkrumah; and in the Pacific Islands with Western Samoa in 1962 as a result of the Mau nationalist movement.

While 1945 was a very significant transition year, Timothy Yates proposes that the 1960s "may prove to have been the greater transition."[4] During this decade of transition and chaos, particularly in North America and Europe, societal norms and values were challenged by the youth in Vietnam War protests, by student riots in Berkeley, Paris and many other campuses, and by Martin Luther King, Jr., and the civil rights movement. A "sexual revolution" and "drug culture" also characterized this period, and the assassinations of Martin Luther King, Jr., Malcolm X, and John and Robert Kennedy further shook up the world. On the political scene, the Cold War between the United States and the USSR (Union of Soviet Socialist Republics) almost exploded with the Bay of Pigs fiasco in 1961 and the Cuban missile crisis the following year, and the Cold War turned the world map into a chess board. The resistance of the white government to dismantle apartheid in South Africa, despite the fact that political independence movements were occurring across Africa, was signaled with the killings in Sharpeville in 1960. Mao Zedong provided leadership for the Cultural Revolution in China in 1966. The Six-Day War in 1967 between Israel and its Arab neighbors set the boundaries that continue to be a source of tension today. The strong hold of the USSR on its satellites was demonstrated by its suppression of the "Prague spring" in Czechoslovakia in 1968. The youth uprising in Mexico was viciously suppressed in the same year.

In the late 1980s, the world was shocked as it witnessed the overthrow of one Communist rule after another, symbolized by the fall of the Berlin Wall in 1989. Some historians consider that year to mark the end of the twentieth century. As the Cold War came to an end with the breakup of the USSR, a new world power was reemerging in the Muslim world. In the 1970s, oil-producing nations in the Middle East united to raise the price of oil significantly in the world market. This economic strength was soon accompanied by growing political and religious power, often in opposition to the United States and Europe. Another group of nations in east and southeast Asia, known as the Asian Tigers, emerged as an economic world power. However, world economic forces had shifted beyond national boundaries to multinationals, and most of the third-world countries[5] found that they had moved from colonialism to a political-economic situation of neocolonialism. By the end of the second millennium, Western Europe formed an economic European Union; China, Vietnam, North Korea and Cuba were the only surviving Communist countries; much of Africa faced the challenges of local wars, poverty and AIDS; and South Africa gained independence under the leadership of Bishop Desmond Tutu and Nelson Mandela.

Relationships between the state and Christianity took many forms. The group called the German Christians identified with Nazi nationalism, while Confessing

Christians risked their lives in opposing this movement. Groups of Christians in South Africa vigorously supported apartheid; other groups of Christians vehemently opposed it. While churches and individual Christians actively or passively endorsed oppressive regimes, the number of martyrs who died for their faith and Christian values of justice and peace was perhaps higher than in any other century.

The Religious Context

Through the twentieth century, the primary perspective of Catholic and Protestant Christianity shifted from dominance and dependence, represented most clearly (for Protestants) at Edinburgh, to opposition to the threat of atheistic communism, and finally to being one religion among others in a pluralistic world, in which the relationship with Islam drew particular focus. Protestantism experienced both tension and rebirth as new religious expressions emerged in what would become distinguished as Evangelical, Conciliar and Pentecostal movements. Catholicism over this period likewise felt the pains and joys of new birth and renewal as the forms of expressing and experiencing Christian faith became much more diverse. The Eastern Orthodox Church (as well as other Christians) suffered under Communism from the Russian Revolution until the fall of the Berlin Wall, on the one hand, while Eastern Orthodoxy spread to all six continents and formed vibrant diaspora communities, on the other.

The missionary and religious optimism of Edinburgh was based on the assumption that Western Europe and Russia would continue as *the* centers of Christianity. Both crumbled fairly quickly during the years after 1917 in the face of Communism and secularization, but Christianity, rather than declining, experienced a religious revival and emerged as a global religion. In 1893, 80 percent of those who professed the Christian faith lived in Europe and North America, while at the end of the twentieth century almost 60 percent lived in Africa, Asia, Latin America and the Pacific. "Christianity began the twentieth century as a Western religion, and indeed *the* Western religion; it ended the century as a non-Western religion, on track to become progressively more so."[6] This demographic shift in Christianity, brought about by the missionary movement, has created two new realities today: a post-Christian West and a post-Western Christianity. The new religious forms of Christianity that are growing most rapidly are the African Initiated Churches and the Pentecostal churches. In addition, Evangelicalism and Catholicism are maintaining steady growth.

As for other world religions, European Judaism was threatened with extinction by the Holocaust, but its continuance was guaranteed by the establishment of the state of Israel. Islam experienced renewal through the twentieth century in a variety of political-religious contexts around the world, with its most significant growth occurring in sub-Saharan Africa. The emergence of many new forms within Hinduism characterized its renewal, which likewise had been intertwined with national independence and more recent political developments in India. Buddhism was also revitalized through its association with cultural loyalty in certain post-colonial contexts, particularly in Sri Lanka and southeast Asia. The external expressions of traditional religions significantly decreased over the century, particularly with the spread of Christianity and Islam, but the internal influence continued to be very meaningful for many. We are still feeling these same dynamics today.

The Institutional Context

Three streams emerged within the nineteenth-century Protestant ecumenical movement from the momentum of the Edinburgh Conference: the Continuation Committee eventually became the IMC in 1921; the Life and Work movement was primarily the fruit of the World Alliance for Promoting International Friendship and had its first conference in 1925; and the Faith and Order movement came from the vision of cooperation and held its first conference in 1927. The second and third developments merged into the World Council of Churches (WCC) in 1948. After much debate, the IMC was merged into the WCC in 1961. The growing tension between the liberal and conservative theological/ missiological perspectives led to the birth of the Lausanne movement in 1974 of those conservative churches and faith traditions that generally refer to themselves as Evangelicals and dissociate themselves from the WCC. The Protestant churches that continue to belong to the WCC usually call themselves Conciliar. The Orthodox Church and the Kimbanguist Church (one of the first AICs), joined the WCC in 1969.

For the Catholic Church in this period, there were five popes, four of whom were quite influential in their own ways. The pivotal person was John XXIII, who, to everyone's surprise, called the Second Vatican Council (1962-1965). This event set into motion major changes in the church both *ad extra* and *ad intra*. Rather than viewing the "world" as totally opposed to God's reign, the church began to "read the signs of the times" and to acknowledge the movement of God's Spirit outside the Catholic Church, leading it to more open and positive attitudes toward other churches, religions, non-Western cultures and society in general. Internally, the new image of church opened up avenues for collegiality on all levels, with laity and clergy working together and local churches forming a communion based not on uniformity but on unity in diversity. Since Vatican II, conservative and progressive camps and perspectives have struggled with each other in shaping the future of the post–Vatican II church. The shift in the center of gravity of Christianity to the non-Western world continues to reshape the institutions of Catholic and Protestant churches alike. Christianity in the twenty-first century will be influenced by their conservative, largely Pentecostal and charismatic forms of Christian life.[7]

In the following presentations of mission in the twentieth century, the year 1991, rather than 2000, will be the closing parameter. In order to gain a more appropriate perspective on history—with a better possibility for objectivity, accuracy and completeness—we have established a chronological "cushion" of

1991. Such an approach, we hold, does not at all distort the descriptions of twentieth-century mission models, but rather enables us to offer a more focused picture of a "moving target," since this missionary period is still in process.

MODELS OF MISSION IN THE CATHOLIC CHURCH: CERTAINTY, FERMENT, CRISIS AND REBIRTH

Robert Schreiter's description of the twentieth-century Roman Catholic missionary movement in terms of four periods provides an excellent general framework for this section.[8] After an initial period of certainty, the decade of the sixties, primarily through the Second Vatican Council, was the key moment of ferment and transition. After a time of crisis, Catholicism experienced a rebirth of its mission theology and practice, which were characterized by developments into diverse streams and expressions of the one Christian mission.

Certainty: From *Maximum Illud* to the Second Vatican Council

After recovering from World War I, the Catholic Church recommenced its missionary efforts with the same mission model of expansion and with the same belief that it had an exclusive claim to the truth. Benedict XV's 1919 encyclical *Maximum Illud*, subtitled *On Spreading the Catholic Faith throughout the World,* was the first of five mission encyclicals issued over the next forty years. It did not provide a theological basis for missionary work, and the goals of mission continued to be the winning of converts *(conversio animarum)* and the establishing of the local church *(plantatio ecclesiae)*. Regarding this latter goal, Cardinal Willem van Rossum,[9] the prominent prefect of the SCPF from 1918 to 1932, carried out the recommendations of Benedict XV[10] and Pius XI[11] to promote the formation of indigenous clergy and the ordination of indigenous bishops.

Another major influence on van Rossum regarding the cause for ordaining local bishops was the prophetic voice of Vincent Lebbe, a Belgian Vincentian missionary in China.[12] Having arrived the year after the anti-foreigner, anti-Christian Boxer Rebellion (1900) in China, Lebbe insisted that the time for Chinese bishops was overdue, that Chinese Christians should not have to become like foreigners in their own society, and that missionaries should distance themselves from European nationalistic interests to the point of missionaries becoming naturalized Chinese citizens in order to identify as closely as possible with the Chinese. On this final point, Stephen Neill compares Lebbe with Hudson Taylor.[13] Pius XI personally ordained the first six Chinese bishops (in the modern period) in 1926, the first Japanese bishop in 1927 and the first Vietnamese bishop in 1933. Pius XI also instituted the annual celebration of World Mission Sunday for the entire church, named Francis Xavier and the Carmelite nun Thérèse of Lisieux patrons of missionary work, and supported the resolution of the Rites Controversy, a process that was officially completed under Pius XII in 1941, almost three hundred years after it began.

As a result of World War I, Europe was not in a position, at least immediately, to revive Catholic missionary efforts abroad. About one-third of French seminarians and missionaries were killed during the war. In addition, accusations of nationalistic affiliations led to the expulsion of European, particularly German, missionaries in many places, and colonial countries were looking for English-speaking missionaries.[14] Due to these factors and to having witnessed the missionary vigor of their Protestant fellow citizens, many Catholics in the United States saw this postwar period as "America's hour" for overseas mission. Aware of the success of John Mott's Student Volunteer Movement for Foreign Missions (SVM) and of the presence of some Catholic student mission movements in Europe, Clifford King[15] and Robert Clark—both seminarians with the Society of the Divine Word (SVD) in Techny, Illinois—were instrumental in founding the Catholic Students' Mission Crusade (CSMC) in 1918. The CSMC over the years drew together thousands of seminarians as well as college and high school students from across the United States for study, prayer and participation in mission.[16] Congregations of men and women began sending out significant numbers of missionaries. In addition, in the 1920s and 1930s, U.S. bishops, the National Council of Catholic Women, the National Catholic Welfare Conference (NCWC) and the CSMC were among the groups involved in building up better relationships with Catholics in Latin America.[17] Over forty-five Catholic mission magazines printed in the United States were in circulation in 1930. The mission education programs of Maryknoll from the 1920s to the 1950s played a major role in shaping the understanding of mission work for U.S. Catholics. In the 1930s, Matthias Braun, SVD, translated and published the major works of German missiologist Joseph Schmidlin—*Catholic Mission History* and *Catholic Mission Theory*.

The establishment in 1925 of the Catholic Medical Mission Board in New York pointed to the importance of linking care of the body and spirit in the Catholic holistic sense of mission. A very influential person in this area was Anna Dengel.[18] The Austrian-born physician began her missionary work in 1920 in Rawalpindi, India, where she heard the call to respond to women's health needs, which could not be adequately addressed by male medical workers due to local cultural-religious customs. To gather further support for medical mission efforts, she came to the United States, where in 1925 she formed the Pious Society to provide medical help where it was most needed. This society became the Society of Catholic Medical Missionaries in 1936—the same year in which Pius XI lifted the ban on women religious becoming physicians. It was the first Catholic congregation of women to work as physicians, surgeons and obstetricians.

In 1942, there were over twenty-seven hundred U.S. Catholic missionaries involved in foreign missionary work, with the strongest concentration (651) in China.[19] As a representative of this latter group, Francis Ford was one of the first four Maryknollers (MM) to leave for China in 1918.[20] After serving for ten years as the head of the mission work in the northeastern part of Kwangtung

(Guangdong) province, he was appointed bishop of this area in 1935. In 1950, Ford was arrested by the Communists and sentenced to prison, where he died in 1952. With *Maximum Illud* as his guide, all his efforts were directed toward the establishment of a self-governing and self-reliant local Chinese church, with its own well-trained clergy, sisters and laity. Ford was one of the first to emphasize the role of religious women in direct evangelization, and furthermore, this was done in an innovative way, which became known as the Kaying method.[21] Instead of living in a large convent, the Maryknoll sisters went two by two to live in Chinese houses, which often also served for the women's catechumenate.

Alongside mission efforts in the areas of health and direct evangelization, Catholic missionaries also continued their tradition in education, hoping to extend a Christian influence on the wider society through its educated elite. While Protestants had founded a number of colleges in China, Catholics focused on establishing a single institution in 1925, which in a few years would be renamed Fu Jen University. Responsibility for this project was initially in the hands of Benedictines from the United States but was later handed on to the Society of the Divine Word, known for its work in the sciences, and the Holy Spirit Missionary Sisters, both congregations founded by Arnold Janssen. Paleontologist Harold Rigney, SVD, was the religious superior of Fu Jen after World War II and Chinese Liberation (1949); he was imprisoned by the Communists in 1952. Through his published memoirs, entitled *Four Years in a Red Hell*,[22] he would become one of the central figures—together with Maryknollers Joan Marie Ryan and Francis Ford, and Canadian-born Passionist Cuthbert O'Gara[23]—in the publicity surrounding the imprisonment of missionaries in China. These missionaries of the Cold War became the heroic images of Christianity against Communism, light against darkness, religiously, politically and economically. The fight against Communism began after the 1930s, particularly in the United States, and became very prominent in the 1950s under the leadership of Catholic senator Joseph McCarthy in the political arena and Bishop Fulton Sheen and Cardinals Francis Spellman and Richard Cushing in the ecclesiastical one.[24] Rigney's release and return to the States in 1955 was highly publicized within this environment. Opposition to Communism by both political and religious sectors soon extended its focus beyond the USSR and China to Korea, Vietnam, Cuba and Latin America.

While most Roman Catholic mission activity was focused outside of Europe and North America, Pius XI in a 1931 encyclical *Quadragesimo Anno* initiated the movement of Catholic Action, calling Catholic laity to address the situation of social-economic depression and unrest "at home." In the United States, Catholic Action influenced the CSMC, NCWC and working relationships between North American and South American Catholics. At this same time, another movement responding to the same situation was begun by a Catholic lay woman, Dorothy Day,[25] who has been called the most influential and significant person in the history of Catholicism in the United States.[26] As a college student, Day had rejected Christianity in favor of radical causes. She then experienced a series of traumatic events in her life, from which she emerged with a commitment to live a radical brand of Christianity. In 1933, with Peter Maurin, she began the *Catholic Worker* newspaper to address societal ills in solidarity with workers and the poor. The Catholic Worker movement grew to include houses of hospitality for the growing numbers of hungry and homeless during the depression years. Dorothy worked tirelessly not only to respond to the daily needs of the poor but to address the systemic evils causing poverty. Her commitment to non-violence was expressed in her protests regarding World War II, the Cold War and the threat of nuclear weapons. Dorothy Day combined her radical social positions, which led to accusations of her being a Communist, with a rather conservative Catholic piety. The Catholic Worker movement had spread throughout the country by the time of her death in 1980.

Catholic mission within the United States also involved the continuation of certain nineteenth-century efforts, particularly with Native Americans and African Americans.[27] In Chapter 7 we highlighted the work of Katherine Drexel and the Sisters of the Blessed Sacrament in this regard. Other congregations that began working within the African American community before 1919 and continued through the twentieth century include the Josephites,[28] the Spiritans, the Society of the Divine Word,[29] the Holy Spirit Missionary Sisters, the Society of the African Missions, the Missionary Servants of the Most Holy Trinity and the Franciscan Handmaids of the Most Pure Heart of Mary. Those who were involved during this same time period in the Native American community include the Jesuits, Benedictines and Ursuline Sisters. A new area of "domestic mission" began with the foundation of the Glenmary Society of Priests, Brothers and Sisters in 1937 by Howard Bishop to work in rural areas where there were very few Catholics. Religious congregations of women that were among the first founded specifically for mission work in the United States include the Mission Helpers of the Sacred Heart and the Religious of Our Lady of Christian Doctrine.

Most Catholic foreign missionaries continued to be celibate men and women—priests, brothers and sisters. One outstanding early exception was the Grail movement, an international women's association founded in Holland in 1921 and officially established in the United States in 1944.[30] In addition, a number of other individual lay persons in the 1920s and 1930s worked with men's and women's missionary congregations, most notably the Columban Society, Franciscan communities and Maryknoll.[31] Pius XII's 1943 encyclical *Mystici Corporis*, followed by his two mission encyclicals, *Evangelii Praecones* (1951) and *Fidei Donum* (1957), encouraged Catholic lay involvement in social action and mission. For example, in response to the specific call of *Fidei Donum* for missionaries in Africa, two lay organizations began in the United States in the 1950s: the Women Volunteers for Africa and Lay Mission Helpers of Los Angeles. In 1958, there were ninety-six Catholic lay missionaries serving overseas,[32] and the first Catholic national conference on lay mission was held in Chicago the following year.

Fidel Castro established the first Communist government in the Western hemisphere in Cuba in 1959. Grave concern over the further spread of Communism, combined with the increased activity of Protestant missionaries in Latin America, motivated the Catholic Church in the United States to devote a significant portion of its financial and personnel resources to Latin America in the 1960s. Within this context, many dioceses responded positively to the 1960 Vatican-endorsed lay missionary program, Papal Volunteers for Latin America. The total number of lay missionaries increased during the 1960s and early 1970s but was small compared with the number of Protestant laity in mission.

Returning to the other side of the Atlantic, one person who offered an alternative approach to mission in the twentieth century was Charles de Foucauld.[33] The early adult years of this Frenchman were spent in wandering both spiritually and geographically—from the life of an aristocrat and a soldier in Morocco to the life of an ascetic in Jerusalem. Foucauld lived for a while in a Trappist monastery in Syria but then left the Trappists and did volunteer work for a community of Poor Clares in Nazareth and Jerusalem. After being ordained in 1901, he went to French Algeria as a hermit to live what he called "the life of Nazareth." Foucauld first went to the oasis in Beni-Abbes but then settled in the mountain area of Tamanrasset. Austerity, penance, prayer and eucharistic devotion characterized Foucauld's life. He also practiced hospitality, bought the freedom of seven slaves, and cared for the wounded from battles between the Arabs and French. The Tuareg people, among whom he lived, considered him a holy person (marabout).[34] Foucauld died in 1916 at the hands of a Tuareg man under uncertain circumstances.[35] While his life and death predate the period covered in this chapter, his life gave the twentieth century a mission model of presence. Foucauld became more widely known after his death through his writings, and two religious congregations were founded according to the rule he had written—The Little Brothers of Jesus (1933) and The Little Sisters of Jesus (1936). These communities continue to live out this model of Christian presence in a wide variety of contexts.

In the midst of the disaster of World War II, Henri Godin and Yvan Daniel wrote a small paperback in 1943 entitled France, pays de mission? (France, a mission country?), in which they described a France without religion.[36] Such a statement shattered the geographical understanding of mission and Christianity. How was the traditional "sender" of mission to become the "receiver"? This sentiment would be echoed later in the phrase "mission on six continents" at the 1963 Commission on World Mission and Evangelism (CWME) conference in Mexico City. Attempts by the French to rebuild bridges between the "official" church and the masses included the efforts of Catholic Action and the Jocist, with their principles of observe, judge and act. However, the powerful image of Charles Foucauld in France also surfaced and inspired Cardinal Emmanuel Suhard to begin the priest-worker movement in 1944—calling priests to leave the rectories and get manual jobs—in order to have Christian presence on the docks and in the factories. While this movement struggled in its early years, it represented an alternative model of mission.

In terms of the pre–Vatican II Catholic theory of mission, the German missiologists (Münster School) developed the conversio animarum principle around the theme of God's salvific will, while the Francophone (French and Belgium) missiologists (Louvain School) developed the *plantatio ecclesiae* principle around the church as the concrete manifestation of God's will. Coming from another area of academia, Wilhelm Schmidt, SVD, linked anthropology with missiology.[37] As an accomplished linguist and ethnologist, he turned his energy to the history of religions and coordinated the efforts of SVD collaborators and other missionaries to collect data. Schmidt is best known for his twelve-volume study of the origin and development of religion and for founding the Anthropos Institute, which continues to foster links between professional anthropological study and missionary practice.

Many of the developments introduced in this section were precursors of changes that were to emerge in the Vatican II and post–Vatican II understanding of church and mission: Lebbe's call for denationalizing mission and de-Westernizing Christianity; Foucauld's example of a mission model of Christian presence; the vision of Pius XI for a church with mission at its center; a developing tradition of Catholic social teachings and action; Dorothy Day's prophetic witness of nonviolence and challenge to structural evil; Catholic Action, Anna Dengel, the Grail movement, Maryknoll sisters in China and lay missionary movements opening doors for greater involvement of and initiative by women and laity in mission and the church; Bishop Ford's vision for an indigenous local church and non-coercive evangelization; the priest-worker movement daring to address a post-Christian Europe as a context for mission; and Wilhelm Schimdt pointing to the essential link of culture and the social sciences with mission.

Ferment: Second Vatican Council

Pope John XXIII convoked the Second Vatican Council in 1962 to be an *aggiornamento* (updating) for the Catholic Church. Eight hundred of the twenty-three hundred bishops attending this global council came from Africa, Asia and Oceania. A preparatory commission, consisting mainly of members of the SCPF, had already begun working on the mission document in 1960. However, after three drafts of the document were not accepted by the council fathers, because it did not sufficiently represent current mission experience or other theological developments of the council, the drafting commission was reorganized under the leadership of Johannes Schütte, the SVD superior general.[38] The *Decree on the Church's Missionary Activity in the Church, Ad Gentes* (AG), was accepted during the final session of the council in 1965.

Robert Schreiter points out three major theological developments in AG and other council documents that define the tensions that would underlie the crisis of Catholic theory and practice of mission in the following twenty years.[39] First, AG begins with *a trinitarian locus for the origin of mission*. The implication is that mission is to be part of the very nature of what it means to be a Christian and to be church. "Mission became, therefore, more than an extending of the perimeters of the church, it was to be something motivating the very heart of the church, not because some command had been laid upon the faithful, but because by being missionary the church was drawn into the life of the Trinity itself."[40] Also, the communal trinitarian image moves mission away from confrontation and toward invitation. While proclamation remains the prominent means of mission, it is to be done in a more dialogical way. Also, Christian presence and witness may be the only form of mission in certain situations (AG 6). Mission became more fundamental but also more vague.

The second major development of the Vatican Council was *an expanded understanding of the church*, a development most clearly found in the decree on the church, *Lumen Gentium* (LG). While there are some vestiges of the hierarchical understanding of the church, which dominated the ecclesiology of the Counter-Reformation and papal pronouncements of the nineteenth century and early twentieth century, the major image of the church presented by LG is that of the church as the pilgrim people of God. With this image, the church's nature is seen as more provisional, imaging a group of people in a common search for the fulfillment of the kingdom or reign of God. In this sense, the church pointed to the kingdom but was not equated with it. Another council document, *The Pastoral Constitution on the Church in the Modern World, Gaudium et Spes* (GS), spelled out the implications of such a shift. The church was now called into a positive dialogue with the world. While the church and membership in it are still important as the visible sign and sacrament of salvation, it is the reign of God, not the church, that is primary, and so the necessity of the church is less well defined. Furthermore, the *Decree on Ecumenism, Unitatis Redintegratio* (UR), opened up the door for new relationships with other Christian churches. This built on the breakthrough statement of the council that the true church of Christ *subsists* in (but is not identical to) the Catholic Church (LG 8).

Third, the Second Vatican Council introduced *a new understanding of the nature of other religions*. AG reaffirmed the theological thread from the patristic period, which acknowledged the value of elements in other religions in preparation for receiving the gospel. However, the *Declaration on the Relationship of the Church to Non-Christian Religions, Nostra Aetate* (NA), took this a step further. This document was initially intended to address the relationship with the Jews, a relationship that had been strained due to the church's ambiguous stance to fascist governments. However, NA expanded its scope to include all world religions. In this context, Christianity is called not only to learn about but also to learn from the religious ways of others. Christians are to "enter with prudence and charity into discussion and collaboration with members of other religions" (NA 2), not with a spirit of superiority but with an attitude of dialogue. While the document certainly affirmed that salvation for all is through Christ and that Christians have the duty to witness to their own faith, it opened the door for the theological debate regarding the role of salvation in other religions and the role of the church in this context. Furthermore, the *Declaration on Religious Liberty, Dignitatis Humanae* (DH), acknowledged that all people should be able in good conscience to seek truth and God freely, without coercion. Again, mission is more open but less clear. In summary, Schreiter asserts, "It seems clear that the frontiers pointed to by questioning the nature of mission, the church, and the relation to other religious traditions marked out the territory that would need to be explored."[41] This questioning contributed to the missionary crisis that would follow.

Crisis: The Decade after the Council

The decade of the sixties was a period of upheaval and tension, which in turn contributed to the missionary crisis. These years witnessed the rise of a youth culture, which questioned traditional authority; the fall of the political status quo, with the rush of more and more colonies toward independence; and an overly optimistic view of the world and humanity, which expressed itself in the theology of secularization. Within Protestantism, the Uppsala Assembly (1968) marked the high point of tension and division between Evangelicals and Conciliars. For Roman Catholics, the updating introduced through the Second Vatican Council brought refreshing new life but also chaos. Liturgical reform and the move toward the use of the vernacular often led to confusion, resistance and abrupt overnight changes; thousands of priests, sisters and brothers left rectories and religious communities; and social and political agendas sometimes fueled further tensions within the church.

Initially, Catholic missionaries felt that their experiences and concerns were reflected in the council documents, and the number of missionaries increased until 1968. However, the impact of the exodus of priests and religious at this time around the world signaled the beginning of a steady decline. In addition, some began questioning the need for missionaries at all. Federico Pagura, as bishop of the United Methodist Church of Panama and Costa Rica, already in 1964 had issued a challenging statement, "Missionary Go Home . . . or Stay."[42] A few years later Ivan Illich called for North American Catholic missionaries to withdraw from Latin America and to focus their efforts on confronting the political and economic policies and structures back home that contributed to maintaining the situation of poverty of their Southern neighbors.[43] In a historically significant address, Ronan Hoffman shocked the U.S. Catholic audience at the 1967 annual meeting of the mission-sending societies with his declaration of the end of the foreign missionary era, as it has been known, and his call for dismantling the current missionary organization and structure, including the SCPF (so that the whole church might become missionary).[44] Furthermore, Hoffman's view that the secular world, not the church, sets the agenda for mission parallels the thought of his Protestant contemporary Johannes Hoekendijk. In 1971, Protestant church leaders John Gatu of Kenya and Emerito Nacpil of the Philippines officially proposed a missionary moratorium. This was not to question the necessity of mission itself but rather developed into a summons to cease sending Western missionaries and, for example, to use financial resources to support indigenous third-world church workers rather than foreign missionaries. While much of this latter discussion took place in Protestant circles, it certainly had its impact on Catholics as well.

Furthermore, the theological developments of the council undermined the security and sureness of the missionary cause. The traditional forms and motivations for mission were being challenged and discarded. If the reign of God is in the world, why do people need to be brought into the church? If other religions are leading people of good conscience to God, why do they need to be invited to be Christians? How can proclamation and dialogue be reconciled?

Men's and women's missionary congregations had founded SEDOS in 1966 as a documentation and resource center for themselves and the wider church. A 1969 SEDOS-sponsored theological conference addressed the basic haunting question: Why mission at all?[45] Of the various conference papers, the one delivered by Johannes Schütte, according to Schreiter, "remains the best articulation of a theological response to the missionary dilemma of that period."[46] Schütte set up the question by using the well-known term *anonymous Christian,* a phrase coined by Karl Rahner, to explain how Christ's grace is at work implicitly in other religions.[47] Schütte's response was eschatological in nature. The goal of mission is to help in bringing everything ultimately together in Christ (Eph 1:10) by proclaiming Christ as the center of human history, by continuing the process of Christ's incarnation into every culture, and by working for peace and reconciliation, which are to be signs of Christ's imminent return and the establishment of his reign.[48] Although the final conference statement offered no breakthrough on the issue of the relationship of Christianity with other religions, it did begin laying a foundation for a new theology of mission. Within this understanding, the church with its more provisional nature is not the starting point but rather an anticipation of a future vision.

Despite programs of development begun in the early sixties by the United Nations and the United States, the oppressive situation of poverty only seemed to worsen in Latin America. When the Conference of Latin American Bishops (CELAM) gathered in 1968 in Medellín, Colombia, to read "the signs of the times" in this context, they developed an agenda beyond development or revolution to the transformation of unjust structures. Beginning with a reflection on and analysis of Latin American reality *(realidad)* they lay the foundation for what would become known as liberation theology. Gustavo Gutiérrez published his ground-breaking work *A Theology of Liberation* in 1971. The Medellín conference was a turning point not only for the Latin American church, but for the entire church. The 1971 Synod of Bishops in Rome discussed the integral relationship between justice and evangelization.

Like the birth of liberation theology, a variety of other movements represented both the turbulence of this period of crisis and hopeful signs of the new shape of mission. While the "preferential option for the poor" was the theme highlighted in the first post-council decade in Latin America, interreligious dialogue became a focus for Catholics in Asia; the interrelatedness of culture, gospel and church for those in Africa; the conversation between Christianity and secularization in Europe and North America; and the role of Christian faith in rapid social-political change in the Pacific Islands. Around the world, Catholic laity were participating more fully in the worship, ministry and mission of the church. The *cursillo* movement and the emergence of basic Christian (ecclesial) communities were signs of new life. Catholics were hearing and studying the Bible in their own language. Religious congregations began their own renewal process. With the 1969 dissolution of *ius commissionis*, according to which missionary congregations had been assigned "missions" or "mission territories" by the SCPF, bishops as heads of local churches now were responsible for mission activity within their own diocese; thus they were the ones to extend an invitation to a congregation to work in their diocese. Mission was not to be defined geographically, and every local church, to be "fully church," was missionary by its very nature.

In the first half of the 1970s, the Catholic Church in Papua New Guinea conducted a self-study — discussion at village, parish and diocesan levels on a variety of topics over a two-year period.[49] Representatives of the Catholic Church held a national gathering in 1975, four months before the country obtained political independence, to reflect upon the results of this process, and they affirmed that, out of many concerns, the primary issue or statement was "We are the church!" Rather than equating the church primarily with those who are foreign, ordained, vowed or full-time employees, the Papua New Guinean Catholics were acknowledging themselves as the pilgrim people of God.

Rebirth: *Evangelii Nuntiandi* to *Dialogue and Proclamation*

The 1974 Synod of Bishops — the third synod after the Second Vatican Council — met in Rome on the theme "Evangelization in the Modern World." The participants were not able to agree on a final document but requested that the pope compose one from their material at a later date. The following year, Paul VI issued the apostolic exhortation *Evangelii Nuntiandi* (EN), which marked the beginning of the rebirth of the Catholic missionary movement. Coming through the moment of crisis and insecurity, EN developed many of the fundamental principles of AG in light of the reflections and experiences of the first post-council decade. In reaffirming the essential missionary nature of the church (EN 14-15), the reign of God became the central theological focus of the theology of mission. The second chapter described the complex nature of evangelization, which includes explicit proclamation, witness of life, incorporation into the church community and the sending out of new evangelizers. Part of the document addressed some concerns regarding liberation theology, inculturation and an emerging consciousness of autonomy by some local churches. At the same time, EN affirmed the experience of the post–Vatican II church in its ground-breaking statements on the evangelization of culture (20), the liberating nature of evangelization (30), popular piety (48) and basic ecclesial communities (58).

In the next fifteen years, a number of documents represented further reflections and refinements on this still emerging understanding of mission. In 1981, SEDOS sponsored a major consultation, the conclusions of which spelled out the "how" of mission in terms of four elements: proclamation, dialogue, inculturation and liberation of the poor.[50] Regional conferences of bishops contributed to this discussion from their particular contexts.[51] The two major themes of the 1979 Third General Assembly of CELAM in Puebla, Mexico, reflected both a more conservative emphasis on development, communion and participation (Part III) and a re-affirmation of Medellín's emphasis on liberation and the preferential option for the poor (Part IV). The Fourth Plenary Assembly of the Federation of Asian Bishops' Conferences (FABC), which was held in Tokyo in 1986, affirmed the essential mission of the laity in living out their baptismal call in Asian societies. The United States Catholic bishops published two documents in 1986. *Economic Justice for All: Catholic Social Teaching and the U.S. Economy* pointed to implications of justice and mission. *To the Ends of the Earth* reminded the U.S. church of its general responsibility for mission. Celebrating its twenty-fifth anniversary, in 1986, the Association of Member Episcopal Conferences of Eastern Africa (AMECEA) in its meeting in Moshi, Tanzania, wrestled with several particular issues of inculturation, such as trial marriages and polygamy.

To commemorate the twenty-fifth anniversary of AG, Pope John Paul II in 1990 issued the encyclical *Redemptoris Missio* (RM). The document focused on mission *ad gentes*, that aspect of mission dedicated to proclaiming the gospel to those who have not yet heard it and to establishing the church where it does not yet exist. Such a Christocentric, ecclesiological emphasis was intended to counter current movements that were deemphasizing, the pope thought, the central place of Christ and the church in salvation history and the importance of mission *ad gentes*. The encyclical also pointed beyond a geographical sense, in that mission extends "beyond the frontiers of race and religion" (25) and into urban areas and the "modern equivalents of the Areopagus" (37), where Christians work in such areas as social communications, peace, development, liberation, scientific research and international relations. RM stands as the third monumental Catholic mission document of the last thirty-five years of the twentieth century. *Ad Gentes* (1965), *Evangelii Nuntiandi* (1975) and *Redemptoris Missio* (1990) will be treated in further detail in Chapters 9, 10 and 11, respectively, as statements of three different mission theologies today.

The most challenging question facing the church and mission at the end of the twentieth century, within both Catholicism and Protestantism, was the question of the relationship of Christianity and other religions, and this continues to be the case today. The thought of Catholic theologians such as Michael Amaladoss,[52] Gavin D'Costa,[53] Jacques Dupuis,[54] Paul Knitter[55] and Aloysius Pieris[56] represents a serious effort to overcome simple exclusivism and simple pluralism. As for the related issue of mission and interreligious dialogue, the Pontifical Council for Interreligious Dialogue and the Congregation for the Evangelization of Peoples (the new name of the SCPF) jointly published in 1991 an official document entitled *Dialogue and Proclamation* (DP).[57] This document offers a more nuanced and somewhat more open presentation on dialogue than that presented in RM. Proclamation and dialogue are both seen "as component elements and authentic forms of the one evangelizing mission of the Church" (DP 2).

Before concluding this section, the latter part of which consists of tracing the mission theology and models through written statements, it is important to remember that Catholic women and men from all six continents were those "on the ground," searching for and finding the expression of mission that was appropriate for their particular context. The well-known names of those who inspire others internationally include Mother Teresa, Bede Griffiths, James E. Walsh, Joseph Freinademetz, Vincent Donovan, Agneta Chang, Oscar Romero, Samuel Ruiz, Francisco Claver, Maura Clarke and Jean Donovan. Such men and women are representatives of the thousands who devoted their lives to serving God's mission both within and outside of their countries of birth. About 45 percent of the U.S. Catholic missionaries who served in the second half of the twentieth century were women. Many lay people—through such organizations[58] as the Maryknoll Association of the Faithful and the Volunteer Missionary Movement—have also served as missionaries. In looking around the room at the annual United States Catholic Mission Association (USCMA) conference, one notices the "graying" of long-term missionaries from religious communities and the influx of lay people in short-term mission. By the end of the second millennium, the majority of Catholic missionaries were born in the Third World. For example, the largest national group within the Society of the Divine Word, consisting of over sixty nationalities, shifted from German (since its beginning in 1875) to Indonesian in 1990. Another indication of the era of post-Western Christianity is the founding of many non-Western missionary societies such as the Missionaries of Guadalupe (Mexico), the Mission Society of the Philippines, the Missionary Society of St. Paul (Nigeria) and the Foreign Mission Society of Korea.[59]

THE INTERNATIONAL MISSIONARY COUNCIL IN PROTESTANTISM

We now describe the twentieth-century missionary movement within Protestantism in two major sections, with 1961 as the significant year separating them: first, the life of the International Missionary Council (IMC); and second, Evangelical and Conciliar Protestants in mission.

To carry on the work of the 1910 World Missionary Conference of Edinburgh, a continuation committee was established with John R. Mott as chairman and J. H. Oldham as secretary. The outbreak of World War I dealt a blow to Edinburgh's optimism and, from later perspective, brought an end to the nineteenth-century missionary movement. However, this committee became the International Missionary Council (IMC) in 1921 and the seed for the transition into the new missionary period within Protestantism. Initially, the society model continued to serve as the primary paradigm, but soon the twentieth century was shaping something new. Similar to what was occurring within the Catholic Church, mission within Protestantism passed through similar stages of certainty, ferment, crisis and rebirth. The following survey of the Protestant missionary models has benefited significantly from the insightful study by Timothy Yates in *Christian Mission in the Twentieth Century,* mentioned early in this chapter.

German and Anglo-Saxon Missionary Activity

One of the early developments came from German mission efforts. In contrast to the Anglo-Saxon ecclesiocentric method promoted by Henry Venn and Rufus Anderson in the nineteenth century, Karl Graul, the Lutheran mission theorist and first director of the Leipzig Mission, laid the foundations for the so-called *Volkskirche* model of mission.[60] The aim of this approach was to create a church grounded in the cultural or racial characteristics of a people *(Volk)*. Two representative missionaries who embodied and promoted this approach are Bruno Gutmann and Christian Keysser.[61] From their mission experience with people of a tribal society—Gutmann among the Chagga people in present-day Tanzania and Keysser among the Kate people in present-day Papua New Guinea—both men stressed the corporate nature of the congregation and church that was to build upon the God-given social relationships of that people. While they were criticized for ignoring the importance of individual conversions, Gutmann saw the necessity of individual faith to "lead to the creation of a godly community, which would provide the groundwork, by being rooted in the gospel, for the whole society and its transformed consciousness."[62] In the 1930s, Karl Barth criticized this approach for its high assessment of nature (and human culture) to the detriment of the essential role of grace, and others accused Gutmann and Keysser of approving the Nazi nationalistic use of the term *Volk* in promoting the Arian race back in their homeland.[63] While Barth's critique pointed out the dangers of the *Volkskirche* model, evident in the Nazi understanding of the *Deutschekirche*, this model did provide a theological basis for a more corporate approach of mission to some people (as seen earlier with the Germanic peoples and nomads of central Asia). It also pointed to the importance of a more positive assessment of human nature and culture, communal relationships and social context in general. It was a precursor to the later question of inculturation.

Another new stream of missionary thought and practice emerged more directly from Edinburgh within the Anglo-Saxon world on both sides of the Atlantic. Two of the most influential people calling for a new understanding of mission in the 1920s were Roland Allen[64] and Daniel Johnson Fleming,[65] who had been missionaries in China and India, respectively. Allen challenged missionaries to follow the example of Paul in planting churches after a comparatively short time, rather than delaying the process in following the policies of Venn and Anderson. Allen's position was, on the one hand, criticized as being too idealistic and as inappropriately trying to apply a New Testament model to very different contexts. On the other hand, his voice reminded and continues to remind missionaries of the danger of perpetuating a mission and a relationship of dependence. Vincent Donovan's *Christianity Re-discovered* has done the same from a Catholic context.[66] In addition, Fleming criticized missionaries for their attitudes of cultural and racial superiority, and he insisted on separating Western culture from indigenous expressions of Christianity.

The IMC conference of 1928 in Jerusalem emphasized a comprehensive approach to mission that would include challenging unjust economic and social structures in building up the kingdom of God. Also, the critiques of Allen and Fleming echoed in the calls of the Christian communities in Asia—China in particular—to be recognized as churches in their own right and for missionaries to work through the churches and not as representatives of mission boards. There were tensions between emphases placed on the role of social development and justice in mission and emphases placed on individual or corporate aspects of mission, the latter position similar to that of Gutmann.

The next major development was the 1932-1933 Laymen's Foreign Missions Inquiry (LFMI), financed by J. D. Rockefeller, sponsored by eight mission boards and their respective denominations in North America, and considered the most extensive study ever of mission by Protestants.[67] The seven massive volumes of data provided an excellent profile of mission in Asia but also pointed out very clearly the growing tension between conservative and liberal theological positions. For example, the China Inland Mission (CIM), the largest Protestant missionary group in China with a thousand missionaries, had withdrawn from China's National Council of Churches in 1926, presumably on theological grounds. Summarizing the information from the LFMI, W. E. Hocking[68] and others on the Commission of Appraisal compiled a book, entitled *Rethinking Missions*,[69] that stirred up an immense amount of controversy. It was criticized for shifting emphases to the social rather than the individual aspects of mission; to the kingdom rather than the church; and, more fundamentally, to Christ as teacher and example rather than as Redeemer (through the cross and the resurrection). The study was valuable for its serious appraisal and critique of the situation of mission and "the firm support and backing given to the younger churches in their search for independence and indigenization."[70]

Mission, Other Religions and Church Unity

The issue of the relationship of Christianity to other religions was a key issue raised at Jerusalem and in the LRMI, and it became the crucial question for mission.[71] After the 1928 conference, discussion of this issue continued through *The International Review of Missions* (IRM), a journal begun by Oldham in 1912. On the one side, the positive assessment of Bantu religion by the famous missionary-anthropologist Henri Junod[72] in recalling Justin Martyr's theology was one example of those who followed the "fulfillment" approach of J. N. Farquhar.[73] On the other side, Julius Richter,[74] the first full professor of missions at the University of Berlin, represented the exclusivist attitude as he insisted that Christianity must oust other religions in order to save their adherents, and Karl Hartenstein, a key figure in German missiology, stood on the side of Tertullian's emphasis of discontinuity between Christianity and other religions.[75]

Hendrik Kraemer, a Dutch lay missionary in Java, Indonesia, and an expert on Islam, was asked by the IMC to write a book to clarify the Christian position on this issue in preparation for the next IMC conference to be held in Tambaram, India, in 1938.[76] In this book,[77] writes Yates, Kraemer "was as eager to escape the liberalism of the LFMI report as he was the dogmatic and creedal orthodoxies of fundamentalism."[78] For many, Kraemer's Christocentric mission theology offered a counterbalance to Hocking's report, and both strands were present in the final Tambaram document.

Representing many missionaries who contributed to energizing and shaping the missionary movement at this time, the names of five from India can be singled out for their creative innovations. Timothy Yates links C. F. Andrews[79] with David Livingstone as "more influential as Christian 'icons' of mission than anyone else of their generation."[80] The British Anglican Andrews began his missionary life as a professor at St. Stephen's College in Delhi, eventually developed mutual lifelong friendships with the Bengali poet Rabindranath Tagore and Mahatma Gandhi, and became an international advocate on behalf of India's poor, particularly indentured laborers in South Africa and Fiji. The second person is E. Stanley Jones, a Methodist missionary from the United States, who broke new ground in the areas of evangelism, interreligous dialogue and peace-making.[81] He established an international ashram movement, was involved in peace initiatives between Japan and the United States, and twice was nominated for the Nobel Peace Prize. Third, V. S. Azariah, the first Indian bishop of the Anglican Church, was a visionary leader for an indigenous church in India and church unity movements throughout south Asia;[82] he is remembered for his gentle call already at Edinburgh for mutual relationships between Western missionaries and indigenous churches. Fourth is the medical missionary Ida S. Scudder, born in India into a missionary family.[83] Under the auspices of the mission board of the Reformed Church of America, she started a nursing school—quite a novel idea in Asia—that became the first graduate school of nursing in India; began roadside dispensaries to administer public health services into rural areas; founded a college to train women doctors; and in 1923 built a new and larger hospital in Vellore (state of Tamil Nadu). Scudder reminds us of Anna Dengel. A sign of the indigenization shift among women in mission is that the 1938 IMC conference "had the largest representation of non-Western Christian women in the history of ecumenical Protestantism."[84] Fifth, D. T. Niles was born in Ceylon (Sri Lanka), which was then part of India, into a family of Congregational and Methodist ministers.[85] Noted for his commitment to ecumenism and evangelism, Niles was a prominent figure in the WCC and in a number of Asian church organizations, and he is remembered for his description of the task of evangelism as "one beggar telling another beggar where to get food."

Despite the criticism of E. Stanley Jones that the Tambaram conference was too centered on the church rather than on the kingdom, the church continued to be emphasized in mission discussions and actions after 1938. The WCC was established in Amsterdam in 1948. A year earlier, the Church of South India was formed when Anglicans, Congregationalists, Methodists and Presbyterians formed an organic unity — the first unification ever of episcopal and non-episcopal churches. V. S. Azariah worked for over twenty years for this historic achievement.

Mission as Presence and Dialogue

The process of recognizing the autonomy and indigenization of the "new churches" accelerated after World War II with the beginning of the end of colonialism. Three British Anglicans were very influential in mission developments in the 1950s. M. A. C. (Max) Warren did missionary work in the northern Muslim area of Nigeria and later became secretary of the Church Missionary Society (CMS).[86] In Warren's general introduction to the Christian Presence book series as its editor, we find his famous image of "taking off one's shoes" when approaching the cultural-religious world of the other, since it is a holy place.[87] Second, Stephen Neill served as a missionary in India, where he was influenced by E. Stanley Jones and was very involved in the formation of the Church of South India.[88] One of the major themes that emerged during his years of teaching, writing and speaking was his commitment to the method of dialogue — a dialogue in which one must stand up for one's own truth *and* not impose it forcefully on the other.[89] The final figure in this trio is Kenneth Cragg, an Islamic scholar whose early missionary years were in the Middle East.[90] He proposed an approach of witness and dialogue to establish a "renewed relationship with Muslims in Christ."[91]

Since the founding of the WCC, there was discussion about its relationship with the IMC. Many saw the linking of the two structures as symbolic of theological integration of mission and church. Max Warren supported cooperation between the two organizations but vehemently opposed integration, because he thought that the conservative and more evangelical mission boards in the IMC would not be comfortable within the vision and bureaucracy of the young WCC. The integration of the WCC and the IMC was approved at the final IMC Assembly in Accra in 1958 and formalized at the WCC meeting in New Delhi in 1961. The WCC created the Division on World Mission and Evangelism (later the CWME) to succeed the IMC. The Orthodox Church brought to the New Delhi meeting its understanding of the importance of church unity, which would in turn lead to mission. It would officially join the WCC in 1969.

While the mission approach of presence continued to have influence after 1960, Donald McGavran (who will be discussed in further detail below) was one of the strongest emerging voices that called for restoring proclamation as the primary method of mission. He did, at the same time, recognize that the presence model was appropriate in certain circumstances.

EVANGELICAL AND CONCILIAR PROTESTANTS IN MISSION

The decade of the sixties with its social and political turbulence — marked by protests, chaos, prophetic voices and the height of the Cold War — was also a time of transition and ferment for church and mission. The Second Vatican Council was shaking and renewing the Catholic Church in a radical way. While some Protestant and Orthodox Christians rejoiced over the potentiality of new life coming from the WCC, others felt less and less at home with these developments, to the point that Protestants would eventually distinguish themselves according to these differences and form two distinct Christian movements, each with its own theology of mission.

One of the first signs that the turbulence of the sixties was likewise stirring within the mission movement was the strong endorsement of the "radical" missiological views of Johannes Hoekendijk[92] during the meeting of the World's Student Christian Federation in Strasbourg in 1960. The main theme of Hoekendijk's thought, which would have an impact on the WCC during the sixties, was that the secular world and not the church was the primary locus of God's activity; that mission should shift from the church to the world, which is in need of shalom; and that the church was important, but only as God's instrument and not as the focus of God's intention.

The new CWME held its first international mission conference in Mexico City in 1963. Moving beyond the previous issue of the relationship between older and younger churches, this gathering pointed to the fact that God's mission was not geographically bounded; rather, one should talk of "mission on six continents." The IRM, which became the official journal of CWME, altered its title from being a review of missions to a review of *mission*, and illustrated the point made by Stephen Neill in 1964 that "the age of missions is at an end; the age of mission has begun."[93] However, this was only one of several profound transitions in mission that were initiated in the sixties.

Evangelical Mission as Proclamation and Church Growth

While there had been significant differences according to conservative/liberal perspectives throughout the nineteenth-century Protestant missionary movement, such as between faith missions and the Social Gospel movement, prominent leaders had been able to maintain sufficient unity and balance. However, new developments in the mid-twentieth century led to further tension. In response to the integration of the IMC into the WCC and the influence of the thought of those like Hoekendijk, the conservative and more fundamentalist churches and mission bodies organized the Berlin Congress on Evangelism and the Wheaton Congress on the Christian World Mission, both in 1966. The primary significance of these two conferences was to give wider visibility to the Evangelical movement and "to offer a biblically based alternative to ecumenism."[94] The number of missionaries from the conservative Evangelical mission bodies was increasing at a much higher rate than the number sent by the liberal, more "ecumenical" ones; by 1960 the total number of missionaries from the former was about sixteen thousand, in comparison to approximately ten thousand from the latter. Another sign of this shift was that by 1966 there were more subscribers to *Christianity Today*, an Evangelical journal started in 1955, than to *The Christian Century*, a more ecumenically inclined journal founded in 1908.[95] The 1968 WCC Assembly in Uppsala (Sweden) echoed much of Hoekendijk's emphasis on the horizontal aspect of mission, with its primary goal being humanization rather than salvation. In response, Donald McGavran[96] raised the Evangelicals' common concern, "Will Uppsala betray the two billion?"[97] The distrust of the Evangelicals for the WCC began in Accra in 1958 and climaxed at Uppsala in 1968.

Sponsored by the Billy Graham Evangelistic Association, the International Congress on World Evangelization at Lausanne (Switzerland) in 1974 "represented a high-water mark for evangelical identity and solidarity in mission and evangelism."[98] Billy Graham, the "foremost Protestant evangelist of the twentieth century"[99] and honorary chairman of the Lausanne Congress, described the significance of Lausanne as no less than the recovery of the spirit of Edinburgh. The major breakthrough was the adoption of a theological consensus contained in the Lausanne Covenant, which affirmed the authority of the Bible and the uniqueness and universality of Christ.[100] John Stott,[101] another strong Evangelical voice within the WCC, was primarily responsible for drafting this as well as later Evangelical statements. While the primacy of proclamation for mission was very clear, the most controversial section of the covenant stated that social justice and evangelism were Christian duties. The rather surprising inclusion of this aspect was the contribution of the so-called radical Evangelicals and many from the Third World, such as René Padilla and Samuel Escobar. The Lausanne Committee for World Evangelization (LCWE) was established to carry on the mandate of the covenant, which continues to be the heart of what has become known as the Lausanne movement.[102] Another organization, the World Evangelical Fellowship (WEF),[103] which had been founded in 1951 to provide an alliance of Evangelical bodies, also has offered a number of important mission-related consultations,[104] sometimes in conjunction with the LCWE.

One particular model, which became prominent for Evangelicals in the United States, is the church growth movement,[105] which traces its beginning to the publication of *The Bridges of God* by Donald McGavran in 1955.[106] Ten years later, the movement established its center at Fuller Theological Seminary in Pasadena, California. In contrast to a traditional "mission station" approach, with its focus on individual conversions and a tendency to isolate individuals from their social context, McGavran proposed evangelizing a whole people through "people movements," the success of which can be demonstrated through statistical numerical growth. His methodology included the "homogeneous unit principle," which presumed that people receive the Christian message most readily if it comes through people who share their cultural, social and linguistic background. In response to those who criticized this latter point for promoting racist or ethnocentric Christian communities, leaders of the church growth movement explain that this principle describes the fact that initially, during what is called the "discipling" stage, mass movements proceed more naturally among like-minded people, and later, during the long-term "perfecting" stage, when the Christian community matures, they will reach out beyond their own cultural/ social boundaries.[107] While McGavran's assumptions formed the theoretical basis for LCWE's cross-cultural mission, further significant modifications have been made by Ralph Winter's work regarding the evangelization of "unreached peoples" and the concrete gathering of data by MARC (Mission Advanced Research and Communication Center), the research branch of World Vision Incorporated. Other "parachurch organizations" (for example, Wycliffe Bible Translators and Campus Crusade for Christ) have also been part of Evangelicals' missionary outreach.[108]

After the 1974 Lausanne conference, the LCWE held a number of smaller follow-up consultations. It sponsored its first major international consultation in Pattaya, Thailand, in 1980—the same year that CWME-WCC sponsored a missionary conference in Melbourne.[109] The occurrence of parallel conferences in the same year was a further indication of the development of two separate and distinct approaches to mission within Protestantism. At the same time, Evangelicals held a series of consultations with Roman Catholics between 1977 and 1984. The second major LCWE missionary conference, held in Manila in 1989 and popularly called Lausanne II, produced the *Manila Manifesto*.[110] This important summary document reaffirms the primacy of proclamation but also includes dialogue, a strong concern for the poor and a more holistic approach. In 1980, conservative Evangelicals contributed 66 percent of the financial support and 88 percent of overseas career personnel for North American mission agencies.[111] The WEF shifted its international headquarters to Singapore in 1987 and elected its first non-Western international director in 1992—indications of the growing international membership in the Evangelical movement.

Conciliar Mission as Wholeness, Pluralism and Enlightenment

The 1968 Uppsala Assembly led Evangelicals to distinguish themselves more distinctly from the WCC. However, the other mainstream within Protestantism, which today is called the Conciliar (ecumenical) movement, traces its line of continuity from Edinburgh to and through Uppsala and to the present. From its perspective, Uppsala was important for bringing mission into the secular world. However, there was a surprising voice from the secular world, when, as we said earlier, the African leader John Gatu initiated a call in 1971 for a moratorium on missionaries, a call that challenged Christian mission itself. This issue would be the focal point at the CWME meeting in Bangkok in 1973 and at the All-African Council of Churches a year later. While the final Bangkok document did address the conference's stated theme of salvation in proposing an integration of vertical and horizontal salvation and a reconciliation of personal salvation and social responsibility, most of its energy focused on the issues underlying the call for a moratorium, that is, the relationship between the North and the

South. The Bangkok meeting was a call for liberation and an end of Western cultural and ecclesiastical dominance, and it marked "the transition from Western mission agency dominance to two-thirds world leadership in the CWME."[112]

After the tumult of its predecessor in Uppsala, the Fifth Assembly of the WCC in Nairobi in 1975 was a moment of reconciliation and of discovering the new direction for mission. "Nairobi marks the beginning of a new phase in the development of ecumenical mission theology, as seen in the attempt to reconcile 'churchly' and 'worldly' approaches to mission."[113] The 1980 CWME conference in Melbourne was important for continuing this process of grounding the Conciliar mission theology through its reflection on mission from the perspective of the kingdom of God. Proclamation was understood in a holistic sense, the church's response to the situation of the poor was highlighted, and the rightful place of the church as an instrument for mission was reaffirmed. In 1982, the WCC Central Committee approved *Ecumenical Affirmation: Mission and Evangelism*—an excellent statement of convergence regarding the meaning of mission—as the result of a wide consultation process. *Ecumenical Affirmation* "may be the single most important ecumenical statement on mission in this period."[114] Later WCC and CWME assemblies, conferences and consultations continued to address specific issues and new concerns of mission, such as "wholistic" evangelism (Stuttgart, 1987); stewardship of creation (San Antonio, 1989); justice, peace and the integrity of creation (Seoul, 1990); and reconciliation (Canberra, 1991).[115]

Over this period of time, the relationship of Christianity to other religions also resurfaced as a central issue of mission. Wilfred Cantwell Smith and John Hick were important figures in the field of the theology of religion during this time. Cantwell Smith, who worked as a missionary in India, held that God is not bringing all people to Christ, but rather is drawing the believers of all religions, through their interactions with each other, toward a fuller awareness of God. John Hick called for a "Copernican revolution" in Christology. As we now know that the earth revolves around the sun, so Christians should move from a Christocentric understanding of Christianity to a theocentric one, that is, a pluralist position or what David Bosch categorizes under relativism.[116] While many Conciliar Protestant missionaries would not endorse the views of these two particular authors, Smith and Hick are representative of a wide range of inclusive and pluralist Christologies that provide the foundation for interreligious dialogue in a pluralistic world. Already before Uppsala, the WCC had established a subunit entitled Dialogue with People of Living Faiths and Ideologies, which during the 1970s held a number of meetings with peoples of other faiths. Through such a process of dialogue between living faith communities, and not just between scholars, the WCC in 1979 published *Guidelines on Dialogue with People of Living Faiths and Ideologies*.[117] In these guidelines, dialogue is neither a substitute nor a deceptive means for mission. On a wider basis, dialogue within Conciliar mission theology was becoming "a new style of ecumenical action and an expression of the Christian's approach to a wide range of activities of witness, service and community relationships in a pluralistic world."[118]

One of the key mission practitioners and theoreticians in the Conciliar ecumenical movement was Lesslie Newbigin.[119] After coming to the Christian faith through the British Student Christian Movement, he studied at Westminster College, Cambridge, and was especially influenced by Presbyterian theologian John W. Oman. Ordained in the Church of Scotland, he served in India as a missionary—for eleven years as a village evangelist, and then as bishop in the Church of South India. Newbigin attended the Tambaram conference and was one of the principal drafters of the breakthrough statement at the IMC Willingen conference of 1952. In 1959, he became general secretary of the IMC and guided its integration into the WCC; he continued to have responsibility for the newly established CWME until he returned to India during the period from 1965 to 1974. Upon his return to England, this preeminent theologian and ecumenical statesman devoted himself to teaching, writing, administration and pastoral work. In response to the secularist and pluralist society in which Newbigin now found himself, he established in 1982 the Gospel and Our Culture program as a forum for a missionary encounter with post-Enlightenment culture in the West.[120] This continuing project is one of many efforts of mission within the present context of the post-Christian West.

MODELS OF MISSION OF THE ORTHODOX CHURCH:
PRESENCE, PROCLAMATION AND ECUMENISM

From the Russian Revolution until Mikhail Gorbachev initiated the new order, the Eastern Orthodox Church in the USSR lived under the repression of Communism. The Orthodox were further constrained after 1945, as this atheistic ideology spread into Eastern and Central Europe and Muslim political and religious influence was renewed in the Middle East. While the church was unable to send out missionaries during these years, its mission activity was carried out in the diaspora through what has been called "the Orthodox presence approach."[121] Emigrants from these countries continued to follow the Orthodox incarnational model of assimilating themselves within their new society, establishing theological faculties, and eventually using the vernacular in their worship, such as English in the United States. At the same time, the focus of the diaspora communities was on serving the immigrants and preserving their religious/cultural identity and faith.

However, during the transitional decade of the 1960s, the Orthodox Church began shifting its interest toward reaching out beyond its own boundaries. Bishop Anastasios Yannoulatos[122] laid the foundation when he started both an Orthodox journal of mission studies in 1959 and an Orthodox missionary society, called *Porefthendes* ("Go ye"), out of the World Organization of Orthodox Youth Movements (Syndesmos) the preceding year. A 1967 consultation, held in Geneva and sponsored by Syndesmos, pointed out the challenge and responsibility the Orthodox Church had for sharing its faith in the West.[123] The Greek Orthodox supported missionary efforts initially in Uganda, Kenya, Korea and

Alaska, and later in other African and Asian countries. The Orthodox consider an important element of mission to be their ecumenical contacts. With significant participation at New Delhi in 1961 and officially joining the WCC in 1969, the Orthodox contributed to the WCC-CWME missionary movement. They later were engaged in particular dialogues with Roman Catholics, Anglicans, Reformed/Lutherans and Southern Baptists.

Established in 1973, an Orthodox Advisory Commission to the CWME organized annual conferences, hosted by local churches, to study Orthodox missionary issues.[124] The fruits of some of these studies over a ten-year period were reedited by Ion Bria into a comprehensive single statement, "Go Forth in Peace: Orthodox Perspectives on Mission," and published by the WCC in 1986.[125] Building upon a strong trinitarian and incarnational theology and a mission ecclesiology, this statement depicts the Orthodox importance placed on common witness, liturgy and mission, proclamation and witness, and mission as "liturgy after the liturgy." The 1988 CWME Orthodox consultation in Neapolis, Greece, marked closer collaboration and reconciliation between the Eastern Orthodox and representatives of the Oriental (non-Chalcedonian) Eastern Churches, including Armenian, Syrian, Jacobite, Coptic and Ethiopian communities. The 1990 CWME Orthodox advisory report of Boston focused on the theology of the Holy Spirit and Mission.[126]

NEW MODELS OF CHURCH AND MISSION

African Initiated Churches and Mission

The phenomenon referred to as African Initiated Churches (AICs)[127] traces its roots to nineteenth-century movements in which African Christians separated themselves from churches established, to varying degrees, by Western missionaries. In the 1880s, Bishop Crowther was aging, Henry Venn had already died, a new spirit of imperialism was flowing, and a new CMS generation entered the scene with different policies, attitudes and an evangelical spirituality. These young missionaries began dismantling and taking over the work of Crowther, and after his death in 1891, Crowther would be replaced by a European bishop. In 1880, a young Yoruba (Nigerian) man, who had received the name of David Brown Vincent at baptism by the CMS, left the CMS. He became a Baptist several years later. In 1888, he played a major role in the establishment of the Native Baptist Church in Lagos, and symbolic of his affirmation of African culture and rejection of Western dominance, he chose the name Mojola Agbebi to replace his Western one.[128] A number of independent churches from Baptist, Anglican and Methodist foundations soon emerged in West Africa. During the same time period in South Africa, some Africans joined the black American African Methodist Episcopal Church (AME) and others formed independent churches with Presbyterian and Congregationalist roots. Agbebi became the first president of the African Communion of Independent Churches in 1913.

After World War I, a number of African Christians who were not officially commissioned by any church were very influential in the rapid spread of the Christian faith in certain areas of Africa; they include William Wadé Harris, Sampson Oppong, Joseph Babalola and Walter Mattita.[129] Most of those who responded positively to their preaching (except in the case of Babalola) joined established churches, but several independent churches also later came into existence as the result of their efforts and influence.

The most famous figure of the AIC movement was Simon Kimbangu.[130] Born in the Belgian Congo (present-day Democratic Republic of the Congo) and baptized by British BMS missionaries, Kimbangu applied to become a catechist, but his application was rejected by the church. Kimbangu then began a public ministry outside the mission church in 1921, a charismatic ministry of preaching and healing. His preaching was characterized by a denunciation of traditional African rituals and beliefs, a questioning of the role of missionaries in the direct intervention of God on behalf of the Africans and a prediction that the end of colonial rule was imminent. Due to this final point, the colonial authorities sentenced Kimbangu to life imprisonment; he died in prison in 1951. Because the government outlawed it, the movement went underground, and, as colonialism collapsed, it reemerged under the leadership of Kimbangu's youngest son as L'Eglise de Jésus-Christ sur las Terre par le Prophète Simon Kimbangu (EJCSK). This AIC, officially recognized in 1959, joined the WCC in 1969 and developed extensive social, medical and agricultural outreach as well as its own theological resources. By the end of the second millennium, EJCSK had over five million members.

While the earlier AICs reflect more of the influence from the missionary-founded churches, those founded since 1980 have been more innovative and charismatic. The continent-wide Organization of African Independent Churches, formed in 1978 and later renamed Organization of African Instituted Churches, became an associate council of the WCC in 1998. David Barrett estimates that in 1997 the AICs had some fifty-five million members in ten thousand distinct denominations.[131] This phenomenal development was part of the overall picture of the rapid emergence of Christian faith in various traditions—Catholic, Conciliar, Evangelical and Pentecostal—throughout Africa during the twentieth century. The number of Christians in Africa increased from 10 million in 1900 to 360 million in 2000.

The AIC movement represents a multitude of indigenous appropriations of the Christian faith in a variety of African contexts and particular world views. For all of them, the word of God—whether it is through the written biblical text or a charismatic person—is of ultimate importance, to such a degree that Andrew Walls calls them "radical biblicists" and compares them with the Anabaptists of Western church history.[132] Common characteristics of the AICs include revelation through prophecy, trances and dreams; the importance of healing within a holistic context; and some identification with Levitical law.

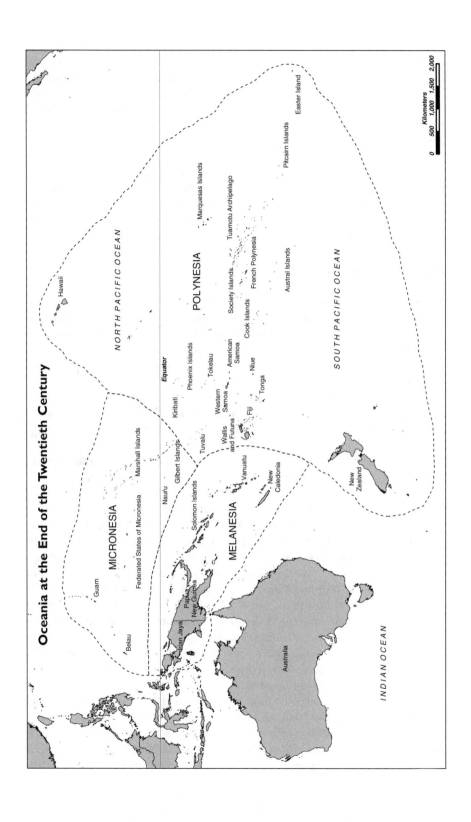

Oceania at the End of the Twentieth Century

NORTH PACIFIC OCEAN

SOUTH PACIFIC OCEAN

INDIAN OCEAN

Equator

MICRONESIA

MELANESIA

POLYNESIA

Belau

Guam

Federated States of Micronesia

Marshall Islands

Nauru

Gilbert Islands

Kiribati

Tuvalu

Phoenix Islands

Tokelau

Hawaii

Marquesas Islands

Tuamotu Archipelago

Society Islands

French Polynesia

Pitcairn Islands

Easter Island

Cook Islands

Austral Islands

Wallis and Futuna

Western Samoa

American Samoa

Fiji

Niue

Tonga

Vanuatu

New Caledonia

Solomon Islands

Papua New Guinea

Irian Jaya

Australia

New Zealand

Kilometers
0 500 1,000 1,500 2,000

Lamin Sanneh describes this contextualization dynamic: "A process of internal change was . . . initiated in which African Christians sought a distinctive way of life through mediation of the spirit, a process that enhanced the importance of traditional religions for the deepening of Christian spirituality. . . . Biblical material was submitted to the regenerative capacity of African perception, and the result would be Africa's unique contribution to the story of Christianity."[133] One aspect of this contribution is that the AICs were able to combine the elements of ritual and hierarchy with the spontaneous and charismatic, elements that Christianity identified with different traditions and that usually were not found in one church.[134] Another example is the emergence of a new Christian theology and practice called earthkeeping, which is a unique form of theological environmentalism.[135]

Other Indigenous Church Movements

Besides the well-known AICs, we present a brief survey, which is only representative, of other indigenous movements around the world. Beginning in the Solomon Islands, Ini Kopuria—a policeman who was educated with the Anglican Melanesian Mission—founded the Melanesian Brotherhood, an indigenous, monastic-type community for missionary outreach in 1925.[136] Making annually renewable promises, the brothers went out in pairs to evangelize beyond the Solomon Islands to present-day Vanuatu, Fiji and Papua New Guinea. In 2000, this movement included over 250 brothers and 150 novices in the two-year training program. Another Solomon Islander, Silas Eto, was the prophet of an indigenous religious movement that synthesized the Melanesian religious-cultural world view with Christianity.[137] In the early 1960s it developed into an independent church, the Christian Fellowship Church, which includes schools, businesses and a theological college. Another type of religious phenomenon, which is more temporary in nature, is the so-called cargo cult, a millenarian-type movement for which the anticipation of the arrival in bulk of Western material goods is a common characteristic.[138] The earliest evidence of these movements, which reflect an indigenous people's attempt to adjust to a rapidly changing cultural/ religious context, was in the 1830s in Samoa, but they became most prevalent among Melanesian peoples of the western Pacific, particularly from the 1940s through the 1970s. Although the cargo cults almost disappeared after 1980, the mentality continues within some independent churches, Evangelical and Pentecostal denominations, and mainline churches.

If we now move to China, we enter a complex religious and ecclesiastical world: first, the Three-Self Patriotic Movement and the Chinese Catholic Patriotic Association representing the government-recognized Protestant and Catholic churches, respectively; second, non-registered Christian groups of the so-called underground church; and third, a variety of people and circumstances between or in combination with the first two identities.[139] While acknowledging new developments within the Catholic Church, one of the most interesting changes is the house-church movement within Protestantism.[140] Refusing to register with the government, small groups of Christians meet in Christian homes. Parallels are drawn to the situation of the early church in the Roman Empire or a dissenting tradition like Puritanism. Although there is no common statement of faith, the groups share a central obedience to the word of God and a belief in the separation of church and state. The house churches are nondenominational and were quite independent in the beginning. However, many now form large networks of house-church groupings with thousands of meeting sites. For this reason, some maintain that this phenomenon has moved beyond the confines of the words *house church* and *movement*, and they propose the term *autonomous Christian communities* to reflect their growth in size and complexity.[141] In some areas, hundreds of people gather in large halls or in churches they have built. The majority of the church workers are lay leaders, including many Bible women, and there is a close relationship with popular Chinese culture and the traditional extended family network. While it is extremely difficult to count the total number of persons in this Christian movement,[142] estimates range from thirty to eighty million. This new image of church and mission is often associated with the "Third Wave" of Pentecostalism, to be described below. In addition to the house-church movement, which also seems to be growing in Vietnam, the Assembly Hall Churches (Little Flock) and the True Jesus Church are two earlier indigenous Chinese movements, each of which numbers over a million.[143]

In the Philippines, the Iglesia Filipina Independiente (or Philippine Independent Church) was founded by Gregorio Aglipay at the turn of the twentieth century. In 1961, however, it entered into full communion with the Protestant Episcopal Church of the United States of America and so now is technically a Conciliar church. The Iglesia ni Cristo (INC), founded by Felix Manalo, is, with three million members, the largest independent church in Asia.[144] Although there is no emphasis on healing or special revelations, the Bible is central, and Manalo claimed that, as the last messenger of God, he had special authority for interpreting the biblical message. The members of this church believe that they represent the true faith of Jesus that was lost in the first century but was reestablished by Manalo as the "leader from the East" prophesied in Isaiah 41:2. Today the church is led by the founder's son, Erano Manalo, and the church is basically unitarian in theology and denies that Jesus was divine. Members of the INC must attend services twice weekly and contribute regularly to the church based on a graduated income scale. They may marry only INC members and may vote only for the candidates endorsed by the church's leadership.[145] Other indigenous Filipino independent movements are quite far from Christian orthodoxy.[146]

In 1999, Roger Hedlund pointed out that while the indigenization of Christianity is a highly discussed topic in the Catholic and Protestant churches, it is "a natural quality of the Churches of the 'Little' Tradition." All over India today, Hedlund says, independent churches are thriving, often with a membership of oppressed peoples who are "finding new identity as disciples of Jesus Christ."[147] While these churches have historical precedents in the nineteenth and early twentieth centuries—for example, in the Christian Revival Movement and the Indian Pentecostal Church of God—a number of newer churches have sprung up in almost every part of the subcontinent. In Madara, one of the most important independent churches is the Apostolic Christian Assembly. Hedlund reports that many educated Hindus participate as observers in the worship, and a large number of baptisms are held weekly. Worship is in Tamil and English and consists of much congregational singing in a Hindu style. There are 144 branches of the church throughout India, with a total membership (in 1997) of almost eighteen thousand.[148] Another independent church in Madras is called the Laymen's Evangelical Fellowship. In Madras City there are thirty worship centers with a total of ten thousand members.[149] Andhra Pradesh, however, is the main center of Indian indigenous Christian movements. Among these are the Assemblies of Brother Bankht Sing, the Bible Mission of Fr. M. Devadas, the Gospel Band and the Independent Christian Believers Gospel Fellowship.[150] Other groups exist in Pune, Punjab and North Gujarat.[151] All in all, says Hedlund, "Christianity has proven to be culturally translatable. Christ is found in an Indian robe in Indian churches of the 'Little Tradition.'"[152]

In his important study of Japanese indigenous churches, Mark Mullins speaks of the emergence of a number of Japanese churches that developed in the twentieth century and that, unlike mainline Christianity brought by missionaries from abroad, paid attention to "the strength and persistence of traditional and popular religious concerns."[153] Of the several churches he names—the Glorious Gospel Christian Church, the Living Christ One Ear of Wheat Church, the Christian Canaan Church, the Japan Ecclesia of Christ, the Sanctifying Christ Church, the Spirit of Jesus Church, the Holy Ecclesia of Jesus—he chooses to elaborate on the last two and also briefly considers the Pentecostal version of "Nonchurch Christianity" called the Original Gospel Movement. Our own focus here is on the Spirit of Jesus Church and the Holy Ecclesia of Jesus.

Murai Jun, the founder of the Spirit of Jesus Church, was born the second son of a Methodist minister and began to study theology at Aoyama Gakuin, a Methodist-affiliated school in Tokyo. During a period of deep depression, he came to the point of committing suicide but was at that moment overpowered by the Holy Spirit and received the gift of tongues, thus relieving him of all doubts and filling him "with new strength and vision for the Christian mission."[154] After pastoring a Pentecostal congregation, and after visiting the True Jesus Church in Taiwan (an indigenous movement that had existed for twenty years), Murai founded the Spirit of Jesus Church, the name of which was given in a revelation to his wife, Suwa. While much of the doctrine and practice of the church is influenced by American Pentecostalism—the stress on Spirit baptism, speaking in tongues, foot washing and "Jesus only" unitarianism—the Spirit of Jesus Church tends to place emphasis on what is referred to in Japan as "the worldly benefits of religion."[155] Thus, sermons focus on the spiritual and material blessings that are to be had by the true believer; the ministry of healing is a prominent feature of the church as well. Although the members of the church are strictly forbidden to practice traditional Japanese ancestor veneration, the church compensates for this by a rite for the baptism of the dead, following the text of 1 Corinthians 15:29. Traditional religious needs are also met by the church in rites of land purification to protect church members from evil spirits and to make it safe to build homes and live in them. "More than anything else," says Mullins, "it is the way Murai and his followers have directly addressed these folk religious concerns that distinguishes the Spirit of Jesus Church from Western pentecostal movements."[156]

In 1946, Otsuki Takeji received a revelation to found a church that was to be called the Holy Ecclesia of Jesus. Otsuki had long been a member of the Holiness Church. As a missionary to Manchuria in the 1930s and 1940s, he had been blessed with a deep experience of Christ. This led him to understand the word of Paul that "It is no longer I who live, but Christ who lives in me" (Gal 2:20) and that, consequently, Christians themselves continue Christ's presence as his body on earth. The Holy Ecclesia of Jesus, therefore, has as its aim to restore Christianity to its apostolic origins and has a particular mission to pray and work for the restoration of the nation of Israel so that the coming eschatological era will be hastened. Otsuki writes that "authentic mission is not to transmit the doctrine or theology of Christianity, but to manifest the living Christ in our lives."[157] Otsuki was struck by the importance of the various names of God, and a solemn part of the church's worship services occurs when, following the direction of the minister, one of God's names (for example, I am God almighty, I am who am, I am the bread of life) is chanted repeatedly by the whole congregation. As Mullins comments, "Given the centrality of the practice, it seems fitting to classify the Holy Ecclesia of Jesus as a form of *nembutsu kirisutokyo*. The tradition of the *nembutsu*, calling on the name of Amida Buddha for protection and salvation, was a practice that began in China and first flourished in Japan during the tenth and eleventh centuries."[158] The church also emphasizes Spirit baptism, healing and the possibility of continuing revelation from God; it is also the only independent movement in Japan that has taken the Apostles' Creed as its own confession of faith.[159] A key tenet of the church's faith is the importance of Israel's conversion for the restoration of all in Christ. However, it does not engage in direct evangelization of the Jews. "In the light of the history of Christian-Jewish relations—persecution, murder, and the holocaust—the Holy Ecclesia of Jesus claims that Gentiles have no right to evangelize the Jews. Their calling is simply to pray for the restoration of Israel and peace in Jerusalem."[160]

These brief and sketchy portraits of indigenous Christian movements in various parts of the world point clearly to two facts about Christianity in the twentieth century: In the first place, as Andrew Walls, Lamin Sanneh and others have pointed out, Christianity itself is "infinitely translatable" and so able to maintain faithfulness to its constants in varying contexts. There is something in Christianity that calls for authentic inculturation and contextualization. Second, however, the existence and continuing vitality of these movements points to the fact that ordinary Christians are ultimately the ones who can both sense the constants and engage the context. This dynamic of Christianity is also revealed in the next understanding of Christianity with which we deal: Pentecostalism.

Pentecostalism and Mission

Pentecostalism, as a millenarian movement emphasizing the baptism and gifts of the Holy Spirit, emerged out of the broader holiness movement.[161] In 1900, holiness preacher Charles F. Parham[162] founded the Bethel Bible School in Topeka, Kansas, to prepare missionaries to evangelize the world before the imminent premillennial return of Christ. Early the following year, Parham and his students received the baptism of the Spirit, accompanied by the gift of speaking in tongues, which was seen as "Bible evidence" of the baptism and which would become the specific trait of Pentecostal doctrine. Parham opened another Bible school in Houston in 1905, where the African American holiness preacher William J. Seymour[163] accepted Parham's teaching and then became the principal leader of the Azusa Street revival in Los Angeles (1906-1909). Unique elements of this latter revival, which would have greater worldwide influence than other early Pentecostal revivals, included its stress on racial reconciliation and the outpouring of the Spirit on the poor. The earliest Pentecostal churches in the United States, which would eventually enroll millions, include the Church of God in Christ, the Church of God based in Cleveland (Tennessee), the Pentecostal Holiness Church and the Assemblies of God.

As a result of these initial revivals in the United States, Canada, England and Scandinavia, some two hundred missionaries were sent out by 1910. In addition, a group of veteran missionaries of the Christian and Missionary Alliance (CMA) in India became Pentecostal. Beginning in the 1920s, the bulk of the missionaries were Bible institute graduates from North America and Great Britain who were sent by an ever-increasing number of Pentecostal mission boards, although many preferred to work independently from any board. As the outpouring of the Spirit was equally on women and men, Aimee Semple McPherson[164] and Lillian Trasher[165] are representative of the major role of women in Pentecostal mission work, as was also true with its predecessor, the holiness movement.

The Pentecostal model of mission highlighted baptism in the Spirit, indigenous church principles, pragmatism in technology and communications, rapid church growth and expectations of "signs and wonders" in proclaiming the gospel.[166] It was this final aspect in particular, along with speaking in tongues and the belief that all the gifts of the Spirit were restored, that distinguished the Pentecostal missionaries from their CMA and holiness contemporaries. Pentecostals continued to emphasize miraculous signs and wonders more than these other missionaries did, and many other Evangelicals basically dismissed the possibility of miracles altogether.[167] In the face of Satanic forces, Pentecostal missionaries aimed to prepare Christians for lifelong "spiritual warfare," which often is initiated by a "power encounter" between God and other spiritual powers. Such encounters, like those between Moses and Pharaoh (Ex 7–12) and between Elijah and the prophets of Baal (1 Kg 18), were recorded earlier in the works of missionaries like Columba, Boniface and Gall in the early Middle Ages.

The nineteenth-century precedents of Pentecostalism in Asia can be traced, on the one hand, to the holiness movement and revival movements in Europe and North America and, on the other hand, to indigenous revival movements with Pentecostal-like phenomena. "Thus, by the time the first Pentecostal missionaries arrived in Asia from the United States in 1907, Pentecostal-like movements and expressions had appeared for almost half a century in various places."[168] Furthermore, separate from its better-known origins in the United States, Pentecostalism emerged independently in 1906 in India, partly under the leadership of the former Methodist missionary Minnie Abrams, and in a girls' school headed by Pandita Ramabai.[169] Pentecostal churches in Asia today reflect more diversity than those in Europe and North America, and they contributed to the growing ranks of non-Western Pentecostals serving as missionaries during the second half of the twentieth century.

Along with classical (denominational) Pentecostals, modern Pentecostalism also includes Neo-Pentecostals (charismatics) and the so-called Third Wave. The charismatic renewal, as the Second Wave of Pentecostalism, began in the 1950s and 1960s in mainline Protestant churches, the Roman Catholic Church and several Orthodox churches, and most of these charismatic movements gained acceptance within their denominations. Whether through their own denominations or independent charismatic churches and mission bodies, the impact of charismatics in mission has been felt around the world.[170] For example, Roman Catholic charismatics promoted the cause of mission through the programs of Evangelization 2000 and mission training at the Franciscan University of Steubenville (Ohio).

Most recently, the Third Wave within Pentecostalism includes neo-charismatics, indigenous groups, and New Apostolic Reformation churches. These Christian bodies, which are not classified as either classical Pentecostals or charismatics, emphasize signs and wonders (without requiring speaking in tongues) as essential for success in ministry. They are as diverse as the cultures and contexts in which they have developed, and many of the indigenous church movements described above would be included here. While at the moment it is difficult clearly to categorize this general Christian development, it is estimated that this Third Wave of Pentecostalism is the largest part of the overall Pentecostal movement in Asia and that on a worldwide basis it outnumbers the first two waves combined.[171]

While the above represents one account of the series of waves of the Pentecostal movement, Kwabena Asamoah-Gyadu of Ghana is representative of those who describe another series of waves.[172] In looking at the history of Christianity in Africa, Asamoah-Gyadu identifies three waves of indigenous Pentecostalism. Beginning at the end of the nineteenth century, the "Spiritual churches," or older AICs, strove to relive the scriptural Pentecostal experience in an African context. Second, the twentieth century brought indigenous classical Pentecostal denominations, such as the Church of Pentecost, founded through the initiative of Ghanaian Peter N. Anim and subsequent collaboration with British missionaries in the 1930s and listed as the largest Protestant denomination in Ghana in

2000. Third, the category of "charismatic ministries," as part of the wider Neo-Pentecostal movement, includes renewal groups within Catholic and Protestant churches, trans-denominational associations like the Full Gospel Business Men's Fellowship International, and some of the AICs founded since the late 1970s. Unlike the first two movements, this Third Wave was very much influenced by foreign forms of Pentecostalism, particularly from North America. However, African ingenuity is constantly at work as Pentecostal faith interacts with African culture.[173] In this account, we see an overlap with the earlier descriptions of Pentecostalism and AICs.

These two presentations reflect the diversity, fluidity, ecumenicity and contextuality of the worldwide Pentecostal movement, as well as the ongoing discussion of how to define and count Pentecostals/Charismatics.[174] No matter what estimate one uses, however, Pentecostals represent the fastest growing body of Christianity today. In looking at other Christian contexts, since the 1950s Pentecostalism has accounted for 80 to 90 percent of Protestant/Pentecostal growth across Latin America, particularly in Chile, Central America and Brazil.[175] Also noteworthy is the Catholic El Shaddai movement, which, though native to the Philippines, has spread into almost every country throughout the world, especially among Filipino immigrants.

While the Conciliar, Catholic, Orthodox and even the Evangelical churches were at times struggling with the motivation and goal of mission during the twentieth century, Pentecostalism has prompted Christian women and men to approach the missionary task with certainty and confidence. The Pentecostal World Conference was established in 1947, and the Pentecostal Fellowship of North America in 1948 (reorganized as the Pentecostal/Charismatic Churches of North America in 1994). Some Pentecostal church bodies have joined the WEF, the LCWE and the WCC. A Roman Catholic and classical Pentecostal dialogue began in 1972 and continues to the present.

At the end of this series of descriptions of mission during the twentieth century, let us look briefly at the developments within the discipline of missiology itself over this same period. Building upon the foundations laid by pioneers like Warneck and Schmidlin, academic institutions established missiological programs and chairs. Catholic faculties developed these initiatives fairly rapidly in Germany, the Netherlands, Switzerland and Rome, while the boom of such Protestant endeavors occurred after World War II in Germany, Scandinavia, the Netherlands and particularly the United States. While missiology was still flourishing in the United States at the end of the twentieth century, many of the traditional chairs of missiology in Europe had been replaced by or joined with chairs in history of religion, ecumenism and contextual theology. After the transitional decade of the sixties, the study of missiology spread worldwide with the establishment of missiology centers in Asia, Latin America, Africa and Oceania.

Early professional organizations included the Deutsche Gesellschaft für Missionswissenschft (German Society of Missionary Science, 1918), Association of Professors of Mission (USA, 1952), the South African Missiological

Society (1968), the International Association for Mission Studies (1972) and the American Society of Missiology (1973). Except for the earlier German society, all of these were ecumenical in membership from their beginnings. Warneck's founding of the scientific journal *Allegemeine Missions Zeitschrift* much earlier (1874) also prompted the establishment of similar periodicals, beginning in Germany, the United States, the Netherlands and Scandinavia. While developing as an academic discipline in its own right, missiology engaged in mutually enriching dialogue with other disciplines, such as biblical studies history, systematic theology, ethics, world religion studies and the social sciences.[176]

CONSTANTS IN THE CONTEXT OF THE TWENTIETH CENTURY

Since the next three chapters paint a detailed picture of the six constants according to three theological/missiological perspectives operative during the final quarter of the twentieth century, we present only a brief sketch of the primary issues at this point.

When Christianity was in its mid-century moment of transition, Stephen Neill pointed out that a satisfactory *ecclesiology* will provide the basis for answering every question facing mission.[177] Within Protestantism, an ecclesiocentric view of mission developed quite strongly before and after the birth of the WCC, despite the concerns of missionaries, like E. Stanley Jones, that such a trend ignored the reign of God. Conciliars and Orthodox strove for more church unity, while the former also gave growing importance to the reign of God. Evangelicals in general focused their energies on establishing vibrant local churches and congregations. Similar dynamics were at work with the Catholic Church, which, through the Second Vatican Council, opened the door for new understandings of itself as more communal and less hierarchical and as a communion of local churches. Points of tension emerge around the role and identity of the church in relation to the reign of God, and how unity is maintained in diversity instead of uniformity. Despite these differences, all of the Christian traditions rediscovered a mission ecclesiology during the twentieth century.

Debate surrounding the Laymen's Foreign Mission Inquiry was basically due to two conflicting *Christologies*,[178] which had begun developing in the nineteenth century. The first represents a low Christology with Christ seen more as a human teacher and example, while the second represents a high Christology with the emphasis on Christ as divine Redeemer and Savior. This divergence was fundamental in shaping the differing perspectives of the Conciliar and Evangelical/Pentecostal Protestants. These two Christological stances, with many variances, also are operative within the Catholic Church. The constants of how one views Christ and the relation of the church to the reign of God directly affect one's understanding of *salvation* and the relationship of Christianity with other religions. Therefore, Evangelicals and Pentecostals hold an exclusivist perspective, with insistence on explicit faith in Christ; Conciliars move toward variances of inclusivist and pluralist perspectives; and, while all three approaches

MISSION IN THE TWENTIETH CENTURY (1919-1991)

Context	Worldwide	Worldwide	Worldwide
Stream of Christianity	Roman Catholic	Orthodox	Conciliar Protestant
Primary model	Modified society model	Presence	Modified society model
Key figures in mission	Pius XI, Lebbe, Dengel, Ford, Catholic Action, Day, Grail, Foucauld, Schmidt, Schütte	Yannoulatos, Bria	Gutmann, Keysser, Allen, Fleming, Hocking, Kraemer, Andrews, Azariah, Scudder, Niles, Warren, Neill, Bosch
Theological typology	Pluralism of approaches	B (emphasis on truth)	C (emphasis on history)
Primary theologians	Rahner, Congar, Lonergan, Gutiérrez, Schillebeeckx	Meyendorf, Zizioulas, Florovsky	Barth, Tillich, Brunner, Hoekendijk, Moltmann

CONSTANTS

Christology	High/low Exclusive, inclusive	High Inclusive, pluralist	Low Inclusive
Ecclesiology	Multiple models Missional	Mystical communion, Sacrament Missional	Herald, servant Missional
Eschatology	Futurist/realized Individual/historical	Realized Individual	Inaugurated Historical
Salvation	Spiritual/holistic	Spiritual	Holistic
Anthropology	Positive	Positive	Positive
Culture	Positive Multiple models	Positive Anthropological model	Positive Multiple models

MISSION IN THE TWENTIETH CENTURY (1919-1991)

Context	Worldwide	Worldwide
Stream of Christianity	Evangelical Protestant	Independent, Pentecostal, Indigenous
Primary model	Modified society model	Pentecostalism, Evangelism
Key figures in mission	Jones, Cragg, McGavran, Graham, Newbigin, Stott	Agbebi, Anim, Kimbangu, Kopuria, Eto, Manalo, Jun, Takeji, Parham, Seymour, McPherson, Trasher, Abrams
Theological typology	A (emphasis on law)	A (emphasis on law)
Primary theologians	Henry, Kantzer, Escobar	Spittler, Fee, McClung, Land, Ma, Kärkkäinen

CONSTANTS

Christology	High Exclusive	High Exclusive
Ecclesiology	Voluntary society	Community mode
	Missional	Missional
Eschatology	Imminent Individual	Imminent; realized: AIC Individual
Salvation	Spiritual	Spiritual
Anthropology	Negative	Negative
Culture	Negative Counter-cultural and translation models	Negative; positive: AIC Counter-cultural model

are present and in tension within the Catholic Church, there seems to be more attraction toward inclusivist and pluralist positions, or what Jacques Dupuis calls an "inclusive pluralism."[179] The relationship of Christianity with world religions poses the most challenging items for the theological and missiological agenda at the beginning of the twenty-first century.

The contrasting *eschatological* perspectives of the nineteenth century between the postmillennialist and amillennialist, on the one hand, and premillennialist, on the other, became a pronounced element that distinguished Conciliars and Evangelicals. The premillennialist perspective was particularly prominent within the Christian traditions of Adventism, the holiness movement, Pentecostalism, fundamentalism and conservative Evangelicalism—traditions that in varying degrees identify themselves as Evangelical. While there have been tendencies toward an almost exclusive emphasis of either the horizontal or vertical levels of salvation, the Catholic Church attempted to hold a both/and rather than an either/or view of the "already" and "not yet" aspects of the reign of God.

Regarding the constant of the attitude toward *culture*, Conciliars had a positive assessment, while Evangelical Protestantism and Pentecostalism held a more guarded negative stance, although Pentecostalism used the culture's technology (for example, the Internet, radio and TV) in remarkable ways. As for the Catholic Church, the Second Vatican Council marked a very significant shift in that culture was embraced as a valued partner in the process of evangelization. While John Paul II has expressed deep appreciation for traditional (that is, non-Western) cultures, he has tended to regard modern secular culture in both the West and the East with more suspicion, often making a distinction between the "gospel of life" and the "culture of death" (that is, abortion, violence, drugs, war and the death penalty). The Orthodox Church continued to value culture highly. Finally, Evangelicals and Pentecostals follow a relatively pessimistic *anthropology*, while Conciliars, Catholics and Orthodox are more optimistic.

It is not as easy to identify the theological constants of the AIC movement because of the tremendous diversity *ad intra*, new categories that don't "fit" so neatly *ad extra* with other Christian traditions, and the lack of a sufficient amount of written theology. For example, while the AIC churches tended to follow a similar path to Evangelicals and Pentecostalism in terms of Christology, salvation and eschatology, they generally maintained a more positive, but not uncritical, assessment of their own culture, traditional religion and the "already" (healing) aspects of God's reign.

Because the twentieth century was a time of turbulence and the intermingling of theologies, all three types of theology, as described by González and Sölle, are found to some degree in Catholicism and Protestantism during this period. While Evangelicals and Pentecostals were strong representatives of Type A theology (emphasis on law), Conciliar Protestants were strong representatives of Type C (emphasis on history). Within Catholicism, RM in general reflected Type A theology, and AG contained both A and B (emphasis on truth). All three streams of Christianity experienced what González called the twentieth century's rediscovery of Type C theology.[180] Liberation and feminist theologies and the emphasis on the reign of God represented this dynamic for Conciliars and Catholics, and people like René Padilla and Samuel Escobar did so for Evangelical Christians. The Orthodox continued to be the clearest expression of Type B theology. The AICs were most strongly representatives of Type A theology, and their concern for culture showed a little influence of Type B theology. However, such efforts as that of earthkeepers and the strong pastoral orientation pointed to the influence of Type C here as well.

IMPLICATIONS FOR THE THEOLOGY OF MISSION TODAY

Since in Part III, particularly in Chapter 12, we draw implications directly from the various forms of mission theology and practice in the twentieth century in spelling out the theology of mission for the twenty-first century, we limit ourselves here to just a few overall observations.

The amazing growth of Christianity in the last century was the result of missionary efforts under many different shapes and forms. This diversity in some cases has led to situations of confusion, competition and contradiction—a situation that points to the scandal of a "divided gospel" and sparks some calls for dialogue among Christian bodies on various levels and "common witness" not only for the sake of the gospel but for our common human family and world. At the same time, since such diversity represents the dedication and ingenuity of faith-filled Christians to participate in the *missio Dei*, the various Christian constituencies have the opportunity to learn from one another. Latin American Evangelicals brought social-justice issues into Lausanne in 1974. John Stott reminded the WCC of its obligations for evangelization at its assembly in Nairobi the following year. The Orthodox brought its mission tradition for church unity and liturgy into the WCC. Such opportunities for mutual enrichment were opened up when the Catholic Church entered into a variety of long-term dialogues with other Christian traditions, situations unheard of before the ecumenical spirit of the Second Vatican Council. How will all this reshape Christianity?

The twentieth century has given birth not only to a global Christianity, but a global Christianity that has its center in the South, not in the North. Demographically, the majority of Christians now live in Latin America, Africa and Asia. By the year 2025, Africa and Latin America will be vying for the title of being the most Christian continent, and the two together will have half of the Christians in the world. "If we want to visualize a 'typical' contemporary Christian, we should think of a woman living in a village in Nigeria or in a Brazilian *favela*."[181] This emerging world Christianity—shaped by the shift in geography, nationality, race, economic status and daily concerns—will for the foreseeable future, according to Philip Jenkins, be "traditionalist, orthodox, and supernatural."[182] The rapid expansion of Pentecostalism and AICs is the clearest and most predominant indicator of this trend. Coming out of a very different political-religious context, but also a key part of this world movement, are remarkable examples of the growth of Christianity in Asia, including China, the Chinese diaspora, Korea and Vietnam.[183] In fact, the single largest congregation in the world is in Seoul, Korea—Yoido Full Gospel Church, pastored by David Paul Yonggi Cho. Writing in 1995, Harvey Cox estimated that membership had already reached 800,000.[184] In this overall process, Christianity will become more and more identified with the poor South rather than the rich North. How will this reshape Christianity?

Another worldwide phenomenon is the reemergence of Muslim power in the political, economic and religious spheres. This movement will most probably continue to have a—if not *the*—major impact on the future of Christianity and the world through the first part of the twenty-first century. Based on their economic strength as oil-producing nations and their political strength, particularly in the Middle East and western Asia, the Muslims have reclaimed their place on the world stage. Tragically, this has led to a series of confrontations—marked by war and violence on all sides—between Muslims and Muslims, Muslims and Western nations, Muslims and Jews, and Muslims and Christians. Regarding the latter, these conflicts are not solely religious ones; rather, they are most often driven by a combination of ethnic, national, economic and religious motivations—as seen, for example, in the brutal Sudan conflict between the light-skinned, Arabic-speaking Muslims in the north and the dark-skinned Christians and traditionalists in the south. Political developments, with threats of war and terrorism, have fueled a "crusading" mentality among many Christian, Muslim and Jewish individuals and nations. How will Christianity participate in the *missio Dei* in these contexts, which call for peace, reconciliation and interreligious dialogue? How will this reshape Christianity?

Part III

CONSTANTS IN CONTEXT: A THEOLOGY OF MISSION FOR TODAY

While mission has ever been faithful to its six constants of Christology, ecclesiology, eschatology, soteriology, anthropology and the dialogue with human culture, it has, as we hope this book so far has demonstrated, taken on new forms and concerns as it has been faithful as well to its ever-changing context. In this third part our aim is to propose a model for mission that is relevant to the context of these turbulent years of our new twenty-first century and the beginning of the third millennium. Our sense is that the model that we propose, mission as prophetic dialogue, while emerging out of the rapid and significant developments in the practice and theology of mission during the last quarter of the twentieth century, is one that both synthesizes and deepens them and gives them new direction.

FROM THE TWENTIETH CENTURY
TO THE TWENTY-FIRST CENTURY IN MISSION

As outlined in the previous chapter, mission theory and practice went through four stages of development during the twentieth century: certainty, ferment, crisis and rebirth. While World War I did dampen the high optimistic spirit of Edinburgh, missionary efforts were resumed fairly soon, with the same dedication and sense of certainty. Basically, such efforts began in continuity with the nineteenth century's society model, which understood mission primarily in terms of the extension of the church—extension either by the conversion of individuals (in the Catholic debate, advocated by the Münster School), or by the establishment of ecclesiastical structures in non-Christian territories (advocated by the Catholic Louvain School). The formation of the IMC in 1921 provided continuity with the nineteenth-century missionary period. However, even during this time of certainty, there were signs that the twentieth-century missionary movement was taking a shape distinct from the previous one. Vincent Lebbe, Charles de Foucauld, Pius XI, Dorothy Day, Anna Dengel, the Grail movement,

Francis Ford, Maryknoll sisters in China, Catholic Action and Wilhelm Schmidt were pointing to new directions and challenges. Within Protestantism, Bruno Gutmann, Christian Keysser, Roland Allen, Daniel Johnson Fleming, W. E. Hocking, Hendrik Kraemer, C. F. Andrews, E. Stanley Jones, V. S. Azariah and Ida S. Scudder are representative of both the tremendous vigor and the budding controversy underlying this initial phase of this new missionary movement.

By mid-century, in the wake of the Second World War, the collapse of colonization and the worldwide rise of independence movements, an amazing renaissance of the world's various religions, the height of the Cold War and the social turmoil of the 1960s, this period of certainty came to an end. The titles of Godin and Daniel's paperback, *France, pays de mission?* (France, a mission country?), and James Scherer's book, *Missionary Go Home*, perhaps best capture the depth of insecurity at this turning point.[1] However, this was also a moment of ferment and transition. For Catholics, and in many ways for all Christians, the Second Vatican Council was a crucial time. Its *Decree on the Church's Missionary Activity (Ad Gentes)* emphasized the essential missionary nature of the church. Its *Dogmatic Constitution on the Church (Lumen Gentium)* characterized the church as the people of God and the universal sacrament of salvation in the world. Its *Declaration on the Relationship of the Church to Non-Christian Religions (Nostra Aetate)* presented a positive attitude—while maintaining the centrality and uniqueness of Christ—toward other religious ways. Its *Pastoral Constitution on the Church in the Modern World (Gaudium et Spes)* taught a holistic anthropology, acknowledged the importance and goodness of culture, and offered a perspective of Christian existence lived in hope of the full inauguration of the reign of God. This phase of ferment and transition within Protestantism occurred with the integration of the IMC within the WCC during the final IMC assembly in Accra in 1957 and the WCC meeting in New Delhi in 1961. This moment represented both the official recognition of the essential bond between church and mission and the beginning of the formal division between conservative and liberal perspectives. The new CWME spoke of "mission on six continents" in Mexico City in 1963, and the "age of missions" ended, while the "age of mission" began. However, this new age, both within Catholicism and Protestantism, would first have to pass through a time of testing and trial.

The period of crisis, which began in the mid-sixties, can be attributed to some of the ideas that came out of the events of ferment and transition. For Catholics, the serious question that missionaries were asking was raised by the 1969 SEDOS conference: Why mission at all? And the general state of change and chaos in the Catholic Church after the Second Vatican Council contributed to the crisis in mission. Johannes Hoekendijk's radical thought at the WCC meeting in Uppsala in 1968 most poignantly highlighted the question of the why of mission within Protestant circles. The call for a missionary moratorium put the final stamp on the crisis. At this same time, Evangelical Protestants had begun to separate themselves from the WCC, and the Lausanne Movement started in 1974; Catholics in Latin America were turning things upside down with their call for a preferential option for the poor at their bishops' conference in Medellín in 1968, and liberation theology was born a few years later. These events symbolized the pain, confusion and divisiveness of this period of crisis, on the one hand, as well as the new life, hope, energy and passion for mission, on the other.

The last quarter of the twentieth century witnessed a rebirth of the missionary movement. Building upon the breakthroughs and foundations of the Second Vatican Council, this new way of approaching mission was more fully developed by Paul VI's *Evangelii Nuntiandi* in 1975 and John Paul II's encyclical *Redemptoris Missio* in 1990. SEDOS, regional bishops' conferences and other official church bodies added to this development. With its assembly in Nairobi in 1975, the WCC began to outline the new direction for Conciliar mission theology, and the CWME conference in Melbourne in 1980 continued this process. Other notable achievements by the WCC and the CWME include the *Ecumenical Affirmation: Mission and Evangelism* in 1982 and *Guidelines on Dialogue with People of Living Faiths and Ideologies* in 1979. After the 1974 Lausanne conference, the LCWE began mapping out the direction of mission for Evangelicals. The WEF, which had been in existence since 1951, and Donald McGavran's church growth movement added their valuable contributions to this process. The LCWE conference of 1989 produced the *Manila Manifesto*, which is a very important summary document of Evangelical theology and practice. The Orthodox church also added its voice to this missionary renewal, beginning with its initial participation in the meeting of the CWME in 1963. The Orthodox Advisory Commission to the CWME, established in 1973, has enabled the Orthodox to clarify and reaffirm their mission theology, both for themselves and for the sake of the wider ecumenical mission efforts. Finally, the rebirth of the missionary movement owes much to newer forms of church and mission through the African Initiated Churches and Pentecostalism. Both of these movements trace their roots to the end of the nineteenth-century missionary period, are very active in mission, and have developed in a wide variety of ways. In the last quarter of the twentieth century, some of them formed official links with other Christian denominations and bodies.

THREE MODELS OF MISSION
IN THE LATE TWENTIETH CENTURY

Throughout these decades of missionary renewal there seem to have been three strains of theological thought that grounded various approaches to mission and both inspired and have been inspired by the major statements of the Catholic, Conciliar Protestant, Orthodox, Evangelical and Pentecostal traditions. These three theological strains have run through all of these ecclesial traditions, and have shaped as well their attitudes toward the six constants of mission referred to throughout this book. A first strain, evident particularly in Vatican II's AG and documents of the Orthodox churches, roots the church's mission in the overflowing communion of the *trinitarian God*. A second, expressed most fully in Paul VI's apostolic exhortation EN and documents of the WCC, focuses on God's patient and freedom-respecting work of establishing *God's reign* among human beings and, indeed, within all of creation. Within this strain there is a particular emphasis on the liberating and justice-establishing activity of God and the church. A third strain, present especially in John Paul II's encyclical RM and the documents of the LCWE and the WEF, emphasizes the *centrality of Christ* and the importance of sharing God's truth with humankind.

A THEOLOGY OF MISSION FOR TODAY:
MISSION AS PROPHETIC DIALOGUE

While there is no strict correspondence to the three types of theology to which we have alluded throughout this book, we might point to the trinitarian missiology of AG and the Orthodox Church as relating to both Type B and Type C theologies. EN's and the Conciliar Protestant focus on the church participating in Jesus' liberating mission of preaching, serving and witnessing to the reign of God points to the theology espoused in Type C. And John Paul II's and the Evangelical emphasis on "Jesus Christ the Only Savior" (RM, chap. I) and the pope's explicit, though not exclusive, link of the church to the reign of God and to salvation (see RM 17 and 55) suggest an affinity with Type A theology.

The purpose of Chapters 9-11 is to sketch out these three perspectives, particularly as they appear in the official statements of the churches[2] and in some theologians, and to sketch briefly how each perspective might articulate each of the six constants of mission on which we have reflected throughout this book. While we believe that all three approaches are valid, we also believe that only a *synthesis* of all three will provide the firmest foundation for the model of mission that we are proposing as the most adequate model for these first years of the twenty-first century: mission as prophetic dialogue. Chapter 12 then shows how the various elements involved in an understanding of mission today—witness and proclamation, liturgical action and contemplation, inculturation, interreligious dialogue, working for justice and commitment to reconciliation—all contribute to a missionary practice that is both dialogical and prophetic, faithful to contemporary context as well as to the constants of Christian faith.

The model of mission that we believe is emerging in our own day is the result of theological reflection on missionary practice in today's multicultural, multireligious, globalized and religiously polarized world, a world in which the center of gravity of Christianity has, at least in terms of population, shifted to the South, and a world in which Christianity may well be becoming more and more Pentecostal, more supernaturalist, more theologically conservative and more religiously assertive.[3] No longer can we conceive of mission in terms of church expansion or the salvation of souls; no longer can we conceive of mission as supporting the outreach of colonial powers; no longer can we understand missionary activity as providing the blessings of Western civilization to "underdeveloped" or "developing" peoples and cultures; no longer can we conceive of mission as originating from a Christianized North and moving toward a non-Christian or a religiously underdeveloped South. Mission today, rather, is something much more modest and at the same time much more exciting—and, indeed, more urgent. It is much more modest because we realize that "the mission is not ours, but God's";[4] it is much more exciting because it is about God's gracious invitation to humanity to share in the dynamic communion that is at the same time God's self-giving missionary life; it is more urgent because in a world of globalized poverty, religious violence and new appreciation of local culture and subaltern traditions, the vision and praxis of Jesus of Nazareth can bring new healing and new light. Mission is about preaching, serving and witnessing to the work of God in our world; it is about living and working as partners with God in the patient yet unwearied work of inviting and persuading women and men to enter into relationship with their world, with one another and with Godself. Mission is dialogue. It takes people where they are; it is open to their traditions and culture and experience; it recognizes the validity of their own religious existence and the integrity of their own religious ends. But it is *prophetic* dialogue because it calls people beyond; it calls people to conversion; it calls people to deeper and fuller truth that can only be found in communion with dialogue's trinitarian ground. Mission today will be done in what David Bosch calls "bold humility,"[5] modeled after mission in Christ's way of humility and self-emptying and bold proclamation of God's "already" and "not yet" reign.

9

Mission as Participation in the Mission of the Triune God (*Missio Dei*)

AD GENTES AND DOCUMENTS OF THE ORTHODOX CHURCHES

Ad Gentes

The Second Vatican Council marks a radical departure from a Roman Catholic ecclesiology that had primarily concerned itself—particularly since the Reformation—with the external and institutional aspects of the church. Church teaching and theological textbooks before the council had emphasized that the church was fundamentally "an unequal society," composed of "the pastors and the flock," and images of the church "were drawn not from biblical sources but from civil society."[1] It was not surprising, then, that understandings of mission emphasized either individual salvation through entrance into the church (Münster School) or the establishment in "mission lands" of the church's hierarchical structures (Louvain School). In contrast, Vatican II's *Dogmatic Constitution on the Church* spoke of the church as a *mystery*, as "the people made one in the unity of the Father, Son and Holy Spirit" (LG 4). The church was now understood as a people, a communion, and mission was conceived as the participation in the dynamic communion of God's triune life, that is, the church was a sacrament of salvation, a sign and instrument of God's saving presence toward and within all of creation. The church of Vatican II, declared Michel Philipon in one of LG's most respected commentaries, is the church of the Trinity.[2]

Despite the fact that Vatican II's document on missionary activity was put together rather hurriedly and like practically all the council documents was the product of a number of compromises,[3] the bishops of the council insisted that its decree on missionary activity be grounded in the same trinitarian theology as that of the document on the church.[4] AG would present a definition of *mission* in the stricter sense of "evangelization and planting of the Church among those peoples and groups where she has not yet taken root" (AG 6). But this idea is presented in the context of the wider and deeper reality that the church, as such, is missionary by its very nature, because it itself is the result of the overflowing love of God, expressed in the mission of the Son and the mission of the Holy Spirit (AG 2). Mission, therefore, is understood fundamentally as rooted in the continual self-giving and self-revelation of God within the history of creation; trinitarian processions are understood not only as movements within the mystery of God, as such, but as God moving in saving love within the world. The church is then understood as the people that God has chosen not only to participate in the saving life of the divine community—"a people made one with the unity of the Father, the Son and the Holy Spirit"—but also to be agent and cooperator in God's outreach to the whole of creation. The church not only "walks in love," but it "glows with an apostolic spirit" (AG 15).

In AG 2, God the Father is pictured as a life-giving fountain of love who freely creates the world and calls humanity in particular to share in the fullness of divine life. God does this by generously pouring out the divine goodness in history (the mission of the Son—AG 3) and never ceasing to do so as history continues (the mission of the Spirit—AG 4). Since humanity is created in God's image and is called to share in God's fullness, the end of God's action is not that men and women are taken up individually; rather, like God in God's innermost mystery, they too are formed into a community, a people, an "icon" of the Trinity. God is a community of Father, Son and Spirit, constantly involved in the world; salvation, human wholeness, is life lived in a community that reflects the community and self-giving that is God.

God's involvement in history was made concrete in Jesus of Nazareth. Through him, God is revealed, not as interfering in human life and curtailing human freedom, but as calling people to greater and more abundant life. As both truly divine and truly human, therefore,

the Son of God walked the way of a true Incarnation that He might make men and women sharers in the divine nature. He became poor for our sakes, though He had been rich, in order that His poverty might enrich us (2 Cor 8:9). The Son of Man came not that he might be served, but that He might be a servant, and give His life as a ransom for the many—that is, for all (see Mk 10:45). (AG 3)

And, in order that this historical deed might have perpetual meaning, "Christ sent the Holy Spirit from the Father . . . to carry out his saving work inwardly" (AG 4) and to form his group of well-meaning but weak followers into a community-in-mission that would mirror the community of overflowing trinitarian life. "Throughout all ages, the Holy Spirit gives the entire Church 'unity in fellowship and in service; He furnishes her with various gifts, both hierarchical and charismatic.' He vivifies ecclesiastical institutions as a kind of soul and instills into the hearts of the faithful the same mission spirit which motivated Christ himself" (ibid., quoting LG 4). Thus God's *exitus* in sending the Son and

Spirit results in a *reditus* in which the church cooperates with God in making God "all in all" (1 Cor 15:28; see AG 2).[5]

In his "Response" to AG in the Abbot edition of the Vatican II documents, Eugene L. Smith observes that the strongly theological first chapter of AG appears to be more of an addition to a practical and juridical reflection than a vision that integrates the whole.[6] While this is basically true, it must be pointed out that this rich trinitarian perspective does indeed show through in various other parts of the document. In paragraphs 10 and 11, for example, the *kenosis* of the incarnation is alluded to when the church is challenged to identify closely with the peoples and cultures among whom it works. In paragraph 13, the "spiritual journey" on which the new convert embarks is described as "being snatched away from sin and led into the mystery of the love of God, who has called him or her to enter into a personal relationship in Christ." At the end of paragraph 20, the trinitarian motif can only be the background for the idea that as the "younger churches" themselves move into mission, their communion with the universal church is thereby strengthened—active cooperation with God's mission binds men and women closer to one another. Finally, in paragraph 42, the council fathers pray that as the church continues in mission, "the nations may be led into the knowledge of the truth as soon as possible (1 Tim 2:4), and that the splendor of God which brightens the face of Jesus Christ may shine upon all peoples through the Holy Spirit (2 Cor 4:6)." Despite the fact, therefore, that much of AG deals with many practical details and offers several other reasons for the church's essentially missionary nature (see, for example, 1, 8, 12, 38), AG has provided a strong, consistent reason of considerable theological depth; that is, the church is in mission because it has been graciously caught up in the *missio Dei*, the very mission of God in creation, redemption and continual sanctification.

Documents of the Orthodox Churches

Documents issued by the Orthodox churches in the last quarter of the twentieth century are unanimous in placing the doctrine of the Trinity at the center of theological thinking about the nature of mission. The 1986 document entitled "Go Forth in Peace: Orthodox Perspectives on Mission" begins with the assertion that while the church's mission is based on the mission of Christ, "a proper understanding of this mission requires in the first place, an application of trinitarian theology."[7] Trinitarian theology points to the radical communal nature of God as such, and this communion overflows into an involvement with history that "aims at drawing humanity and creation in general into this communion with God's very life."[8] God's very nature, therefore, is missionary.[9] It is not primarily about "the propagation or transmission of intellectual convictions, doctrines, moral commands, etc.,"[10] but rather about the inclusion of all creation in God's overflowing, superabundant life of communion. Sent by the Spirit, Jesus' ministry is not so much as a teacher or example but to be "a bearer of this divine life that aims at drawing the world into the way of existence that is to be found in the trinity."[11]

The church's missionary nature derives from its participation in this overflowing trinitarian life. Orthodox theology emphasizes the notion of *theosis*— literally "deification." Through baptism, Christians share the very life of God. This is particularly expressed in the members of the church becoming members of Christ's body, extensions, as it were, of Christ's identity and activity in the world.[12] Because of this, "we do not have the option of keeping the good news to ourselves."[13]

This identity as members of Christ's body and sharers in God's communal life is renewed and re-created as the church celebrates the liturgy, particularly as it celebrates the Eucharist. As Christians participate in communal prayer, singing and ritual action, and as they experience their unity through the communion of the one bread and one cup, they are caught up anew in God's life and life giving. As the document "Go Forth in Peace" puts it:

> The liturgy is not an escape from life, but a continuous transformation of life according to the prototype of Jesus Christ, through the power of the Spirit. . . . The liturgy does not end when the eucharistic assembly disperses. "Let us go forth in peace"; the dismissal is a sending off of every believer to mission in the world where he or she lives and works, and of the whole community into the world, to witness by what they are that the kingdom is coming.[14]

THEOLOGIANS AND MISSIOLOGISTS

In his commentary on chapter I of AG, Yves Congar points out that the trinitarian perspective of Vatican II's decree on missionary activity, as well as the trinitarian perspective of the council's document on the church to which AG is so intimately connected, is based on three theological traditions.[15] In the first place, the dynamic trinitarian perspective of AG is rooted in the theology of the "divine missions" developed by St. Augustine and the great thirteenth-century Scholastics such as Alexander of Hales, Bonaventure, Albert the Great and Thomas Aquinas. This perspective is further developed, Congar says, by the missionary ecclesiology of Cardinal Pierre de Bérulle in the seventeenth century, an ecclesiology characterized by missiologist André Rétif as based on Bérulle's rich insights into the close connection between the interior processions of the Trinity and their external missions in the world.[16] In the third place, Congar says, the decree's emphasis on the Trinity is influenced "at least in a general way" by the twentieth-century Protestant missionary thinking; Congar cites in a footnote Lesslie Newbigin's 1963 work on the trinitarian foundations of mission.[17] This Protestant influence is expressed as well by Joseph Masson in his own commentary on AG; it is becoming clear, he says, that Vatican II's decree on missionary activity "is the result of a series of official documents, scientific researches of theologians and missiologists, and the lived experience *(presa di coscienza vissuta)* of the whole people of God today, both Catholics and other Christians."[18] It is here that we see a vital connection between the council's dynamic trinitarian theology of mission and the theology that founded much of the Protestant thinking on mission in the latter part of the twentieth century.

This influence of Protestant mission theology on AG, we believe, was significant for the development of the trinitarian perspective in the years after the council. Such influence has its origin in the trinitarian theology of Karl Barth, and in particular in an important paper that Barth gave at the 1932 Brandenburg Mission Conference. At this conference, says Norman Thomas, Barth rejected the idea of mission as a human activity of witness and service, the work of the *church*, and insisted that it was primarily *God* who engages in mission by sending God's self in the mission of the Son and the Spirit. "The church can be in mission authentically only in obedience to God as *missio*."[19] Barth's idea was taken up by Karl Hartenstein, who in 1934 coined the term *missio Dei* and distinguished it from the *missio ecclesiae,* the mission of the church that takes its existence from its participation in God's mission, which is always accomplished in trinitarian fashion.[20]

Although the exact term was not used, *missio Dei* became the key idea in the 1952 meeting of the IMC in Willingen, Germany, where Hartenstein played a key part, along with Wilhelm Andersen and Lesslie Newbigin. Mission, said the final document, "comes from the love of God in His active relationship with [humanity]."[21] Rather than anchoring mission in the context of ecclesiology or soteriology, says David Bosch, Willingen followed Barth and Hartenstein and situated it in the context of the doctrine of the Trinity—which was, for an official document, an "important innovation."[22] As Bosch summarizes Willingen's message:

> The classical doctrine of the *missio Dei* as God the Father sending the Son, and God the Father and the Son sending the Spirit was expanded to include yet another "movement": Father, Son and Holy Spirit sending the church into the world. . . . Willingen's image of mission was mission as participating in the sending of God. Our mission has no life of its own: only in the hands of the sending God can it truly be called mission, not least since missionary initiative comes from God alone.[23]

The result of this, therefore, is that mission is not a task that is one among several in which the church should be engaged; mission, rather, belongs to the very purpose, life and structure of the church—its "royal charter."[24]

There was present at Willingen, however, an interpretation of the *missio Dei* that actually militated against this powerful ecclesiological interpretation and actually *excluded* the church's involvement. If God is the primary missionary, and if God works in the whole world, then it is the *world* that sets the agenda for the church, not the church that is the sign and instrument of God's presence in the world. Chief among those who developed this more secularized notion of *missio Dei* was the Dutch theologian Johannes Hoekendijk. For Hoekendijk, *missio Dei* means that God needs no help in "articulating himself"; the church's missionary efforts only get in the way. If anything, the church simply points to what God is doing in the world; that is all.[25] Such a perspective reached its peak at the 1968 meeting of the WCC at Uppsala, Sweden, where the church was often ridiculed and where the church itself was seen as an arena for mission, "together with centers of power, revolutionary movements, universities and urban areas."[26]

It is most likely because of this secular interpretation of the *missio Dei*—and, as we shall see in the following chapter, the emergence of liberation theology— that the rich trinitarian theology of mission articulated by AG did not make a stronger impact at the time on the Catholic missiological scene. Since the 1980s, however, there has been a genuine renewal in trinitarian theology in Catholic, Protestant, Evangelical and Pentecostal theology, and it is possible to say that the understanding of mission as rooted in the trinitarian mission of God in the world is once again at the forefront of missiological thinking.

For Catholics, at least, this general renewal in trinitarian theology can be traced back to Karl Rahner's 1967 essay on the Trinity in which he makes the observation (and this despite the trinitarian perspectives of LG and AG) that "Christians are, in their practical life, almost mere 'monotheists,'" and that "should the doctrine of the Trinity have to be dropped as false, the major part of religious literature could well remain unchanged."[27] Rahner's trinitarian theology took as its starting point the saving work of God in the missions of the Son and the Spirit, insisting that Christians know God's nature as trinitarian communion (what he calls the "immanent Trinity") not from speculation or arcane revelation but from their experience of God in Jesus and in the Spirit (the "economic Trinity"). Indeed, says Rahner in a famous dictum, *"The 'economic' Trinity is the 'immanent' Trinity and the 'immanent' Trinity is the 'economic' Trinity."*[28] At the same time, Karl Barth's mighty trinitarian theology has been revived and further developed by the German theologian Eberhard Jüngel,[29] and Jürgen Moltmann has also written creatively and somewhat provocatively on the Trinity's revelation in history through the death of Jesus on the cross, together with an ecclesiology that incorporates both the trinitarian and *missio Dei* perspectives.[30]

The 1980s and 1990s saw the publication of a number of important works on the Trinity, many of which were linked explicitly to ecclesiology and the church's mission. Brazilian theologian Leonardo Boff linked the unity in diversity of the trinitarian communion with God's action for justice in the world. For Boff, God is both model and agent for liberation, equality and justice in a world marked by sin and oppression; to be church is to share God's life and to be on God's side.[31] Catherine Mowry LaCugna emphasized the importance of the economic Trinity in her ground-breaking study *God for Us: The Trinity and Christian Life.* "An immanent trinitarian theology," she writes, "cannot be an analysis of what is 'inside' God, but a way of thinking and speaking about the structure or pattern of God's self-expression in salvation history." And what it means to be church is to participate in that saving action of God: "The mission, the 'being sent forth' of every Christian, is the same as the mission of Christ and the Spirit: to do the will and work of God, to proclaim the good news of salvation, to bring peace and concord, to justify hope in the final return of all things to God."[32]

In her elegant re-imagining of God images and God language in feminist perspective, Elizabeth Johnson also begins from God's revelation in human experience and constructs a doctrine of God that is thoroughly trinitarian. She writes:

> The power of an interpersonal communion characterized by equality and mutuality, which [the Trinity] signifies, still flashes like a beacon through the dark night, rather than shining like a daytime sun. . . . Yet the central notion of the divine Trinity, symbolizing not a monarch ruling from isolated splendor but the relational character of Holy Wisdom points inevitably in that direction, toward a community of equals related in mutuality.[33]

From among several equally significant works,[34] we mention finally David S. Cunningham's 1998 volume *These Three Are One: The Practice of Trinitarian Theology*. Cunningham emphasizes the point that our trinitarian *faith*, if genuine, will radically change the way we live; this is because it challenges contemporary understandings of the individual and helps us open up to otherness and diversity. Trinitarian faith—participating, that is, in God's rich, "polyphonic" life—will lead us toward peacemaking, inclusion and new forms of authority. Cunningham does not deal with the missiological implications of his work, but they are fairly obvious and quite important.[35] At least one missiologist has reflected on the implications of Cunningham's work as a theological foundation for inculturation.[36]

In the last several years there has appeared a good number of specifically *missiological* works—Catholic, Conciliar Protestant, Evangelical and Pentecostal—that have given new life and depth to the notion that mission is fundamentally about the participation in God's mission in the world through the sending of the Son and the Spirit. In a 1998 article, British missiologist Anthony Gittins speaks eloquently about the nature of mission being rooted in God's "bountiful, boundless, expansive, outgoing goodness." Mission is, says Gittins, God's job description, describing "both what God does and who God is," and Christians engage in mission not by doing this or that particular kind of work or going to this or that place, but by being conformed "to the mission and ministry of Jesus (which is the extension of the *missio Dei*, the mission of God)."[37] Robert J. Schreiter, in several places in the last few years, has indicated that the trinitarian understanding of the *missio Dei* might hold out a new direction for mission theology. In a summary of an important meeting held in 2000 under the auspices of SEDOS, Schreiter remarked how many of the speakers at the symposium referred to the *missio Dei* and suggested that it might be coming back into use today with a different sense than it had in the 1950s with Barth and

Hartenstein. "In view of the many difficult, seemingly intractable issues mission is facing—conflict, interreligious violence, growing poverty and hunger, loss of local control, erosion of the physical environment—there seems to be a growing awareness that it is not that we carry out mission, but rather that we participate in what is first and foremost God's work." This does not mean, Schreiter insists, that our missionary work should withdraw commitment from social justice or social engagement; it rather points to a new spirituality in the face of what seems an overwhelming challenge: our task is to cooperate with God's presence in the world, not go it alone.[38] At a symposium reflecting on the task of mission for the twenty-first century, Schreiter again emphasized the rootedness of mission in *God's* work and the church's identification with that work as constitutive of its identity.[39] He further spoke of the explicitly trinitarian character of mission and its importance for a new understanding of mission in our new century. First, he said, the unity in diversity of the Trinity will be a key for a theology of religious and cultural pluralism that is the mark of postmodern thought and civilization. Second, trinitarian existence provides a strong theological foundation for mission as a dialogical process of giving and receiving, proclaiming and learning, speaking out prophetically and opening oneself for critique.[40]

In a 1998 article, Stephen Bevans presents a trinitarian approach to mission that lays particular emphasis on the mission of the Holy Spirit. Following the insights of Frederick Crowe, Elizabeth Johnson and John V. Taylor, Bevans argues for a temporal and experiential priority of the Spirit as the Mystery of the Father's love "inside out" in the world, a presence that is given a concrete "face" in the ministry, death and resurrection of Jesus. Bevans writes:

> I propose that the church will live out its mission worthily only to the extent that it allies itself with and is transformed by the Spirit's power. If the Spirit is the first way that God sends and is sent, the Spirit's activity becomes the foundation of the church's own missionary nature. If the church is to express its nature, therefore, it needs first to look at the Spirit's activity. Its task is, like that of Jesus, both to follow the Spirit's lead and to be the concrete 'face' of the Spirit in the world.[41]

Gittins, Schreiter and Bevans are all Catholics. Among Protestants, Evangelicals and Pentecostals, there is also a strong emphasis on the trinitarian nature of the mission of God as the foundation for the church's mission. Thomas Thangaraj, an Indian missiologist teaching at Emory University in the United States, begins his theology of mission from the experience of being human: to be human is to be engaged in a *missio humanitas*, a movement of responsibility, solidarity and mutuality. Such a mission is understood as the image of the *missio Dei*, made concrete both in the *missio Christi* and the *missio ecclesiae*, and transformed by Christian faith into cruciform responsibility, liberative solidarity and eschatological mutuality.[42] Mennonite missiologist Wilbert Shenk insists that any renewal in the church today is inexorably linked to the "recovery of the *priority* of mission," a priority that is constitutive of the church. "The character of the mission of God," writes Shenk, "is defined by the ministry of God's messiah, Jesus the servant, whose servanthood was empowered by the Holy Spirit."[43] Very much along the same lines is British missiologist Andrew Kirk, who explains that God's mission is based on the very nature of God as such—a community of love and mutuality that overflows into the world in a presence that calls humanity to equality, mercy, mutuality, compassion and justice. Kirk envisions the church as elected (not for privilege but for responsibility) to live out God's missionary nature, and so essential is this that, should the church cease to be missionary, "it has not just failed one of its tasks; it has ceased being church."[44]

In two important works of missionary ecclesiology, Darrell Guder and Craig van Gelder express the same urgency for the church to be aware of its missionary nature through its partnership with God in the world. Guder summarizes:

> The *missio Dei* has always been the gospel, good news about God's goodness revealed in God's Word through Israel's experience, leading up to its climax and culmination in Jesus Christ. . . . The Father sends the Son. This exclusive focus upon God as the subject of his mission is essential to the gospel, for it makes it clear that humans, in their lostness, find hope in what God has done for them, not in what they might imagine they can do for themselves. . . . God's mission continues as that call takes shape in the apostolic community, the church.[45]

Guder and van Gelder are also deeply involved in a movement entitled The Gospel and Our Culture Network and, with a number of their colleagues, have published several studies that are rooted in the trinitarian, *missio Dei* perspective. One of these, a collaborative effort entitled *Missional Church*, is also a full-blown missionary ecclesiology and has been an important contribution to the contemporary discussion.[46]

Much of the renewal in trinitarian theology in the West owes its inspiration to Orthodox theology. As Orthodox theologian Timothy (Kallistos) Ware puts it, the doctrine of the trinity "is not a piece of 'high theology' reserved for the professional scholar, but something that has a living, *practical* importance for every Christian."[47] The mutual openness of Father and Son, Son and Spirit, Spirit and Father as a model of relationship, the constitutive nature of relationship for personal identity, the inclusion of diversity in community—all these vital truths and practices are rooted in trinitarian reality and existence. Theologians like Valdimir Lossky, John Meyendorf and John Zizioulas have helped theologians in the West understand the Trinity as an ec-static communion of persons, always involved in the world, always inviting all of creation to share in the triune life of communion-in-mission.[48] Such an understanding of God as Trinity is at the basis of the Orthodox theology of mission as well.

While we can speak of the church as Christ-centered, says prominent Orthodox missiologist Archbishop Anastasios Yannoulatos, this can only be understood authentically if it is understood in a trinitarian way. "The one-sidedness of the Western type of Christocentrism was often caused by the restriction of the image of Christ to the so-called 'historical Jesus.' But the Christ of the church is the eternal word . . . who is ever-present in the church through the Holy Spirit, risen and ascended. . . . The faith and experience of the church are summed up in the phrase: the Father, through the Son, in the Holy Spirit, creates, provides, saves." The Trinity, says Yannoulatos, is a loving communion of persons, and to be church means to share in that dynamic life of love: "By sharing the life of the risen Christ, living the Father's will moved by the Holy Spirit, we have a decisive word and role in shaping the course of humankind."[49]

In his pioneering systematization of Orthodox mission theology, James J. Stamoolis quotes M. A. Siotis's "definition"[50] of the church as "not an institution" but "a new life with Christ and in Christ, guided by the Holy Spirit." Stamoolis then points out two important aspects of this "definition." First, he says, Siotis understands the church as constituted not by structures (hierarchy), but by activity. Second, this activity is characterized by an extension of *God's activity* in the world, although the church's activity cannot be equated with the *missio Dei* as such, for God's mission is carried on outside of and independently of the church. Nevertheless, to be church is to share in that mission by virtue of one's participation in the life of Christ, and to be guided, like him, by the Holy Spirit.[51] This is why, as Vsevolod Spiller has said, "the Church *as such* is mission."[52]

Stamoolis also points out, as do Orthodox theologians in general, how central the liturgy (the Eucharist) is to an Orthodox understanding of mission.[53] Liturgy is always the entrance into the presence of the triune God and always ends with the community being sent forth in God's name to transform the world in God's image. Mission is conceived, in other words, as "the liturgy after the liturgy," the natural consequence of entering into the divine presence in worship.[54] Stamoolis speaks of the liturgy as a "method" for mission. It is the source of Christian witness because at liturgy women and men open themselves to the Spirit through communion in the Lord's body and blood. And just as the Spirit is invoked in the epiclesis of the Eucharistic Prayer to change the gifts of bread and wine into Christ's body and blood, Orthodox theology maintains that "it is not only upon the gifts that the priest prays the Spirit will descend, but upon the congregation as well."[55] As Orthodox liturgical theologian Alexander Schmemann expresses it, the Eucharist transforms the church into what it is, "transforms it into mission."[56]

MISSIO DEI AND THE SIX CONSTANTS OF MISSION

How might this trinitarian/*missio Dei* foundation for mission interpret the six constants that we have proposed? In general, it would do so through a combination of Type B and Type C theologies. While, on the one hand, any centrality accorded to understanding God as Trinity might seem to fall within a more

Mission as Participation in the Mission of the Triune God

Stream of Christianity	Roman Catholic	Orthodox	Conciliar Protestant
Theological typology	C/B (emphasis on history and truth)	C/B (emphasis on history and truth)	C/B (emphasis on history and truth)
Primary documents	Ad Gentes	"Go Forth in Peace"	Willengen document, "Ecumenical Affirmation: Mission and Evangelism"
Theologians/ missiologists	Rahner, L. Boff, Johnson, LaCugna, Cunningham, Gittins, Schreiter, Bevans	Ware, Lossky, Siotis, Meyendorf, Zizioulas, Yannoulatos, Stamoolis, Schmemann, Oleska, Voulgarakis	Barth, Hartenstein, Hoekendijk, Thangaraj, Shenk, Kirk, Guder, van Gelder, Newbigin

CONSTANTS

Christology	Spirit Christology Exemplar (subjective) model Inclusive, pluralist
Ecclesiology	Servant, mystical communion, sacrament Communion-in-mission People of God, pilgrim people, body of Christ, creation of Spirit Missional
Eschatology	Inaugurated/realized Historical/individual
Salvation	Holistic
Anthropology	Primarily positive Social, communitarian, cosmic
Culture	Critically positive Anthropological and moderate counter-cultural models

academic approach to theology, still Orthodox theology, theologians influenced by it (for example, LaCugna), and Karl Rahner all point to the fact that the doctrine of the Trinity is a practical doctrine with many concrete ramifications for Christian life. It took shape not so much out of the speculations of Greek-inspired philosophy but in the struggle of the early church to "bring to speech" its experience of Jesus as revealing the mystery of God and the Spirit inspiring faith and guiding the community. And such experience persists today. David Cunningham even speaks of how trinitarian faith both originates and results in *practice*. Quoting Wittgenstein, Cunningham argues that *"practice* gives the words their sense" and that doctrines such as the Trinity "draw their meaning from, and are ultimately intended to have some effect on, the practices of the believing community."[57] S. Mark Heim points to the doctrine of the Trinity as holding the solution to Christians' contemporary dilemma regarding the uniqueness and absoluteness of Jesus as universal savior and the experience of insight and validity in other religions. It is precisely the divine diversity in unity that is the ground of a true pluralism of religious ends as well as the ground of the confession of Jesus' unique role in God's gracious saving action in the midst of creation.[58] So, while there may be some elements of Type B theology in this approach—and certainly understanding God as Trinity takes some philosophical sophistication and hard thinking—we believe that a trinitarian/*missio Dei* foundation for mission falls in the more practical realm of Type C. In many ways it is an elaboration of Irenaeus's insight that the Son and the Spirit are the Father's two hands within history.[59]

A *Christology* rooted in a trinitarian understanding of God could certainly avoid the temptation of a focus on Christ that is too narrow, on what some theologians have called a "Christomonism." On the one hand, Jesus could be understood as not focusing on himself but on the reign of God, on the Father (see Mt 11:25-27; Mk 1:15; Lk 18:18-19; Jn 12:44-45; 14:9; 17:1-8). On the other hand, a *Spirit Christology* would emphasize both the central role of the Spirit in Jesus' mission (see Mt 3:13-4:1; Lk 3:21-22; 4:1, 16-19) and the Spirit's presence before Jesus' coming and in places beyond the boundaries of the church (see AG 4, GS 22, RM 29). Jesus is, at it were, the "face" of the Spirit, who is "God inside out" in the world. He is the agent par excellence of the Spirit's work of stirring up prophecy; re-creating; restoring life; and bringing healing, reconciliation and forgiveness.[60] As the "face" of the Spirit, Jesus can be confessed as the unique bearer of God's salvation; at the same time, Jesus does not exhaust God's saving presence and saving activity. Orthodox theologian Michael Oleksa makes the point that the Christian, while knowing where Christ is, can never be certain where he is not.[61] And Lesslie Newbigin writes that "the Spirit who thus bears witness in the life of the Church to the purpose of the Father is not confined within the limits of the Church. It is the clear teaching of the Acts of the Apostles, as it is the experience of missionaries, that the Spirit goes, so to speak, ahead of the Church."[62]

A number of theologians today speak about the paschal character of the Trinity's life and mission. The mutual giving and receiving that is constitutive of the divine communion is mirrored, first, in the sending of the Spirit into the world. Through the Spirit, in other words, God's mystery is turned "inside out" and so is fully present within the warp and woof of cosmic and historical processes. In a second move of self-giving, God's mystery is present in the historical person of Jesus through the self-emptying of the eternal Logos (Phil 2:6-11). Orthodox theologian Elias Voulgarakis speaks of God's mission as God's *kenosis* in the world for the sake of the world's unity.[63] Such an understanding leads to an interpretation of Jesus' death and resurrection as part and parcel of that full self-giving, one that Jesus completes by sending, from the cross, the Spirit into the world (Jn 19:34; see also the Easter refrain *Vidi Aquam*), and, on the evening of his resurrection, sending the Spirit upon the church (Jn 20:22). Like Jesus, the church is sent by the Father (Jn 20:21) in the power of the Spirit, to spend itself for the life of the world (see Jn 6:33; 10:10).[64]

A trinitarian-inspired *ecclesiology* speaks of the church as a communion-in-mission. On the one hand, the church is understood as a *communion*; it is "a people made one with the unity of the Father, the Son, and the Holy Spirit" (LG 4). As David Cunningham has pointed out, the Trinity challenges us to think differently not only about God but about ourselves. We are not so much *individuals*, as our Western culture in particular would have it, but, as images of God, deeply social and communal in nature.[65] The perfect communication and self-giving that is God's very self is the church's deepest reality, since Christians have undergone *theosis* and participate in the divine nature (see 2 Pet 1:4). At a mysterious and yet very real level, the church is fully one, even though divided, because God is one; in the same way the church is fully catholic, because God exists and lives in a rich diversity. Like a complex fugue or polyphonic motet, God's unity is constituted by diversity and God's diversity is rooted in unity of will and purpose; the church is the church inasmuch as it has been included in that harmony. What the church is in its deepest reality, it is called to be in its every aspect. The building of a vibrant community life, therefore, where real sharing, mutuality, justice, service and solidarity take place, is of the church's essence as a sign and foretaste of its own destiny and that of all creation. In the same way, a real sense of local autonomy and cultural identity needs to be fostered, as well as a sense of communion with other local churches and Christians of other cultural groups. Within the inevitably multicultural reality of the church today, not the uniformity of monarchy but the unity in diversity of the Trinity is to be the goal. In the same way, the church participates in God's holiness and is called to make itself holy—both in the sense of being set apart, different from the world in which it lives, and in the sense of reflecting God's excellence in the community of its members.

The church's apostolicity reveals the fact that as rooted in trinitarian life it also sees itself as a communion-*in-mission*. Like the Trinity, it is "missionary by its very nature" (AG 2), because it takes its very identity from the mission of the Son and the Spirit and is founded on the "apostles" who were called with the whole church to share that mission in the world. As Moltmann has expressed succinctly, "It is not that the church 'has a mission' but the very reverse; . . . the mission of Christ creates its own church."[66] So the church's inner unity moves it to be a sign and instrument of unity in the world; its catholicity calls it to be a sign and instrument of diversity in unity for all to see. In the same way, the church's holiness is an impetus to point to the holiness of creation and to call all people to authentic life in God. The church's holiness is not for itself but for the world, as "bearers—not exclusive beneficiaries."[67]

The image of the church that resonates most closely with its trinitarian foundation would most likely be that of people of God. The church community, participating in God's life, is God's special people, a people living God's life of communion in a covenant of relation and love, a people convinced of its fundamental equality through its common baptism in the name of the triune God. But as communion-in-mission, this image takes on a dynamic meaning as God's people on pilgrimage, God's people chosen not for themselves but for God's purposes, God's people respectful of the Spirit's workings outside their own boundaries but committed to sharing the full implications of God's covenant with all humanity (see LG 13-17). But two other major images of the church in the New Testament, body of Christ and creation of the Spirit, would also figure prominently in any trinitarian missionary ecclesiology. Christians baptized in the name of the Trinity are configured to Christ's death and resurrection (Rom 6:1-11) and become one body with him through participation in the Eucharist (1 Cor 10:14-17); their closeness in Christ is expressed through the unity and diversity of gifts for service, and so the church lives as the Lord's presence in the world, sharing and continuing his mission of making concrete the Spirit's work. As the Acts of the Apostles emphasizes, it is the Spirit who leads the early community to its realization as church, as its members cross boundaries that perhaps even Jesus never dreamed of in his own ministry.

Church structures, finally, are at the service of this communion-in-mission.While not everyone in the church proceeds by the same path (see LG 32), all share equally in the dignity of God's people, and all are called in their own way to ministry and mission. It is this trinitarian unity in diversity that grounds any leadership in the church. Ordained ministry is not something *quantitatively* different from any other ministry, but it finds its *qualitative* difference in the peculiar service of ordering the whole community by coordinating the community's ministries, presiding at its worship and guarding its faith.[68] As such, ecclesial leadership is real possession of authority, but, as the root of the word suggests, it is an exercise of augmenting *(augere)* and calling women and men to true responsibility or "authorship" in their Christian lives. All authority is to be exercised in dialogue, with care for participation, subsidiarity and collegiality.

A trinitarian *eschatology* would be focused particularly on the "already" aspect of Christian life. In baptism and Eucharist, Christians are incorporated into the divine life and experience a foretaste of the world's destiny of full communion with God, with one another and with all of creation. To experience salvation is to experience this communion fully; to experience damnation is to decide to be forever isolated from anyone or anything else. Any future fulfillment, in terms of "general eschatology" or "personal eschatology," is not qualitatively different from the present state of the world or a person bathed in God's grace. As Aquinas says so succinctly, present grace is "the seed of future glory."[69] Life after death, says S. Mark Heim, "is not an addendum to this life, but an unveiling and ratification of its actual character."[70] As Orthodox theologians emphasize, participation in the liturgy is an eschatological event. "The Eucharist is always the End," writes Schmemann, "the sacrament of the *parousia*."[71] In the Eucharist one experiences already, through ritual and communion, the destiny of all creation.

Nevertheless, since Christian existence is participation as well in God's ongoing mission of calling creation to its fulfillment, a trinitarian eschatology would be one where the "not yet" aspect of God's plan would also have a place. The continuation of Schmemann's sentence quoted above insists that, while the Eucharist *is* the sacramental participation in the *parousia*, it is, nevertheless, "always the *beginning*, the *starting point*: now the mission begins, 'We have seen the true Light, we have enjoyed life eternal,' but this Life, this Light, are given us in order to 'transform' us into Christ's witnesses in the world."[72] History continues after the liturgy, and the church has been transformed to bear God's witness within it. Through the Spirit, Christians in liturgy "proclaim the death of the Lord until he comes" (1 Cor 11:26).

S. Mark Heim insists on the centrality of trinitarian faith for the uniquely Christian understanding of *salvation*. While *moksha,* nirvana, total peace through full submission to God's will and perfect union with the One are valid and achievable religious ends, Christians seek the religious end of communion with the triune God that at the same time puts them in communion with one another and with the whole of created reality. Heim sees damnation as a real possibility for human beings who systematically refuse to open up to any other reality but themselves, but he argues that there is a variety of levels of relationship with God, all grounded in the Trinity's unity in diversity and diversity in unity. Salvation, as such, however, is something that comes only through Christ (explicitly or implicitly acknowledged) and consists in participation in God's triune communal life and mission. In line with our eschatological reflections in the previous paragraphs, salvation is something that is operative *now* as we live in the presence of God's grace in the Spirit through Christ (again, explicitly or implicitly acknowledged), and yet it is something toward which we continually move in this life, and into which we grow more deeply as we move beyond this life. The question is not, Heim insists, the validity of other religious ends, but rather what end most accords with the deepest desires of human and creaturely existence. This is why mission exists, to proclaim and witness to the world the "depths of the riches" (Rom 11:33) of God's love, and the availability of that love as the Spirit speaks to human hearts and as Christ reveals that love through his life of authentic service "unto the end" (Jn 13:1). And since communion with God can never be separated from communion with human beings and with all of creation, the sense of a holistic salvation is not lost. Communion with other human beings means justice and reconciliation, and communion with the entire created world means a commitment to creation's integrity.[73]

In a wonderful passage at the end of his two-volume systematic theology, Robert Jensen expresses this trinitarian understanding of salvation in terms of musical harmony:

> The last word to be said about God's triune being is that he "is a great fugue." Therefore, the last word to be said about the redeemed is Jonathan Edwards's beautiful saying . . . : "When I would form an idea of a society in the highest degree happy, I think of them . . . sweetly singing to each other." The point of identity, infinitely approachable and infinitely to be approached, the enlivening *telos* of the Kingdom's own life, is perfect harmony between the conversation of the redeemed and the conversation that God is. In the conversation God is, meaning and melody are one. The end is music.[74]

Such an understanding of salvation, of course, presupposes an *anthropology* that emphasizes both humanity's radical social nature and its unbreakable connection with the whole of the created world. First of all, human beings image God in that they only find their fulfillment in relationship and communion. The great myth, in the light of trinitarian theology, is the modern understanding of the person as a completely autonomous individual. Africans are much closer to the truth with their phrase "I am because we are" than are modern Westerners with the idea "I think, therefore I am." Personhood is not grounded on personal experience and personal achievement; it is always something that one receives from another. Community is not something that a group of individuals contract to make; it is something that exists prior to each individual and happens when people acknowledge the bond that binds them together. Mission in the light of trinitarian existence is the call to work with God in creating a human community that reflects God's perfect self-giving and self-receiving, a community of equality, mutuality and justice.

At the same time, trinitarian faith calls us to recognize the interconnectedness of everything in the universe. Everything is related to everything else, and this means that an anthropology in the light of the Trinity can never be one that is anthropocentric. Humanity may be described in one sense as the pinnacle of God's creation, but such distinction, to follow what Lesslie Newbigin calls the "logic of election,"[75] is never for itself but for the whole. The more one is gifted, the more responsibility one holds. On the other hand, however, since everything is indeed related to everything else, humanity is also *part* of the whole. Just as God is present and active in every created particle in the universe, so those who are called to participate in this presence and activity need to recognize their interconnectedness and responsibility for all that exists.

Trinitarian faith certainly sees the human person as fallen and sinful. S. Mark Heim points out that Western theology, inspired by Augustine, and Eastern theology, inspired by Irenaeus and Origen, have two different understandings of human sinfulness. For Augustine and the West, Adam's fall incurred moral guilt that was passed down generation to generation through original sin. The more legal development of the West through Tertullian (Type A theology) eventually led to the brilliant theology of atonement of Anselm of Canterbury and the Reformation and Counter-Reformation's theology of justification. Human beings stand before God as guilty, and through Christ that guilt is covered up (Luther) or taken away (Trent). Eastern theology, however, understood sin as the loss of capacity for relation with God, with the subsequent loss of capacity for eternal life.[76] Irenaeus, as we saw in Chapter 2, conceived of Adam's fall more as a misdirection and enslavement. Humanity, says Irenaeus, was created in God's image and called to grow into God's likeness. Tragically, Adam turned humanity away from this direction, but Christ, through his death and resurrection and sending of the Spirit, set it back on the path of growth toward full recapitulation at the end of time.

A trinitarian understanding of mission could, in fact, favor either of these explanations of human sinfulness. It seems to us, however, that the Eastern understanding, particularly that inspired by Irenaeus, is one more consistent with the love of God expressed in God's loving, missionary nature, and one that is more resonant with the relationality that is at the heart of God and God's presence in the world. The triune God, and the church participating in God's life and mission, calls humanity to abundant life. Humanity without the full understanding of the depths of God's love (again, an understanding that is either explicit or implicit) is lost and needs to be found, blind and needs to see.

Finally, an understanding of mission rooted in the Trinity looks upon *culture* in a most favorable way. As AG expresses it, through God's "secret presence" (AG 9) in history and culture, there are distributed "treasures . . . among the nations of the earth" (AG 11), in which the "seeds of the Word" are hidden (AG 9). When missionaries, like Jesus, are truly in relationship with God's Spirit, that Spirit will impel them to discover those seeds as they practice "sincere and patient dialogue" (AG 11) with the cultures and times in which they find themselves. In a 2001 article, Stephen Bevans attempted to sketch out the trinitarian foundations for the process of inculturation. The thesis of the article was that Christians "must promote the inculturation of the gospel because, ultimately, *God* promotes the inculturation of the gospel."[77] In terms of the economic Trinity, the Spirit's mission points to the fact that God is always and everywhere "inside out" in the world; all creation, therefore, is holy, because it is constantly touched by "the finger of God's right hand" as the Pentecost Sequence "Veni, Sancte Spiritus" expresses it. That mysterious presence of the Spirit is made concrete by God's incarnation in Jesus, pointing to the lengths that God will go to communicate God's love to humanity, and pointing to the sacredness of human history, human endeavors and human flesh: "*Caro/Cardo*: the flesh, the concrete, the particular, the ordinary is the way to God. In an even more radical way, whatever is good in God's creation is material for human response, expression and celebration. Inculturation is a natural and inevitable response to incarnation."[78] But the immanent Trinity is also a foundation for inculturation and points to the holiness of culture. First, says Bevans, the communal, relational and dialogical life of the Trinity points to the need for mission itself to be the same. So much of mission involves the task of *attending* to the peoples and cultures in which the gospel is being proclaimed, being evangelized, so to speak, by the cultural treasures found there. Second, the unity in diversity that is the Trinity is a witness to the need for a diversity of cultures so that the full richness of Christ can be discovered.[79] Finally, Bevans suggests, as has David Cunningham, that, seen through the lens of trinitarian faith, Christians can discern "in the fabric of God's creation, historical events and human culture, certain 'triune marks' — what the tradition calls *vestigia Trinitatis* — that help us understand what God is like."[80] Thus culture, for eyes of faith, becomes a way of deepening in a fully human and contextual way, human knowledge of and relation with the Mystery that is ineffable and yet closer to us than we are to ourselves.

At the same time, it is clear that culture has its limits and is often thoroughly ambiguous. A trinitarian perspective of communion and relationship will be prophetic over against any forms of culture that do not acknowledge human dignity and equality or all of creation's interrelatedness. And incarnation's sharp particularity reveals that God's saving presence in the Spirit has particular parameters. "Not everything concrete in culture holds the 'secret presence.' Jesus is, as it were, God's standard, against which the rest of concrete expressions are measured and in relation to which they are validated."[81]

CONCLUSION

Richly theological, thoroughly ecumenical, eminently practical, basing the foundation of mission on the fact that Christians participate in the trinitarian life and mission of God is, of all three theological foundations that we discuss in this third part, the most promising. Such a trinitarian grounding is in tune with some of the most important theology being done today, and it acknowledges unabashedly the centrality of the trinitarian mystery in Christian life and theology. Christology is an integral part of mission from this perspective, but there is room as well for the work of God's Holy Spirit to lead men and women further into God's unfathomable mystery and to allow Christians to recognize God's surprising presence outside of exclusively Christian parameters. Mission is the basic and most urgent task of the church, not because without human action so many might not reach some kind of fulfillment, but because to be Christian is to become part of God's life and God's vision for the world. David Bosch gives this trinitarian perspective his wholehearted approval: "Mission has its origin in the heart of God. God is a fountain of sending love. This is the deepest source of mission. It is impossible to penetrate deeper still; there is mission because God loves people."[82]

There are dangers, however, within this approach, to which the secularized, churchless theology of the 1960s starkly attests. There is a danger of Christ's integral, even central role in God's mission being eclipsed by a naive understanding of the priority of the Spirit.[83] There is a danger, as well, that the emphasis on the Holy Spirit in the trinitarian mission might lead to a denial of the uniqueness and absoluteness of Jesus Christ and of the superiority of fulfillment that God offers in salvation in and through him. Finally, there is a danger that the particular *ecclesial* nature of mission might be seen as trivial or unnecessary and that conversion to Christ or to God's purposes in him would not include membership in a community of faith. But while these are real dangers, we do not believe they are intrinsic to the conviction that mission is ultimately rooted in God's own nature and saving work. The dialogue with the world and with human beings that this understanding of mission implies is, to our minds, a *sine qua non* of doing mission today. As we will see, one can hold a strong position about the trinitarian foundation of mission and still profess the centrality of Jesus' Lordship and the necessity of the church. This notion can only be enriched by the other approaches to mission that are part of the synthesis of mission as prophetic dialogue.

10

Mission as Liberating Service
of the Reign of God

EVANGELII NUNTIANDI AND THE DOCUMENTS
OF THE WORLD COUNCIL OF CHURCHES

Evangelii Nuntiandi

Instead of taking as a point of departure the grand doctrine of the Trinity and the wide sweep of God's plan of salvation as the ground of the church's mission—and perhaps in response to the virtual explosion of liberation theologies in Latin America and subsequently throughout the world[1]—Paul VI's 1975 apostolic exhortation *Evangelii Nuntiandi* (EN) anchors its theology of mission in the second major theological strain to which we have pointed. EN begins with the concrete ministry of Jesus and his preaching of the kingdom or reign of God. This preaching "sums up the whole mission of Jesus" (EN 6) and points to the fact that Jesus is the "first and greatest evangelizer" (EN 7). The church's role in evangelization—whether in terms of its pastoral activity, its reevangelization of those who no longer believe, or its first proclamation of the gospel to those who have never heard of Christ (see EN 49-58)—comes from its vocation to prolong and continue Jesus' mission in the world (EN 15).

Jesus' work as an evangelizer, the pope insists, was the proclamation of the kingdom or reign of God, "and this is so important that, by comparison, everything else becomes 'the rest,' which is 'given in addition.' Only the Kingdom therefore is absolute, and it makes everything else relative" (EN 8; the reference is to Mt 6:33). It is of this kingdom that Jesus speaks in his parables, witnesses to in his works of healing and nourishment, and embodies in the very mystery of his person. Key to an understanding of this kingdom is the notion of salvation, which Jesus makes available to everyone he meets, on the sole condition that the person open up fully to God's love by undergoing "a total interior renewal . . . a radical conversion, a profound change of mind and heart" (EN 10). This salvation is for the whole person; a proper understanding of the kingdom and its salvation demands an anthropology that sees all people as needing not only internal and spiritual healing, but external and physical healing as well, as they are drawn together into a community of disciples. Nevertheless, while the pope accepts the idea that God's salvation is "liberation from everything that oppresses man" (EN 9), he insists that it cannot be reduced to only that; "it must envisage the whole man, in all his aspects, right up to and including his openness to the absolute, even the divine Absolute" (EN 33). This is the first appearance of the word *liberation* in an official Catholic document, and it clearly reflects the influence of the theology of liberation that was so important in the 1970s.

The community of disciples that gathered around the Twelve took its identity from a common faith in the crucified and risen Jesus. It began to realize that Jesus' words "I must proclaim the good news of the kingdom of God" now applied to itself as its own "grace and vocation," its "deepest identity" (see EN 14). In other words, the early church began to realize gradually what is clear to us today; that is, it had come into existence through faith in the risen Lord for one main purpose: "in order to evangelize, that is to say in order to preach and teach, to be the channel of the gift of grace, to reconcile sinners with God, and to perpetuate Christ's sacrifice in the Mass, which is the memorial of his death and glorious Resurrection" (EN 14).

Mission, in other words, is what it means to be church, because to be church means to share in the mission of Jesus, which was to preach, to serve and to witness with his whole heart to the kingdom of God. This idea is expressed in another way as the pope reflects on the complex nature of the evangelization process. Evangelization begins with the "silent proclamation of the Good News" as Christians witness by their life together, by their solidarity with the local culture and by the efforts of men and women of all faiths "for whatever is noble and good," by their fidelity to values "that go beyond current values, and their hope in something that is not seen and that one would not dare imagine" (EN 21). As people begin to ask questions about their motives for such behavior, Christians answer with a specific proclamation of the gospel: "The Good News proclaimed by the witness of life sooner or later has to be proclaimed by the word of life. There is no true evangelization if the name, the teaching, the life, the promises, the Kingdom and the mystery of Jesus of Nazareth, the Son of God are not proclaimed" (EN 22).

Evangelization then enters a third stage as men and women express further interest in the gospel message, attach themselves to the church as catechumens and, through baptism, are incorporated visibly into the community of believers and celebrate with the community the full sacramental life of the church (EN 23). But the pope goes on to insist that there is a fourth stage to the evangelization process, one that is integral to the whole: the person who has been evangelized and incorporated into the church goes on to evangelize others by witness and, eventually, new proclamation. Paragraph 24 says it clearly: "Here lies the touchstone of evangelization: it is unthinkable that a person should accept the Word and give himself to the kingdom without becoming a person who bears witness to it and proclaims it in his turn." Here is the inner reason for mission: incorporation into the church, which exists as the continuing presence and activity of Jesus in the world, the continuation of Jesus' mission of preaching, serving and witnessing to the kingdom of God.

Toward the end of the apostolic exhortation, when the pope speaks of the role of the Holy Spirit as the "principal agent of evangelization" (EN 75), some elements of the trinitarian approach of AG are hinted at. And in several places the document anticipates in some way the motives for mission that John Paul II will articulate more fully in RM (EN 53, 78). Nevertheless, the motive for mission in EN remains quite distinct:

> The Church remains in the world when the Lord of glory returns to the Father. She remains as a sign—simultaneously obscure and luminous—of a new presence of Jesus, of his departure and of his permanent presence. She prolongs and continues him. And it is above all his mission and his condition of being an evangelizer that she is called upon to continue. For the Christian community is never closed in upon itself. The intimate life of this community . . . only acquires its full meaning when it becomes a witness, when it evokes admiration and conversion, and when it becomes the preaching and proclamation of the Good News. Thus it is that the whole Church receives the mission to evangelize, and the work of each individual member is important for the whole. (EN 15)

Documents of the World Council of Churches

While documents from the WCC also point to the roots of mission in the trinitarian reality of God's mission in the world,[2] and while never flinching from the centrality of preaching Christ,[3] their main emphasis in the last quarter of the twentieth century was on the church's identity as the witness to and embodiment of the reign of God. The particular focus of these documents is on the church's mission of liberation and its commitment to justice, peace and the integrity of creation.

In many ways these documents represent a position of moderation compared with what the WCC had issued in the decade or so previously. In the 1960s, as we have seen in Chapters 8 and 9, particularly under the leadership of Johannes Hoekendijk, the WCC had developed a radical position out of the trinitarian, *missio Dei*–oriented ideas rooted in Karl Barth, Karl Hartenstein and the 1952 conference at Willingen. At a 1960 WSCF conference in Strasbourg, Hoekendijk challenged his young audience "to move out of the traditional Church structure in open, flexible groups" and "to begin radically to desacralise the Church."[4] As the decade of the 1960s developed, mission was seen almost exclusively in terms of working for justice in the world. In the famous phrase of the 1968 Uppsala Assembly, it is the *world*, not the church, that writes the agenda for mission.[5] However, by the next WCC assembly in Nairobi, Kenya, in 1975, the tide had turned somewhat toward a more balanced understanding of mission, one that was not church-centered but that understood the church as intimately connected to God's mission of establishing God's reign within God's creation.

The Nairobi assembly spoke about the church's mission as confessing and proclaiming the whole gospel to the whole person throughout the whole world by the whole church. To preach Christ today, in other words, inevitably involves "the responsibility to participate in the struggle for justice and human dignity, the obligation to denounce all that hinders human wholeness, and a commitment to risk life itself."[6] It is the work of every person in the church, which is dedicated to the transformation and renewal of every people, culture and situation. The centrality of the reign of God for mission, however, was developed more fully by the 1980 meeting of the World Conference on Mission and Evangelism in Melbourne, Australia, under the theme "Your Kingdom Come." The origins of the church's mission is in Jesus' mission of proclaiming the reign of God, for that same mission has been entrusted to it. Like Jesus' recognition that God's Spirit had anointed him "to preach the good news to the poor" (Lk 4:18), so the church's understanding of its own vocation to proclaim the reign of God is one that commits it to a gospel of liberation and justice:

> The Church of Jesus Christ is commissioned to disciple the nations, so that others may know that the kingdom of God has already drawn near and that its signs and first fruits can be seen in the world around the churches, as well as in their own life. Mission that is conscious of the kingdom will be concerned for liberation, not oppression; justice, not exploitation; fulness, not deprivation; freedom, not slavery; health, not disease; life, not death. No matter how the poor may be identified, this mission is for them.[7]

The 1982 WCC ecumenical affirmation on mission and evangelism also links mission with the church's sharing and continuing in the kingdom ministry of Jesus. Mission, it says, "ensues from the nature of the Church as the Body of Christ, sharing in the ministry of Christ as Mediator between God and His Creation," the very heart of which "is the proclamation of the kingdom of God inaugurated in Jesus the Lord, crucified and risen." Mission centered on the reign of God is described as complex and multifaceted. It involves a vital liturgical life, a commitment to evangelism and a "daily lifestyle in solidarity with the poor, through advocacy even to confrontation with the powers that oppress human beings."[8] In a reference to the 1975 document "Confessing Christ Today," the affirmation insists that the preaching of the gospel is directed to all areas of life: it must be the *whole* gospel preached to the *whole* person and to the *whole* world. Jesus' teaching about the reign of God was a teaching about "God's loving lordship over all human history," and so mission cannot be limited "to a supposedly private area of life. . . . The Good News of the kingdom is a challenge to the structures of society (Eph 3:9-10; 6:12) as well as a call to individuals to repent."[9] Connecting the trinitarian nature of mission to this holistic vision, the 1982 document quotes Nairobi: "The transfiguring power of the Holy

Trinity is meant to reach into every nook and cranny of our national life. . . . The Evangelistic Witness will also speak to the structures of this world; its economic, political and societal institutions."[10]

In 1989, at the fourth World Conference on Mission and Evangelism in San Antonio, Texas, the same connection was made between a trinitarian-rooted understanding of mission and one that emphasized the liberating power of the reign of God. The first section of the conference's final document, "Turning to the Living God," opens with the double affirmation that "at the very heart of the church's vocation in the world is the proclamation of the kingdom of God inaugurated in Jesus the Lord, crucified and risen . . . and made present among us by the Holy Spirit" and that "the Triune God, Father, Son and Holy Spirit, is a God in mission, the source and sustainer of the church's mission. The church's mission cannot but flow from God's care for the whole creation, unconditional life for all people and concern for unity and fellowship with and among all human beings."[11] There cannot be a "material gospel" and a "spiritual gospel"; these have to be one, "as was true of the ministry of Jesus. . . . There is no evangelism without solidarity; there is no Christian solidarity that does not involve sharing the message of God's coming reign."[12] Also significant in San Antonio was that, for the first time at a missionary conference, the idea of ecological concern and action was given major attention as an integral part of the church's mission, thus widening Nairobi's idea of the *whole* gospel to include care for "the integrity of creation."[13]

At the 1996 Conference on World Mission and Evangelism in Salvador, de Bahia, Brazil, a strong link was again made between the understanding of mission as the participation primarily in God's mission and the wider understanding of what God's mission entails. The conference focused mainly on the importance of culture in the proclamation of the gospel but, as a foundation for this, spoke of the need not to view the gospel in a narrow, one-dimensional way. The work of mission, it said, quoting the 1910 Edinburgh conference, is urgent and needs to be done now, and it affirmed that "it is still the church's primary calling to pursue the mission of God in God's world through the grace and goodness of Jesus Christ. Yet this mission, history-long, worldwide, cannot be seen today in narrow ways—it must be an every-member mission, from everywhere to everywhere, involving every aspect of life in a rapidly changing world of many cultures now interacting and overlapping."[14]

The Eighth Assembly of the WCC, celebrating its fiftieth anniversary in 1998, was held in Harare, Zimbabwe, with the theme "Together on the Way: Being Together under the Cross in Africa." The Assembly Message concluded with these powerful words:

> We are challenged by the vision of a church
>   that will reach out to everyone,
>   sharing,
>   caring,
>   proclaiming the good news of God's redemption,
>   a sign of the kingdom and a servant of the world.

We are challenged by a vision of a church,
    the people of God on the way together,
    confronting all divisions of race, gender, age or
       culture
    striving to realize justice and peace,
    upholding the integrity of creation.
. . . .

We journey together as a people of prayer.
    In the midst of confusion and loss of identity,
    we discern signs of God's purpose being fulfilled
    and expect the coming of God's reign.
. . . .

We expect the healing of human community,
the wholeness of God's entire creation.[15]

THEOLOGIANS AND MISSIOLOGISTS

The idea that the church takes its mission from its relationship to the kingdom or reign of God was certainly not a new one in the last third of the twentieth century. The great Methodist churchman and missionary E. Stanley Jones, for example, is well known for insisting on the priority of the kingdom in the church's mission, and he reacted to what he thought was a too church-centered approach at the 1938 Tambaram meeting of the IMC.[16] Already in the 1930s and 1940s, theologians were reflecting on a new eschatological turn in Protestant ecclesiological thinking. "The mission of the Church flows from her nature," writes Richard McBrien in a summary of these theologians; "namely, she exists to orient the present world toward the future Kingdom where God will be all in all. The Church, then, is the instrument of the Kingdom, *but it is not itself the Kingdom.*"[17] In an article appearing in English in 1951, Lutheran theologian Krister Skydsgaard argued that the church receives its entire identity from the reign of God, and even though it is already manifest in the church, the church awaits its full and final inauguration. At that time, the age of the church will come to an end and the church itself will cease to exist: "the age of signs will give way to the age of sight."[18] In 1954, Anglican theologian J. A. T. Robinson could write, "Just as the NT bids us have as high a doctrine of the ministry as we like, as long as our doctrine of the Church is higher, so it commands us to have as high a doctrine of the Church as we may, provided our doctrine of the Kingdom is higher."[19]

A major Catholic voice in this discussion was that of New Testament scholar Rudolf Schnackenburg. In 1959, Schnackenburg published *Gottes Herrschaft und Reich (God's Rule and Kingdom)*, in which he makes three vital distinctions. First, he suggests that the word *reign* expresses better the dynamic meaning of the Greek *basilea* than does the word *kingdom*. God's reign is a relationship, not a place; it is not something that comes into existence gradually. God rules already, and one day God will rule fully and completely. Second, Schnackenburg distinguishes between the reign of Christ, which is present now, and the reign of God, which is the full realization of Christ's reign at the parousia, when Christ will hand over everything to the Father (1 Cor 15:27-28). Third, the church itself must be distinguished from the reign of Christ and the reign of God. This is not to say that the church does not participate in the reign of God; it does so proleptically. But it is the people of God "imperfectly assembled . . . incompletely under the reign of Christ, and still awaiting that reign's completion at its King's coming."[20]

The Second Vatican Council reflects this scholarship, if somewhat ambiguously. In LG 5 we read that the church receives from Christ through the Spirit "the mission to proclaim and among all peoples the kingdom of Christ and of God," and "becomes itself the initial budding forth of that kingdom." But this cautious distinction was actually a big step. In fact, it was in an effort to "make precise and give theological background" to this paragraph of the document on the church that Hans Küng developed his chapter on the foundation of the church in his now-classic 1967 book *The Church.*[21] Küng begins his theology of the church with Jesus' preaching of the nearness of the reign of God. "This fact," he says, "is at the very heart of Jesus' preaching. . . . This approaching kingdom of God is the centre and horizon of his preaching and teaching, whatever the precise interpretation put on the idea of 'nearness' may be."[22] While Jesus did not found the church in his lifetime by any specific juridical act, he did, nevertheless, lay a foundation for the emergence of the church after his death and resurrection by such acts as the establishment of the Twelve, the community of disciples and the experience of shared meals together. But the church, Küng insists, is a post-resurrection reality, coming into existence as the disciples proclaimed their faith in Jesus' resurrection and saw themselves as the heirs to his ministry of the reign of God. Because theirs was the task of witnessing to that reign, Küng speaks about similarities and differences between the reign of God and the church:

> The Church is not a preliminary stage, but an *anticipatory sign* of the definitive reign of God: a sign of the reality of the reign of God already present in Jesus Christ. . . . The meaning of the Church does not reside in itself, in what it is, but in what it is moving towards. It is the reign of God which the Church hopes for, bears witness to, proclaims. . . . The Church is devoted entirely to its service.[23]

The year before the publication of Küng's book, Richard P. McBrien published his doctoral dissertation on Bishop J. A. T. Robinson in which, despite some fundamental criticisms, he strongly endorsed Robinson's emphasis on the fact that the church is always subordinate to God's reign as it carries out its mission in service to the world.[24] In 1969, McBrien published his own groundbreaking work in ecclesiology, provocatively entitled *Do We Need the Church?*

McBrien's answer to his question was very clear: *no*, if we conceive of the church as centered on itself, along the lines of a pre-Copernican or pre-Einsteinian cosmology or physics; *yes*, if by the church we mean a church that is centered on its divine election to be the sign and instrument of the reign of God. "The world, in the final accounting, needs a Church which, as a revolutionary community, never rests until the principles of the Gospel of Jesus Christ are everywhere realized and extended."[25] The church, says McBrien, must become a servant church, standing for "the highest ideals of the Gospel, standing at the forefront in the struggle for peace, racial justice, and the alleviation of poverty."[26] It is this linking of kingdom-centeredness with the commitment for justice and liberation that will constitute the further development of this theological foundation for the church's mission, fueled by the heady optimism of the time just after the council, the promise of secularization and the revolutionary activism of the 1960s.

In August 1968, the Conference of Latin American Bishops (CELAM) met in Medellín, Colombia, to reflect together on how to implement the ideas of Vatican II in the Latin American context. Taking their lead from Vatican II's document on the church in the modern world and the call of Pope John XXIII to read "the signs of the times," the documents produced by the Medellín conference employed a method that began with an analysis of a particular situation (justice, peace, education, youth, and so on), continued with a brief theological reflection in the light of the scriptures and church teaching, and concluded by stating a number of pastoral commitments. This method indicated a new way of understanding the church and of understanding the church's mission. The church was not to be centered on itself or on its own concerns, but on its mission in the very concrete world of Latin American reality; mission was conceived not only as the proclamation of the gospel but as a commitment to justice, genuine development and liberation.[27] This was a turning point, not just in the Latin American church but in the church at large, for it marks the beginnings of what would become liberation theology. Medellín anticipated what the Synod of Bishops meeting in Rome in 1971 was to say about justice: that it was a "constitutive dimension of the preaching of the Gospel, or, in other words, of the Church's mission for the redemption of the human race and its liberation from every oppressive situation."[28]

In 1971, Peruvian theologian Gustavo Gutiérrez, who had been present at Medellín as a theological advisor, published one of the first and perhaps the most widely known work of the new liberation theology—*A Theology of Liberation*. To articulate a theology that is a "critical reflection on Christian praxis in the light of the Word," Gutiérrez pulls together the work of the European political theologians Metz, Moltmann and Pannenberg; the creative interpretation of Marxism by his fellow Peruvian José Carlos Mariátegui; the insights of post–Vatican II theology; and the experience of the Latin American people.[29] Liberation theology starts with the experience of the poor and works not only toward understanding their reality, but toward liberating them from any kind of oppression, liberating them for their own participation in the drama of history and liberating them from the personal and structural bonds of sin.[30] Theology is at the service of mission, and it is committed to witnessing to and bringing about justice.

Gutiérrez links the often-cited image of the church as the sacrament or sign of salvation (for example, LG 1, 48; GS 42, 43, 45, 92; AG 2, 5) to the nature of the church as taking its mission from preaching, serving and witnessing to the reign of God. Explaining the notion of the church as sacrament, Gutiérrez says that one understands the church "only in relation to the reality which it announces. . . . Its existence is not 'for itself,' but rather 'for others.' Its center is outside itself; it is in the work of Christ and his Spirit."[31] Gutiérrez links this other-directedness of the church to its witness to the reign of God: "Since the Church is not an end in itself, it finds its meaning in its capacity to signify the reality in function of which it exists. Outside of this reality the Church is nothing; because of it the Church is always provisional; and it is towards the fulfillment of this reality that the Church is oriented: this reality is the kingdom of God, which has already begun in history."[32] The task of the church today, Gutiérrez continues, is both *annunciation* and *denunciation*: announcing the good news of God's reign involves at the same time denouncing and working against any oppression or injustice. The church's missionary task stands or falls on its solidarity with the world's marginalized and victims of injustice.

Gutiérrez's perspective is developed in depth in an important book by Mexican ecclesiologist Alvaro Quiroz Magaña.[33] After tracing the main aspects of the theology of liberation as it had developed in the preceding two decades in Latin America, Quiroz Magaña develops a "basic horizon" from which one can understand the "ecclesiology of liberation" by linking the idea of the missionary nature of the church to the church's sacramental nature and also to the church's emergence as the community that continues Jesus' mission of preaching, serving and witnessing to the reign of God. Such a church will be church in a new way in the context of Latin America, one that is "in solidarity with the poor and oppressed who seek their liberation," one that "is sign and servant of the Reign of God as it makes itself the church of the poor, the church of the people."[34] Quiroz Magaña goes on to re-image the three Pauline images of the church—people of God, body of Christ, creation of the Spirit—in the light of the church's missionary, liberating task. He speaks of the four traditional marks of the church from such a perspective as well: unity must never dodge conflict, catholicity emphasizes the particular situation of the poor, holiness calls the church to constant conversion and apostolicity is done in faithfulness to the church's missionary nature of liberation. In a final chapter, Quiroz Magaña treats office in the church, emphasizing the pivotal importance of the basic ecclesial communities for understanding the nature of ministry, whether ordained, religious or lay. As Leonardo Boff would say, such communities have "reinvented the church." Such small communities, in other words, have pointed out new and dynamic ways of living the gospel in fidelity to the reign of God.[35]

Protestant ecclesiology, especially the ecclesiology of Wolfart Pannenberg and Jürgen Moltmann, has also focused on the eschatological nature of the church in relation to the reign of God. In 1969, Pannenberg published a collection of essays entitled *Theology and the Kingdom of God* in which he offers a strong critique of the Protestant ecclesiology as focused too much on the church as a *congregatio sanctorum* or *fidelium*. He points out that such an understanding of the church "usually tended toward the distorted notion that the Christian community is primarily concerned with itself and with the piety and salvation of its members."[36] The church *is* a communion with Christ, says Pannenberg, but not in a static, church-centered sense. Rather, communion with Christ points to the fact that Jesus' central concern was the proclamation of God's reign. "Within the context of proclamation and expectation of God's Kingdom, the idea of communion with Christ reveals its genuine meaning and avoids privatized notions of religious communion."[37] The church, in other words, is concerned not with itself, but with the world and the future God is working out within it; missionary activity, therefore, needs to strengthen and develop Christian communities "so that they may become progressive examples of, and forces for, human dignity in their societies."[38] Moltmann has already been cited in the previous chapter as developing a strong trinitarian understanding of the church; while this is true, his early work on the theology of hope emphasized the eschatological nature of all Christian theologizing and practice. In the same way, his 1977 volume of ecclesiology, while it admits influence by the theology of the *missio Dei*, also shows the influence of Latin American liberation theology and has a lengthy chapter on the church and its relationship to the reign of God. "In provisional finality and in final provisionality, the church . . . witness[es] to the kingdom of God as the goal of history in the midst of history. In this sense the church of Jesus Christ is *the people of the kingdom of God*."[39]

Both Pannenberg and Moltmann, as we have already indicated, exerted considerable influence on the development of Latin American liberation theology. In addition, liberation theology, articulated originally by Catholic theologians like Gutiérrez, Boff and Segundo, found expression in Latin American Conciliar and Evangelical Protestants and even, to a certain extent, among Latin American Pentecostals.[40] In 1970, several years before Gutiérrez and Latin American liberation theology burst upon the theological scene, James Cone wrote that "the event of the kingdom today is the liberation struggle in the black community."[41] Participation in the struggle, Cone writes a few pages later, "is the defining characteristic of the church." For Cone, the church has a threefold task: it must proclaim the reality of divine liberation; it must actively share in the liberation struggle; and it must itself be a visible manifestation that the gospel is a reality "of the irruption of God's kingdom."[42] Justo González speaks of the church as a *mañana* people—not in the sense that the church is fixed on some "pie in the sky," but that it is a radically eschatological reality. There is no conflict between a commitment to justice and a commitment to evangelism, for our proclamation of Jesus' Lordship is only credible if we live what we proclaim. "To love our neighbor, to do justice, to announce peace, to care for the widow and the orphan—all these are not things we do beyond or apart from proclaiming the good news. They are a necessary part of the good news. Evangelism must be grounded on the spirituality of the Reign of God or it is not the good news of Jesus Christ."[43] The centrality of the reign of God is also in evidence in other forms of liberation theology, such as those of Africans and feminists.[44]

Since the epochal events of 1989 and the demise of Communism in Europe and the Soviet Union, some of the utopian vision and Marxist analysis of the theology of liberation have needed major refocusing. Robert Schreiter, in dialogue with some of the literature in this regard, suggests that a post-socialism liberation theology needs to focus on the liberating aspects of popular religiosity, on deepening spirituality, and on particularly marginalized groups such as women, the indigenous and (in Latin America especially) those of African descent. In addition, he says, the tasks of a theology of liberation need to be more clearly delineated in an age of globalization and neo-liberal capitalism: there is need of resistance, denunciation, critique, advocacy and reconstruction.[45] In an age of one multinational economic system (capitalism) and one superpower (the United States), globalization is the context in which the church's mission is lived and worked out. The church's commitment to justice needs to be articulated and practiced in critical collaboration with the emerging global "culture." The church needs to celebrate the unity of the globalized world and the new consciousness of human rights and dignity that the communications revolution has ushered in. But it also needs to stand firm for the vision of God's reign as a reign of justice, dignity and equality; it needs to use the miracles of communication to mobilize support against any abuse of status or power; and it needs to proclaim the possibility and fact of God's reconciling justice active in what has become a world of politically and religiously motivated violence.

The context of liberation theology has certainly changed, but its need today is greater than ever.[46] At the 2002 World Mission Institute in Chicago, liberation theologian and scripture scholar Pablo Richard emphasized the fact that, after the fall of Communism, the age of the great prophets of liberation theology is over, and that we are now in the age of apocalyptic. Rather than the call for liberation coming from the prophetic professional theologians seeking great, systemic change, Richard said, the call now comes from the grassroots, through little acts of resistance. In this way the situation is similar to Israel under Greek and Roman rule in the two centuries before Christ, and similar as well to the early Christian church, living as a tiny suspected minority within the vast and powerful Roman Empire.[47]

Catholic and Protestant missiology alike have been deeply affected by the understanding of mission as participation in Jesus' mission in service of God's reign and by the emergence of the theology of liberation. Indian missiologist Michael Amaladoss insists that one of mission's most important aspects in our contemporary world is its commitment to social justice and the change of unjust social structures. As theologians have reflected on this changed theory and praxis of mission, Amaladoss explains, they have proposed a paradigm shift in theological understanding. "The focus of mission is not the Church, but the Reign of God: the church is indeed to be built up, but as the servant of God's Reign. . . . While the Reign of God will be fully realized only on the last day and will be

God's gratuitous gift, it is also our task and we are called to contribute to its building up in history through creative development and through struggle for liberation from oppressive structures."[48] And Amaladoss writes, "In . . . humble service to the Reign of God, Christians have in the vision of Jesus a constant challenge to conversion."[49] In an article originally published in 1992, Amaladoss calls for the notion of prophecy as the theological foundation for mission in our day, but a prophecy always in service of the reign of God. This means that mission, like the reign of God itself, has a much wider focus than the church, whose "proclamation will be authentic and fruitful only insofar as it becomes transparent to the action of the Word and the Spirit"[50] as they lead the church toward its final destiny. Mission as service to the reign of God means that it is "a call to conversion, *a challenge to change*, an invitation to realize the Reign of God, an urge to enter into the creative dynamism of God's action in the world, making all things new."[51]

In his widely read introduction to missiology, the late Dutch Protestant missiologist Johannes Verkuyl speaks of the kingdom of God as the goal of the *missio Dei* and affirms that among all the various images in the Bible that describe God's purposes in the world, the image of the kingdom of God is the clearest. God's goal in the world is to establish the *basilea*, and this kingdom makes present "a total salvation, one which covers the whole range of human needs and destroys every pocket of evil and grief affecting mankind."[52] For Verkuyl, the reign of God includes an acknowledgment of Jesus' Messiahship and Lordship. As he writes elsewhere, "There is no Kingdom without the King."[53] Second, a call to God's reign is a call to conversion, although conversion is not so much a matter of sorrow and remorse as it is beginning to "think again." It involves "a total reorientation of one's thinking, will, and emotions and results in a new style of living and new conduct."[54] Third, the "messianic Kingdom" necessarily includes the "messianic People";[55] conversion to God's reign always includes a communal dimension. Full consciousness of what God's reign entails will mean entrance into the church; but any acceptance of God's purposes in this world will bind women and men closer together in community. This third point leads to a fourth, which is that God's reign always includes a commitment to struggle for justice at every level.

In 1992, Verkuyl presented what might be considered a fifth ramification of kingdom-centered theology. In an essay in a Festschrift for missiologist Arthur F. Glasser, Verkuyl rehearses the four implications sketched out above and then speaks of the importance of dialogue with other religions as a direct consequence of missionary activity grounded in and directed by the biblical symbol of the reign of God. While the breadth of the kingdom of God beyond the church should not compromise Christian faith in Jesus' unique Lordship, nevertheless, says Verkuyl, it does point to the presence of a genuine general revelation and the universality of God's offer of grace to humanity:

Who could fail to see evidence of the clemency of God in the fact that the great religions have created forms of human community that have provided for a certain amount of regularity and order in the lives of whole peoples? Who could fail to recognize the presence of God's compassion in the humanizing of social relationships brought about by the great religious systems of the world? Who would dare to deny the workings of God's mercy in the development of ideas and the refinement of human thought inspired by these religions?[56]

Verkuyl notes that "missiology is more and more coming to see the kingdom of God as the hub around which all mission work revolves."[57] Verkuyl mentions the works of Max Warren, Hans Jochen Margull, D. T. Niles and Ludwig Wiedenmann. We could also mention the essays of Raymond Fung, Daniel von Allmen and John V. Taylor.[58]

THE REIGN OF GOD AND THE SIX CONSTANTS OF MISSION

Particularly in its form as liberation theology, this second theological foundation for mission as participation in Jesus' mission of preaching, serving and witnessing to the reign of God is an outstanding example of Type C theology. But even in its more general form, this theology is rooted in history and in the church's commitment to action within it, in imitation of Jesus' own action of preaching about God's love and mercy, bringing comfort and healing to those who suffer, and witnessing to God's inclusiveness by his association with those deemed unworthy of God's concern and compassion. Mission conceived as sharing and continuing Jesus' mission is a "feet-on-the-ground theology,"[59] constantly scrutinizing "the signs of the times," and rooted in Christian experience. Mission done in the light of the reign of God is always about transformation; liberation theologians have helped the church see that genuine transformation must always be about liberation, whether at the level of economic justice, structural realignment or personal conversion. While a trinitarian theology of mission begins from a doctrine hammered out in dialogue with Hellenistic culture, a kingdom-oriented mission theology has direct recourse to scripture—in fact, to the central theme in Jesus' ministry.

Christology, therefore, will focus first and foremost on the "historical Jesus" as presented in the gospel narratives. As Küng and the majority of exegetes have argued, preaching, serving and witnessing to the already-present but not yet fully inaugurated reign of God was the main preoccupation of Jesus' mission. Jesus, as Edward Schillebeeckx has argued, saw himself as the eschatological prophet, the one whose task was to announce by word and deed and in his very person the imminent fulfillment of God's promises to Israel. It was for this reign that Jesus lived, and he was handed over to death because of his convictions about the radical transformation of the religious and political world that the reign of God demanded.[60] The focus of such a Christology will be on Jesus' humanity, a humanity through which women and men encountered the fullness of God. Dedicated completely to the witness to God's reign, Jesus

MISSION AS LIBERATING SERVICE OF THE REIGN OF GOD

Stream of Christianity	Roman Catholic	Conciliar Protestant
Theological typology	C (emphasis on history)	C (emphasis on history)
Primary documents	*Evangelii Nuntiandi* Medellín document	"Confessing Christ Today" "Your Kingdom Come"
Theologians/ missiologists	Schnackenburg, Küng, McBrien, Gutiérrez, Quiroz Magaña, Freire, L. Boff, Segundo, Magesa, Hines, Richard, Amaladoss	Skydsgaard, Robinson, Pannenberg, Moltmann, Cone, González, Verkuyl, Warren, Margull, Niles, Wiedenmann, Fung, von Allmen, Taylor

CONSTANTS

Christology	Low Liberation Inclusive, pluralist
Ecclesiology	Herald, servant, sacrament of salvation People of God, pilgrim people, body of Christ, creation of Spirit Missional
Eschatology	Inaugurated Historical
Salvation	Holistic Liberation
Anthropology	Positive Communal
Culture	Primarily positive Praxis and moderate counter-cultural models

himself is totally theocentric; he never focuses on himself. The irony, however, says Roger Haight, is that "what he presents to the world is a God who is anthropocentric. God's cause is the cause of human existence. God is a God who is for humanity, as creator and thus one who is intrinsically interested and concerned about the well being of what God creates." God is "like Jesus."[61] And the Christian community, reflecting on this fact and on its own tradition of prayer, began to understand that Jesus *himself* was, in the language of its surrounding culture, *consubstantial* with God, was "of one being with the Father," in the words of the Nicene Creed (DS 125-126). Because Jesus *re-presented* God in his praxis of the reign of God, we can confess Jesus *both* as fully human and fully divine, as the Council of Chalcedon concluded (DS 300-303).

Such a Christology "from below" is matched by an *ecclesiology* that is equally so. Jesus' mission was centered on God's reign, not on the foundation of a church. Jesus can certainly be said to have instituted the Twelve as a symbol of the coming restoration of Israel; Simon or Cephas (Peter) certainly seems to have exercised some kind of leadership or spokesmanship role within this group; and Jesus certainly had about him a number of disciples, both women and men. Since it is so well attested to in the New Testament (Mk 14:22-25; Mt 26:26-29; Lk 22:14-20; 1 Cor 11:23-25), we can affirm that Jesus foresaw his death and bade his disciples remember him when they "broke bread." But, as Küng and others have argued, he did not juridically found a church during his lifetime.[62] It was only as the early community recognized its own vocation to share and continue Jesus' mission, particularly as it crossed the boundaries at Antioch and faced the new horizon of a worldwide mission, that the church as such emerged in Christians' consciousness (see Chapter 1).

Such an understanding of the church points to its radical missionary nature, for it is only in mission that the church continues to be what it is. This missionary nature, then, should begin to shape the way the church is imaged (people of God, body of Christ, and so forth), and how it is structured. Everything in the church serves its mission. Like Jesus, the church's cause is human existence and all of creation. Jesus' kingdom ministry of healing, forgiveness and inclusion is at the center of its life.

That the church gets its meaning not from itself but from the reign of God toward which it moves implies an *eschatology* that is dynamic and oriented toward the future. While Jesus preached the reign of God as already fulfilled in himself (Lk 4:21), and while the early community understood that the kingdom's presence could be found within it (for example, see Acts 2:16-21), nevertheless Jesus understood that the complete inauguration of God's reign was still in the undetermined future (for example, see Mt 24:1-25:26). Paul's conviction was that Christ is the firstfruits of the destiny of creation (1 Cor 15:20-20) and that the Spirit lavished upon the community the pledge of future fulfillment (Rom 8:23; 2 Cor 1:22; 5:5). The church takes its identity from this future and, as many theologians say, will dissolve into the greater reality of the kingdom at its final inauguration.[63] The church is the pilgrim people of God, and on the way to its destiny it calls all humanity to the plenitude of grace to which it is called and in which it already participates (LG 13-16; 48-51).

While individual eschatology is not precluded in this particular model of mission, much more important are the concerns of general eschatology—the goal of history, the communal nature of life under God's rule of compassion and love. Such a perspective fits in well with some of the utopian visions of the future that are generated in the theology of liberation. Utopia, writes Gutiérrez, involves both a "denunciation" of the existing order and an "annunciation" of the new society and transformed social order that will inevitably be established in the future. But, he says (referring to the work of Paulo Freire), "between the denunciation and the annunciation is the time for building, the historical *praxis*. . . . If utopia does not lead to action in the present, it is an evasion of reality."[64] Focus on the future, in other words, poises the church for its liberating, missionary task.

Jesus' own *praxis* of the reign of God reflects the relational and holistic aspects of *salvation*. His parables about God's lavish, even extravagant, love and forgiveness (for example, see Mt 20:1-16; Lk 15:4-32; Mt 18:21-35) paint a picture of God's reign as a community of forgiven and forgiving women and men. Jesus' healing of the blind, the lame, the deaf, the unclean, his exorcisms, and his association with sinners, the poor and women, paint a picture of a future in which all creation lives with God in peace and harmony (see Mt 11:2-6; Lk 4:18-19 [Is 61:1-3; Is 35:1-10]). As Gutiérrez explains it, salvation involves liberation from sin, whether individual or structural, and this spills over into societal transformation, political responsibility and economic stability. Salvation is both individual and communal, for creation is called to participate in "a kingdom of truth and life, a kingdom of holiness and grace, a kingdom of justice, love and peace," as the Preface for the Feast of Christ the King so beautifully expresses it.

Such salvation is offered to all, for all are called to be members of God's chosen people (LG 13), and God's Spirit is present in mysterious ways in both history and in human religions, guiding all to the reality of the paschal mystery (GS 22). God's Spirit has sown the "seeds of the Word" (RM 28) in all the world's religions, and so, through Christ, they can be true vehicles of God's saving love. Ultimately, it is not to the church that people are called, but to the reign of God; the reign of God is a reality wider than the church or explicit knowledge of and faith in Christ, and it is in the grace of that reign that people find its fulfillment, whether or not they are members of the church. Where there is commitment to peace, justice and the integrity of God's creation, there is the grace of the kingdom, and there people find salvation "already" but "not yet" present.

While the individual is certainly respected and honored in this model of mission, its *anthropology* is much more communal than individual. The reign of God is about God's working in *history*, and its goal is the transformation of *creation*. Persons are defined, writes José Ignacio González Faus, by their dual openness to communion with others, on the one hand, and to transcendence, on the other. Such openness, however, is only fulfilled within a community of freedom and love. If either of these is missing, community will be self-seeking and oppressive to others.[65] Human beings find their fulfillment, in other words, as they assert their freedom and work in love to make their brothers and sisters free as well. Liberation theology insists that humanity shines particularly brightly in the world's poor; they are a sign that being human is not a matter of what a person (or society) *has*, but rather what kind of person (or society) he or she *is*. Paulo Freire is famous for his dictum that the tragedy is that the poor, once liberated, often become oppressors themselves.[66] Being human means, therefore, to be concerned with justice and committed to service.

Liberation theologians also emphasize the structural realities of sin; they insist that much more insidious than individual transgressions are those actions and attitudes that construct or maintain networks that systematically oppress and marginalize whole groups of people or scar God's creation in a way that future generations are deprived of its wonder and resources. In the light of the preponderance of structural evil in the world, humans are seen as captives of sin rather than corrupt actors with full freedom of deliberation. Salvation comes as a liberation, as a breakthrough and triumph of the Spirit over the complex web of injustice and blindness in which human beings are enmeshed.

In the same way that God's Spirit sows the seeds of the word among the world's religions, God's presence is always and everywhere within human *culture* (see RM 28). As noted above, God's reign is wider than the church, and so the wholeness that that reign brings is found in the efforts of human beings to make sense of their world. God's presence in culture, however, is not static; it is a presence that beckons all people to work in partnership with God for the full humanization and liberation of thought forms, traditions and customs.[67] Culture, while generally good, can be coopted by the structures of oppression and exclusion, and is often, if not always, in need of prophetic correction in the light of the values of God's reign.

CONCLUSION

Mission as participation in Jesus' mission in service of God's reign is a powerful, dynamic model of mission. It points clearly to the truth that evangelization as a holistic process of announcing, serving and witnessing to the reign of God is constitutive of the church's "deepest identity" (EN 14). It also harmonizes well with the theology of liberation, one of the most influential theological developments in theology in the twentieth century. Perhaps even more than the trinitarian model of mission discussed previously, it recognizes that any dialogue with the world needs to be one that is truly prophetic and that takes the side of the world's poor and excluded majority, one that is involved in the warp and woof of human and cosmic history.

Church documents and theologians, however, as we will see in the next chapter, have cautioned that such an understanding of mission, particularly in terms of its focus on justice, can lead to an understanding of mission as mere humanization and development work. Pope John Paul II has strongly cautioned in RM that any understanding of God's reign must necessarily include the church. Nevertheless, the focus on the reign of God and its "centrifugal" vision is a truly necessary perspective for mission today. Mission in service of the reign of God will prove to be a key ingredient in the development of our model of mission as prophetic dialogue.

11

Mission as Proclamation
of Jesus Christ as Universal Savior

REDEMPTORIS MISSIO AND THE DOCUMENTS
OF THE EVANGELICAL AND PENTECOSTAL CHURCHES

Redemptoris Missio

On the occasion of the twenty-fifth anniversary of AG and the fifteenth anniversary of EN, Pope John Paul II issued his eighth encyclical, *Redemptoris Missio* (RM). Perhaps even more than the other two mission documents we have discussed, this encyclical quite consciously asks the question "why mission?" And while it certainly incorporates the trinitarian basis of AG (see RM 1, 7, 22, 23, 32) and devotes an entire chapter to the continuation of Jesus' mission of proclaiming the reign of God by the church (RM 12-20), another motive surfaces as primary: the obligation to proclaim the truth of the newness of life found in Jesus Christ. This is expressed most clearly at the beginning of the first chapter: "The Church's universal mission is born of faith in Jesus Christ" (RM 4), followed by a quotation from the Christological section of the Nicene-Constantinopolitan Creed. The same idea is expressed in paragraph 5: the "fundamental reason why the Church is missionary by her very nature" is that in Jesus is found "the definitive self-revelation of God." And toward the end of the chapter, the question is asked explicitly: "*Why mission?* Because to us, as to Saint Paul, 'this grace was given, to preach to the Gentiles the unsearchable riches of Christ' (Eph. 3:8). . . . The Church, and every individual in her, may not keep hidden or monopolize this newness and richness which has been received from God's bounty in order to be communicated to all humanity" (RM 11).

Cardinal Josef Tomko stated that one of the reasons the encyclical was written was to speak out against a Christology developed by some theologians that was obscuring the notion of Christ's unique mediatorship between God and humankind,[1] and one can certainly see Tomko's statement justified as the encyclical develops. The pope insists from the start that it is only through faith in Jesus Christ that mission can be understood and can find a basis (RM 4). Reflecting on the origins of the church, the pope points out that from the very beginning there was a clear affirmation that "Christ is the one Saviour of all, the only one able to reveal God and lead to God." It is perhaps significant that the first text of scripture quoted in the first chapter is from Acts 4, verses 10 and 12. The latter verse reads: "And there is salvation in no one else, for there is no other name under heaven given among men and women by which we must be saved." This rather "exclusive"[2] Christology is modified somewhat in other parts of the chapter, however. Indeed, it is affirmed several times in other parts of the encyclical that God's grace through the Holy Spirit "offers everyone the possibility of sharing in the Paschal Mystery in a manner known to God" (RM 6, 10, 28, quoting GS 22), and that the "seeds of the Word" are sown within the experience of humankind (RM 56). Nevertheless, the pope emphasizes again and again the uniqueness of the reality of Christ. No one can come to communion with God except through him (RM 5); he has absolute and universal significance and is history's center and goal (RM 6). Mission issues from faith in Christ, and is "an accurate indicator of our faith in Christ and his love for us" (RM 11). And even though interreligious dialogue is an intrinsic part of mission, it "should be conducted and implemented with the conviction that *the Church is the ordinary means of salvation* and that *she alone* possesses the fulness of the means of salvation" (RM 55).

Christians have the fullness of the truth, and because of this they are obliged to share it. But this is not the whole reason, according to the encyclical, that the church is essentially missionary. Proclamation of the name of Jesus Christ is the "permanent priority of mission," the pope says in paragraph 44, not only because of "Christ's explicit mandate," but also because men and women should not be deprived of the truth, the good news that they are "loved and saved by God." All peoples have a *right* to the fullness of truth, and so the church must be in mission. The urgency of mission comes from the fact that, while the fullness of life is found only completely with faith in Christ, there are vast numbers who do not know him or who have ceased to care (RM 3). Because of this, "we cannot be content when we consider the millions of our brothers and sisters, who like us have been redeemed by the blood of Christ but who live in ignorance of the love of God. For each believer, as for the entire Church, the missionary task must remain foremost, for it concerns the eternal destiny of humanity and corresponds to God's mysterious and merciful plan" (RM 86).

The rhetoric of RM is, in many ways, quite different from the two great mission documents that it commemorates. Its Christocentrism, however, is very deliberate; the church in the late 1980s saw itself challenged by a worldwide resurgence of religious identity among practitioners of non-Christian religions, on the one hand, and by what it considered a dangerous tendency to pluralism and indifferentism among many Christian theologians, missiologists and even missionaries, on the other. Its perspective of the centrality and uniqueness of Christ and of the church's obligation to offer all humanity the fullness of its truth is also evident in the papal documents issued after the various regional synods that took place in the 1990s, especially in the document issued by the Congregation for the Doctrine of the Faith in 2000, *Dominus Iesus*.[3] The ultimate purpose of this theology of Christian mission, however, is very much the same as AG's trinitarian emphasis and EN's kingdom perspective: to ground the church's mission in the saving love of God, who graciously has called men and women to cooperate in its manifestation. RM, nevertheless, presents a very clear and comprehensive statement of the third strain of theological thought that is proposed to ground the theology of mission as it found fresh life in the last quarter of the twentieth century: the centrality and truth of the person of Jesus Christ.

Evangelical Documents

While this emphasis on proclamation of the truth found in the person and work of Jesus finds resonance in Conciliar Protestant and Orthodox theology as well,[4] it is in Evangelical and Pentecostal theology that the more Christocentric approach of RM finds its closest parallel.[5] "To evangelise," says the Lausanne Covenant, "is to spread the good news that Jesus Christ died for our sins and was raised from the dead according to the Scriptures (1 Cor 15:3, 4), and that as reigning Lord he now offers the forgiveness of sins (Acts 2:32-39) and the liberating gift of the Spirit to all who repent and believe (Jn 20:21)." It is "the proclamation of the historical, biblical Christ as Saviour (1 Cor 1:23; 2 Cor 4:5) and Lord, with a view to persuading people to come to him personally and so be reconciled to God (2 Cor 5:11, 20)."[6]

Mission is urgent, because only in Christ can women and men find salvation.[7] Even though "everyone has some knowledge of God through his general revelation in nature"[8] and although "the religions which have arisen do sometimes contain elements of truth and beauty," human sin has placed the world "under the control of the evil one."[9] Unless women and men come to an "explicit acceptance of [Christ's] work through faith,"[10] they "condemn themselves to eternal separation from God (2 Thes 1:7-9)."[11] In the past, confesses the *Manila Manifesto*, Christians have approached those of other faiths with "attitudes of ignorance, arrogance, disrespect and even hostility." Such an attitude was wrong, but Christians still need "to bear positive and uncompromising witness (1 Tim 2:5-7) to the uniqueness of our Lord . . . in all aspects of our evangelistic work including inter-faith dialogue."[12]

While reconciliation with other people is not in itself reconciliation with God, and while social action is not evangelism and political liberation is not salvation, the Lausanne Covenant nevertheless insists that evangelism and social responsibility are both Christian duties. When persons are converted to Christ, the new life of God's reign that they experience calls them "not only to exhibit but also to spread its righteousness (Mt 5:20; 6:33) in the midst of an unrighteous world."[13] Yet at the same time, the Lausanne Covenant insists that "in the church's mission of sacrificial service evangelism is primary."[14] A joint consultation of the LCWE and the WEF on the relation of evangelism and social responsibility speaks eloquently about social activity as a *consequence* of evangelism, as a *bridge* to evangelism and as *accompanying* evangelism as a partner;[15] and the 1989 *Manila Manifesto* speaks of the essential *incarnational* nature of the church's mission: "It necessitates entering humbly into other people's worlds, identifying with their social reality, their sorrow and suffering, and their struggles for justice against oppressive powers (Phil 2:5-8)."[16] But what remains the driving force behind mission in Evangelical theology is the centrality of Christ and the proclamation of his name: "Proclaim Christ until He Comes" was the theme of Lausanne II in Manila; and a statement on the evangelization of Jews affirms that "sharing the Good News of Jesus Christ with lost humanity is a matter of prime obligation for Christian people, both because the Messiah commands the making of disciples and because love of neighbor requires effort to meet our neighbor's deepest need."[17]

From 1977 to 1984 Evangelicals and Catholics held dialogues on issues involved in mission.[18] Although they were not able to agree on everything—especially in terms of the role of the church and church authority—they nevertheless agreed that a number of "strong incentives urgently impel Christians to the task of mission": to further the glory of God, to proclaim the Lordship of Christ, to proclaim Christ's victory over evil, to proclaim the graciousness of salvation and to hasten the Lord's return.[19] In 1993 and 1997 there were additional dialogues sponsored by the Roman Catholic Church and the WEF, the second of which concentrated on the nature of the church and its mission. The communiqué that was issued at the end of this second meeting acknowledged that Roman Catholics and Evangelicals agreed on the importance of the missionary nature of the church and understood this commitment to mission as flowing "from a deep conviction regarding the uniqueness and all-sufficiency of Christ's person and work."[20] Where Evangelicals and Catholics parted company, however, was in the way that Christ's salvation is granted. For Evangelicals, one is "lost" if one does not have explicit knowledge of and make an act of explicit faith in Jesus Christ as Lord. For Catholics, God's Spirit works in "ways known only to God" to lead women and men of sincerity and good will to a participation in the paschal mystery (see GS 22).

Although it was in no way an official event, a group of relatively liberal Evangelical theologians and relatively conservative Catholic theologians met together in the early 1990s and issued, on March 4, 1994, a statement entitled "Evangelicals and Catholics Together: The Christian Mission in the Third Millennium" (ECT).[21] The statement acknowledges the connection between Catholics and Evangelicals as the "most evangelistically assertive and most rapidly growing" Christian communities in the world today and calls for a common understanding and working together, despite the fact that, especially in Latin America and increasingly in Eastern Europe, "the relationship between these communities is marked more by conflict than cooperation, more by animosity than by love, more by suspicion than by trust, more by propaganda and ignorance than by respect for the truth."[22] Nevertheless, the members from each group affirmed together that "Jesus Christ is Lord" and that such an affirmation "is the first and final affirmation that Christians make of all reality."[23] They expressed their hope "that all people will come to faith in Jesus Christ as Lord and Savior," a hope that "makes necessary the church's missionary zeal."[24] And, although there is much over which Evangelicals and Catholics still contend, the group pledged to witness together when possible, because "bearing witness to the saving power of Jesus Christ and his will for our lives is an integral part of Christian discipleship."[25]

In October 1999, the Missions Commission of the WEF held a major consultation in Foz do Iguassu, Brazil, and issued what it called the *Iguassu Affirmation*.[26] The document called for a commitment to the trinitarian foundation of mission, but it is very clear that such trinitarian emphasis needs to be rooted profoundly in the centrality and uniqueness of Jesus Christ. The first of nine declarations at the beginning of the document says that "Jesus Christ is Lord of the church and Lord of the universe. Ultimately every knee will bow and every tongue confess that Jesus is Lord. The Lordship of Christ is to be proclaimed to the whole world, inviting all to be free from the bondage of sin and the dominion of evil in order to serve the Lord for his glory." This is followed by a second declaration that "the Lord Jesus Christ is the unique revelation of God and the only Savior of the world. Salvation is found in Christ alone. God witnesses to himself in creation and in human conscience, but these witnesses are not complete without the revelation of God in Christ."[27]

Pentecostal Documents

While it is important to understand that there really are Pentecostalism*s* rather than one general Pentecostalism,[28] and while it is important as well to recognize that the Pentecostal churches differ in significant ways from Evangelical churches, we may nevertheless speak of Evangelicals and Pentecostals (particularly the classical Pentecostals and those of the Third Wave) as siblings or cousins.[29] Pentecostalism, it is generally acknowledged, emerged out of the nineteenth-century radical Evangelicalism known as the holiness movement; it has remained basically Evangelical in doctrine, "confessing belief in the Trinity (the large majority), the inspiration and infallibility of Scripture, justification by faith, substitutionary atonement of Christ, and other historic doctrines of the Christian faith,"[30] like Jesus' virginal birth.

Unlike Roman Catholics, of course, and similar to both Conciliar Protestants and Evangelicals, Pentecostals have no Magisterium to issue formal and official statements of doctrine or policy—they are famous, in fact, for their opposition to "man-made creeds and dead rituals."[31] Nevertheless, groups like the Assemblies of God did issue a "Statement of Fundamental Truths" in 1916,[32] and Walter Hollenweger offers a collection of "Declarations of Faith" from various Pentecostal bodies in the appendix to *The Pentecostals*.[33] In all of these statements one finds a strong belief in God as Trinity and an implicit belief in Jesus Christ as the one and only Savior (the creed of the Pentecostals of Italy

explicitly confesses the fact that regeneration is only through faith in Christ—
soltanto per fede in Cristo).[34]

Of particular interest to us, however, are several documents resulting from
dialogues with the Roman Catholic Church, on the one hand, and the World
Alliance of Reformed Churches, on the other. While these dialogues were quite
controversial within the ranks of Pentecostals themselves (particularly the dialogue with Roman Catholics), and while, as the most recent document of Pente-
costal/Roman Catholic dialogue says, they represent the voice of individuals,
the Pentecostal signers of these documents believe that what they express about
Pentecostalism is what is held by the majority of Pentecostals worldwide.[35] Because of this, we believe that these documents—five in all—represent a fairly
"official" Pentecostal perspective. If nothing else, they represent the perspectives of some of the most important Pentecostal theologians of the twentieth
century—among others David Du Plessis, Cecil M. Robeck, Edith Blumhoffer,
Gary B. McGee, Walter Hollenweger, David Daniels and Steven Land—as well
as eminent Catholic and Reformed ecumenists and theologians such as Hervé
Legrand, Kilian McDonnell, Karl Müller and Bishop Basil Meeking (Catholics), and Henry Wilson, Anthea Butler, Silvia Rostango and Abival Pires da
Silveira (Reformed).

Walter Hollenweger, the acknowledged "dean of Pentecostal studies," has
suggested that the dialogue between Pentecostals and Roman Catholics has been
"one of the most important events in the religious scene" of our time.[36] It began
in 1972, has produced four documents so far, and is still in progress at this
writing some thirty years later. A first "quinquennium" focused mainly on "the
phenomena of Pentecostalism"; a second focused on "faith and experience,
hermeneutics, speaking in tongues, healing, tradition, the church as communion, Mary, and ministry." A third, from 1985 to 1988, produced the "highly
acclaimed report . . . *Perspectives on Koinonia*." The fourth phase of the dialogue took a full seven years to complete and resulted in 1997 in a document
that deals with the thorny issues of evangelization, proselytism and common
witness.[37] It is the content of this fourth document that is especially important
for our reflections here.

Paragraph 8 of "Evangelization, Proselytism and Common Witness" points
out that "both Pentecostals and Catholics recognize as an essential part of the
mission of the Church the call to evangelize" (EPCW 8), because "proclaiming
God's reconciliation of the world through Christ is central to the Church's faith,
life and witness (cf. 2 Cor 5:18-19)" (11). Jesus Christ, paragraph 117 explains,
is the unique witness to God, and the Spirit comes from God the Father to witness to Jesus Christ, a witness "rooted in the apostles' experience of Jesus who
is the image of the Father sent in the power of the Spirit to return all to the
source, the Father. Disciples are empowered by the Holy Spirit to proclaim the
Gospel (Acts 1:8; 4:20)" (117).

Paragraph 13 emphasizes that Pentecostals are particularly concerned to proclaim "Jesus Christ as Saviour and Lord resulting in a personal, conscious acceptance and conversion of an individual; a 'new birth' as in John 3:3," particularly

in light of the fact that we live in the "'last days' before Christ returns." Quoting EN 27 and referring to Ephesians 2:8 and Romans 1:16, the document acknowledges that both Catholics and Pentecostals "agree that 'evangelization will . . . always contain—as the center and at the same time the summit of its dynamism—a clear proclamation that, in Jesus Christ, the Son of God made man, who died and rose from the dead, salvation is offered to all humankind, as a gift of God's grace and mercy'" (13). And, referring to Acts 4:12, the document insists that both groups of Christians "believe that there is only one Name whereby we can be saved" (21). Nevertheless, the document also acknowledges that, while all are saved through the death of Christ, Catholics have a more positive approach to other religions while Pentecostals, "like many of the early Christians, tend to point out the demonic elements in other religions" (21).

Although there seems to be a growing convergence between Catholics and Pentecostals regarding Christians' role in society, EPCW still points to the fact that, for Catholics, the process of evangelization is a more complex activity, involving not only proclamation but also commitment to inculturation and social-justice activity. Pentecostals, on the other hand, "make a sharper distinction . . . between the proclamation of the Gospel to those they consider 'unsaved' and the discipling of believers or promotion of Christian values in society" (15). Nevertheless, Pentecostals also have a strong sense of responsibility for the welfare of the whole person, and this is seen in the centrality of healing in Pentecostal theology and Pentecostals' concern for the social welfare of their members, especially in the Third World (40). While Pentecostals certainly recognize the centrality of proclamation of the person and message of Jesus in their understanding of mission, in other words, they are deeply committed at the same time to social justice—although this commitment is expressed more in action than as a result of explicit theological reasoning. Fully thirty paragraphs are devoted to the question of social justice (37-67), and, as the document puts it quite eloquently: "Pentecostals and Catholics believe Jesus Christ to be the Lord of the Kingdom. He came to proclaim, and in our preaching and understanding, the Kingdom of God and social justice should never be separated" (66).

In 2001, the journal of the Society for Pentecostal Studies, *Pneuma*, published the final report of the five-year dialogue, from 1996 to 2000, between "Representatives of the World Alliance of Reformed Churches and Some Classical Pentecostal Churches and Leaders."[38] "If there is a center to the Pentecostal message," the document points out, "it is the Person and work of Jesus Christ. From the beginning of the Pentecostal Movement, its central message has referred to Jesus Christ as Savior, Sanctifier, Spirit Baptizer, Healer and Coming King. In fact, Pentecostal practice strives to conform to the biblical injunction that the yardstick of Christ must judge those things ascribed to the Holy Spirit" (WSCW 17). This centrality of Christ in Pentecostal thought—a fact that might be surprising to some in view of Pentecostals' emphasis on the work of the Holy Spirit in the gift of tongues, other bodily manifestations (such as "holy laughter") and healing—is emphasized once more a little further on in the document where we read that both Pentecostals and Reformed Christians "agree that God has revealed God's Self decisively in Jesus Christ, the One in whom the fullness of the Godhead dwells" (19).

Where there is disagreement between Pentecostals and Reformed, it lies in the exclusivity of Christ's "Person and work" in regard to God's saving work, through the Spirit, in the world. Some Pentecostals have indeed begun to be more open to the possibility to "the role of the Spirit in creation and culture to reveal God and to accomplish God's just and holy will." However, this openness does not go as far as saying that "there is saving grace outside the ministry of the Gospel" (21). Nevertheless, both churches believe that Jesus is the Way, the Truth and the Life (22), and members of the Reformed tradition are seeking ways by which, "without diminishing the unique role of Jesus Christ in God's saving plan . . . , the role of the Spirit in culture" is understood "more expansively and positively than solely as a preparation for the ministry of the Gospel" (21). While Pentecostals and *some* Reformed do not accept that salvation is found outside explicit faith in Jesus Christ, some in the Reformed tradition are less strict in this, believing the Spirit to be acting in and through other cultures and other religious ways.

Once again, though, both traditions see mission as multidimensional and not just limited to witness and proclamation of Jesus' name. Both have a wide understanding of God's mission as embracing the whole person and will insist that the church is the servant of God's reign (78-95). Pentecostals, nevertheless, still insist on the important duty of proclamation and are convinced that "human culture stands in alienation from God and God's Truth" (68). Because of this, "the ministry of the Gospel is meant to liberate people from captivity to that which is godless in culture" (68).

In 1970, in preparation for what has resulted from thirty years of substantial Pentecostal/Roman Catholic dialogue, Catholics and Pentecostals agreed that the "essence of Pentecostalism" was "the personal and direct awareness and experiencing of the indwelling of the Holy Spirit by which the risen and glorified Christ is revealed and the believer is empowered to witness and worship."[39] These somewhat "official" documents resulting from dialogue certainly show how this Christocentric focus—in the power of the Spirit—is operative within the Pentecostal churches.

THEOLOGIANS AND MISSIOLOGISTS

Both RM and Evangelical and Pentecostal documents, while often trinitarian and kingdom-oriented, nevertheless maintain a very strong Christocentric focus. It is this centering on Christ, and on his role as unique and universal Savior, that is characteristic of this third strain of mission theology. Christian theology, of course, has always been centered on Jesus Christ, but the emphasis of this theology has emerged with particular urgency in light of the challenges in the last several decades to the validity of mission in general, and to the uniqueness and absoluteness of Jesus Christ as universal Savior in particular. The WCC's turn to "humanization" as the goal of missionary work; the writings of John Hick and Paul Knitter, who have argued for the "myth of Christian uniqueness"; calls to abandon missionary proclamation, evangelism and efforts of conversion in favor of conversation and dialogue; certain versions of the theology of liberation that seemed to abandon notions of sin in favor of human justice as the goal of the church's mission—these were all factors that provoked major Evangelical congresses in Berlin, Germany, and Wheaton, Illinois (both in 1966), the Lausanne movement in 1974 and the papal documents EN and RM in 1975 and 1991.[40] Much of the Christocentric perspective expressed in Roman Catholic documents in the last decades, as well as in Evangelical documents in the last thirty years, has been developed as a defense of the uniqueness and absoluteness of Jesus Christ and of the continuing importance of the dimension of proclamation or evangelism in missionary work. This position is not in *opposition* to a fuller trinitarian perspective or a more justice-oriented perspective afforded by focus on the reign of God, but it has been articulated in a way that attempts to avoid the real dangers inherent in both perspectives. Unfortunately, however, it can sometimes seem to fall into the opposite danger of a narrow exclusivism and mistrust of human existence, human culture and human experience. While this Christocentric perspective needs to be a vital part of a twenty-first century theology of mission, it needs both to temper and to be tempered by the two other perspectives that we discussed in the last two chapters.

The pluralist proposals of Hick and Knitter caused a furor in Catholic, Protestant, Evangelical and Pentecostal theological circles. Carl Braaten's *No Other Gospel!* was a strong denunciation of the pluralist position from the Conciliar Protestant side, and Harold Netland's *Dissonant Voices: Religious Pluralism and the Question of Truth* challenged it from the perspective of Evangelical Christian theology.[41] One of the most important Catholic contributions—although it contained essays by Protestants and Evangelicals like M. M. Thomas, Jürgen Moltmann, Rowan Williams, Christoph Schwöbel and John Milbank—was the volume edited by Gavin D'Costa and provocatively entitled *Christian Uniqueness Reconsidered: The Myth of a Pluralistic Theology of Religions.*[42] In this volume D'Costa and a number of others call into serious question both the *idea* of religious pluralism and its inherent *truth*. In the first place, the pluralist perspective, as presented by many theological pluralists at least, seems to propose not a genuine regard for the uniqueness of individual religious ways but a new absolutism and theological imperialism. Ultimately, they argue, Hick's and Knitter's brand of pluralism is really a version of exclusivism, although this time the dominating position is that of Enlightenment rationality rather than Christian universal claims. Second, while the authors believe in the value of today's pluralist religious world, they also believe that abandoning every religion's claim to uniqueness would, in effect, eviscerate every religion's identity. Dialogue is *dialogue* precisely because religious women and men believe passionately in their own religious experience and traditions. Christians, in other words, should not abandon too easily their faith in Jesus' Lordship and their obligation to share that faith with the world.

In 1996, under the direction of Sebastian Karotemprel and an international team of Catholic mission scholars, there appeared a book that was intended to serve as a "foundational course in missiology" for theological students throughout the Catholic world, aptly titled *Following Christ in Mission*.[43] The book had been in preparation since 1993 and was clearly intended to be a reflection on mission in the light of the official teaching of the Catholic Church, particularly that of RM with its signal Christological emphasis.

In the opening article, which provides a general introduction to the science of missiology, noted German missiologist Karl Müller points out that *mission* or *evangelization* could be understood both in a "broad meaning as the mission of the Church in its totality" and in a "specific meaning as the clear and unambiguous proclamation of Jesus Christ." Nevertheless, "essentially, Christ is the only foundation for mission. No matter how Scripture is turned or twisted, Christ remains central (cf. RM 4-11). He is the Alpha and the Omega, the center and goal of all creation. 'For all the names in the world given to men, this is the only one by which we can be saved' (Acts 4:12)." And so, "the main purpose of mission theology is to proclaim the name of Jesus to those who do not yet know him."[44]

In an essay on the trinitarian foundation of mission, Adam Wolanin of the Gregorian University in Rome acknowledges that the theology of the Trinity had been neglected in the past, but that Vatican II and theology since then have recognized the connection between the missionary nature of the church and its rootedness in the Trinity. Nevertheless, Wolanin offers a particularly *Christological* understanding of the Trinity in this essay. Referring to RM's observation that the waning of missionary activity is due to a crisis of faith (RM 2), Wolanin says that that lack of faith is precisely the "non-acceptance of the unique salvific value of Christ's redemptive mission which is ultimately based on the Holy Trinity. In other words, the denial of the validity of Christ's *missionary mandate* has its roots in the denial of Christ himself as the Son of God." Jesus is key to understanding God in God's full salvific, trinitarian reality: "It is from the *salvific Trinity*, and more precisely from the mission of Jesus Christ and the Holy Spirit, that we come to know the true foundation of this same mission, and consequently, of the Church's mission as well."[45] Citing Lutheran theologian Carl Braaten, Wolanin points to the fact that there is mutual connection between the doctrine of the Trinity and Christology. We can only understand the Trinity by seeing it through the lens of Christology; we can only properly understand Christology through the lens of God's communal, overflowing trinitarian nature.

Other chapters in the book also emphasize the centrality of the proclamation of Jesus Christ to the church's missionary enterprise. Because some mission thinkers are neglecting Jesus' uniqueness today, "Christian mission," writes Karotemprel, "is essentially related to the Church's understanding of Jesus Christ and the salvific value of his death and resurrection. Its content and method are

determined by Christology and soteriology."[46] Pointing to the continuing necessity of proclamation, Jesús López-Gay says that the "proclamation of Jesus Christ
cannot be substituted by purely temporal and human programs; the Gospel continues to be the center of missionary activity."[47] And, while some theologians
propose a "theocentric" proclamation of the reign of God through interreligious
dialogue and cooperation with other religions, "such a position is theologically
untenable. Jesus believed that the kingdom of God was present in himself and
his ministry, present in 'mystery.'"[48] Once again, it is important to emphasize
that while the book neither denies nor is opposed to trinitarian or reign of God
perspectives of mission—indeed, it clearly endorses them—it presents them in
a way that does not jeopardize the centrality of Jesus for evangelization, for
interpretations of God's reign and for understanding the church.

In 2000, a major missiological congress was held at the Pontifical Urban
University in Rome to inaugurate the International Association of Catholic
Missiologists and as part of the celebration of the church's Jubilee Year. Significantly—particularly because the congress was held just one month after the
publication of the Congregation for the Doctrine of the Faith's declaration *Dominus Iesus* (DI), which reiterated in no uncertain terms the Vatican's concern for
theological relativism and a loss of Christocentrism—the theme of the congress
was "Who Do You Say That I Am? Missiological and Missionary Responses in
the Context of Religions and Cultures." Subsequently, in 2001, the proceedings
of the congress were published as *Cristologia e Missione oggi* (Christology and
mission today).[49] The congress was no slavish repetition of the Magisterium's
teaching on the centrality in Christ in mission but was rather an attempt to reflect more fully and more deeply on the church's insistence on the uniqueness
and absoluteness of Christ expressed in RM and most recently in DI. Major
papers were delivered by Walter Kasper, president of the Pontifical Council for
Christian Unity, who anchored an understanding of the unicity and universality
of Christ in the Christian doctrine of monotheism, and by eminent theologian
Claude Geffré, who proposed the concept of "concrete universal" as a way of
understanding how the human being Jesus could have universal meaning. For
Geffré, it is important not to confuse the universality of *Christ* with the universality of *Christianity*. Christianity exists to promote the former, not to promote
itself. It is, therefore, a religion of dialogue: "This is not a question of tolerance
in an age of interreligious dialogue. This is a question of nature."[50] Other papers
delivered by Asians (Indians), Africans and Latin American theologians also
insisted on the constitutive nature of dialogue, inculturation and commitment to
justice for the church's mission, and they called for cultural and pastoral sensitivity in presenting Christianity's truth in their respective contexts. As one
speaker, George Karakunnel, put it:

> The Church certainly cannot abandon the foundational experience of Jesus
> Christ, the Word Incarnate, the Son of God who came into the World for
> the salvation of all. The Church by its vocation feels duty bound to pro-
> claim Jesus Christ as the Saviour. But at the same time, the Church that

lives in a pluralistic world cannot disregard the Spirit of God working in all human persons, in all cultures and religions.[51]

The balance that the congress tried to achieve was expressed well by one of its chief organizers and editors of its proceedings, Sebastian Karotemprel, who wrote in the book's introduction that

> Christian mission, on the one hand, can no longer be exclusivistic in its approach, as during the period of mission during the colonial period. It can no longer be ecclesiocentric in its approach so as to deny or underestimate the presence of the *Logos* and the Spirit in the world continuing their mysterious work of bringing salvation to all believers. On the other hand, it cannot be reduced to the promotion of the values of the kingdom of God, with little emphasis on the proclamation of Jesus Christ and the call to enter the community of the Church. Again, Christian mission cannot be presented as purely soteriocentric in a horizontal sense of the word, namely human promotion, thereby reducing Christian mission to a secular project.[52]

In the aftermath of the Fourth Assembly of the WCC, in Uppsala, Sweden, in 1968, German Evangelical Peter Beyerhaus of the University of Tübingen wrote a small but important book that sets forth the Evangelical position on mission over against the WCC's drift toward a more "horizontal" understanding of mission, which shied away from evangelism and the clear confession of Jesus as the world's only Savior. While Beyerhaus uses the language of the Trinity and the reign of God, he vigorously asserts that "mission occurs when—and only when—it is directed toward putting man's existence, through a conscious decision of faith, under Christ's lordship and His effective spiritual power." Mission, says Beyerhaus, is *"participation in the restoring, exorcising, and regenerating activity of the triune God."*[53] It is an activity that begins with the sending of the Son into history and is continued by confronting humanity with God's offer of grace in the crucified and risen Lord. Mission's goal is the return of Christ and the full inauguration of God's reign. "Mission occurs, then, *primarily* in the proclamation of the redemptive act of Jesus Christ's kingly lordship in all new and, as yet, untouched areas of life."[54]

Printed in the appendix of Beyerhaus's book is the "Frankfurt Declaration" (1970), of which Beyerhaus was the principal author. Theses one, two and three read as follows:

- Christian mission discovers its foundation, goals, and the content of its proclamation solely in the commission of the resurrected Lord Jesus Christ and his saving acts as they are reported by the witness of the apostles and early Christianity in the New Testament.
- The first and supreme goal of mission is the *glorification* of the name of the one *God* throughout the entire world and the proclamation of the lordship of Jesus Christ.

- Jesus Christ is our Saviour, true God and true man, as the Bible proclaims him in his personal mystery and his saving work, is the basis, content, and authority of our mission. It is the goal of this mission to make known to all people in all walks of life the gift of his salvation.[55]

Another prominent Evangelical missiologist who was disenchanted with Uppsala was John R. W. Stott. Stott expressed the unease of Evangelical leaders like Donald McGavran, Arthur F. Glasser and Buana Kibangi when he said: "I do not see this assembly very eager to obey its Lord's command. The Lord Jesus Christ wept over the city which rejected him. I do not see this Assembly weeping similar tears" over those millions of people who were without Christ and so were perishing.[56] Stott went on to become one of the chief architects of the Lausanne conference of 1974. He championed an understanding of mission that, while including concern for justice and the poor of the world, regarded evangelism or the proclamation of Jesus Christ as mission's primary task. In a small book published just a year after Lausanne, Stott expressed his position eloquently: "Anything which undermines human dignity should be an offence to us. But is anything so destructive of human dignity as alienation from God through ignorance or rejection of the gospel? And how can we seriously maintain that political and economic liberation is just as important as eternal salvation."[57] Nevertheless, a concern for justice is extremely important in Stott's mind; for him, mission must keep in balance both the Great Commission and the Great Commandment.

In the chapter on evangelism, Stott expounds on what the proclamation of the gospel is by first stating what it is not. It is not, in the first place, to be defined by the gospel's *recipients*. It is not a question, in other words, of *mission* being for nonbelievers and *evangelism* being for people once evangelized but who no longer practice their faith. Evangelism is about the proclamation of Christ as Lord to those who are near or those who are far. Second, evangelism cannot be defined in terms of *results*. Again, evangelism is the proclamation of the good news; it is not about being successful or being a failure at converting women and men to it. Nor, finally, is evangelism to be defined in terms of its *methods*. How the gospel is proclaimed is not the issue; evangelism is only concerned that it *is* proclaimed—by word, by deed, by film, by music, by drama, by fiction, by a transformed life. What, then, is evangelism? It is the preaching of the gospel, the good news; and "all concur that in a single word, God's good news is Jesus."[58]

One of the leading Evangelical mission theologians today is Charles van Engen, who teaches at Fuller Seminary's School of World Mission in Pasadena, California. In his 1991 book *God's Missionary People*, van Engen speaks about the essential missionary nature of the church in general and of the local community in particular. For him, as for many other missiologists today, the church gets its commission to preach the gospel from its participation in Jesus' mission to preach, serve and witness to the reign of God. Van Engen's interpretation of the reign of God, however, is particularly Christological; in this way it is quite similar to Pope John Paul II's treatment of God's reign in chapter II of RM. The church is the covenant community of the King, community ruled by the King, the central locus of the King's rule, the anticipatory sign of the rule of the King; its mission is to spread the knowledge of the rule of the King.[59] As van Engen expresses it in summary:

> The missionary Church grows, not toward some human utopia, nor toward individual salvation, perfect fellowship or spiritual identification with the values of justice, truth, joy and love. The Church points to something far more magnificent—the rule and reign of the King over the cosmos. . . . Thus as the Church emerges it moves toward Christ as *Alpha* and *Omega* (Rev. 1:8), the One who is both King of all and Head of the Church.[60]

In a 1996 collection of essays, van Engen presents a definition of mission that is both trinitarian and kingdom-oriented. Notice, however, that in the following extract the name *Jesus Christ* appears three times:

> Mission is the people of God intentionally crossing
>   barriers
> from church to nonchurch, faith to nonfaith,
> to proclaim by word and deed
> the coming kingdom of God
> in Jesus Christ;
> this task is achieved by means of the church's
>   participation
> in God's mission of reconciling people
> to God, to themselves, to each other, and to the world,
> and gathering them into the church
> through repentance and faith in Jesus Christ
> by the work of the Holy Spirit
> with a view to the transformation of the world
> as a sign of the coming of the kingdom
> in Jesus Christ.[61]

In an essay on the uniqueness of Christ in contemporary theological and missiological discussion in the same 1996 collection, van Engen notes that in the generally used terminology of *exclusivist, inclusivist* and *pluralist,* the last two terms are generally regarded as positive in today's culture, while the term *exclusivist* has taken on negative connotations. Because of this, and because his own Evangelical faith in Jesus' universality and uniqueness allies him with the exclusivist paradigm, van Engen seeks to develop a new paradigm—or perhaps a new name for the exclusivist paradigm—that expresses more positively how Evangelicals regard Christ. This "evangelist" paradigm, he says, has as its starting point that "Jesus Christ is Lord." Furthermore, it speaks of human nature as "fallen," and so defines mission as "calling people in multiple cultures to conversion, confession, and new allegiance, personally and corporately, to Jesus Christ as Lord."[62] Whether or not this position is a real advance over the exclusivist position, van Engen's point about the negativity of the terminology is well taken. In any case, Evangelicals are struggling today to maintain their strong Christocentric position over against the fact of religious pluralism and the contemporary resurgence of non-Christian religions. Another prominent Evangelical theologian, Clark Pinnock, has embraced an inclusivist position and has been disowned by many of his fellow Evangelicals; Harold Netland, on the other hand, has tried to maintain a real respect for other religious ways while at the same time trying to develop an authentic Evangelical theology of religions.[63]

A final example of Evangelical Christocentric missiology is Samuel Escobar, a Peruvian Baptist who teaches missiology both in Peru and in the United States. Escobar, along with fellow Latin Americans Orlando Costas and René Padilla, was an important figure at Lausanne and has been the advocate of a missiology of "radical discipleship," which sees action for justice as an integral and indeed constitutive part of evangelism.[64] In a presentation at the 1999 Iguassu conference, Escobar acknowledged that Evangelical missiological thought has been thoroughly Christological because it has been grounded in a Christocentric understanding of the spiritual life. Nevertheless, what is called for today, he believes, is a theology of mission that is rooted in the triune God—not in a way that would "detract from a Christ-centered stance but to look at our Lord the way Scripture presents him in relation to the Father and the Spirit."[65] Ever since the Berlin conference in 1966, Evangelicals have been searching for a new Christological paradigm; there is a sense, expressed by John Stott at Berlin, that a more trinitarian interpretation of John 20:21 might be a more profound and more challenging form of the Great Commission than Matthew 28:18. Jesus' own mission was rooted in his obedience to the Father and carried out by the direction of the Holy Spirit. It was not a triumphalistic entry of a king but the humble ministry of a son and servant. While it is necessary to preach Jesus the Christ, the Jesus who is preached is one who leads his disciples to service in turn. Drawing on the work of René Padilla, Escobar characterizes Jesus' mission as "fishing for the kingdom":

> It is conversion to Jesus which stands as the basis upon which the Christian community is formed. Mission also includes "compassion" as a result of immersion among the multitudes. It is neither a sentimental burst of emotion nor an academic option for the poor, but definite and intentional actions of service in order to "feed the multitude" with the bread *for* life, as well as bread *of* life. Mission includes "confrontation" of the powers of death with the power of the Suffering Servant, and thus "suffering" becomes a mark of Jesus' messianic mission and a result of this power struggle and of human injustice.[66]

At the same time, Escobar affirms the typically Evangelical stances of the atoning work of Jesus, Jesus' absoluteness in the face of other religions, and wariness of any compromising of the gospel in the face of popular religious practices (syncretism). Regarding these latter two issues, however, Escobar is quite nuanced; he avers that Evangelicals have much to learn from biblical evaluations of other religions. Quoting Argentinean theologian José Míguez Bonino, he believes that a Christological focus *within* a trinitarian focus can be the best guide, for the Word and Spirit are present within the movements of history. "It is no less true, however, that Christian theology cannot disengage the Word and the Spirit of God from the 'flesh' of the son of Mary. . . . By Jesus one measures all presumed presence of that God in human history."[67]

As David Bundy has asserted, "It is clear that the genre of systematic theology within Pentecostalism is still in its earliest phases."[68] Indeed, as Pentecostal theologian Russell P. Spittler has remarked, "Pentecostals have been better missionaries than theologians,"[69] and, at least up until relatively recently, Pentecostal theology was done more in the genre of the sermon, the testimony or the hymn.[70] Frank Macchia comments, "Theology was catechism and, in a movement suspicious of formal training, was considered the 'least of the gifts.'"[71] Rather than a systematic investigation of the basic doctrines of Christian faith (Trinity, Christology, ecclesiology, and so on), Pentecostal theologizing has centered on issues that needed to be hammered out as the Pentecostal movement developed into a tradition,[72] such as the meaning of tongues, the controversies of the "Jesus only" or "oneness" movement, and the controversies about the "finished work" of Christ.[73]

Pentecostalism has nonetheless produced a good number of first-rate theologians and missiologists. The Society for Pentecostal Studies has existed since 1970; since 1979 it has published *Pneuma* as its journal. In addition, the *Journal of Pentecostal Theology* began in 1992, and a number of other significant Pentecostal journals are published online. Several Conciliar Protestant and Catholic theologians, influenced by the Neo-Penteocostal or charismatic movement, have also contributed significantly to a growing reflection on the Pentecostal experience of Christianity.

In an important editorial reflection on the Roman Catholic document *Dominus Iesus*, Pentecostal theologian Frank Macchia takes strong exception to the claim by the Congregation for the Doctrine of the Faith that the true church of Christ is somehow identical (as the document interprets LG's *subsistit*) with the Church of Rome. Despite this critique, however, Macchia applauds the Christocentric aspects of the document, pointing out that foundational to the document is "an important truth that prevents the gospel from being dissolved into a general religious aspiration."[74] Jesus is the incarnate Word of God, he affirms with the document, not "one of the many faces that the Logos has assumed" (DI 9); as such, says Macchia, quoting paragraph 15 of the document, Jesus is "the 'exclusive, universal, and absolute' source of salvation for the world"[75] and not simply one way to salvation among many others. What we have here is the editor of one of the premier Pentecostal theological journals taking a firm stand against any pluralistic reading of the Christ event. With DI, Macchia affirms that Jesus Christ is "the key, the center, and the purpose" (DI 13) of the entire sweep of human history.[76]

This Christocentric emphasis in Pentecostalism is also expressed by Finnish Pentecostal theologian Veli-Matti Kärkkäinen, who emphasizes that, contrary to what many non-Pentecostals think, Pentecostalism is "not centered on the Holy Spirit more than on Christ," despite the fact that its spirituality is strongly charismatic. "The classic 'five-fold gospel,' or as it soon came to be known, 'full gospel,' of Pentecostalism depicted Jesus Christ in his role as Savior (or justifier), baptizer with the Spirit, sanctifier, healer and soon-coming King."[77] According to David R. Nichols, Christ is "the central figure of all Christian reality," and truths about him are central to any thinking about Christianity.[78] In words that are reminiscent of both RM and DI, Nichols insists that it is the ministry of *Jesus*, "and no one else," which "is propagated by the Holy Spirit in the present."[79]

Pentecostalism even includes an extreme form of Christocentrism in the "one-ness" or "Jesus only" branch of the tradition, a theology embraced by one-fourth of Pentecostals throughout the world.[80] The majority of Pentecostals, however, are strongly trinitarian in their doctrinal expression and look upon it as modalism or Sebellianism. As Catholic theologian Ralph del Colle interprets it, "The Pentecostal-charismatic experience is intrinsically trinitarian in structure." Del Colle suggests that through "the pneumatic effusion of Spirit-baptism the Christian is empowered with the Holy Spirit in the mission of Jesus to the glory of God the Father."[81] As Pentecostal theologian Simon Chan implies, however, such a trinitarian dynamic still has a strong Christocentric focus (as is certainly implied in what del Colle says as well). Chan argues that "the action of the Spirit makes possible the ongoing traditioning of Christ the Truth in the church."[82] Catholic theologian Donald Gelpi points very much in the same direction. For Gelpi, "when the charismatic experience is consciously trinitarian, one experiences the gift of the Spirit in one's ability to acknowledge Jesus as the incarnate Son of God who reveals historically to men the love of their heavenly Father."[83]

Such a trinitarian, charismatic understanding of Jesus' centrality in Christian faith necessarily leads to an understanding of mission as an essential and constitutive part of Christian faith. Gary McGee has stated that "the history of Pentecostalism cannot be properly understood apart from its missionary vision,"[84] and this can be said as well of Pentecostal theology. For Pentecostals, the experience of salvation naturally leads to sharing that experience with others. In Steven J. Land's powerful words, salvation is "*eschatological trinitarian passion*," a "passion for the God who is at work in all things to move history toward the consummation."[85] Speaking in tongues is not ultimately for oneself; it is always for others. At its best, the baptism of the Spirit and the accompanying gift of tongues are understood as empowerment for Christian witness, the center of which is witness to the Lordship of Jesus as the Christ.[86] As William J. Seymour puts it memorably, the point is not to "go from this meeting and talk about tongues, but [to] try to get people saved."[87]

As the documents resulting from dialogue with Roman Catholics and the churches of the Reformed tradition point out, the Pentecostal view of mission is not the proclamation of a mere "spiritualizing" (that is, otherworldly) message. Pentecostals do not necessarily speak about social justice or get explicitly involved in political or social issues (although they are doing both more and more).[88] Nevertheless, their strong community life and strict lifestyle (no gambling, drinking, using tobacco) do serve the survival and advancement of the poor in very concrete ways.[89]

As Allan Anderson has argued convincingly, Pentecostals all over the world have been able to inculturate Christianity to a great degree, to the extent that it cannot really be seen as "a predominantly western movement."[90] Engagement with the culture—both in terms of utilizing popular culture and religiosity and subjecting it to strong critique in the light of the Bible—seems to be part and parcel of the way Pentecostals do mission.[91] While most Pentecostals would identify with the exclusivist view that salvation is available only through explicit faith in Christ, Veli-Matti Kärkkäinen, referring to an article by Amos Yong, concludes that "the global presence of Pentecostal-Charismatic Christianity, the privileged place of the Spirit and experience in their theology and the growing internationalization of mission challenges Pentecostal-Charismatics to deepen their understanding of the role of the Spirit in the world,"[92] and among the world's religions. Pentecostal understandings of mission also include a strong sense of reconciliation among people of various classes and races. As is well known, William J. Seymour's Azusa Street revival included women and men of African American, Indian, Latino, white and Asian racial and cultural backgrounds and was heralded as a foretaste of a fast-approaching Eschaton. As one bystander put it: "The color line was washed away by the blood."[93] Finally, Pentecostal worship is suffused with mission. The purpose of tongues, as we have already noted, is to empower the recipient for witness and service, and, according to Simon Chan, "Eucharistic worship does not end in cozy fellowship, but in costly mission in the world."[94]

CHRISTOCENTRISM AND THE SIX CONSTANTS OF MISSION

The theology of RM, bolstered by the strict interpretations of DI, and the Christocentrism of Evangelical and Pentecostal mission theology, all with their emphasis on the absolute necessity of Christ for salvation, point to the inclusion of this strain of missiological thought within the perspectives of Type A theology. There is no question that Catholic, Evangelical and Pentecostal theology of this sort appreciates the richness of a trinitarian, *missio Dei* approach to mission and that an understanding of mission as the prolongation of Jesus' mission in service to the reign of God is integral to its development. Nevertheless, the openness of the trinitarian approach to the validity of other religious ways, and to the constitutive dimension of working for the justice of God's reign, while not entirely absent from this perspective—and in fact quite prominent in some

MISSION AS PROCLAMATION OF JESUS CHRIST AS UNIVERSAL SAVIOR

Stream of Christianity	Roman Catholic	Evangelical and Protestant churches
Theological typology	A (emphasis on law)	A (emphasis on law)
Primary documents	*Redemptoris Missio, Dominus Iesus*, Evangelical and Roman Catholic Dialogue on Mission, EPCW	"The Lausanne Covenant," the *Manila Manifesto*, the *Iguassu Affirmation*, Evangelical and Roman Catholic Dialogue on Mission, EPCW
Theologians/ missiologists	Tomko, Karotemprel, Müller, Wolanin, López-Gay, Kasper, Geffré, Dulles, Kroeger	Netland, Beyerhaus, Stott, McGavran, Glasser, Kibangi, van Engen, Escobar, Costas, Padilla, Bonino, Fernando, Robeck, Kärkkäinen, Macchia

CONSTANTS

Christology	High Satisfaction theory Inclusive	High Substitutionary atonement theory Exclusive
Ecclesiology	Hierarchical communion Missional	Free association of members Missional
Eschatology	Futurist/inaugurated Individual	Futurist Individual
Salvation	Spiritual Only through the church	Spiritual
Anthropology	Negative	Negative
Culture	Negative Translation and counter-cultural models	Negative Translation and counter-cultural models

parts of RM and in the thought of some Latin American Evangelicals and Pentecostals—is clearly subordinate to the proclamation of Jesus Christ (for both Evangelicals and Catholics), his atoning death (particularly for Evangelicals and Pentecostals) and his explicit connection with the institutional church (especially for Catholics).

It will be no surprise that the *Christology* of this approach is a "high" Christology. Jesus is the preexistent *Logos*; he is fully and completely human but also fully and completely divine. While Jesus' praxis of the reign of God (his teachings, miracles, inclusivity) is certainly important, the emphasis is on the fact that he is the *autobasilea*, the fulfillment of the message that he preaches. "Since the 'Good News' is Christ, there is an identity between the message and the messenger, between saying, doing and being. His power . . . lies in his total identification with the message he announces: he proclaims the 'Good News' not just by what he says or does, but by what he is" (RM 13). The kingdom of God is summed up in the identity of the King (as van Engen says). Jesus is Son of the Father; the Spirit is the Spirit of Jesus. Klaus writes, "Jesus is the clearest picture of God and His mission the world has ever seen."[95]

Perhaps more prominent in Evangelical and Pentecostal theology than in the theology of RM, but present there as well, is the notion of the death of Jesus as atoning and sacrificial. Rather than an emphasis on Jesus' death as a result of his ministry with the marginal people of his society and his insistence on a more human-centered interpretation of the law, this theology would tend to accept Anselm of Canterbury's understanding of Jesus' death as making satisfaction for sin or Luther's "penal substitution" theory. Only through Christ, therefore, does God become reconciled with the world; only by explicit faith in him can men and women find access to that reconciliation. "In [Christ], and only in him, are we set free from all alienation and doubt, from slavery to the power of sin and death" (RM 11); "there is only one Saviour and only one gospel" (Lausanne Covenant).[96] Catholic evaluations of the possibility of salvation without explicit knowledge of and faith in Christ, through allegiance to the various world religions, are more positive than Evangelical and Pentecostal theology, but such an approach does not take away the urgency of mission. For Evangelicals and Pentecostals, women and men are "lost" without faith in Christ; for Catholics that faith can be expressed implicitly, as people open up to God's Spirit who leads them "in ways known to God" (GS 22; RM 10) toward participation in the paschal mystery.

As the Evangelical–Roman Catholic dialogues on mission have pointed out, perhaps where Catholics differ most radically from Evangelicals and Pentecostals is in the area of *ecclesiology*. Evangelicals and Pentecostals have tended to focus on individual conversion and faith in Christ; an Evangelical understanding of church is very much that of a free association of believers. Schleiermacher's dictum about the priority in Protestantism of relation to Christ over relation to the church is seen with particular clarity here.[97] Nevertheless, Charles van Engen has developed an ecclesiology that emphasizes the local congregation's missionary nature. At the Iguassu congress Sri Lankan theologian Ajith Fernando spoke about the church in words that call to mind Cyprian's image of the church quoted in LG 4: a "mirror of the Trinity," a biblical community that lives a prophetic lifestyle in the midst of the world.[98] In a forward-looking article in the Pentecostal journal *Pneuma*, Simon Chan attempts to propose a Pentecostal ecclesiology that has as its basic principle that "the primary locus of the work of the Spirit is not in the individual Christian but in the church."[99]

Pope John Paul II's ecclesial vision in RM includes the vision of AG about the missionary nature of the church. An entire chapter of RM is devoted to the reign of God and its relationship to both Jesus and the church. The pope is decidedly cautious, however, about accepting current understandings of the reign of God that would emphasize secular values of liberation and justice and so downplay the close ties that God's reign has with both Jesus and the concrete church. Although the church is not an end in itself, finding its identity in the missionary service of the reign of God (RM 18-20), it already participates in the fullness of that reign through communion with the person of the risen Christ. Both RM and DI say quite clearly that the salvation won in Jesus is most fully available only through communion with the Roman Catholic Church: *"The Church is the ordinary means of salvation* and . . . *she alone* possesses the fullness of the means of salvation" (RM 55); "the ecclesial communities which have not preserved the valid Episcopate and the genuine and integral substance of the Eucharistic mystery, are not Churches in the proper sense; however, those who are baptized in these communities are, by Baptism, incorporated in Christ and thus are in a certain communion, albeit imperfect, with the Church" (DI 17). We have already noted Pentecostal theologian Frank Macchia's strong disagreement with this position, and we have certainly heard the same disagreement from a number of Evangelical colleagues as well.

Traditionally, Evangelical and Pentecostal ecclesiologies have been "low" ecclesiologies, in that the human dimension of the church is emphasized over the divine. This is matched by an *eschatology* that is future oriented, and one that makes the mission of the church urgent. As the Lausanne Covenant states: "We believe that the interim period between Christ's ascension and return is to be filled with the mission of the people of God (Mt. 28:20; Acts 1:8-11), who have no liberty to stop before the end."[100] There seems to be a trend in Evangelical—and even Pentecostal—ecclesiology, however, that would advocate a "higher" ecclesiology that recognizes the reign of God as present in some inchoate way. As van Engen expresses it, for example, the church is the "place" where Christ's rule prevails and is an anticipatory sign of that rule's universal fullness. The reign of God is much more than this, however, and points to the church's missionary nature, but van Engen's ecclesiology certainly gives central place to the church as mission's chief instrument and goal.[101] In this, van Engen's position is similar to the Catholic one. Pope John Paul II emphasizes that while the church is not an end in itself, it is at the same time ordered to the fullness of God's reign and is both a sign and instrument of its full inauguration (RM 18). Avery Dulles, commenting on the relation between church and kingdom at a theological symposium on RM, acknowledged that the church is not to

be identified totally with the reign of God. But neither is it totally to be separated from it. "In the eyes of believers, it should be obvious that the kingdom of
God cannot be adequately realized apart from the Church. Missionary activity,
in seeking to achieve an inner conversion of hearts and minds to Christ the
King, serves the Church."[102]

In terms of individual eschatology, Roman Catholics who espouse this theological perspective would insist that, while salvation is *possible* for all through
the secret workings of the Spirit, missionary proclamation is necessary to ensure that as many as possible can participate in the "means of salvation" available through membership in the church. DI goes so far as to speak of non-
Christians being in "a gravely deficient situation in comparison with those who,
in the Church, have the fullness of the means of salvation" (22). While salvation
is offered to all, the possibility is that it may not be achieved by all, despite
God's universal salvific will, the Spirit's mysterious presence, or even external
membership in Christ's church (22). For Evangelicals and Pentecostals, however, human beings are "lost without Christ," and "other religions and ideologies are not alternative paths to God, and . . . human spirituality, if unredeemed
by Christ, leads not to God but to judgement, for Christ is the only way."[103] It is
this eschatological destiny of human beings without Christ that fuels much of
Evangelicals' and Pentecostals' zeal for mission. As John Stott remarks in a
commentary on the Lausanne Covenant regarding the destiny of those who reject Christ, "The prospect is almost too dreadful to contemplate; we should be
able to speak of hell only with tears."[104]

What is the *salvation* that is found, in this perspective, only in the name and
person of Jesus Christ? While Catholics, Evangelicals and Pentecostals admit
that salvation includes dimensions of economic and social justice and of political, social and individual liberation (the "horizontal" dimension), their emphasis is on the reconciliation with God through Christ (the "vertical" dimension).
"The content of the message of salvation is Jesus Christ himself, the way to
reconciliation with the Father" (EPCW 23). For Evangelicals and Pentecostals,
this reconciliation has been achieved through Jesus' "atoning death"; the implication is that the reconciliation is of persons in their individuality. Catholics in
RM and Evangelicals and Pentecostals articulate their position very much in
contrast to interpretations of salvation that seem to exaggerate the "horizontal"
dimension of salvation. RM points out that, while there are understandings of
salvation and mission in circulation that are "'anthropocentric' in the reductive
sense of the word, inasmuch as they are focused on man's earthly needs," such
understandings are not consonant with the teaching of the church. On the contrary, even though such "kingdom values" are to be promoted, full salvation has
a transcendent dimension. Like the reign of God, salvation "is not of this world
. . . is not from the world" (Jn 18:36) (see RM 17). Sebastian Karotemprel writes:
"Salvation . . . consists in the gradual transformation of the inner person into the
image and likeness of the Creator, to an authentic humanity. This is a gradual
and lifelong process; here is the ground for the unity of the human vocation,

salvation and fulfillment."[105] As John Stott insists, salvation ultimately consists neither in physical health nor economic and social liberation, although it does include both. Rather, salvation is "personal freedom": freedom *from* judgment to a relationship with God as sons and daughters, freedom *from* self-centeredness and *for* self-giving service, and freedom *from* eternal death and *for* eternal glory.[106] Thus, salvation is ultimately about service, about identifying with God's saving mission in the world.

Such an understanding of salvation implies an *anthropology* that is certainly holistic but that places its main emphasis on human beings' transcendent, spiritual dimension. Full humanity is achieved not only through economic security or political autonomy, but also and most fundamentally through communion with God in Christ and transformation by the gospel. This is because, as Catholics, Evangelicals and Pentecostals acknowledge, human beings are sinners and so are in need of a restoration of right relation with God as well as with other human beings and all of creation. Catholics speak of this originally sinful state as injury and disorder, the weakening of human nature; Evangelicals and Pentecostals speak of it as distorting every part of human nature.[107] In paragraph 58 of RM, the pope quotes a phrase from the 1979 CELAM meeting in Puebla, Mexico, noting that "the best service we can offer to our brother is evangelization, which helps him to live and act as a son of God, sets him free form injustices and assists his overall development." The human being, in other words, is best served by a spiritual fulfillment, one that opens up to material fulfillment as well—but the spiritual must come first. Although reconciliation with others is not to be equated with reconciliation with God, and although social action and political liberation are not to be equated with evangelism and salvation, the Lausanne Covenant insists that both "evangelism and socio-political involvement are part of our Christian duty. For both are necessary expressions of our doctrines of God and man."[108] But the nourishment to the spiritual side of human beings, evangelism, "remains primary."[109]

While Catholics, Evangelicals and Pentecostals call for an urgent witness throughout the entire world, there is also a sense that the gospel cannot be imposed upon people; nor ought it be preached in ways that insult or offend human dignity. In RM in particular, Pope John Paul emphasizes the fact that the gospel needs to be preached "in a way that respects consciences, does not violate human freedom" (RM 8; see also RM 3). The acceptance of Jesus Christ will only enhance human freedom, the pope insists: *"The Church proposes; she imposes nothing"* (RM 39). In the report on the Catholic/Evangelical dialogue on mission, there is a section that condemns any "unworthy witness" in no uncertain terms.[110] This emphasis on human dignity is also expressed in the conviction expressed in both RM and in Evangelical and Pentecostal documents that all peoples are worthy to hear the message of the gospel. Commitment to preach Jesus Christ to the ends of the earth rests on a conviction of the fundamental equality of the members of the entire human family. In the document on evangelization and proselytism that was issued by Catholics and Pentecostals, there is a condemnation of "every form of force, coercion, compulsion, mockery or intimidation of a personal, psychological, physical, moral, social, economic, religious or political nature" (EPCW 93).

Connected to this notion of human dignity is the importance of *culture* as the context and even as the means of authentic evangelization. RM has a section completely devoted to the importance of inculturation and recognizes it as an integral part of the missionary task (RM 52-54). Evangelicals and Pentecostals have become sensitive to culture, as well, and recognize that without a knowledge of the culture and concrete situation of peoples to be evangelized the gospel may well fall on deaf ears. As a WEF consultation in Wheaton, Illinois, in 1983 stated:

> Culture is God's gift to human beings. God has made people everywhere in His image. As Creator, He has made us creative. This creativity produces cultures. Since every good gift is from above and since all wisdom and knowledge comes from Jesus Christ, whatever is good and beautiful in cultures may be seen as a gift of God (James 1:16-18). Moreover, where the Gospel has been heard and obeyed, cultures have become further ennobled and enriched.[111]

Juan Sepúlveda, a Pentecostal from Chile, points to Pentecostalism's ability "to translate the Protestant message into the forms of expression of the local popular culture"[112]—a sign that Pentecostals regard culture with some positive esteem.

But, as the WEF statement quoted above continues, cultures are also "infected with evil" because of the pervasiveness of human sin,[113] and, for Pentecostals, "human culture stands in alienation from God and God's Truth" (WSCW 68). Cultures are regarded as deeply ambiguous and need to be either confronted by the gospel or enriched or fulfilled by it. Any inculturation of the gospel will only take place through the employment of a translation or counter-cultural model.[114] Cultures are vital to engage as one preaches Christ; but they are in no way as important a locus for God's presence as is the Word proclaimed.

CONCLUSION

The great advantage of this strain of missionary theology is to be found in its power to motivate Christians to undertake explicit evangelizing and cross-cultural missionary work. It is no accident that the majority of mission-oriented congregations and cross-cultural missionaries are Christians who belong to Evangelical or Pentecostal churches—and that these are the churches which are growing most rapidly today. It is to this fervor and enthusiasm in missionary work that Pope John Paul II calls Catholics as well. To our minds, any renewal in understanding mission today needs to drink deeply from these more

Christocentric sources. In addition, this theology of mission presents a clear and unequivocal statement of the particularity of Christ and of Christian faith.

Nevertheless, such a Christocentric perspective is in danger of neglecting a truly trinitarian dimension of Christian mission and is prone to a certain "spiritualizing" of conversion and religious life that can easily fall prey to the maintenance of the status quo, particularly in situations of widespread injustice and oppression. RM and many Evangelical and Pentecostal documents recognize this danger, however, and rightly call attention to the wider trinitarian and reign-of-God perspectives' danger of compromising the newness and truth of the gospel and of undermining the whole motivation for missionary commitment. This makes this perspective necessary for inclusion in the construction of a notion of mission conceived as prophetic dialogue.

12

Mission as Prophetic Dialogue

The three preceding chapters have presented an overview of three strains
that grounded mission theology in the last quarter of the twentieth century: mission as participation in the life and mission of the Trinity; mission as continuation of the mission of Jesus to preach, serve and witness to the justice of God's
"already" but "not yet" reign; and mission as the proclamation of Christ as the
world's only savior. These three strains are, we believe, elements of a synthesis
that would serve well as an underlying theology of mission for these first years
of the twenty-first century and the third millennium. We propose to call this
synthesis *prophetic dialogue*.[1]

Mission today should first and foremost be characterized as an exercise of
dialogue. Just as the interior life of God is a perfect communion of gift and
reception, identity and openness to the other, communion in relationship and
communion in mission, so the church that is called into being by that mission
must be a community that not only gives of itself in service to the world and to
the peoples of the world's cultures but learns from its involvement and expands
its imagination of the depths of God's unfathomable riches. And just as the
triune God's missionary presence in creation is never about imposition but always about persuasion and freedom-respecting love, mission can no longer proceed in ways that neglect the freedom and dignity of human beings. Nor can a
church that is rooted in a God that saves through self-emptying think of itself as
culturally superior to the peoples among whom it works. Mission, as participation in the mission of the triune God, can only proceed in dialogue and can only
be carried out in humility.

But, to advert to the famous phrase of David Bosch, the humility of God and
of the church in mission must also be a "bold humility."[2] The Spirit is sent as
holy mystery "inside out" in the world, and Jesus is sent as the concrete, incarnate "face" of that mystery, so that the world might be released from the sin in
which it is so utterly enmeshed. As Genesis attests, almost from creation's beginning it has been in need of reconciliation, and God's choice of Israel as a
blessing for all the communities of the earth (see Gen 12:3) needed constantly

348

to be maintained through prophets who not only affirmed God's love and Israel's universal vocation, but also brought Israel to task for its faithlessness to God and injustice to those who were powerless within it. In the "fullness of time" (Gal 4:4) God's prophetic Word became flesh (Jn 1:14) in Jesus of Nazareth. He too affirmed God's unimaginable, unbounded love through his words, deeds and personal witness (see RM 14), but he also stretched his culture's religious imagination through a "wineskin-breaking ministry"[3] of attention to and inclusion of those on the margins of his society and an interpretation of the Law that emphasized its focus on human wholeness and authenticity. Jesus' Spirit-inspired mission was the proclamation and embodiment of the reign of God, and it called for every kind of justice. His death on account of his faithfulness to his mission and his resurrection to new life as the "firstfruits" (1 Cor 15:20) and promise of new life for all humanity—indeed for all creation—were the reasons why the early community of disciples proclaimed him Lord and Messiah (Acts 2:36) and were convinced that only in him could women and men find the fullness of God's salvation (see Acts 4:12).

Christian mission, then, is participation in the dialogical life and mission of the Trinity. But that dialogue is one that is *prophetic*. As the Roman Catholic bishops of Asia have expressed it, mission (in Asia, but from our perspective, in the whole world) needs to be done in a threefold dialogue: with the poor, with culture and with other religions.[4] It needs to share the life of the poor—who are in any case the majority of its members—and speak out against what keeps them that way; it needs to appreciate and critique human culture and guard it against any encroaching leveling of cultural differences; and it needs to engage the truth of other religions while maintaining the conviction that Jesus is the Way, the Truth and the Life (Jn 14:6). Mission rooted in the Trinity's unity in diversity will be able to maintain the validity of all religions' "ends" while testifying in humility to the overwhelming wealth found in the Christian religious "end" of intimate communion with God, with others and with all of creation.[5] Mission rooted in the Trinity will testify to the faith that "communion is the first and last word of the mystery of God and the mystery of the world," a communion so rich that Orthodox theologians can say that "the holy Trinity is our social program."[6]

Mission, as we have attempted to develop throughout this book, is the church's witness in faith to certain *constants*—the person and work of Jesus Christ, ecclesial existence in eschatological hope of a salvation that embraces the whole of humanity and of human culture—always within particular and ever-changing *contexts*. Throughout the centuries the church has maintained its identity as church because it has been faithful—albeit at times more faithful than others—to God's leading Spirit. At its origins, this Spirit led it beyond the boundaries of Judaism in an encounter with Greek and Hellenistic culture in the West and with Persian culture in the East; at a time of crumbling empire, mission was carried out by monastic communities; in cultures of Islamic rule, mission was lived out in witness and dialogue; at a time of unimaginable expansion of Europe's horizons, new ways emerged to deal with oppressed peoples and rich cultures; in a time of colonialism, church and state worked hand in glove at times for the sake of the gospel, but at times the church worked *against* the state for the sake of the gospel as well. In the last century Roman Catholicism and Conciliar Protestantism experienced a dramatic decrease in enthusiasm for mission, but then, in the century's last decades, interest in mission experienced a modest but solid rebirth. We believe that this rebirth in Christian mission commitment—with its elements of trinitarian vision, focus on the justice of God's reign and witness to the uniqueness of Jesus Christ—might be best characterized in this new century as a commitment to prophetic dialogue. It must be *prophetic* because the church is obligated to preach always and everywhere, "in season and out of season" (2 Tim 4:2), the fullness of the gospel in all its integrity. And it must be *dialogue* because the imperative—rooted in the gospel itself[7]—to preach the one faith in a particular *context*. Without dialogue, without a willingness to "let go" before one "speaks out,"[8] mission is simply not possible.

This final chapter attempts to outline in more detail how this model of mission for the twenty-first century might be conceived by reflecting in some depth on the multidimensional understanding of mission that is evident in missiological thought today. If in the past mission might have been understood somewhat "monaurally" as working for the salvation of souls or planting the church or preaching Jesus Christ, mission today is understood more "stereophonically" as involving a number of elements, all of which are integral to the "evangelizing mission of the church."[9] What these elements are composed a large part of missiological discussion in the last third of the twentieth century.

In 1981 an important seminar was organized by SEDOS that focused on the future of mission. In the remarkable document that summarized the seminar's proceedings, four "principal activities" of the church's mission were singled out: proclamation, dialogue, inculturation and liberation of the poor.[10] Three years later, a slightly different but complementary list of activities was offered by the Vatican's Secretariat for Non-Christians (as it was then called).[11] Mission here is described as a "single but complex and articulated reality," having as its principal elements (1) presence and witness, (2) commitment to social development and human liberation, (3) liturgical life, prayer, and contemplation, (4) interreligious dialogue, and (5) proclamation and catechesis.[12] In RM, Pope John Paul II speaks about witness, proclamation, inculturation, interreligious dialogue, working for development and doing deeds of charity (RM 41-60). Documents of the WCC, Evangelicals and Pentecostals have also recognized that mission is multidimensional, although documents of the first are perhaps closer to Catholic thought than the latter two, and although documents from the WCC place less emphasis than Catholics, Evangelicals and Pentecostals on direct gospel proclamation.[13] David J. Bosch, J. Andrew Kirk, Anthony Gittins, Donal Dorr and Samuel Escobar have all reflected in their work on the multidimensional nature of the missionary task. In addition, Robert J. Schreiter has emphasized reconciliation as an important component of and indeed an overarching category with which to understand Christian missionary activity.[14] While all these elements are quite different, Stephen Bevans and Eleanor Doidge have proposed a synthesis that tries to take into account both the diversity of the elements proposed and their similarity to one another. For Bevans and Doidge, "there are six essential components of God's mission in which the church is called to share": (1) witness and proclamation, (2) liturgy, prayer and contemplation, (3) commitment to justice, peace and the integrity of creation, (4) the practice of interreligious dialogue, (5) efforts of inculturation, and (6) the ministry of reconciliation.[15]

In speaking about the content of mission as prophetic dialogue, this chapter reflects on the six elements or components suggested by Bevans and Doidge and attempts to link these various elements that speak to the present-day, twenty-first-century context with the various constants that we have discerned in missionary practice and theology down through the centuries. It will be obvious to

MISSION AS PROPHETIC DIALOGUE	
Primary model	Baptism as a call to mission "Single but complex reality"
Components	Witness and proclamation Liturgy, prayer and contemplation Justice, peace and the integrity of creation Interreligious dialogue Inculturation Reconciliation
Theological typology	B/C (emphasis on contextual nature of truth and history)
CONSTANTS	
Christology	Spirit Christology Exemplar (subjective) and liberation models Inclusive and modified pluralist
Ecclesiology	Servant, herald, sacrament Communion-in-mission Pilgrim people of God Missional
Eschatology	Historical and communal
Salvation	Holistic All of creation
Anthropology	Communal and cosmic
Culture	Critically positive Anthropological, praxis and moderate counter-cultural models

readers that our own preference is a theology that is a combination of Types B and C. As *dialogue*, it appreciates human experience and human reason that is characteristic of Type B; as *prophetic* dialogue, it appreciates Type C's suspicion of human structures of ecclesiastical, political and patriarchal power and its commitment to liberative praxis.

WITNESS AND PROCLAMATION AS PROPHETIC DIALOGUE

"The first means of evangelization," wrote Paul VI, "is the witness of an authentically Christian life" (EN 41); "proclamation," says DP, "is the foundation, summit and center of evangelization" (10).[16] Jesus' own mission was characterized by both words and deeds, and each explained the other. Jesus' parables and teachings were prophetic utterances that often went against the grain of accepted religious wisdom and practice; his healings and exorcisms were parables in action, and his practice of including those on the margins of society as disciples and in table fellowship was a powerful witness to his teaching's validity (see DP 56-57). Jesus' missionary mandate for the church is expressed in its Lucan version in terms of both witness and proclamation: "Penance and the remission of sins is to be preached to the nations. You are witnesses of this" (Lk 24:47-48); "you are to be my witnesses in Jerusalem, throughout Judea and Samaria, yes, even to the ends of the earth" (Acts 1:8). In the Matthean version the emphasis may seem to be more on "making disciples of all nations" (Mt 28:19) and teaching these disciples all that Jesus taught (see Mt: 28:20), but what Jesus taught was more a way to live (accepting forgiveness, being forgiving, creating a new family structure, being compassionate toward those who suffer)[17] than a particular set of doctrines. Perhaps the church's greatest problem today is that its witness does not measure up to its teaching; it does not always "practice what it preaches." As Paul VI wrote in an often-quoted sentence, contemporary men and women listen more willingly to witnesses than to teachers, and if they listen to teachers, it is because they are witnesses (see EN 41). Witness and proclamation belong together. The authenticity of Christians, the vitality of the Christian community, the institutional integrity of the church, the common witness of believers from differing traditions—all point to the life-giving power and authenticity of the message and Person the church proclaims. The message of the gospel and the story of Jesus explain the reasons for the church's life together and the activity in its community and in the entire world. As Evangelical theologian John W. Stott expresses it, "If . . . there should be no presence without proclamation, we must equally assert that there should be no proclamation without presence."[18]

What Catholics call witness and proclamation, Conciliar Protestants, Evangelicals and Pentecostals often speak of as evangelism, although Evangelicals and Pentecostals might focus more on the proclamation aspect in their own definition of evangelism. David J. Bosch, however, provides a comprehensive definition of evangelism that not only includes witness and proclamation but links this specifically *evangelical* dimension of the church's mission to the other elements as well. For Bosch, evangelism is

> that dimension and activity of the church's mission which, by word and deed and in the light of particular conditions and a particular context, offers every person and community, everywhere, a valid opportunity to be directly challenged to a radical reorientation of their lives, a reorientation which involves such things as deliverance from slavery to the world and its powers; embracing Christ as Savior and Lord; becoming a living member of his community, the church; being enlisted into his service of reconciliation, peace and justice on earth; and being committed to God's purpose of placing all things under the rule of Christ.[19]

When we use the terms *witness* and *proclamation* in these reflections, therefore, we mean very much the same as what Bosch and other Protestant thinkers mean by *evangelism.*

Witness

At its Sixth General Assembly in Vancouver, British Columbia, the WCC described witness as "those acts and words by which a Christian or community gives testimony to Christ and invites others to make their response to him."[20] Thus witness here involves proclamation, for neither can really be separated from the other. For our purposes in this reflection, however, we speak of witness more in terms of lifestyle and presence, what is sometimes referred to in Evangelical circles as lifestyle evangelism[21] and what appears in Catholic papal teaching as a distinct, initial phase in the evangelization process (EN 21; RM 42-43). This kind of witness can be that of individual Christians, of a local Christian community, of the institutional church and/or of Christian communities bearing witness together.

First of all, and perhaps most basic, witness is about individuals of faith living their lives in the light of that faith. This witness can be the extraordinary type of a Charles de Foucauld, who pioneered the idea of a ministry of presence,[22] or that of an Albert Schweitzer or a Mother Teresa, but it is also the witness of persons who live their ordinary lives with integrity. As Pope John Paul II puts it eloquently, "The missionary who, despite all his or her human limitations and defects, lives a simple life, taking Christ as the model, is a sign of God and of transcendent realities. But everyone in the Church, striving to imitate the Divine Master, can and must bear this kind of witness. . . . In many cases it is the only possible way of being a missionary" (RM 42). The witness to others of a person of prayer, a faithful spouse, a patient and loving parent, a meticulous carpenter, a physician willing to listen to patients, a cancer victim filled with hope or living out his or her days in faithful resignation (like the late Cardinal Joseph Bernardin), a lawyer who does extra *pro bono* work, a dedicated organic farmer, a person who engages in business with ethical integrity, a person doggedly struggling with an addiction, a poor parent valiantly supporting his or her family—these are people (and, of course, many more examples could be mentioned) whose faith-inspired lives bring new life wherever they are; they raise questions about their motives and their visions in people's minds. Personal witness prepares the way for authentic proclamation of the gospel.

Second, witness is carried on corporately by individual faith communities. Lesslie Newbigin speaks persuasively of the local Christian congregation as a "hermeneutic of the gospel," meaning that it is oftentimes only in the local community where the gospel is truly lived that people encounter what the gospel is really about.[23] As Pentecostal missiologist Byron D. Klaus puts it: "One might ask how the gospel can be credible and powerful enough that people would actually believe that a man who hung on a cross really has the last word in human affairs. Undoubtedly, the only answer, the only hermeneutic of the gospel, is a congregation of people who believe it and live by it (Phil 2:15-16)."[24]

In his provocative book about the early expansion of Christianity, sociologist Rodney Stark points to the strong witness of the Christian community as Christians risked their lives to nurse people during devastating plagues; how their attitudes toward marriage, children and women were very appealing to women especially; and how their strict morality was an inspiration in what had become a very unstable and corrupt world.[25] It is true that Christianity spread, as D. T. Niles characterized it, by "one beggar telling another beggar where to find bread." Indeed, Stark stresses the person-to-person communication that we spoke of in Chapter 3, a dynamic that points to the importance of proclamation. Nevertheless, the validity of the community was found in the *life* of the community itself: "see how they love one another." A famous passage from the anonymous *Letter to Diognetus* from the middle of the second century C.E. points to a kind of witness that seems to be very relevant today. While Christians lived in the midst of the world and in some respects seemed quite ordinary, they also lived in a way that was strikingly different:

> They live in their own native lands, but as aliens; as citizens they share all things with others; but like aliens suffer all things. . . . They are treated outrageously and behave respectfully to others. When they do good, they are punished by evildoers; when punished, they rejoice as if being given new life. They are attacked by Jews as aliens, and are persecuted by Greeks; yet those who hate them cannot give any reason for their hostility.[26]

Today, the witness that the local community gives must also be one that is "in the world but not of the world"[27] as a community of "resident aliens," a "contrast community"[28] that nevertheless loves the world and is deeply involved in it.[29] In EN Pope Paul VI gives a fine example of the power of the witness that a local community can give:

> Take . . . a handful of Christians who, in the midst of their own community, show their capacity for understanding and acceptance, their sharing

of life and destiny with other people, their solidarity with the efforts of all for whatever is noble and good. Let us suppose that, in addition, they radiate in an altogether simple and unaffected way their faith in values that go beyond current values, and their hope in something that is not seen and that one would not dare to imagine. Through this wordless witness these Christians stir up irresistible questions in the hearts of those who see how they live: Why are they like this? Why do they live in this way? What or who is it that inspires them? Why are they in our midst? Such a witness is already a silent proclamation of the Good News and a very powerful and effective one. Here we have an initial act of evangelization. (EN 21)

Members of The Gospel and Our Culture Network, the Center for Parish Development and the participants in the Ekklesia Project speak of a "missional church" that is primarily a witness to the possibilities of life in Christ, a church that draws people not so much by explicit word as by a lived Christian authenticity. They speak of a number of "practices" that need to be "cultivated," such as worthy celebration of the sacraments, reconciliation, hospitality and community decisions by discernment.[30] As C. Norman Kraus puts it in summary: "The life of the church *is* its witness. The witness of the church *is* its life. The question of authentic witness is the question of authentic community."[31]

A third aspect of witness is institutional in nature. The church is more than a local community; its nature as a *catholic* church (at least in the Roman, Anglican, Lutheran and several other traditions) points to its more universal nature. And as the small communities grow, the church takes on both an institutional structure and *has* institutions—schools, hospitals, agencies, orphanages.[32] In the first place, therefore, the *leaders* of the institution need to witness by the quality of their leadership, their integrity and their faith-filled lives to the truth of the gospel. Such moments of institutional gospel witness—like the emergence of the Confessing Church in Hitler's Germany, the issuing of the *Kairos Document* by the churches of South Africa (both exercises of common witness as well, as we will discuss below), the stance of the Catholic Church in the Philippines against the Marcos regime in 1986 and the process employed by the United States Catholic Bishops in the development of their two landmark pastoral letters on peace and the economy in the 1980s—are examples of powerful institutional witness. The ongoing scandal in the Catholic Church, in contrast, regarding sexual abuse by the Catholic clergy and the subsequent years of coverup by several bishops, serves just as powerfully as a counter-witness to the truth and richness of a life lived according to Jesus' example. Second, institutional witness is given through the presence of various church-sponsored institutions. Many young people have been attracted to Christianity through the witness of dedicated teachers in Christian schools throughout the world, particularly in those places where institutions of learning were almost nonexistent. In the same way, Christian hospitals that are more than places of physical healing offer a witness to the healing power of love in Jesus' name. It is only when these institutions lose their charism as *Christian* institutions that they either make no difference at all to people or become counter-signs that cater to the rich or breathe a "culture" (for example, the schools for Native Americans in the United States and Canada or the "dormitories" and "convents" for aboriginal children in Australia) that can hardly be said to be life-giving. But the potential for true witness to the gospel remains very great.

Fourth and finally, we can speak of common witness, that is, the witness that various Christian traditions can render by working together. Anyone who has been engaged in the church's mission work knows that one of the most serious obstacles to evangelization throughout the world is the scandalous separation of Christian communities, their rivalry and even enmity, and their practice of gaining members in ways that "contradict the spirit of Christian love, violate the freedom of the human person and diminish trust in the Christian witness of the church."[33] While full communion among these communities is still in the future and will only come about by God's grace, it is already possible to witness to the unity that we share as Christians who have, at least in many cases, shared a common baptism, a common creed in its essentials and many theological positions as well. The possibilities that the various church documents offer for common witness are manifold. Churches witness together when they pray together, work together for justice, offer common counter-cultural witness, help support each other's worthy efforts, engage together in artistic ventures, exchange professors, participate in theological education and scholarly research, work together in projects that foster inculturation, share resources and personnel in common Bible translations, witness to the gospel in times of persecution and participate as Christians in interfaith dialogue. As the *Manila Manifesto* pointedly stated, "If the task of world evangelization is ever to be accomplished, we must engage in it together."[34] That common engagement itself will be an eloquent witness to the gospel's power to unite and reconcile Jew and Greek, slave and free, male and female, Asian and African, rich and poor. As Catholics and Pentecostals said in their document on evangelization, proselytism and common witness, "Why do we do apart what we can do together?" (EPCW 129).

Witness is a fine example of mission as prophetic dialogue. On the one hand, witness never imposes the Christian message; people are attracted to it and will perhaps ask questions about it. Often, particularly through the institutional witness of the church's education and healing ministries, other religious and secular groups will be inspired to engage in such activities, and so work for God's reign continues even though the church itself does not expand in membership. As a person or a Christian community lives in contact with another religion or another context, is open to it and learns from it—indeed, is in some sense *evangelized* by it ("mission in reverse")[35]—a tremendous witness is given. On the other hand, witness is often counter-cultural, as Lesslie Newbigin and members of The Gospel and Our Culture Network insist. In a culture of individualism, for example (like that in North America), Christians witness to the fact that community is more than a support group or a place for personal growth but rather is a communion in which individuals can find their deepest human identity. Or in cultures where ethnicity and racial identity divide people, the church strives to be a place of inclusion where ethnicity and race are valued but are not divisive. Witness is also witness to a *person*, Jesus Christ; it is lived testimony to a *message*, the Christian story and Christian gospel; and it is a *way of life* that often acts in ways against the grain of accepted cultural or traditional behavior. True Christian witness, no matter the level, always has a prophetic edge.

Witness is extremely sensitive to the *contextual* nature of the church's mission. As times change, the need of the church to witness differently and creatively changes with them.[36] The early community required a witness to the integrity of the Jewish scriptures and so opposed Marcion's rejection of them. In the context of Roman and Hellenistic culture, the community required a witness to the new reality that had been accomplished in Christ, and so the church was a beacon of respect for life, greater respect for women (within the context of strong patriarchy) and respect for Hellenistic culture and learning. As the church expanded into Syrian and Persian cultures, it witnessed to the integrity of the gospel despite marginalization and persecution. As the world's boundaries were expanded in the fifteenth century, the church witnessed to the dignity of all women and men, despite their race and color. The nineteenth century brought missionary witness through institutions of learning and healing, and the twentieth century called the church to witness to justice and to the sanctity of human cultures. Of course, none of this witness was perfect, and more often than the church would like to admit it engaged in counter-witness, as ample historical studies point out.[37] But the church has witnessed to the gospel, however imperfectly, throughout history. Witness is also connected to a number of the *constants* in the church's missionary task. In witness we see the importance of the *ecclesial* nature of Christian mission; we see a certain *anthropology* of human freedom operative; and we see a positive attitude to *culture* in practice. And witness, as we have said, is not simply witness to an idea; it is a witness to a *person*, "the name, the teaching, the life, the promises, the Kingdom and the mystery of Jesus of Nazareth, the Son of God" (EN 22). Proclamation, which follows naturally from true Christian witness, will articulate this name as a prophetic answer to questions in dialogue.

Proclamation

> Proclamation is the communication of the Gospel message, the mystery of salvation realized by God for all in Jesus Christ by the power of the Spirit. It is an invitation to a commitment of faith in Jesus Christ and to entry through baptism into the community of believers which is the Church. This proclamation can be solemn and public, as for instance on the day of Pentecost . . . or a simple private conversation. . . . It leads naturally to catechesis which aims at deepening this faith. (DP 10)

Proclamation, in the first place, as Mortimer Arias has pointed out, is the act of communicating the gospel *about* Jesus and the gospel *of* Jesus.[38] It tells the story of Jesus, his life, ministry, death and resurrection, and it introduces this man whose life and person were so transparent of God. This is the gospel *about* Jesus. But proclamation also tells of the gospel *of* Jesus—how his parables called his disciples to be forgiving, how his miracles called them to be agents of healing and wholeness, how his exorcisms called them to be opposed absolutely to evil in every form, how his inclusive lifestyle called them to be inclusive. Proclamation is not simply the communication of a story that is past. Jesus Christ is alive, and his message continues to challenge unjust secular and religious structures, to console and hearten those who grieve or struggle, to condemn evil in today's complex globalized, religiously polarized and vindictive world. Furthermore, proclamation is an invitation to join the community of disciples, the church. As Methodist New Testament scholar John Knox once wrote, the difference between the world before Jesus and the world after he lived is that "now there is a group of people who believe in him and what God did and is doing through him. They make a difference. The world is different if there is a genuine Church in it."[39] Proclamation involves inviting those who believe in the gospel of and about Jesus to join in making that gospel visible and audible in the world.

In the apostolic exhortation EN, Pope Paul VI remarked that proclamation, which he says consists of *kerygma* (that is, proclaiming Christ to non-Christians, unbelievers or the unchurched), preaching or catechesis, "occupies such an important place in evangelization that it has often become synonymous with it." Nevertheless—and this in many ways is a major point in the document—"it is only one aspect of evangelization" (EN 22). This being acknowledged, however, it must also be acknowledged, as Pope John Paul II insists in RM, that proclamation remains "the permanent priority of mission" (RM 44). The explicit proclamation of the person and message of Jesus Christ, or at least the burning intention to do so, is what ultimately makes mission *mission*. Although the other elements that we discuss in this chapter are equally *constitutive* of the church's participation in God's mission, without the practice or intention of introducing others into a relation with God through and in Jesus, the church's missionary activity remains just that—the *church's* activity and not participation in *God's* activity.

This being said, another "however" needs to be introduced at this point. DP points out that the Second Vatican Council, "when dealing with missionary work, mentions solidarity with mankind, dialogue and collaboration, before speaking about witness and the preaching of the Gospel (cf. AG 11-13)" (DP 75). As the late Archbishop Marcello Zago once pointed out, "Proclamation presupposes and requires a dialogue method in order to respond to the requirements of those to be evangelized and to enable them to interiorize the message received."[40] The prophetic activity of explicitly proclaiming Christ, in other words, must always be done in a context of respectful dialogue: the "permanent priority" of mission is proclamation in dialogue.

DP devotes an entire section, therefore, to the "manner of proclamation." In the first place, the document reminds Christians that the task of proclaiming the gospel is never done in a context in which there is no trace of God's presence—there can be no such thing, in other words, as a *tabula rasa* approach to missionary work. This is because "the Holy Spirit, the Spirit of Christ, is present and active among the hearers of the Good News even before the Church's missionary action comes into operation." Even those hearing the gospel for the first time, continues the document, may have already responded to God implicitly, "a sign of this being the sincere practice of their own religious traditions." This means that they have already, through the Spirit, participated in some way in the "paschal mystery of Jesus Christ (cf. GS 22)" (DP 68). Evangelical Anglican theologian Andrew Kirk would agree, at least to the first premise. For it to be authentic, Christians need to be aware that "evangelism is God's work long before it is our work. The Father prepares the ground, the Son gives the invitation and the Spirit prompts the person to respond in repentance and faith to the good news."[41]

It is because of this prior activity of God's Spirit and the possible implicit acceptance of God's grace that "the Church seeks to discover the right way to announce the Good News." Taking as an example the "divine pedagogy," practiced by Jesus in his own ministry, DP reflects that "Jesus only progressively revealed to his hearers the meaning of the Kingdom. . . . Only gradually, and with infinite care, did he unveil for them the implications of his message, his identity as the Son of God, the scandal of the Cross." And so, in imitation of its Master, "the Church's proclamation must be both progressive and patient, keeping pace with those who hear the message, respecting their freedom and even their 'slowness to believe' (EN 79)" (DP 69).

DP goes on to list a number of other qualities that should characterize missionary proclamation. It must be a *confident* proclamation, not because it is our word, but because it is testimony to God's Word and to the Spirit's continuing presence in all places and at all times. It must be *faithful* to the message transmitted by the church, that is, one that is "deeply ecclesial (EN 60)." It must be *humble*, both in the sense that those who proclaim have been chosen to do so by grace (the servant quality of election is something on which Lesslie Newbigin insisted[42]) and in the sense that those who proclaim are imperfect vehicles in every sense of the word. Proclamation, says DP, must be *respectful* and *dialogical*, especially in the realization that God has already been at work before the missionaries' arrival; and it must be *inculturated* by a prior attitude of respect for the cultural and religious context in which the gospel is being preached, and by efforts to make the message "not only ineligible . . . but . . . conceived as responding to their deepest aspirations, as truly the Good News they have been longing for (cf. EN 20, 62)" (DP 70).

Several other points need to be made about proclamation. First, while it is true that what was said above about the mutuality of witness and proclamation—for example, Bosch writes that "it is the 'Word made flesh' that is the gospel. The deed without the word is dumb; the word without the deed is empty"[43]—we believe that authentic witness has a certain priority over proclamation. Certainly this is true temporally, as Paul VI suggests (EN 21); we would argue, however, that it is also true missiologically. If an individual person or a church community cannot provide authentic witness to the gospel (not *perfect*, but authentic), that person or community has no right to proclaim the gospel and to invite others into fellowship. There is no doubt that it is not the missionary but the Spirit who is the "principal agent of evangelization" (EN 75), and there is no doubt that the gospel is most often transmitted not by "official" missionaries but by its own power and by ordinary men and women of faith.[44] Nevertheless, because of so much "malpractice" by the church's missionaries in the past, contemporary mission thinkers insist on holiness of life and authenticity of Christian practice as a *sine qua non* for proclaiming the gospel.[45] As the CWME conference in San Antonio pointed out, "no matter how eloquent our verbal testimony, people will always believe their eyes first." Hundreds of years earlier, theologians of the University of Salamanca in Spain insisted that *signs* (authentic Christian life) must accompany proclamation; no one, they said, had an obligation to accept the proclamation of the gospel if signs did not accompany it![46]

Second, proclamation is *always* an invitation; it "should never deteriorate into coaxing, much less into threat."[47] As Pope John Paul put it forcefully, *"The Church proposes; she imposes nothing"* (RM 39). The church calls for conversion and invites people into the community of faith in order to join the church in its task of preaching, serving and witnessing to God's reign coming into the world. Pressure tactics are proselytism, not evangelization. Such an attitude of invitation again points to the dialogical nature of the prophetic task of proclamation. The Catholic/Pentecostal dialogue on evangelization, proselytism and common witness is eloquent against crude proselytism and for the promotion of authentic religious freedom (see EPCW 68-116).

In the third place, the proclamation of the gospel today should most often, if not always, be an answer to a question. The proclaimer is, as indicated above, first of all the witness. As Paul VI has said, if witness is authentic, people will ask questions (EN 21). Ray Finch, former superior general of the Maryknoll Fathers and Brothers, suggests that perhaps the best scripture text to ground mission today might be 1 Peter 3:15: "Should anyone ask you the reason for this hope of yours, be ever ready to reply, but speak gently and respectfully."[48] Finch's reflections focus more on proclamation being a testimony to personal and communal hope rather than the transmission of a particular content, and he emphasizes the gentle and respectful *manner* of proclaiming the gospel truth. Nevertheless, we might also point to the fact that the "reason for our hope" is not offered as a first move or as a monologue but as a response in what should be an ongoing conversation. As the popular quip goes, "Christ is the answer. But what is the question?" Cardinal Francis George once remarked in a conversation at our theological school, Catholic Theological Union, that the first task of evangelization is *listening*. Those who proclaim need to listen carefully to people's real questions.

Finally, as Finch emphasizes and as David Bosch expressed eloquently in one of his last published essays, proclamation needs to be done out of weakness and vulnerability.[49] Rather than seeing proclamation as the humble activity of one beggar telling other beggars where to find bread, says Finch, we often proclaim from a position of superiority more similar to the rich giving bread to a beggar out of their surplus. Bosch reminds us of Kosuke Koyama's famous distinction between doing mission with a "crusading mind" and doing mission with a "crucified mind."[50] Even as an answer to a question, even out of a deep respect for a religion or context, proclamation will not always be enthusiastically received. To be a prophet is almost inevitably to suffer. But Christians are still called upon to give a reason for their hope, to preach whether convenient or inconvenient. In today's world of new religious consciousness and suspicion of "missionizing," proclamation can only be done authentically if it is done as an exercise of prophetic dialogue.[51]

From what we have said so far, it is clear that the act of proclamation, like that of witness, takes seriously the *context* in which the church proclaims the person and message of Jesus. Once again, a survey of the history of mission, as we have seen in Chapters 3-8, shows that the "age-old story" has always been told with new understandings and new emphases as the age demands. After Arius's questioning of Jesus' divinity, the preaching of the gospel needed to underline that Jesus was indeed the *incarnate God*. In the turmoil of the Reformation it was necessary to focus on an understanding of *salvation* that was not dependent on human works, but on God's grace. This was recognized especially by Protestants, but also, in their own way, by Catholics. In times of colonization and exploitation, the gospel needed to include a clear word about the *humanity* of all peoples and all races. In an age of globalization, the gospel must be one that honors local *cultures* and *contexts* and stands fiercely on the side of justice. In a postmodern world, special focus must be given to the proclamation of Jesus as the world's only true savior, despite the real validity of other religious ways. But proclamation is always about Jesus Christ; it is always about the inbreaking of God's reign of mercy and justice and reconciliation; it always recognizes the dignity and the tragedy of the human person; it is always an invitation to a faith community. Our prophetic proclamation of the constants of the gospel, today more than ever, needs to be done with a deep conviction of the importance of context. Our witness and our proclamation need to be accomplished as prophetic dialogue.

LITURGY, PRAYER AND CONTEMPLATION
AS PROPHETIC DIALOGUE

We don't often think about our personal or communal prayer as mission. Liturgical or individual prayer is something between ourselves and God; it is praise and adoration of God; it is asking forgiveness for our corporate and personal failings and sins; it is about asking God to be present with healing and reconciliation and power in our lives, in the lives of others and in the events of the world in which we live. Perhaps there is a missionary aspect in this last petitionary sense of prayer, but otherwise Christian prayer is its own justification. Lutheran liturgical theologian Gordon Lathrop's words about liturgy are valid for less formal Christian prayers as well: "In a certain sense, their very existence is itself enough. The meeting for worship is its own end." Indeed, whenever we try to *use* liturgy or prayer for another end, we seem to diminish its importance. Liturgy and prayer "are astonishing gifts, and they are enough."[52]

Yes, says Lathrop, but no. "Like every gift of God, the gift of the assembly for worship [and, we add, the gifts of prayer and contemplation] also keeps on giving more widely and more surprisingly than we expected. It turns inside out."[53] The church, says Robert Hawkins, "lives from the center with its eyes on the borders."[54] The church is most the church when it is assembled for worship; the Christian is most a Christian when he or she is in attentive dialogue with God; prayer and liturgy are the *center* of Christian life, and yet that center will only hold if Christian eyes are not on the center but on its periphery. Prayer and liturgy are "the summit toward which the activity of the Church is directed; at the same time [they are] the fountain from which all her power flows" (SC 10). In liturgical practice and prayer and contemplation, we discover who we are as God's people, "but also and primarily we discover who God is in this act."[55] And, as we have argued in this book, God is always a missionary God, a God whose being is active, saving love in the mysterious presence through the Spirit in creation and the redeeming ministry of Jesus of Nazareth. To encounter God at the center is to participate in God's life at the boundaries; to participate in God's boundary-crossing mission is to be drawn always to the center. A life of liturgical celebration and personal prayer and contemplation is constitutive of the church in mission.

Liturgy

In a seminal essay, Thomas Schattauer proposes that there are three possible relationships between liturgy and mission: "inside and out," "outside in," and "inside out."[56] Schattauer argues that while all three approaches are valid in some sense, only the third way that liturgy and mission relate—"inside out"—is truly adequate. While we believe that Schattauer is basically correct in this judgment, we believe that his purpose might be better served if each one of these approaches is understood more positively. Liturgy is both "inside and out" in that, in liturgy, "God acts to empower the Church for mission," or, as Walter C. Huffman nicely puts it, "worship becomes a 'ritual rehearsal' for ministry."[57] Liturgy is also "outside in" in that events in the world, other peoples and cultures and social locations need to be in constant dialogue with the Christian assembly, stretching it beyond its comfort level and affording it an opportunity to grow in its vision. And liturgy is also "inside out" in that, on the one hand, it is in the church assembled that God's mission is constantly being accomplished in forming *this* community into a prophetic sign of God's reign; on the other hand, liturgy needs always to be done with a missionary intent, recognizing that the word proclaimed, the meal shared, the vocation being celebrated, the reconciliation being offered are moments of evangelization—for the evangelized and the unevangelized in the congregation alike.

First, then, Christian liturgy on the "inside" empowers and equips the Christian community for mission on the "outside." As our colleague Richard Fragomeni once put it in a presentation at the 2000 Chicago World Mission Conference, we do *liturgy* in order to *worship*: liturgy is done within the Christian community in order that the Christian community can worship the triune God through its life in the world, offering itself through work and service as a "living sacrifice" (Rom 12:1). "Liturgy," to quote Vatican II's document on the liturgy once again, "marvelously fortifies the faithful in their capacity to preach Christ" (SC 2) because it is the fountain from which all the church's power flows (SC 10). Perhaps the richest source of missionary service in the liturgy is the celebration of the Eucharist. In his study of the fundamental link between the Eucharist and mission from the church's earliest beginnings, New Testament scholar John Koenig describes "how these early table ministries helped to define and fuel the outreach ministries of Jesus' disciples."[58] "The eucharist," writes the USCC, "is the primary proclamation of the love Christ showed by his death and resurrection. It is the heart of the Gospel. Like those who first ate and drank at the table of the Lord, we who gather today at that table have no choice but to proclaim his Gospel to all. The eucharist nourishes our mission spirituality and strengthens our commitment to give of ourselves and our resources to . . . all peoples of the earth" (TEE 58). The entire movement of the eucharistic liturgy culminates in the sending forth of the community at the end of the service: we are nourished by the bread of the Word and share the bread and cup of the Lord's body and blood in order to become ourselves God's Word and Christ's presence "in the midst of the world, for the life of the world,"[59] as the document of the Evangelical Lutheran Church of America, *The Use of the Means of Grace*, puts it. The document expresses the movement of the liturgy in this beautiful passage:

> We gather in song and prayer, confessing our need of God. We read Scriptures and hear them preached. We profess our faith and pray for the world, sealing our prayers with the sign of peace. We gather an offering for the poor and the mission of the Church. We set our table with bread and wine, we give thanks and praise to God, proclaiming Jesus Christ, and eat and drink. We hear the blessing of God and are sent out in mission to the world.[60]

Indeed, says Pentecostal theologian Simon Chan, "Eucharistic worship does not end in cosy fellowship, but in costly mission to the world."[61]

Other sacramental celebrations also challenge the church and nourish it for its work of mission. Baptism is the sacrament par excellence of mission, and every baptismal liturgy is a prayer and a challenge for all Christians present to renew their own baptismal call. The mission received at baptism is sealed by the Spirit in the sacrament of confirmation. The sacrament of reconciliation is not simply about the forgiveness of sins done in the past. Its grace is not just given *retrospectively* but *prospectively*: it calls us to live a life truly worthy of our calling (2 Thess 1:11; Eph 4:1), and it gives us the strength to do it. Those who are ordained and those who marry—and the community gathered to celebrate with them—are called through the rites to be themselves sacraments—signs and instruments—of the triune God's presence and love in the world. Orthodox liturgical theologian Alexander Schmemann speaks of the Eucharist, but it could just as well be said that the liturgy itself transforms "'the Church into what it is'—transforms it into mission."[62] Finally, one cannot participate in the daily Liturgy of the Hours, alone or in community, without being formed by the worldwide and evangelical perspective of the hymns, the psalms, the readings and the prayers.

Liturgy, secondly, is celebrated "outside in." Our celebrations together equip, nourish, challenge and empower us for God's service in the world, but what is going on in the world also needs to be brought inside to enlarge our vision and challenge our often set ways. True, as Schattauer objects, such an approach either can be used as a strategy to reach the unchurched through "relevant" Seeker Services that use symbols, songs and techniques from the secular world or can be a way to galvanize people into action according to certain "liberal" social or political agendas.[63] But it can also be a way to open up peoples' minds to other cultures (say, with a guest presider from Africa or Latin America, or the use of Filipino or Kiswahili songs) or other perspectives of faith (say, a testimony by a Muslim or a Jew). Gilbert I. Bond writes movingly about how a Chicago congregation was shaken and changed as it began to invite "outsiders" from the neighborhood to participate in one of the community's ritual practices, the love feast. The liturgy became not only a means of evangelization, but it gave the entire community a new vision of what it was as church. "If we carried the logic of our most powerful, liturgical enactments to their conclusion, we could define our practice of encountering the stranger in an effort to create the conditions that would enable us to wash one another's feet. Receiving from those we were supposed to serve, from those outside of our community, stretched, painfully, the boundaries of our understanding of ourselves and our perception of others."[64] Letting the "outside" in evangelizes the liturgical assembly, so that the assembly can better be church in the world.

Third, and perhaps most important, liturgy is celebrated "inside out." Liturgy is never celebrated for its own sake; it is always performed with an "eye to the borders." The aim of the liturgy is always to be transformed in an encounter with the missionary God, so that the liturgy never really ends—so that life becomes, as the Orthodox love to say, the "liturgy after the liturgy."[65]

In addition, because of its aesthetic and symbolic power as an icon and foretaste of the reign of God,[66] the liturgy is a witness as well to those not part of the worshiping community. James A. Stamoolis speaks of how the Orthodox liturgy evangelizes both by its beauty and by its strangeness, and he recounts a popular story of how, during the evangelization of Russia, Prince Vladimir of Kiev was converted when he observed the liturgy being celebrated.[67] The method of Orthodox missionary work was marked by the missionaries first building a church and then establishing a liturgical community. Often these missionaries were monks who were "first of all a liturgical community" that offered "the model of sharing, common action, repentance and forgiveness, all centered on the celebration of the presence of the risen Lord among those who believe in him."[68] We might point out, however, that if the liturgy is not celebrated worthily, or if the community's liturgy—however beautiful—does not really match its performance of "liturgy after the liturgy," it will provide only a counter-witness.

An image of the church that was deeply etched on Lesslie Newbigin's mind was one he recalls from his long service as a missionary to India. Often, he remembers, he was asked to speak to Hindus and Muslims in a village before conducting a service with the Christian community itself:

> I have often stood at the door of a little church, with the Christian congregation seated on the ground in the middle of a great circle of Hindus and Muslims standing around. As I have opened the Scriptures and tried to preach the Word of God to them, I have always known that my words would carry little weight, would only be believed, if those standing around could recognize in those seated in the middle that the promises of God were being fulfilled; if they could see that this new community in the village represented a new kind of body in which the old divisions of caste and education and temperament were being transcended in a new form of brotherhood. If they could not see anything of the kind, they would not be likely to believe.[69]

Newbigin's image, however, brings up one more aspect of liturgy as celebrated "inside out." Montfort Father Donald G. LaSalle reflects on the fact that the space in which he presides at Sunday liturgy from May to October every year is a "church without walls," an outdoor space in front of a grotto of Our Lady of Lourdes, and that he can see people attending the Mass who are both literally and figuratively "on the edges of the assembly."[70] LaSalle discovered through conversation with these people who stood at the back, sat on the grass or leaned against a convenient tree that they were "not simply indulging in a Catholic preference for the back row," but were often "the seekers and the hesitant, the curious, and those who are passing by. Some of them have been alienated from the church and are cautiously testing the waters. Some are in the process of healing from past hurts. Some come once and are not seen again; others come back."[71] His point is that as Christians gather to celebrate the Eucharist, not all are solid members of the community: the unchurched might once in a while go to church; members of other faiths or people with no faith at all might be attending church with relatives or friends. And this makes liturgy a context for evangelization. How the assembly welcomes the stranger (not too indifferently or not too warmly), with what reverence the scriptures are proclaimed, with what intensity the music is played and sung, with what sense prayer is experienced in the congregation (pivotal in Thomas Merton's conversion was his witnessing a Catholic community, especially a young girl, at prayer; Harvey Cox reports that often visitors to the Azusa Street revival "came to scorn and stayed to pray"[72]), with what care the presider preaches, gestures and prays—all these are ways to witness to the love of God and the good news of the gospel. In the same way, weddings, baptisms and funerals can be moments not just for community renewal and celebration for those of faith, but positive moments of evangelization. The community needs to be aware of this, and, *a fortiori*, so does its leader. To prepare liturgy with this reality in mind, to make sure to acknowledge newcomers when it seems appropriate, to make sure prayers of the faithful are inclusive and wide-ranging—all these things are exercises of a truly *missionary* liturgical community, one that has been drawn "inside out" by the liturgy.

Liturgy is mission in prophetic dialogue. It needs to be celebrated with deep awareness of the *context* of the community—its experiences, its culture, its social location(s), its struggles and its victories. It needs to be celebrated with an "eye to the borders," recognizing that for one or two or more in the congregation, the liturgical action can be a moment of evangelization (whether they are part of the community already or those "on the edge"). It needs to be the product of dialogue within the community in terms of its preparation; it cannot just be determined by the clerical presider or performed as a "canned" ceremony. But liturgy is neither theater nor entertainment. It is an exercise of prophetic truth. The scriptures illumine the community, but they also challenge it; the beautiful moment of all coming forth to receive bread and wine—the rich, the poor, the sinful, the struggling, whites, blacks, Latinos/as, Asians, women, men—is a call to be what is being signified, and a proclamation of the future that is even now breaking into the world. The liturgy revolves around "proclaiming the death of the Lord until he comes" (1 Cor 11:26) and so is radically *Christological*; in fact, Christ himself is the principal actor in the liturgical action (SC 7). It is deeply *ecclesial*, since the assembly, as Christ's body, is the celebrant. It is *eschatological*, because even though the church waits "until he comes," it experiences in sign the eschatological banquet and eschatological shalom. This eschatological sign points to the nature of *salvation* as communal and dialogical and is based on a profound *anthropology* of human wholeness. Finally, liturgy, when done well, is a celebration of the holiness of *culture*, from the vestments worn to the language used to the music and gestures that are sung and performed.

Prayer and Contemplation

In 1927, the Roman Catholic Church proclaimed two saints as patrons of the church's missionary work. The first, Francis Xavier, seems a natural choice. His tireless work in India, Japan and his dreams of China mark him as one of the most dynamic missionaries the church has known. The second patron, however, Thérèse of Lisieux, popularly called the Little Flower, might not seem such an obvious choice. She was a Carmelite nun, living a cloistered and contemplative life; never once did she leave France after entering the convent at age fifteen, and she died at twenty-four from the effects of tuberculosis. And yet, as became apparent in her autobiography, which was published soon after her death, Thérèse was a woman who was passionately concerned about evangelization. She lived her quiet life in prayer—in word and deed—for the sake of the church's mission, especially among non-Christians. "But O my Beloved," she wrote, "one mission alone would not be sufficient for me, I would want to preach the Gospel on all the five continents simultaneously and even to the most remote isles. I would be a missionary, not for a few years only but from the beginning of creation until the consummation of the ages."[73] As Mary Frohlich writes, one of Thérèse's most striking images was a comparison of herself "to a barely glimmering candlewick which, although placed in a dark corner of the sacristy, can be used to light thousands of candles, filling the whole church with light."[74] Through prayer for missionaries and the church's boundary-crossing missionary work, through a life lived intentionally as an offering for God's work in the world, and through a practice of contemplation that was able to discern the value of the smallest action, Thérèse of Lisieux witnesses to the value of prayer and contemplation for missionary work.

Wayne Teasdale, a Christian *sannyasi* (an ascetic or holy man in Hinduism) who is a "monk in the world," writes about his early years in Hundred Acres Monastery in New Hampshire: "When I first lived in a monastery, I learned very quickly that monastic life did not afford more escape from the world than any other place. Rather, it presented a deeper encounter with it. The monastic life is not a rejection of the world; it is a decision to engage with this world from a different dimension, from the enlarged perspective of love, as perceived by the Gospel in its utter simplicity and clarity."[75] A cloister or a monastery, to borrow an image from Roger S. Arnold, is like the telephone booth in the British TV science-fiction series "Dr. Who." It might seem like a closed-in, small space, but once inside it one discovers the whole world. There is a standing joke in our religious congregation, the Society of the Divine Word, that if you want to know what is going on in our society or in the world in general, just ask the Holy Spirit Sisters of Perpetual Adoration, the contemplative branch also founded by our founder, St. Arnold Janssen. Even though they are on the "inside," their concern in terms of their prayer and contemplation is definitely on the "outside." Such "missionary contemplation" continues a tradition that we have seen exemplified by Leoba, by Clare of Assisi and by the beguines and Quakers.

What this also means, we believe, is that the life of prayer of anyone can be a truly missionary act, whether a lay person fully engaged in a profession, an ordained minister or religious involved in pastoral or teaching ministry of whatever kind, a retired person with some leisure, or a person suffering or recuperating from an illness. No matter who we are, we can get in touch with the "monastery within," the "inner monk."[76] Prayer for those engaged in the church's work of crossing boundaries, for peoples struggling with injustice and poverty, for fragile communities of faith, for victims of human-caused or natural disasters—this is a valid way of being caught up in the saving and redeeming mission of God in the world. Prayer is aligning oneself with God's purposes in the world; it is opening ourselves up so that God's will may be done in us and in God's creation; it transforms us into more available partners with God's work.

This is exemplified in the Pentecostal conviction that the gift of praying in tongues is not for oneself but rather is an empowerment for service and witness in the world. When we pray, Jesus will surely come, as he promises, into our hearts. But, as Gordon Lathrop says, "when he comes, he will bring with him all those who belong to him. That is a great crowd. If it is truly Christ who comes, your heart will be filled with all the little and needy ones of the earth."[77]

Contemplation, too, can be missionary activity. Wayne Teasdale relates how the acquisition of a "contemplative attitude," by which we relate to the world "on a deeper level of attention,"[78] leads those who cultivate it to authentic Christian involvement with the needs of the world: with the homeless, those of other religions, those who work for political change for the world's marginalized and oppressed. If we were to see the world through God's eyes, which in many ways is the essence of contemplation, we would understand, as Michel Quoist writes,

> That everything is linked together,
> That all is but a single movement of the whole of
>   humanity and
>   Of the whole universe toward the Trinity. . . .
> [We] would understand that nothing is secular, neither
>   things nor
> people, nor events.[79]

Robert Schreiter emphasizes the importance of cultivating the "contemplative attitude" for those who are engaged in the "arduous and often unsuccessful" work of reconciliation—indeed, we might add, the "arduous and often unsuccessful work" of any boundary-crossing ministry. As part of the development of a life of spirituality and interiority, Schreiter recommends the practice of contemplative prayer because it "allows one at once to acknowledge one's own wounds . . . and to learn to wait, watch, and listen."[80]

Prayer and contemplation, like liturgy, involve dialogue and prophetic utterance and also action. Prayer can never be a monologue; it has to be in touch with both God's will and the world's and the church's deepest needs. But it also involves the "speaking forth" that is at the heart of prophecy; it calls us to speak and align ourselves with God's purposes, discerned through the practice of a "contemplative attitude" in the quiet of a monastery or the tumult of the world. Prayer and contemplation are never disembodied; they take place in a particular *context* and have a definite focus. In today's world of growing Pentecostal and charismatic communities, prayer is spontaneous, joyful and even ecstatic. But we see in every prayer style the constant focus on *Jesus Christ* and his own prayer in the Spirit to the Father; we see an *ecclesiology*, since prayer, no matter how private or individual, is always with other Christians and for the world. That prayer is linked to bodily expression points to a profound *anthropology* that resists simple body/spirit dichotomies. In sum, liturgy, prayer and contemplation are powerful ways for Christians to participate in God's mission within God's creation, "as we wait in joyful hope for the coming of our Lord, Jesus Christ."[81]

JUSTICE, PEACE AND THE INTEGRITY OF CREATION
AS PROPHETIC DIALOGUE

"Action on behalf of justice and participation in the transformation of the world fully appear to us as a constitutive dimension of the preaching of the Gospel, or, in other words, of the Church's mission for the redemption of the human race and its liberation from every oppressive situation."

"If you want peace, work for justice."

"We discern two types of injustice: socio-economic-political injustice . . . and environmental injustice."

"Because the earth is the Lord's, the responsibility of the church towards the earth is a crucial part of the church's mission."[82]

These four quotations point to two important truths in the church's contemporary understanding of mission. First, the quotations indicate that working for justice in the world is an integral part of the church's missionary work, equal in importance to witnessing to and proclaiming the gospel and to establishing Christian communities of shared faith, friendship and worship. Second, they make clear that justice is a wide concept, ranging from economic and political liberation to basic human rights, to peace activism, to commitment to working for ecological stability and environmental sustainability. Like the prophets of the Hebrew scriptures, and like Jesus' ministry in the New Testament, the church's mission is about cooperating with God in the call of all people always and everywhere, to justice, peace and the integrity of creation.

Justice

Down through the ages the church has been noted for its care of the poor and those on the margins of society, and this has always been seen as part of the church's missionary outreach. In the New Testament, Paul calls on Christians from all parts of the Mediterranean world to contribute to the welfare of poor Christians in the Jerusalem church (see Rom 16:24-28; 1 Cor 16:1; Gal 2:10); Christians within the Roman Empire distinguished themselves in caring for the sick during a number of plagues that took the lives of significant portions of the population in the second and third centuries;[83] monasteries were well known as places of hospitality and refuge during the cataclysmic events of the great migrations during the fifth, sixth and seventh centuries; Christians like Elizabeth of Hungary, Elizabeth of Portugal, Margaret of Scotland, Francis of Assisi, John of God and John Woolman have witnessed to the inseparable connection between love of God and love of neighbor in Christian life. Whether it was in Marie de la Incarnation's establishment of schools in New France, Vincent de Paul's and Louise de Merillac's ministry to the poor in France, Peter Claver's care of slaves off the coast of Colombia, Martin de Porres's generosity to the poor of Lima, Peru, or William Carey's educational efforts in India, sharing the faith has always been seen as sharing resources with the poor and marginalized.

In the late twentieth century, however, this commitment to aiding the poor and marginalized, while still continuing throughout the world and still considered extremely valuable (for example, in the inspiring ministry of Albert Schweitzer and Mother Teresa) underwent what missiologist Eloy Bueno has called an "epistemological leap."[84] Because of a number of factors in the development of secular society and in the understanding of the churches, it has become increasingly clear that it is not enough merely to minister *to* the poor and marginalized through works of charity. Because of new understandings of human dignity and equality that emerged in the Enlightenment, because of new insights into the systemic causes of poverty in socialist and Marxist thought, because of a gradually developing social consciousness within the churches (such as Rauschenbusch's Social Gospel movement in Protestantism and a growing body of social teaching in Catholicism), and because of the shift of the center of gravity of Christianity from the wealthy North to the poor South, it became apparent that the mission of the church was to be involved not only in the *alleviation* of human suffering and exclusion but also in the eradication of their roots. Not only was the church to engage in the corporal works of mercy through charitable service, but it was also to be involved in human development, the practice and establishment of justice and the struggle for liberation. The Evangelical and Pentecostal churches tended to hesitate in this regard, because they did not want to compromise the spiritual nature of the proclamation of the gospel, but by the 1980s they too saw an integral connection between the Great Commission and the Great Commandment.[85] The two, Evangelicals said in an important declaration, are related in three ways: as a *consequence of*, as a *bridge to*, and as a *partner with* evangelism or the proclamation of the gospel.[86] Today it is clear among *all* the churches that churches are called to speak *to* and *for* the poor and marginalized, to empower them to speak with their own voice, and to be *with* them in an option of solidarity and praxis: "The Kingdom of God and social justice should not be separated" (EPCW 66). In addition, the churches today recognize that if they are to preach and work for justice in any credible manner, they themselves must be communities where justice is practiced and clearly visible.

First, then, the church today is called to participate in that aspect of God's mission that speaks to and for the world's poor and marginalized.[87] What the church speaks *to* the world's poor and marginalized (or as some would even say today, the excluded[88]) is the good news that God is a God of justice, that God does not and will not tolerate exploitation and is working in the world through the Spirit to bring about a society that is just and inclusive. Throughout history the powerful have tried again and again to coopt God for their own unjust purposes, but the prophetic tradition in the religion of Israel resisted this at every turn. When Israel was oppressed by Egypt, God came to its rescue with "strong hand and outstretched arm" (Dt 11:2); when their own people of wealth oppressed the poor of the land, God spoke powerful words of condemnation through the prophet Amos (Amos 2:6-8); when God's people were in exile, God spoke words of comfort and hope through the prophets we call Second and Third Isaiah.

And God's Spirit is fully manifested in Jesus, whose "inaugural discourse" at the synagogue in Nazareth spoke, in the words of Third Isaiah, of bringing good news to the poor, proclaiming liberty to captives, giving the blind sight and prisoners freedom in a new "year of favor," a new just and inclusive society (see Lk 4:18-19 and Is 61:1-2). In the last quarter of the twentieth century this tradition of the God of justice was rediscovered by the theology of liberation. The image of God in this theology rejected the idea that God is on the side of the "powers that be," serving as the ultimate foundation for the status quo of classism, sexism, racism, and political and economic oppression. God, rather, is radically, passionately on the side of the poor, the oppressed, the excluded and the disenfranchised, and is calling all of humanity to be partners in God's work. Liberation theologian Ronaldo Muñoz writes that this "God of our discovery contrasts sharply with the God of punishment and passive resignation—whom we now begin to recognize as having been imposed by dominant groups and by agents of the church having ties to the same."[89]

What the church speaks *for* the poor and marginalized is a word of justice and liberation within a world dominated by what Paul called the "principalities and powers" (see Eph 6:12; Col 2:15) and that Walter Wink has interpreted as not so much spiritual demons but as the intangible power, often a mixture of good and bad, of global corporations, national governments, various ideological expressions like capitalism or socialism, or sociological trends like globalization.[90] Even though the church is a spiritual reality, it nevertheless is also a visible reality (see LG 8); therefore, it has a certain public presence, whether as a local community or an area institution, even in parts of the world where it has an almost negligible presence. How exactly the church should engage the powers is something for each community to decide, but there needs to be both a moment of "unmasking," when the truth of injustice is told, and a moment of constructive suggestion, when the principles of the gospel and Christian social doctrine are presented. Because the "principalities and powers" in this world are often not wholly evil (for example, corporations often want to do good as well as make profits; some aspects of globalization are good and should be encouraged), both honest dialogue and truthful, prophetic critique need to be used. Examples of the church speaking *for* the poor and marginalized in the world might be formal exercises like papal or episcopal teaching on justice in the Catholic Church, statements of the WCC or the LCWE, or the group of South African theologians and church officials who issued the *Kairos Document* in the 1980s; there are also many agencies of the churches, like the Vatican's Pontifical Council for the Pastoral Care of Migrants and Itinerant Peoples, the organization Caritas, or pressure groups like the Africa Faith and Justice Network or the Center of Concern in the United States. Martin Luther once called the church the "mouth house"[91] of God, that is, the concrete way that God's word is spoken in the world. The church's commitment to speaking on behalf of the world's excluded is the way that the God of justice is heard in the world.

Second, the justice mission of the church is one of empowerment. This does not mean, it is important to say, that the more powerful church shares its power with those who have little or none; that would be more paternalism and merely patronizing. Rather, *empowerment*, as we understand it here, means the ministry of conscientization, of assisting people toward self-awareness of their own power, subjectivity, strengths and capabilities. Ultimately this means that the goal of the church's commitment to justice is not to remain a spokesperson *for* the poor and marginalized, but to work in such a way that they discover *their own voice* and speak within their culture, their traditions, and their humanity. Donal Dorr tells of two trips to South Africa as part of a training team for South African activists. On the first trip, in 1982, Dorr was overcome with the awareness of how pervasive and powerful the apartheid regime was. He thought that it would be "very difficult to have any real hope that liberation could be achieved without massive military intervention from the outside." Seven years later, however, he sensed that, somehow, the atmosphere had completely changed. Even though Nelson Mandela had not yet been released from prison and the political oppression was almost worse than ever, somehow "those who had struggled for liberation were now assured of victory. It was clear to all that it was just a matter of time until the oppressive government would give up and the 'New South Africa' would come into being."[92] As people become more certain of their own power, of their own right to justice and, most fundamental, of their own goodness and dignity as human beings, the outcome of the struggle for justice is assured—indeed, it is in some ways already won.

Third, the church is called to be *with* the poor through an option of both solidarity and praxis, what has come to be called the "preferential option for the poor." Some have objected to this idea, arguing that God loves all people equally, and therefore so should the church, but proponents of the option for the poor insist that "far from being a sign of particularism and sectarianism," it "manifests the universality of the church's being and mission."[93] In order to *ensure*, in other words, that God's love and empowerment reaches all peoples, a special, preferential commitment to the poor and the marginalized must be made. Without such intentional commitment, it becomes easy for the church to overlook or disregard the plight of the poor, who are so often unheard and unseen. Such an ecclesial affirmative-action plan makes sure that those who are most in need get the attention that they deserve.

As Donal Dorr explains, opting for the poor calls for both *solidarity* and *analysis/action* (often simply called praxis).[94] Solidarity with the poor and the marginalized involves sharing the lifestyle of the poor as much as possible in particular circumstances. Christians are called to a "simple lifestyle,"[95] living with what we need rather than with what we want, avoiding the empty consumerism that is rampant in a globalized world. Christians are called to listen to the voices of the poor and marginalized, to vote for their concerns, to contribute to causes that promote their development, to cultivate a spirituality of patience, for example, while waiting in line (something the poor spend a lot of time doing). Above all, solidarity involves letting go of the way of the powerful and relying more and more completely on God. "It is to renounce any likelihood of political success in the conventional sense, and even to re-define radically the very notion of success. It is a decision to find joy and fulfillment in ways that are incomprehensible in conventional terms."[96] But solidarity is not enough for the church, or at least for some of its members actively committed to its mission of justice. The option for the poor involves an analysis with the poor of the causes of their poverty or exclusion and the formulation of plans of action to resist or overcome those causes. This, then, leads back to analysis and reflection in a never-ending cycle of action and reflection. The praxis aspect of the option for the poor is to be done principally by the poor and marginalized themselves. "This means," writes Dorr, "that those who have opted to be in solidarity with them often have to 'hold back.' And when they do intervene it should be to encourage or facilitate the disadvantaged people themselves in articulating their own experience and in planning realistic action."[97]

But the credibility of the church in its mission of justice inevitably depends on its own authentic living out of justice. As the 1971 Synod of Bishops acknowledges: "While the Church is bound to give witness to justice . . . everyone who ventures to speak to people about justice must first be just in their eyes. Hence we must undertake an examination of the modes of acting and of the possessions and lifestyle found within the Church itself."[98] In a number of short paragraphs, therefore, the synod outlines some of the ways that the church is called to be evangelized *ad intra* so that it might more credibly evangelize *ad extra*. Human rights must be preserved in the church; those who work in the church, including priests and religious, should receive a fair wage and "that social security which is customary in their region." Lay people should have a share in the administration of church property, and "women should have their own share of responsibility and participation," not only in society but also within the church. The church should guarantee the free expression of thought, and when one is accused in the church, the person has a right to know the accuser and a right to a proper defense. All members of the church—clergy and lay— should have a say in the decision-making processes in the church. As the 1989 *Manila Manifesto* stated, "The church is intended by God to be a sign of his kingdom (Lk 12:32), that is an indication of what human community looks like when it comes under his rule of righteousness and peace (Rom 14:17)."[99] And so the justice that the church lives within itself is a first and fundamental step toward effective proclamation and witness of God's justice among all peoples.[100]

Peace

The church's mission of justice is intrinsically linked to its mission of cultivating and preserving peace among the peoples and nations in the world. Frustration and rage over repeated injustices—as witnessed in our own days in Chechnya, Kosovo, Chiapas and Palestine—are the cause of much of the world's violence, and the greed of the great powers to control land and resources unjustly have been the cause of many of the major wars of history. Today, with the continued proliferation of nuclear weapons, not only among the world's major powers, but also among medium powers like India, France, Pakistan and Israel, global war itself is an unthinkable injustice, since it would mean the deaths of tens of millions of people and the destruction of the environment in ways that we can hardly imagine. As the U.S. bishops expressed it in their 1983 pastoral letter, *The Challenge of Peace,* itself a marvelous exercise of the church's mission of proclaiming the gospel and challenging the United States to work for peace and justice:

> The crisis of which we speak arises from this fact: nuclear war threatens the existence of our planet; this is a more menacing threat than any the world has known. It is neither tolerable nor necessary that human beings live under this threat. But removing it will require a major effort of intelligence, courage, and faith. As Pope John Paul II said at Hiroshima: "From now on it is only through a conscious choice and through a deliberate policy that humanity can survive."[101]

The first thing that the church can do to promote peace is to help the peoples of the world make that "conscious choice" and help to develop that "deliberate policy." Although the church has certainly condoned war in the past—preaching the crusades, blessing troops and battleships—it also has a strong tradition of calling for peace. Peace, shalom, was the dream of the Bible (see, for example, Is 2:2-5; 9:5-6; 48:18; Ez 37:26; Rev 21). Jesus himself was a man of peace (for example, see Mt 5:21-26, 38-48; 26:52), and the reign of God that he preached was the fulfillment of Israel's eschatological hopes for peace (see Lk 4:18-19; Mt 11:2-6; Is 60:1-11). For two hundred years the early Christian community resisted entering Roman military service, but even when Christians did join the army, there is a tradition that some refused to fight for unjust causes.[102] In the midst of the crusades, Francis of Assisi certainly proved himself an instrument of God's peace, as have many Christians from George Fox and John Woolman to Dorothy Day and Peter Maurin. As Andrew Kirk points out, even Augustine's theory of just war is really one of justified war; the just-war theory "is not an attempt to sanitize the general use of lethal violence, but to show how *unjustified* it is in most circumstances."[103] Both Pope Paul VI and John Paul II have given major addresses on peace every year on World Peace Day, January 1. Such teaching of the churches (and lobbying efforts of U.S. groups like the Conference of Major Superiors of Men and the Leadership Conference of Women Religious) needs to continue, even if it sometimes seems like a voice crying in the wilderness. It is an important, constant reminder that violence and war are *never* the answer that will serve humanity in the long run.

Second, as we have already intimated above with the mention of Fox, Woolman, Day and Maurin, the church can support the efforts of its prophets for peace. Pacifism has always been a minority position in the church, but it has always been present, and we need to listen to prophetic words and react to prophetic witness with openness and honesty. The efforts of the Catholic Worker Movement and the Fellowship of Reconciliation, the movement for the closing of the School of the Americas in Fort Benning, Georgia, in the United States, the witness of the Mennonite tradition, and the voices of people like Daniel Berrigan and Michael Baxter are important, if always controversial, aspects of the church's mission for peace.

Third, Christians can participate in the fourfold pastoral response outlined by the U.S. bishops in their 1983 pastoral. In the first place, Christians can develop and participate in educational programs that will form their consciences to be more sensitive to issues of violence, war and peace. Second, they can develop a "reverence for life" that is kin to the "seamless garment" approach to ethical behavior articulated by the late Joseph Cardinal Bernardin of Chicago. Third, the bishops ask Catholics, "other Christians and everyone of good will" to join them in "continuing prayer for peace . . . within ourselves, in our families and community, in our nation, and in the world." Fourth, the bishops recognize that "prayer, by itself is incomplete without penance," and so, drawing on a longstanding Catholic tradition, they suggest that "every Friday should be a day significantly devoted to prayer, penance, and almsgiving for peace."[104]

Finally, since tension within and between religions is the source of so much violence in the world (such as Northern Ireland, Sri Lanka, Indonesia, Israel and Palestine), the church's commitment to interreligious dialogue—a topic that we will take up more fully in the next section of this chapter—can be a way to foster better understanding and to reduce suspicions among people of differing religious beliefs. As religions participate in common efforts for justice and liberation in particular (the dialogue of action), people of faith can come to the realization that *they* are not each others' enemies but have a common enemy in the "principalities and powers" that, if unchecked, can continue to create an atmosphere of injustice and uphold the spiral of violence. If Philip Jenkins is correct in predicting that Christianity in the future will tend to take on a more militant attitude, particularly in Africa and Asia,[105] we believe that one of Christian mission's biggest challenges will be to help people to understand that the gospel has its roots in God's shalom, Jesus' call for nonviolence and the Bible's vision of new heavens and a new earth. Such a challenge can only be met if the church offers its prophetic message to the world in a spirit of authentic dialogue.

Integrity of Creation

Although it has long been recognized that issues of ecology are integrally connected to issues of justice and peace,[106] there has not been much reflection on how the preservation of the integrity of creation is linked to the church's mission.[107] There is no question, however, that it is. The Christian vision of salvation is of new heavens and a new earth (Is 66:22; Rev 21:1). Sins of injustice and greed, Walter Brueggemann writes, not only do violence to human beings, but also to the earth and all earth's creatures.[108] The call of the church to repentance and new vision, therefore, is a call to ecological responsibility. In the words of novelist Rudy Wiebe, "You repent, not by feeling bad but by *thinking different*."[109] Mission witnesses to, proclaims, celebrates and works for a new way of thinking about and seeing human beings, earth's creatures and the created universe itself. Prophets such as Francis of Assisi, Hildegard of Bingen, John Woolman and Pierre Teilhard de Chardin have pointed to the holiness of all of creation; it is urgent that the church follow in these prophets' footsteps.

In one of the few sustained reflections on mission and the integrity of creation, Andrew Kirk offers several suggestions as to how the church might live out its mission of preaching, serving and witnessing to ecological justice. Our suggestions here are inspired by his.[110] First, Christians themselves need to live in ways that persuade others to adopt a lifestyle that uses fewer of the world's resources, particularly those resources which take away opportunities for peoples in societies that are not as affluent as those of the West. Commitment to recycling waste, driving automobiles less, driving vehicles that are fuel efficient and using energy sources sparingly and wisely are practices that Christians can cultivate and proclaim. In addition, churches and church institutions such as schools, hospitals and seminaries can support efforts to build and remodel buildings so that they are ecologically sound. Second, Christians individually and the churches as institutions can support and promote legislation that enhances the sustainability of the environment. The move to drill for oil, for example, in wilderness areas of the United States or plans to harvest timber in Philippine forests need careful evaluation and even strong opposition. Third, the church and, again, Christians individually can support and promote the development of organic farming. In the United States at the moment, organic produce tends to cost more than produce grown with chemical fertilizers, but that is because U.S. Americans have not gotten used to buying products produced more naturally. In Europe, however, organic produce is being sold much more cheaply, due in part to the influence of the Green Parties and higher ecological consciousness. What might seem like a small thing, and in some instances a small sacrifice, is an important step for the renewal and preservation of the earth. Finally, the Christian mission for the preservation of God's creation finds expression in the support of any kind of initiative for the development or protection of wildlife areas, national parks and other places of natural beauty. God has gifted all of humanity with the wonders of scenic majesty and abundant plant and animal life, and human beings are called not only to enjoy these fully but also to ensure that God's creation can keep its freshness for coming generations.

It is sometimes argued that a ministry of ecological responsibility is only a concern of first-world countries that can afford the luxury of protecting their natural resources. People in Asia, Africa or Latin America may need to cut timber and hunt rare animals simply to survive. While this is certainly true, it must be emphasized that third-world peoples have recognized the long- and short-term dangers of unwise exploitation of the natural world. African, Latin American and Asian Roman Catholic bishops have recognized the importance of the cultivation of environmental justice and responsibility for their regions of the world.[111] In a remarkable book, Zimbabwean missiologist and ecological activist Marthinus Daneel tells the moving story of the "war of the trees" waged against the ravaged environment of Zimbabwe in the last several decades in a cooperative effort of Shona practitioners of traditional religion and a number of local AICs. For a number of years these local religious people have planted over a million trees a year to combat the effects of the long war of liberation and shifting populations. Daneel writes that as he faced the drought and deforestation of his boyhood land,

> African holism became the hermeneutic for theological reorientation. Saving souls was important, I thought. But never at the expense of the salvation of all creation. In my situation conversion had little significance if it did not translate into full environmental stewardship. . . . The biblical concept of a new heaven and a new earth no longer seemed merely a new dispensation to be ushered in by God, but a challenge to be realised in this existence.[112]

Daneel writes compellingly of how interfaith dialogue combined with environmental activism (what we call dialogue of action) was a powerful practice of authentic Christian missionary activity. Christian concern for the environment illumined Shona spirituality; traditionalist perspectives on the environment moved Christian faith and action to new and deeper levels of commitment to Christ the Earthkeeper.

To conclude this section, it is important to reflect briefly on how a commitment to justice, peace and the integrity of creation is understood as prophetic dialogue and to point out which of the missiological constants it illuminates. It is certainly clear that the prophetic dimension of mission is paramount here; committing oneself to justice, peace and ecological integrity demands prophetic living, prophetic speech and prophetic action individually, communally and institutionally. Great prophets of peace, justice and ecology are among the thousands of martyrs of our times—Martin Luther King, Jr., Oscar Romero, Chico Mendes, Steve Biko, Felix and Mary Barreda, to name only a few. But true prophets are inspired not by anger but by love, and so prophetic witness, word and action need to be founded on the love of the trinitarian God. They need to try to understand people's motives, to persuade with facts. They can never—or at least only in extreme cases—employ violence. They need to establish authentic relationships with people who are often unwilling pawns in the hands of global corporations and greedy politicians. Evil needs to be confronted, but Christians need to listen, to study and to reflect in order to know where evil truly lurks.

The "epistemological leap" described by Eloy Bueno has thrown new light on the nature of *salvation*. Human beings are called by God to a human wholeness that includes the possibilities of participating in a society that is just and peaceful not only in the sense of the absence of violence but also the absence of the *causes* of injustice. The emergence of ecological consciousness of the last three decades has stretched the notion of salvation even further to include not only *human* well-being, but the well-being of all of creation as well. The spiritual wholeness that the gospel brings is neither disembodied nor dematerialized but reflects the love of a God who expresses the divine identity in total solidarity with creation. *Anthropology*, therefore, is central to this element of mission; indeed, it was the emergence of the subject in Enlightenment thinking that sowed the seeds for conceptions of human dignity and "inalienable rights" to "life, liberty and the pursuit of happiness," as the United States Declaration of Independence puts it, and on which the social consciousness of the churches, having discovered deep echoes of this in the Bible, is founded. But again, the ecological revolution has "de-centered" the human person in philosophical, political and theological thought, and this too has found resonance in a rereading of the scriptures. We must pursue justice and peace in our world with a sense of the interconnectedness of all things. God's entire creation, not the human person, is the measure of all things. Finally, a commitment to human and cosmic welfare points to an *eschatology* that is both already being realized and yet to reach its final fulfillment. Eschatological fulfillment that is only a future "pie in the sky when you die" cannot measure up to the message of Israel's scriptures and the teachings of Jesus. A world of justice, peace and creation's integrity is important now, because the future, in God's mysterious plan, is what we make of it now. But, on the other hand, it is only the God of Jesus through the Spirit who will inaugurate the new age. The kingdom of "truth and life . . . holiness and grace . . . justice, love and peace"[113] is the kingdom *of God*.

INTERRELIGIOUS DIALOGUE AS PROPHETIC DIALOGUE

"Dialogue is . . . the norm and necessary manner of every form of Christian mission, as well as of every aspect of it, whether one speaks of simple presence and witness, service or direct proclamation. Any sense of mission not permeated by such a dialogical spirit would go against the demands of true humanity and against the teachings of the Gospel."[114] These powerful and challenging words from the 1984 Roman Catholic document on dialogue and mission point to the fact that dialogue with those of other religious ways (and for that matter with those who are not members of any religious group or who do not subscribe to any religious doctrine) is not a tack that the church has been forced to take in order to "get along" in the aftermath of Western colonialism, the worldwide renaissance of the world's religions, or the spread of postmodern secularism. Nor is dialogue to be interpreted from these words to be a subtle tactic or strategy to proclaim the name and message of Jesus Christ to believers. Dialogue *is*, of course, the only option in today's globalized and polycentric world; it *does* and *must* include a moment of proclamation—of each partner to the other. In no way does dialogue *replace* proclamation or the necessity of an invitation to Christian conversion. But, most profoundly, dialogue is today "the norm and necessary manner of every form of Christian mission" because Christian mission is participation in the mission of *God*, and God's being and action is dialogical. God's self-revelation shows a communion in dialogue in which Mystery, "inside out" in the world, is made concrete in Jesus of Nazareth, and God's way of revealing through Spirit and incarnate Word is always one that treats humanity and all of creation with freedom and respect. God, writes John Oman, "does not force His mystery on us."[115] Rather, as DP puts it, "God, in an age-long dialogue, has offered and continues to offer salvation to humankind." And so, "in faithfulness to the divine initiative, the Church too must enter into a dialogue of salvation with all men and women."[116]

Dialogue is possible because the presence of God's saving grace is not confined to the church alone. It is significant that at the Second Vatican Council the traditional dictum "outside the church there is no salvation" was never used. The council, rather, spoke of the possibility of salvation for all people of good will, whether they have faith in God or not (LG 16), of other religious ways as possessing "a ray of that Truth which enlightens all men" (NA 2), and of the presence of the Holy Spirit who "in a manner known only to God, offers to every man the possibility of being associated with this paschal mystery" (GS 22). As *Ecumenical Affirmation: Mission and Evangelism* puts it, the attitude of dialogue "springs from the assurance that God is the creator of the whole universe and that he has not left himself without witness at any time or any place. The Spirit of God is constantly at work in ways that pass human understanding and in places that to us are least expected."[117] While these admissions are rather new in general church teaching, they are not completely new to theology. A strict interpretation of "outside the church there is no salvation" seemed to be the majority position in Christian thinking, but there was always a minority opinion that emphasized the presence of salvation outside Israel's covenant (in the "cosmic covenant" with Noah) and witnessed to in the tradition of "pagan saints" in the Hebrew scriptures,[118] the prophets (Is 19:21, 25; Mal 1:11) and the ministry of Jesus (the centurion, Mt 8:10; the Canaanite woman, Mt 15:28). Justin Martyr, Clement of Alexandria, the East Syrian monks Adam and Alopen, Thomas Aquinas, Ramón Lull, E. Stanley Jones, Max Warren and Stanley Samartha are only a few of the major voices in this tradition, which also found voice in the Roman Magisterium.[119]

Ecumenical Affirmation: Mission and Evangelism points out one of the major motives for dialogue: the discovery in the knowledge of the other new depths and possibilities in oneself. While such a motive might be interpreted as an abandonment of the missionary task of specific Christian witness and proclamation, S. Mark Heim explains that such openness actually is involved in a genuine missionary encounter. "The missionary's conviction," he writes, "that she brings a transforming message to the new context is or should be balanced by the recognition that the transforming of that message itself is a new gift that is returned from the context. It is a gift that can be given only from that particular place." Real dialogical encounter with a context or religion, in other words, leads Christians to a discovery of the "fullness of Christ"; this, says Heim, is "the complementary side" of explicit Christian witness and the invitation to conversion.[120] It is precisely why dialogue is so essential in Christian missionary service. Dialogue indeed presents us with a non-threatening moment on both sides for prophetic confession of faith; it allows us to know other religions not as abstract systems but as ways of life lived by persons with whom we can actually become friends and partners; and it helps us deepen our knowledge as such of the other religion. But first and foremost, it provides a way to discover the fullness of our own faith, so that, paradoxically, we can offer it to others with a bolder humility and a humbler boldness.

Approaches to dialogue in the last several decades have been based on how various Christian theologies estimated the presence of grace outside explicit knowledge and faith in Christ.[121] One approach, which scholars have called *exclusivism,* or the *replacement model,* is espoused by more conservative Christians, perhaps more in past times than at present. This position would hold that only Christians possess religious truth and the means of salvation. If one would engage in dialogue from this perspective, it would only be in order to understand other religions so as to preach the gospel to them more effectively. A second approach, dubbed *inclusivism* or the *fulfillment model,* is held by Christians who believe that salvation is available to all people of good will, and even in some way through their religions, but that such grace ultimately comes solely through Jesus Christ. From this perspective dialogue is important both to enrich the understanding of one's own and the other's faith and to help the other see that behind his or her own faith lies a reality that can bring what is already believed to full completion. Third, there is the *pluralist* understanding of the availability of salvation, called alternately the *mutuality model* or the *acceptance model.* Whereas exclusivism and inclusivism are Christocentric in their outlook, pluralism is theocentric or soteriocentric. Rather than focusing on the saving power of Christ, pluralist theologies focus on God (in whatever way God is named) or on the salvation that is available through conscientious religious practice. Here dialogue is important so that *all* religions can get beyond themselves to the one reality that they all point toward but never fully articulate.

S. Mark Heim, however, has proposed quite a different approach to the issue. Acknowledging that he is a "convinced inclusivist,"[122] his position is one that, he contends, is nevertheless even more pluralist. The pluralist position espoused by theologians like John Hick and Paul Knitter, Heim argues, is, if truth be told, an exclusive one. This is not in the sense, of course, that salvation is found only in Jesus Christ, but in the sense that, beyond all the individual religions, there is one perspective that is true. What this seemingly pluralist (all religions are paths up the same mountain) but crypto-exclusivist (there is only one truth) position fails to recognize is the integrity of religious ways in themselves and the fact that they may not *really* be after the same *kind* of final fulfillment. (Heim quotes Catholic scholar Joseph Augustine Di Noia, who quotes a rabbi saying that "Jesus Christ is the answer to a question I have never asked."[123])

In order, therefore, to do justice to the Christian tradition that Jesus is the full revelation of God and the world's only savior, to our human experience that genuine grace and goodness are actively present not only among the followers of other religions but are mediated through the various religious systems themselves, and to the integrity of each religious system in itself, Heim suggests that the theology of religions speak not of *salvation* as a religion's goal but of the various *religious ends* of the world's faiths. He further suggests that, as mediators of their religious ends, all religions (or at least the "great" religions—Heim is not completely clear on this point) are valid. *Nirvana* is the religious end of Buddhism, in other words, and if one follows the eightfold path, *nirvana* will be reached—and by no other way. Complete absorption into the One is possible by following the disciplines of Hinduism—and this religious end can be reached by no other way. The religious end of Christianity, and *only* Christianity, is *salvation*, which Heim defines as a perfect communion of human beings with God, each other and God's creation, and this can only be reached through faith in Jesus Christ and following him as a disciple. And so, for Heim, "the question is not 'Which single religious tradition alone delivers what it promises?' Several traditions may be valid in that sense. The truly crucial questions become 'Which religious end constitutes the fullest human destiny?' and 'What end shall *I* seek to realize?'"[124]

Heim's proposal regarding the validity of religious ends seems to dovetail with contemporary attempts to recognize how Christians should understand themselves in relation to Judaism.[125] Vatican II repudiated the idea that all Jews were guilty of Christ's death and deplored "the hatred, persecutions, and displays of anti-Semitism directed against the Jews at any time and from any source" (NA 4). Thus NA became the "Magna Carta" of a profound development of the Catholic Church's relationship with Judaism that had begun before the council with John XXIII and had advanced "with the extraordinary example of John Paul II, along with years of patient and responsible work in local and national dialogues."[126] In the mainline Protestant churches as well, a number of dialogues and statements have been issued on this topic.[127]

The major development has been the overcoming of the idea of *supercessionism*—the notion that Christianity has now "fulfilled" Judaism and, in effect, "made it obsolete and superfluous,"[128] and that the Christian church has now "replaced Israel as God's chosen people."[129] While such a position is deeply ingrained in both church teaching and Christian theology, it has been argued by some contemporary Jewish, Protestant and Catholic scholars that supercessionism is neither scripturally based nor theologically accurate.[130] It is true, certainly, that the New Testament laid the groundwork for the later supercessionist theologies of Justin Martyr, Origen and Tertullian. Luke Timothy Johnson, however, maintains that the anti-Jewish texts were written at the time when Christianity was little more than one Jewish sect polemicizing *other* Jewish interpretations of the meaning of Jesus in the context of Judaism. Even the Letter to the Hebrews, which Cardinal Avery Dulles has called "the most formal statement on the status of the Sinai covenant under Christianity," is written within this atmosphere of sibling competition.[131] Johnson's argument is bolstered by the 2001 statement of the Pontifical Biblical Commission entitled "The Jewish People and Their Sacred Scriptures in the Christian Bible":

The New Testament . . . expresses at one and the same time its attachment to the Old Testament revelation and its disagreement with the synagogue. This discord is not to be taken as "anti-Jewish sentiment," for it is

disagreement at the level of faith, the source of religious controversy between two human groups that take their point of departure from the same
Old Testament faith basis, but are in disagreement on how to conceive the
final development of that faith. Although profound, such disagreement in
no way implies reciprocal hostility.[132]

The document goes on to point out how Paul, in chapters 9-11 in the Letter to
the Romans, shows how the only attitude Christians should have for Jews is that
of "respect, esteem, and love;" for in the end "all Israel will be saved" (Rom
11:26). As John Paul II said during his visit to the synagogue in Mainz, Germany, the Covenant with Israel "has never been abrogated by God (see Rom
11:29)."[133]

Not only does the New Testament not support a supercessionist, anti-Jewish
reading, but such a reading is one that also lacks "theological imagination."[134]
In the first place, to conceive of election as an exclusive claim on God's revelation flies in the face of the church's teaching about the presence of grace and
salvation outside the boundaries of Christianity. Christians' claims about God's
unique revelation in Jesus Christ, in other words, do not negate the fact that
grace continues to be present in other religious ways. With reference to Judaism
in particular, this means that God has *not* rejected the Jewish people. On the
contrary, God's original covenant with Israel is now "extended to the Christian
community as well."[135] Second, as Johnson puts it, "the internal claims of Jews
and Christians are markedly different and do not cancel each other."[136] Rather
than define Christianity over against Judaism, which still remains a valid way
of understanding God's presence and action within history, Christians should
focus on the many things that the two traditions have *in common,* on the one
hand (for example, God's graciousness in election and God's command to help
the poor), and on what is uniquely *Christian,* on the other. Rather than focusing
on Jesus as the "new Moses," for example—which would imply that Moses'
importance is now surpassed—Jesus might be better understood as the "new
Adam," the one who brings about a "new creation." As Johnson suggests, "Christians understand the 'promise of Abraham' not in terms of the flourishing of the
people on the land, but as the eschatological gift of the Holy Spirit poured out
on all flesh and capable of transforming human freedom itself (Acts 2:17-39;
2 Cor 3:17-18)."[137]

Because of the rethinking that has gone on among some Christians about
their identity in the light of Judaism, certain Catholic scholars have proposed
that "dialogue, not conversion, should be the Catholic goal in relations with
Jews."[138] Mission is not something for which Jews are a "target"; rather, Christians and Jews are called to work together as "partners in waiting," to "witness
and work for God's reign together."[139] This newer perspective on Judaism, however, is not shared by all Christians. Catholics such as Cardinal Avery Dulles,
Scott Hahn and John Echert, and Evangelicals like Richard J. Mouw and A. Albert
Mohler, Jr., would tend to espouse a more "fulfillment" theology and point to the
need to continue efforts of preaching to Jews with a view to conversion.[140] And

Gerald H. Anderson, in his 2003 Sherer Lecture on world mission at the Lutheran School of Theology in Chicago, emphasized the importance of a mission today that witnesses to *all* who have not yet come to know the good news of the gospel—including Jews. Nevertheless, no one, we believe, would deny that the Jewish people hold a very particular place in God's own missionary work of salvation, and that, to use the language of Mary C. Boys, "Ecclesia" needs to change its "posture" in relation to "Synagoga."[141]

The plurality of valid religious ends, argues Heim, is actually part of the dynamism of Christianity itself. Christian doctrine has as its center the doctrine of God as a communion of persons, each of whom is distinct from the other, but all of whom partake in a unity in which all equally share and that is greater together than each of the distinct persons. It is this dynamic of unity in diversity and diversity in unity that grounds the validity of religious ends, but it establishes two facts as well. The first is that religious ends which mirror the communal nature of God are more likely to constitute "the fullest human destiny" and so are most worthy to pursue. From this perspective—which is, of course, a perspective of faith—Christianity has a certain "superiority" over other religions. Second, however, is that since all religions have valid religious ends as Mystery, Spirit and Word are each distinct, they need one another and so need to commit themselves to dialogue in imitation of the continuing dialogue *(perichoresis)* of the Trinity. Christianity, even though perhaps most adequate for the fullness of life, is still a partial expression of that fullness, and so can discover new depths in what it is through genuine dialogue with Judaism, Buddhism, Islam, traditional religions, and so on. As Christianity enters into dialogue, it comes—as do all the other faiths—with a conviction of its truth and a readiness to confess it. But it also comes with a recognition that it has much to learn from other faiths and other traditions. Dialogue is thus at the same time a deeply prophetic activity. It is clearly an integral part of the mission of the church as it participates in the mission of the Trinity (see DP 9; RM 55).

DP proposes that there are four forms of interreligious dialogue that Christians can practice. First, and as Marcello Zago says, "above all else,"[142] there is the "dialogue of life." Often, people of other faiths simply do not mix with one another or form friendships with one another, even though they live in the same neighborhoods, send their children to the same schools and shop in the same stores. Commitment to a dialogue of life, however, would help people of different faiths *intentionally* to get to know one another as human beings, as neighbors and as fellow citizens. As people begin to see one another not in the abstract but with concrete faces and personalities, many of the fears and tensions that so often exist between practitioners of different religions can be dissolved. German missiologist Theo Sundermeier speaks of the importance for mission today of *Konvivenz*, a genuine sharing of self, life and experience with others.[143] Such a dialogue of life is the foundation for any other kind of dialogue.

Second, there is the dialogue of action about which we have spoken already in connection with joint action for justice, peace and the integrity of creation. While not downplaying religious commitments and religious differences, when people of different faiths set their eyes on the common goal of social, political or ecological justice they can work for values that are common in practically all religions. We have seen how interfaith cooperation in the "war of the trees" in Zimbabwe affected both Shona religious traditionalists and Christians of AICs. Archbishop Zago mentions an example of interfaith cooperation in Senegal where the minority Christian population rose in the esteem of the Muslim minority.[144]

Third, we can speak of the dialogue of theological exchange. This is a form of dialogue usually done by experts or officials of particular religions; it can be either an exchange of information or a mutual wrestling with a particular religious topic, for example, eschatology, or, for Jews, Christians and Muslims, the role of Jesus.

DP names a fourth kind of interreligious dialogue, dialogue of religious experience. Again, this may most often be engaged in by experts, but it is a way of dialogue accessible to the ordinary religious practitioner. All religions have a spirituality and forms of prayer, and an exchange about the meaning and practice of these can lead to a deeply mutual enrichment. Much of the work of the two sessions of the Parliament of the World's Religions (Chicago, 1993, and Cape Town, 2000) was on this level of spirituality and prayer. Although it was not exactly dialogue in the formal sense, the meetings of Pope John Paul II with leaders of various religions in Assisi in 1986 and 2000, and their praying together in their own distinct ways, was somewhat akin to this kind of dialogue. *Ecumenical Affirmation: Mission and Evangelism* suggests another form of interreligious dialogue for Christians who come from cultures shaped by another faith. This is an intra-church and even intra-personal dialogue that can take place among Christians as they try to understand themselves as both Christians, with ties to a catholic tradition and scriptures coming out of the Jewish and Hellenistic world views, and members of their own cultural and social contexts. This intra-Christian dialogue is also an effort of inculturation, the element of mission that we will take up in the next section.

Interreligious dialogue is indeed prophetic dialogue. As *dialogue* it demands attentive listening, conversation skills, empathy, study, respect. As *prophetic,* it demands honesty, conviction, courage and faith. So often dialogue is depicted as a search for a "lowest common denominator" or for a greater reality beyond particular religious expressions or practices. What experience has shown, however, is that real dialogue does not take place when everyone is "being nice" or "politically correct." What theologian David Tracy says in an often-quoted paragraph about conversation can easily be said of dialogue as a prophetic practice:

> Conversation is a game with some hard rules: say only what you mean; say it as accurately as you can; listen to and respect what the other says, however different or other; be willing to correct or defend your opinions if challenged by the conversation partner; be willing to argue if necessary, to confront if demanded, to endure necessary conflict, to change your mind if the evidence suggests it. . . . In a sense they are merely variations of the transcendental imperatives elegantly articulated by Bernard

Lonergan: "Be attentive, be intelligent, be responsible, be loving, and, if necessary, change."[145]

In the coming decades of the twenty-first century, the church's promotion of interreligious dialogue may be one of its greatest missionary services in a world that may very well resort to confrontation and violence—quick fixes—rather than God's method of patient listening and gentle yet unmistakable commitment to truth. Rather than being on the side of an arrogant, militant brand of Christianity, the church will be authentic if it consistently follows the way of its Master, who could be astounded at the faith of people whom others in his culture counted as unreligious and unworthy of notice (see Mt 15:21-28; Lk 7:1-10, 24-30; Jn 4:4-42).

As an integral part of missionary activity, dialogue focuses on the missionary constant of the *centrality of Jesus Christ*, even while it recognizes the presence of the Spirit, and of "seeds of the Word" in those women and men of good will with whom they meet in the dialogue of life, with whom they work in the dialogue of action, and with whom they share in the dialogue of theological exchange and the dialogue of spirituality. If, as we do, those who dialogue accept the position of S. Mark Heim that *salvation* is a particularly Christian religious end, they will understand salvation to be radically relational and available at least in germ in the here and now, although only to be fully realized in the *eschatological* future. The dialogical commitment presupposes an *anthropology* that conceives of the human person in whatever context as open to God's grace as it is present through God's all-embracing Spirit. Dialogue, like inculturation, is an element that is most sensitive to the *contextual* nature of mission. But in its faithfulness to the divine method of dialogue, it never loses sight of the gospel's *constants*.

INCULTURATION AS PROPHETIC DIALOGUE

As much of the second part of this book has shown, mission has always engaged in what is today called the process of inculturation or contextualization. Some of the great figures in the church's history are those who have in some way taken seriously and treated with respect the context in which the gospel has been witnessed to and proclaimed: Peter and Paul, Justin Martyr, Origen, Benedict, Boniface, Leoba, Francis of Assisi, Clare, Ramón Lull, Matteo Ricci, Bartolomé de las Casas, Vincent Lebbe, Charles de Foucauld, Lesslie Newbigin, Mother Teresa, William J. Seymour. In the sixth century, Gregory the Great wrote to Augustine of Canterbury in Britain, instructing him not to destroy the local shrines completely but rather to adapt them to Christian worship; in the ninth century Cyril and Methodius preached the gospel in the language of the Slavs and invented an alphabet in order to translate the scriptures; at the beginning of the modern era, Martin Luther and the Reformers saw the urgent need for accessible scriptures in local languages; and the newly established SCPF in

Rome spoke of how foolish it would be to transport France, Spain or Italy to China—missionaries were called to bring not European culture but the *faith*. There is no doubt that missionaries in the past also imposed European culture and disparaged local culture; the so-called *tabula rasa* approach is very much in evidence throughout the church's history. But, as scholars like Andrew Walls, Lamin Sanneh and Kwame Bediako have pointed out, there is within the gospel itself a dynamic that is "infinitely translatable"[146]; it has even helped to *preserve* the cultures of receivers despite the unworthiness of its bearers. For Pentecostals, Allan Anderson argues, the "emphasis on 'freedom in the Spirit' has rendered the movement inherently flexible in different cultural and social contexts."[147]

For a number of reasons, however, the necessity for a truly inculturated presentation and interpretation of the gospel became clearer than ever before in the last quarter of the twentieth century and continues to be an integral element of mission today. In theology in general, there has been a gradual discovery that theology draws not only on the traditional sources of scripture and tradition but also on human experience. In fact, human experience or context has assumed a certain priority in theological thinking, because Christians can only read the scriptures and interpret tradition from a particular "place," and scripture and tradition, while absolutely normative, are nevertheless at bottom the products of particular experiences of Israel, the early Christian community and the church in various contexts throughout history. As the last vestiges of the great modern missionary era were dismantled, people in former European colonies began to rediscover their own cultures—and often the values of the religions in which those cultures are grounded. Often this cultural renaissance was paired with a religious renaissance and the emergence of nationalism. This led to a real dissatisfaction with traditional theologies, and the realization dawned in both First and Third Worlds that what had pretended to be a *universal* theology was in fact one that *universalized* theological expression according to what amounted to a local theology developed in Europe. Even more fundamental was the shift from understanding human culture in a classicist manner (culture is a norm up to which one must live in order to be "cultured") to understanding culture empirically (culture is a set of meanings and values that inform a way of life—*any* way of life). It was in terms of a more classicist understanding of culture that traditional theology had developed; when culture is taken as an empirical reality, a certain equality among the world's cultures is recognized, and so theology can be in dialogue not just with one normative culture but with any culture in the world.

Such "external" factors revealed within the gospel itself a dynamic of "translatability" or "inculturation." Doctrines such as the incarnation, the sacramentality of the world, the nature of divine Revelation as personal encounter rather than propositional truth, the catholicity of the church and the nature of God as Trinity (self-diffusive in the world, a community of dialogue, a community of unity in diversity) all were discovered to point to the fact that contextualization or inculturation is a theological and missiological imperative.[148] In 1969, Paul VI could exclaim on a visit to Kampala, Uganda, that "you may, and you must, have an African Christianity"; in 1974, the Asian bishops emphasized that the primary task of evangelization in Asia is the building up of the local church and spoke of a threefold dialogue with Asian poverty, religions and cultures. Evangelical theologian David Hesselgrave insists that "contextualization . . . is not simply nice. It is a necessity."[149]

In our discussion of the missionary constant of culture in Chapter 2, we pointed out six models that Stephen Bevans has discerned to be operative in the inculturation efforts of the church in various situations throughout the world. No one of these models—translation, anthropological, praxis, synthetic, transcendental or counter-cultural—is absolute; that is, there is no one model that can be used at all times and in all situations. Each one has a certain validity within certain types of context. For example, the anthropological model seems most appropriate in situations where the culture has been systematically disparaged, as in Africa or parts of Asia; the counter-cultural model seems most appropriate in secularized postmodern Europe or North America. The primary task of the person who would inculturate the gospel is to be in *dialogue* with the context in which the gospel is to be preached or the Christian life interpreted, and to *listen* and *discern* how best to connect the unchanging aspects of Christian faith with the changing and challenging aspects of a particular experience, culture, social location or social changes in a specific place or within a specific people. Inculturation, in other words, is done best in prophetic dialogue. Roger Schroeder has described this dynamic as "entering someone else's garden."[150] On the one hand, persons of faith need to have a healthy respect for the culture as containing the "seeds of the word," as charged with "immanent transcendence." On the other hand, Christians need to realize that the gospel will always have some kind of counter-cultural edge to it. Prophetic dialogue also takes place as individual expressions of local theology, Christian life and church order enter into dialogue with other local theologies, ways of living and ways of ordering the church in the wider church. Andrew Walls speaks eloquently of both an "indigenizing" principle and a "pilgrim" principle within the gospel.[151] "The faith of Christ," he says, "is infinitely translatable, it creates 'a place to feel at home.' But it must not make a place where we are so much at home that no one else can live there. Here we have no abiding city. In Christ all poor sinners meet, and in finding themselves reconciled with him, are reconciled to each other."[152]

Vietnamese American theologian Peter C. Phan has recently expressed five convictions about inculturation that are worth noting here. First, Phan says, inculturation will be "the most urgent and most controversial issue in mission for decades to come," particularly given the fact that Christianity is now truly a world Christianity and the church is now truly a world church. Second, current ideas and practices of inculturation are currently being challenged as understandings of inculturation and culture itself are undergoing significant revision within theology, missiology and anthropology. Third, inculturation will benefit greatly from a broader appreciation of popular religiosity, the religion of ordinary women and men. Fourth, a deeper understanding of mission history will provide "useful lessons on the process of inculturation and the role of popular religion within it." And finally, on the success or failure of inculturation will hang the future of the church.[153]

Inculturation is proving in many ways to be an exciting task, but it has also proven to be, as Pope John Paul II has pointed out, a "lengthy" and a "difficult and delicate task" (see RM 52; EIA 62). It is also a task that, if engaged in seriously, causes pain—pain that is ultimately liberating and life-giving, but pain nevertheless. Those who have been "objects" of the church's mission some-times must struggle painfully to recover and reclaim identities that were wrongly taken from them in the name of the gospel. Those who have worked as cross-cultural missionaries, many times for long years and with considerable sacri-fice, may be forced to confront the fact that their understanding of Christianity was conditioned by colonial expansionism, racism and assumptions of Western cultural superiority. It is perhaps the risk and the pain involved in the process of inculturation that have made the actual results of inculturation so meager, de-spite the many eloquent testimonies about its importance.

Stephen Bevans has suggested that a spirituality of inculturation is needed to guide Christians through the heady but difficult task of allowing Christian faith and local contexts to encounter one another authentically. He calls this a spiri-tuality of "letting go" and "speaking out," and it is one that functions differently for "outsiders" and "insiders." For outsiders, the main spiritual task in the inculturation process is letting go—of superiority, of power, of illusions that they understand a culture, of illusions that theirs is the true understanding of Christianity. Only after years of listening, learning and being evangelized by the context in which they live as strangers and guests might they dare speak out with suggestions for inculturation or with critiques of the context. For insiders, in contrast, the main spiritual task is to speak out—to have confidence in them-selves and in their own understandings of their cultural and/or social context, and to risk ways of encounter between gospel and context. Only very slowly should they heed criticism of their culture and let go of their intuitions and instincts. It is, again, in such prophetic dialogue that local communities and their leadership—whether insiders or outsiders—will discover new ways of living, witnessing to and proclaiming the good news of healing, reconciliation and new life.[154]

Inculturation is certainly an exercise in prophetic dialogue. It needs, first of all, to be profoundly dialogical, because a context is not always easily readable on the surface. Years of listening, years of learning from a culture's traditions, the hard work of conversing with both grassroots people and academic stud-ies—these are all essential for both insiders and outsiders in any pastoral situa-tion. At the same time, not everything in a culture is good; some things might even need to be denounced as evil and eradicated from a culture. Experience must be honored, but biases can distort perceptions as well. The gospel finds resonances and obstacles in every context. Ironically, says Darrell Whiteman, "good contextualization offends."[155]

Inculturation is rooted in a *Christology* that recognizes the "seeds of the word" in every historical and cultural situation. It is strongly *ecclesial* in that it honors the values and customs of the local church, and yet it is open for correction by other local churches and available to enter into critical conversation with those churches. Inculturation is the work of communities, not individuals, and so besides the ecclesial implications of such a conviction, there is present an *anthropology* that recognizes the deep social nature of humanity and recognizes also the goodness of human experience and the human process of culture making. *Salvation* is somehow about human and cultural integrity and wholeness; *eschatology* is not the waiting for a future dismantling of the efforts of human beings but the present realization that God's vision is taking shape as people discover how their own deepest dreams coincide with God's vision of the future. *Culture*, whether prized as "holy ground" in the anthropological model or looked on with some suspicion, as in the counter-cultural model, is still regarded as of utmost importance for theology and Christian life. Human beings are not abstract creatures; they are radically cultural beings.

RECONCILIATION AS PROPHETIC DIALOGUE

The "ministry of reconciliation" (2 Cor 5:19) might have very well been included in our reflections on the ministry of justice, peace and the integrity of creation, since issues of justice, the conditions for the cessation of violence and the full blossoming of peace (shalom) and involvement in healing the wounds of creation are all included in this sixth element of mission. However, as Robert Schreiter argues forcefully, the particular *context* of the world and the church today calls special attention to the praxis (for example, action-reflection-action) of reconciliation as a newly emerging paradigm of mission. At the dawn of the era that Schreiter has called the "rebirth of mission" for the Catholic Church, the SEDOS conference of 1981 helped missionaries focus on new approaches to missionary work in the wake of the seismic theological shifts articulated by the Second Vatican Council. This conference, as we have noted earlier in this chapter, suggested that mission in the final decades of the twentieth century should be lived out in the practice of four interconnected ministries: proclamation, dialogue, inculturation and liberation.[156] Schreiter points out that while proclamation showed the continuity with previous missionary eras, the ministries of dialogue, inculturation and liberation were the fruits that the church had discovered at Vatican II and "constituted new avenues of being in mission, avenues that marked the road of accompaniment."[157] While the SEDOS conference's endorsement of proclamation as an integral part of mission affirmed the constant of the centrality of Jesus Christ in the church's missionary work, the endorsement of dialogue, inculturation and liberation was a response to a changed and changing context in the post-colonial, late-twentieth century and expressed the constants of eschatology, salvation, anthropology and culture in new and exciting ways. This was the era, as Schreiter says frequently, of mission as "incarnation," "accompaniment" and "solidarity."[158]

But the context has changed in the twenty-first century, especially if one dates the close of the twentieth-century era at 1989, with the fall of Communism and the beginning birth pangs of a "New World Order."[159] What marks the context of this time is the phenomenon of globalization, which in its compression of space and time through communications technology and rapid and easily accessible transportation, has connected the peoples in the world as never before in history and has provided new levels of human, educational, economic and political possibilities. Globalization also threatens, perhaps as never before, to exclude whole peoples from economic and political participation and to extinguish traditional languages and cultures. In reaction and resistance to globalization, however, there is the emergence as well of new ethnic identities, the strengthening of old ones and a renaissance in religiosity. There is nothing near to a uniform *global culture* except in the most superficial sense of that term. Benjamin R. Barber has characterized the movement of globalization as a confrontation between "jihad and McWorld," a confrontation that pits culture-leveling global tendencies over against angry and defensive local reactions. Samuel Huntington, in a controversial article and subsequent book, prophesies that the world is poised for future conflicts not between great national powers but between competing "civilizations."[160] The twentieth century was branded "the most terrible of centuries" by intellectual historian Isaiah Berlin,[161] but the death and violence that erupted to unspeakable levels as the century ended (Rwanda, Burundi, Bosnia-Herzogovina, Kosovo, East Timor, the AIDS crisis) seem very likely to continue into the present as Israel and Palestine continue to be trapped in a deadly dance of violence, India and Pakistan face each other with nuclear weapons over another unnegotiable situation in Kashmir, terrorists—often religious extremists—threaten to hold the whole world hostage, the United States seems bent on asserting world leadership by military domination, the AIDS pandemic seems likely to wipe out almost half of the population of Africa, and refugees the world over are proliferating. In addition, the deliverance of South Africa from apartheid and the stabilization of countries like Argentina, Chile and Mexico have unearthed the unspeakable acts of violence of those regimes. In addition, investigations are being held (most recently in Mexico) to discover the truth behind the lies told for years by these "national security" states, and indigenous peoples in every part of the world (for example, aboriginals in Australia and Native Americans and African Americans in North America) are demanding recognition of and compensation for the damage done by majority populations to their traditional ways of life and their cultures.

It is because of this changed context in the world that Schreiter proposes that reconciliation be considered a new model of mission. Like the inclusion of proclamation in the new paradigm of mission proposed by the 1981 SEDOS conference, the praxis of reconciliation does not supplant the notions of dialogue, inculturation and liberation that that conference set forth. But the context of the times does point to the importance of a special focus today on a way of doing mission that has reconciliation as a central missionary focus as the church preaches, serves and witnesses to the "already" but "not yet" reign of the triune God. The possibility of reconciliation is one of, if not the most compelling way of expressing the meaning of the gospel today. In the midst of unspeakable violence, unbearable pain and indelible scars on people's memory, the church as God's minister of reconciliation proclaims that in Christ and in his community, healing is possible. This is news that is almost too good to be true, but it can become credible through a Christian community that is committed to giving itself over to the possibility and living it out in the authenticity of its life.

Reconciliation takes place at a number of different levels, and the church needs to be involved, according to its capacity, at every one. In the first place, there is the *personal* level of reconciliation. The violence done to women by abusive spouses and the sexual abuse of children by members of families and family friends leaves terrible emotional scars on the victims, scars that may take a lifetime to heal, but with God's grace and the mediating help of a minister, therapist or friend, healing is possible. Healing is possible as well for victims of violent crimes; for those who have suffered devastating loss in hurricanes, floods or other natural disasters; and for couples who have gone through the throes of divorce. While much of this might be classified as pastoral work inside the Christian community, a missionary vision will inspire Christians to find ways to make the church's ministry of personal reconciliation available as well to those who are "unchurched," to people of other faiths and to people who do not affiliate themselves with a particular religion or set of doctrines. Such availability and openness are simply for the sake of those who suffer, with "no strings attached;" but such ministry cannot but be a witness to God's reconciling love in Jesus and perhaps provide an opportunity, when asked, to proclaim one's motives and faith explicitly.

A second level of reconciliation might be called *cultural* reconciliation. Some members of the church might be called to be present to women and men of cultural groups whose cultural identity has been ignored, disparaged or stolen from them altogether. Such ministry is a delicate one of being present and yet not getting in the way, affirming without being patronizing, spending many hours listening and gaining trust. Australian theologian Gerard Goldman tells of long hours spent listening to stories of aboriginal people about the experiences in the "dormitories" (for boys) and "convents" (for girls). He marveled at the healing that took place as deeply wounded people were asked, for the first time in their lives, to tell their stories.[162] Eleanor Doidge reflects on years of Native American ministry:

> The true measure of our commitment and integrity will be tested and purified in our ability to remain faithful to the truth and not abandon the people in their time of anger and mistrust. This can take a long time, years, in fact. Are there people today prepared to set down their tents and work to build honest relationships where the truth can be told and trust can be reestablished?[163]

A third level is *political* reconciliation. Here we have in mind national commitments like the establishment and accomplishment of the Truth and Reconciliation Commission presided over by Nelson Mandela and chaired by Archbishop

Desmond Tutu in South Africa, or similar inquiries in Argentina, Chile and Guatemala. In South Africa, it was very clear through the presence of Archbishop
Tutu that the church was in the thick of the process. This might not be so evident
in other places in the world, but the church can be present in many auxiliary ways,
and it can always be present to refugees and victims who have escaped genocide
or "ethnic cleansing." Reconciliation is also needed in situations of violence among
local ethnic groups, which are smaller in scale but still devastating. For example, missionaries like Bishop Doug Young in Papua New Guinea are involved on various levels to facilitate efforts to reconcile enemies engaged in
modern-day tribal fighting, in which guns have replaced bows and arrows.[164]

Last but certainly not least, there is reconciliation *within* the church itself. To
speak only for the needs in the Roman Catholic Church, there is reconciliation
needed for divorced Catholics, who often in the past were excluded (sometimes
brutally by both clergy and family members) from full participation in the sacramental life of the church. Women today in the Catholic Church find themselves more and more alienated from church leadership, and not just because of
the church's stance on women's ordination. There are many other ways that
women can actively participate in ministry and decision-making in the church.
Yet time and time again one hears stories of women who have been victims of a
clericalism or sexism that refuses to acknowledge their dignity as persons and
belittles their considerable pastoral gifts. Anyone who works in the church's
multicultural ministry will have heard stories, as well, of how church leadership
has paid scant attention to the customs and religious practices of certain cultural
groups in the church. And, while various Christian bodies struggle with the
morality of homosexuality, the church needs to develop adequate pastoral practices in order to include and be reconciled with those of homosexual orientation, many of whom have deep faith in Jesus' Lordship and yet have suffered
greatly from the leadership and membership of the churches they love. The
Catholic Church at present is still reeling from the shocking revelations in 2002
of bishops involved in covering up multiple instances of sexual abuse by priests
of children and adolescents, especially boys, often reassigning the perpetrators
to parish work after a leave of absences or attempts at therapy. The church must
find ways to help those who have been abused to come to healing, forgiveness
and wholeness. And the hierarchy must restore its credibility by opening up the
church to the voice and vote of the laity.

While the church must be wholly committed to this ministry of reconciliation on every level, it needs to realize nevertheless that its ministry is just that:
ministry. Its commitment to reconciliation must recognize, as Schreiter says,
that it is God and God *alone* who accomplishes the work of reconciliation within
people's hearts. The church proclaims reconciliation as a possibility and works
as a mediator of that possibility, but it cannot bring it about itself. "The enor-
mity of the misdeeds of the past is so great that it overwhelms the human imagination to consider how they might ever be overcome. Who can undo the consequences of a war or of centuries of oppression? Who can bring back the dead? . . .
A new possibility of life can be given to those who have suffered, but ultimately

no wrongdoer can give that back; it will have to come from the source of all life."[165] What this means as well is that reconciliation is a process that is neither initiated by the wrongdoer nor brought about by his or her apology or repentance. Rather, reconciliation happens through God's amazing grace working within victims, filling them with the courage to put closure on their brokenness. "The victim is not restored to a *status quo ante*, but is brought to a new place from which the victim can come to see the world and its brokenness from God's own perspective, as it were, that is, from a perspective of grace and mercy."[166]

Schreiter insists that, before all else, the ministry of reconciliation is a *spirituality* rather than a *strategy;* it necessarily involves the cultivation of a vibrant relationship with God through contemplation.[167] Nevertheless, he has sketched out several "elements" for a strategy of reconciliation in general, and for the church's missionary involvement in particular.[168] Christians, he says, can create communities of reconciliation—safe havens of truth, of care, of concern, of prayer, of genuine participation and solidarity. Christians can and must, in the second place, engage in the moral reconstruction of broken societies through a process of keen discernment of needs and a generous involvement in conflict mediation, offering hospitality and emergency aid to those in need, and helping people connect with the wider world. It can develop ways of celebrating the sacrament of reconciliation that allow truth to be told, guilt to be acknowledged and accepted, and pardon to be offered by the church spokespersons and the victims themselves. Schreiter recommends a collection that gives twelve case histories of the church's involvement in reconciliation activities. These case histories are encouraging, but the book itself acknowledges sadly that such efforts of reconciliation are all too uncommon. Such an acknowledgment leads Schreiter to articulate a fourth and final strategy for the church: not to be afraid. "To the extent to which the Church succumbs to either fear or guilt is the extent to which it fails in its ministry of reconciliation. Churches should be trusting enough in the reconciling grace of God to admit their own failings and find ways of working toward reconciliation."[169]

The church's ministry of reconciliation is without a doubt a ministry of prophetic dialogue. The witness and proclamation to victims of injustice and violence that reconciliation is a possibility and that it is thoroughly God's work are actions that take real courage. Reconciliation is undoubtedly a counter-cultural movement, a call to envision not a repaired world but a new creation. At the same time, reconciliation is mediated through Christians who are in solidarity with the world's victims, who, as Eleanor Doidge says, stand with people even when those people vent their anger and frustration on those offering their help and support. Working for reconciliation is nothing if not deeply dialogical and empathetic.

The church's proclamation of reconciliation is a proclamation of the *centrality of Jesus Christ*, in whom the world was reconciled to God (2 Cor 5:19). It is deeply *ecclesial* in that, while it is the work of face-to-face relationship, it happens within the safe place of a community of truth, trust and mutuality. It offers a powerful view of *salvation* as breaking in upon human beings, offering healing and wholeness, offering a new vision of what the world can be, offering forgiveness without denying the importance of consequences. Reconciliation does not "forgive and forget"; it does not "just move on" or "get on with life." It remembers and still rages, laments and grieves. But it does so with the grace of wholeness, *salus*. Obviously, there is a profound *anthropology* at work here, as well as an *eschatology*. In some cases, healing is based on a new appreciation and celebration of a people's *cultural* heritage. Reconciliation, in sum, is a way of doing mission in today's very particular *context* while still remaining faithful to mission's age-old *constants*.

CONCLUSION

What seems evident at the conclusion of this reflection on the six elements of mission today is how they are all distinct from one another and yet intricately intertwined as well. A witness that is not a witness to justice, that is not sufficiently inculturated so as to be understood as good news, that is not evident in the church's life of prayer and ritual action, or that is not of a community that is reconciled and reconciling—such a witness is no witness at all. One could say the same about an inculturation that is not involved in the issues of justice, that is not sensitive to the integrity of creation, that is not a clear proclamation of the Lordship of Christ; or about a praxis of reconciliation that is insensitive to culture and injustice, that is not ritually acted out, that is not anchored in a vibrant community, and so on.

The point is that there is *one* mission: the mission of God that is shared, by God's grace, by the church. It has *two* directions—to the church itself *(ad intra)* and to the world *(ad extra)*. Mission to the church itself is necessary so that the church can shine forth in the world for what it is, a community that *shares* the identity of Christ as his body (see Gal 2:20; Phil 1:21; 1 Cor 10:16-17; Mt 10:40; Jn 20:21). Mission to the world points to the fact that the church is only the church as it is called to *continue* Jesus' mission of preaching, serving and witnessing to God's reign in *new* times and places (Mt 28:18-20; Mk 16:15-16; Lk 24:44-47; Acts 1:8). Mission has a basic threefold structure of word *(kerygma)*, action *(diakonia)* and being *(koinonia* or *martyria)*. Thus mission shares and continues the threefold office of Christ as priest, prophet and servant-king (see LG 10-12). It has four fields of activity—pastoral work, the new evangelization of reaching the unchurched, the transformation of the world and the evangelization of those who have not heard the gospel or among whom the church is not fully viable (mission *ad gentes)*. And, as we have seen in this chapter, it has six elements, all distinct and yet interconnected.

Mission today is a "single, complex reality" (RM 41). In its singleness it remains faithful to what has always been constant: the centrality of Jesus Christ, the importance of the church, the urgency of the message in the light of the world's end, the proclamation of salvation, the importance of the human person and human culture. But as a complex reality the one mission needs to be sensitive to the various movements of culture, thought, politics and spiritual sensitivity that make up the context in which mission is lived out. Today, we believe, mission needs to be acknowledged first of all as *God's* work and as a dedication to preaching, serving and witnessing to the reign of God as lived, preached and embodied in Jesus of Nazareth. It needs to be open and determined, sensitive and courageous. As the church witnesses and proclaims, prays and celebrates, works for justice for humanity and for creation, is open to people of other faith perspectives and to the context in which people live, is available as God's instrument of reconciliation—in other words, as the church lives out its radical *missionary* nature—our conviction is that *prophetic dialogue* best names the service to which God is calling it in these first years of a new century and a new millennium. *Prophetic dialogue,* in other words, is the phrase that best summarizes a theology of mission for today, keeping the church *constant* in this *context.*

Concluding Reflections

On Being Constant in Today's Context

One of the most important things that Christians need to know about the church is that *the church* is not of ultimate importance. This was the first sentence of the introduction to Part I, and we hope by now that its profundity is clear. What *is* of ultimate importance is the reign of God, and it is from the church's commitment to preach, serve and witness to that reign that the church receives and maintains its identity. To preach, serve and witness to the reign of God is to preach, serve and witness to the gospel *about* and *of* Jesus, and it is to participate as well in the very life of the triune God. The point of the church is not the church. The church can only be church if it is poised toward the kingdom, continuing to embody the ministry of Jesus as the face of the Spirit, sharing in the abundant trinitarian life God shares in history. The church is missionary by its very nature.

The church is the reign of God's sacramental presence in the world and so is intimately, inextricably bound up with humanity, history and cosmos. Its presence, if it is participating in God's mission authentically, is always in a particular context, always seeking to communicate the gospel in terms of a particular culture, in a particular language, with the advantages and limitations of a particular age. It was not enough for the church to stay connected with Jewish thought forms and symbols. We see in the Acts of the Apostles how God's Spirit led the early community beyond its prejudices and preconceptions to embrace a religious practice that was wholly inconceivable to it, or even to its Lord during his earthly life. But fidelity to God's mission pushed it into new context after new context, and to the extent that the church was attentive to those contexts it was faithful to its Lord and his Spirit. Whether in India at the dawn of Christianity, Roman North Africa, Hellenistic Asia Minor, Persia, the Germanic frontier, China of the T'ang Dynasty, Latin America of the Spanish conquistadors, nineteenth-century colonial Africa or twentieth-century postmodern secular Europe, the church's mission has mirrored the values, the discoveries, the prejudices and the dreams of every age and every situation in which it found itself. The Spirit has led the church to do mission through the witness of its martyrs' courage, its monks' and nuns' example, its mendicants' zeal, its beguines' lives in common, its Jesuits' loyalty and creativity, its Reformers' boldness, its Pentecostals' fervor. Corrupt papal power, the meddling of kings, the blindness of colonial greed and the narrowness of Eurocentrism have certainly hindered God's mission and the church's work, but the gospel has been preached. The church is all too human and even sinful, but it is also a mystery "imbued with the hidden presence of God," and it continues to preach, serve and witness to Jesus and his gospel of the reign of God in the power of the Spirit. The history of the Christian movement is nothing if not the history of Christians struggling to be faithful to God's Spirit as that Spirit is made manifest in new and surprising ways in new and surprising contexts. We hope that Part II of this work has made the radical contextual nature of Christianity clear.

But we hope that Christians' fidelity to the gospel has been made clear as well. Whether in ancient Persia, eighth-century China, twelfth-century Italy, sixteenth-century Paraguay or nineteenth-century West Africa, the center of preaching, serving and witnessing to God's reign has remained Jesus Christ. Such fidelity to Christ has constituted the church, which lives in eschatological hope until its Lord's return and which offers healing and wholeness to all of humanity and indeed to all of creation. Sometimes this has been done without regard to cultural sensitivity, but in a surprising number of instances it was, and the great miracle is that the gospel has today become rooted in almost all parts of the world. The church's mission has been lived out in the concrete circumstances of particular contexts but also in fidelity to the constants of the gospel and the church's rich and diverse traditions of theology, liturgical practice and Christian life.

Today we recognize that the missionary era begun in the fifteenth century, within the Age of Discovery, has come to an end. We are faced with a challenge to the constants of the gospel in a new context. With the collapse of colonialism, the renaissance of the religions of the world, the recession of Christianity in Europe and the overall shift in the center of gravity within Christianity, migrations of the Third World to the First, the advent of rapid transport, satellite communication, and the emergence of globalization, a new age of mission has begun. Jesus Christ is no less central, the church's missionary nature has not been altered, the gift of God's grace is still offered to all creation. But the way that mission is carried on must change.

The theology of mission we have offered in this book has its theological roots in the missionary rebirth at the end of the twentieth century and is in continuity with those roots. Christians today must recognize at a deep level that first and foremost they share *God's* mission. They must recognize their service of the reign of God and God's justice as constitutive of their identity as church. They must confess the absoluteness and uniqueness of Jesus Christ while pondering the implications of the Spirit's apparent presence within the traditions and practices of other religious ways.

In a world of spatial and temporal compression, human rights and recognition of religions' truth, liberal Christians may be tempted to blunt the edge of

Christianity's prophetic tradition and settle for a witness that engages in respectful dialogue but that really espouses liberal, Enlightenment or post-Enlightenment causes. In a world of increasing religious violence, Pentecostal fervor and ecological peril, a more conservative third-world church—already the majority of Christians—may be tempted to choose a vigorous, prophetic style of Christian witness and communication and neglect some of the values of tolerance and dialogue that Western modernity has given us as a precious heritage. The position we have articulated in this book, however, is that to yield to one or the other of these temptations would be to be unfaithful to the complex context of today. Mission must by all means be *dialogical,* since it is nothing else finally than the participation in the dialogical nature of the triune, missionary God. But it must be *prophetic* as well, since, at bottom, there can be no real dialogue when truth is not expressed and clearly articulated.

Only by preaching, serving and witnessing to the reign of God in bold and humble prophetic dialogue will the missionary church be constant in today's context.

Notes

Introduction

1. Harvie Conn, *Eternal Word and Changing Worlds: Theology, Anthropology and Mission in Trialogue* (Grand Rapids, Mich.: Zondervan, 1984).
2. David J. Bosch, *Transforming Mission: Paradigm Shifts in Theology of Mission* (Maryknoll, N.Y.: Orbis Books, 1991); J. Andrew Kirk, *What Is Mission? Theological Explorations* (Minneapolis, Minn.: Fortress Press, 2000); Wilbert R. Shenk, *Changing Frontiers of Mission* (Maryknoll, N.Y.: Orbis Books, 1999). Stephen Bevans attempted to outline a theology with a "missiological imagination" in his address at the Catholic Theological Society of America meeting in Milwaukee, Wisconsin, in June 2001 (see "Wisdom from the Margins: Systematic Theology and the Theological Imagination," *Proceedings of the Catholic Theological Society of America* 56 [2002], 21-42).
3. Dale T. Irvin and Scott W. Sunquist, *History of the World Christian Movement*, vol. 1, *Earliest Christianity to 1453* (Maryknoll, N.Y.: Orbis Books, 2001). See also Wilbert R. Shenk, ed., *Enlarging the Story: Perspectives on Writing World Christian History* (Maryknoll, N.Y.: Orbis Books, 2002); Justo L. González, *The Changing Shape of Church History* (St. Louis, Mo.: Chalice Press, 2002).
4. Justo L. González, *Christian Thought Revisited: Three Types of Theology*, 2d ed. (Maryknoll, N.Y.: Orbis Books, 1999); Dorothee Sölle, *Thinking about God: An Introduction to Theology* (London: SCM Press; Philadelphia: Trinity Press International, 1990).
5. Gerald H. Anderson et al., eds., *Mission Legacies: Biographical Studies of Leaders of the Modern Missionary Movement* (Maryknoll, N.Y.: Orbis Books, 1994); Gerald H. Anderson, ed., *Biographical Dictionary of Christian Missions* (New York: Macmillan, 1998).

Part I. Introduction

1. This beautiful phrase is a quotation from Cyprian of Carthage, *De oratione dominica* 23 (PL 4, 533). The note also refers to Augustine *Serm.* 71, 20, 33 (PL 38, 463f.) and St. John of Damascus, *Adv. Iconol.* 12 (PG 96, 1358D).
2. Paul VI, Opening Address of the Second Session of Vatican II, in *Enchiridion Vaticanum* (Bologna: Edizioni Dehoniane, 1968), 97.
3. "The Church is necessary so long as the social and political life of man does not provide the ultimate human fulfillment that the Kingdom of God is to bring in human history. In this way we see that the Church is not eternal, but is necessary for the time this side of the Kingdom" (W. Pannenberg, *Theology and the Kingdom of God* [Philadelphia: The Westminster Press, 1969], 83); "One day the Church will have completed her earthly task and will be absorbed in the eschatological kingdom of Christ or of God" (R. Schnackenburg, *God's Rule and Kingdom* [New York: Herder and Herder, 1963], 301). Commenting on the title of Chapter VII of *Lumen Gentium*, Otto Semmelroth writes: "Clearly it is the Church herself whose eschatological character we are discussing. She herself confesses that she is something provisional, destined to be done away with" (H. Vorgrimler, ed., *Commentary on the Documents of Vatican II* [New York: Herder and Herder, 1967], 1:281); "When the Kingdom comes, then the age of the Church, which is the age of signs and is itself under the sign 'till he come,' will have passed. Then we shall be in the age of direct sight" (K. Skydsgaard, quoted in J. Haughey, "Church and Kingdom: Ecclesiology in the Light of Eschatology," *Theological Studies* 29/1 [March 1968]: 80). To be fair, however, not all theologians would agree with this view. Avery

Dulles, for example, has written in more than one place that he sees the church *fulfilled* in the inauguration of the reign of God rather than *dissolved* (*Models of the Church* [Garden City, N.Y.: Image Books, 1978], 217). More recently, Dulles has written that "the glorious consummation described in Revelation, chapter 21 . . . far from doing away with the Church, establishes it as the new Jerusalem. . . . If the city contains no temple, that is because the entire city is a holy reality, suffused with God's transfiguring presence" ("The Church and the Kingdom," in E. Laverdiere, ed., *A Church for All Peoples: Missionary Issues in a World Church* [Collegeville, Minn.: The Liturgical Press, 1993], 16-17).

4. "Theses on the Local Church: A Theological Reflection in the Asian Context," Thesis 2.1, in J. Gnanapiragasam and F. Wilfred, eds., *Being Church in Asia: Theological Advisory Commission Documents (1986-92)* (Quezon City, Philippines: Claretian Publications, 1994), 45.

5. A. Hastings, "Mission," in K. Rahner, ed., *Encyclopedia of Theology: The Concise Sacramentum Mundi* (New York: Crossroad, 1975), 968. See also R. D. Haight, "Mission: The Symbol for Understanding the Church Today," *Theological Studies* 37/4 (December 1976): 620-651.

6. E. Brunner, *The Word in the World* (London: SCM Press, 1931), 11. As Donald G. Miller comments: "Without flame, no fire; without mission, no Church!" ("Pauline Motives for the Christian Mission," in G. H. Anderson, ed., *The Theology of the Christian Mission* [Nashville, Tenn.: Abingdon Press, 1961], 79).

7. Frans J. Verstraelen, "Africa in David Bosch's Missiology: Survey and Appraisal," in W. Saayman and K. Krtizinger, eds., *Mission in Bold Humility* (Maryknoll, N.Y.: Orbis Books, 1996), 8, 39. See also J. Blauw, *The Missionary Nature of the Church* (New York: McGraw-Hill, 1962), 112. Blauw speaks of mission as "a boundary notion which indicates that Christ's dominion knows no geographical boundaries either."

8. Throughout this book, *mission* will be equated with *evangelization*. We believe we are justified in this equation since both can have the more general meaning of the church's ministry *ad intra* (or its work of ministry to itself, so that it can be a sign and credible witness of what it stands for) and *ad extra* (or its work outside itself, persuading people to membership or promoting the values of God's reign in the world). Although David Bosch has some reservations about such an identification, he admits that it occurs to a certain extent in *Evangelii Nuntiandi* (see David J. Bosch, *Transforming Mission: Paradigm Shifts in Theology of Mission* [Maryknoll, N.Y.: Orbis Books, 1991], 409-420; see also Karl Müller, *Mission Theology: An Introduction* [Nettetal, Germany: Steylerverlag, 1987], 66). The 1991 document entitled *Dialogue and Proclamation* also makes the identification in speaking of the church's "evangelizing mission" (DP 8).

9. Dialogue was a major concern of Paul VI's first encyclical, *Ecclesiam Suam*, but it does not play a large part in the pope's understanding of evangelization in *Evangelii Nuntiandi*. It has only been in more recent years that dialogue has been recognized as "one of the integral elements of the Church's evangelizing mission" (DP 9). See also RM 55.

10. R. H. Matzken, "Standing under the Missionary Mandate," in F. J. Verstraelen, A. Camps, L. A. Hoedemaker and M. R. Spindler, eds., *Missiology: An Ecumenical Introduction* (Grand Rapids, Mich.: Eerdmans, 1995), 175. See 1 Cor 5:18.

11. Stephen Neill, *Creative Tension* (London: Edinburgh House Press, 1959), 81.

12. Bosch, 512. See also Blauw's discussion of Neill's dictum in Blauw, 121-122.

13. Lucien Legrand, *Unity and Plurality: Mission in the Bible* (Maryknoll, N.Y.: Orbis Books, 1990), xii.

1. "Missionary by Its Very Nature"

1. Martin Kähler, *Schriften zur Chrstiologie und Mission* (Munich: Chr. Kaiser Verlag, 1971; originally published in 1908), 190; quoted in David J. Bosch, *Transforming Mission: Paradigm Shifts in Theology of Mission* (Maryknoll, N.Y.: Orbis Books, 1991), 16.

2. Jürgen Moltmann, *The Church in the Power of the Spirit* (New York: Harper & Row, 1977), 206.

3. See Carroll Stuhlmueller and Donald Senior, *The Biblical Foundations for Mission* (Maryknoll, N.Y.: Orbis Books, 1983), 157.

4. Martin Hengel, *Between Jesus and Paul: Studies in the Earliest History of Christianity* (London: SCM Press, 1983), 53, quoted in Bosch, 15.

5. For example, see Stuhlmueller and Senior, 255-256; Mark Allan Powell, *What Are They Saying about Acts?* (Mahwah, N.J.: Paulist Press, 1991), 47, citing Gerhard Krodel, *Acts* (Minneapolis, Minn.: Augsburg, 1986); Luke Timothy Johnson, *The Acts of the Apostles*, Sacra Pagina 5 (Collegeville, Minn.: The Liturgical Press, 1992), 1; Jacques Dupont, *The Salvation of the Gentiles* (New York: Paulist Press, 1979), 9.

6. Lucien Legrand, *Unity and Plurality: Mission in the Bible* (Maryknoll, N.Y.: Orbis Books, 1990), 91; Stuhlmueller and Senior, 255; John Stott, *The Spirit, the Church and the World: The Message of Acts* (Downers Grove, Ill.: InterVarsity Press, 1990), 5.

7. Legrand, 92.

8. We have already referred to Senior and Stuhlmueller's ground-breaking work, as well as to the important work of Lucien Legrand. Bosch's *Transforming Mission* has a chapter on the New Testament in general and has a chapter each on the Gospel of Matthew, Luke-Acts and the writings of Paul. See also Carlos F. Cardoza-Orlandi, *Mission: An Essential Guide* (Nashville, Tenn.: Abingdon Press, 2002), 49-70; Marion Soards, "Key Issues in Biblical Studies and Their Bearing on Mission Studies," *Missiology: An International Review* 24/1 (January 1996): 93-109. Classic studies in this area are Johannes Blauw, *The Missionary Nature of the Church: A Survey of the Biblical Theology of Mission* (New York: McGraw-Hill, 1962), and Ferdinand Hahn's *Mission in the New Testament* (London: SCM, 1965). For an Evangelical perspective, see William J. Larkin, Jr., and Joel F. Williams, eds., *Mission in the New Testament: An Evangelical Approach* (Maryknoll, N.Y.: Orbis Books, 1998); Arther F. Glasser, with Charles E. van Engen, Dean S. Gilliland and Shawn B. Redford, *Announcing the Kingdom: The Story of God's Mission in the Bible* (Grand Rapids, Mich.: Baker Academic, 2003); and the collected articles in Ralph D. Winter and Steven C. Hawthorne, eds., *Perspectives on the World Christian Movement*, 3d ed. (Pasadena, Calif.: William Carey Library, 1999). For a Pentecostal perspective, see Byron D. Klaus, "The Mission of the Church," in Stanley M. Horton, ed., *Systematic Theology* (Springfield, Mo.: Logion Press, 1995), 568-581. For a more extensive bibliography, see M. R. Spindler and P. Middlekoop, *Bible and Mission: A Partially Annotated Bibliography* (Leiden: Brill IIMO, 1981); Donald Senior, "Bible," in K. Müller, T. Sondermeier, S. Bevans and R. Bliese, eds., *Dictionary of Mission: Theology, History, Perspectives* (Maryknoll, N.Y.: Orbis Books, 1997), 44-47.

9. Lesslie Newbigin, "The Logic of Election," in *The Gospel in a Pluralistic Society* (Grand Rapids, Mich.: Eerdmans; Geneva: WCC Publications, 1989), 80-88. See also George R. Hunsberger, *Bearing the Witness of the Spirit: Lesslie Newbigin's Theology of Cultural Plurality* (Grand Rapids, Mich.: Eerdmans, 1998), 45-112; John T. Pawlikowski, "Judaism," in Müller et al., 236-240.

10. Hans Küng, *The Church* (New York: Sheed and Ward, 1967), 74-75.

11. Mortimer Arias, *Announcing the Reign of God: Evangelization and the Subversive Memory of Jesus* (Philadelphia: Fortress Press, 1984), 2.

12. For this helpful distinction, see David Lowes Watson, "Christ All in All: The Recovery of the Gospel for Evangelism in the United States," in George R. Hunsberger and Craig van Gelder, eds., *The Church between Gospel and Culture: The Emerging Mission in North America* (Grand Rapids, Mich.: Eerdmans, 1996), 189-190. Watson attributes the distinction to Arias, 8-12; see also "Missional Vocation: Call and Sent to Represent the Reign of God," in Darrell L. Guder, ed., *Missional Church: A Vision of the Sending of the Church in North America* (Grand Rapids, Mich.: Eerdmans, 1998), 87-90.

13. Martin Hengel, *Acts and the History of Earliest Christianity* (Philadelphia: Fortress Press, 1980), 126.

14. Johnson, 16.

15. Stephen G. Wilson, *The Gentiles and the Gentile Mission in Luke-Acts* (Cambridge: Cambridge University Press, 1963), 261-262.

16. For a survey of opinions on Luke's historical reliability, see Wilson, 255-257. See also Powell, 80-95; Johnson, 3-7.

17. Wilson, 267.

18. Hengel, *Acts and the History of Earliest Christianity,* 60.

19. Johnson, 7.

20. Wilson, 255. Wilson calls Luke "a pastor and a historian rather than a theologian." His point is well taken, but it seems he thinks of a theologian in stricter, perhaps more "intellectual" terms.

21. Powell, 57.

22. Johnson, 1.

23. Dupont, 13.

24. Robert W. Wall, "The Acts of the Apostles," *The New Interpreter's Bible* (Nashville, Tenn.: Abingdon Press, 2002), 10:5.

25. Although we have read widely in more recent scholarship and have expanded the number of stages discernible in Acts, this section owes its original inspiration to David Stanley's essay "Kingdom to Church" in his book *The Apostolic Church in the New Testament* (Westminster, Md.: The Newman Press, 1966), 1-37. Stanley's essay was first published in 1955 (in *Thelogical Studies* 16, 1-29), but it is still correct in its basic direction. Where ecclesiology would most sharply disagree with him some forty years later would be in his too-close identification of the church with the reign of God. In taking the "stages approach" to the emergence of the church, we are taking an approach similar to, yet at the same time significantly different from, that of Gerhard Lohfink in his essay "Hat Jesus eine Kirch gestiftet?" *Theologische Quartalschrift* 161 (1981): 81-97. For a summary of Lohfink's development, see Francis Schüssler Fiorenza, *Foundational Theology: Jesus and the Church* (New York: Crossroad, 1984), 137-140.

26. See Arias, 1-12; Küng, *The Church,* 54-79; Walter Kasper, *Jesus the Christ* (London: Burns and Oates; New York: Paulist Press, 1976), 72-88; Edward Schillebeeckx, *Jesus: An Experiment in Christology* (New York: Vintage Books, 1981), 115-178; Michael Fahey, "The Church," in Francis Schüssler Fiorenza and John Galvin, eds., *Systematic Theology: Roman Catholic Perspectives* (Minneapolis, Minn.: Fortress Press, 1991), 2:16-19; John Fuellenbach, *Church: Community for the Kingdom* (Maryknoll, N.Y.: Orbis Books, 2002), 6-12. Bosch says that God's reign was "undoubtedly central to Jesus' entire ministry" and quotes Stuhlmueller and Senior's remark that the reign of God is for Jesus "the starting point and context for mission" (Bosch, 31-32, quoting Stuhlmueller and Senior, 144). On the Jesus movement as a movement within Judaism, see John H. Elliot, "The Jewish Messianic Movement: From Faction to Sect," in Philip F. Esler, ed., *Modeling Early Christianity: Social-Scientific Studies of the New Testament in Its Context* (London and New York: Routledge, 1995), 75-95; Markus Bockmuehl and Michael B. Thompson, *A Vision for the Church: Studies in Early Christian Ecclesiology* (Edinburgh: T & T Clark, 1997); Haim G. Perelmuter, *Siblings: Rabbinic Judaism and Early Christianity at Their Beginnings* (Mahwah, N.J.: Paulist Press, 1989); Mary C. Boys, *Has God Only One Blessing? Judaism as a Source of Christian Understanding* (Mahwah, N.J.: Paulist Press, 2000).

27. There is, of course, a vast literature on Jesus' ministry. For more scholarly treatment, see Kasper; Schillebeeckx; John Fuellenbach, *The Kingdom of God* (Maryknoll, N.Y.: Orbis Books, 1995); Elisabeth Schüssler Fiorenza, *In Memory of Her: A Feminist Reconstruction of Christian Origins* (New York: Crossroad, 1983). For other perspectives from the Third World, see Albert Nolan, *Jesus before Christianity* (Maryknoll, N.Y.: Orbis Books, 1992); George Soares-Prabhu, "The Kingdom of God: Jesus' Vision of a New Society" and "Good News to the Poor! The Social Implications of the Message of Jesus," in D. S. Amalorpavadass, ed., *Indian Church in the Struggle for a New Society* (Bangalore, India: NBCLC, 1981), 579-608 and 609-626. Carlos Bravo, "Jesus of Nazareth, Christ the Liberator," in I. Ellacuría and J. Sobrino, eds., *Mysterium Liberationis* (Maryknoll, N.Y.: Orbis Books, 1993), 420-439. Although it was written over three decades ago, Andrew Greeley's *The Jesus Myth* (New York: Doubleday, 1971) remains, in our minds, a splendid introduction to Jesus' ministry.

28. See Schillebeeckx, 154-172.

29. On the reasons for Jesus' arrest and execution, see Schillebeeckx, 272-319; Bravo, 432-436; Jon Sobrino, *Jesus the Liberator: A Historical-Theological View* (Maryknoll, N.Y.: Orbis Books, 1993), 219-232; M. Thomas Thangaraj, *The Crucified Guru: An Experiment in Cross-Cultural Christology* (Nashville, Tenn.: Abingdon Press, 1994), 99; Elizabeth A. Johnson, *Consider Jesus: Waves of Renewal in Christology* (New York: Crossroad, 1990), 57-59; idem, "Jesus and Salvation," in P. Crowley, ed., *The Catholic Theological Society of America: Proceedings of the Forty-Ninth Annual Convention* (1994), 1-18.

30. Wilson, 28. See also Wilson's more recent work, *Related Strangers: Jews and Christians 70–170 C.E.* (Minneapolis, Minn.: Fortress Press, 1995). In the Introduction to this work Wilson summarizes his (and, I believe, contemporary scholarship's) conclusion: "Jesus . . . was wholly embedded in the Judaism of his day and thought he was going to precipitate the restoration of Israel. That he would found a religion called Christianity, which would become competitive with the Judaism he knew, was a thought that never entered his mind" (xv). Scholars, however, are not unanimous on this. James LaGrand, for example, argues that Jesus did indeed carry on a Gentile mission in continuity with such a mission in the Old Testament (see James LaGrand, *The Earliest Christian Mission to 'All Nations' in the Light of Matthew's Gospel* [Grand Rapids, Mich.: Eerdmans, 1999]; see also Glasser et al., 217-219).

31. Stuhlmueller and Senior, 142.

32. See Küng, 70-79; R. Collins, "The Twelve," in D. N. Freedman, ed., *The Anchor Bible Dictionary* (New York: Doubleday, 1992), 6:670-671; R. P. Meye, *Jesus and the Twelve* (Grand Rapids, Mich.: Eerdmans, 1968), 192-209; J. D. Quinn, "Ministry in the New Testament," in *Lutherans and Catholics in Dialogue IV: Eucharist and Ministry* (Washington, D.C.: United States Catholic Conference; New York: USA National Committee of the Lutheran World Federation, 1970), 69-100; Karl Rahner, *Foundations of Christian Faith: An Introduction to the Idea of Christianity* (New York: Seabury, 1978), 332-335; Francis Schüssler Fiorenza; L. Wostyn, *Doing Ecclesiology: Church and Mission Today* (Quezon City: Claretian Publications, 1990); Raymond E. Brown and K. P. Donfried, eds., *Peter in the New Testament* (Minneapolis, Minn.: Augsburg; New York: Paulist Press, 1973); Schillebeeckx, 320-397.

33. Wilson says that the fact that Luke put these words on the lips of the risen Jesus reflects his and the early community's belief that the subsequent mission to the Gentiles and the emergence of the church were indeed mandated expressly by Jesus. See Wilson, *Gentiles*, 258. What the narrative of Acts suggests, however, is that the community was not at all aware of such an explicit directive. Luke, writing in the 80s, when the Gentile mission was in full swing and Jerusalem had been destroyed, was certainly convinced that what had emerged as the church was according to the will of God and happened at the direction of the Lord Jesus. As Wilson explains it, however dubious historically it may be to attribute the Gentile mission to an express command of the risen Jesus, "and however much it may create tensions with the later narrative of Acts, this commission was fundamental to Luke's way of thinking. . . . The Gentile mission did not originate as a bright idea of the early Church, nor did it occur unexpectedly or by accident; it was rooted in the words of Jesus, as a promise in his earthly ministry and as a command after the Resurrection" (ibid., 243). This is perhaps an example of one of those "lacunae and loose ends" that Luke leaves as a testimony to his own honesty about the historical facts (see ibid., 267). Jesus' words, therefore, serve as a theological justification to what will happen in the narrative, but Luke does not subsequently alter the "real facts" that show the community's hesitation about the direction in which the Spirit was leading them.

34. Ibid., 257.

35. Küng, 72-73; Wostyn, 29; Collins.

36. See D. L. Tiede, "The Exaltation of Jesus and the Restoration of Israel in Acts 1," *Harvard Theological Review* 75 (1986): 278-286; Arther M. Wainwright, "Luke and the Restoration of the Kingdom to Israel," *Expository Times* 89 (1977-1978), 76-79.

37. Stanley, 8.

38. See Wilson, *Gentiles,* 110. Although he explains this position and cites several scholars (Wickenhauser, Rengstorf, Beardslee and E. Schweizer) who espouse it, Wilson himself

believes that it was not Luke's intention to speak of such an imminent fulfillment. However, given the fact that Luke does trace a development of the church's consciousness, particularly in regard to the Gentile mission, such a development from a narrow, imminent expectation to a more inclusive understanding of God's reign makes eminent sense as Lucan theology.

39. James G. Dunn, *The Acts of the Apostles* (Peterborough, U.K.: The Epworth Press, 1996), 10.

40. Ibid., 18.

41. Luke Timothy Johnson, 45; Stanley, 10.

42. Luke Timothy Johnson, 60, 62-63.

43. Stanley, 15.

44. Robert C. Tannehill, *The Narrative Unity of Luke-Acts: A Literary Interpretation*, vol. 2, *The Acts of the Apostles* (Minneapolis, Minn.: Fortress Press, 1994), 27.

45. Ibid., 28.

46. See James G. Dunn, *Unity and Diversity in the New Testament: An Inquiry into the Character of Earliest Christianity* (Philadelphia: Fortress Press, 1977), 239: "It is evident that *the earliest community in no sense felt themselves to be a new religion, distinct from Judaism.* There was no sense of a boundary line drawn between themselves and their fellow Jews. They saw themselves simply as a fulfilled Judaism, the beginning of eschatological Israel. And the Jewish authorities evidently did not see them as anything very different from themselves: they held one or two eccentric beliefs (so did other Jewish sects), but otherwise they were wholly Jewish. Indeed we may put the point even more strongly: . . . the earliest Christians were not simply Jews, but in fact continued to be quite 'orthodox' Jews." See also Stanley, 14 and 16.

47. See Dunn, *Unity and Diversity*, 237-239. See also Wall, 74, and Filipe Gómez, "Mission History from the Beginnings to the Modern Period," in Sebastian Karotemprel, ed., *Following Christ in Mission* (Bombay: Pauline Publications, 1995), 163.

48. Dunn, *Acts*, 79.

49. Legrand, 93.

50. Ibid., 95; Dunn, *Acts*, 84; Wall, 112.

51. Hengel, *Acts and the History of Earliest Christianity,* 72.

52. Ibid., 73.

53. Wilson, *Gentiles*, 141-142; Dunn, *Acts*, 83-84.

54. Luke Timothy Johnson, 119. See also Wilson, *Gentiles*, 138.

55. R. P. C. Hanson, *The Acts of the Apostles*, New Clarendon Bible (Oxford: Oxford University Press, 1967), 102, quoted in Wilson, *Gentiles*, 136.

56. See Hengel, *Acts and the History of Earliest Christianity,* 72.

57. John J. Kilgallen, "The Function of Stephen's Speech (Acts 7:2-53)," *Biblica* 70 (1989): 173-193. Kilgallen shows how Luke constructed the speech to tie together a number of themes in Luke's two-volume narrative. Pablo Richard remarks briefly on how the speech is a Lucan construction but is nevertheless an accurate reconstruction of the prophetic theology of the Hellenists (*El movimiento de Jesús: Después de su resurrección y antes de la Iglesia* [Quito, Ecuador: Editorial "Tierra Nueva," 1998], 79).

58. Stott, 130-131.

59. Kilgallen, 182.

60. Ibid., 192.

61. Stanley, 18; see Hengel, *Acts and the History of Earliest Christianity*, 73.

62. Wilson, *Gentiles*, 136.

63. Luke Timothy Johnson says that the fact that the stoners lay their cloaks at Saul's feet during Stephen's stoning hints at the fact that Saul himself was the author of the plot against Stephen (see Johnson, 143-144). That this might indeed be the case seems to be borne out by the fact that Saul appears to be the spirit behind the "great persecution" (8:1) that broke out in the aftermath of Stephen's killing (see 8:3).

64. Dunn, *Acts*, 104.

65. See Dunn, *Unity and Diversity*, 235-266.

66. See Wilson, *Gentiles*, 144-145.

67. Luke Timothy Johnson, 141.

68. Stott, 147.

69. Luke Timothy Johnson, 151; Wall calls the Samaritans, as well as the Ethiopian eunuch whose story follows, the "Outcasts of Israel" (see Wall, 141).

70. Wilson, *Gentiles*, 171-172.

71. Stott, 160.

72. Luke Timothy Johnson, 160.

73. Ibid.

74. Tannehill, 109. In notes 16 and 17 Tannehill refers to the commentaries of Ernst Haenchen (*The Acts of the Apostles: A Commentary*, trans. Bernard Noble and Gerald Shinn [Philadelphia: The Westminster Press, 1971], 310), who notes the ambiguity of the term *eunuch,* and of Hans Conzelmann (*Acts of the Apostles*, trans. James Limburg, A. Thomas Kraabel, and Donald H. Juel, Hermeneia [Philadelphia: Fortress Press, 1987], 68), who notes the reference to both the man's physical condition and his social position. See also C. J. Martin, "A Chamberlain's Journey and the Challenge for Interpretation for Liberation," *Semeia* 47 (1987): 105-135; Justo L. González, *Acts: The Gospel of the Holy Spirit* (Maryknoll, N.Y.: Orbis Books, 2001), 114.

75. Dunn, *Acts*, 114. Dunn adds: "Isa. 11.11-12 seems to regard it [Ethiopia] as one of 'the corners of the earth' (cf. Zeph. 3.10), and Ethiopians were regarded by Homer as the 'last of men.'"

76. Ibid.; Tannehill, 108-110; Hengel, *Acts and the History of Earliest Christianity,* 79.

77. Luke Timothy Johnson, 186.

78. Ibid.

79. Wilson, *Gentiles*, 177.

80. Dunn, *Acts*, 135.

81. Ibid.

82. See Stott, 185.

83. Wilson, *Gentiles*, 176.

84. Dunn, *Acts*, 134.

85. Tannehill, 137.

86. Ibid., 129-131.

87. Luke Timothy Johnson, 198; see also González's comments on the text, 134-136.

88. Andrew F. Walls, *The Missionary Movement in Christian History: Studies in the Transmission of Faith* (Maryknoll, N.Y.: Orbis Books, 1996), 52. In another place Walls plays down the conversion of Cornelius in favor of the move in Antioch: "Certainly, some non-Jews—the household of Cornelius is the example featured in Acts (10:1-11:18)—learned about Jesus, but Cornelius belonged to the fairly small community of Gentiles in Palestine itself who had been attracted to Jewish religion and morality" (Andrew F. Walls, "Old Athens and New Jerusalem: Some Signposts for Christian Scholarship in the Early History of Mission Studies," *International Bulletin of Missionary Research* 21/4 [October 1997]: 146). The admission of Cornelius probably plays a more significant role in Acts than Walls intimates and was probably accepted with more agonizing than the text expresses. However, what Walls points to is the move in Antioch beyond a *Jewish* conception of Jesus (after all, Cornelius and his household were baptized "in the name of Jesus *Christ*). As Walls points out, and as we cite him below, the innovation in Antioch was to present Jesus not as "Christ"—Messiah, "Anointed One" or "Smeared One"—but as "Lord"—*Kyrios*—which was not a Jewish but a Hellenistic title of divinity (see Walls, "Old Athens and New Jerusalem," 146).

89. Raymond E. Brown and John P. Meier, *Antioch and Rome: New Testament Cradles of Catholic Christianity* (New York: Paulist Press, 1983), 12. Josephus spoke of Antioch as "the third greatest city in the Roman Empire (*War* 3.2.4, no. 29). In note 1 it is indicated that W. Meeks and R. Wilken (*Jews and Christians in Antioch* [Missoula, Mont.: Scholars Press, 1978], 1) prefer "the more general statement that Antioch was 'one of the three or four most important

cities in the Roman Empire.'" Rodney Stark lists Antioch as the fourth largest city of the empire, after Rome, Alexandria and Ephesus, with a population of 150,000 (Rodney Stark, *The Rise of Christianity* [San Francisco: HarperCollins, 1997], 131).

90. Some manuscripts have the word "Greeks" in verse 20, and some have "Hellenists." Commentators are divided as to what the correct reading is. Tannehill gives a succinct summary of the range of opinions (146 n. 1) and himself opts for the word "Greeks," although he says it has a wider range of meaning than just "Gentiles." As indicated in the text, it could include Gentiles converted to Judaism, and Jews of Greek birth and culture. The text certainly seems to contrast the disciples preaching "to none but Jews" (11:19) and "even to the Greeks" (11:20). Also, it would seem that since Antioch was the birthplace of the church's world mission, aimed at both Jews and Gentiles, the intimation that Gentiles were included in the Hellenists' (that is, the group of Stephen's) evangelization would make eminent sense.

91. Hengel, *Acts and the History of Earliest Christianity*, 99.

92. Tannehill, 146-147.

93. Dunn says that the relative brevity of the breakthrough at Antioch (which he says is even more momentous in terms of its consequences than the breakthrough at Caesarea) ironically attests to its importance in Luke's mind. "It was so important that it had to be securely interwoven into the history of the movement's steady expansion, and the revolutionary shift to the Gentiles validated beforehand by the critically scrutinized and divinely approved breakthrough at Caesarea" (*Acts*, 153; see also 154). Wilson (*Gentiles*, 261) quotes Haenchen (93) approvingly: "Luke the historian does not sketch the frequently broken line of the real development of the Gentile mission, but its ideal curve."

94. Walls, *The Missionary Movement in Christian History*, 34.

95. Ibid., 35.

96. Stanley, 22.

97. Luke Timothy Johnson, 205.

98. Stott, 205.

99. Hengel, *Acts and the History of Earliest Christianity,* 103.

100. Moltmann, 142. Wall (176) would concur with Moltmann. He believes that the term *Christian* refers to a *theological* difference betweeen the Jerusalem and Antioch communities. González acknowledges that the term *Christian* could have been a derisive one but suggests that it is more probable that it was taken by Christians themselves to indicate that they were "slaves of Christ." González also notes that "the first person known to have employed the word 'Christianity' to refer to the new faith was a bishop of Antioch, Ignatius, in the early second century" (see González, 139).

101. As Dale T. Irvin and Scott W. Sunquist point out, however, the church's expansion at this stage was "without worldly power." They write: "Eventually Christians would march under imperial banners to conquer new cities and nations in the name of Christ. But the earliest Christian missionaries from Jerusalem went out as refugees and victims of persecution, an experience that offers a sharp contrast to the imperial armies that brought the message of other universal lords and emperors to these same cities before and after them. These first Christians had expansionist tendencies without worldly power. That legacy would eventually be eclipsed, but it could never be entirely forgotten by the wider Christian movement" (Dale T. Irvin and Scott W. Sunquist, *History of the World Christian Movement,* vol. 1, *Earliest Christianity to 1453* [Maryknoll, N.Y.: Orbis Books, 2001], 26).

102. David Bosch takes issue with the position that "the Jews' rejection of Jesus forms a decisive presupposition for the Gentile mission" and insists that "Luke wrote his two-volume work for the benefit of Jews as much as Gentiles" (Bosch, 92). In this he is in line with contemporary scholars like Stuhlmueller and Senior, Tannehill and Johnson. Luke Timothy Johnson, for example, writes that Luke's ultimate conclusion is that the Gentile mission is not a new mission after the rejection of the Jews but the *continuation* of the mission to the Jews (Johnson, 8-9). See Boys, 149-159.

103. Dunn, *Acts*, 159; Tannehill, 159.

104. On the textual problem in 12:25, see Stott, 215.

105. Ibid., 222; Dunn identifies the area in which Pisidian Antioch was located as the "underbelly of modern Turkey" (*Acts*, 171).

106. Stanley, 25.

107. Legrand contrasts Paul's attitude, "which is always tinged with nostalgia," with Luke, "for whom the arrival of the nations is welcomed and joyously described" (128). A close reading of Acts, however, suggests that even Luke was not so sanguine about the rejection of Israel. That God had *not* rejected Israel, in fact, was a major reason for writing the two-volume work. See, e.g., Bosch, 115.

108. Luke Timothy Johnson, 268; Wilson, *Gentiles*, 192.

109. Tannehill, 187; for the significance of the term *laos*, see Werner Ustorf, "'People' (Volk), 'Nation,'" in Müller et al., 350-354.

110. Luke Timothy Johnson, 268.

111. Ibid., 286.

112. Wilson, *Gentiles*, 237; see also Wilson, *Related Strangers*, 66.

113. See, for example, Wilson, *Gentiles*, 237-238.

114. See Brown and Meier, 2-8.

115. Dale T. Irvin, *Christian Histories, Christian Traditioning: Rendering Accounts* (Maryknoll, N.Y.: Orbis Books, 1998).

116. Dunn, *Unity and Diversity*, 244.

117. Ibid., 266.

118. On this, see Y. Congar, *Diversity and Communion* (Mystic, Conn.: Twenty-Third Publications, 1984), 9-12.

119. Walls, *The Missionary Movement in Christian History*, 22. In an analysis of the *Didache*, Eugene Laverdiere also speaks to this missionary and inclusive nature of the church from a different though, we believe, quite complementary perspective. *Didache*, Laverdiere argues, is a document from a community in Antioch that "was separatist from the beginning"—in a first stage with other Jews from Gentiles, in a second from other Jewish communities, in a third from other Christian communities that included Gentiles. Consequently, says Laverdiere, the Eucharist they *thought* they were celebrating was not authentic. This was because such a celebration "would have opened the community to all God's people, including the Gentiles. . . . With that they would have become a community among others in a Church that was catholic in principle and missionary in reality. Instead, they remained a community turned in on itself until it disappeared" (Eugene Laverdiere, *The Eucharist in the New Testament and the Early Church* [Collegeville, Minn.: The Liturgical Press, 1996], 143, 145). If the church is not both missionary and inclusive, it seems, it cannot be the church.

120. Moltmann, 360. The quotation is from A. A. Van Ruler, *Theologie van het Apostolaat* (Nijkerk: Callenbach, 1954), 20.

2. "You Are Witnesses of These Things"

1. Andrew F. Walls, "The Gospel as Prisoner and Liberator of Culture," in *The Missionary Movement in Christian History: Studies in the Transmission of Faith* (Maryknoll, N.Y.: Orbis Books, 1996), 3-15.

2. For example, Walls writes in "Culture and Coherence in Christian History": "Christianity . . . has throughout its history spread outwards, across cultural frontiers, so that each new point on the Christian circumference is a new potential Christian centre. And the very survival of Christianity as a separate faith has evidently been linked to the process of cross-cultural transmission" (in Walls, *The Missionary Movement in Christian History*, 22).

3. "The Gospel as Prisoner and Liberator of Culture," in ibid., 6.

4. Ibid., 7.

5. Ibid., 6.

6. The meaning of Jesus Christ, of course, should *always* be understood within the context of his trinitarian identity as incarnate Word of the Father and the "face" of the Holy Spirit

in history. This will be evident as the various aspects of Christology are developed throughout the book.

7. Justo L. González, *Christian Thought Revisited: Three Types of Theology*, rev. ed. (Maryknoll, N.Y.: Orbis Books, 1999).

8. Dorothee Sölle, *Thinking about God: An Introduction to Theology* (London: SCM Press; Philadelphia: Trinity Press International, 1990).

9. Avery Dulles, *Models of Revelation* (New York: Doubleday, 1983), 30. For a discussion of models, see Stephen B. Bevans, *Models of Contextual Theology*, rev. and exp. ed. (Maryknoll, N.Y.: Orbis Books, 2002), 28-33.

10. Sölle, 7: "This division has its problems, because there are always overlaps, connections, cross-fertilizations everywhere, and established 'schools' in no way determine the field; nevertheless it seems to me to be useful."

11. González, 16.

12. For a presentation of the paradigms in general terms, see Sölle, 7-21.

13. How these preferences play themselves out will become evident in the course of the book. In Part III we speak of mission as "prophetic dialogue," a way of doing mission that takes into account Type B's appreciation of human experience and human reason and Type C's suspicion of human structures of power and its commitment to liberative praxis.

14. Philip Jenkins, *The New Christendom: The Coming of Global Christianity* (Oxford and New York: Oxford University Press, 2002).

15. Ibid., 22.

16. Ibid., 20-22.

17. Ibid., 33-36.

18. See, for example, the discussion of Douglas John Hall, *Professing the Faith* (Minneapolis, Minn.: Fortress Press, 1993), 366-370.

19. Ibid., 51. Tertullian first expressed this distinction in *Against Praxeas*, 25.

20. Thomas Aquinas, ST III, 2-26; Jean Calvin, *The Institutes of the Christian Religion*, Book II, Chapters XII-XVII; Karl Barth, *Church Dogmatics,* vol. 1, part 2, *The Doctrine of the Word of God* (Edinburgh: T & T Clark, 1956), 132-171; Donald G. Bloesch, *Jesus Christ: Savior and Lord* (Downers Grove, Ill.: InterVarsity Press, 1997); Donald Macleod, *The Person of Christ* (Downers Grove, Ill.: InterVarsity Press, 1998). See also Jaroslav Pelikan, *The Christian Tradition,* vol. 3, *The Growth of Medieval Theology (600-1300)* (Chicago and London: The University of Chicago Press, 1978), 144-157; *Catechism of the Catholic Church*, 422-511; Alister E. McGrath, *Christian Theology: An Introduction* (Oxford: Blackwell Publishers, 1994), 270-308; Walter Kasper, *Jesus the Christ* (London: Burns and Oates; New York: Paulist Press, 1976), 163-229.

21. Sölle, 111-112; J. J. Mueller, *What Is Theology?* (Wilmington, Del.: Michael Glazier, 1988), 56-58; Karl Rahner, "The Two Basic Types of Christology," *Theological Investigations 13* (New York: Seabury, 1975), 213-223.

22. Karl Rahner, however, insists that, however normative, the Chalcedonian formula is just that—a formula. "Thus we have not only the right but the duty to look at it as an end *and a beginning*" ("Current Problems in Christology," *Theological Investigations 1* [Baltimore, Md.: Helicon Press; London: Darton, Longman and Todd, 1961], 150). Such an understanding is just the opposite of what we have attributed to Type A understandings of Chalcedon's definition. See also S. Mark Heim, *The Depth of the Riches: A Trinitarian Theology of Religious Ends* (Grand Rapids, Mich.: Eerdmans, 2001), 141-144.

23. Jaroslav Pelikan, *The Christian Tradition,* vol. 1, *The Emergence of the Catholic Tradition (100-600)* (Chicago: University of Chicago Press, 1971), 147.

24. Andrew F. Walls, "Old Athens and New Jerusalem: Some Signposts for Christian Scholarship in the Early History of Mission Studies," *International Bulletin of Missionary Research* 21/4 (October 1997): 150. Sölle, 122, also notes the juridical nature of Anselm's discussion.

25. Pelikan, *The Christian Tradition,* vol. 3. The reference is to Bernard's *Epistles* 190.8.20 (PL 182:1069).

26. Pelikan, 3:133.

27. Around this question there has emerged a vast literature. See, for example, Alan Race, *Christians and Religious Pluralism: Patterns in the Christian Theology of Religions* (London: SCM Press, 1983). See also Harold Coward, *Pluralism: Challenge to World Religions* (Maryknoll, N.Y.: Orbis Books, 1985); Aloysius Pieris, "Speaking of the Son of God," in *Jesus, Son of God, Concilium* 153/3 (1982), 65-70; and Mariasusai Dhavamony, "Theology of Religions," in Sebastian Karotemprel, ed., *Following Christ in Mission* (Bombay: Pauline Publications, 1995), 245-255. A good summary of the three approaches is presented by J. van Lin, "Models for a Theology of Religions," in F. J. Verstraelen, A. Camps, L. A. Hoedemaker and M. R. Spindler, eds., *Missiology: An Ecumenical Introduction* (Grand Rapids, Mich.: Eerdmans, 1995), 177-193. Perhaps the most magisterial discussion of the entire issue of grace and salvation outside Christianity is presented by Jacques Dupuis, *Toward a Christian Theology of Religious Pluralism* (Maryknoll, N.Y.: Orbis Books, 1997), 180-201. For a solid Evangelical perspective, see Harold Netland, *Dissonant Voices: Religious Pluralism and the Question of Truth* (Grand Rapids, Mich.: Eerdmans, 1991); and idem, *Encountering Religious Pluralism: The Challenge to Christian Faith and Mission* (Downers Grove, Ill.: InterVarsity Press; Leicester, UK: Apollos, 2001). In his brilliant *The Depths of the Riches*, S. Mark Heim argues that the threefold distinctions are inadequate and even contradictory. J. Andrew Kirk finds the terminology inadequate and proposes instead positions of "particularity," "generality" and "universality" (see *What Is Mission?: Theological Explorations* [Minneapolis, Minn.: Fortress Press, 1999], 127-130).

28. See, for example, Dupuis, 53-157.

29. "The Lausanne Covenant," 3, in James A. Scherer and Stephen B. Bevans, eds., *New Directions in Mission and Evangelization 1: Basic Statements 1974-1991* (Maryknoll, N.Y.: Orbis Books, 1992), 254.

30. *Manila Manifesto,* affirmation 7, in Scherer and Bevans, 293.

31. Van Lin, 180-181. See the *Manila Manifesto*, paragraph 3, in Scherer and Bevans, 297.

32. Avery Dulles, *Models of the Church* (Garden City, N.Y.: Image Books, 1974). In 1987 Dulles published an expanded edition of this work (Garden City, N.Y.: Image Books) which included a sixth model, "Community of Disciples." This, however, was "not a model among others, but a synthesis of points important in the other models" (Dennis M. Doyle, *Communion Ecclesiology* [Maryknoll, N.Y.: Orbis Books, 2000], 18). Here, therefore, we will confine ourselves to Dulles's classic five models.

33. Sölle, 148.

34. David J. Bosch, *Transforming Mission: Paradigm Shifts in Theology of Mission* (Maryknoll, N.Y.: Orbis Books, 1991), 369.

35. "Instr. S. C. De Propag. Fide 1659 [ad Vicarios App. Societatis Mission. Ad Exteros]," *Collectanea S. Congregationis de Propaganda Fide seu Decreta Instructiones Rescripta pro Apostolicis Missionisbus*, vol. 1, *1622-1866* (Rome: Ex Typographia Polyglotta S. C. De Propaganda Fide, 1907), N. 135, 42.

36. See David M. Stowe, "Anderson, Rufus," in Gerald H. Anderson, ed., *Biographical Dictionary of Christian Missions* (New York: Macmillan Reference, USA, 1997), 20; Wilbert R. Shenk, "Venn, Henry," in Anderson, 698.

37. See McGrath, 470; see also Bosch, 504-510.

38. González, 36, referring to Tertullian, *Apology*, 48, and *Against Marcion*, 3.24.

39. Type A eschatology might lend itself to what David Bosch calls the "extreme eschatologization of mission" (see Bosch, 504-506). On the nature of "apocalyptic," see Christopher Rowland, "Apocalyptic and Mission," in Karl Müller et al., eds., *Dictionary of Mission: Theology, History, Perspectives* (Maryknoll, N.Y.: Orbis Books, 1997), 30-33; Robert G. Clause, "Millennial Thought," in A. Scott Moreau, ed., *Evangelical Dictionary of World Missions* (Grand Rapids, Mich.: Baker Books, 2000), 627-628.

40. Bosch, 504; see his longer development of Protestant (Lutheran) orthodoxy on 248-252.

41. Ibid., 504. Bosch's longer development of Pietism is found on 252-255.

42. See McGrath, 472-473.

43. *Catechism of the Catholic Church*, 1030-1032.

44. On the influence of Dante, see McGrath, 468, and Jacques LeGoff, *The Birth of Purgatory* (Chicago: The University of Chicago Press, 1984), 334-355.

45. Without a doubt, one of the most famous of these is William Carey's 1792 tract *An Enquiry into the Obligations of Christians to Use Means for the Conversion of the Heathens*. Catholics will remember sermons (as we do) that spoke about the millions of heathen that would perish if the gospel were not preached to them before their death, and articles in such periodicals as Maryknoll's *The Field Afar*.

46. The reference is to the great, terrifying poem used until the reform of the Roman Catholic liturgy in the 1960s, as the "sequence" of the Requiem Mass or Mass for the Dead. The sequence no doubt was the product of the medieval eschatological imagination, and doubtless as well was the source of that imagination for generations of Christians as well. Even the melody is evocative and used often in music to signal the presence of death, for example, in Berlioz's *Symphonie Fantastique* or Liszt's "Dance of Death."

47. To give just one example of this, see Dana L. Robert, "American Women and the Dutch Reformed Missionary Movement," in Willem Saayman and Klippies Kritzinger, eds., *Mission in Bold Humility: David Bosch's Work Considered* (Maryknoll, N.Y.: Orbis Books, 1996), 98. Robert writes about Mary Lyon, foundress of Mt. Holyoke Seminary in Mt. Holyoke, Massachusetts: "The passion of her life was foreign missions. . . . She was steeped in the theology of the New Divinity, the modified Calvinism expounded by the followers of Jonathan Edwards. It was Edwards's followers who launched America's foreign mission movement. . . . [Lyons] taught a weekly class based on Edwards's *History of the Work of Redemption*. The theology of the New Divinity was evangelical, believing that without a commitment to Jesus Christ, persons would suffer eternal damnation."

48. See Dietrich Wiederkehr, "Eschatology," in Müller et al., 126-131.

49. J. D. Gort, "Human Distress, Salvation and Mediation of Salvation," in Verstraelen, Camps, Hoedemaker and Spindler, 195.

50. Bosch, 393.

51. See Thomas F. O'Meara, *Thomas Aquinas, Theologian* (Notre Dame, Ind.: University of Notre Dame Press, 1997), 150. See also 3 Sent. D. 13, q. 1, a. 1, ad 5: "The light of glory [in heaven] is the same as grace in its consummate stage; [it is] the same grace energizing us in the acts of our life" (quoted in O'Meara, 150).

52. Bosch, 394.

53. Ibid. On "pre-evangelization," see Alfonso M. Nebreda, *Kerygma in Crisis* (Chicago: Loyola University Press, 1965).

54. Sölle, 102-103.

55. John R. W. Stott, *Christian Mission in the Modern World* (London: Falcon, 1975), 100. The quotation from the Lausanne Covenant is from paragraph 5 (see Scherer and Bevans, 255).

56. McGrath, 374.

57. This is a simplification of one of the most complex issues in the history of theology: the interrelationship of grace and freedom. This issue has its origins in Augustine's controversies with the Pelagians and is a prominent theme in Luther, Calvin, the Jansenist controversy and the controversy *De Auxiliis* between the "Thomists" and "Molinists." See, for example, John W. Oman, *Grace and Personality*, 3d ed., rev. (Cambridge, UK: Cambridge University Press, 1925), 3-90; Pelikan, 1:294-331; Karl Rahner, *Sacramentum Mundi* 2 (London: Burns and Oates, 1968), 418-420; Bernard J. F. Lonergan, *Grace and Freedom: Operative Grace in the Thought of St. Thomas Aquinas* (London: Darton, Longman and Todd; New York: Herder and Herder, 1971).

58. González, 22.

59. Ibid., 87. As we will see in the next section, Neoplatonism is the guiding philosophy behind Type B theology. González observes that, although Augustine generally typifies Type A, he is influenced at several points by Type B thinking. The notion of the spiritual nature of

the soul, and thus of a radical dualism in humanity, met with stiff resistance but eventually won out and became an integral part of this more legalistic view of God's salvific work.

60. Garry Wills, however, offers a somewhat revisionary reading of Augustine's attitude toward sexuality. Referring to Peter Brown's 1967 biography of Augustine (*Augustine of Hippo* [Berkeley and Los Angeles: University of California Press, 1967]), Wills says that "he did not harp on sexual sin in preaching to his congregation. Greed, violence, and deception were greater concerns in the sermons. In his pastoral life, he was hardly a scourge of sexual sin. . . . His own experience did not make him intolerant but compassionate" (Garry Wills, *Saint Augustine* [New York: Penguin Books, 1999], 135).

61. Roots of this attitude go back to Aristotle (see *Politics* 1:5 and *The Republic* 1:13). For specific examples of how this attitude affected evangelization in Latin America, Africa and Asia (Philippines), see Gustavo Gutiérrez, *Las Casas: In Search of the Poor of Jesus Christ* (Maryknoll, N.Y.: Orbis Books, 1993), 218-220; José Ignacio González Faus, "Anthropology: The Person and the Community," in Ignacio Ellacuría and Jon Sobrino, eds., *Mysterium Liberationis: Fundamental Concepts of Liberation Theology* (Maryknoll, N.Y.: Orbis Books, 1993), 511-512; David L. Edwards, *Christianity: The First Two Thousand Years* (Maryknoll, N.Y.: Orbis Books, 1997), 530; José M. de Mesa, "Doing Theology as Inculturation in the Asian Context," in James A. Scherer and Stephen B. Bevans, eds., *New Directions in Mission and Evangelization 3: Faith and Culture* (Maryknoll, N.Y.: Orbis Books, 1999), 124-125.

62. Quoted in Yves Congar, *Lay People in the Church* (Westminster, Md.: Newman Press, 1957), 7, 9. The first part of the quotation (up until the ellipsis) appears in Latin and is our own translation. Congar notes: "From our angle of interest here two things are particularly noticeable in this passage: the lay position is presented as a concession, and its general tendency is to deny that the laity, concerned in temporal things, have any active part in the sphere of sacred things" (9).

63. See Vitor Westhelle, "Conquest and Evangelization in Latin America: Three Missionary Models and a Common Presuppostion," in Stephen Bevans, SVD, and Roger Schroeder, SVD, eds., *Word Remembered, Word Proclaimed: Selected Papers from Symposia Celebrating the SVD Centennial in North America* (Nettetal: Steylerverlag, 1997), 89-107.

64. Robert J. Schreiter, *The New Catholicity: Theology between the Global and the Local* (Maryknoll, N.Y.: Orbis Books, 1997), 29. Schrieter refers to Jens Loenhoff, *Interkulturelle Verständigung. Zum Problem grenzüberschreitender Kommunikation* (Oplade: Leske und Budrich, 1992), 144.

65. Bernard Lonergan, *Method in Theology* (London: Dartman, Longman and Todd, 1972), xi.

66. Benjamin R. Barber, *Jihad vs. McWorld* (New York: Times Books, 1995).

67. Bevans, *Models of Contextual Theology*.

68. *Praescription of Heretics*, 7. See González, 6. Richard R. Niebuhr cites Tertullian as the classic representative of "Christ against Culture" (see *Christ and Culture* [New York: Harper Torchbooks, 1975; originally published in 1951], 51-55).

69. See Darrell Whiteman, "Contextualization: The Theory, the Gap, the Challenge," *International Bulletin of Missionary Research* 21/1 (January 1997): 2. We owe the reference to "Christian Shen as American Shen" to Rev. Sai Aung Win, general secretary of the Swlishan Baptist Mission in Myanmar, in a conversation at Overseas Ministries Study Center in fall 1997.

70. See Allan R. Tippett, "Christopaganism or Indigenous Christianity?" in Charles H. Kraft and Tom N. Wisley, *Readings in Dynamic Indigeneity* (Pasadena, Calif.: William Carey Library, 1979), 400-421. Today this suspicion is increasingly rare, as even more conservative Evangelical theologians move out of the more rigid forms of Type A thinking. The trajectory of Type A theology, however, seems to point to a more suspicious or, as we point out below, negative understanding of culture in its encounter with Christian faith.

71. See, for example, Stanley Hauerwas and William Willimon, *Resident Aliens: Life in the Christian Colony* (Nashville, Tenn.: Abingdon Press, 1989).

72. AD 2000 and Beyond closed its international office in early 2001. Its vision and work, however, are continued by projects like Joshua Project II. For more information, see the AD 2000 and Joshua Project II websites.

73. Daniel Boorstin, *The Creators: A History of Heroes of the Imagination* (New York: Vintage Books, 1993), 47.

74. Ibid., 48.

75. González, 7-8.

76. Ibid., 8.

77. Ibid., 9. The reference is to Clement's *Stromata*, 1.5. We are using the term *Platonic philosophy* in a rather loose manner here. Clement and Origen are probably most influenced by what is called Middle Platonism, which is a mixture of Plato's thought with some elements of Stoicism. Origen might also reflect some of the elements of the more mystical Neoplatonism. Plotinus, the founder of Neoplatonism, was Origen's contemporary in Alexandria.

78. Walls, "Old Athens and New Jerusalem," 149.

79. González, 25.

80. David Tracy, *The Analogical Imagination: Christian Theology and the Culture of Pluralism* (New York: Crossroad, 1981), 380.

81. David Tracy, "The Uneasy Alliance Reconceived: Catholic Theological Method, Modernity and Postmodernity," *Theological Studies* 50/3 (1989): 548-570.

82. González, 78; Sölle points out how this is true particularly in liberal theology, which insists that the "truth of scripture cannot be opposed to reason" (47).

83. The phrase is the title of one of José de Mesa's books, *In Solidarity with the Culture* (Quezon City, Philippines: Maryhill School of Theology, 1991).

84. See González, 107-113.

85. Ibid., 84. González claims that the reason Type A theology in the West did not get caught up in such minutiae was because of a different political climate. With the shift of the center of the empire to the East, the West was freer to disregard imperial claims. In the East, however, approval of the emperor was more and more frequently sought for orthodoxy, and the development of theological positions became ways that political parties claimed imperial power. In the fifth century in particular, after the West had been weakened by invasions of Germanic peoples, the East followed its own course without much objection from the West, and more and more theological subtleties were developed.

86. In his great pioneering work of systematic theology, *On First Principles*, Origen gives reflections on the incarnation using the example of a colossal statue. The divine essence, he says, so far exceeds our grasp that it is as though we humans are ants trying to see the entirety of an immense statue. While we may be awed by the statue's size, because we cannot really see it we are not really affected by it. If, however, we would be presented with a version of the statue that would meet our own limitations of sight, we perhaps would be affected by the statue's beauty and perfection. Such a scaling down of the immense statue, says Origen, is what God has done in the incarnation. When we see Jesus, we indeed see God in all God's majesty and ineffability, but in a way that our mortal intellects can grasp, understand and respond to. Through the humanity of Jesus, therefore, we are able to find illumination and thus contemplate once more the One from whom we have been separated through the Fall (see González, 37-38).

87. Robert Ellsberg, "St. Mechtild of Hackeborn," in *All Saints* (New York: Crossroad, 1997), 505. Ellsberg gives as a reference Carol Walker Bynum, *Jesus as Mother: Studies in the Spirituality of the High Middle Ages* (Berkeley and Los Angeles: University of California Press, 1982).

88. Walter Kasper, *Jesus the Christ* (London: Burns and Oates; New York: Paulist Press, 1976), 31, quoting *The Christian Faith* (Kasper quotes from the German version, 2:43; the English translation is found in H. R. Macintosh and J. S. Stewart, eds., *The Christian Faith* [Philadelphia: Fortress Press, 1928], 385, §94. This version reads, "The constant potency of His God-consciousness, which was a veritable existence of God in Him").

89. Albert Schweitzer, *The Quest for the Historical Jesus: A Critical Study of Its Progress from Reimarus to Wrede* (Baltimore, Md.: Johns Hopkins University Press in association with the Albert Schweitzer Institute, 1998; first English edition, 1910; first German edition, 1906).

90. Peter Abelard, *Christian Theology*, 4.62. *Corpus Christianorum. Continuatio medievalis.* 12:292. Quoted in Pelikan, 3:128.

91. Peter Abelard, *Problems of Heloise*, 6. PL 178:686. Quoted in Pelikan, 3:128.

92. González, 105.

93. Douglas John Hall, *Professing the Faith* (Minneapolis, Minn.: Fortress Press, 1993), 428-429; see also Sölle, 123; Brian A. Gerrish, "The Protest of Grace: John McLeod Campbell on the Atonement," *Tradition in the Modern World* (Chicago: University of Chicago Press, 1978), 71-98; Stephen Bevans, *John Oman and His Doctrine of God* (Cambridge, UK: Cambridge University Press, 1992), 108-111.

94. Clement of Alexandria, *Stromata*, V, 13. Quoted in Dupuis, 66.

95. Clement of Alexandria, *Stromata*, I, 15. Quoted in Dupuis, 68.

96. Dupuis, 102-109, 120-129.

97. Karl Rahner, "Anonymous Christians," in *Theological Investigations* 6 (Baltimore, Md.: Helicon, 1969), 390-398; "Anonymous Christianity and the Missionary Task of the Church," in *Theological Investigations* 11 (New York: Seabury, 1974), 161-178; "Observations on the Problem of the 'Anonymous Christians,'" in *Theological Investigations* 14 (New York: Seabury, 1976), 280-294; "On the Importance of Non-Christian Religions for Salvation," in *Theological Investigations* 18 (New York: Crossroad, 1983), 288-295.

98. For example, John Paul II quotes this sentence in DEV 53 and in RM 6, 10 and 28.

99. World Conference on Mission and Evangelism, "Mission in Christ's Way," 26, in Scherer and Bevans, 1:78.

100. Paul F. Knitter, *No Other Name? A Critical Survey of Christian Attitudes to World Religions* (Maryknoll, N.Y.: Orbis Books, 1985); "Catholic Theology of Religions at the Crossroads," *Concilium* 183/1, 99-107; *One Earth, Many Religions* (Maryknoll, N.Y.: Orbis Books, 1995).

101. Dupuis, 385-390; Bosch, 474-489; William R. Burrows, "The Absoluteness of Christianity," in Müller et al., 1-6; Heim.

102. Clement of Alexandria, *Stromata*, I, 5, 3, quoted in Dupuis, 67; ibid., VI, 8, quoted in Dupuis, 67.

103. Dupuis, 67-68.

104. Origen, *Commentary on the Gospel of John*, 1.34.246, 1.37.269. Quoted in Dhavamony, 251.

105. Walls, "Introduction," *The Missionary Movement in Christian History*, xvii.

106. Frederick E. Crowe, "Son of God, Holy Spirit, and World Religions: The Contribution of Bernard Lonergan to the Wider Ecumenism," Chancellor's Address II, Toronto, Regis College, 1985, 21.

107. Bosch, 489.

108. Quoted in Gustavo Gutiérrez, *A Theology of Liberation* (Maryknoll, N.Y.: Orbis Books, 1973), 261.

109. Alexander Schmemann, *Church, World, Mission* (Crestwood, N.Y.: St. Vladimir's Seminary Press, 1979), 213.

110. Cyprian, *On the Lord's Prayer*, PL 4:553, quoted in LG 4.

111. Henri de Lubac, *Corpus Mysticum: l'eucharistie et l'Église au Moyen Age*, 2d ed. (Paris: Aubier, 1949).

112. Paul VI, "Opening Address of the Second Session of Vatican II," in *Enchiridion Vaticanum* (Bologna: Editioni Dehoniane, 1968), 97.

113. Origen, *On First Principles*, 2 and 3; see González, 39.

114. Adolf Harnack, *What Is Christianity?* (New York: Harper Torchbooks, 1957), 51, quoted in González, 115-116.

115. Rudolf Bultmann, "New Testament and Mythology," in H. W. Bartsch, ed., *Kerygma and Myth: A Theological Debate* (New York: Harper Torchbooks, 1961), 1-44.

116. Paul Tillich, *Systematic Theology*, vol. 3 (3 vols. in 1 ed.) (Chicago: University of Chicago Press, 1967); vol. 2 (ibid.), 118-138.

117. Roman Missal, Embolism after the Lord's Prayer in the order of the celebration of the Eucharist.

118. Bosch, 395.

119. Ibid., 396.

120. Bosch mentions in this connection the thought of Johannes Hoekendijk in the 1960s, as well as the thought of Emmanuel Mesthene and Richard Schaull at the Geneva Conference on Church and Society in 1966 (ibid.). Pope Paul VI addressed some of these issues as well in his 1975 apostolic exhortation *Evangelii Nuntiandi*.

121. R. B. Tollinton, *Alexandrine Teaching on the Universe* (New York: Macmillan, 1932), 159, quoted in González, 67.

122. González, 93; see Pelikan's discussion about how faith is the fulfillment of reason in Jarislav Pelikan, *Christianity and Classical Culture: The Metamorphosis of Natural Theology in the Christian Encounter with Hellenism* (New Haven, Conn.: Yale University Press, 1993), 214-230.

123. González, 77-78.

124. Walls, "Old Athens and New Jerusalem," 149, referring to Origen's letter to Gregory Thaumaturgus (=*Philokalia* xiii), 2.

125. Claude Marie Barbour, Kathleen Billman, Peggy DesJarlait and Eleanor Doidge, "Mission on the Boundaries: Cooperation without Exploitation," in Susan B. Thistlethwaite and George F. Cairns, eds., *Beyond Theological Tourism: Mentoring as a Grassroots Approach to Theological Education* (Maryknoll, N.Y.: Orbis Books, 1995), 72-91. See also Stephen Bevans, Eleanor Doidge and Robert Schreiter, eds., *The Healing Circle: Essays in Cross Cultural Mission. Presented to the Rev. Dr. Claude Marie Barbour* (Chicago: CCGM Publications, 1999).

126. Niebuhr, 83-115.

127. See Schreiter, 62-83, for a perceptive discussion on syncretism.

128. González, 11, 120-121.

129. Ibid., 11-13.

130. Ibid., 11-12, 15.

131. Ibid., 15.

132. See, e.g., ibid., 72-73, 75.

133. See ibid., 107-145.

134. Irenaeus, *Against Heresies*, 4, *prol*; see González, 151 n. 28.

135. González, 28.

136. Irenaeus, *Against Heresies*, 3.16.6, quoted in González, 42.

137. Leonardo Boff, *Jesus Christ Liberator: A Critical Christology for Our Time* (Maryknoll, N.Y.: Orbis Books, 1978); Jon Sobrino, *Christology at the Crossroads: A Latin American Approach* (Maryknoll, N.Y.: Orbis Books, 1978).

138. Sölle, 114.

139. González, 40.

140. Irenaeus, *Against Heresies*, 3.18.6, quoted in González, 40.

141. González, 41.

142. Gustav Aulén, *Christus Victor* (New York: Macmillan, 1969).

143. Sölle, 124. The quotation is from Louise Schrottroff, Barbara von Wartenberg-Potter and Dorothee Sölle, *Das Kreutz—Baum des Lebens* (Stuttgart, 1987), 10-11.

144. Sölle, 132.

145. Hendrik Kraemer, *The Christian Message in a Non-Christian World* (London: Edinburgh House Press, 1947 [1938]); see Timothy Yates, *Christian Mission in the Twentieth Century* (Cambridge: Cambridge University Press, 1994).

146. Aloysius Pieris, *An Asian Theology of Liberation* (Maryknoll, N.Y.: Orbis Books, 1988), 45-50.

147. Jacob Kavunkal, "Eschatology and Mission in Creative Tension: An Indian Perspective," in Saayman and Kritzinger, 77.

148. González, 42, referring to Irenaeus, *Against Heresies*, 3.19.3.

149. Irenaeus, *Against Heresies*, 3.24.1, quoted in Pelikan, *The Christian Tradition*, 1:156.

150. Irenaeus, *Against Heresies*, 3.3.1, quoted in Pelikan, *The Christian Tradition*, 1:118.

151. See Lode Wostyn, *Doing Ecclesiology: The Church and Mission Today* (Quezon City, Philippines: Claretian Publications, 1990), 43-60; Stephen Bevans, "A Spirituality of American Priesthood, Part I: Resources for Leadership in a Missionary Church," *Emmanuel* 108/4 (May 2002): 195-196.

152. Gutiérrez, *A Theology of Liberation*.

153. Leonardo Boff, *Ecclesiogenesis: The Base Communities Reinvent the Church* (Maryknoll, N.Y.: Orbis Books, 1986); see also the quotation from Boff in Sölle, 151.

154. González, 29, 44.

155. Ibid., 44-45.

156. Pierre Teilhard de Chardin, *The Phenomenon of Man* (New York: Harper & Row, 1965); idem, *The Divine Milieu* (New York: Harper & Row, 1965); Ursula King, *Spirit of Fire: The Life and Vision of Teilhard de Chardin* (Maryknoll, N.Y.: Orbis Books, 1996); Christopher Mooney, *Teilhard de Chardin and the Mystery of Christ* (New York: Harper & Row, 1966).

157. González, 133.

158. See Rosemary Radford Ruether, "Ecojustice at the Center of the Church's Mission," *Mission Studies* 16/1/31 (1999): 111-121.

159. Sölle, 138-140; McGrath, 470.

160. Bosch, 509.

161. González, 39-46.

162. Bosch, 399.

163. Ibid., 397.

164. Ibid., 400.

165. Gort, 209.

166. Irenaeus, *Against Heresies*, 2.18.3, quoted in González, 157 n. 52.

167. Gutiérrez, *A Theology of Liberation,* 265-272.

168. Sölle, 49-52.

169. Sölle speaks of liberation theology in terms of "Christ against culture" and "Christ and culture in paradox" (Sölle, 21, chart).

Part II
3. Mission in the Early Church (100-301)

1. For excellent background on this period, see Dale T. Irvin and Scott W. Sunquist, *History of the World Christian Movement*, vol. 1, *Earliest Christianity to 1453* (Maryknoll, N.Y.: Orbis Books, 2001), 1-153. Regarding the new emphasis on the second and third centuries, see Justo L. González, *The Changing Shape of Church History* (St. Louis, Mo.: Chalice Press, 2002), 35-40.

2. Karl Rahner, "Toward a Fundamental Theological Interpretation of Vatican II," *Theological Studies* 40 (1979), 716-727.

3. For a concise discussion of parallel shifts in ecclesiology within other Christian denominations, see David J. Bosch, *Transforming Mission: Paradigm Shifts in Theology of Mission* (Maryknoll, N.Y.: Orbis Books, 1991), 368-373.

4. One of several works to begin remedying this situation is James Stamoolis, *Eastern Orthodox Mission Theology Today* (Maryknoll, N.Y.: Orbis Books, 1986).

5. Samuel Hugh Moffett, "Early Asian Christian Approaches to Non-Christian Cultures," *Missiology: An International Review* 15/4 (1987): 473-486; idem, *A History of Christianity in Asia*, vol. 1, *Beginnings to 1500* (San Francisco: Harper Collins, 1992). More recent books that

have also contributed in this area are John C. England, *The Hidden History of Christianity in Asia: The Churches of the East before 1500* (Delhi: ISPCK; Hong Kong: CCA, 1996); and Ian Gillman and Has-Joachim Klimkeit, *Christians in Asia before 1500* (Ann Arbor, Mich.: University of Michigan Press, 1999).

6. Bosch, 202-205. Bosch only had the benefit of Moffett's 1987 article, since Moffett's book appeared after *Transforming Mission* was published.

7. The first volume, *Earliest Christianity to 1453,* was published by Orbis Books in 2001; volume 2 is forthcoming.

8. Philip Jenkins, *The Next Christendom: The Coming of Global Christianity* (New York: Oxford University Press, 2002), 15.

9. See Moffett, *Christianity in Asia*, 46-51.

10. See ibid., 57-58.

11. Ibid., 94.

12. See ibid., 77-80.

13. For fuller treatment of this topic, see ibid., 24-44. For a brief summary with a slightly different interpretation, see Irvin and Sunquist, 93-95.

14. Moffett, *Christianity in Asia*, 79.

15. See Julian Saldanha, *Patterns of Evangelization in Mission History* (Bandra-Bombay: St. Paul Publications, 1988), 18.

16. See Moffett, "Early Asian Christian Approaches," 478-485.

17. See Moffett, *Christianity in Asia*, 100-101.

18. Wayne Meeks, *The First Urban Christians: The Social World of the Apostle Paul* (New Haven, Conn.: Yale University Press, 1983), 11; see also Ramsay MacMullen, *Roman Social Relations* (New Haven, Conn.: Yale University Press, 1983), 28-56.

19. James C. Russell, *The Germanization of Early Medieval Christianity: A Sociohistorical Approach to Religious Transformation* (New York: Oxford University Press, 1994), 100.

20. Stephen Neill, *A History of Christian Missions*, rev. ed. (New York: Penguin Books, 1986; originally published in 1964), 25.

21. See David Max Eichhorn, *Conversion to Judaism: A History and Analysis* (New York: Ktav Publishing House, 1965), 33-66; Joseph Rosenbloom, *Conversion to Judaism: From the Biblical Period to the Present* (Cincinnati, Ohio: Hebrew Union College Press, 1978), 35-64.

22. See Neill, 25. Without denying this, recent study has contributed another factor that quite possibly the number of Hellenized Jews from the Diaspora who also become Christians is much larger than previously assumed (see Rodney Stark, *The Rise of Christianity* [San Francisco: Harper Collins Publishers, 1996], 69-70).

23. See Per Beskow, "Crossing the Frontiers in the Second Century," in Peter Beyerhaus and Carl Hallencreutz, eds., *The Church Crossing Frontiers: Essays on the Nature of Mission* (Uppsala: Gleerup, 1969), 32.

24. See Stark, 49-71. After reviewing the positions of Stark and his critics on this point, Michael Slusser supports Stark's conclusions in "Did the Early Christian Mission to the Jews Really Succeed?" presented at the 2001 conference of the Catholic Theological Society of America. Slusser's paper is a version of a lecture given at the University of Bonn in November 2000 under the auspices of Sonderforschungsbereich 534: Judentum-Christentum: Konstituierung und Differenzierung in Antike und Gegenwart.

25. For a further description of this religious context of the Roman Empire, see Hubert Jedin and John Dolan, eds., *History of the Church,* vol. 1, *From the Apostolic Community to Constantine* (New York: Seabury Press, 1980), 86-98.

26. Stark, 74; for further development, see 73-94.

27. Bosch, 192.

28. Ignatius of Antioch, *To the Smyrnaeans* 8, in Francis Glimm, Joseph Marique and Gerald Walsh, trans., *The Fathers of the Church, the Apostolic Fathers* (New York: Christian Heritage, 1947).

29. Jedin and Dolan, 275. For a further description of this early development of the catechumenate, see Michel Dujarier, *A History of the Catechumenate* (New York: Sadlier, 1979), 30-76.

30. Neill, 39.

31. Stark, 6; for further development, see 3-27.

32. Eusebius, *Church History*, III, 37, in Philip Schaff and Henry Wace, eds., *Nicene and Post-Nicene Fathers*, vol. 1, second series (Peabody, Mass.: Hendrickson Publishers, 1994).

33. *Didache*, XI, 1-6, in Glimm, Marique and Walsh, *The Fathers of the Church, the Apostolic Fathers*.

34. Michael Green, *Evangelism in the Early Church* (Grand Rapids, Mich.: Eerdmans, 1970), 170.

35. See Irvin and Sunquist, 118-128.

36. Justo González, *Christian Thought Revisited: Three Types of Theology*, rev. ed. (Maryknoll, N.Y.: Orbis Books, 1999), 13.

37. Justin Martyr, *First Apology,* 46, in Walter Burghardt, John Dillon and Dennis McManus, eds., *Ancient Christian Writers*, vol. 56 (Mahwah, N.J.: Paulist Press, 1997).

38. Tertullian, *On Prescription against Heretics*, 7, in Alexander Roberts and James Donaldson, eds., *Ante-Nicene Fathers*, vol. 3 (Peabody, Mass.: Hendrickson Publishers, 1994).

39. Moffett, *Christianity in Asia*, 36.

40. Clement of Alexandria, *Stromateis,* I, 28 (3), in *The Fathers of the Church*, vol. 85, *Clement of Alexandria, Stromateis, Books 1-3*, trans. John Ferguson (Washington, D.C.: The Catholic University of America Press, 1991). Other authors (e.g., Pelikan) call this work *Stromata.*

41. Green, 172.

42. Ramsay MacMullen, "Two Types of Conversion to Early Christianity," in *Conversion, Catechumenate, and Baptism in the Early Church*, vol. 11 of *Studies in Early Christianity*, ed. Everett Ferguson (New York and London: Garland Publishing, 1993), 36. Originally published in *Vigiliae Christianae* 37 (1983): 174-192.

43. See Adolf von Harnack, *The Mission and Expansion of Christianity in the First Three Centuries*, trans. and ed. James Moffatt, vol. 1 of 1908 edition (New York: Harper & Brothers, 1962), 210, 366-367; Irvin and Sunquist, 69-73, 82-85, 109-111, 137-140.

44. Eusebius, *Church History*, IV, 15.

45. Ibid., V, 1 (41).

46. See Elizabeth Clark, *Women in the Early Church*, vol. 13 of *Message of the Fathers of the Church* (Wilmington, Del.: Michael Glazier, 1983), 97-98.

47. Tertullian, *Apology,* 50 (12), in Rudolph Arbesmann, Emily Daly and Edwin Quain, trans., *The Fathers of the Church, Tertullian: Apologetical Works and Minucius Felix: Octavius* (New York: Fathers of the Church, 1950).

48. For a very interesting sociology of religion perspective, see Stark, 163-189.

49. Origen, *Against Celsus*, III, 55, in Alexander Roberts and James Donaldson, eds., *Ante-Nicene Fathers*, vol. 4 (Peabody, Mass.: Hendrickson Publishers, 1994).

50. Green, 173.

51. See Stark, 20-21.

52. See ibid., 30-31; for a sociological analysis, see 32-47.

53. Ibid., 208.

54. See Green, 207-223.

55. Meeks, 29; for further elaboration, see 29-30, 75-77.

56. Stark, 160-161.

57. See ibid., 16-19.

58. For a description of this dynamic from a strong opponent to Christianity, see Origen, *Against Celsus*, III, 9 and 55.

59. See Beskow, 30.

60. Ibid., 31.

61. See Bosch, 191-192.

62. See Harnack, 147-198, 367-368.

63. Bosch, 192. See Green, 178-193.

64. See Stark, 83-88.

65. *Letter to Diognetus* 5, in Glimm, Marique and Walsh, *The Fathers of the Church, the Apostolic Fathers.*

66. Stark, 161.

67. See Walter Liefeld, "Women and Evangelism in the Early Church," *Missiology: An International Review* 15/3 (July 1987): 293-295.

68. Stark, 100.

69. Ibid., 105.

70. Rosemary Ruether and Eleanor McLaughlin, *Women of Spirit: Female Leadership in the Jewish and Christian Traditions* (New York: Simon and Shuster, 1979), 32.

71. See Stark, 97-99.

72. Tertullian, *To His Wife,* II, 4, in *Ancient Christian Writers* 13 (Westminster, Md.: The Newman Press, 1951).

73. Ibid., II, 7. See also 1 Pet 3:1-2; *Apostolic Constitutions,* I, 10, in Alexander Roberts and James Donaldson, eds., *Ante-Nicene Fathers,* vol. 7 (Peabody, Mass.: Hendrickson Publishers, 1994).

74. See Stark, 111-115.

75. See Green, 207-223.

76. Barbara Reid, "Women in the New Testament," in *Dictionary of Mission: Theology, History, Perspectives,* eds. Karl Müller, Theo Sundermeirer, Stephen Bevans, and Richard Bliese (Maryknoll, N.Y.: Orbis Books, 1997), 482.

77. Origen, *Against Celsus,* III, 55.

78. We think of such women as Lydia, the textile saleswoman from Thyatira (Acts 16:14).

79. Tabitha in Acts 9:36-39.

80. For example, see Ben Witherington III, *Women in the Earliest Churches,* Society for New Testament Studies Monograph Series 59 (Cambridge: Cambridge University Press, 1988), 5-182; Reid, 480-490.

81. See Reid, 480-481.

82. Ibid., 481.

83. Witherington, 115 and n. 187.

84. Acts 21:9. See ibid., 151-152.

85. Maximilla was a preacher and prophetess within the Montanist movement and actually became the de facto leader of the movement with the death of Montanus.

86. Witherington, 194; see also Ruether and McLaughlin, 37ff.

87. Ibid., 195.

88. Tertullian, *On Baptism,* 17, in Roberts and Donaldson, *Ante-Nicene Fathers,* vol. 3.

89. See Ruether and McLaughlin, 38.

90. See ibid., 74.

91. Elizabeth Schüssler Fiorenza, *In Memory of Her: A Feminist Theological Reconstruction of Christian Origins* (New York: Crossroad, 1983), 183.

92. See Ruether and McLaughlin, 56.

93. Roger Gryson, *The Ministry of Women in the Early Church,* trans. Jean Laporte and Mary Louise Hall (Collegeville, Minn.: The Liturgical Press, 1976), 41.

94. See Witherington, 5-23.

95. Reid, 488.

96. E. Glenn Hinson, *The Evangelization of the Roman Empire* (Macom, Ga.: Mercer University Press, 1981), 87.

97. Stark, 208.

98. Jenkins, 17.

99. Bosch, 197.

100. See ibid., 198-199.

101. Beskow, 34-35.

102. See Bosch, 199-201.

103. See Hinson, 73-95.

104. See Bosch, 190-213.

105. See ibid., 210-211; Charles Kannengieser, "Origen, Augustine and Paradigm Changes in Theology," in *Paradigm Change in Theology*, ed. Hans Küng and David Tracey, trans. Margaret Köhl (New York: Crossroad, 1989), 125-126.

106. *A Letter from Origen to Gregory* 1, in Roberts and Donaldson, *Ante-Nicene Fathers*, vol. 4.

107. See Bosch, 211.

108. Andrew Walls, "Old Athens and New Jerusalem: Some Signposts for Christian Scholarship in the Early History of Mission Studies," *International Bulletin of Missionary Research* 21/4 (October 1997): 148-149.

109. See Stamoolis; Bosch, 205-213.

110. Bosch, 208.

111. For example, see Tertullian, *Ad Martyras,* 3; and *De Corona,* both found in Roberts and Donaldson, *Ante-Nicene Fathers*, vol. 3.

112. For example, see Tertullian, *Ad Martyras,* 1.

113. *Tertullian, De exh. pers.*, 1, reference in Hinson, 20.

114. For a more detailed development of this theme, see Hinson, 21-29.

115. See C. Philip Slate, "Two Features of Irenaeus' Missiology," *Missiology: An International Review* 23/4 (October 1995): 432-435.

116. Ibid., 439. For further discussion of his understanding of salvation, see Terrance Tiessen, *Irenaeus of the Salvation of the Unevangelized*, ATLA Monograph Series 31 (Metuchen, N.J.: Scarecrow Press, 1993).

117. Irvin and Sunquist, 63.

118. Moffett, *Christianity in Asia*, 53.

119. Bosch, 472.

120. For example, see Kathleen Hughes and Mark Francis, eds., *Living No Longer for Ourselves: Liturgy and Justice in the Nineties* (Collegeville, Minn.: The Liturgical Press, 1991).

121. Alexander Schmemann, "The Missionary Imperative in the Orthodox Tradition," in Gerald Anderson, ed., *The Theology of Christian Mission* (London: SCM Press, 1961), 255-256.

122. Thomas H. Schattauer, ed., *Inside Out: Worship in an Age of Mission* (Minneapolis, Minn.: Fortress Press, 1999), 13.

123. Schüssler Fiorenza, 199.

4. Mission and the Monastic Movement (313-907)

1. For excellent background on this period, see Dale T. Irvin and Scott W. Sunquist, *History of the World Christian Movement*, vol. 1, *Earliest Christianity to 1453* (Maryknoll, N.Y.: Orbis Books, 2001), 155-381.

2. See ibid., 260-270.

3. Ibid., 196.

4. John Stewart, *Nestorian Missionary Enterprise: The Story of a Church on Fire* (Edinburgh: T & T Clark, 1928), 16.

5. For further description of the situation of Armenia during the period from 300 to 1000, see Irvin and Sunquist, 206-208, 281-282.

6. For further description of Christian life during this period of early Islam, see ibid., 273-278.

7. Samuel Hugh Moffett, *A History of Christianity in Asia,* vol. 1, *Beginnings to 1500* (San Francisco: Harper Collins, 1992), 100.

8. Ibid., 101.

9. Ibid.

10. For a detailed historical account of these events from a more Western perspective, see Hubert Jedin and John Dolan, eds., *History of the Church*, vol. 2, *The Imperial Church from Constantine to the Early Middle Ages* (New York: Seabury Press, 1980), 93-121, 463-474. For a more cross-cultural perspective, see Moffett, 168-215.

11. Described the unity of Christ as one person *(hypostasis)* and one nature *(physis)*, both God and man.

12. Defined the unity of Christ as one person *(prosopon)* in two natures *(physis)*, human and divine.

13. The Council of Chalcedon tried to resolve the theological controversy with a compromise formula for describing the unity of Christ as one person *(hypostasis)* in two natures *(physis)*, using the "Monophysite" word for "person" and the "Dyophysite" insistence on two natures.

14. See Moffett, 202.

15. Samuel Moffett, "Early Asian Christian Approaches to Non-Christian Cultures," *Missiology: An International Review* 15/4 (October 1987): 481.

16. It is possible that this was done a bit later by Yeshuyab III (650-660); see Moffett, *Christianity in Asia*, cf. 257 and 269.

17. Ibid., 257.

18. See ibid., 266; Irvin and Sunquist, 203.

19. Irvin and Sunquist, 204.

20. Ibid., 310.

21. Ibid.

22. Ibid.

23. For further description of Christianity in China at this time, see Nicolas Standaert, ed., *Handbook of Christianity in China*, vol. 1, *635-1800, Handbook of Oriental Studies,* vol. 15/1 (Leiden: Brill, 2001); Li Tang, *A Study of the History of Nestorian Christianity in China and Its Literature in Chinese* (Frankfurt am Main: Peter Lang, 2001); and Frederick W. Norris, *Christianity: A Short Global History* (Oxford: OneWorld, 2002), 45-46, 86-89.

24. See Moffett, *Christianity in Asia*, 293.

25. For further references regarding these documents, the monument, paintings, letters and other East Syrian materials from central Asia and China, see John C. England et al., eds., *Asian Christian Theologies: A Research Guide to Authors, Movements, Sources* (Maryknoll, N.Y.: Orbis Books; Delhi: ISPCK/Claretian Publishers, 2002), 1:10-26.

26. Irvin and Sunquist, 317.

27. A prominent example of such political connections was Issu, the son of a Persian priest-missionary and himself an East Syrian priest and general in the Chinese army, well known for both his charitable works and his military standing (see Moffett, *Christianity in Asia*, 300).

28. Ibid.

29. John Kaserow, "Christian Evaluations of Buddhism" (Ph.D. diss., University of St. Michael's College, 1976), 716.

30. See Moffett, *Christianity in Asia*, 302-314.

31. For source of information, see ibid., 313 and n. 106.

32. Ibid., 312. In the appendix, Moffet shows that the translation of the Chang'an monument reveals both how Chinese it is and how much it resembles the confession of Nicea.

33. Ibid., 351.

34. Ibid., 354.

35. See Irvin and Sunquist, 313-314.

36. John C. England, *The Hidden History of Christianity in Asia: The Churches of the East before 1500* (Delhi: ISPCK; Hong Kong: CCA, 1998), 102-107.

37. See Moffett, *Christianity in Asia*, 361.

38. Irvin and Sunquist, 321.

39. Stewart, 17.

40. Moffett, "Early Asian Christian Approaches," 481.

41. See ibid., 484.

42. T. V. Philip, "The Missionary Impulse in the Early Asian Christian Tradition," *PTCA Bulletin* 10/1 (1997): 12.

43. Wolfgang Hage, "Der Weg nach Asien: Die ostsyrische Missionskirche," in Knut Schäferkiek, ed., *Kirchengeschichte als Missionsgeschichte*, Bd II/1, *Die Kirche des früheren Mittelalters* (Munich: Chr. Kaiser Verlag, 1978), 360.

44. Moffett, *Christianity in Asia*, 75-77.

45. Athanasius, *Vita S. Antonii*, 3.

46. While the mission aspect was in general less pronounced than in other monastic movements, for a presentation on mission and Egyptian monasticism, see Anastasios Yannoulatos, "Monks and Mission in the Eastern Church during the Fourth Century," *International Review of Mission* 58/2 (April 1969): 212-218.

47. See Moffett, *Christianity in Asia*, 77-78.

48. See Irvin and Sunquist, 216-217.

49. Ibid., 297.

50. Andrew F. Walls, *The Cross-Cultural Process in Christian History* (Maryknoll, N.Y.: Orbis Books, 2002), 91.

51. For further discussion of the context and content of the "conversion" of Constantine, see Irvin and Sunquist, 160-165.

52. For an excellent study of this process, see Ramsay MacMullen, *Christianity and Paganism in the Fourth to Eighth Centuries* (New Haven, Conn.: Yale University Press, 1997).

53. The majority of the Germanic peoples followed the Arian teaching that Jesus Christ was not God but one of the highest creatures. Ulfilas and other monks of the Greek East had initially introduced the Christian faith with an Arian perspective to East Gothic tribes. On the one hand, this easily fit into their traditional Germanic religious world of different spirits and beings, and on the other hand, it avoided the complex issues regarding the nature and person of Jesus Christ. In the face of a movement to form an alliance of Arian Christian Germanic tribes against non-Arian Christians, Clovis would become the defender of the latter.

54. See Irvin and Sunquist, 237-239.

55. Norris says, however, that Charlemagne crowned himself (see Norris, 74).

56. See Irvin and Sunquist, 299-304.

57. Andrew Walls, "Translation and the Fullness of Christ," *International Bulletin of Missionary Research* 21/4 (October 1997): 150.

58. For an excellent description, see James C. Russell, *The Germanization of Early Medieval Christianity: A Sociohistorical Approach to Religious Transformation* (New York: Oxford University Press, 1994), 107-133.

59. Ibid.

60. See Irvin and Sunquist, 166-172.

61. For a discussion of the Arian-Nicene controversy, see ibid., 173-183.

62. As noted in Chapter 3, the catechumenate process is interrelated with the understanding and praxis of church, baptism and mission. For a concise history of the catechumenate after Constantine into the early Middle Ages, see Michel Dujarier, *A History of the Catechumenate: The First Six Centuries* (New York: Sadlier, 1979), 77-119.

63. For further background behind the *filioque* controversy, see Irvin and Sunquist, 339-340, 369-371, 444-445.

64. Jedin and Dolan, 213.

65. The importance placed on the Christian conduct and missionary obligation of the laity is evident in the preaching of such people as Chrysostom, Ambrose and Augustine (see ibid., 214 and n. 184).

66. David J. Bosch, *Transforming Mission: Paradigm Shifts in Theology of Mission* (Maryknoll, N.Y.: Orbis Books, 1991), 202.

67. For a description of the origins of monasticism of the Latin West, see Jedin and Dolan, 374-393.

68. Ibid., 378-379.

69. See Irvin and Sunquist, 230-231.

70. John Henry Newman, *Historical Sketches*, vol. 2 (Westminster, Md.: Christian Classics, 1970; first published in the 1830s), 452.

71. Bosch, 233.

72. Kenneth Scott Latourette, *A History of the Expansion of Christianity,* vol. 1, *The First Five Centuries* (New York: Harper & Brothers Publishers, 1937), 218 and n. 258.

73. See J. T. Addison, *The Medieval Missionary: A Study of the Conversion of Northern Europe, A.D. 500-1300* (New York and London: International Missionary Council, 1936), 78-79.

74. See Russell, 156-162.

75. Christopher Dawson, *Religion and the Rise of Western Culture* (New York: Sheed and Ward, 1950), 54.

76. Ibid., 62.

77. Bosch, 233. G. S. M. Walker discusses his description of Columban "as a missionary through circumstance, a monk by vocation" in "St. Columban: Monk or Missionary?" in G. J. Cuming, ed., *The Mission of the Church and the Propagation of the Faith* (London: Cambridge University Press, 1970), 39-44.

78. Eleanor Duckett, *The Wandering Saints of the Early Middle Ages* (New York: W. W. Norton & Company, 1959), 85-86.

79. Regarding the date of Easter, the Celtic monks wanted to preserve the more ancient custom, which actually corresponded with the earlier one of the West before it had been modified in 342. As for the shape of the tonsure, which went from ear to ear according to Celtic custom, it seems preference for one's cultural tradition was at stake.

80. For a commentary on the Rule of St. Benedict, see Emmanuel Heufelder, *The Way to God: According to the Rule of Saint Benedict* (Kalamazoo, Mich.: Cistercian Press, 1983).

81. Newman, 410.

82. For an interesting sociohistorical description, see Russell, 183-208.

83. Venerable Bede, *The Ecclesiastical History of the English Nation*, Book I, chap. XXX.

84. Depending on one's theological and historical perspective, such an appropriation of the Christian faith may or may not be considered an appropriate Christian expression. For example, see Russell, 185-192.

85. Dawson, 66.

86. See Bosch, 235.

87. Rosemary Ruether and Eleanor McLaughlin, eds., *Women of Spirit: Female Leadership in the Jewish and Christian Traditions* (New York: Simon and Schuster, 1979), 105.

88. See Rudolf, Monk of Fulda, "Life of St. Leoba," in *Anglo-Saxon Missionaries in Germany*, trans. and ed. C. H. Talbot (New York: Sheed and Ward, 1954), 222.

89. For example, in most (if not all) of the eight hundred vernacular languages of present-day Papua New Guinea, there is no word or separate category for "religion" within the holistic religious-cultural world view.

90. See Jedin and Dolan, 487.

91. Ernst Benz, *The Eastern Orthodox Church: Its Thought and Life*, trans. Richard and Clara Winston (Chicago: Aldine Publishing Company, 1957), 89.

92. See ibid., 107-110.

93. See Yannoulatos, 218-223.

94. See Jedin and Dolan, 508.

95. See Irvin and Sunquist, 248-250.

96. Ibid., 366.

97. See Jedin and Dolan, 504.

98. For example, see Richard Sullivan, "Early Medieval Missionary Activity: A Comparative Study of Eastern and Western Methods," in *Christian Missionary Activity in the Early Middle Ages* (Aldershot, Great Britain; Brookfield, Vt.: Variorum, 1994), 17-35.

99. Bosch, 230.

100. See Dawson, 47-48.

101. Ibid., 56.

102. Moffett, *Christianity in Asia*, 354.

103. Alexander Schmemann, "The Missionary Imperative in the Orthodox Tradition," in G. Anderson, ed., *The Theology of the Christian Witness* (New York: McGraw-Hill, 1961), 256.

104. Martin of Braga, who was a missionary with the Germanic Sueves, convinced the Council of Braga in 572 to require three weeks of preparation. In the eighth century, Boniface instructed catechumens for two months or longer. Later in that century, in face of the forced baptisms of Charlemagne, Alcuin insisted on a preparation of between seven and forty days.

105. For elaboration, see Justo L. González, *Christian Thought Revisited: Three Types of Theology*, rev. ed. (Maryknoll, N.Y.: Orbis Books, 1999), 94-106.

106. Bosch, 214.

107. Regarding its implications for mission, see ibid., 217-219.

108. Bosch, 236.

109. Russell, 184.

110. Ibid., 184 and n. 4.

111. Bosch, 233.

112. Richard Sullivan, "The Medieval Monk as Frontiersman," in *Christian Missionary Activity in the Early Middle Ages*, 39.

113. See Walls, "Translation," 150.

114. See Douglas Hayward, "Contextualizing the Gospel among the Saxons," *Missiology: An International Review* 22/4 (October 1994): 439-453.

115. Moffett, *Christianity in Asia*, 125.

116. Philip, 11.

117. Ibid.

118. Ibid., 10.

119. Bosch, 204.

120. Irvin and Sunquist, 198.

121. Sullivan, "Medieval Monk as Frontiersman," 38.

122. P. G. Henry, "Monastic Mission: The Monastic Tradition as Source for Unity and Renewal Today," *The Ecumenical Review* 39 (1987): 271-281.

123. See MacMullen, 99-102.

124. Russell, 162.

125. Andrew F. Walls, *The Missionary Movement in Christian History* (Maryknoll, N.Y.: Orbis Books, 1996), 20.

5.   Mission and the Mendicant Movement (1000-1453)

1. For excellent background for this period, see Dale T. Irvin and Scott W. Sunquist, *History of the World Christian Movement*, vol. 1, *Earliest Christianity to 1453* (Maryknoll, N.Y.: Orbis Books, 2001), 383-506.

2. For a good description of the crusades within the wider context of the history of Christianity and Islam, see ibid., 395-405; Rollin Armour, Sr., *Islam, Christianity, and the West: A Troubled History* (Maryknoll, N.Y.: Orbis Books, 2002), 61-79.

3. See Irvin and Sunquist, 440-449.

4. For a concise description and discussion of the Renaissance period, see *New Encyclopaedia Britannica, Micropaedia*, 1986 ed., s.v. "Renaissance"; *Macropedia*, s.v. "Europe—The Emergence of Modern Europe, 1492-1648."

5. Kenneth Scott Latourette, *A History of the Expansion of Christianity*, vol. 2, *The Thousand Years of Uncertainty* (New York: Harper & Brothers Publishing, 1938), 317.

6. For a further discussion of the social context and the theology, see M.-D. Chenu, *Nature, Man, and Society in the Twelfth Century: Essays on New Theological Perspectives in the Latin West*, eds. and trans. Jerome Taylor and Lester Little (Chicago: University of Chicago Press, 1968), 239-269.

7. Beginning in the second half of the twelfth century in southern Italy, the Humiliati were mostly artisans, laborers and social outcasts who were committed to preaching and the simplicity of life. Although they were excommunicated in 1184 for their unorthodox doctrine, many of them were reconciled in 1201 as long as they preached by giving witness to faith and morals and did not preach doctrine. Eventually, the male branch was suppressed by Pius V in 1571. There are still a few of the women's communities in Italy.

8. Also known as the Poor Men of Lyons, the Waldensians were founded in the mid-twelfth century in southern France by Peter Waldo, a wealthy merchant who felt the call to leave everything and become an itinerant preacher. Although they initially received qualified papal approval, they were not accepted by many of the hierarchy and clergy. Eventually, some of them drifted beyond the boundaries of official church doctrine and were confronted through the Inquisition (see Irvin and Sunquist, 411-412).

9. While recognizing the shortcomings and abuses, Brooke also points to often over-looked effective pastoral ministry of the parish clergy in the eleventh- and twelfth-century towns (C. N. L. Brooke, "The Missionary at Home: The Church in the Towns, 1000-1250," in G. J. Cuming, ed., *The Mission of the Church and the Propagation of the Church* [London: Cambridge University Press, 1970], 59-83).

10. For a more detailed description of the Gregorian reform, see Hubert Jedin and John Dolan, eds., *History of the Church,* vol. 3, *The Church in the Age of Feudalism* (New York: Herder and Herder, 1969), 351-403.

11. For a more detailed description of the origins of the various monastic renewal and reform movements, see ibid., 320-332, 453-465.

12. See ibid., 464-465.

13. See Latourette, 430-431.

14. *Apostolica* is synonymous with mission, and therefore the adjective is better translated today in English as "evangelical" rather than literally "apostolic."

15. Catharism was a revival of ancient dualistic Gnosticism, in which the followers attempted to live a perfectly pure life in sharp contrast to the totally corrupt earthly world. For more background, see Hubert Jedin and John Dolan, eds., *History of the Church,* vol. 4, *From the High Middle Ages to the Eve of the Reformation* (New York: Herder and Herder, 1970), 98-104; Irvin and Sunquist, 412-414.

16. Simon Tugwell, ed., *Early Dominicans: Selected Writings,* The Classics of Western Spirituality (Ramsey, N.J.: Paulist Press, 1982), 9-10.

17. For further discussion of the event, see Jedin and Dolan, *History,* 3:404-417; Irvin and Sunquist, 390-393.

18. For further discussion of this event, see Jedin and Dolan, *History,* 4:401-425.

19. Ibid., 380.

20. E. Randolph Daniel, *The Franciscan Concept of Mission in the High Middle Ages* (Lexington, Ky.: University of Kentucky Press, 1975), 5.

21. Frederick W. Norris, *Christianity: A Short Global History* (Oxford: One World, 2002), 108.

22. For an excellent description of the context and world view into which Francis was born, see Jacques le Goff, "Francis of Assisi between the Renewals and Restraints of Feudal Society," *Concilium* 149 (1981), 3-10.

23. "Minor" was chosen as a term of humility.

24. Leonhard Lehmann, "Essential Elements of Franciscan Mission according to Chapter 16 in the Rule of 1221," in *Spirit and Life,* vol. 6, *Mission in the Franciscan Tradition* (St. Bonaventure, N.Y.: Franciscan Institute, 1994), 35.

25. For a concise summary and discussion of the various accounts of the meeting of Francis with the sultan, see Francis de Beer, "St. Francis and Islam," *Concilium* 149 (1981), 11-20.

26. For a further discussion of various opinions regarding the place of martyrdom in Francis's motivation, see ibid., 13-20.

27. Walbert Bühlmann, "Francis and Mission according to the Rule of 1221," in *Spirit and Life,* 6:93.

28. Mary Motte, "In the Image of the Crucified God: A Missiological Interpretation of Francis of Assisi," in Dale Irwin and Akintunde Akinade, eds., *The Agitated Mind of God: The Theology of Kosuke Koyama* (Maryknoll, N.Y.: Orbis Books, 1996), 79.

29. The earlier rule represents the second step in the three-part development of the final Franciscan rule. First of all, the rule of 1209 or 1210, the simple pattern of life, was orally accepted by Pope Innocent III, but the original text was lost over time. Second, the rule of 1221—also called the "Regula non bullata" or the "earlier rule"—incorporated and expanded the first edition. Finally, the rule of 1223—the "Regula bullata" or the "later rule"—is the edited and revised version that received official papal approval on November 29, 1223.

30. For the complete text of chapter 16, see Regis Armstrong and Ignatius Brady, eds. and trans., *Francis and Clare: The Complete Works*, The Classics of Western Spirituality (Ramsey, N.J.: Paulist Press, 1982), 121-122. For a concise missiological commentary on chapter 16, see Bühlmann, 87-107; Lehmann, 35-45. For a more detailed study of the historical context of Francis's approach to Islam and how this approach is reflected in chapter 16, see J. Hoeberichts, *Francis and Islam* (Quincy, Ill.: Franciscan Press, 1997), 1-134.

31. See Bühlmann, 97.

32. See Cajetan Esser, "Saint Francis and the Missionary Church," trans. Ignatius Brady, in *Spirit and Life*, 6:22-23.

33. Motte, 81.

34. Esser, 23.

35. For a more detailed commentary and reflection on the event, see Margaret Carney, *The First Franciscan Woman: Clare of Assisi and Her Form of Life* (Quincy, Ill.: Franciscan Press, 1993), 36-39; Joy Prakash, "The Conversion of St. Clare (Part II)," *Tau: A Journal of Search into the Vision of Francis* 19 (March 1994): 8-15.

36. Recent significant works include Regis Armstrong, ed. and trans., *Clare of Assisi: Early Documents*, The Classics of Western Spirituality (Mahwah, N.J.: Paulist Press, 1988); Marco Bartoli, *Clare of Assisi*, trans. Sr. Frances Teresa (Quincy, Ill.: Franciscan Press, 1993); Carney; Sr. Frances Teresa, *This Living Mirror: Reflections on Clare of Assisi* (Maryknoll, N.Y.: Orbis Books, 1995).

37. Carney, 19.

38. See Frances Ann Thom, "Clare of Assisi: New Leader of Women," in Lillian Thomas Shank and John A. Nichols, eds., *Medieval Religious Women*, vol. 2, *Peaceweavers,* Cistercian Studies Series no. 72 (Kalamazoo, Mich.: Cistercian Publications, 1987), 199.

39. Angelyn Dries, "Mission and Marginalization: The Franciscan Heritage," *Missiology: An International Review* 26/1 (January 1998): 8.

40. For further comment on the significance of Clare's image of the mirror for mission, see ibid., 8-10.

41. Ibid., 244. For a concise development of this thought, see Margaret Carney, "Clare and the Franciscan Missionary Charism," *New Serafika: The Franciscan Magazine for South Africa* (April 1995), 22-25.

42. Thom, 200.

43. See Bartoli, 158-175.

44. For a more detailed history of the Poor Clares, see Lazaro Iriate, *Franciscan History: The Three Orders of St. Francis of Assisi*, trans. Patricia Ross (Chicago, Ill.: Franciscan Herald Press, 1982), 439-473; William Short, *The Franciscans* (Collegeville, Minn.: Liturgical Press, 1990), 22-25, 71-85.

45. Dries, 11.

46. The beghards were the male counterpart of the beguines. For an in-depth study of both, see E. W. McDonnell, *The Beguines and Beghards in Medieval Culture: With Special Emphasis on the Belgian Scene* (New Brunswick, N.J.: Rutgers University Press, 1954).

47. See ibid., 5-7; Dennis Devlin, "Feminine Lay Piety in the High Middle Ages: The Beguines," in Lillian Thomas Shank and John A. Nichols, eds., *Medieval Religious Women*, vol. 1, *Distant Echoes*, Cistercian Studies Series no. 71 (Kalamazoo, Mich.: Cistercian Publications, 1984), 184-185.

48. See Jedin and Dolan, *History*, 4:244-246.

49. See Caroline Walker Bynum, *Holy Feast and Holy Famine* (Berkeley and Los Angeles: University of California Press, 1987); Devlin, 186-193; Robert Ellsberg, *All Saints: Daily Reflections on Saints, Prophets, and Witnesses for Our Time* (New York: Crossroad, 1997), 271; McDonnell.

50. See McDonnell, 299-319.

51. Ibid., 343-344; see also B. M. Kienzle and P. J. Walker, eds., *Women Preachers and Prophets through Two Millennia of Christianity* (Berkeley and Los Angeles: University of California Press, 1998).

52. Devlin, 189.

53. See Caroline Walker Bynum, *Jesus as Mother: Studies in the Spirituality of the High Middle Ages* (Berkeley and Los Angeles: University of California Press, 1882), 228-247; Ellsberg, 320-322.

54. See Devlin, 189-192.

55. Carney, *First Franciscan Woman*, 214. For an interesting reflection on Clare and the beguine mystic, Mechthild of Magdeburg, see Mary Schmiel, "Medieval Sisters' Voices: Clare and Mechthild," *Tau: A Journal of Search into the Vision of Francis* 19 (December 1994): 124-129.

56. Lazaro Iriate, "Clare of Assisi: Her Place in Female Hagiography," trans. Ignatius McCormick, *Greyfriars Review* 3 (August 1989): 180.

57. For a more detailed history of the Third Order, see Iriate, *Franciscan History*, 475-542; Short, 87-103. For a history of the Franciscan Sisters of the Third Order, see Raffaele Pazzelli, *The Franciscan Sisters: Outlines of History and Spirituality*, trans. Aidan Mullaney (Steubenville, Ohio: Franciscan University Press, 1993).

58. Pazzelli, 27.

59. See ibid., 38-51.

60. See ibid., 52-62.

61. For a further description of the history of the Friars Minor up to 1517, see Iriate, *Franciscan History*, 31-168; Short, 40-57.

62. See Iriate, *Franciscan History*, 51-57.

63. See Jedin and Dolan, *History*, 4:240-246.

64. For example, see Daniel, 76-100.

65. Chap. 16, ln. 10.

66. For further information and bibliography, see Iriate, *Franciscan History*, 126-129.

67. Stephen Neill, *History of Christian Missions*, rev. ed. (New York: Penguin Books, 1986), 114-115.

68. Scholars debate if Lull's mysticism was influenced by the Sufis (see Latourette, 322 and n. 59).

69. For a further description of the Franciscan missionaries within a context that also includes a balanced view of the East Syrian Christians, see Samuel Hugh Moffett, *A History of Christianity in Asia*, vol. 1, *Beginnings to 1500* (San Francisco: Harper Collins, 1992), 406-420, 456-459.

70. For a further presentation of Franciscan theological scholarship, see Iriate, *Franciscan History*, 149-163; Kenan Osborne, ed., *The History of Franciscan Theology* (St. Bonaventure, N.Y.: The Franciscan Institute, 1994). For a treatment of the accomplishments of Roger Bacon and Ramón Lull in terms of the intellectual conversion aspect of mission in the Middle Ages, see Daniel, 55-75.

71. Daniel, 121.

72. Ibid., 127.

73. For an excellent in-depth account of the context, life and work of Dominic, see M.-H. Vicaire, *Saint Dominic and His Times*, trans. Kathleen Pond (New York: McGraw-Hill, 1964). For a concise picture, see Tugwell, 6-27.

74. Tugwell, 11.

75. For an in-depth study of this development, based on current scholarship, see Simon Tugwell, "Notes on the Life of St. Dominic," *Archivum Fratrum Praedicatorum* 65 (1995): 6-35, 142-145.

76. For a detailed history of the foundation in Prouille, see Vicaire, 115-136.

77. Suzanne Noffke, "The Evolution of Dominican Common Life for Women," in *Common Life: In the Spirit of St. Dominic* (River Forest, Ill.: Parable, 1990), 58.

78. Mary of God Kain, OP, *Commentary of the Basic Constitution of the Nuns* (p. 6), delivered June 5, 1984, quoted in ibid., 60.

79. For references, see Noffke, 59.

80. McDonnell, 344.

81. For example, a group of beguines in Augsburg adopted the Third Order rule in the late fourteenth century. See Noffke, 61 n. 15.

82. See Tugwell, *Early Dominicans,* 30.

83. Ibid.

84. See Ellsberg, 188-190; Suzanne Noffke, trans. and introduction, *Catherine of Siena: The Dialogue*, The Classics of Western Spirituality (Ramsey, N.J.: Paulist Press, 1980).

85. Teresa of Avila and Catherine of Siena were named in 1970 and Thérèse of Lisieux in 1997.

86. Susan A. Muto, "Foundations of Christian Formation in the *Dialogue* of St. Catherine of Siena," in Shank and Nichols, 2:276.

87. See Tugwell, *Early Dominicans*, 179-370.

88. Ibid., 35.

89. Ibid., 40 n. 30.

90. McDonnell, 7.

91. For interesting discussions of the distinctions between the two orders and their possible influences upon each other in the earliest days of their development, see Christopher Dawson, *Religion and the Rise of Western Culture* (New York: Sheed & Ward, 1950), 256-261; Tugwell, *Early Dominicans*, 16-24; Tugwell, "Notes on the Life of St. Dominic," 80-82.

92. Thomas Aquinas, *Summa Theologiae*, P.I., q. 1, a. 4 resp.

93. Bonaventure, Proem. in I *Sentent.*, q. 3; *Opera Omnia* I, 13.

94. Dawson, 261.

95. For a concise history and extensive bibliography, see James Stamoolis, *Eastern Orthodox Mission Theology Today* (Maryknoll, N.Y.: Orbis Books, 1986), 24-34, 179-180; also see Irvin and Sunquist, 375-378.

96. John Meyendorff, "Orthodox Missions in the Middle Ages," in *History's Lessons for Tomorrow's Missions* (Geneva: World's Student Christian Federation, 1960), 103.

97. Stamoolis, 26.

98. Moffett, 376.

99. For an excellent treatment of this five-hundred-year history of the church in Asia, see ibid., 374-512.

100. Ibid., 405.

101. See ibid., 406-414, 456-459.

102. See ibid., 453-454, 431-434; Irvin and Sunquist, 461-463.

103. See Jean-Paul Wiest, "Learning from the Missionary Past," in Edmond Tang and Jean-Paul Wiest, eds., *The Catholic Church in Modern China: Perspectives* (Maryknoll, N.Y.: Orbis Books, 1993), 182. This election also had the political advantage of placing a Mongol of the powerful empire of the East in a key position (see Moffett, 432).

104. Moffett, 476.

105. See John C. England, *The Hidden History of Christianity in Asia: The Churches of the East before 1500* (Delhi: ISPCK; Hong Kong: CCA, 1998), 91-101.

106. See Moffett, 503-509.

107. For a further description of Christianity in Armenia during this time, see Irvin and Sunquist, 451-452, 492-493.

108. See ibid., 470-475.

109. For a further description of Christianity in India during this time, see ibid., 495-496; Moffett, 498-503.

110. Irvin and Sunquist, 504.

111. Thomas Aquinas, *Summa Theologiae* II-2, q. 10, a. 8.

112. Justo González, *A History of Christian Thought,* vol. 2, *From Augustine to the Eve of the Reformation* (Nashville, Tenn.: Abingdon Press, 1971), 98-99.

113. Ellsberg, 433.

114. Irvin and Sunquist, 421.

115. Karl Rahner, "Theology: History," in *Sacramentum Mundi* (New York: Herder and Herder, 1970), 6:243.

116. Chenu, 253.

117. See ibid., 255.

118. Although this theological school was primarily developed by Dominicans, it should not be interpreted literally, since some Dominicans were among its primary opponents.

119. See González, 231-238.

120. Friedrich Wetter, "Franciscan Theology," in *Sacramentum Mundi,* 2:347.

121. Roger Schroeder, "Women, Mission, and the Early Franciscan Movement," *Missiology: An International Review* 28/4 (October 2000): 419.

122. Ibid.

123. Motte, 82.

124. Claude Marie Barbour, "Seeking Justice and Shalom in the City," *International Review of Mission* 73/291 (1984): 304.

125. See Hoeberichts, 137-196.

126. Saskia Murk-Jansen, *Brides in the Desert: The Spirituality of the Beguines* (Maryknoll, N.Y.: Orbis Books, 1998), 112.

127. Ibid., 115.

6. Mission in the Age of Discovery (1492-1773)

1. For excellent background on this period, see Dale T. Irvin and Scott W. Sunquist, *History of the World Christian Movement,* vol. 2, *1453-2000* (Maryknoll, N.Y.: Orbis Books, forthcoming), parts I-III.

2. See Kenneth Scott Latourette, *A History of the Expansion of Christianity,* vol. 3, *Three Centuries of Advance* (New York: Harper & Brothers Publishing, 1939), 66-71, 359, 367-371.

3. For a description of the missionary activity in Africa (excluding Ethiopia) from the fifteenth to the eighteenth centuries, see Adrian Hastings, *The Church in Africa, 1450-1950* (Oxford, Great Britain: Clarendon Press, 1994), 71-129. For a concise summary and comment, see Andrew F. Walls, *The Cross-Cultural Process in Christian History* (Maryknoll, N.Y.: Orbis Books, 2002), 92-94.

4. See Irvin and Sunquist, chap. 2.

5. Frederick W. Norris, *Chistianity: A Short Global History* (Oxford: OneWorld, 2002), 167.

6. Latourette, 17.

7. For a concise summary of the social-political, religious and ecclesial (Roman Catholic) context of Brazil from 1500 to the 1970s, see Eduardo Hoornaert, "The Church in Brazil," in Enrique Dussel, ed., *The Church in Latin America: 1492-1992* (Maryknoll, N.Y.: Orbis Books, 1992), 185-200.

8. See Peter G. Gowling, *Islands under the Cross: The Story of the Church in the Philippines* (Manila: National Council of Churches in the Philippines, 1967); John Leddy Phelan, *The Hispanization of the Philippines: Spanish Aims and Filipino Responses, 1565-1700* (Madison, Wis.: University of Wisconsin Press, 1959).

9. For a concise description of this context from a religious-cultural perspective, see Juan Schobinger, "The Amerindian Religions," in Dussel, 23-42.

10. For example, the extreme difference between the consciousness of an oral culture and a literate culture would very much affect the missionary efforts (see Ana Maria Pineda, "Evangelization of the 'New World': A New World Perspective," *Missiology: An International Review* 20/4 [October 1992]: 151-161).

11. Schobinger, 23.

12. The most extreme depopulation occurred in Hispaniola (Haiti and the Dominican Republic), where there were not more than three hundred indigenous people by 1540. For a summary of the discussion around this question, see Gustavo Gutiérrez, *Las Casas: In Search of the Poor of Jesus Christ* (Maryknoll, N.Y.: Orbis Books, 1993), 461-464. For a broader discussion, see Charles C. Mann, "1491," *The Atlantic Monthly* 289/3 (March 2002), 41-53.

13. For example, see Justo González, "Voices of Compassion," *Missiology: An International Review* 20/4 (October 1992): 163-173.

14. Quoted from the reports of Las Casas, in Gutiérrez, 29.

15. While many of the Franciscans would eventually join the Dominicans in their defense of the indigenous peoples, some Franciscans defended the *encomenderos* because they were chaplains for the settlers and also because there was sometimes bitter rivalry between the two orders (see González, 172 n. 1).

16. For a collection of and theological commentary on his writings, see George Sanderlin, ed. and trans., *Witness: Writings of Bartolomé de Las Casas* (Maryknoll, N.Y.: Orbis Books, 1992); and Gutiérrez.

17. Aristotle, *Politics* I, 5. For discussion, see Gutiérrez, 291-295.

18. Ibid., 184.

19. See ibid., 302-303.

20. See Gutiérrez, 329.

21. See Enrique Dussel, "The Real Motives for the Conquest," *Concilium*, no. 6 (1990), 40.

22. González, 164.

23. Quoted in Mario A. Rodríguez León, "Invasion and Evangelization in the Sixteenth Century," in Dussel, *The Church in Latin America*, 50.

24. See Virgil Elizondo, *Guadalupe: Mother of the New Creation* (Maryknoll, N.Y.: Orbis Books, 1997), and *La Morenita: Evangelizer of the Americas* (San Antonio: Mexican American Cultural Center, 1980); Gary Riebe-Estrella, "*La Virgen*: A Mexican Perspective," *New Theology Review* 12/2 (May 1999): 39-47; Jeanette Rodriguez, *Our Lady of Guadalupe: Faith and Empowerment among Mexican-American Women* (Austin, Tex.: University of Texas Press, 1994).

25. See Latourette, 100.

26. Johannes Meier, "The Religious Orders in Latin America: A Historical Survey," in Dussel, *The Church in Latin America*, 380.

27. Casiano Floristán, "Evangelization of the 'New World': An Old World Perspective," *Missiology: An International Review* 20/4 (October 1992): 140.

28. Harry Kelsey, "European Impact on the California Indians, 1530-1830," *The Americas* 41 (Washington, D.C., 1985), 511; also found in J. S. Cummins, ed., *Christianity and Missions, 1450-1800, An Expanding World*, vol. 28 (Aldershot, Great Britain: Ashgate/Variorum, 1997), 276.

29. For opposing assessments of his missionary work, see Don DeNevi and Noel Francis Moholy, *Junipero Serra: The Illustrated Story of the Franciscan Founder of California's Missions* (New York: Harper & Row, 1985), and George Tinker, *Missionary Conquest: The Gospel and Native American Cultural Genocide* (Minneapolis, Minn.: Fortress Press, 1993), 42-68.

30. For a concise historical survey of the reductions, see Margarita Durán Estragó, "The Reductions," in Dussel, *The Church in Latin America*, 351-362.

31. See ibid., 352-353.

32. Ibid., 357.

33. Indians would be tied to this large stone or tree trunk and flogged as a punishment for those crimes that carried a public sentence. Women were whipped on the back and men on the

buttocks. For example, a woman could receive twenty-five strokes if she refused to do her communal work of spinning thread or did not meet the weekly quota (see ibid., 358, 360).

34. Nineteenth-century examples include the Congregation of the Immaculate Heart of Mary in China, the Society of the Missionaries of Africa in North Africa and the Spiritans in East Africa.

35. For a further critical discussion of these general developments, see Ruth Liebowitz, "Virgins in the Service of Christ: The Dispute over an Active Apostolate for Women during the Counter-Reformation," in Rosemary Ruether and Eleanor McLaughlin, eds., *Women of Spirit: Female Leadership in the Jewish and Christian Traditions* (Eugene, Ore.: Wipf and Stock Publishers, 1998), 131-152. On the Ursulines in particular, see Linda Lierheimer, "Preaching or Teaching? Defining the Ursuline Mission in Seventeenth-Century France," in Beverly Mayne Kienzle and Pamela J. Walker, eds., *Women Preachers and Prophets through Two Millennia of Christianity* (Berkeley and Los Angeles: University of California Press, 1998), 212-226.

36. David J. Bosch, *Transforming Mission: Paradigm Shifts in Theology of Mission* (Maryknoll, N.Y.: Orbis Books, 1991), 214-238.

37. Rodríguez León, 53.

38. Erick Langer and Robert Jackson, eds., *The New Latin American Mission History* (Lincoln, Neb.: University of Nebraska Press, 1995).

39. See C. R. Boxer, "A Note on Portuguese Missionary Methods in the East: Sixteenth to Eighteenth Centuries," *The Ceylon Historical Journal* 10 (Dehiwala, Sri Lanka) (1965): 77-90; also found in Cummins, 161-174.

40. Francis Xavier was named the patron of missions by Pope Pius XI in 1927.

41. See Andrew Ross, *A Vision Betrayed: The Jesuits in Japan and China, 1542-1742* (Maryknoll, N.Y.: Orbis Books, 1994), 16, 19-20.

42. Andrew Ross, "Alessandro Valignano, SJ," *Missiology: An International Review* 27/4 (October 1999): 507.

43. Letter of November 5, 1549, quoted in Stephen Neill, *A History of Christian Missions*, rev. ed. (New York: Penguin Books, 1986), 133.

44. See Ross, *Vision Betrayed*, 27.

45. The first period occurred during the seventh to tenth centuries during the T'ang dynasty (see Chap. 4) and the second during the thirteenth and fourteenth centuries under the Mongol Empire (see Chap. 5).

46. For a further discussion of this encounter, see Ross, *Vision Betrayed*, 34-42.

47. Ross, "Valignano," 511.

48. Ross, *Vision Betrayed*, 128.

49. Ibid., 135.

50. Ibid., 42.

51. The sacred cotton thread, worn over the left shoulder and under the right armpit, is bestowed on boys, normally between the ages of eight and twelve, of the three upper castes of Hinduism during an initiation rite. After the entire initiation ritual, the boy is conferred with the status of "twice-born" *(dvija)* and now has the right to study the Hindu sacred scriptures.

52. Philip Jenkins, *The Next Christendom: The Coming of Global Christianity* (New York: Oxford University Press, 2002), 183-184.

53. For an excellent study of de Rhodes's *Cathechismus*, see Peter Phan, *Mission and Catechesis: Alexandre de Rhodes and Inculturation in Seventeenth-Century Vietnam* (Maryknoll, N.Y.: Orbis Books, 1998).

54. See ibid., 100-101.

55. Ibid., 101.

56. For an interesting study of this organization of catechists by de Rhodes within the wider context of the role of catechists in Roman Catholic missionary work, see John T. Boberg, "The Catechists in the Missions" (Ph.D. diss., Pontifical Gregorian University, Rome, 1969).

57. *Sacra Congregatio de Propaganda Fide, Collectanea* 10/300 (Rome, 1907), 103.

58. For a detailed study of the Rites Controversy, see George Minamiki, S.J., *The Chinese Rites Controversy from Its Beginning to Modern Times* (Chicago: Loyola University Press, 1985). For a concise summary of the Rites Controversy from the seventeenth into the twentieth century, see Peter De Ta Vo, "Chinese Rites Controversy," in *New Catholic Encyclopedia,* 2d ed.

59. For a description and analysis of the Rites Controversy from a Dominican perspective, see Fidel Villarroel, "The Chinese Rites Controversy: Dominican Viewpoint," *Philippiniana Sacra* 28/82 (1993), 5-61.

60. For a Dominican viewpoint of this situation, see ibid., 38-43.

61. Jenkins, 32.

62. See Ross, *Vision Betrayed*, 202-204.

63. See ibid., 204-206.

64. Ibid., 205.

65. William Burrows, "A Seventh Paradigm? Catholics and Radical Inculturation," in Willem Saayman and Klippies Kritzinger, eds., *Mission in Bold Humility: David Bosch's Work Considered* (Maryknoll, N.Y.: Orbis Books, 1996).

66. See Bosch, 244-245.

67. James A. Scherer, *Gospel, Church, and Kingdom: Comparative Studies in World Mission Theology* (Minneapolis, Minn.: Augsburg, 1987), 65.

68. Andrew Walls, "A History of the Expansion of Christianity Reconsidered: The Legacy of George D. Day," *Occasional Papers,* no. 8 (New Haven, Conn.: Yale Divinity School Library, 1996), 17.

69. See Paul E. Pierson, "Moravian Missions," in A. Scott Moreau, ed., *Evangelical Dictionary of World Missions* (Grand Rapids, Mich.: Baker Books, 2000), 660-661.

70. Bosch, 255.

71. For a concise and fine summary of Puritan mission theology, see Bosch, 258-260.

72. Ibid., 257.

73. See Ernst Benz, "Pietist and Puritan Sources of Early Protestant World Missions (Cotton Mather and A. H. Franke)," *Church History* 20 (Indialantic, Fla.) (1951), 28-55; also found in Cummins, 315-342.

74. Bosch, 261.

75. For a description of the church in Ethiopia from the fifteenth to eighteenth centuries, see Hastings, 130-169.

76. The Christian history of the Soyo Kingdom near the mouth of the River Zaire used to be considered primarily as an example of political opportunism. However, the Kongolese Christianity, which emerged as a result of the efforts of Capuchin missionaries, is now being recognized as having been a genuinely African church (Walls, *Cross-Cultural Process*, 93). For further description of the Kongo church during this time period, see Hastings, 73-77, 79-118, 123-129, 635-639 (extensive bibliography). For an in-depth study of the indigenous nature of Kongolese Christianity, see Richard Gray, *Black Christians and White Missionaries* (New Haven, Conn.: Yale University Press, 1990).

77. Gutiérrez, 190; for a fuller theological elaboration of this issue, see 99-191.

78. See ibid., 244-248.

79. Las Casas, *Tratado comprobatorio*, 1552, *Obras escogidas* 5:357b, cited in ibid., 273.

80. See Volker Küster, *The Many Faces of Jesus Christ* (Maryknoll, N.Y.: Orbis Books, 2001), 41-46.

81. See James B. Nickoloff, "A 'Church of the Poor' in the Sixteenth Century: The Ecclesiology of Bartolomé de Las Casas' *De unico modo,*" *Journal of Hispanic/Latino Theology* 2/4 (May 1995): 26-40.

82. For a further discussion of these issues regarding adult baptism, see Floristán, 141-142.

83. David Brading, "Prophet and Apostle: Bartolomé de Las Casas and the Spiritual Conquest of America," *New Blackfriars* 65/774 (1984), 532; also found in Cummins, 136. Note that for Las Casas, predestination is not fate but an expression of divine knowledge (see Gutiérrez, 252-256).

84. Brading, 532. "Apostolic" is understood here as "creating a Church, initiating entire Indian communities into the practice and devotions of medieval Catholicism" and "seeking to bring sacramental grace to those in darkness."

85. F. J. Verstraelen, A. Camps, L. A. Hoedemaker and M. R. Spindler, eds., *Missiology: An Ecumenical Introduction* (Grand Rapids, Mich.: Eerdmans, 1995), 217.

86. Gutiérrez, 184.

87. Justo González, *A History of Christian Thought*, vol. 3, *From the Protestant Reformation to the Twentieth Century*, rev. ed. (Nashville, Tenn.: Abingdon Press, 1987), 222.

88. Phan, 129. For a detailed summation of Phan's assessment and approach to each of the Vietnamese religious traditions, see 82-96.

89. Aylward Shorter, *Toward a Theology of Inculturation* (London: Geoffrey Chapman, 1988), 162.

90. Bosch, 261.

91. Ibid.

92. Gutiérrez, 271.

93. Ibid., 270.

94. Burrows, 133.

7. Mission in the Age of Progress (1792-1914)

1. For excellent background on this period, see Dale T. Irvin and Scott W. Sunquist, *History of the World Christian Movement*, vol. 2, *1453-2000* (Maryknoll, N.Y.: Orbis Books, forthcoming), Part IV.

2. Kenneth Scott Latourette, *A History of the Expansion of Christianity* (New York: Harper & Brothers, 1937-1945). Volumes 4, 5 and 6 cover the "Great Century," which he delineates as 1800-1914.

3. David J. Bosch, *Transforming Mission: Paradigm Shifts in Theology of Mission* (Maryknoll, N.Y.: Orbis Books, 1991), 274.

4. Building upon the Renaissance and rationalism, the Enlightenment era began in the seventeenth century. However, it was more fully developed through eighteenth-century philosophers—such as Rousseau, Voltaire, Kant and Hume—who asserted the autonomy of the individual and the capability of human reason to discover truth. The Enlightenment rejected external sources of truth, including the authority of divine revelation or religious institutions. For further description, see S. C. Burchell, *Age of Progress* (New York: Time-Life Books, 1966).

5. For a stirring article on how the Catholic Church was still struggling with this paradigm shift in Europe in the year 2000, see Peter Hünermann, "Evangelization of Europe? Observations on a Church in Peril," in Robert J. Schreiter, ed., *Mission in the Third Millennium* (Maryknoll, N.Y.: Orbis Books, 2001), 57-80.

6. Bosch, 303.

7. See Max Warren, *Social History and Christian Mission* (London: SCM Press, 1967), 54-57.

8. Bosch, 312.

9. Anne Wind, "The Protestant Missionary Movement from 1789 to 1963," in F. J. Verstraelen, A. Camps, L. A. Hoedemaker and M. R. Spindler, eds., *Missiology: An Ecumenical Introduction* (Grand Rapids, Mich.: Eerdmans, 1995), 239.

10. Roger Hedlund, *Roots of the Great Debate in Mission: Mission in Historical and Theological Perspective* (Bangalore, India: Theological Book Trust, 1993), 21.

11. For a very interesting study of the impact of this experience on John Wesley and some implications for today, see W. Harrison Daniel, "The Young John Wesley as Cross-Cultural Witness: Investigations into Wesley's American Mission Experience and Implications for Today's Mission," *Missiology: An International Review* 28/4 (October 2000): 443-457.

12. For a more detailed picture of mission and Protestantism between 1763 and 1787, see Charles Chaney, "The Missionary Situation in the Revolutionary Era," in R. Pierce Beaver,

ed., *American Missions in Bicentennial Perspective* (Pasadena, Calif.: William Carey Library, 1977), 14-31.

13. Wind, 238.

14. Andrew F. Walls, "Missionary Societies and the Fortunate Subversion of the Church," *Evangelical Quarterly* 88/2 (1988): 141-155.

15. Bosch, 280.

16. See Joe L. Coker, "Developing a Theory of Missions in Serampore: The Increased Emphasis upon Education as a 'Means for the Conversion of the Heathens,'" *Mission Studies* 18/1/35 (2001): 42-60.

17. For example, see A. Christopher Smith, "William Carey, 1761-1834: Protestant Pioneer of the Modern Mission Era," in Gerald Anderson et al., eds., *Mission Legacies: Biographical Studies of Leaders of the Modern Missionary Movement* (Maryknoll, N.Y.: Orbis Books, 1994), 245-254.

18. Ibid., 253.

19. For example, the Society for the Propagation of the Gospel in Foreign Parts, a Protestant ecclesiastical agency, was founded in London in 1701, and the American Society for Propagating the Gospel among the Indians and Others in North America, an independent mission agency, was officially recognized in 1787.

20. Bosch, 328.

21. Ibid., 330.

22. See Wilbert Shenk, "Henry Venn, 1796-1873: Champion of Indigenous Church Principles," in Anderson et al., 541-547.

23. See R. Pierce Beaver, "Rufus Anderson, 1796-1880: To Evangelize, Not Civilize," in Anderson et al., 548-553.

24. See Andrew F. Walls, "Samuel Ajoyi Crowther, 1807-1891: Foremost African Christian of the Nineteenth Century," in Anderson et al., 132-139; Lamin Sanneh, "The CMS and the African Transformation: Samuel Ajayi Crowther and the Opening of Nigeria," in Kevin Ward and Brian Stanley, eds., *The Church Mission Society and World Christianity, 1799-1999* (Grand Rapids, Mich.: Eerdmans; Richmond, Surrey, U.K.: Curzon Press, 2000), 173-197.

25. Andrew Walls, *The Missionary Movement in Christian History: Studies in the Transmission of the Faith* (Maryknoll, N.Y.: Orbis Books, 1996), 102; for further description, see 102-110.

26. See Lamin Sanneh, *Abolitionists Abroad: American Blacks and the Making of Modern West Africa* (Cambridge, Mass.: Harvard University Press, 1999), 126-129, 150-167, 242-243.

27. Andrew F. Walls, *The Cross-Cultural Process in Christian History* (Maryknoll, N.Y.: Orbis Books, 2002), 144; for further information on this aspect of Crowther's mission approach, see 143-147. In order to get a glimpse of the "conversation" between Christianity and Islam within the context of Sierra Leone, Lamin Sanneh offers a description of and reflection on a format debate held in Freetown in 1888 on the topic "Is Christianity or Islam best suited to promote the true interests of the Negro race?" (see Lamin Sanneh, *Piety and Power: Muslims and Christians in West Africa* [Maryknoll, N.Y.: Orbis Books, 1996], 67-84).

28. Walls, *Missionary Movement*, 87.

29. For example, see Allan Davidson, "Semisi Nau—A Pacific Islander Missionary," *Missiology: An International Review* 27/4 (October 1999): 481-486; Doug Munro and Andrew Thornley, *The Covenant Makers: Islander Missionaries in the Pacific* (Suva, Fiji: Pacific Theological College, Institute of Pacific Studies, The University of the South Pacific, 1996).

30. See Andrew F. Walls, "David Livingstone, 1813-1873: Awakening the Western World to Africa," in Anderson et al., 140-147.

31. Ibid., 141.

32. See William Hutchinson, *Errand to the World: American Protestant Thought and Foreign Missions* (Chicago: The University of Chicago Press, 1987), 91-124.

33. See Bosch, 311-312.

34. See J. Herbert Kane, "J. Hudson Taylor, 1832-1905: Founder of the China Inland Mission," in Anderson et al., 197-204.

35. See Joel Carpenter, "Moody, D(wight) L(yman)," in Gerald Anderson, ed., *Biographical Dictionary of Christian Missions* (New York: Simon and Schuster Macmillan, 1998), 470-471.

36. See Dana Robert, "Arthur Tappan Pierson, 1837-1911: Evangelizing the World in This Generation," in Anderson et al., 28-36.

37. See C. Howard Hopkins, "John R. Mott, 1865-1955: Architect of World Mission and Unity," in Anderson et al., 79-84.

38. See Kathleen Bliss, "J. H. Oldham, 1874-1969: From 'Edinburgh 1910' to the World Council of Churches," in Anderson et al., 570-580.

39. See H. McKennie Goodpasture, "Robert E. Speer, 1867-1947: Affirming the Finality of Christ," in Anderson et al., 563-569.

40. See Lesslie Newbigen, "W. A. Visser 't Hooft, 1900-1985: 'No Other Name,'" in Anderson et al., 117-122.

41. Bosch, 321.

42. Hutchinson, 91.

43. See Dana Robert, "Adoniram Judson Gordon, 1836-1895: Educator, Preacher, and Promoter of Missions," in Anderson et al., 18-27.

44. Hutchinson, 93.

45. William Richey Hogg, *Ecumenical Foundations* (New York: Harper & Brothers, 1952), 45.

46. Gerald H. Anderson, "American Protestants in Pursuit of Mission: 1886-1986," in Verstraelen et al., 384-385.

47. J. Hunter, quoted in ibid., 387.

48. Dana L. Robert, *American Women in Mission: A Social History of Their Thought and Practice* (Macon, Ga.: Mercer University Press, 1996), 37.

49. Ibid., 93.

50. Ibid., 114.

51. Ibid., 136.

52. See ibid., 167-169.

53. See Catherine B. Allen, "Charlotte (Lottie) Moon, 1840-1912: Demonstrating 'No Greater Love,'" in Anderson et al., 205-215.

54. Robert, *American Women in Mission*, 191.

55. Ibid., 200-201.

56. R. Pierce Beaver, *All Loves Excelling: American Protestant Women in World Mission* (Grand Rapids, Mich.: Eerdmans, 1968), 143.

57. Robert, *American Women in Mission*, 269.

58. For historical background, see Robert S. Ellwood, "World's Parliament of Religions," in Mircea Eliade, gen. ed., *The Encyclopedia of Religion* (New York: Macmillan, 1987), 15:444-445.

59. W. R. Hogg, "The Rise of Protestant Missionary Concern, 1517-1914," in Gerald Anderson, ed., *The Theology of the Christian Mission* (New York: McGraw-Hill, 1961), 111.

60. Bosch, 337.

61. See Andrew F. Walls, "Alexander Duff," in Anderson, *Biographical Dictionary of Christian Missions,* 187-188.

62. See Hans Kasdorf, "Gustav Warneck, 1834-1910: Founder of the Scholarly Study of Missions," in Anderson et al., 373-382.

63. See Karl Müller, SVD, "Joseph Schmidlin, 1876-1944: Pioneer of Catholic Missiology," in Anderson et al., 402-409.

64. In opposition to those who wanted to limit the pope's authority, Ultramontanism represented the perspective of those who looked southward "beyond the mountains" (the Alps) to the pope for the focus of centralized ecclesiastical authority. Ultimately, the declaration by the First Vatican Council did not satisfy the Ultramontanes in that the council was quite restrictive of the pope's exercise of infallibility. See, for instance, Michael A. Fahey, "Church," in Elisabeth Schüssler Fiorenza and John P. Galvin, eds., *Systematic Theology: Roman Catholic*

Perspectives, vol. 2 (Minneapolis, Minn.: Fortress Press, 1991), 50-58; Patrick Granfield, *The Limits of the Papacy* (New York: Crossroad, 1987), 68-73.

65. Bosch, 262.

66. See Robert Schreiter, "Gregory XVI," in Anderson, *Biographical Dictionary of Christian Missions*, 260.

67. See Mary Motte, "Javouhey, Anne-Marie," in Anderson, *Biographical Dictionary of Christian Missions*, 330.

68. See Marc Spindler, "Libermann, François Marie Paul," in Anderson, *Biographical Dictionary of Christian Missions*, 399.

69. See Angelyn Dries, "Duchesne, Rose Philippine," in Anderson, *Biographical Dictionary of Christian Missions*, 187.

70. Ibid.

71. See Robert, *American Women in Mission*, 322-332.

72. See Adrian Hastings, "Lavigerie, Charles Martial Allemande," in Anderson, *Biographical Dictionary of Christian Missions*, 387.

73. See Stephen Neill, *Colonialism and Christian Missions* (London: Lutterworth, 1966), 349.

74. See Marc Nikkel, "Comboni, (Anthony) Daniel," in Anderson, *Biographical Dictionary of Christian Missions*, 146-147.

75. See Mary Motte, "Drexel, Katherine," in Anderson, *Biographical Dictionary of Christian Missions*, 185.

76. See Jean-Paul Wiest, "Walsh, James A(nthony)" and "Price, Thomas Frederick," in Anderson, *Biographical Dictionary of Christian Missions*, 715, 548.

77. See Barbara Hendricks, MM, "The Legacy of Mary Josephine Rogers," *International Bulletin of Missionary Research* 21/2 (April 1997): 72-80.

78. For excellent studies of Christianity in Oceania, see Ian Breward, *A History of the Churches in Australasia*, The Oxford History of the Christian Church (Oxford: Oxford University Press, 2001); John Garrett, *To Live among the Stars* (1985), *Footsteps in the Sea* (1992), *Where Nets Were Cast* (1997) (Suva: Institute of Pacific Studies; and Geneva: World Council of Churches).

79. Robert Entenmann, "Christian Virgins in Eighteenth-Century Sichuan," in Daniel H. Bays, *Christianity in China: From the Eighteenth Century to the Present* (Stanford, Calif.: Stanford University Press, 1996), 180-193.

80. See Arnulf Camps, "Policy and Practice in Catholic Missions in Asia," in *Studies in Asian Mission History, 1956-1998* (Leiden: Brill, 2000), 139-154.

81. James Stamoolis, *Eastern Orthodox Mission Theology Today* (Maryknoll, N.Y.: Orbis Books, 1986), 28.

82. See ibid., 28-31; Paul Garrett, "Glukharev, Makarii (Mikhail Yakovlevich)," in Anderson, *Biographical Dictionary of Christian Missions*, 245.

83. Frederick W. Norris, *Christianity: A Short Global History* (Oxford: OneWorld, 2002), 224.

84. See Stamoolis, 33-34; Paul Garrett, "Innocent Veniaminov (Ivan Popov-Veniaminov)," in Anderson, *Biographical Dictionary of Christian Missions*, 320.

85. See Stamoolis, 35-40; Paul Garrett, "Kasatkin, Nikolai (Ivan Dmitriyevich)," in Anderson, *Biographical Dictionary of Christian Missions*, 354-355.

86. See Stamoolis, 41-42.

87. See ibid., 42-43.

88. See ibid., 58-60.

89. See Johannes van den Berg, *Constrained by Jesus' Love* (Kampen: Koch, 1956), 98-102, 156-159, 172-176.

90. Bosch, 287.

91. See van den Berg, 100-101, 157-158, 174-175.

92. Bosch, 289.

93. See ibid.

94. Van den Berg, 193-194.
95. Bosch, 290.
96. Ibid., 291.
97. Hutchinson, 113.
98. Bosch, 295.
99. Hutchinson, 65.
100. James S. Dennis, *Christian Missions and Social Progress: A Sociological Study of Foreign Missions*, vol. 1 (New York: Fleming H. Revell, 1897), 23.
101. Van den Berg, 150.
102. For example, see Lamin Sanneh, "The Yogi and the Commissar: Christian Missions and the African Response," *International Bulletin of Missionary Research* 15/1 (1991): 2-11; idem, "Christian Missions and the Western Guilt Complex," *The Christian Century* 104/11 (1987): 330-334; Walls, *Missionary Movement*, 85-101.
103. Wilbert Shenk, *Changing Frontiers of Mission* (Maryknoll, N.Y.: Orbis Books, 1999), 150.
104. Van den Berg, 159.
105. Bosch, 331.
106. Charles Edward Van Engen, *The Growth of the True Church: An Analysis of the Ecclesiology of Church Growth Theory* (Amsterdam: Radopi, 1981), 272.
107. Bosch, 332.
108. Shenk, *Changing Frontiers of Mission*, 151.
109. Walls, "Missionary Societies," 154.
110. Bosch, 313.
111. James Moorhead, "Searching for the Millennium in America," *Princeton Seminary Bulletin* 9/30, quoted in ibid.
112. See Bosch, 315-319.
113. Ibid., 315.
114. See ibid., 319-325.
115. See Justo González, *A History of Christian Thought,* vol. 3, *From the Protestant Reformation to the Twentieth Century,* rev. ed. (Nashville, Tenn.: Abingdon Press, 1987), 377-382.
116. Bosch, 321.
117. See ibid., 322.
118. See James Patterson, "Robert P. Wilder, 1863-1938: Recruiting Students for World Mission," in Anderson et al., *Mission Legacies,* 71-78.
119. Bosch, 324.
120. Ibid., 325.
121. See Robert, *American Women in Mission*, 411-415.
122. Ibid., 188.
123. Aylward Shorter, *Toward a Theology of Inculturation* (London: Geoffrey Chapman, 1988), 167.
124. See ibid., 168-172.
125. See Karl Müller, SVD, "Janssen, Arnold," in Anderson, *Biographical Dictionary of Christian Missions*, 328.
126. The official theology allowed for baptism not only by water but also by blood and by desire. The third means provided an opening for people being saved outside explicit faith in Christ and membership in the church. The operative theology was found in the plethora of missionary magazines (e.g., *Little Messenger* and *The Field Afar*) and devotional prayer books, and in the personal motivations of missionaries.
127. González, 3:386, 3:410.
128. See ibid., 3:386.
129. Justo González, *Christian Thought Revisited: Three Types of Theology*, rev. ed. (Maryknoll, N.Y.: Orbis Books, 1999), 113.
130. Ibid., 118.

131. Ibid., 115.

132. Bosch, 302; see Hutchinson, 44f.

133. For example, see Neill, *Colonialism*; idem, "Evangelization and Civilization: Protestant Missionary Motivation in the Imperialistic Era," *International Bulletin of Missionary Research* 6 (April 1982): 50-65.

134. See Frances F. Hiebert, "Beyond a Post-Modern Critique of Modern Missions: The Nineteenth Century Revisited," *Missiology: An International Review* 25/3 (July 1997): 268-272; Albert de Jong, "Church, Colonialism and Nationalism in Tanzania," in Frans Wijsen and Peter Nissen, eds., *'Mission Is a Must': Intercultural Theology and the Mission of the Church* (Amsterdam: Rodopi, 2001), 61-77.

135. See Hiebert, 260.

136. Lamin Sanneh, *Translating the Message: The Missionary Impact on Culture* (Maryknoll, N.Y.: Orbis Books, 1989), 1.

137. See ibid., 101-117.

138. Sanneh, "Christian Missions and the Western Guilt Complex," 331.

139. Sanneh, "The Yogi and the Commissar," 2.

140. Peter Berger, *The Sacred Canopy* (Garden City, N.Y.: Doubleday, 1967), 3-51.

141. Walls, *Missionary Movement*, 100-101.

142. For example, see A. Christopher Smith, "A Tale of Many Models: The Missiological Significance of the Serampore Trio," *Missiology: An International Review* 20/4 (October 1992): 479-500; Ralph D. Winter, "William Carey's Major Novelty," *Missiology: An International Review* 22/2 (April 1994): 203-222.

143. See Dwight P. Baker, "William Carey and the Business Model of Mission," in Jonathan J. Bonk, ed., *Between Past and Future: Evangelical Mission Entering the Twenty-first Century* (Pasadena, Calif.: William Carey Library, 2003), 167-202.

144. Shenk, *Changing Frontiers of Mission*, 142.

8. Mission in the Twentieth Century (1919-1991)

1. For excellent background on this period, see Dale T. Irvin and Scott W. Sunquist, *History of the World Christian Movement,* vol. 2, *1453-2000* (Maryknoll, N.Y.: Orbis Books, forthcoming), Part V.

2. David J. Bosch, *Transforming Mission: Paradigm Shifts in Theology of Mission* (Maryknoll, N.Y.: Orbis Books, 1991).

3. Andrew F. Walls, *The Cross-Cultural Process in Christian History* (Maryknoll, N.Y.: Orbis Books, 2002), 64.

4. Timothy Yates, *Christian Mission in the Twentieth Century* (Cambridge: Cambridge University Press, 1994), 163.

5. While the term *Third World* is controversial, we will use it rather than another term, such as *Two-Thirds World,* because theologians from this part of the world in general prefer the "Third World" designation (see Stephen B. Bevans, *Models of Contextual Theology*, rev. and exp. ed. [Maryknoll, N.Y.: Orbis Books, 2002], 145 n. 1).

6. Walls, 64.

7. See Philip Jenkins, *The Next Christendom: The Coming of Global Christianity* (New York: Oxford University Press, 2002), 6-10. While most scholars accept the correctness of Jenkins's demographic facts, Peter Phan, for example, has voiced critique of some aspects of Jenkins's interpretation of the theology of the Third World (see Peter C. Phan, "The Next Christianity," *America* 188/3 [February 3, 2003], 9-11).

8. Robert J. Schreiter, "Changes in Roman Catholic Attitudes toward Proselytism and Mission," in James A. Scherer and Stephen B. Bevans, eds., *New Directions in Mission and Evangelization 2: Theological Foundations* (Maryknoll, N.Y.: Orbis Books, 1994), 113-125.

9. See Willi Henkel, OMI, "Rossum, Willem van," in Gerald Anderson, ed., *Biographical Dictionary of Christian Missions* (New York: Simon and Schuster Macmillan, 1998), 578-579.

10. See Josef Metzler, OMI, "Benedict XV," in Anderson, 54.

11. See Josef Metzler, OMI, "Pius XI, 1857-1939: The Missionary Pope," in Gerald Anderson et al., eds., *Mission Legacies: Biographical Studies of Leaders of the Modern Missionary Movement* (Maryknoll, N.Y.: Orbis Books, 1994), 55-61.

12. See Jean-Paul Wiest, "The Legacy of Vincent Lebbe," *International Bulletin of Missionary Research* 23/1 (January 1999): 33-37.

13. Stephen Neill, *A History of Christian Missions* (London: Penguin Books, 1964), 412.

14. See Angelyn Dries, OSF, *The Missionary Movement in American Catholic History* (Maryknoll, N.Y.: Orbis Books, 1998), 86.

15. See Angelyn Dries, OSF, "King, Clifford J.," in Anderson, 365.

16. See Dries, *Missionary Movement*, 87-92.

17. See ibid., 95-100.

18. See ibid., 104-106; Angelyn Dries, OSF, "Dengel, Anna," in Anderson, 175.

19. Ibid., 304 n. 2.

20. See Jean-Paul Wiest, "Francis X. Ford, M.M., 1892-1952: Maryknoll Pathfinder in China," in Anderson et al., 232-241.

21. Ibid., 238. For a brief description and missiological reflection on this approach by Maryknoll sisters, see Angelyn Dries, "American Catholic 'Woman's Work for Woman' in the Twentieth Century," in Dana L. Robert, ed., *Gospel Bearers, Gender Barriers: Missionary Women in the Twentieth Century* (Maryknoll, N.Y.: Orbis Books, 2002), 138-140.

22. Harold Rigney, SVD, *Four Years in a Red Hell* (Chicago: Henry Regnery Company, 1956).

23. See Robert E. Carbonneau, CP, "'It Can Happen Here': Bishop Cuthbert O'Gara, CP, and the Gospel of Anticommunism in Cold War America," *Mission Studies* 15/2/30 (1998): 119-146.

24. See Dries, *Missionary Movement*, 161-168.

25. See Robert Ellsberg, *All Saints: Daily Reflections on Saints, Prophets, and Witnesses of Our Time* (New York: Crossroad, 1997), 519-521; Sandra Yocum Mize, "Unsentimental Hagiography: Studies on Dorothy Day and the Soul of American Catholicism," *U.S. Catholic Historian* 16/4 (Fall 1998): 36-57.

26. Ellsberg, 519.

27. See Dries, *Missionary Movement*, 27-38. For the most complete history of African American Catholicism in the United States, see Cyprian Davis, *The History of Black Catholics in the United States* (New York: Crossroad, 1990).

28. For an in-depth study of the mission ecclesiology of the founder of the Josephites, see Jamie Theresa Phelps, "The Mission Ecclesiology of John R. Slattery: A Study of an African-American Mission of the Catholic Church in the Nineteenth Century" (Ph.D. diss., Catholic University of America, 1989).

29. See Joseph D. Simon, SVD, "The African American Apostolate and the Society of the Divine Word," in Stephen Bevans and Roger Schroeder, eds., *Word Remembered, Word Proclaimed: Selected Papers from Symposia Celebrating the SVD Centennial in North America* (Nettetal, Germany: Steyler Verlag, 1997), 135-152.

30. See Dries, "American Catholic 'Woman's Work for Woman,'" 136-138. An entire issue of *U.S. Catholic Historian* is devoted to the theme "Grailville: Women in Community, 1944-1994" (*U.S. Catholic Historian* 11/4 [Fall 1993]).

31. See Dries, *Missionary Movement*, 119-120.

32. Ibid., 176.

33. See David A. Kerr, "Foucauld, Charles Eugène de," in Anderson, 219-220.

34. For a very interesting study of Foucauld from a Muslim perspective, see Ali Merad, *Christian Hermit in an Islamic World: A Muslim's View of Charles de Foucauld*, trans. Zoe Hersov (Mahwah, N.J.: Paulist Press, 1999).

35. Although the circumstances are not completely clear, it appears that Foucauld was shot in the process of being robbed.

36. Henri Godin and Yvan Daniel, *France, pays de mission?* (Paris: Editions du Cerf, 1943).

37. See Ernest Brandewie, *When Giants Walked the Earth: The Life and Times of Wilhelm Schmidt, SVD*, Studia Instituti Anthropos 44 (Fribourg, Switzerland: University Press Fribourg, 1990). For a biographical article, see Louis J. Luzbetak, SVD, "Wilhelm Schmidt, S.V.D., 1868-1954: Priest, Linguist, and Ethnologist," in Anderson et al., 475-485.

38. See Heribert Bettscheider, "The Legacy of John Schuette, S.V.D.," trans. Louis J. Luzbetak, *International Bulletin of Missionary Research* 27/1 (January 2003): 29-33.

39. Schreiter, "Changes in Roman Catholic Attitudes toward Proselytism and Mission," 116.

40. Ibid., 117.

41. Ibid., 120.

42. Gerald H. Anderson and Thomas F. Stransky, eds., *Mission Trends No. 1* (New York: Paulist Press; Grand Rapids, Mich.: Eerdmans, 1974), 115-116.

43. See Ivan Illich, "The Seamy Side of Charity," *America* 116 (January 21, 1967), 88-91.

44. See Ronan Hoffman, "The Changing Nature of Mission," *Washington Service* 19/1, special issue (1968), 5-12.

45. The proceedings of this conference were edited by SEDOS and published as *Foundations of Mission Theology*, trans. John Drury (Maryknoll, N.Y.: Orbis Books, 1972).

46. Schreiter, "Changes in Roman Catholic Attitudes toward Proselytism and Mission," 121.

47. The phrase *anonymous Christians* later will be criticized in light of further developments of thought in this area, and Schreiter points out that the phrase does not convey the intent and subtlety of Rahner's discussion (see Robert Schreiter, CPPS, "Rahner, Karl," in Anderson, 556).

48. See Schreiter, "Changes in Roman Catholic Attitudes toward Proselytism and Mission," 121.

49. *Self Study of the Catholic Church in Papua New Guinea* (Goroka, Papua New Guinea: Self Study Secretariate, 1973-1975).

50. The proceedings and final statement of this seminar are found in Mary Motte and Joseph Lang, eds., *Mission in Dialogue* (Maryknoll, N.Y.: Orbis Books, 1982).

51. For excerpts of the following cited statements from bishops' conferences, see James A. Scherer and Stephen B. Bevans, eds., *New Directions in Mission and Evangelization 1: Basic Statements 1974-1991* (Maryknoll, N.Y.: Orbis Books, 1992), 99-111, 128-148.

52. Michael Amaladoss, *Making All Things New: Dialogue, Pluralism, and Evangelization in Asia* (Maryknoll, N.Y.: Orbis Books, 1990); idem, "Pluralism of Religions and the Proclamation of Jesus Christ in the Context of Asia," in Richard C. Sparks, ed., *Proceedings of the Fifty-sixth Annual Convention* (The Catholic Theological Society of America, 2001), 1-14.

53. Gavin D'Costa, *Theology and Religious Pluralism: The Challenge of Other Religions* (London: Basil Blackwell, 1986); idem, *The Meeting of Religions and the Trinity* (Maryknoll, N.Y.: Orbis Books, 2000).

54. Jacques Dupuis, *Toward a Christian Theology of Religious Pluralism* (Maryknoll, N.Y.: Orbis Books, 1997); idem, *Christianity and the Religions: From Confrontation to Dialogue* (Maryknoll, N.Y.: Orbis Books, 2002).

55. Paul F. Knitter, *No Other Name? A Critical Survey of Christian Attitudes toward the World Religions* (Maryknoll, N.Y.: Orbis Books, 1985); idem, *Jesus and the Other Names: Christian Mission and Global Responsibility* (Maryknoll, N.Y.: Orbis Books, 1996).

56. Aloysius Pieris, *Love Meets Wisdom: A Christian Experience of Buddhism* (Maryknoll, N.Y.: Orbis Books, 1988); idem, *An Asian Theology of Liberation* (Maryknoll, N.Y.: Orbis Books, 1988).

57. For an excellent commentary and the complete text of both *Dialogue and Proclamation* and *Redemptoris Missio*, see William Burrows, ed., *Redemption and Dialogue: Reading Redemptoris Missio and Dialogue and Proclamation* (Maryknoll, N.Y.: Orbis Books, 1993).

58. For a list of (and number of missionaries sent by) such lay organizations in the United States, see *U.S. Catholic Mission Handbook 2000* (Washington, D.C.: USCMA, 2000), 20-22. For a more extensive listing including additional volunteer avenues, see *Response: Directory of Volunteer Opportunities*, annual publication by the Catholic Network of Volunteer Service (Washington, D.C.). Available on the CNVS website.

59. For a listing of missionary institutes, see *Annuario Pontificio* (Rome: Polyglot Press, 2001), 1280-1286. For a history of and reflection on Asian Catholic mission societies, see James H. Kroeger, *Asia-Church in Mission* (Quezon City, Philippines: Claretian Publications, 1999).

60. See Hans-Werner Gensichen, "Graul, Karl," in Anderson, 257.

61. For Bruno Gutmann, see Ernst Jäschke, "Bruno Gutmann, 1876-1966: Building on Clan, Neighborhood, and Age Groups," in Anderson et al., 173-180. For Christian Keysser, see Yates, 44-49.

62. Yates, 42.

63. Later on, from a different perspective, the principal critic of the *Volkskirche* model would be Johannes Hoekendijk. Particularly in the German edition of his dissertation with an added appendix, Hoekendijk developed his argument that the church usually prefers *Volk* rather than *Gesellschaft* (society) as its sociological reference point, that is, tradition rather than revolution, and therefore the church misses the opportunity to learn from the worldwide revolutionary ferment (see *Kirche und Volk in der deutschen Missionswissenschaft* [Munich: Chr. Kaiser Verlag, 1967]).

64. Roland Allen's most widely known work is *Missionary Methods: St. Paul's or Ours?* (London: Robert Scott, 1912). For a biographical article, see Charles Henry Long and Anne Rowthorn, "Roland Allen, 1868-1947: Missionary Methods: St. Paul's or Ours?" in Anderson et al., 383-390.

65. See Lydia Huffman Hoyle, "Daniel Johnson Fleming, 1877-1969: A Large Heart in the Narrow Way," in Anderson et al., 486-493.

66. Vincent Donovan, *Christianity Re-discovered* (Maryknoll, N.Y.: Orbis Books, 1978).

67. Yates, 59.

68. See Leroy S. Rouner, "Hocking, William Ernest," in Anderson, 295-296.

69. W. E. Hocking, ed., *Rethinking Missions: A Laymen's Inquiry after One Hundred Years* (New York: Harper & Brothers, 1932).

70. Yates, 93.

71. See ibid., 94-124.

72. See Norman E. Thomas, "Junod, Henri Alexandre," in Anderson, 347-348.

73. See Eric Sharpe, "J. N. Farquhar, 1861-1929: Presenting Christ as the Crown of Hinduism," in Anderson et al., 290-296.

74. See Hans-Werner Gensichen, "Richter, Julius," in Anderson, 569.

75. See Gerold Schwarz, "Karl Hartenstein, 1894-1952: Mission with a Focus on 'The End,'" in Anderson et al., 591-601.

76. See Libertus A. Hoedemaker, "Hendrik Kraemer, 1888-1965: Biblical Realism Applied to Mission," in Anderson et al., 508-515.

77. Hendrik Kraemer, *The Christian Message in a Non-Christian World* (London: Edinburgh House Press, 1938).

78. Yates, 116.

79. See Eric Sharpe, "C. F. Andrews, 1871-1940: The Most Trusted Englishman in India," in Anderson et al., 316-323.

80. Yates, 74.

81. One of Jones's most widely known works is *The Christ of the Indian Road* (New York: Abingdon Press, 1925). For a biographical article, see Richard W. Taylor, "E. Stanley Jones, 1884-1973: Following the Christ of the Indian Road," in Anderson et al., 339-347.

82. See Susan Billington Harper, *In the Shadow of the Mahatma: Bishop V. S. Azariah and the Travails of Christianity in British India* (Grand Rapids, Mich.: Eerdmans, 2000). For a

biographical article, see Carol Graham, "V. S. Azariah, 1874-1945: Exponent of Indigenous Mission and Church Unity," in Anderson et al., *Mission Legacies*, 324-329.

83. See Dorothy Clark Wilson, "Ida S. Scudder, 1870-1960: Life and Health for Women in India," in Anderson et al., 307-315.

84. Robert, *Gospel Bearers, Gender Barriers*, 12.

85. See Creighton Lacy, "D. T. Niles, 1908-1970: Evangelism, the Work of Disrupting People's Lives," in Anderson et al., 362-370.

86. See F. W. Dillistone, "Max Warren, 1904-1977: Disciplined Intercession That Embraced the World," in Anderson et al., 616-623. For a fine, recent study of Warren's letters around this theme, see Graham Kings, *Christianity Connected: Hindus, Muslims and the World in the Letters of Max Warren and Roger Hooker*, Mission 31 (Zoetermeer, The Netherlands: Boekencentrum, 2002).

87. For example, see Warren's introduction to John V. Taylor, *The Primal Vision: Christian Presence amid African Religion* (Philadelphia: Fortress Press, 1963), 10.

88. Of Neill's many works, two particularly well-known ones are *Creative Tension* (London: Edinburgh House Press, 1959) and *A History of Christian Missions*. For a biographical article, see Christopher Lamb, "Stephen Neill, 1900-1984: Unafraid to Ask Ultimate Questions," in Anderson et al., 445-451.

89. See Yates, 145-149.

90. One of Cragg's most widely known works is *Sandals at the Mosque: Christian Presence amid Islam* (New York: Oxford University Press, 1959). For a biographical article, see David A. Kerr, "Cragg, Albert Kenneth," in Anderson, 157.

91. Kerr, 157; see also Yates, 150-155.

92. See Libertus A. Hoedemaker, "The Legacy of J. C. Hoekendijk," *International Bulletin of Missionary Research* 19/4 (October 1995): 166-170.

93. Neill, *A History of Christian Missions,* 572.

94. James A. Scherer, *Gospel, Church, and Kingdom: Comparative Studies in World Mission Theology* (Minneapolis: Augsburg Press, 1987), 167.

95. Yates, 195-196.

96. See George G. Hunter, III, "Donald A. McGavran, 1897-1990: Standing at the Sunrise of Missions," in Anderson et al., 516-522.

97. Donald McGavran, "Will Uppsala Betray the Two Billion?" *Church Growth Bulletin* 4/5 (May 1968): 1.

98. Scherer, 167.

99. Richard V. Pierard, "Graham, William ('Billy') Franklin," in Anderson, 255.

100. For a concise presentation of the mission theology of the *Covenant*, see Scherer, 167-177. For the entire statement, see Scherer and Bevans, *New Directions in Mission and Evangelization 1*, 253-259.

101. Graham Kings, "Stott, John R(obert) W(almsley)," in Anderson, 644.

102. See Jim Reapsome, "Lausanne Movement," in A. Scott Moreau, gen. ed., *Evangelical Dictionary of World Missions* (Grand Rapids, Mich.: Baker Books, 2000), 563-564.

103. See David M. Howard, "World Evangelical Fellowship," in Moreau, 1027-1028.

104. For the texts of these consultations, with particular relevance for mission, see Scherer and Bevans, *New Directions in Mission and Evangelization 1*, 268-273, 276-291, 306-312.

105. See C. Peter Wagner, "Church Growth Movement," in Moreau, 199-200.

106. Donald McGavran, *The Bridges of God: A Study in the Strategy of Missions* (New York: Friendship Press, 1955).

107. See Scherer, 177-178; Yates, 217-218.

108. See Scherer, 185-187; see also J. W. Nyquist, "Parachurch Agencies and Mission," in Moreau, *Evangelical Dictionary of World Missions*, 722-723.

109. For commentary on the mission theology of these Evangelical consultations after the first Lausanne conference, see ibid., 177-195. For the excerpts or complete texts of these documents, see Scherer and Bevans, *New Directions in Mission and Evangelization 1*, 260-291.

110. For the complete text of the *Manila Manifesto*, see Scherer and Bevans, *New Directions in Mission and Evangelization 1*, 292-305.

111. Yates, 211. For detailed personnel data, see Robert T. Coote, "The Uneven Growth of Conservative Evangelical Missions," *International Bulletin of Missionary Research* 4/3 (July 1982): 118-123.

112. Scherer, 124.

113. Ibid., 126.

114. Scherer and Bevans, *New Directions in Mission and Evangelization 1*, 36. For the entire statement, see 36-51.

115. For brief commentary and excerpts or complete texts, see ibid., 52-88.

116. Bosch, 482.

117. For commentary, see Scherer, 159-163.

118. Ibid., 163.

119. Of Newbigin's many writings, his most well-known works include *The Open Secret: Sketches for a Missionary Theology* (Grand Rapids, Mich.: Eerdmans, 1978); *Foolishness to the Greeks: The Gospel and Western Culture* (London: SPCK, 1986); and *The Gospel in a Pluralist Society* (Geneva: WCC Publications; Grand Rapids, Mich.: Eerdmans, 1989). For more on Newbigin, see Michael W. Goheen, *"As the Father Has Sent Me, I Am Sending You": J. E. Lesslie Newbigin's Missionary Ecclesiology* (Zoetermeer, The Netherlands: Boekencentrum, 2001); George R. Hunsberger, *Bearing the Witness of the Spirit: Lesslie Newbigin's Theology of Cultural Plurality* (Grand Rapids, Mich.: Eerdmans, 1998); and Geoffrey Wainwright, *Lesslie Newbigin: A Theological Life* (New York: Oxford University Press, 2000). For a brief biographical article, see Charles C. West, "Newbigin, J(ames) E(dward) Lesslie," in Anderson, 491.

120. Yates, 243; see 239-244.

121. James J. Stamoolis, *Eastern Orthodox Mission Theology Today* (Maryknoll, N.Y.: Orbis Books, 1986), 74.

122. See Luke A. Veronis, "Anastasios Yannoulatos: Modern-Day Apostle," *International Bulletin of Missionary Research* 19/3 (July, 1995): 122-128.

123. Stamoolis, 76.

124. See Scherer and Bevans, *New Directions in Mission and Evangelization 1*, xv.

125. For the complete text of "Go Forth in Peace," see ibid., 203-231.

126. For the complete texts of these 1988 and 1990 documents, see ibid., 232-250.

127. Although this movement often is called *African Independent Churches*, we use the term *African Initiated Churches*, which they have used for themselves since 1970.

128. See Matthews A. Ojo, "Agbebi, Mojola (David Brown Vincent)," in Anderson, 7.

129. See Andrew F. Walls, *The Missionary Movement in Christian History: Studies in the Transmission of the Faith* (Maryknoll, N.Y.: Orbis Books, 1996), 87-88. For a broader description of this phase in the movement, see Adrian Hastings, *The Church in Africa, 1450-1950* (Oxford, Great Britain: Clarendon Press, 1994), 504-525.

130. Werner Ustorf, "Kimbangu, Simon," in Anderson, 364-365.

131. David B. Barrett, "African Initiated Church Movement," in Moreau, 43.

132. Walls, *Missionary Movement*, 116.

133. Lamin Sanneh, *West African Christianity: The Religious Impact* (Maryknoll, N.Y.: Orbis Books, 1983), 180.

134. Walls, *Missionary Movement*, 118.

135. Barrett, 44.

136. See Roger Schroeder, "Melanesian Brotherhood," in Robert Benedetto, gen. ed., *New Westminster Dictionary of Church History* (Louisville, Ky.: Westminster John Knox Press, forthcoming).

137. Gary Trompf, "Eto, Silas," in Anderson, 202.

138. See Roger Schroeder, "Cargo Cults," in Benedetto.

139. See Edmond Tang and Jean-Paul Wiest, eds., *The Catholic Church in Modern China: Perspectives* (Maryknoll, N.Y.: Orbis Books, 1993); Alan Hunter and Kim-Kwong Chan, *Protestantism in Contemporary China* (Cambridge: Cambridge University Press, 1993).

140. See Che Bin Tan, "Chinese House Church Movement," in Moreau, 180; Hunter and Chan, 81-88.

141. Hunter and Chan, 81.

142. See Tony Lambert, "Counting Christians in China: A Cautionary Report," *International Bulletin of Missionary Research* 27/1 (2003): 6-10.

143. See Stanley M. Burgess, "Charismatic Movements," in Scott W. Sunquist et al., eds., *A Dictionary of Asian Christianity* (Grand Rapids, Mich.; Cambridge, U.K.: Eerdmans, 2001), 133.

144. Roger E. Hedlund, "Indian Instituted Churches: Indigenous Christianity Indian Style," *Mission Studies* 16/1/31 (1999): 28. Jeffrey Mann points out that the church will not release any membership information and that estimates of membership are from three to ten million members worldwide (see Jeffrey Mann, "Iglesia ni Cristo (INC)," in Sunquist, 360).

145. Mann, 360.

146. See Leonardo N. Mercado, "Notes on Christ and Local Community in Philippine Context," *Verbum SVD* 21/3 and 4 (1980): 303-315. Hilario Moncado founded the Filipino Federation of America to protest exploited Filipino *sacadas* or farm workers in the United States, and it eventually grew into the Equifrilibricum World Religion, Inc., whose members live a very strict moral life, eschewing dancing, smoking, gambling and drinking liquor. Another indigenous group, the Iglesia Watawat ng Lahi, has its headquarters in a barrio of Calamba in the province of Laguna. They are headed by a group of fifteen Philippine national heroes, the foremost of which is Philippine writer and martyr José Rizal, who speaks through the community's board of directors. In 1965 Ruben Ecleo incorporated the Philippine Benevolent Missionary Association, a cult-like organization that has its headquarters on Dinagat Island in the Mindanao province of Surigao del Norte. In 2002, however, Ecleo was arrested and accused of murdering his third wife and a number of members of her family, and this has obviously caused great disillusionment among his followers.

147. Hedlund, 37.

148. Ibid., 33-34.

149. Ibid., 34.

150. Ibid., 34-35.

151. Ibid., 36.

152. Ibid., 37. For more information on Indian indigenous Christianity, see Roger E. Hedlund, ed., *Christianity Is Indian: The Emergence of an Indigenous Community* (Delhi: ISPCK, 2001).

153. Mark R. Mullins, *Christianity Made in Japan: A Study of Indigenous Movements* (Honolulu: University of Hawaii Press, 1998), 96.

154. Ibid., 97.

155. Ibid., 101.

156. Ibid., 102.

157. Quoted in Ibid., 107.

158. Ibid., 108.

159. Ibid., 110-111.

160. Ibid., 115.

161. This is the thesis in particular of Vinson Synan, *The Holiness-Pentecostal Tradition: Charismatic Movements in the Twentieth* Century (Grand Rapids, Mich.: Eerdmans, 1997). For an excellent concise description, see Gary B. McGee, "Pentecostal Movement," in Moreau, 739-742.

162. Gary B. McGee, "Parham, Charles Fox," in Anderson, 515-516.

163. Gary B. McGee, "Seymour, William Joseph," in Anderson, 613-614. See also Harvey Cox, *Fire from Heaven: The Rise of Pentecostal Spirituality and the Reshaping of Religion in the Twenty-first Century* (Cambridge, Mass.: Da Capo Press, 1995), 45-65; and Synan, 84-106.

164. Judith Lingenfelter, "McPherson, Aimee Semple," in Moreau, 608.

165. Roberta R. King, "Trasher, Lillian," in Moreau, 969.

166. Gary B. McGee, "Pentecostal Missions," in Moreau, 738-739.

167. Ibid., 738.

168. Gary B. McGee, "Pentecostalism," in Sunquist et al., 647.

169. Ibid., 648; see also Gary B. McGee, "Abrams, Minnie F." and "Ramabai Dongre Medhavi (Pandita Ramabai Sarasvati)," in Anderson, 3, 557. For an excellent summary and basic bibliography on Pentecostalism in Asia, see ibid., 646-650. See also Synan, 136.

170. Kenneth D. Gill, "Charismatic Missions," in Moreau, 173-175. See Synan, 129-142; David Martin, *Pentecostalism: The World Their Parish* (Oxford: Blackwell Publishers, 2002); and Cox, 161-162.

171. See Burgess, 132; and Peter Wagner, "A Third Wave?" *Pastoral Renewal* 8/1 (July-August 1983), 1-5.

172. Kwabena Asamoah-Gyadu, "Pentecostalism in Africa and the Changing Face of Christian Mission: Pentecostal/Charismatic Renewal Movements in Ghana," *Mission Studies* 19/2/38 (2002): 14-39.

173. For example, see Ogbu Kalu, "Pentecostal and Charismatic Reshaping of the African Religious Landscape in the 1990s," *Mission Studies* 20/1/39 (2003): 84-111.

174. For example, see Allan Anderson, "Diversity in the Definition of 'Pentecostal/Charismatic' and Its Ecumenical Implications," *Mission Studies* 19/2/38 (2002): 40-55.

175. See Jenkins, 63-66.

176. For an excellent article on this development, see James A. Scherer, "Missiology as a Discipline and What It Includes," in Scherer and Bevans, *New Directions in Mission and Evangelization 2*, 173-187. For a more detailed and comprehensive study, see Jan A. B. Jongeneel, *Philosophy, Science, and Theology of Mission in the Nineteenth and Twentieth Centuries*, 2 vols. (Frankfurt am Main: Peter Lang, 1995, 1997); J. Verkuyl, *Contemporary Missiology: An Introduction,* trans. and ed. Dale Cooper (Grand Rapids, Mich.: Eerdmans, 1978); and *Missiology: An International Review* 24/1 (January 1996), an entire issue that addresses the theme "Mission Studies: Taking Stock, Charting the Course."

177. See Yates, 127.

178. Ibid., 71, 91.

179. See Dupuis, *Christianity and the Religions*, 87-95.

180. Justo L. González, *Christian Thought Revisited: Three Types of Theology*, rev. ed. (Maryknoll, N.Y.: Orbis Books, 1999), 125-145.

181. Jenkins, 2.

182. Ibid., 8.

183. See ibid., 69-72. For an excellent description of these developments within the Catholic Church in Asia, see Thomas C. Fox, *Pentecost in Asia: A New Way of Being Church* (Maryknoll, N.Y.: Orbis Books, 2002).

184. Synan, 287; Cox, 219-226. Cox says that the church hoped to reach a membership of one million by the year 2000. At this writing we have not been able to verify that this number has been reached. Some critics point out, however, that the numbers are inflated because not everyone continues to attend services regularly.

Part III. Introduction

1. Henri Godin and Yvan Daniel, *France, pays de mission?* (Paris: Editions du Cerf, 1943); James A. Scherer, *Missionary Go Home: A Reappraisal of the Christian World Mission* (Englewood Cliffs, N.J.: Prentice-Hall, 1964).

2. Technically speaking, only the Roman Catholic tradition has official, "magisterial" documents. But the Conciliar Protestant, Orthodox and Evangelical traditions do possess important, quasi-official statements that recommend themselves to the members of their various bodies because of their innate wisdom and as products of a consensus of respected representatives of their traditions. On the "weight" of such statements, see James A. Scherer and Stephen B. Bevans, "Introduction and Overview: Statements on Mission and Evangelization, 1974-1991," in James A. Scherer and Stephen B. Bevans, eds., *New Directions in Mission and Evangelization 1: Basic Statements 1974-1991* (Maryknoll, N.Y.: Orbis Books, 1992), ix-xx.

3. See Philip Jenkins, "The Next Christianity," *Atlantic Monthly* 290/3 (October 2002), 53-72; and idem, *The Next Christendom: The Coming of Global Christianity* (New York: Oxford University Press, 2002).

4. Lesslie Newbigin, *Trinitarian Faith and Today's Mission* (Richmond, Va.: John Knox Press, 1964), 78. Newbigin is quoting the final statement of the IMC's Ghana assembly of 1957/1958. The actual quotation is this: "The Christian world mission is Christ's not ours" (see Norman Thomas, ed., *Classic Texts in Mission and World Christianity* [Maryknoll, N.Y.: Orbis Books, 1995], 113-114).

5. David J. Bosch, *Transforming Mission: Paradigm Shifts in Theology of Mission* (Maryknoll, N.Y.: Orbis Books, 1991), 489.

9. Mission as Participation in the Mission of the Triune God *(Missio Dei)*

1. Pius X, "Vehementer Nos" (February 11, 1906), quoted in Michael A. Fahey, "Church," in Francis Schüssler Fiorenza and John Galvin, eds., *Systematic Theology: Roman Catholic Perspectives* (Minneapolis, Minn.: Fortress Press, 1991), 32.

2. Michel Philipon, "La Trés Sainte Trinité et L'Église," in G. Barauna, ed., *L'Église de Vatican II*, vol. 2, Unam Sanctam 51b (Paris: Les Éditions du Cerf, 1966), 296.

3. Karl Müller, *Mission Theology: An Introduction* (Nettetal, Germany: Steyler Verlag, 1987), 44. Though the document itself was indeed put together in haste, it was the product of a long development. See Suso Brechter, "Decree on the Church's Missionary Activity," in Herbert Vorgrimler, ed., *Commentary on the Documents of Vatican II*, vol. 4 (New York: Herder and Herder; Montreal: Palm Publishers, 1969), 87-111.

4. Yves Congar, "Principes Doctrinaux (nos. 2 à 9)," in Johannes Schütte, ed., *Vatican II: L'Activité Missionaire de l'Église*, Unam Sanctam 67 (Paris: Les Éditions du Cerf, 1967), 185.

5. On the *exitus/reditus* scheme, see James A. Weisheipl, *Friar Thomas D'Acquino: His Life, Thought and Works* (Garden City, N.Y.: Doubleday, 1974), 70-71; see also Bernard Lonergan, *Divinarum Personarum: Conceptionem Analogicam* (Rome: Gregorian University Press, 1959), 223.

6. Eugene L. Smith, "'Response' to *Ad Gentes*," in Walter M. Abbott, ed., *The Documents of Vatican II* (New York: Guild Press, America Press, Association Press, 1966), 631.

7. Orthodox Advisory Group to the WCC-CWME, "Go Forth in Peace: Orthodox Perspectives on Mission," in James A. Scherer and Stephen B. Bevans, eds., *New Directions in Mission and Evangelization 1: Basic Statements 1974-1991* (Maryknoll, N.Y.: Orbis Books, 1992), 203.

8. Ibid., 204.

9. "Final Report of CWME Orthodox Advisory Group" (Boston, 1990), 5, in Scherer and Bevans, 243.

10. "Go Forth in Peace," 204.

11. Ibid., 205.

12. "Final Report of CWME Consultation of Eastern Orthodox and Oriental Orthodox Churches" (Neapolis, Greece, 1988), in Scherer and Bevans, 235.

13. "Go Forth in Peace," 221.

14. Ibid., 226.

15. Congar, 186.

16. André Rétif, "Trinité et Mission d'aprés Bérulle," *Neue Zeitschrift für Missionswissenschaft* 13 (1957): 1-8.

17. Lesslie Newbigin, *The Relevance of Trinitarian Doctrine for Today's Mission* (London: Edinburgh Press, 1963). The book is perhaps better known today as *Trinitarian Faith and Today's Mission* (Richmond, Va.: John Knox Press, 1964).

18. Joseph Masson, *L'Attività missionaria della chiesa* (Torino: Elle Di Ci, 1967), 29. Masson cites many of the theologians that we discuss in the following paragraphs, many of whom are the architects of the theology of *missio Dei* that found its full expression at the Willingen conference in 1952.

19. Norman Thomas, Introduction to the extract from Barth's Brandenburg paper in *Classic Texts in Mission and World Christianity*, ed. Norman Thomas (Maryknoll, N.Y.: Orbis Books, 1994), 104.

20. See Gerold Schwarz, "Karl Hartenstein, 1894-1952, Missions with a Focus on 'The End,'" in Gerald Anderson et al., eds., *Mission Legacies: Biographical Studies of Leaders of the Modern Missionary Movement* (Maryknoll, N.Y.: Orbis Books, 1994), 591-601; Jürgen Schuster, "Karl Hartenstein: Mission with a Focus on the End," *Mission Studies* 19/1/37 (2002): 53-82.

21. The Willingen document, quoted in Thomas, 103. Thomas substituted "humanity" for "men" (in the original) for the sake of horizontal inclusivity.

22. David J. Bosch, *Transforming Mission: Paradigm Shifts in Theology of Mission* (Maryknoll, N.Y.: Orbis Books, 1991), 390.

23. Ibid.

24. The Willingen document, quoted in Thomas, 104. For the terms *purpose, life* and *structure,* see Thomas, 103.

25. See Bosch, 392.

26. Roger Bassham, *Mission Theology: 1948-1975. Years of Worldwide Creative Tension. Ecumencial, Evangelical and Roman Catholic* (Pasadena, Calif.: William Carey Library, 1979), 81. See also James A. Scherer, *Gospel, Church, and Kingdom: Comparative Studies in World Mission Theology* (Minneapolis, Minn.: Augsburg, 1987), 119-121.

27. Karl Rahner, *The Trinity* (New York: Herder and Herder, 1970), 10-11. The German original appears as Chapter 5, "Die dreifaltige Gott als transzendeter Urgrund der Heilsgeschichte," in Johannes Feiner and Magnus Löhrer, eds., *Mysterium Salutis: Grundriss heilsgeschtlicher Dogmatik* (Einsiedeln, Switzerland: Benzinger Verlag, 1967).

28. Rahner, *The Trinity,* 22. The italics are Rahner's.

29. Eberhard Jüngel, *The Doctrine of the Trinity: God's Being Is in Becoming* (Grand Rapids, Mich.: Eerdmans, 1976). See Ted Peters, *God as Trinity: Relationality and Temporality in Divine Life* (Louisville, Ky.: Westminster/John Knox Press, 1993), 90-96.

30. Jürgen Moltmann, *The Crucified God* (New York: Harper & Row, 1974); idem, *The Trinity and the Kingdom: The Doctrine of God* (New York: Harper & Row, 1981); idem, *The Church in the Power of the Spirit* (Minneapolis, Minn.: Fortress Press, 1993; first English edition, 1977), esp. 10-11, 64.

31. Leonardo Boff, *Trinity and Society* (Maryknoll, N.Y.: Orbis Books, 1988).

32. Catherine Mowry LaCugna, *God for Us: The Trinity and Christian Life* (San Francisco: HarperSanFrancisco, 1991), 225, 401-402.

33. Elizabeth A. Johnson, *She Who Is: The Mystery of God in Feminist Discourse* (New York: Crossroad, 1992), 223.

34. Even in this note we can only mention a few: Michael Downey, *Altogether Gift: A Trinitarian Spirituality* (Maryknoll, N.Y.: Orbis Books, 2000); Patricia A. Fox, *God as Communion: John Zizioulas, Elizabeth Johnson, and the Retrieval of the Symbol of the Triune God* (Collegeville, Minn.: The Liturgical Press, 2001); Anne Hunt, *The Trinity and the Paschal Mystery: A Development in Recent Catholic Theology* (Collegeville, Minn.: The Liturgical Press, 1997); David Coffey, *Deus Trinitas: The Doctrine of the Triune God* (New York: Oxford University Press, 1999); S. Mark Heim, *The Depth of the Riches: A Trinitarian Theology of Religious Ends* (Grand Rapids, Mich.: Eerdmans, 2001). See also Catherine M. LaCugna, "Philosophers and Theologians on the Trinity," *Modern Theology* 2/3 (April 1986): 169-181; and idem, "Current Trends in Trinitarian Theology," *Religious Study Review* 13/2 (April 1987): 141-147; David S. Cunningham, "Trinitarian Theology since 1990," *Reviews in Religion and Theology*, no. 4 (November 1995): 8-16; and idem, "What's [Not] New in Trinitiarian Theology," *Reviews in Religion and Theology,* no. 1 (February 1997): 14-20.

35. David S. Cunningham, *These Three Are One: The Practice of Trinitarian Theology* (Malden, Mass.: Blackwell Publishers, 1998).

36. Stephen Bevans, "Inculturation and SVD Mission: Theological Foundations," *Verbum SVD* 42/3 (2001): 259-281.

37. Anthony J. Gittins, "Mission: What's It Got to Do with Me?" *The Living Light* 34/3 (Spring 1998): 8, 11.

38. Robert J. Schreiter, "Epilogue: Mission in the Third Millennium," in Robert J. Schreiter, ed., *Mission in the Third Millennium* (Maryknoll, N.Y.: Orbis Books, 2001), 155-156.

39. Robert J. Schreiter, "Mission for the Twenty-First Century: A Catholic Perspective," in Stephen Bevans and Roger Schroeder, eds., *Mission for the Twenty-First Century* (Chicago: CCGM Publications, 2001), 34.

40. Ibid., 36-39.

41. Stephen B. Bevans, "God Inside Out: Toward a Missionary Theology of the Holy Spirit," *International Bulletin of Missionary Research* 22/3 (July 1998): 102.

42. M. Thomas Tangaraj, *The Common Task: A Theology of Christian Mission* (Nashville, Tenn.: Abingdon Press, 1999).

43. Wilbert R. Shenk, *Changing Frontiers of Mission* (Maryknoll, N.Y.: Orbis Books, 1999), 7, 19.

44. J. Andrew Kirk, *What Is Mission?: Theological Explorations* (London: Darton, Longman and Todd, 1999), 28, 30.

45. Darrell L. Guder, *The Continuing Conversion of the Church* (Grand Rapids, Mich.: Eerdmans, 2000), 47-48; see also Craig van Gelder, *The Essence of the Church: A Community Created by the Spirit* (Grand Rapids, Mich.: Baker Books, 2000), 27-44.

46. Darrell L. Guder, ed., *Missional Church: A Vision for the Sending of the Church in North America* (Grand Rapids, Mich.: Eerdmans, 1998), esp. 81-82. In many ways, this volume could be discussed under the second heading of this chapter, since one finds here a strong emphasis on the reign of God as the reason for the church's missionary existence. We have chosen to mention it here, if only briefly, because The Gospel and Our Culture Network has as its principal inspiration the life and work of Bishop Lesslie Newbigin, who very clearly has developed a trinitarian approach to mission. See Newbigin, *Trinitarian Faith and Today's Mission*; and idem, *The Open Secret: An Introduction to the Theology of Mission* (Grand Rapids, Mich.: Eerdmans, 1995; originally published in 1978).

47. Timothy Ware, *The Orthodox Church* (Baltimore, Md.: Penguin Books, 1963), 216.

48. Vladimir Lossky, *The Mystical Theology of the Eastern Church* (Crestwood, N.Y.: St. Vladimir's Seminary Press, 1976; originally published in 1944); John Meyendorf, *Trinitarian Theology East and West* (Brookline, Mass.: Holy Cross Orthodox Press, 1977); John Zizioulas, *Being as Communion* (Crestwood, N.Y.: St. Vladimir's Seminary Press, 1985).

49. Anastasios of Androussa, "Thy Will Be Done: Mission in Christ's Way," in James A. Scherer and Stephen B. Bevans, *New Directions in Mission and Evangelization 2: Theological Foundations* (Maryknoll, N.Y.: Orbis Books, 1994), 29, 37.

50. We put *definition* in quotation marks because, as noted theologian Sergius Bulgakov has insisted, "there can . . . be no satisfactory and complete *definition* of the Church. 'Come and see'—one recognizes the Church only by experience, by grace, by participation in its life" (Sergius Bulgakov, *The Orthodox Church* [London: Centenary Press, 1935], 12, quoted in James J. Stamoolis, *Eastern Orthodox Mission Theology Today* [Maryknoll, N.Y.: Orbis Books, 1986], 103).

51. Stamoolis, 123.

52. Vsevolod Spiller, "Missionary Aims and the Russian Ordthox Church," *International Review of Mission* 52 (1963): 197-198, quoted in Stamoolis, 116.

53. See Ware, 269-314; Alexander Schmemann, "The Missionary Imperative in the Orthodox Tradition," in Gerald H. Anderson, ed., *The Theology of the Christian Mission* (Nashville, Tenn.: Abingdon Press, 1961), 250-257; Calvin E. Shenk, "The Ethiopian Orthodox Church's Understanding of Mission," *Mission Studies* 4/1/7 (1987): 4-20; Ion Bria, "Dynamics of Liturgy in Mission," *International Review of Mission* 82 (1993): 317-325; Ion Bria, "The Liturgy after the Liturgy," *International Review of Mission* 67 (1978): 86-90.

54. See Bria, "The Liturgy after the Liturgy."

55. Stamoolis, 99.

56. Schmemann, 256.

57. Cunningham, *These Three Are One*, 1 (and again without reference on p. 3) and 15. The quotation from Ludwig Wittgenstein is from *Culture and Value*, ed. G. H. Von Wright and Heikki Nyman (Chicago: The University of Chicago Press, 1980), 85.

58. Heim, esp. 167-207.

59. Irenaeus, *Against Heresies*, 4, *prol*. See Justo L. González, *Christian Thought Revisited: Three Types of Theology* (Maryknoll, N.Y.: Orbis Books, 1999), 151-152 n. 28.

60. See Bevans, "God Inside Out," 102-103. For an introduction to Spirit Christology, see Ralph del Colle, *Jesus and the Spirit: Spirit Christology in Trinitarian Perspective* (Oxford: Oxford University Press, 1994).

61. Michael James Oleksa, "Orthodox Missiological Education for the Twenty-First Century," in J. Dudley Woodberry, Charles van Engen and Edgar J. Elliston, eds., *Missiological Education for the Twenty-first Century: The Book, the Circle and the Sandals* (Maryknoll, N.Y.: Orbis Books, 1996), 86.

62. Newbigin, *Trinitarian Faith and Today's Mission*, 49.

63. Elias Vulgarakis, "Mission and Unity from a Theological Point of View," *Prorefthendes* 7 (1965): 32, quoted in Stamoolis, 112. See also Heim, 151, where he discusses Raimon Panikkar's idea of the cross in the Trinity.

64. See Anne Hunt, *The Trinity and the Paschal Mystery: A Development in Recent Catholic Theology* (Collegeville, Minn.: The Liturgical Press, 1997).

65. Cunningham, *These Three Are One*, 8.

66. Moltmann, *The Church in the Power of the Spirit*, 10.

67. Newbigin, *Trinitarian Faith and Today's Mission*, 32.

68. Stephen Bevans, "The Service of Ordering: Reflections on the Identity of the Priest," *Emmanuel* 101/7 (September 1995): 397-406; idem, "Entrusted to Us: Theses on Christian Ministry," *Emmanuel* 106/1 and 2 (January-February and March 2000): 15-25, 83-93.

69. Thomas Aquinas, quoted in Thomas F. O'Meara, *Thomas Aquinas, Theologian* (Notre Dame, Ind.: University of Notre Dame Press, 1997), 150. See also 3 Sent. D. 13, q. 1, a. 1, ad 5: "The light of glory [in heaven] is the same as grace in its consummate stage; [it is] the same grace energizing us in the acts of our life" (quoted in O'Meara, 150).

70. Heim, 103.

71. Schmemann, 255.

72. Ibid.

73. Heim, 49-77.

74. Robert Jensen, *Systematic Theology,* vol. 2, *The Works of God* (Oxford: Oxford University Press, 1999), 369. The quotation from Edwards is from *Miscellanies*, 188.

75. Lesslie Newbigin, *The Gospel in a Pluralist Society* (Grand Rapids, Mich.: Eerdmans, 1989), 80-88.

76. Heim, 67-74.

77. Bevans, "Inculturation and SVD Mission," 260-261.

78. Ibid., 272.

79. This is a point made forcefully by Andrew Walls, Lamin Sanneh and S. Mark Heim. See Andrew F. Walls, *The Missionary Movement in Christian History: Studies in the Transmission of Faith* (Maryknoll, N.Y.: Orbis Books, 1996), xviii; Lamin Sanneh, *Translating the Message: The Missionary Impact on Culture* (Maryknoll, N.Y.: Orbis Books, 1989); Heim, 136-148.

80. Bevans, "Inculturation and SVD Mission," 275.

81. Ibid., 272.

82. Bosch, 392.

83. See RM 21-30; see also F. Dale Bruner's concerns in "The *Son* Is God Inside Out: A Response to Stephen B. Bevans, S.V.D," *International Bulletin of Missionary Research* 22/3 (July 1998): 106-108.

10. Mission as Liberating Service of the Reign of God

1. This is suggested by Antonio M. Pernia, "Mission for the Twenty-First Century: An SVD Perspective," in Stephen Bevans and Roger Schroeder, eds., *Mission for the Twenty-First Century* (Chicago: CCGM Publications, 2001), 11; and by Jozef Cardinal Tomko, "Mission for the Twenty-First Century: The Perspective of the Magisterium," in Bevans and Schroeder, 24.

2. See, for instance, Joint Working Group, "Christian Witness—Common Witness" (1980), 15-19, in James A. Scherer and Stephen B. Bevans, eds., *New Directions in Mission and Evangelization 1: Basic Statements 1974-1991* (Maryknoll, N.Y.: Orbis Books, 1992), 18-20; World Council of Churches Seventh Assembly, "Come Holy Spirit" (Canberra, Australia, 1991), 61, in Scherer and Bevans, 85; "Report from the Ecumenical Conference on World Mission and Evangelization" (Salvador, de Bahia, Brazil, 1996), in James A. Scherer and Stephen B. Bevans, *New Directions in Mission and Evangelization 3: Faith and Culture* (Maryknoll, N.Y.: Orbis Books, 1999), 197.

3. "Confessing Christ Today," World Council of Churches Fifth Assembly (Nairobi, Kenya, 1975), in Scherer and Bevans, *New Directions in Mission and Evangelization 1,* 3-11.

4. Johannes Hoekendijk, quoted in Lesslie Newbigin, *The Open Secret: An Introduction to the Theology of Mission,* rev. ed. (Grand Rapids, Mich.: Eerdmans, 1995), 8.

5. Ibid., 9.

6. "Confessing Christ Today," 57, in Scherer and Bevans, *New Directions in Mission and Evangelization 1,* 10.

7. World Conference on Mission and Evangelism, "Your Kingdom Come" (Melbourne, Australia, 1980), 16, in Scherer and Bevans, *New Directions in Mission and Evangelization 1,* 29.

8. WCC Central Committee, *Ecumenical Affirmation: Mission and Evangelism* (1982), 6, in Scherer and Bevans, *New Directions in Mission and Evangelization 1,* 39.

9. Ibid., 14, in Scherer and Bevans, *New Directions in Mission and Evangelization 1,* 42.

10. Ibid., 15, in Scherer and Bevans, *New Directions in Mission and Evangelization 1,* 42. See also the document's lengthy reflection on the connection between preaching the gospel and commitment to the poor, 31-36, in Scherer and Bevans, *New Directions in Mission and Evangelization 1,* 46-48.

11. World Conference on Mission and Evangelism, "Mission in Christ's Way: Your Will Be Done" (San Antonio, Texas, 1989), I.I.1., in Scherer and Bevans, *New Directions in Mission and Evangelization 1,* 73-74. The theme of the stewardship of creation would be taken up in more detail in 1990 in Seoul, Korea (see *Now Is the Time: Final Document and Other Texts,* World Convocation on Justice, Peace and the Integrity of Creation, Seoul, Korea, 5-12 March, 1990 [Geneva: WCC-JPIC Office, 1990]).

12. "Mission in Christ's Way," 5, in Scherer and Bevans, *New Directions in Mission and Evangelization 1,* 74, quoting WCC Central Committee, "Ecumenical Affirmation: Mission and Evangelism," also in Scherer and Bevans, *New Directions in Mission and Evangelization 1,* 33.

13. See Section III of "The Earth Is the Lord's," in Fredrick R. Wilson, ed., *The San Antonio Report: Your Will Done—Mission in Christ's Way* (Geneva: WCC Publications, 1990).

14. "Report from the Ecumenical Conference on World Mission and Evangelization" (Salvador, de Bahia, Brazil, 1996), in Scherer and Bevans, *New Directions in Mission and Evangelization 3,* 197.

15. WCC Eighth Assembly, "Together on the Way: Being Together under the Cross in Africa: The Assembly Message," 3.6. Available online.

16. See Richard W. Taylor, "E. Stanley Jones, 1884-1973: Following the Christ of the Indian Road," in Gerald H. Anderson et al., eds., *Mission Legacies: Biographical Studies of Leaders of the Modern Missionary Movement* (Maryknoll, N.Y.: Orbis Books, 1994), 344-345.

17. Richard P. McBrien, *The Church in the Thought of Bishop John Robinson* (Philadelphia: The Westminster Press, 1966), 48. McBrien cites F. M. Braun, *Aspects nouveaus du*

problème de l'Eglise (Fribourg: Libaraire de l'Université, 1941), who was influenced himself by F. Holmström, *Das eschatologische Denken der Gegenwart* (Gütersloh, 1936).

18. Kirster E. Skydsgaard, "The Kingdom of God and the Church," *Scottish Journal of Theology* 4 (1951): 383-397. The original article was published in German in 1950. See John Haughey, "Church and Kingdom: Ecclesiology in the Light of Eschatology," *Theological Studies* 29/1 (1968): 79-80.

19. J. A. T. Robinson, "Kingdom, Church and Ministry," in K. M. Carey, ed., *The Historical Episcopate in the Fulness of the Church*, 2d ed. (London: Dacre Press, 1960; originally published in 1954), 17. Quoted in McBrien, 53 n. 30.

20. Haughey, 81. See Rudolf Schnackenburg, *God's Rule and Kingdom* (New York: Herder and Herder, 1963).

21. Hans Küng, *The Church* (New York: Sheed and Ward, 1967), 78. Somewhat unexplainedly, Küng leaves out the last two sentences of LG 5 when he quotes it, but it is clear from his development that the council's cautious distinction between church and reign of God is operative in his thinking.

22. Ibid., 45.

23. Ibid., 96; see also 43-104.

24. McBrien, 151.

25. Ibid., 228-229.

26. Ibid., 218.

27. Phillip Berryman, *Liberation Theology* (Oak Park, Ill.: Meyer Stone Books, 1987), 22-24.

28. Synod of Bishops, "Justice in the World" (1971), in David J. O'Brien and Thomas A. Shannon, *Catholic Social Thought: The Documentary Heritage* (Maryknoll, N.Y.: Orbis Books, 1991).

29. Gustavo Gutiérrez, *A Theology of Liberation* (Maryknoll, N.Y.: Orbis Books, 1973), 13.

30. Ibid., 36-37.

31. Ibid., 260.

32. Ibid., 261. After this sentence there is a reference (281 n. 23) to an essay by Karl Rahner in which Rahner says: "The Church, if only she be rightly understood, is living always on the proclamation of her own provisional status and of her historically advancing elimination in the coming Kingdom of God" (Karl Rahner, "The Church and the Parousia of Christ," *Theological Investigations* 6 [Baltimore, Md.: Helicon Press, 1969], 298).

33. Alvaro Quiroz Magaña, *Ecclesiologia en la teología de la liberación* (Salamanca: Ediciones Sigueme, 1983). English translation by authors.

34. Ibid., 152.

35. Leonardo Boff, *Ecclesiogenesis: The Base Communities Reinvent the Church* (Maryknoll, N.Y.: Orbis Books, 1986), esp. 45-60. For a discussion of how the reign of God functions in the theology and ecclesiology of other liberation theologians, see Antonio M. Pernia, *God's Kingdom and Human Liberation: A Study of G. Gutierrez, L. Boff and J. L. Segundo* (Manila: Divine Word Publications, 1988); and Roger Haight, *An Alternative Vision: An Interpretation of Liberation Theology* (Mahwah, N.J.: Paulist Press, 1985), 162-232.

36. Wolfhart Pannenberg, "The Kingdom of God and the Church," in *Theology and the Kingdom of God* (Philadelphia: The Westminster Press, 1969), 75.

37. Ibid., 76.

38. Ibid., 98.

39. Jürgen Moltmann, *The Church in the Power of the Spirit* (New York: Harper & Row, 1977), 196.

40. Notably José Miguez Bonino, *Doing Theology in a Revolutionary Situation* (Philadelphia: Fortress Press, 1975); René Padilla, "Liberation Theology [II]," *The Reformed Journal* (July 1983): 14-18; Orlando E. Costas, *Liberating News: A Theology of Contextual Evangelization* (Grand Rapids, Mich.: Eerdmans, 1989); Samuel Escobar, *La fe evangelica y las teologías*

de la liberación (El Paso, Tex.: Casa Bautsita de Publicaciones, 1987). See also Guillermo Cook, ed., *New Face of the Church in Latin America* (Maryknoll, N.Y.: Orbis Books, 1994).

41. James H. Cone, *A Black Theology of Liberation* (Maryknoll, N.Y.: Orbis Books, 1986; originally published in 1970), 125.

42. Ibid., 130-131.

43. Justo L. González, *Mañana: Christian Theology from a Hispanic Perspective* (Nashville, Tenn.: Abingdon Press, 1990), 167.

44. For African theologies of liberation, see, for example, *The Kairos Document: Challenge to the Church*, rev. 2d ed. (Grand Rapids, Mich.: Eerdmans, 1986); Laurenti Magesa, "Christ the Liberator in Africa Today," in Robert J. Schreiter, ed., *Faces of Jesus in Africa* (Maryknoll, N.Y.: Orbis Books, 1991), 151-163; Emmanuel Martey, "Liberation Theologies, African," in Virginia Fabella and R. S. Gugirtharajah, eds., *Dictionary of Third World Theologies* (Maryknoll, N.Y.: Orbis Books, 2000), 127-129 (includes a short bibliography as well). For feminist liberation theology, see Mary E. Hines, "Community for Liberation—Church," in Catherine M. LaCugna, ed., *Freeing Theology: The Essentials of Theology in Feminist Perspective* (San Francisco: HarperSanFrancisco, 1993), 161-184.

45. Robert J. Schreiter, *The New Catholicity: Theology between the Global and the Local* (Maryknoll, N.Y.: Orbis Books, 1997), 108-110. See also Pablo Richard, "La Iglesia de los pobres en la decada de los noventos," *Pasos* 28 (1990): 10-19; idem, "La teología de la liberación en la nueva conyuntura," *Pasos* 34 (1991): 1-8; Juan José Tamayo, *Presente y futuro de la teología de la liberación* (Madrid: San Pablo, 1994); José Comblin, *Called for Freedom: The Changing Context of Liberation Theology* (Maryknoll, N.Y.: Orbis Books, 1998).

46. See Schreiter, *The New Catholicity*, and Comblin; see also Robert J. Schreiter, "Globalization and Reconciliation: Challenges to Mission," and María Carmelita de Freitas, "The Mission of Religious Men and Women in Latin America Today: A Liberating Mission in a Neoliberal World," in Robert J. Schreiter, ed., *Mission in the Third Millennium*, 121-143 and 88-116; Paulo Suess, "The Gratuitousness of the Presence of Christ in the Broken World of Latin America," *Mission Studies* 17, 1/2, 33/34 (2000): 68-81; Edênio Valle, "Mission for the Twenty-First Century in Latin America: A View from the Perspective of the Missionary Religious Life," in Bevans and Schroeder, 129-148; Stephen Bevans, "Partner and Prophet: The Church and Globalization," in Heribert Bettscheider, ed., *Reflecting Mission, Practicing Mission: Divine Word Missionaries Commemorate 125 Years of Worldwide Commitment*, vol. 1 (Nettetal, Germany: Steyler Verlag, 2001), 91-110; *Spiritus*, Edición Hispanoamericana, 38/1, 196 (March 1997), issue entitled *La globalización: Nuevos desafíos para la misión*.

47. Pablo Richard, at the World Mission Institute, Chicago, Illinois, April 26, 2002.

48. Michael Amaladoss, *Making All Things New: Dialogue, Pluralism and Evangelization in Asia* (Maryknoll, N.Y.: Orbis Books, 1990), 180.

49. Michael Amaladoss, *Life in Freedom: Liberation Theologies from Asia* (Maryknoll, N.Y.: Orbis Books, 1997), 142.

50. Michael Amaladoss, "Mission as Prophecy," in Scherer and Bevans, *New Directions in Mission and Evangelization 2*, 72. The article originally appeared in French in *Spiritus*, 128 (September 1992): 263-275.

51. Ibid., 68.

52. Johannes Verkuyl, *Contemporary Missiology: An Introduction* (Grand Rapids, Mich.: Eerdmans, 1978), 197.

53. Johannes Verkuyl, "The Biblical Notion of the Kingdom: Test of Validity for Theology of Religion," in Charles van Engen, Dean S. Gilliland and Paul Pierson, eds., *The Good News of the Kingdom: Mission Theology for the Third Millennium* (Maryknoll, N.Y.: Orbis Books, 1993), 77. We will avert to this article briefly in what follows, but it might be appropriate to call attention to the entire volume in terms of a missiological discussion on the reign of God as the foundation for mission. The volume is a Festschrift in honor of the distinguished Evangelical missiologist Arthur F. Glasser, himself a major proponent of this approach.

54. Verkuyl, *Contemporary Missiology*, 200.

55. Ibid.

56. Verkuyl, "The Biblical Notion of the Kingdom," 75.

57. Verkuyl, *Contemporary Missiology*, 203.

58. Max Warren, *The Truth of Vision: A Study in the Nature of Human Hope* (London: Canterbury Press, 1948); Hans Jochen Margull, *Hope in Action: The Church's Task in the World* (Philadelphia: Muhlenburg Press, 1962); D. T. Niles, *Upon the Earth: The Mission of God and the Missionary Enterprise of the Churches* (New York: McGraw-Hill, 1962); Ludwig Wiedenmann, *Mission und Eschatologie: Eine Analyse der neueren deutschen evangelischen Missionstheologie* (Paderborn: Verlag Bonifacius-Druckerei, 1965); Raymond Fung, "Good News to the Poor—A Case for a Missionary Movement," Daniel von Allmen, "The Kingdom of God and Human Struggles," John V. Taylor, "The Church Witnesses to the Kingdom," all in *Your Kingdom Come: Mission Perspectives*, report on the World Conference on Mission and Evangelism, Melbourne, Australia, May 12-25, 1980 (Geneva: WCC Publications, 1980), 83-92, 120-132, 133-144.

59. Leonardo Boff, *Feet-on-the-Ground Theology: A Brazilian Journey* (Maryknoll, N.Y.: Orbis Books, 1987).

60. Edward Schillebeeckx, *Jesus: An Experiment in Christology* (New York: Vintage Books, 1981), 107-397. See also Jacques Dupuis, *Who Do You Say I Am?: Introduction to Christology* (Maryknoll, N.Y.: Orbis Books, 39-56; Walter Kasper, *Jesus the Christ* (London: Burns and Oates; New York: Paulist Press, 1976), 65-99; John P. Meier, *A Marginal Jew: Rethinking the Historical Jesus,* vol. 2, *Mentor, Message, and Miracles* (New York: Doubleday, 1994), 237-1038.

61. Roger Haight, *Jesus: Symbol of God* (Maryknoll, N.Y.: Orbis Books, 1999), 116, 88. This last quotation refers to Juan Luis Segundo, *Christ in the Spiritual Exercises of St. Ignatius* (Maryknoll, N.Y.: Orbis Books, 1987), 22-26.

62. Besides Küng, cited above, see Frances Schüssler Fiorenza, *Foundational Theology: Jesus and the Church* (New York: Crossroad, 1984), 61-192.

63. For example, Otto Semmelroth, commenting on LG 48, says that "the title reads 'The Eschatological Nature of the Pilgrim Church and Her Union with the Heavenly Church.' Clearly it is the Church herself whose eschatological character we are discussing. She herself confesses that she is something provisional, destined to be done away with" (in Herbert Vorgrimler, ed., *Commentary on the Documents of Vatican II*, vol. 1, *Dogmatic Constitution on the Church,* Commentary on Chapter VII [New York: Herder and Herder, 1967], 281). See also the remarks of Skydsgaard, Rahner and Pannenberg referred to above.

64. Gutiérrez, 234.

65. José Ignacio González Faus, "Anthropology: The Person and the Community," in I. Ellacuría and J. Sobrino, *Mysterium Liberationis* (Maryknoll, N.Y.: Orbis Books, 1993), 519-520.

66. Paulo Freire, *Pedagogy of the Oppressed* (New York: Seabury Press, 1974).

67. See Stephen Bevans, *Models of Contextual Theology*, 2d ed. (Maryknoll, N.Y.: Orbis Books, 2002), 75-76.

11. Mission as Proclamation of Jesus Christ as Universal Savior

1. Jozef Tomko, "Proclaiming Christ the World's Only Saviour," *L'Osservatore Romano* (April 15, 1991): 4. See also Cardinal Tomko's reflections on the background and content of the encyclical in "Mission for the Twenty-First Century: The Perspective of the Magisterium," in Stephen Bevans and Roger Schroeder, eds., *Mission for the Twenty-First Century* (Chicago: CCGM Publications, 2001), 24-31.

2. The term *exclusive* (along with the terms *inclusive* and *pluralist*) allude to the widely accepted typology for Christology proposed by Alan Race in *Christians and Religious Pluralism: Patterns in the Christian Theology of Religions* (London: SCM, 1993). S. Mark Heim describes the three terms as follows: "Christian exclusivists believe that the Christian tradition

is in sole possession of effective religious truth and offers the only path to salvation. Christian inclusivists affirm that salvation is available through other traditions because the God most decisively acting and most fully revealed in Christ is also redemptively available within or through those traditions. Christian pluralists maintain that various religious traditions are independently valid paths to salvation and Christ is irrelevant to those in other traditions, though serving Christians as *their* means to the same end" (S. Mark Heim, *The Depth of the Riches: A Trinitarian Theology of Religious Ends* [Grand Rapids, Mich.: Eerdmans, 2001], 3 n. 1). We will discuss this typology, and its critiques, more fully in the final chapter of this book.

3. See the various documents: "Ecclesia in Africa," "Ecclesia in Europa," "Ecclesia in America," "Ecclesia in Asia," and "Ecclesia in Oceania" (all available online). See particularly the entire chapters devoted to the centrality of Christ in the the the latter three documents. See Congregation for the Doctrine of the Faith, "Dominus Iesus," also available online.

4. "Confessing Christ Today," World Council of Churches Fifth Assembly (Nairobi, Kenya, 1975), in James A. Scherer and Stephen B. Bevans, eds., *New Directions in Mission and Evangelization 1: Basic Statements 1974-1991* (Maryknoll, N.Y.: Orbis Books, 1992), 3-11; "Mission and Evangelism," 41 (in Scherer and Bevans, 50); Orthodox Advisory Group to the WCC-CWME, "Go Forth in Peace: Orthodox Perspectives on Mission" (in Scherer and Bevans, 204-206); "Final Report of CWME Consultation of Eastern Orthodox and Oriental Orthodox Churches" (in Scherer and Bevans, 233).

5. See Samuel Escobar, "Missionary Dynamism in Search of Missiological Discernment: An Evangelical Perspective on Mission," *Evangelical Review of Theology* 23/1 (January 1999): 75.

6. "The Lausanne Covenant," 4, in Scherer and Bevans, 255.

7. LCWE, "Consultation on World Evangelization" (Pattaya, Thailand, 1980), in Scherer and Bevans, 275.

8. "The Lausanne Covenant, 3, in Scherer and Bevans, 254.

9. LCWE, *Manila Manifesto* (Manila, 1989), A.3, in Scherer and Bevans, 296.

10. Ibid.

11. "The Lausanne Covenant," 3, in Scherer and Bevans, 254.

12. *Manila Manifesto*, A.3, in Scherer and Bevans, 297.

13. "The Lausanne Covenant," 5, in Scherer and Bevans, 255.

14. Ibid., 6, in Scherer and Bevans, 256.

15. LCWE and WEF, "Consultation on the Relation of Evangelism and Social Responsibility" (Grand Rapids, 1982), 4 (C), in Scherer and Bevans, 278-279.

16. *Manila Manifesto*, A.4, in Scherer and Bevans, 297.

17. WEF, "The Christian Gospel and the Jewish People" (Willowbank, 1989), IV.19, in Scherer and Bevans, 310-311.

18. See Basil Meeking and John Stott, eds., *The Evangelical-Roman Catholic Dialogue on Mission 1977-1984: A Report* (Grand Rapids, Mich.: Eerdmans, 1986). Although the Catholics represented in this dialogue were sponsored by the Vatican's Pontifical Council (then Secretariat) for Promoting Christian Unity, "the Evangelical participants in this Dialogue on Mission did not come as official representatives of any denomination," but as "individuals who were interested in developing greating understanding between Roman Catholics and Evangelicals while discussing a topic which was very important to both sides." The result of these dialogues was not an official document, but rather the report cited above (see Thomas P. Rausch, ed., *Catholics and Evangelicals: Do They Share a Common Future?* [Mahwah, N.J.: Paulist Press, 2000], 27).

19. Meeking and Stott, 35.

20. George Vandervelde, "Introduction," *Evangelical Review of Theology* 23/1 (January 1999): 9. See the text of the communiqué, "Evangelicals and Catholics Converse about Church and Mission," ibid., 12.

21. The statement is printed in Charles Colson and Richard John Neuhaus, eds., *Evangelicals and Catholics Together: Toward a Common Mission* (Dallas, Tex.: Word Publishing, 1995), xv-xxxiii.

22. Ibid., xvi.

23. Ibid., xviii.

24. Ibid., xix.

25. Ibid., xxviii.

26. This affirmation, along with commentaries and all the papers given at the consultation, can be found in William D. Taylor, ed., *Global Missiology for the Twenty-first Century: The Iguassu Dialogue* (Grand Rapids, Mich.: Baker Academic, 2000).

27. Ibid., 17-18. The commitment to the trinitarian foundation of mission is found on 19.

28. Cecil M. Robeck, "Making Sense of Pentecostalism in a Global Context," paper presented at the twenty-eighth annual meeting of the Society for Pentecostal Studies, Springfield, Mo., 1999, quoted in Allan Anderson, "Diversity in the Definition of 'Pentecostal/Charismatic' and Its Ecumenical Implications," *Mission Studies* 19/2/38 (2002): 40-41; Veli-Matti Kärkkäinen, *Christology: A Global Introduction* (Grand Rapids, Mich.: Eerdmans, 2003), 89.

29. Regarding the distinction between classical Pentecostals, Neo-Pentecostals/Charismatics and Third Wave Pentecostalism, see Gary B. McGee, "Pentecostalism," in Scott W. Sunquist, ed., *A Dictionary of Asian Christianity* (Grand Rapids, Mich.: Eerdmans, 2001), 646-650, esp. 646. Frank Macchia speaks of Evangelicals and Pentecostals as "siblings," and Wonsuk Ma speaks of them as "cousins." See Frank Macchia, "The Struggle for Global Witness: Shifting Paradigms in Pentecostal Theology," and Wonsuk Ma, "Biblical Studies in the Pentecostal Tradition: Yesterday, Today, and Tomorrow," in Murray W. Dempster, Byron D. Klaus and Douglas Peterson, eds., *The Globalization of Pentecostalism: A Religion Made to Travel* (Oxford: Regnum Books International, 1999), 12 and 62.

30. Gary B. McGee, "Pentecostal Movement," in A. Scott Moreau, ed., *Evangelical Dictionary of World Missions* (Grand Rapids, Mich.: Baker Books, 2000), 739. See also Walter J. Hollenweger, *The Pentecostals* (Peabody, Mass.: Hendrickson Publishers, 1972), 312; Gary B. McGee, "Historical Background," in Stanley M. Horton, ed., *Systematic Theology*, rev. ed. (Springfield, Mo.: Logion Press, 1995), 9. Regarding Pentecostalism's "holiness" lineage, see Vinson Synan, *The Holiness-Pentecostal Tradition: Charismatic Movements in the Twentieth Century* (Grand Rapids, Mich.: Eerdmans, 1997).

31. The phrase is quoted in Harvey Cox, *Fire from Heaven: The Rise of Pentecostal Spirituality and the Reshaping of Religion in the Twenty-First Century* (Cambridge, Mass.: Da Capo Press, 1995), 75.

32. See Synan, 159.

33. Hollenweger, 513-522.

34. Ibid., 520.

35. "Evangelization, Proselytism and Common Witness: The Report from the Fourth Phase of the International Dialogue (1990-1997) between the Roman Catholic Church and Some Classical Pentecostal Churches and Leaders," *Pneuma* 21/1 (Spring 1999): 12 (para. 3). We are, of course, assuming that what is expressed in this fourth document of Pentecostal/Roman Catholic dialogue is true of all three previous documents in the dialogue and of the dialogue between Pentecostals and the Reformed Churches as well. We see no reason not to do so.

36. Walter J. Hollenweger, "Roman Catholics and Pentecostals in Dialogue," *Pneuma* 21/1 (Spring 1999): 135. Regarding Hollenweger as "dean," see Cox, ix.

37. See Veli-Matti Kärkkäinen, "Evangelization, Proselytism, and Common Witness: Roman Catholic-Pentecostal Dialogue on Mission, 1990-1997," *International Bulletin of Missionary Research* 25/1 (January 2001): 16. The documents are published in *Pneuma* 21/2 (Fall 1990): 85-95, 97-115, 117-142; and (the fourth) in 21/1 (Spring 1999): 11-51.

38. "Word and Spirit, Church and World, the Final Report of the International Dialogue between Representatives of the World Alliance of Reformed Churches and Some Classical Pentecostal Churches and Leaders, 1996-2000 (WSCW)," *Pneuma* 23/1 (Spring 2001): 9-43.

39. Quoted in Anderson, 49.

40. See Timothy Yates, *Christian Mission in the Twentieth Century* (Cambridge: Cambridge University Press, 1994), 194-209; John Hick, ed., *The Myth of God Incarnate* (London: SCM Press, 1977); John Hick, *God and the Universe of Faiths* (New York: St. Martin's Press, 1973); Paul F. Knitter, *No Other Name? A Critical Survey of Christian Attitudes toward the*

World Religions (Maryknoll, N.Y.: Orbis Books, 1985); John Hick and Paul F. Knitter, eds., *The Myth of Christian Uniqueness: Toward a Pluralistic Theology of Religions* (Maryknoll, N.Y.: Orbis Books, 1987); Leonard Swidler, ed., *Toward a Universal Theology of Religon* (Maryknoll, N.Y.: Orbis Books, 1988); Leonardo N. Mercado and James J. Knight, eds., *Mission and Dialogue: Theory and Practice* (Manila: Divine Word Publications, 1989); Jacques Dupuis, *Toward a Christian Theology of Religious Pluralism* (Maryknoll, N.Y.: Orbis Books, 1997); Sacred Congregation for the Doctrine of the Faith, "Instruction on Certain Aspects of the 'Theology of Liberation'" (1984), in Roger Haight, *An Alternative Vision: An Interpretation of Liberation Theology* (Mahwah, N.J.: Paulist Press, 1985), 269-291; Congregation for the Doctrine of the Faith, "Instruction on Christian Freedom and Liberation" (1986) (Washington, D.C.: United States Catholic Conference, 1986); Peter Beyerhaus, *Missions: Which Way? Humanization or Redemption* (Grand Rapids, Mich.: Zondervan, 1971); John R. W. Stott, *Christian Mission in the Modern World* (Downers Grove, Ill.: InterVarsity Press, 1979).

41. Carl E. Braaten, *No Other Gospel! Christianity among the World's Religions* (Minneapolis, Minn.: Fortress Press, 1992); Harold Netland, *Dissonant Voices: Religious Pluralism and the Question of Truth* (Grand Rapids, Mich.: Eerdmans, 1991).

42. Gavin D'Costa, ed., *Christian Uniqueness Reconsidered: The Myth of a Pluralistic Theology of Religions* (Maryknoll, N.Y.: Orbis Books, 1990). The book's title refers, of course, to the title of the volume edited in 1987 by John Hick and Paul Knitter, *The Myth of Christian Uniqueness*.

43. Sebastian Karotemprel et al., eds., *Following Christ in Mission: A Foundational Course in Missiology* (Boston: Pauline Books and Media, 1996).

44. Karl Müller, "Missiology: An Introduction," in Karotemprel et al., 26, 33, 38.

45. Adam Wolanin, "Trinitarian Foundation of Mission," in Karotemprel et al., 50, 53.

46. Sebastian Karotemprel, "Christological and Soteriological Foundations of Mission," in Karotemprel et al., 66.

47. Jesús López-Gay, "Proclamation," in Karotemprel et al., 132.

48. Mariasusai Dhavamony, "Theology of Religions," in Karotemprel et al., 360.

49. G. Colzani, P. Giglioni and S. Karotemprel, eds., *Cristologia e Missione oggi* (Rome: Urbaniana University Press, 2001).

50. Walter Kasper, "The Unicity and Universality of Jesus Christ," in Colzani, Giglioni and Karotemprel, 35-45; Claude Geffré, "La prétention du Christianism à l'universel: implications missiologiques," in ibid., 47-65. The quotation is from 55.

51. George Karakunnel, "The Uniqueness of Jesus Christ in Indian Theological Reflection," in Colzani, Giglioni and Karotemprel, 109.

52. Sebastian Karotemprel, "Introduction: Christology and Mission Today," in Colzani, Giglioni and Karotemprel, 27.

53. Beyerhaus, 68.

54. Ibid., 67-68.

55. Ibid., 113-115.

56. John R. W. Stott, quoted in N. Goodall, *The Uppsala Report 1968* (Geneva: WCC Publications, 1968), 26, quoted in Yates, 198.

57. Stott, *Christian Mission in the Modern World,* 35.

58. Ibid., 44.

59. Charles van Engen, *God's Missionary People: Rethinking the Purpose of the Local Church* (Grand Rapids, Mich.: Baker Book Company, 1991), 104, 108-112.

60. Ibid., 113.

61. Charles van Engen, *Mission on the Way: Issues in Mission Theology* (Grand Rapids, Mich.: Baker Books, 1996), 26-27.

62. Ibid., 177-178.

63. Clark Pinnock, *A Wideness in God's Mercy: The Finality of Jesus Christ in a World of Religions* (Grand Rapids, Mich.: Zondervan, 1992); Harold Netland, *Encountering Religious Pluralism: The Challenge to Christian Faith and Mission* (Downers Grove, Ill.: InterVarsity Press, 2001).

64. See van Engen, *Mission on the Way*, 138.

65. Samuel Escobar, "Evangelical Missiology: Peering into the Future at the Turn of the Century," in Taylor, 114.

66. Ibid., 116. The work of Padilla referred to here is "Bible Studies," *Missiology: An International Review* 10/4 (1982): 319-338.

67. Ibid., 118, quoting Josè Míguez Bonino, *Faces of Latin American Protestantism* (Grand Rapids, Mich.: Eerdmans, 1997), 120.

68. David Bundy, "The Genre of Systematic Theology in Pentecostalism," *Pneuma* 15/1 (Spring 1993): 101. See also Paul W. Lewis, "Reflections of a Hundred Years of Pentecostal Theology," *Cyberjournal for Pentecostal Charismatic Research* 12 (January 2003), online.

69. Russell P. Spittler, "Suggested Areas for Further Research in Pentecostalism," *Pneuma* 5/2 (Fall 1983): 39, quoted in Macchia, 9.

70. Cox, 201.

71. Macchia, 10.

72. Synan, ix.

73. See Lewis.

74. Frank Macchia, "Dominus Jesus: A Pentecostal Perspective" (editorial), *Pneuma* 22/2 (Fall 2000): 171.

75. Ibid.

76. DI, quoted in Ibid., 172.

77. Kärkkäinen, *Christology*, 16. Other Pentecostals, however, would only attribute to Christ *four* titles: Savior, Baptizer, Healer and coming King. The title of Sanctifier would be denied by the "finished work" advocates, who would deny that there is another stage of sanctification that differs from the stage of justification (see Lewis, 3). The set of four titles of Jesus is the basis for the "Foursquare Gospel" that goes back to nineteenth-century evangelist A. B. Simpson but was developed by Aimee Semple McPherson with her four "corners": salvation, the Holy Ghost baptism attested by tongues, divine healing and the second coming of Christ (Synan, 201).

78. David R. Nichols, "The Lord Jesus Christ," in Horton, 291.

79. Ibid., 324.

80. On this minority theological tradition, see Synan, 156-157, and Kerry D. Roberts, "The Holy Trinity," in Horton, 145-177.

81. Ralph del Colle, "Oneness and Trinity: A Preliminary Proposal for Dialogue with Oneness Pentecostalism," paper read at the twenty-sixth annual meeting of the Society of Penteocstal Studies, March 9-13, 1996, Toronto, Canada, quoted in Veli-Matti Kärkkäinen, "Trinity as Communion in the Spirit: Koinonia, Trinity, and Filioque in the Roman Catholic-Pentecostal Dialogue," *Pneuma* 22/2 (Fall 2000): 209.

82. Simon Chan, "Mother Church: Toward a Pentecostal Ecclesiology," *Pneuma* 22/2 (Fall 2000): 190.

83. Donald Gelpi, *Pentecostalism: A Theological Viewpoint* (New York: Paulist Press, 1971), 101-102.

84. Gary B. McGee, "Early Pentecostal Missionaries—They Went Everywhere Preaching the Gospel," in L. Grant McClung, Jr., ed., *Azusa Street and Beyond: Pentecostal Missions and Church Growth in the Twentieth Century* (South Plainfield, N.J.: Bridge, 1986), 33.

85. Steven J. Land, "The Triune Center: Wesleyans and Pentecostals Together in Mission," *Pneuma* 21/2 (Fall 1999): 211, 209.

86. L. Grant McClung, Jr., "'Try to Get People Saved': Revisiting the Paradigm of an Urgent Missiology," in Demster, Klaus and Peterson, 48.

87. William J. Seymour, quoted in Byron D. Klaus, "The Mission of the Church," in Horton, 583.

88. For example, see Cox, 161-184; see also David Martin, *Pentecostalism: The World Their Parish* (Oxford: Blackwell Publishers, 2002), and Veli-Matti Kärkkäinen, "Mission, Spirit and Eschatology: An Outline of a Pentecostal-Charismatic Theology of Mission," *Mission Studies* 16/1/31 (1999): 80-83.

89. Martin, 161. Martin also writes: "The converts are not necessarily better off, because they may on occasion have been marginalized and squeezed out of the local system by sheer hardship. But they are, one way or another, on tip-toe edge, picking up new vibrancies which may help them to survive immiseration or to grasp new opportunities. They are helped to survive and/or to initiate change by new priorities and disciplines, by a sense of responsibility, by concern with cleanliness and health. They are also assisted by the restoration of peace in the home and the return of males to their family responsibilities. They acquire networks of mutual support, and these are especially advantageous when they move to the larger urban centers" (130).

90. Allan H. Anderson, "The Gospel and Culture in Pentecostal Mission in the Third World," *Missionalia* 27/2 (August 1999): 221.

91. See ibid.; Cox, 128; Martin, 49, 142, 152, 160.

92. Kärkkäinen, "Mission, Spirit and Eschatology," 86. The article by Yong is "'Not Knowing Where the Wind Blows . . . ': On Envisioning a Pentecostal/Charismatic Theology of Religions," in *Purity and Power: Revisioning the Holiness and Pentecostal/Charismatic Movements for the Twenty-First Century*, Society of Pentecostal Studies Annual Meeting (Cleveland, Tenn.), 2:1-21. The article is also published in *Journal of Pentecostal Theology* 14 (April 1999): 81-112. Yong has since published *Beyond the Impasse: Toward a Pneumatological Theology of Religions* (Grand Rapids, Mich.: Baker Academic, 2003).

93. Quoted in Cox, 58.

94. Chan, 189.

95. Klaus, 585.

96. "The Lausanne Covenant," 3, in Scherer and Bevans, 254.

97. See Friedrich Schleiermacher, *The Christian Faith* (Philadelphia: Fortress Press, 1976), §24, 103. Schleiermacher's thesis is that "the anthithesis between Protestantism and Catholicism may provisionally be conceived thus: the former makes the individual's relation to the Church dependent on his relation to Christ, while the latter contrariwise makes the individual's relation to Christ dependent on his relation to the Church."

98. Ajith Fernando, "The Church: The Mirror of the Trinity," in Taylor, 239-256.

99. Chan, 180.

100. "The Lausanne Covenant," 15, in Scherer and Bevans, 259.

101. Van Engen, *God's Missionary People*, 101-118.

102. Avery Dulles, "The Church and the Kingdom," in Eugene LaVerdiere, ed., *A Church for All Peoples: Missionary Issues in a World Church* (Collegeville, Minn.: The Liturgical Press, 1993), 27.

103. *Manila Manifesto,* Affirmations 4 and 7, in Scherer and Bevans, 293. See also WSCW, 72: "Pentecostals and many Reformed find it impossible to accept the idea that salvaton might be found outside Jesus Christ."

104. John Stott, ed., *Making Christ Known: Historic Mission Documents from the Lausanne Movement, 1974-1989* (Grand Rapids, Mich.: Eerdmans, 1996), 18.

105. Karotemprel, "Christological and Soteriological Foundations of Mission," 69.

106. Stott, *Christian Mission in the Modern World*, 82-108.

107. Meeking and Stott, 39-40.

108. "The Lausanne Covenant," 5, in Scherer and Bevans, 255.

109. Ibid., 6, in Scherer and Bevans, 256.

110. Meeking and Stott, 89-91.

111. WEF, "Consultation on the Church in Response to Human Need" (Wheaton, Ill., 1983), 20, in Scherer and Bevans, 286.

112. Juan Sepúlveda, quoted in Anderson, "The Gospel and Culture in Pentecostal Mission in the Third World," 221.

113. WEF, "Consultation on the Church in Response to Human Need," 21, in Scherer and Bevans, 286.

114. See Stephen B. Bevans, *Models of Contextual Theology*, 2d ed. (Maryknoll, N.Y.: Orbis Books, 2002), 117-137.

12. Mission as Prophetic Dialogue

1. The phrase *prophetic dialogue* was suggested at the Fifteenth General Chapter of our religious congregation, the Society of the Divine Word. While we acknowledge our debt to the General Chapter for the terminology, we also acknowledge that we have developed the idea in a slightly different way in this chapter (see *In Dialogue with the Word Nr. 1* [Rome: SVD Publications, 2000], esp. 30-32).

2. David J. Bosch, *Transforming Mission: Paradigm Shifts in Theology of Mission* (Maryknoll, N.Y.: Orbis Books, 1991), 489.

3. The phrase is from William R. Burrows, *New Ministries: The Global Context* (Maryknoll, N.Y.: Orbis Books, 1980), 37-51. Bosch speaks of the nature of Jesus' "boundary-breaking" ministry in *Transforming Mission*, 30.

4. See, for example, the 1974 document "Evangelization in Modern Day Asia," in Gaudencio Rosales and Catalino Arévalo, eds., *For All the Peoples of Asia: Federation of Asian Bishops' Conferences Documents from 1970-1991* (Maryknoll, N.Y.: Orbis Books; Quezon City, Philippines: Claretian Publications, 1992), 11-25. See also Jonathan Yun-ka Tan, "Towards Asian Liturgical Inculturation," *FABC Papers* 89 (December 1999).

5. This, in a nutshell, is the provocative thesis of S. Mark Heim, *The Depths of the Riches: A Trinitarian Theology of Religious Ends* (Grand Rapids, Mich.: Eerdmans, 2001). See the slightly fuller explanation in Chapter 9, and in the section "Interreligious Dialogue as Prophetic Dialogue" in this chapter.

6. Leonardo Boff, "The Trinity," in Ignacio Ellacuría and Jon Sobrino, eds., *Mysterium Liberationis: Fundamental Concepts of Liberation Theology* (Maryknoll, N.Y.: Orbis Books, 1993), 391, 392.

7. See Stephen Bevans, *Models of Contextual Theology*, rev. and exp. ed. (Maryknoll, N.Y.: Orbis Books, 2002), 11-15.

8. See Stephen Bevans, "Letting Go and Speaking Out: A Spirituality of Inculturation," in Stephen Bevans, Eleanor Doidge and Robert J. Schreiter, eds., *The Healing Circle: Essays in Cross-Cultural Mission* (Chicago: CCGM Publications, 2000), 133-146.

9. See Pontifical Council for Inter-Religious Dialogue and Congregation for the Evangelization of Peoples, *Dialogue and Proclamation*, 2, in William R. Burrows, ed., *Redemption and Dialogue: Reading* Redemptoris Missio *and* Dialogue and Proclamation (Maryknoll, N.Y.: Orbis Books, 1993), 94. The document quotes an important earlier document, "The Attitude of the Church toward Followers of Other Religions (Reflections and Orientations on Dialogue and Mission)," *AAS* 76 (1984): 816-828. In the paragraphs that follow, we are following closely a portion of the essay by Stephen Bevans and Eleanor Doidge, "Theological Reflection," in Barbara Kraemer, ed., *Reflection and Dialogue: What MISSION Confronts Religious Life Today?* (Chicago: Center for the Study of Religious Life, 2000), 37-48, esp. 48. We owe the image of "monaural" and "stereophonic" sound to our friend and colleague Robert Schreiter, who proposed it in a symposium on the document *Dominus Iesus* held at Catholic Theological Union in September 2000. The six elements developed in the following pages have been published in shorter versions in Stephen B. Bevans, SVD, "Unraveling a 'Complex Reality': Six Elements of Mission," *International Bulletin of Missionary Research* 27/2 (April 2003): 50-53, and Roger Schroeder, "Mission as Prophetic Dialogue: The Six Components of Mission," paper delivered at the ACLRI Mission Network Annual Conference, Melbourne, Australia, May 16, 2003 (available online).

10. "Agenda for Future Planning, Study, and Research in Mission," in William Jenkinson and Helene O'Sullivan, eds., *Trends in Mission: Toward the Third Millennium* (Maryknoll, N.Y.: Orbis Books, 1991), 399-414.

11. It is now called the Pontifical Council for Inter-Religious Dialogue.

12. "The Attitude of the Church toward the Followers of Other Religions: Reflections and Orientations on Dialogue and Mission," *Bulletin. Secretariatus pro non christianis* 56:13 (1984/2). Quoted in DP 2.

13. See, for example, "Report from the Ecumenical Conference on World Mission and Evangelization" (Salvador, de Bahia, Brazil, 1996), in James A. Scherer and Stephen B. Bevans, eds., *New Direction in Mission and Evangelization 3: Faith and Culture* (Maryknoll, N.Y.: Orbis Books, 1999), 196-234; "The Iguassu Affirmation," in William D. Taylor, ed., *Global Missiology for the Twenty-first Century: The Iguassu Dialogue* (Grand Rapids, Mich.: Baker Academic, 2000), 15-21; and WSCW, 74.

14. Bosch; J. Andrew Kirk, *What Is Mission? Theological Explorations* (Minneapolis, Minn.: Fortress Press, 2000); Anthony J. Gittins, *Reading the Clouds: Mission Spirituality for New Times* (Ligouri, Mo.: Ligouri Publications, 1999); idem, "Kiribatizing Christianity: A Local Church Discovers Itself," *Mission Studies* 16/2/32 (1999): 71-99; Donal Dorr, *Mission in Today's World* (Maryknoll, N.Y.: Orbis Books, 2000); Samuel Escobar, *Changing Tides: Latin America and World Mission Today* (Maryknoll, N.Y.: Orbis Books, 2002); Robert J. Schreiter, "Reconcilation as a Model of Mission," *Neue Zeitschrift für Missionswissenschaft* 52 (1996): 243-250; idem, "Globalization and Reconciliation: Challenges to Mission," in Robert J. Schreiter, ed., *Mission in the Third Millennium* (Maryknoll, N.Y.: Orbis Books, 2001), 121-143.

15. Bevans and Doidge, 38-39.

16. See Pontifical Council for Inter-Religious Dialogue and Congregations for the Evangelization of Peoples, *Dialogue and Proclamation*, in William R. Burrows, ed., *Redemption and Dialogue: Reading* Redemptoris Missio *and* Dialogue and Proclamation (Maryknoll, N.Y.: Orbis Books, 1993), 93-118.

17. See, for example, Bruce J. Malina, *The Social Gospel of Jesus: The Kingdom of God in Mediterranean Perspective* (Minneapolis, Minn.: Fortress Press, 2001); Richard A. Horseley and Neil Asher Silberman, *The Message and the Kingdom: How Jesus and Paul Ignited a Revolution and Transformed the Ancient World* (Minneapolis, Minn.: Fortress Press, 1997); Albert Nolan, *Jesus before Christianity* (Maryknoll, N.Y.: Orbis Books, 1976).

18. John W. Stott, *Christian Mission in the Modern World* (Downers Grove, Ill.: InterVarsity Press, 1975), 55.

19. Bosch, 420.

20. World Council of Churches Sixth Assembly, "Witnessing in a Divided World" (1983), in James A. Scherer and Stephen B. Bevans, eds., *New Directions in Mission and Evangelization 1: Basic Statements 1974-1991* (Maryknoll, N.Y.: Orbis Books, 1992), 55-56.

21. See Timothy K. Beougher, "Lifestyle Evangelism," in A. Scott Moreau, ed., *Evangelical Dictionary of World Missions* (Grand Rapids, Mich.: Baker Books, 2000), 578-579. While emphasis here is put on lifestyle, Beougher still describes it as "using the channels of relationships to share the gospel through both words and deeds" (578).

22. See Chapter 8, "Models of Mission in the Catholic Church," herein.

23. Lesslie Newbigin, *The Gospel in a Pluralist Society* (Grand Rapids, Mich.: Eerdmans, 1989), 222-233.

24. Byron D. Klaus, "The Mission of the Church," in Stanley M. Horton, ed., *Systematic Theology*, rev. ed. (Springfield, Mo.: Logion Press, 1995), 573.

25. Rodney Stark, *The Rise of Christianity* (San Francisco: HarperSanFrancisco, 1997).

26. *Letter to Diognetus* 5.5; 5.15-16, quoted in Darrell L. Guder, ed., *Missional Church: A Vision for the Sending of the Church in North America* (Grand Rapids, Mich.: Eerdmans, 1998), 120.

27. Ibid., 6.3.

28. See Stanley Hauerwas and William H. Willimon, *Resident Aliens: Life in the Christian Colony* (Nashville, Tenn.: Abingdon Press, 1989); Gerhard Lohfink, *Jesus and Community* (Philadelphia: Fortress Press, 1984).

29. See Michael Goheen, "Is Lesslie Newbigin's Model of Contextualization Anticultural?" *Mission Studies* 19/2/38 (2002): 136-158.

30. Guder, 142-182. See also *The Center Letter*, published by the Center for Parish Development (1525 E. 55th Street, Suite 201, Chicago, IL 60615; missionalchurch.org), and Inagrace

T. Dietterich and Laceye Warner, *Missional Evangelism*, The Ekklesia Project, Pamphlet 7 (Eugene, Ore.: Wipf and Stock Publishers, 2002).

31. C. Norman Kraus, *The Authentic Witness: Credibility and Authority* (Grand Rapids, Mich.: Eerdmans, 1978), 156, quoted in Guder, 182. See also Philip D. Kenneson, *Life on the Vine: Cultivating the Fruit of the Spirit in Christian Community* (Downers Grove, Ill.: InterVarsity Press, 1999).

32. See Victor Turner, *The Ritual Process: Structure and Anti-Structure* (Ithaca, N.Y.: Cornell University Press, 1969). See also A. H. Mathias Zahniser, *Symbol and Ceremony: Making Disciples across Cultures* (Monrovia, Calif.: MARC, 1997); and Antony J. Gittins, *A Presence That Disturbs: A Call to Radical Discipleship* (Ligouri, Mo.: Ligouri/Triumph, 2002), 69-90.

33. Orthodox Consultation on Mission and Proselytism (Moscow, 1995), quoted in "Report from the Ecumenical Conference on World Mission and Evangelism," in Scherer and Bevans, *New Directions in Mission and Evangelization 3*, 232.

34. *Manila Manifesto*, 9, in Scherer and Bevans, *New Directions in Mission and Evangelization 1*, 301. See also Stephen B. Bevans, "Common Witness," in Karl Müller et al., eds., *Dictionary of Mission: Theology, History, Perspectives* (Maryknoll, N.Y.: Orbis Books, 1997), 72-73.

35. See the essays in Bevans, Doidge and Schreiter; see also Claude Marie Barbour, Kathleen Billman, Peggy DesJarlait and Eleanor Doidge, "Mission on the Boundaries: Cooperation without Exploitation," in Susan B. Thistlethwaite and George F. Cairns, eds., *Beyond Theological Tourism: Mentoring as a Grassroots Approach to Theological Education* (Maryknoll, N.Y.: Orbis Books, 1995), 82-83; and Anthony J. Gittins, *Bread for the Journey: The Mission of Transformation and the Transformation of Mission* (Maryknoll, N.Y.: Orbis Books, 1993), 55-71.

36. For a clear development of this, see Fredrick W. Norris, *Christianity: A Short Global History* (Oxford: OneWorld, 2002).

37. For example, see the suggestive remarks of Francine Cardman in the *Proceedings of the Catholic Theological Society of America* 56 [2001], 175-176.

38. Mortimer Arias, *Announcing the Reign of God: Evangelization and the Subversive Memory of Jesus* (Philadelphia: Fortress Press, 1984).

39. The quotation is from Joseph Komonchak, "Christians Must Make a Difference," *The Tablet* (September 28, 2002), 4. Komonchak makes the reference to Knox in the article.

40. Marcello Zago, OMI, "The New Millennium and the Emerging Religious Encounters," *Missiology: An International Review* 28/1 (January 2000): 17.

41. Kirk, 73.

42. On this crucial point, see Newbigin, 80-88; see also idem, *The Open Secret: An Introduction to the Theology of Mission*, rev. ed. (Grand Rapids, Mich.: Eerdmans, 1995), 17-18. See also George R. Hunsberger, *Bearing the Witness of the Spirit: Lesslie Newbigin's Theology of Cultural Plurality* (Grand Rapids, Mich.: Eerdmans, 1998), 45-112. Pentecostal missiologist Byron D. Klaus also makes this point (see Klaus, 568-569).

43. Bosch, 420.

44. This is something often pointed out by Andrew Walls (see, for example, Andrew F. Walls, *The Missionary Movement in Christian History: Studies in Transmission of Faith* [Maryknoll, N.Y.: Orbis Books, 1996], 87).

45. See WCC, *Ecumenical Affirmation: Mission and Evangelism*, 13, in Scherer and Bevans, *New Directions in Mission and Evangelization 1*, 41; LCWE and WEF, "Consultation on Simple Life-Style," 4, in Scherer and Bevans, *New Directions in Mission and Evangelization 1*, 270; EN 76; RM 90-91.

46. World Conference on Mission and Evangelization, "Mission in Christ's Way, Your Will Be Done" (San Antonio, Tex., 1989), 22, in Scherer and Bevans, *New Directions in Mission and Evangelization 1*, 78. Jesús López-Gay, "Proclamation," in Sebastian Karotemprel et al., eds., *Following Christ in Mission* (Boston: Pauline Books and Media, 1996), 131.

47. Bosch, 413.

48. Ray Finch, "Missionaries Today," *Origins* 30/21 (November 2, 2000): 327-332.

49. David J. Bosch, "The Vulnerability of Mission," in James A. Scherer and Stephen B. Bevans, eds., *New Directions in Mission and Evangelization 2: Theological Foundations* (Maryknoll, N.Y.: Orbis Books, 1994), 73-86.

50. Ibid., 83-84. See Kosuke Koyama, *No Handle on the Cross: An Asian Meditation on the Crucified Mind* (Maryknoll, N.Y.: Orbis Books, 1976).

51. Josef Neuner, "A New Theology of Proclamation," in James H. Kroeger and Peter C. Phan, eds., *The Future of the Asian Churches: The Asian Synod and Ecclesia in Asia* (Quezon City, Philippines: Claretian Publications, 2002), 92-101.

52. Gordon W. Lathrop, "Liturgy and Mission in the North American Context," in Thomas H. Schattauer, ed., *Inside Out: Worship in an Age of Mission* (Minneapolis, Minn.: Fortress Press, 1999), 201.

53. Ibid.

54. Robert D. Hawkins, "Occasional Services: Border Crossings," in Schattauer, 187.

55. Don E. Saliers, *Worship as Theology: Foretaste of Glory Divine* (Nashville, Tenn.: Abingdon Press, 1994), 27, quoted in Gilbert I. Bond, "Liturgy, Ministry, and the Stranger: The Practice of Encountering the Other in Two Christian Communities," in Miroslav Volf and Dorothy C. Bass, eds., *Practicing Theology: Beliefs and Practices in Christian Life* (Grand Rapids, Mich.: Eerdmans, 2002), 138.

56. Thomas H. Schattauer, "Liturgical Assembly as Locus of Mission," in Schattauer, *Inside Out,* 1-21.

57. Evangelical Lutheran Church of America, *The Use of the Means of Grace: A Statement on the Practice of Word and Sacrament* (1977), principle 51, quoted in Schattauer, *Inside Out,* 6; Walter C. Huffman, "Liturgical Space: Faith Takes Form," in Schattauer, *Inside Out,* 111.

58. John Koenig, *The Feast of the World's Redemption: Eucharistic Origins and Christian Mission* (Harrisburg, Pa.: Trinity Press International, 2000), xii.

59. Evangelical Lutheran Church of America, *The Use of the Means of Grace,* application 51b, quoted in Schattauer, "Preface," in Schattauer, *Inside Out,* viii.

60. Ibid., application 34b, quoted in Paul Westermeyer, "Music: Poured Out for the World," in Schattauer, *Inside Out,* 127.

61. Simon Chan, "Mother Church: Toward a Pentecostal Ecclesiology," *Pneuma* 22/2 (Fall, 2000): 189. For additional sustained reflection on the missionary implications of the Eucharist, see Koenig; and Gittins, *Bread for the Journey.*

62. Alexander Schmemann, "The Missionary Imperative in the Orthodox Tradition," in Gerald H. Anderson, ed., *The Theology of the Christian Mission* (Nashville, Tenn.: Abingdon Press, 1961), 256.

63. Schattauer, "Liturgical Assembly as Locus of Mission."

64. Bond, 147.

65. See James J. Stamoolis, "Orthodox Theology of Mission," in Moreau, 715.

66. Daniel C.-I. Ciobotea, "Unity and Mission: An Orthodox Perspective," *International Review of Mission* 78/309 (January 1989): 33. See also Schattauer, "Liturgical Assembly as Locus of Mission," 11.

67. James J. Stamoolis, *Eastern Orthodox Mission Theology Today* (Maryknoll, N.Y.: Orbis Books, 1986), 99-100, 55.

68. Ciobotea, 33.

69. Lesslie Newbigin, *Is Christ Divided? A Plea for Christian Unity in a Revolutionary Age* (Grand Rapids, Mich.: Eerdmans, 1961), 24, quoted in Michael Goheen, *"As the Father Has Sent Me, I Am Sending You": J. E. Lesslie Newbigin's Missionary Ecclesiology* (Utrecht, The Netherlands: Boekencentrum, 2001), 30.

70. Donald G. LaSalle, Jr., "At the Threshold of the Assembly: Liturgy, the New Evangelization, and the New Millennium," *Liturgical Ministry* 8 (Fall 1999): 183.

71. Ibid.

72. Thomas Merton, *The Seven Storey Mountain* (New York: Harcourt, Brace and Company, 1948), 207-208; Harvey Cox, *Fire from Heaven: The Rise of Pentecostal Spirituality*

and the Reshaping of Religion in the Twenty-First Century (Cambridge, Mass.: Da Capo Press, 1995), 59.

73. Thérèse of Lisieux, *Story of a Soul: The Autobiography of St. Thérèse of Lisieux*, 3d ed., trans. John Clarke (Washington, D.C.: ICS Publications, 1996), 192-193.

74. Mary Frohlich, "Mission Patrons," in Müller et al., 313.

75. Wayne Teasdale, *A Monk in the World: Cultivating a Spiritual Life* (Novato, Calif.: New World Library, 2002), 1.

76. Ibid., xxiii-xxiv.

77. Lathrop, 202.

78. Teasdale, 21.

79. Michel Quoist, *Prayers* (New York: Sheed and Ward, 1963), 14-15.

80. Robert J. Scheiter, "Mission for the Twenty-First Century: A Catholic Perspective," in Stephen Bevans and Roger Schroeder, eds., *Mission for the Twenty-first Century* (Chicago: CCGM Publications, 2001), 35.

81. Roman Catholic Order of the Mass, Embolism after the Lord's Prayer.

82. Synod of Bishops, "Justice in the World" (1971), "Introduction," in David J. O'Brien and Thomas A. Shannon, eds., *Catholic Social Thought: The Documentary Heritage* (Maryknoll, N.Y.: Orbis Books, 1992), 289; Paul VI, "Message for World Day of Peace," *Origins* 1/29 (January 6, 1972): 491; Leonardo Boff, "Social Ecology: Poverty and Misery," in David G. Hallman, ed., *Ecotheology: Voices from South and North* (Maryknoll, N.Y.: Orbis Books, 1994), 243; Frederick R. Wilson, *The San Antonio Report: Your Will Be Done, Mission in Christ's Way* (Geneva: WCC Publications, 1990), 54.

83. Stark, 73-94.

84. Eloy Bueno, *La iglesia en la encrucijada de la misión* (Estella, Spain: Editorial Verbo Divino, 1999), 241.

85. Stott, *Christian Mission in the Modern World*, 15-34.

86. "The Grand Rapids Report on Evangelism and Social Responsibility: An Evangelical Commitment" (1982), 4.c, in John R. W. Stott, ed., *Making Christ Known: Historic Mission Documents from the Lausanne Movement, 1974-1989* (Grand Rapids, Mich.: Eerdmans, 1997), 181-182.

87. *Poor* and *marginalized* are used here to refer to those people who are economically poor, or who are marginal, peripheral or simply disregarded by society as unimportant or worthless. These might include migrants, refugees, women, disabled, indigenous groups, certain racial or tribal groups, children, the aged or homosexuals. Very often, however, these peripheral or excluded groups are also economically poor, and so not educated; often they are also the perpetrators and/or victims of crimes and violence.

88. Kirk, 99; see also Schreiter, "Globalization and Reconciliation," 125.

89. Ronaldo Muñoz, "God the Father," in Ignacio Ellacuría and Jon Sobrino, eds., *Mysterium Liberationis: Fundamental Concepts of Liberation Theology* (Maryknoll, N.Y.: Orbis Books, 1993), 405.

90. Walter Wink, *Naming the Powers: The Language of Power in the New Testament* (Minneapolis, Minn.: Fortress Press, 1984); idem, *Unmasking the Powers: The Invisible Forces That Determine Human Existence* (Minneapolis, Minn.: Fortress Press, 1986); idem, *Engaging the Powers: Discernment and Resistance in a World of Domination* (Minneapolis, Minn.: Fortress Press, 1992). Here I am following Donal Dorr's reflections in Dorr, 115-117.

91. Quoted in Jann E. Boyd Fullenwieder, "Proclamation: Mercy for the World," in Schattauer, *Inside Out*, 24.

92. Dorr, 117.

93. Congregation for the Doctrine of the Faith, "Instruction on Christian Freedom and Liberation," 68, quoted in U.S. Bishops, *To the Ends of the Earth: A Pastoral Statement on World Mission* (New York: The Society for the Propagation of the Faith, 1987), para. 49, 25.

94. Dorr, 155-156; for a discussion of praxis, see Bevans, *Models of Contextual Theology*, 88-89.

95. LCWE and WEF, "Consultation on Simple Life-Style."

96. Dorr, 153.

97. Ibid., 156.

98. "Justice in the World," in O'Brien and Shannon, 295.

99. *Manila Manifesto*, 8, in Scherer and Bevans, *New Directions in Mission and Evangelization 1*, 300.

100. A contemporary example of working for justice in the church is the formation of Voice of the Faithful (and its counterpart, Voice of the Ordained) in 2002 in response to the clergy sexual abuse scandal (see David Gibson, *The Coming Catholic Church* [San Francicso: HarperSanFrancisco, 2003]).

101. U.S. Bishops, *The Challenge of Peace: God's Promise and Our Response* (1983), in O'Brien and Shannon, 492. The quotation is from John Paul II, "Address to Scientists and Scholars," *Origins* 10 (1981): 621.

102. E.g., the tradition of St. Maurice and members of the Theban Legion. See Robert Ellsberg, *All Saints: Daily Reflections on Saints, Prophets and Witnesses for Our Time* (New York: Crossroad, 1997), 411-412.

103. Kirk, 148.

104. *The Challenge of Peace*, IV.B.1-4, in O'Brien and Shannon, 552-556; the quotations are from 555. For Cardinal Bernardin's "seamless garment" theory of ethics, see Thomas G. Fuechtmann, ed., *Consistent Ethic of Life* (Kansas City, Mo.: Sheed and Ward, 1988).

105. Philip Jenkins, *The Next Christendom: The Coming of Global Christianity* (New York: Oxford University Press, 2002), 163-190.

106. E.g., Paul VI, *Octogesima Adveniens*, 21, in O'Brien and Shannon, 273; "Justice in the World," in O'Brien and Shannon, 289; LCWE and WEF, "Consultation on Simple Life-Style," 2, in Scherer and Bevans, *New Directions in Mission and Evangelization 1*, 269; WCC, "Justice, Peace and the Integrity of Creation" (1990), in Scherer and Bevans, *New Directions in Mission and Evangelization 1*, 82-83. Thomas Thangaraj quotes Orthodox theologian Constantin Voicu: "A better environment will never exist without a more just social order" (see Thomas Thangaraj, *The Common Task: A Theology of Christian Mission* [Nashville, Tenn.: Abingdon Press, 1999], 92, quoting Constantin Voicu, "Orthodox Theology and the Problems of the Environment," *The Greek Orthodox Theological Review* 38/1-4 [1993]: 175).

107. See Kirk, 166, 262 n. 6. In note 6 Kirk presents a general bibliography on environmental justice written from a Christian perspective. For a specific *mission* perspective, see Heidi Hadsell, "Ecology and Mission," in Müller et al., 114-117; Rosemary Radford Ruether, "Ecojustice at the Center of the Church's Mission" and Larry Rasmussen, "Global Ecojustice: The Church's Mission in Urban Society," *Mission Studies* 16/1/31 (1999): 111-121 and 123-135.

108. Walter Brueggemann, "The Uninflected *Therefore* of Hosea 4:1-3," in Fernando F. Segovia and Mary Ann Tolbert, eds., *Reading from This Place*, vol. 1, *Social Location and Biblical Interpretation in the United States* (Minneapolis, Minn.: Fortress Press), 231-249.

109. Rudy Wiebe, *The Blue Hills of China* (Toronto, Canada: McClelland & Stewart, New Canadian Library Edition, 1995), 258.

110. See Kirk, 180-183.

111. See, e.g., Special Synod for Africa (1994), Proposition 55, in Africa Faith and Justice Network, ed., *African Synod: Documents, Reflections, Perspectives* (Maryknoll, N.Y.: Orbis Books, 1996), 106; Federation of Asian Bishops' Conferences, Final Statement of the Seventh Plenary Assembly, "A Renewed Church in Asia: A Mission of Love and Service," II.D, *FABC Papers* 93, 7; Fourth General Conference of Latin American Bishops, "Conclusions," 169-177, in Alfred T. Hennelly, ed., *Santo Domingo and Beyond* (Maryknoll, N.Y.: Orbis Books, 1993), 119-122.

112. Marthinus L. Daneel, *African Earthkeepers: Wholistic Interfaith Mission* (Maryknoll, N.Y.: Orbis Books, 2001), 10.

113. Roman Catholic Liturgy, Preface to the Eucharistic Prayer, Feast of Christ the King.

114. Secretariat for Non-Christians, "The Attitude of the Church Towards the Followers of Other Religions: Reflections and Orientations on Dialogue and Mission," 29, quoted in U.S. Bishops, *To the Ends of the Earth*, para. 40, 22.

115. John W. Oman, *Vision and Authority*, 2d ed. (London: Hodder and Stoughton, 1928), 225.

116. DP 38. For a survey of Roman Catholic documents on dialogue, see James H. Kroeger, "A Church Walking in Dialogue: Interreligious Dialogue Milestones," in *Becoming Local Church* (Quezon City, Philippines: Claretian Publications, 2003), 87-107.

117. WCC, *Ecumenical Affirmation: Mission and Evangelism*," 43, in Scherer and Bevans, *New Directions in Mission and Evangelization 1*, 50.

118. See Jacques Dupuis, *Toward a Christian Theology of Religious Pluralism* (Maryknoll, N.Y.: Orbis Books, 1997), 34-37.

119. For a detailed study of the history of the church's openness to other religious ways, see ibid.

120. Heim, 138. The reference to the "fullness of Christ" is to Ephesians 4:13. Of this, Andrew Walls (who inspired Heim in his own thinking) writes: "It is as though Christ himself actually grows through the work of mission" (Walls, xvii).

121. For what follows, see Allan Race, *Christians and Religious Pluralism: Patterns in the Christian Theology of Religions* (London: SCM Press, 1993), and Paul F. Knitter, *Introducing Theologies of Religions* (Maryknoll, N.Y.: Orbis Books, 2002). For a thumbnail sketch of exclusivism, inclusivism and pluralism, see also Heim, 3 n. 1.

122. Heim, 8.

123. Joseph Augustine Di Noia, "Jesus and the World Religions" (available online), quoted in Heim, 4.

124. Heim, 4.

125. This phrasing is according to the point made by Luke Timothy Johnson, "Christians and Jews: Starting Over—Why the Real Dialogue Has Just Begun," *Commonweal* 103/2 (January 31, 2003): 15: "I do not hope to answer the question of how Christians should think about Jews, because I think it is the wrong way to put the question. Instead, I hope to suggest a way that Christians might begin to think of themselves with reference to Jews." See also the title of Mary C. Boys's recent book: *Has God Only One Blessing? Judaism as a Source of Christian Self-Understanding* (Mahwah, N.J.: Paulist Press, 2000).

126. Donald Senior, "Rome Has Spoken: A New Approach to Judaism," *Commonweal* 103/2 (January 31, 2003): 20.

127. Boys, 247-266.

128. Senior, 22.

129. Johnson, 15.

130. See, for example, the articles of Johnson and Senior and the book of Mary Boys cited above, as well as John Pawlikowski, *Jesus and the Theology of Israel* (Wilmington, Del.: Michael Glazier, 1989), and John T. Pawlikowski and Hayim Goren Perelmuter, eds., *Reinterpreting Revelation and Tradition: Jews and Christians in Conversation* (Franklin, Wis.: Sheed and Ward, 2000).

131. Avery Dulles, "'Covenant and Mission,'" *America* 187/12 (October 21, 2002), 10. See Johnson, 16.

132. Pontifical Biblical Commission, "The Jewish People and Their Sacred Scriptures in the Christian Bible" (2001), 87, available online.

133. John Paul II, quoted in Senior, 20.

134. Johnson, 17.

135. Senior, 23.

136. Ibid.

137. Ibid., 18.

138. Mary C. Boys, Philip A. Cunningham and John T. Pawlikowski, "Theology's 'Sacred Obligation': A Reply to Cardinal Avery Dulles on Evangelization," *America* 187/12 (October 21, 2002), 13.

139. See Boys, 258-261. The call to witness together is present in an important address by Tommaso Federici in 1977 at a meeting in Venice, Italy, of the International Jewish-Catholic

Dialogue (II, 10-11 [quoted in Boys, 261]). The quotation is from a document of the United Methodist Church, quoted on 261.

140. Dulles, 9.

141. See the illustration in Boys, 246, and 247-278.

142. Zago, 10.

143. Theo Sundermeier, "Theology of Mission," in Müller et al., 429-451.

144. Marcello Zago, "Mission and Interreligious Dialogue," *International Bulletin of Missionary Research* 22/3 (July 1998): 100.

145. David Tracy, *Plurality and Ambiguity: Hermeneutics, Religion, Hope* (New York: Harper & Row, 1987), 19.

146. Walls, 25.

147. Allan H. Anderson, "The Gospel and Culture in Pentecostal Mission in the Third World," *Missionalia* 27/2 (August 1999): 221.

148. The foregoing paragraphs are a summary of the first chapter of Bevans, *Models of Contextual Theology.* See also Robert J. Schreiter, *Constructing Local Theologies* (Maryknoll, N.Y.: Orbis Books, 1985).

149. Paul VI, "Closing Discourse to All-Africa Symposium," quoted in Aylward Shorter, *African Christian Theology* (Maryknoll, N.Y.: Orbis Books, 1975), 20; see José M. de Mesa, "Doing Theology as Inculturation in the Asian Context," in Scherer and Bevans, *New Directions in Mission and Evangelization 3*, 118; David J. Hesselgrave, *Communicating Christ Cross-Culturally: An Introduction to Missionary Communication* (Grand Rapids, Mich.: Zondervan, 1978), 85.

150. Roger Schroeder, "Entering Someone Else's Garden: Cross-Cultural Mission/Ministry," in Bevans, Doidge and Schreiter, 147-161.

151. Walls, 3-15.

152. Ibid., 25.

153. Peter C. Phan, *In Our Own Tongues: Asian Perspectives on Mission and Inculturation* (Maryknoll, N.Y.: Orbis Books, 2003), xii.

154. Bevans, "Letting Go and Speaking Out."

155. Darrell Whiteman, "Contextualization: The Theory, the Gap, the Challenge," *International Bulletin of Missionary Research* 21/1 (January 1997): 2.

156. Jenkinson and O'Sullivan, 399-414.

157. Schreiter, "Globalization and Reconciliation," 137.

158. Ibid., 136; Robert J. Schreiter, "Mission as a Model of Reconciliation," *Neue Zeitschrift für Missionswissenschaft* 52 (1996): 243-250; Robert J. Schreiter, *The New Catholicity* (Maryknoll, N.Y.: Orbis Books, 1997), 124-126.

159. Schreiter quotes historian Eric Hobsbawm, "who has dubbed the twentieth century 'the short century,'" since it began with the Great War in 1914 and ended with the tearing down of the Berlin Wall in 1989 (see Schreiter, "Globalization and Reconciliation," 122).

160. Benjamin R. Barber, *Jihad vs. McWorld* (New York: Times Books, 1995); Samuel P. Huntington, *The Clash of Civilizations and the Remaking of World Order* (New York: Simon and Schuster, 1996); Scott C. Alexander, "The 'Clash of Civilizations' and the Dialogue Imperative: A Self-Fulfilling Prediction?" *Chicago Studies* 41/2 (Summer 2002): 192-208.

161. Quoted in Schreiter, "Mission for the Twenty-First Century," 34.

162. Gerard Goldman, "'Remembering Ian, Alan Goldman, and Memelma'—Using Narrative as an Approach to Aboriginal Reconciliation in Australia" (Doctor of Ministry Thesis, Catholic Theological Union, Chicago, 1999).

163. Eleanor Doidge, "Accompaniment: Mission in the Heart of God," in Bevans, Doidge and Schreiter, 172.

164. Douglas W. Young, "Reconciliation: 'Breaking Down the Wall of Hostility,'" *Verbum SVD* 41/1 (2000): 137-149; idem, "Nonviolent Alternatives among the Enga of the Papua New Guinea Highlands," *Social Alternatives* 16/2 (April 1997): 42-45; idem, *Our Land Is Green*

and Black: Traditional and Modern Methods for Sustaining Peaceful Intergroup Relations among the Enga of Papua New Guinea (Goroka, Papua New Guinea: Melanesian Institute, forthcoming).

165. Schreiter, "Globalization and Reconciliation," 140. This article is a fine, recent summary of Schreiter's thought as it has developed over the last decade; see also idem, *The Ministry of Reconciliation: Spirituality and Strategies* (Maryknoll, N.Y.: Orbis Books, 1998), 6-19.

166. Schreiter, "Globalization and Mission," 141.

167. Schreiter, *The Ministry of Reconciliation*, vi; idem, "Mission for the Twenty-First Century," 35.

168. Schreiter, *The Ministry of Reconciliation*, 105-130; idem, "Globalization and Mission," 141-142.

169. Schreiter, *The Ministry of Reconciliation*, 129.

Index

Abelard, Peter, 51, 52, 53, 59, 60
Abgar VIII, 75, 78
acceptance model, the, 380
accommodational approach, the: examples of, in Asia, 184–91; Jesuits and, 194; in New France, 182, 183; in nineteenth-century mission, 231; the Rites Controversy and, 192–94
Accra conference (WCC, 1958), 261
Acts, book of: on Antioch, 25–27; conclusions regarding its view of mission, 30–31; on Cornelius and his household, 23–25; on mission before Pentecost, 14–16; on the mission to the Gentiles, 27–30; overview of, 11–13; on Pentecost, 16–18; on Samaria, 21–22; on Stephen, 18–21
Adam (East Syrian bishop, missionary), 105, 111
adaptation model. *See* accommodational approach, the
Addai, 75, 79
Ad Gentes: on the church and history, 66; on culture, 302; overview of, 249–50, 282; three theological bases of, 289–90; the triune God and, 286–88
AD 2000 and Beyond, 49, 412n.72
Africa: Crowther and, 213; independent churches in, 265–68; Javouhey and, 223; Livingstone and, 214; mission in the early church in,

113–15; nineteenth-century Catholic mission to, 224–25; the slave trade and, 172–73; tendency to diminish the will to resist Western culture in, 237
African Americans, 225, 247, 314
African Communion of Independent Churches, 266
African Initiated churches, 242, 265–68, 377
Agbebi, Mojola, 265
Aglipay, Gregorio, 269
AIDS, 241, 390
Alaska, 227–28
Albert the Great, 157, 167
Albigensians, the, 153
Alcuin of York, 126, 131
Alexander of Hales, 152
Alfonso VI, 138
All-African Council of Churches, 262
Allen, Robert, 256, 257
Allgemeine Missions Zeitschrift, 221, 275
Alopen, 105, 111
Amaladoss, Michael, 254, 315–16
American African Methodist Episcopal Church, 265
American Baptist Foreign Mission Society, 212
American Board of Commissioners for Foreign Missions, 212, 218, 231, 234
American Society for Propagating the Gospel among the Indians and Others in North America, 433n.19
American Society of Missiology, 275

amillennialism, 233, 234
Anabaptists, 173, 196
ancestor veneration, 108, 190, 193, 270
Andersen, Wilhelm, 290
Anderson, Allan, 340, 386
Anderson, Gerald H., 383
Anderson, Rufus, 42, 231, 232, 234
Andhra Pradesh, India, 270
Andrews, C. F., 258
Anglo-Saxon missionary activity, 256–57
Anglo-Saxon monasticism, 124–25
Anim, Peter N., 273
anonymous Christianity, 53, 252, 439n.47
Anselm of Canterbury, 39, 44, 64, 133, 302, 342
Anthony of Padua, 150, 152
anthropological model, the, 48
anthropology: the Age of Progress and the attitude toward, 230; basic questions that define, 34; the Catholic Church on, 345; comparison of Las Casas and the conquest approach on, 200; Ephraem the Syrian and, 134; inculturation and, 388; interreligious dialogue and, 385; Jesuits in Asia on, 202; liturgy and, 366; prayer and, 368; Protestantism in the Age of Discovery on, 203; reconciliation and, 394; the reign-of-God approach on, 320; social action and, 377–78; summary of the early church on, 95; summary of

467

pacifism, 374–75
Padilla, René, 261, 279, 337
paganism, 135
Pagura, Federico, 251
Palladius, 120
Pannenberg, Wolfhart, 312, 313–14, 399n.3
Pantaenus, 78, 85
Papal Volunteers for Latin America, 248
Parham, Charles F., 272
Parliament of the World's Religions, 384
Pastoral Constitution on the Church in the Modern World. See *Gaudium et Spes*
paternalism, 181, 216
Patrick, St., 114, 120
patronato system, the, 174–75, 191–92
Pattaya conference (LCWE, 1980), 262
Paul, St.: in Antioch, 28; Barnabas and, 26–27; the Jerusalem council and, 29; Stephen's death and, 20; on women, 90–91
Paul III, Pope, 177
Paul VI, Pope: on the church as the people of God, 56; definition of mission by, 8; on dialogue, 400n.9; *Evangelii Nuntiandi* and, 253; on the first means of evangelization, 352; on inculturation, 386–87; on mission and the church's identity, 7; on peace, 374; on proclamation, 358, 359, 360; on the reign of God, 305; on salvation, 69
Pax Romana, 80
peace, 307, 373–75, 383–84
Pelagians, 131
penitential movement, the, 148, 155
Pentecost, 16–18
Pentecostal Fellowship of North America, 274

Pentecostal/Charismatic Churches of North America, 274
Pentecostals: anthropology of, 345; Christocentrism and, 338–40, 342; on culture, 346; ecclesiology of, 342–43; eschatology of, 43, 343; on evangelism, 352; growth of, 242; inculturation and, 386; liberation theology and, 314; overview of twentieth-century Christology of, 275; overview of twentieth-century soteriology of, 275; overview of twentieth-century view of culture of, 278; the poor and, 370; recent documents on proclamation, 327–30; on salvation, 344; summary of views of, 272–74; on titles of Christ, 456n.77; the Trinity in recent missiology of, 293–94; women and, 219
people of God, 56, 299
peregrinatio pro Christo, 121, 124
Perpetua, 86
Persian Church, the, 103–4.
    See also East Syrian Church
Persian Empire, the, 99–100
Peter, St., 16–17, 24, 29
Phan, Peter C., 387–88, 437 n.7
Philip, St., 21–22
Philipon, Michel, 286
Philippine Benevolent Missionary Association, 443 n.146
Philippines, the, 162, 174, 269
Philo, 50, 95
Pieris, Aloysius, 65, 254
Pierson, A. T., 217
Pietism, 43, 196, 208, 209
pilgrimage, 121, 142
Pinnock, Clark, 337
Pious Society, the, 245
Pius VI, Pope, 209
Pius VII, Pope, 209

Pius IX, Pope, 58, 222, 225, 235
Pius X, Pope, 58, 222
Pius XI, Pope, 244, 246, 249
Pius XII, Pope, 41, 55
plantatio ecclesiae, 249
Platonic thought, 50
Platonism, 50, 59, 331, 412 n.77
pluralism: critical response to, 331; dialogue and, 380; Heim on, 452–53n.2; liberation theology and, 65; Smith's and Hick's Christologies and, 263; Type B theology and, 53–54; van Engen on, 336
Plütschau, Henry, 196
Polikin, Isaias, 228
Polycarp, 61, 83, 85
Pontifical Council for Interreligious Dialogue, 254
Pontifical Institute for Foreign Missions, 222–23
poor, the: Asian bishops on, 349; Elizabeth of Hungary and, 148; God and, 370–71; history of the church's relation to, 369; Las Casas and, 200; Pentecostals and, 340; shifting attitudes toward, 370; solidarity with, 372–73; term discussed, 462n.86. *See also* poverty
Poor Clares, 145–46, 151, 178
Porefthendes, 264
postmillennialism, 233, 234
Poullart-des-Places, Claude-François, 223
poverty: the church's response to, in the late nineteenth century, 207; Clare of Assisi and, 145; Francis of Assisi and, 143; Illich on, 251; in Latin America, 252; liberation theology and, 312–15, 321; monasticism and, 128; SEDOS on, 254. *See also* poor, the
Powell, Mark Allan, 12

secular holiness, 148
SEDOS, 252, 253, 389
Semmelroth, Otto, 399n.3, 452n.63
Senior, Donald, 14, 402n.26
Sepúlveda, Juan Ginés de, 176, 197, 346
Serampore College, 211
Serampore Trio, the, 211–12
Seventh-Day Adventism, 233
sexual abuse scandal, 463n.99
sexuality, 46
Seymour, William J., 272, 339, 340
Sheen, Bishop Fulton, 246
Shenk, Wilbert, 1, 232, 238, 293–94
signs of the times, 243
sin, 58–59, 301–2, 321
Siotis, M. A., 295
Sisters of St. Joseph of Cluny, 222, 223
Sisters of the Blessed Sacrament, 225
Skydsgaard, Krister, 310, 399n.3
slavery, 172–73, 175, 176, 177, 213, 225
Slavic peoples, 128
Slusser, Michael, 416n.24
Smith, Eugene L., 288
Smith, Wilfred Cantwell, 263
Sobrino, Jon, 63
social action, 369–78. See also justice; praxis; social responsibility
Social Gospel movement, 207, 217, 231, 370
social responsibility, 325–26
La Société des Missions étrangères de la Province de Quebec, 226
Society for Pentecostal Studies, 338
Society for the Propagation of the Gospel in Foreign Parts, 433n.19
society model, the, 206, 210–12, 222–26, 238
Society of Catholic Medical Missionaries, 245

Society of Foreign Missions (Paris), 191–92
Society of the Divine Word, 246, 255
Society of the Sacred Heart of Jesus, 224
Sölle, Dorothee, 2, 35–36, 41, 64, 408n.10
soteriology. See salvation
South African Missiological Society, 274–75
Southern Baptist Convention, 219
Spain, 174–75
special revelation, 40
Speer, Robert, 217, 234
Spellman, Francis Cardinal, 246
Spener, Philipp Jakob, 196
Spiller, Vsevolod, 295
Spirit Christology, 297
Spiritans. See Holy Ghost Fathers/Spiritans
Spiritual Exercises, 195
Spittler, Russell P., 338
Sri Lanka, 104
Stamoolis, James J., 295, 364
Stanley, David, 16–17, 20, 402n.25
Stark, Rodney, 82, 83, 87–88, 89, 90, 354
Stephen, St., 19–21
Stephen of Perm, 160
Stoicism, 38
Stott, John: on the connection between salvation and social liberation, 45; on the Ethiopian eunuch, 22; on hell, 344; the Lausanne Covenant and, 261; on Philip, 21; on the primary task of mission, 335; on salvation, 345; on Stephen, 19; the WCC and, 279
Student Volunteer Movement for Foreign Missions, 217
Stuhlmueller, Carroll, 14, 402n.26
Sublimis Deus, 177
Suárez, Francisco, 202
Sufism, 426n.68

Suhard, Emmanuel Cardinal, 248
Sullivan, Richard, 134–35
Sundermeier, Theo, 383
Sunquist, Scott W., 2, 104, 105, 406n.101
supercessionism, 381–82
Swedish Missionary Society, 212
sword-and-cross approach, 141–42, 159
Syllabus of Errors, 209, 222, 235
syncretism, 61, 338
Synod of Bishops (1974), 253, 373
synthetic mode, the, 48
Syrian Church. See East Syrian Church

tabula rasa approach, 178, 183, 185, 192, 194, 201, 230, 231
Tambaram conference (IMC, 1938), 258–59
Tamerlane, 162
T'ang dynasty, 105, 108, 110, 129
Tannehill, Robert, 22, 25
Taoism, 108
Tatian the Assyrian, 78, 79
Taylor, Hudson, 219, 233
teachers, 85, 110
Teasdale, Wayne, 367, 368
technology, 390
Teilhard de Chardin, Pierre, 55, 62, 67–68, 69–70
Tekakwitha, Kateri, 182
Teresa, Mother, 255, 353
Teresa of Avila, 427n.85
terrorism, 390
Tertullian: Christology of, 39; contemporary implications of the thought of, 98; on culture, 48; on the discontinuity between Christian faith and secular philosophy, 84; eschatology of, 42–43; Greek philosophy and, 96; on interreligious marriage, 90; on martyrdom, 86; on

The American Society of Missiology Series, published in collaboration with Orbis Books, seeks to publish scholarly work of high merit and wide interest on numerous aspects of missiology—the study of Christian mission in its historical, social, and theological dimensions. Able proposals on new and creative approaches to the practice and understanding of mission will receive close attention from the ASM Series Committee.

PREVIOUSLY PUBLISHED IN
THE AMERICAN SOCIETY OF MISSIOLOGY SERIES